THE OFFICIAL®
PRICE GUIDE TO
Paperbacks
& Magazines

FROM THE EDITORS
OF THE HOUSE OF COLLECTIBLES

Consulting Editors
Charles and Donna Jordan

FIRST EDITION

THE HOUSE OF COLLECTIBLES
NEW YORK, NEW YORK 10022

T5-CCJ-510

Important Notice. The format of *The Official Price Guide Series,* published by *The House of Collectibles,* is based on the following proprietary features: *All facts and prices are compiled through a nationwide sampling of information* obtained from noteworthy experts, auction houses, and specialized dealers. *Detailed "indexed" format* enables quick retrieval of information for positive identification. *Encapsulated histories* precede each category to acquaint the collector with the specific traits that are peculiar to that area of collecting. *Valuable collecting information* is provided for both the novice as well as the seasoned collector: How to begin a collection; how to buy, sell and trade; care and storage techniques; tips on restoration; grading guidelines; lists of periodicals, clubs, museums, auction houses, dealers, etc. *An average price range* takes geographic location and condition into consideration when reporting collector value. *An inventory checklist system* is provided for cataloging a collection.

All of the information, including valuations, in this book has been compiled from the most reliable sources, and every effort has been made to eliminate errors and questionable data. Nevertheless the possibility of error, in a work of such immense scope, always exists. The publisher will not be held responsible for losses which may occur in the purchase, sale, or other transaction of items because of information contained herein. Readers who feel they have discovered errors are invited to *write* and inform us, so they may be corrected in subsequent editions. Those seeking further information on the topics covered in this book are advised to refer to the complete line of Official Price Guides published by The House of Collectibles.

TABLE OF CONTENTS

ACKNOWLEDGMENT

We would like to extend our thanks to our assistant, Galina Kolev, who has helped us tremendously in our research and preparation of this book.

NOTE TO READERS

MARKET REVIEW

Both paperback and magazine collecting are specialized hobbies. No one who considers himself a collector will attempt to build a collection of either interest without having clear direction. While this has always been the case, the degree of specialization in both hobbies has become more extreme, and this is evident in the current year's price performances. While many collectors still attempt to build a full set of *Life* or *National Geographic* magazines, they are now well outnumbered by those who collect magazines topically, looking for articles and/or covers on certain celebrities or favorite subjects. The presence of a good article or cover art on a heavily collected celebrity assures a strong price. This form of specialization has had such influence on the market that values of many magazines are now established strictly by content rather than title, age or other considerations.

PAPERBACKS

Science fiction and mysteries continue to claim the greatest numbers of active collectors. Mystery paperbacks have been the leaders in this hobby for more than a decade, in terms of overall interest and market activity. They are of course ideal for the collector, as mysteries were among the first paperbacks published and therefore span the entire lifetime of paperback books. Science fiction was only occasionally published in paperback format before 1950. Though the major mystery authors are well represented by groups of devoted fans and collectors, shifts in popularity do occur. This was noticeable by the popularity of television's presentation of "Mike Hammer." Mickey Spillane's works enjoyed a particularly successful year on the collector market, with increased competition and price gains.

The writings of Agatha Christie, the most prolific mystery novelist, also do well. Here again, theatrical exposure has encouraged greater collecting activity. Film versions of her novels, such as *Murder on the Orient Express,* generated widespread interest in many of her lesser-known works. This led to their reissuing, and to higher market values for the original paperback editions, some of which were by then 30 years old or more.

The paperbacks registering the strongest overall value gains this past year were those with motion picture covers. Many of these, while authored by novelists with relatively little reputation or collector following, have achieved prices in the $10 to $15 range. This included works dating as recently as the early 1970s. Of course there are many hundreds of such paperbacks and collector enthusiasm is not nearly as fervent for some as for others. The success of the motion picture is not a vital factor, as some of the highest prices are being obtained for films that literally died at the box office. The most relevant consideration is the star or stars pictured on the cover. Any paperback with Natalie Wood, Marlon Brando, Marilyn Monroe, or other heavily collected celebrity on the cover is automatically of strong value in the current market. In the cases of some popular celebrities there are few paperbacks picturing them, and thus the level of competition for those available is intensified. This is true of Jayne Mansfield, who appears on the cover of *Will Success Spoil Rock Hunter?* Most of her films were not published in paperback form as they were created solely as screenplays. There are quite a few paperbacks picturing Elizabeth Taylor, but still the prices are going rather high. Of course when a movie paperback has interior photos in addition to a cover picture it will draw even greater interest.

Closely related to the motion picture paperback is the television paperback. These are far less in number and totally nonexistent for many of the most popular programs. Yet those that are available, going back to the 1950s and continuing to the present day, have considerable hobbyist following. Often a television paperback does not contain a story or script but rather a history of the show, biographies of its performers and miscellaneous information of interest to fans of the program.

MAGAZINES

It would appear from present indications that interest in magazine artwork will become a dominant force in this hobby. It is not an entirely new territory, as fans of Norman Rockwell have been collecting his *Post* covers for decades. Today, however, it is not the traditionally famous illustrators who are at the center of attention, but those who may be termed "newly discovered." Premium prices paid for magazines with their covers and/or interior artwork would undoubtedly surprise the general public as they are far from household names. This phenomenon is partly a spillover from comic book collecting. Many of the favorite comic book artists such as Frazetta, Ward, Kirby, Andriola, etc., did some magazine illustrating. These individuals have gained such stature in the comic book hobby that all of their work, in whatever medium, is eagerly sought after. As it was nearly all *freelanced,* it can turn up anywhere. Bill Ward, for example, did covers for cartoon and joke books during the 1950s. Frank Frazetta illustrated articles for men's magazines including *Cavalier.* The potential presence of work by these illustrators, or others with a collector following, makes it worthwhile to carefully inspect all backdate magazines carrying artwork.

Among subject groups, theatrical magazines scored extremely well over the past year. Once again this is a clear instance of buying competition coming simultaneously from at least two directions. Early issues of the historic motion picture magazines such as *Photoplay, Silver Screen, Screen World* and others are collected by movie memorabilia hobbyists as well as magazine collectors. If these were the only buyers, one would probably find a situation in which issues from the 1920s sold for 10 times as much as those from the 1940s or 1950s. In fact, many late issues are nearly as valuable as the early ones. Prices are high on late issues (and advancing rapidly) because of competition from fans of various stars, who want the issues with their covers or photo spreads. As each issue of a typical film magazine carried articles on a dozen stars, plus a color cover, there are few issues that fail to include a heavily collected celebrity. Of course the cover is the major point of interest; a good Gable, Harlow, Garbo, or Garland cover from the 1930s can result in a higher than normal market price, despite the fact that these stars were very frequently featured on magazine covers. In the case of a star seldom portrayed on magazine covers, such as John Wayne (who had few covers before the 1950s), the price can go still higher. Interestingly enough, motion picture magazines traditionally carried a far higher percentage of female star portraits on their covers. It was not until around 1960 that the number of male stars pictured on covers achieved a balanced ratio.

As far as the pulps are concerned, most of the more celebrated early titles were already in the higher price category but nevertheless scored healthy gains. The newcomer to magazine collecting might be surprised to find issues of pulps from the 1920s and 1930s commanding $100, $200 and more. While they are certainly not to everyone's taste, the cult of pulp collecting is very active and its enthusiasts willingly pay these lofty sums. There is an undeniable scarcity factor associated with pulps, as their poor quality paper led to more rapid deterioration. Some of the early issues are very hard to find, and almost never in a reasonable state of preservation.

ABOUT THE PRICES IN THIS BOOK

All prices in this book are *retail* prices—that is sums charged by dealers in paperbacks and magazines when they sell to the public. When selling *to* a dealer, you receive what amounts to a *wholesale* price, which of course will be considerably lower.

The prices represent *averages* and were compiled from dealers' lists, advertisements, shop offerings, and auction sale results.

Within the market, there will be many cases of items selling above' and below the prices shown. Obviously there is a sharp difference in price between buying from a recognized specialist dealer, and buying at a garage sale or Salvation Army store. But even among the full-time dealers who make a living selling paperbacks and magazines, there are differences in price. One dealer may have more customers for certain types of paperbacks or magazines than another, and his prices will probably reflect this. Prices can also change because of fads, trends, or news events, and this can make a published price outdated very quickly. In the magazine field, everything with M*A*S*H covers or articles has been going up strongly. If you used the prices of two or three years ago as a guide in buying, you'd swear you were being overcharged. This is just one of many such examples, magazines with Joan Collins or Victoria Principal on the cover. With paperbacks of course it's a matter of the author's current popularity and also the popularity of his or her type of writing. There, too, trends and rapid price changes are fairly common.

When a dealer's price seems excessively high, stop and consider whether you might be able to buy the identical item (in identical condition) for less elsewhere. Usually you can find it in the stock of another dealer. It pays to check around. You will either save some money or, at the least, you'll confirm the fact that the item has risen substantially in value throughout the trade.

When a price is surprisingly *low,* this could be a genuine bargain (the seller might not realize its true value), or it could be in poor condition with pages missing or some other serious defects. You will need to examine the item thoroughly to find out. Most of the full-time professional dealers are very well informed about values, so don't expect to get too many bargains from them!

HOW TO USE THIS BOOK

In the PAPERBACKS section, all titles are arranged alphabetically by *author.* The title is given, followed by the publishing company, publisher's serial number (if any), and date (if it appears in the book). Occasionally, other pertinent information is furnished. The letters ED indicate that the author acted as an editor on that particular title, which will generally be in the nature of an anthology (works of various other authors). ND means no date (the book was issued without a publication date).

In the MAGAZINE section, all titles are listed alphabetically and then, within the listings for each, chronologically by issue dates. Notes are given on the contents or covers of many of the magazines. In nearly all cases where an issue carries a premium value it is because of the content or cover noted. For example a 1950s magazine with a Marilyn Monroe story would automatically carry a higher value than an ordinary issue of the same magazine from the same era.

In all cases, for paperbacks and magazines, prices are based on copies in *very good* condition. Copies in very good condition will show evidence of handling and very minor defects as are common with used paperbacks and magazines. There will be no pages or covers missing, no clippings removed, no heavy stains, no bad wrinkling or creasing, no pen scribbling, no discoloration of the front cover. Copies in *mint* or *near mint* condition, which show virtually no indication of having been handled, naturally sell for higher prices. The premium on such copies varies. By the same token, copies in less than very good condition sell for lower prices than those shown in the listings.

Each listing in *The Official Price Guide to Paperbacks and Magazines* carries *three* accompanying prices. The first two prices represent the current range at which the item was selling at the time of compilation. A range is used rather than a single price to compensate for the normal variations in prices from one seller to another. The third price is the current *year average* (C/Y Avg.), a price to be used for quick reference.

Paperbacks

HISTORY OF PAPERBACKS

While mass-market paperbacks belong to the twentieth century, their roots date far back into history—almost from the earliest days of publishing.

The concept of inexpensive books for people who were just readers and not book collectors was a very obvious one. All during the Middle Ages (500–1500 A.D.), while books were being handwritten, it was impossible to produce inexpensive volumes. The labor cost automatically caused a high price, even if a book was small and modestly bound. When printing was developed around 1450, the stage was set for large-scale distribution and cost-cutting. At first, the opportunity to make inexpensive books was bypassed. Johann Gutenberg and other pioneer printers took a typical craftsman's pride in their work. They wanted to make their books as fine and impressive as possible, like works of art. Within 50 years of the invention of printing, however, printers with sharp business sense started thinking of the mass market. Why sell 50 books for the equivalent of $10 each if you could sell 1,000 for the equivalent of $2 each?

The first publisher of low-price books intended for large distribution was a Venetian named Aldus Manutius. In the late 1490s, Manutius began putting out a series of titles which he called "pocket classics." These were the forerunners to modern pocket books though, of course, they do not resemble modern paperbacks too closely in physical appearance.

Nearly all of Manutius' books were Greek and Latin classics, printed in the original language. They sold fabulously and he became wealthy. But as soon as they reached the market, competitors brought out imitations. Before long, publishers in all parts of Europe were issuing small-format handy books.

There was still some room for improvement—or, at least, for further cost-cutting. As the art of printing progressed, type was cast in smaller sizes and it became possible to print smaller and even more inexpensive volumes. The masters at this trade in the seventeenth century were the Elzevirs of Holland. They put out more than a thousand books, in extremely small size (about 4½″ × 2½″). The Elzevir line was more diverse than Manutius. It comprised not only of classics but many other types of books as well, including cookbooks and modern writings.

No important advance in low-price, mass-distribution books was made in the eighteenth century. The Elzevirs were undoubtedly considered the ultimate to which low cost books could be carried, and publishers just went along imitating them. One development of some significance during the eighteenth century was the increasing use by some publishers of paperboard bindings covered in colored paper. These appeared not only on pocket-size volumes but works of standard size. By using such a binding, the cost of calf or other leather was eliminated, and the retail price was brought down somewhat. This led eventually (in the 1820s) to the use of cloth and buckram bindings, and in a way it also led to the concept of paperbacks.

In the nineteenth century the book market expanded as never before. It was revolutionized by the Industrial Age, the steam-driven printing press, and a much higher rate of literacy among the public. Also, many more people were coming out of the poverty ranks in the nineteenth century and could afford to buy reading matter. Some publishers took a novel approach, which for a while proved very successful. Instead of issuing all books in hardcover, they brought out some in monthly parts, just like magazines. Each part had a soft cover, and the reader could collect all the parts and have a whole book. It was like buying a book in installments. When the total price was added up, these books cost just as much and sometimes more than a hardbound volume. But they sold better, because readers bought them who could not afford to immediately spend the money for a hardback. Many of Charles Dickens' novels came out originally as part-issued books—and are great favorites of collectors today.

The first true paperbacks in the English language were issued in Germany. Their publisher was Christian von Tauchnitz, one of the industry's giants in the nineteenth century. Just like many modern publishers of paperbacks. Tauchnitz bought the rights to popular books from their original publishers. He then issued them in soft paper bindings in various languages. There were French language versions for France, Dutch for Holland, English for Britain and America, etc. The Tauchnitz books were small in size, just slightly over six inches tall, but usually much thicker than the average present-day paperbacks. Through wars and depressions Tauchnitz carried on, and it seemed that no rival could give the firm serious competition.

The great strides in paperback publishing of the twentieth century might never have occurred without the Black Friday stock market crash of 1929. Suddenly, the market for hardcover books collapsed; hardly anyone could afford them. The situation was no brighter in Europe than in America when the Great Depression began. In 1931 an English publisher, Albatross Books, launched an ambitious paperback program. Like Tauchnitz, the plan was to issue each title in a number of translations and sell it to the entire western hemisphere. Albatross scored such success that Tauchnitz, rather than try to compete, sold out to Albatross just three years later. For a while it seemed as though Albatross would have an iron-grasp monopoly on paperbacks.

Then, the following year (1935), Penguin Books was born. Penguin started virtually on a shoestring, but soon became the leading English paperback house. Unlike its predecessors, it concentrated on the English-language market and published mostly classics. Penguin is still flourishing today, having put many thousands of titles into print. During the 1960s it began diversifying, issuing lines of nonfiction paperbacks that were liberally illustrated and carried high (for the time) cover prices. The industry concept of "quality paperback," a book equal to a hardcover volume in everything but the binding, was inspired largely by Penguin.

In America, a unique kind of paperback was being published from as early as 1919. These were the *Little Blue Books* of Haldeman-Julius, whose headquarters was in Gerard, Kansas. With World War I over and millions of servicemen returning to civilian life, Haldeman-Julius felt this was the ideal time for marketing *very* inexpensive reading matter. His *Little Blue Books* originally sold for a nickel each. Later the price went up to ten cents. Most of them contained from 40 to 70 pages printed on the lowest grade of paper and stapled at the spine. They had no illustrations. Titles included classics, biographies, history, and how-to-books (including one on *How to Write Blue Books*). Will Durant, the noted historian, started out by writing for Haldeman-Julius, but most of the firm's other authors were not that gifted. *Little Blue Books* became a national craze. But other publishers paid little attention to them, as they were sold almost exclusively by mail and were not considered competition. They stopped publishing in 1964.

Following *Little Blue Books,* the next major step in American paperbacks was made by Charles Boni of New York. In 1929 he set up Paper Books, and sold his books by subscription and in book clubs. His second series was called Boni Books, dating from the 1930s. However, in 1917, the Boni's started the Modern Library classic reprints, which became Bennett Cerf's Random House. They were of very high quality, often illustrated by top artists, and never condensed or abridged.

In 1937, a firm called Modern Age Books got into the paperback sweepstakes. Also in that same year, American Mercury Books was founded, and published some novels of Agatha Christie among its paperbacks. American Mercury Books was headed by Lawrence Spivak, who later became a TV personality.

As the depression dragged on and war clouds loomed once again, it looked as though paperbacks would rule the publishing trade for many years to come—though no one realized just how big the paperback industry would eventually become. In 1939 the first Pocket Books were published—those familiar volumes whose trademark was a little figure of a kangaroo on the cover. Pocket Books became the largest paperback publishing house up to that time. The company, headed by Robert deGraff, brought out new titles with machine-gun-like rapidity. They literally swarmed on the newsstands and in shops. The standard price for Pocket Books was 25 cents, and it was hard to find anyone in the country who did not own at least a few of them. They became so well known that "pocket books" gradually crept into the language as an alternate name for "paper backs." Many people still refer to all paperbacks as "pocket books."

The years following World War II brought many new publishers into the paperback business. Hardcover books were once again selling fast, but there was not an established market for paperbacks—so both types of books poured into the bookshops. Until the 1960s, the usual arrangement was for paperback publishers to buy the softcover rights to already-published hardcover works. Very few original books came out in paperback. Then, from the 1960s onward, many paperback houses switched from issuing reprints to putting out new works. Today there are many more original works being published in paperback.

PAPERBACK VALUES: HOW MUCH? AND WHY?

If your exposure to the world of out-of-print paperbacks has chiefly been in shops where every title is a dollar apiece, or three for $2.50, some of the values in this book might stun you. The fact is that many old, used, out-of-print paperbacks rank as prime collectors' fare and are valued accordingly. A price of $10, $15 or even $25 for a volume originally selling for 25 cents isn't particularly unusual. On the other hand, there are *millions* of used paperbacks that don't deserve any stiffer price than one dollar apiece, or three for $2.50.

What you find basically in the one dollar apiece shops is a conglomeration of non-collected authors, seventeenth and eighteenth repressings of popular works, and books that WOULD be somewhat valuable if a previous owner hadn't mangled the life out of them. Tucked in amongst them, occasionally, will be a prize plum: a book that you can pick up for the low price of one dollar and resell for $5 or $10.

Nonetheless, this type of shop is not regarded as a first-rate hunting grounds for serious collectors. Some goodies will surface there but you might not be able to carry on any really devoted collecting with the purchases from such shops. The cream of the crop does not gravitate toward little neighborhood shops but rather to the more specialized dealers—some of whom operate shops, some just issue lists.

Amongst the stocks of specialized dealers you will find very early paperbacks from the vintage years of the 1930s and 1940s, FIRST editions (not late reprints) of works by avidly collected authors, and all sorts of things that seldom turn up elsewhere. These are the collectors' delights, and mostly it is hobbyists—not readers—who buy them. If you're principally interested in a certain Agatha Christie blood-curdler for reading, there's no point in paying a hefty premium to get the elusive, much-coveted first edition. It reads just as well in a reissue or anthology.

Understandably, then, it is collectors who are responsible for the values of valuable paperbacks. Readers look for the cheapest copy they can get; collectors want the earliest, scarcest, most pride-boosting specimen for their shelves. The continual competition among collectors drives up the prices, and that is why certain early or especially desirable editions will fetch high sums. It's just the old law of supply and demand at work with its own special twist. Paperbacks were always printed in larger quantities per edition than hardbound books, even back in the 1930s and early 1940s. There was a very extreme difference in original retail prices, between soft and hard covers, in that era. Today, a paperback novel can go for $3 or $4 as against a possible $12 or $15 for a hardbound. Forty-odd years ago, the average paperback was 25 cents and the average novel was $2.50, which meant the paperback sold for only *one tenth* as much. So you know the paperbacks of those days were being ground out in enormously large numbers.

But they didn't survive in enormously large numbers.

Quite the reverse as a matter of fact. As a result of paying such a minimal price for them, most readers were more than content to treat them as "disposable." Mystery story addicts usually bought one a week, read it, and unsentimentally tossed it into the trash can the following week. The destruction rate was not only high, but rapid. Some copies managed to escape the incinerator's fires for a while, as they were passed along to Aunt Mildred after the original purchaser had finished with them. Those that got passed around to several more hands were the rarities. And, of course, they deteriorated in the process. Nobody treated a 25-cent mystery chiller like a string of pearls.

For a 1930s or early 1940s paperback to have survived is one thing. To have survived in presentable shape is quite another. So you will find that quite a value spread exists on the earlier, scarcer books, when it comes to condition. If you just want a certain edition for your library and are willing to take whatever comes along—stained, battered, pulverized —it won't be too costly. But if you're determined to get a decently preserved specimen, you could pay a premium just for the condition.

Most collectors are at least a *bit* fussy about condition, and are becoming more so as the hobby grows progressively refined and so-phisticated. Paperback collecting is a relatively new pastime, insofar as old and rare editions are concerned. Given another five or ten years, it's well within the scope of possibility that the *huge* premiums for fine condition—as are willingly paid by collectors of stamps, coins, etc.—will apply to paperbacks as well.

In a sense, this is still the ground floor of the hobby with the elevator set to ascend. Sure, you might have to pay $10 for a book today that would have cost only $3 in the 1970s. But compared to most hobbies, the values of old and rare paperbacks seem very, very modest. Hardly any of them bring as much as $50, which certainly can't be said of comic books, posters, prints, campaign buttons, or most other things that hobbyists collect. Don't forget that in the 1960s, when comic book collecting got started, many people said that $75 or $100 was awfully high for an Action #1—which today is in the multi-thousand range. It COULD happen with paperbacks, too, though of course there's no guarantee.

COLLECTING PAPERBACKS

Almost everybody has collected paperbacks at one time or another, in the sense of accumulating them. Maybe you've put certain ones away after reading them on the chance that they'd be worthwhile to read again in a couple of years . . . after they fade from vivid memory. Maybe you just stashed them away with the intent of donating them to charity. In the strict sense of the term, this is not *collecting*. It's saving, hoarding, pack-ratting, or lots of other things, but not real collecting.

Collecting is the impulse to buy and save without reading as your main purpose. The postage stamp collector does not mail letters with his stamps, and the paperback book collector—while he might sometimes read his books—is after loftier pursuits.

Most paperback collectors fall into one of three groups:

AUTHOR collectors, SUBJECT collectors, or PUBLISHER collectors.

Of these, the author collectors are by far the majority. They want to build complete sets of the paperback editions of works by their favorite authors, and they want them (usually) in the first editions rather than later reissues. If that means going after scarce and more expensive books, so much the better. The presence of those first editions means more class for their collection, plus the good possibility that it will increase in value through the years. The more desirable a paperback is, the more likely it will continue to rise in price. Some collectors have even made tidy profits reselling their collection, though investment in the strict sense is the goal of very, very few of them.

SUBJECT collectors approach the hobby with a broader target in mind. Instead of narrowing themselves down to a specific author, they want books of various different authors—perhaps of *any* authors so long as they fall into a given subject category. With paperbacks, the chief subject collection categories are: MYSTERY, SCIENCE FICTION, ADVENTURE, OLD WEST, ROMANCE, HISTORICAL, and SLEAZE ("sleaze" being a general category including all paperback novels with super-spicy cover art).

A subject collection will grow somewhat faster than an author collection. It can even grow too fast and get out of hand, so it's smart to set some kind of guidelines before becoming too deeply involved. If your chosen field is simply "mystery," there are at least 100,000 paperbacks that fall into that category. (You don't really want to collect 100,000 paperbacks, do you? At roughly eight ounces apiece that's 25 tons of books.) If the available selection is too great, it's really worse than having too few to choose from. And this is precisely what will happen if you collect along general subject lines without fencing yourself in a bit. How do you do that? By deciding not to buy any title issued after 1950, for example. Or figuring out a list of half a dozen authors to stay with. Or buying only books that have at least 400 pages in them. Maybe you want to collect paperbacks by the covers, which is becoming more and more popular all the time.

The PUBLISHER collectors are very, very specialized. Sometimes, author and subject collectors do not comprehend the motives behind PUBLISHER collecting. But, in fact, publisher collecting is the ONE approach to paperback collecting that bears very strong resemblance to other collecting hobbies. In publisher collecting, you try to assemble a set of the books of a given publisher, maybe all of his books, or just his mysteries (for example) if his mysteries were a separate and distinct series with their own serial numbers. Then it's a game of "filling in the blanks" as your collection grows. The blanks will usually be the scarcer, harder to get titles. This kind of collection lines up very well on shelves, as the serial numbers follow each other in consecutive order and prove —even to a non-collector—that you've got something more than just a bunch of books.

You're the only one who can make the ultimate decision on what sort of collection is right for *you*.

BUYING PAPERBACKS

You might be accustomed to buying your paperbacks at the drugstore. As a collector you won't necessarily be avoiding that source; tomorrow's hot collectible is today's freshly published title, and there's no better way to get it than for the cover price. If you're building an author collection and the author is still turning them out, you certainly want to get his latest titles immediately. Any stalling around and you might find "second impression" or "third printing before publication" or other distressing words on the reverse side of the title-page.

You won't be turning your back on the drugstore, but most of your acquisitions as a collector will be made from secondhand sources. In collector parlance, "secondhand" is not a derogatory word. It simply means that you are not the first owner of the book. And, obviously, you cannot be, if it was issued in 1944 and you were born in 1956. Virtually every collector's item, including the Hope Diamond, is secondhand. Or third, or fourth, or fifth. The amount of traveling it's done is not so important as the condition, though.

Where are the secondhand sources?

Your own attic might be one of them. Or try the lawn sales, the thrift bazaars, flea markets, junkshops, or anywhere that used merchandise is offered. You will find paperbacks in just about every secondhand store amidst the pop-up toasters and moth-nibbled fashions. On a higher level, there are the secondhand bookshops and specialist dealers who issue catalogues of out-of-print paperbacks. Dealing in old, scarce paperbacks has become a thriving business these days, so there are plenty of individuals pursuing it. Check the classified ad pages of collecting publications such as *Hobbies, Collectors News,* and *The Antique Trader Weekly* (among numerous others) for names and addresses of dealers who have lists. Some of them will make a small charge for their lists, which can usually be deducted from your first order. In any case, if you're going to be a serious *collector* of paperbacks instead of just a *reader,* you need to get as many *current* lists as you possibly can. Each dealer's stock is different. What you find on the list of one dealer bears no relation to what is contained in another's list. Get them all, read them all, and make your selections accordingly.

Buying through the mail is becoming the accepted thing in paperback collecting. Not everyone has a used paperbacks shop close by. Even if such a shop is within your sphere of travel, it may not carry the type of titles or the authors that interest you. In buying through the mail, you can rest assured of finding every possible book that you might want to buy, though it may take a little time to locate a particular title. There is no such thing as a paperback you can't find if you really look diligently —how much you're going to pay for it is another point.

The listings in this book show the current average prices for thousands of paperbacks in *very good* condition. Obviously there are many others which could not be listed in the available space. Even on those which we do list, we advise you to shop around a little from one dealer to another unless you're extremely anxious to make the purchase. Instead of buying a second or third edition, you might be able to locate a first edition at just about the same price. In the case of books valued at $15, $20 or $25, one dealer might be several dollars higher or lower than another on a copy in the *identical* grade of condition. So, keep up with the lists and other literature of dealers.

In reading a dealer's list, make sure you clearly understand what it says. Every dealer—no matter how meticulously he compiles his lists —receives orders from some people who think they're getting something other than the listed title. They mistake the name of one author for that of another, the title of one book for the title of another; they overlook the fact that the book is listed as the 8th or 9th edition; they ignore references to poor condition, and so on.

As yet there is no uniform way for a dealer's pricelist to be arranged. You will receive some lists in which the books are all arranged in groups by author (as is the practice followed in *The Official Price Guide to Paperbacks and Magazines).* Others have the listings set up by publisher, and instead of running alphabetically by author they work sequentially by the serial numbers of the books. On such a list, Avon #2 follows Avon #1, regardless of whether the authors are the same or even if the books bear any relation in subject matter. When a list is arranged in that fashion, fiction and non-fiction can be mixed together.

Regardless of how a list is laid out, though, it will usually carry the essential information needed by a collector in making his decision of whether or not to buy: author, title, publisher, publisher's serial number (for that book), year of publication, edition number (first, second, etc.). Any information beyond this is considered gravy, such as the number of pages or what sort of cover it has. Since most dealers try to squeeze as many titles as possible into their lists, brevity in describing them is the rule. Almost all descriptions are one-liners, with abbreviation being the order of the day. But you will quickly come to realize that ND means No Date, ED means Editor, 1st is First Edition, R is a Reprint, AN or ANT is an Anthology and so forth.

It is not wise to make any assumptions when reading a dealer's list or contemplating a possible order. If the dealer fails to state that a book is the first edition, you should not (under normal circumstances) presume that it is, just because it was published in the right year to be a first edition. With the vast majority of popular paperbacks, additional printings hit the stands in the same year as the first printing. Keep in mind that the dealer is trying to sell his books. You can generally count on him to mention everything favorable about them. He is not too likely to omit calling attention to a first edition.

When you buy paperbacks in a shop, you might find that all titles are arranged by author with the subjects mixed . . . or arranged by subject . . . or not arranged in any way, shape or form. A non-arranged or "loose" stock is the sure sign of a shop that isn't catering too strongly to collectors. Most collectors just won't patronize that kind of establishment, as they don't have all day to search through 50,000 or 100,000 books. The prices do tend to be lower when the stock is jumbled together, however, so if you're a beginner, you might want to browse.

If the stock is neatly arranged, if the books are not too dusty, and the overall physical condition of the books looks acceptable, this is likely to be a shop that does ample business with collectors. Within a few minutes the owner will be able to tell you—or you'll be able to tell yourself—whether a given title is in stock. In this kind of shop, the scarce titles might be encased in vinyl or mylar bags, and there will probably be a no-nonsense sign reading "THIS IS NOT A LIBRARY," or words to that effect. In other words: whether you buy it or not, don't read it on the premises.

When you're buying in person, you have to do the same sort of work that goes into preparing a dealer's list. You won't have anybody telling you whether or not it's a first edition, so you'll need to look. Also, note the condition. Once your collection has grown beyond the formative stage, you may want to carry a checklist with you of the titles already in your possession to avoid duplication. It is very difficult, if you own several hundred or more books, to keep track of all of them by memory.

PAPERBACK CARE AND STORAGE

As collector's items go, paperback books are very easy to take care of. This might seem hard to believe when you survey the general condition of old, used paperbacks and see every conceivable sort of damage. It looks as though paperbacks are very, very fragile and likely to fall prey to just about any kind of potential harm. Actually, 99% of the wear and tear in evidence on used paperbacks could have been—and should have been—prevented, with a little care exercised on the part of former owners. If you exercise that kind of care, there is no reason why you should experience any difficulty in keeping your paperbacks in the best grade of condition—or, at least, no worse than the condition in which you acquired them.

Most things that go wrong with the physical condition of paperbacks do so because of accident or abuse. Left to itself, a paperback will not get wrinkled, stained, or soiled. The cover will not fall off and the pages will not come loose. One thing that does happen with age is discoloration of the pages, and there is really not much you can do to prevent this, especially since most old paperbacks are already pretty discolored. You will notice discoloration (browning or yellowing) in paperbacks much more than in hardcovered books, simply because a lower grade of paper was used. The older the book, the worse this problem is apt to be, not because of age but economic considerations. In the very earliest days of paperbacks (late 1930s) every possible corner was cut to reduce their cover prices, including the use of really bad paper. Publishers were aiming for the read-it-and-discard-it market, not giving any thought to the possibility that some readers might want to save their paperbacks. This line of reasoning led also to the use of cheap glues to hold the pages to the spine, in many cases with no staples and hardly ever with stitching. You guessed it: the book was not programmed for a long and happy life. The situation gradually changed, though, and today we've reached the point where paperbacks are manufactured just about as well as hardcovered books . . . though of course the lack of a hard binding makes them somewhat more vulnerable to bruises and bangs.

These poor quality papers were high in two elements that spell slow death to paper: wood pulp and acid. Acidity makes paper turn a different color; too much wood pulp causes paper to become very stiff and, eventually, brittle.

If you buy a paperback in good condition (no serious problems), it can be kept in a bookcase or on a wall unit shelf, so long as it stands upright, not lying down on the side—and not tipped-over books resting diagonally against each other. A book has to stand upright to stay in good condition. Lying flat is more harmful (potentially) for a paperback than for a hardcovered book, though it's not recommended for either. If the book has a laminated or "glossy" cover, it can stick to the shelf or to another book, or whatever it's resting on. Letting books tip over is bad, as this splays out the pages and causes the spine to weaken: If left that way too long, they can become permanently out of shape.

Along those lines, it should be unnecessary to point out that books must not be jammed into shelves. Too many owners make the effort to utilize every inch of a bookcase or other storage unit, cramming and jamming. A paperback collection is best kept in a bookcase with adjustable shelves. Since paperbacks are smaller than hardbacks, you will be able to add an extra shelf or two within the case and utilize your available space in that fashion—which beats cramming.

Do not position your bookcase or wall shelving near a source of heat or moisture, such as an air conditioning unit, window, heating duct, stove, or fireplace. To make sure you've taken every possible precaution, determine if there are overhead plumbing pipes in the room and get the bookcase away from them, just in case. Generally speaking, it is better not to situate your library on the top floor of a house, unless there is an attic overhead. If the roof is directly overhead, the upper floor will be damper than the lower and this could cause problems. And by all means rule out the cellar as a possible storage area, as it will be damper still.

Do not attempt to repair your books with cellophane tape or any other kind of tape, no matter how "invisible" it may be, unless the book is so badly damaged that the value couldn't be hurt any further. If the laminated cover of a paperback is soiled it can be wiped with a damp cloth and then dried, but be sure to avoid getting the pages wet. Soiling inside the book may possibly be removed with a pencil eraser, depending on its nature. You should assume, when buying a soiled book, that it cannot be cleaned up.

SELLING PAPERBACKS

Your paperbacks are worth money. Paperback books always have some kind of value, if they're complete (no pages or covers missing) and in a good state of preservation. Even if a book is only valued for reading purposes, this can still be translated into dollars and cents, or, at the least, cents. So—never throw away a paperback. Sell it! If you aren't able to sell it to a secondhand bookshop, sell it as part of your next lawn or garage sale. If you can't sell it at all, put it away for the future. It isn't going to consume much space and, who knows, it might increase in value within the coming years. Maybe by then you'll be stampeded with offers for it.

With your better-grade paperbacks—the old, scarce titles by popular authors—you generally will not find a problem selling to dealers. The dealers regularly buy these books to replenish their stocks and are receptive to anyone who has them for sale at a reasonable sum. The price, of course, is the keynote to whether you'll be chalking up a sale or packing them back in the carton for the return trip home. If you compare a dealer's buying prices against the prices listed in this book, you're apt to be disappointed. But unless you sell directly to collectors, it would be very difficult for you—as a non-dealer—to obtain these prices. When you sell paperbacks to a dealer, you're selling at what amounts to a wholesale price.

What is the wholesale price?

That depends on the book, its condition, its age, and how much the dealer really wants or needs it. It may also depend a little on how good a salesman you are. If the book is quite recent, published say within the past five years, it most likely ranks as a "reading" book rather than a "collecting" book, at least at this point in time. This means the dealer would probably offer it on his shelves at a discount from the original cover price, rather than the premium over the cover price that he would apply to an old or scarce title. The wholesale price is always calculated on his selling price—never on the book's cover price, which may be far out of line with its current value as a secondhand book.

You will find that most dealers in secondhand paperbacks will buy the recent discount-from-cover-price material only if they can get it at a very favorable price. Chances are, they already have some copies of that particular title on hand, with opportunities to get more every day. They aren't going to stretch for something that just isn't worth stretching for. If a dealer is going to sell a book for one dollar, the odds are that he'll pay you 25 cents in cash for it. But if you want to trade, he might do much better for you, taking two or three of your books in trade for one of his.

If you have old, scarce, desirable paperbacks to sell, you will do better than 25 cents on the dollar vs. the dealer's selling price. For a book worth $10, you should be able to get no less than $4 from most dealers and possibly as much as $5. Of course, the condition must be good, and it must be the sort of book for which the particular dealer has some demand among his clientele. If he's selling science fiction, he probably won't want Mickey Spillane no matter your selling price. Selling by mail is a good idea as you reach dealers who specialize in the precise type of books you have and will pay you top dollar.

GRADING PAPERBACKS

An ever present factor in the price of a used paperback is its physical condition. With collectors (as opposed to readers) comprising a growing segment of the market for used paperbacks, condition is more important today than ever. Most collectors are willing to pay a premium for books in the best condition, and dealers are well aware of this. On the other hand, if a book is damaged, it is quite likely no collector will want it and the ultimate purchaser will be just a reader. The beginning collector should waste no time learning the grading terminology, as he will then be able to visualize the condition of any paperback offered in a dealer's list. He should likewise learn to apply the grading principles himself, to grade books found on browsing expeditions and those already in his possession. The apparent bargain that turns up at a flea market or lawn sale will likely prove quite the reverse, unless the book has been correctly graded.

Paperbacks are of course found in every conceivable state of condition. On the whole their condition is somewhat lower than that of hardcovered books of a similar age. The lack of a hard binding exposes their pages to greater wear and possible injury. The covers, being soft, can easily become creased or torn. The covers of a paperback are much more likely to be loose, or missing, than the covers of a hardcovered book. Additionally, paperbacks tend to receive rougher treatment. Their small convenient size encourages them to be carried in pocket or purse, to be read on the train or bus, while hardcovered volumes normally remain safely at home. As most owners do not intend to keep them after reading, no great respect is paid to the handling of them. Page corners are routinely bent down to mark the reader's place, and underlinings are made to note passages. Quite often the paperback also serves as a notation pad or a handy vehicle for doodling. You will find many in which phone numbers have been jotted, and even grocery lists. As paperbacks are far more frequently read while dining or snacking than hardcovered books, they will carry more stains. One collector reported finding a whole strip of bacon in a used paperback, but obviously this is an extreme case. Paperbacks pass through more hands than hardcover books, too. Most people do not routinely give away their hardcover books, but paperbacks are swapped and given away regularly. This means they are handled more often and that contributes to deterioration.

It is important to distinguish between deterioration caused by handling or accident, and natural deterioration. Presence of the first constitutes damage to one degree or another, as it could have been prevented. Presence of natural deterioration is not looked upon as damage, as it will be common to virtually all copies of that particular book. Natural deterioration is the effect of age on a paperback book. Paperbacks as a species do not age very gracefully. The earliest ones were printed on a low grade of paper, and even as recently as the 1960s most paperback novels utilized mediocre paper. Paperbacks dating from the late 1930s to late 1940s, especially those with a cover price of 10 cents, will show considerable natural deterioration. If judged on their appearance, one would guess them to be much older. The pages have become discolored and usually quite brittle. Almost always the staples, if any were used in binding the book, are rusty and the rust has stained some pages. While the condition of such books may be unappealing to some collectors, it would be unfair to term them "damaged." Natural deterioration of early paperbacks could have been prevented only by long storage in an acid-free, humidity-controlled environment. Their original owners, who invested 10 cents in them, were certainly not about to take such measures. Thus the collector can expect, at the very best, to locate copies that have suffered no damage in addition to their natural deterioration.

Paperback collecting has come a long way in applying grading standards to price, but there is still no universal formula for this in the hobby. You cannot say that a *G* (good) copy is worth 30% less than a *VG* (very good), or that an *M* (mint) should bring twice as much as an *F* (fine). A VG is unquestionably worth more than a G, and an M always outsells an F or VF (very fine), assuming we are talking about the exact same edition of the exact same book. If the editions are different, or there are any other variations, condition alone may not dictate which is worth more. For example, a "third impression" in VG condition might outsell a sixteenth impression in F, depending on circumstances. Actually the M (mint) grade is seldom used, as so few paperbacks can measure up to it. Even if you examine paperbacks that have come straight from the distributor, many will grade less than M. An M paperback prior to 1950 is just about unheard of.

Today you will find many used paperbacks with repairs of various kinds, which is rather a recent phenomenon. Before collectors started buying paperbacks heavily, few repaired specimens were seen. The dealers did not bother attempting repairs, nor did the parties who sold used paperbacks to dealers. It was presumed that damage would not deter a potential customer, as the customer would be a reader and not a collector. Also, used paperbacks were much less expensive then, and the labor required in making repairs was considered unrewarding. Now it is quite a different picture. Most of the same kinds of repairs found on used hardcover books are likewise found on paperbacks. The most common is reglued covers. Paperbacks should always be examined for possible repairs as well as unrepaired damaged. The basic attitude toward repairs is that they do not increase the value but they do serve a cosmetic purpose in improving the appearance of a damaged or deteriorated book. The danger lies in paying a VF price for a book which is really a G, but gives the appearance of being VF thanks to skilled repair. Some collectors do their own repairs.

The following are the major grades into which paperbacks fall, along with the usual characteristics of each grade. Refer to the Glossary for detailed explanations of the various types of damage.

M (Mint). Fresh, clean, and perfect in every respect. For the majority of out-of-print paperbacks, no mint copies exist.

VF (Very Fine). The highest grade of condition in which it is reasonable to expect used paperbacks to be found (the term Near Mint, used in comic book collecting, is seldom applied to paperbacks). A VF copy gives the appearance of being unused, though it may have very minor soiling on the covers or along the edges of pages. The presence of a dealer's rubber stamp or other marking on the front cover, or front flyleaf, does not disqualify it from a VF ranking. Nor does the presence of a former owner's bookplate on the inside front cover. A few page corners may be lightly creased. If the book is printed on low quality paper, and is rather old, it will have interior discoloration. The cover should not be discolored.

F (Fine). Identical in many respects to VF but with some evidence of use and handling. The cover may be lightly faded from sun exposure. There may be minor chips missing from the covers. If a chip is wider than ⅛th of an inch it is not considered minor, and the book should not be classified as F. The cellophane overlay on the covers is intact. There is no staining, no repairs, no "spine roll."

VG (Very Good). For most collectors, VG copies are perfectly acceptable when priced accordingly. If the cover is creased, the book cannot rate higher than VG, even if sound in other respects. However to earn the VG grading, rather than a lesser one, the crease should be fairly light and no more than 3 inches in length. It should not run from the top to the bottom of the cover. A bit of the cellophane may be missing from the cover. This is the highest grade in which repairs can be encountered; repaired books are not included in the F or VF grades. The repair must be minor or else the grade will be less than VG. There is no water staining in a VG book, no cover shrinkage, but the book may have slight spine roll or looseness.

G (Good). This is the lowest grade that most collectors will tolerate, and many will tolerate it only if the book is hard to find. Essentially a G book is a reading copy but passable for collecting if one is not disturbed by signs of use and abuse. The pages of a G graded book will likely be discolored but not brittle. Both the front and back covers, as well as spine, will have pieces missing, but if the pieces are really large the book should be demoted to FR (fair) or lower. Spine roll will be noticeable, the book will be rather loose but not detached from its covers, the covers are apt to be creased more heavily than one would expect of a VG rated book. This is the highest grade in which water staining may be present, and to grade G it must not be severe. Water staining is, to a collector, one of the most objectionable forms of damage.

FR (Fair). A reading copy, complete with all pages and both covers, but sub-standard for collecting purposes. The typical FR graded book lacks all of its cellophane cover lamination. The book is quite loose in its covers, the covers are badly creased, there is moderate to severe staining, repairs have been made with cellophane tape on the covers and/or pages.

P (Poor). The lowest grade. There should be no pages missing in a P graded book, meaning it is acceptable for reading, but it will be very noticeably damaged. These books normally sell for 10% to 20% of the VF price.

PAPERBACK LISTINGS

	Current Price Range		C/Y Avg.
☐ **Aarons, Edward,** *Assignment: Budapest,* Gold Medal 971	4.00	5.25	4.50
☐ *Assignment: Burma Girl,* Gold Medal 1091	3.85	4.85	4.00
☐ *Assignment: Zoraya,* Gold Medal 979	4.00	5.25	4.50
☐ **Aarons, Edward,** *State Department Murders,* Gold Medal R2260, no date	1.50	2.25	1.87
☐ *Terror In The Town,* MacFadden 60-356. 1968, second edition	1.75	2.50	2.12
☐ *Terror In The Town,* Manor 95321, 1974, fourth edition	1.35	1.85	1.50
☐ *They All Ran Away,* MacFadden 75-307, 1970	1.35	1.85	1.50
☐ **Aarons, Will B.,** *Assignment Mermaid,* Gold Medal 1-4203, first edition	1.35	1.85	1.50
☐ *Assignment 13th Princess,* Gold Medal 1-3919, first edition	1.35	1.85	1.50
☐ **Abbey, Kieran,** *Beyond The Dark,* Dell Map 93, 1945	2.75	3.75	3.25
☐ **Abbot, Anthony,** *About Murder Of The Circus Queen,* Popular 159, 1948	6.00	8.00	6.37
☐ *About Murder Night Club Lady,* Green Dragon 27, no date	8.00	11.00	8.50
☐ *The Creeps,* Dell Map 88, 1945	10.00	14.00	11.25
☐ *Murder Of The Clergman's Mistress,* Popular 286, 1950	5.75	7.75	6.00
☐ **Adams, Cleve F.,** *Contraband,* Signet 902, 1951	2.00	2.75	2.37
☐ *Contraband,* Signet 1298, 1956, third edition	3.00	4.00	3.50
☐ *The Crooking Finger,* Dell Map 104, 1946	7.00	10.00	7.50
☐ *No Wings On A Cop,* Handi-Book 112, 1950	5.75	7.75	6.75
☐ *Private Eye,* Signet D2588, 1964, second edition	1.50	2.25	1.87

	Current Price Range		C/Y Avg.

☐ *Sabotage,* Signet 936, 1952, third edition **2.00** **2.75** **2.37**

☐ *Sabotage,* Signet 1419, 1957, fourth edition **1.50** **2.25** **1.87**

☐ *Sabotage,* Penguin 522, 1944, second edition ...., **5.00** **7.00** **6.00**

☐ *What Price Murder,* Popular Library 456, 1952 .... **4.00** **5.50** **4.75**

☐ **Adams, Clifton,** *A Noose For the Desperado,* Gold Medal 50 1375 .... **4.00** **5.00** **4.55**

☐ *Killer in Town,* Dell A199 .... **4.25** **5.25** **4.75**

☐ **Adams, Joey,** *Cindy and I,* Popular Library G371 .... **6.00** **8.00** **7.00**

☐ **Adams, John Paul,** *We Dare You To Solve This,* Berkley 766 .... **4.50** **5.50** **4.75**

☐ **Adams, Richard N.,** *Social Change in Latin America Today,* Vintage V196 ... **4.25** **5.25** **4.50**

☐ **Adams, Samuel H.,** *Tambay Gold,* Dell 20, no date **4.00** **6.00** **4.85**

☐ **Addams, Charles,** *Addams and Evil,* Pocket Books 50063, 1965 .... **7.00** **10.00** **8.25**

☐ *Home Bodies,* Pocket Books 50062, 1964 .... **7.00** **10.00** **8.25**

☐ *Night Crawlers,* Pocket Books 50060 **7.00** **10.00** **8.25**

☐ **Addams, Kay,** *Strangest Sin,* Beacon #8444Y **1.60** **2.00** **1.80**

☐ **Adler, Bill,** *Letters From Camp,* MacFadden 35-113 (interior illustrations by Sid Hoff, 1962) **6.00** **8.00** **6.75**

☐ **Aherne, Owen,** *An Affair to Remember,* Avon T182 (photo cover picturing Cary Grant and Deborah Kerr, interior photos from motion picture) **8.00** **11.00** **9.00**

☐ *Man On Fire,* Avon T177 (photo cover picturing Bing Crosby, Inger Stevens, E.G. Marshall, interior photos from motion picture) **8.00** **11.00** **9.25**

☐ **Ahlers, Arvel W.** *Ansco Guide To Picture Fun Made Easy,* Popular Library PC1021 **3.50** **4.25** **3.80**

☐ **Alain (no first name),** *Yoga For Perfect Health,* Pyramid 659 .... **4.00** **5.25** **4.45**

	Current Price Range		C/Y Avg.

☐ **Albee, George S.,** *By the Sea,* Avon F102 . . . .   4.00   5.25   4.45

☐ **Albert, Marvin,** *Come September,* Dell K101 (photo cover picturing Rock Hudson and Gina Lollobrigida) 5.00   7.00   5.75

☐   *The Long White Road,* Pyramid 532 (cover artwork by Crair, interior artwork by Patricia Window) 4.00   5.00   4.50

☐   *Party Girl,* Gold Medal 808 (photo cover picturing Robert Taylor and Vicki Gaye) 5.00   7.00   6.00

☐   *Pillow Talk,* Gold Medal 918 (photo cover picturing Doris Day, Rock Hudson and Tony Randall) 5.00   7.00   6.00

☐   *That Jane From Maine,* Dell 296 (photo cover picturing Doris Day, Jack Lemmon, Ernie Kovacs, Garry Moore, Dave Garroway and Bill Cullen) 6.00   8.00   7.00

☐ **Albrand, Martha,** *After Midnight,* Dell Map 396, no date 3.00   4.00   3.50

☐   *After Midnight,* Dell Map 396, 1950 . .   2.00   2.75   2.87

☐   *A Call From Austria,* Pyramid X-1496, 1966 . . . .   1.75   2.50   2.12

☐   *A Day In Monte Carlo,* Ace G-563, no date 2.00   2.75   2.37

☐   *A Day In Monte Carlo,* Avon V2431, 1972 . . . .   1.25   1.75   1.60

☐   *Desperate Moment,* Dell 651, 1953 . .   2.00   2.75   2.37

☐   *A Door Fell Shut,* Signet T3331, 1967   1.75   2.50   2.12

☐   *The Linden Affair,* Berkley G487, 1960   2.00   3.00   2.50

☐   *Manhattan North,* Avon V2483, 1973   1.25   1.75   1.50

☐   *The Mask Of Alexander,* Pyramid X-1387, 1966 . . . .   1.85   2.50   2.12

☐   *Meet Me Tonight,* Ace G-542, 1965 . .   1.85   2.50   2.12

☐   *Nightmare In Copenhagen,* Pyramid X-1386, 1966 . . . .   1.85   2.50   2.12

☐   *No Surrender,* Pocket 247, 1944, third edition 2.00   3.00   2.50

☐   *None Shall Know,* Award A257X, 1967   1.75   2.50   2.12

☐   *Remembered Anger,* Avon 14464, 1973 . . . .   1.25   1.75   1.50

		Current Price Range		C/Y Avg.
☐	*Rhine Replica,* Avon V2466, 1972 ...	1.25	1.75	1.50
☐	*Wait For the Dawn,* Dell Map 544, 1951	3.25	4.75	3.50
☐	*Wait For The Dawn,* Avon 14696, 1973	1.50	2.00	1.75
☐	*Without Orders,* Award A258S, 1967	1.75	2.50	2.12
☑	*Without Orders,* Armed D-96, 1944 ..	6.50	9.00	7.25
☐	**Albright, William F.,** *From the Stone Age To Christianity,* Anchor 100 (cover artwork by Fransconi)	4.00	5.00	4.50
☐	**Alcott, Louisa M.,** *Little Women,* Dell 296 (photo cover picturing Elizabeth Taylor, June Allyson, Janet Leigh, Margaret O'Brien and Mary Astor)	5.00	7.00	6.00
☐	**Aldiss, Blish, and Harrison** (ED), *Decade The 1950's,* Pan 25034, 1977	2.25	3.50	2.50
☐	(ED), *Nebula Award Two,* Pocket 75114, 1968	2.25	3.50	2.50
☐	*The Airs Of Earth,* Nel 20975, 1975, second edition	3.00	4.00	3.00
☐	(ED), *All About Venus,* Dell 0085, 1968	1.75	2.50	2.12
☐	*Bow Down To Nul,* Ace F-382, no date	2.00	3.00	2.50
☐	*Brothers Of The Head,* Pierrot 01, second edition, 1977, illustrated	8.00	11.00	8.50
☐	*Cryptozoic,* Sphere 1104, 1974, fourth edition	2.00	3.00	2.50
☐	*Cryptozoic!* Avon V2295, 1969	1.75	2.50	2.12
☐	*Dark Light-Years,* Signet D2497, 1964	2.50	3.75	2.50
☐	*Dark Light-Years,* Signet T4586, 1971 second edition	1.50	2.00	1.75
☐	*Dark Light-Years,* 4 square 1437, 1966	2.75	4.00	2.87
☐	*Earthworks,* Signet P3116, 1967	2.00	2.75	2.37
☐	*Earthworks,* 4 Square 1741, 1967 ...	2.75	4.00	2.87
☐	*Earthworks,* Nel 022218, 1974, second edition	1.50	2.00	1.75
☐	*The Eighty-Minute Hour,* Pan 24547, 1975	2.00	2.75	2.37
☐	*Enemies Of The System,* Panther 04996, 1981, second edition	2.50	3.25	2.87
☐	(ED), *Evil Earth,* Avon 44636, 1979 ..	2.00	2.75	2.37
☐	*Frankenstein Unbound,* Crest Q2473, 1975	1.50	2.00	1.75
☐	(ED), *Galactic Empires 2,* Orbit 7909, 1976	2.00	3.00	2.50

		Current Price Range		C/Y Avg.
☐	*Galaxies Like Grains Of Sand,* Signet T4781, second edition	1.00	1.50	1.25
☐	*Galaxies Like Grains Of Sand,* Signet S1815, 1960	2.00	3.00	2.50
☐	*Greybeard,* Signet F2689, 1965	3.00	4.25	3.00
☐	*Greybeard,* Signet Q5141, second edition	1.50	2.00	1.75
☐	*Intangibles, Inc.,* Corgi 08626, 1971 . .	2.00	3.00	2.50
☐	*Intangibles, Inc.,* Corgi 10044, 1975, second edition	1.75	2.50	2.12
☐	*The Interpreter,* Nel 014576, 1973, second edition	2.00	3.00	2.50
☐	*The Long Afternoon Of Earth,* Signet T4557, second edition	2.00	3.00	2.50
☐	*No Time Like Tomorrow,* Signet S1683, 1959	4.00	5.50	4.75
☐	*No Time Like Tomorrow,* Signet 4605, second edition	1.25	1.75	1.50
☐	*Non-Stop,* Pan 24638, 1976	2.00	2.75	2.37
☐	(ED), *Penguin Science Fiction,* Penguin 1638, 1961, second edition	2.75	3.50	3.12
☐	*The Primal Urge,* Sphere 10987, 1972, second edition	2.00	3.00	2.50
☐	*Report On Probability A.,* Sphere 1101, 1973, second edition	1.75	2.50	2.12
☐	*Report On Probability A.,* Lancer 74677, no date	2.00	3.00	2.50
☐	*The Saliva Tree,* Sphere 10898, 1968	2.00	3.00	2.50
☐	*The Saliva Tree,* Sphere 1102, 1973, third edition	1.75	2.50	2.12
☐	*Starship,* Signet D2271, 1963, second edition	2.00	3.00	2.50
☐	*Starship,* Avon V2321, 1969	1.25	1.75	1.50
☐	*Starswarm,* Signet D2411, 1964	2.00	3.00	2.50
☐	*Starswarm,* Signet 4558, third edition	1.75	2.50	2.12
☐	*Starswarm,* Signet T4558, 1971, second edition	1.75	2.50	2.12
☐	**Aldrich, Ann,** *We Walk Alone,* Gold Medal 509, 1956, second edition	5.50	7.50	6.00
☐	**Alexander, David,** *Dead Man Dead,* Dell D362 (cover artwork by Maguire)	4.25	5.25	4.50

	Current Price Range		C/Y Avg.

☐ **Alexander, Robert J.,** *Today's Latin America,* Anchor 327 .... 3.50 4.25 3.50

☐ **Algren, Nelson,** *The Man With the Golden Arm,* Cardinal C31 (photo cover picturing Frank Sinatra, Kim Novack and Eleanor Parker) 6.00 8.00 6.50

☐ **Allan, Jack,** *Good Time Girl,* Newstand Library U148, 1960 .... 1.50 2.00 1.75

☐ **Allan, Nick,** *The End Zone,* Brandon 1064 .... 4.00 5.00 4.25

☐ **Allen, Eric,** *Like Wild,* Monarch 345 (cover artwork by Ericson) 4.75 5.75 5.00

☐ **Allen, Steve,** *Mark It and Strike It,* Hillman 60-100 (photo cover picturing the author) 6.00 8.00 6.75

☐ **Allingham, Margery,** *The Allingham Case-Book,* Manor 12248, 1974, second edition 1.25 1.75 1.50

☐ *The Allingham Case-Book,* MacFadden 95-178, 1972 .... 1.25 1.75 1.50

☐ *Black Dudley Murder,* MacFadden 50-147, 1962 .... 2.50 3.75 2.37

☐ *Black Dudley Murder,* MacFadden 60-254, 1966, second edition 1.75 2.50 2.12

☐ *The Black Dudley Murders,* Manor 95257, 1973, third edition 1.50 2.00 1.75

☐ *Black Plumes,* Bestseller B33, no date 2.50 3.50 3.00

☐ *Black Plumes,* Manor 95277, 1973, second edition 1.25 1.75 1.50

☐ *Cargo of Eagles,* Manor 15321, 1976 1.25 1.75 1.50

☐ *Cargo Of Eagles,* MacFadden 75-271, 1969 .... 1.75 2.50 1.50

☐ *Cargo Of Eagles,* Manor 95299, 1973, second edition 1.25 1.75 1.50

☐ *The China Governess,* MacFadden 60-199, 1964 .... 2.50 3.50 2.50

☐ *The China Governess,* Penguin C2312, 1967, second edition 2.00 3.00 2.50

☐ *The China Governess,* Manor 15314, no date 1.25 1.75 1.50

☐ *Crime At Black Dudley,* Penguin C770, 1963, fifth edition 2.25 3.00 2.62

	Current Price Range		C/Y Avg.
☐ *The Crime At Black Dudley,* Penguin 770, 1961, fourth edition	2.50	3.50	3.00
☐ *The Crime At Black Dudley,* Penguin 770, 1977, twelfth edition	1.75	2.50	2.12
☐ *Dancers In Mourning,* MacFadden 75-436, 1971, third edition	1.25	1.75	1.50
☐ *Dancers In Mourning,* MacFadden 50-136, 1962	2.00	2.50	2.25
☐ *Deadly Duo,* Manor 12341, 1975	1.50	2.00	1.75
☐ *Deadly Duo,* Manor 95291, 1973, second edition	1.00	1.50	1.25
☐ *Deadly Duo,* Avon G1238, 1964, third edition	2.00	2.50	2.25
☐ *Deadly Duo,* Avon F-114, 1961	3.00	4.50	3.12
☐ *Deadly Duo,* MacFadden 75-297, 1970	1.25	1.75	1.50
☐ *Death Of A Ghost,* Penguin 503, 1946, fourth edition	5.00	7.25	6.12
☐ *Estate Of Beckoning Lady,* MacFadden, 75-468, 1972, third edition	1.25	1.75	1.50
☐ *Estate Of Beckoning Lady,* MacFadden, 50-155, 1962	2.50	3.50	3.00
☐ *The Fashion In Shrouds,* Pocket 329, 1945	7.00	10.75	6.87
☐ *The Fear Sign,* MacFadden 50-115, 1963, second edition	2.00	3.00	2.50
☐ *The Fear Sign,* MacFadden 60-323, 1968, third edition	1.75	2.50	2.12
☐ *The Fear Sign,* Manor 12419, 1976 . .	1.25	1.75	1.50
☐ *Flowers For The Judge,* Penguin 459, 1961, seventh edition	3.50	4.50	4.00
☐ *Mystery Mile,* MacFadden 60-129, 1963	1.35	1.85	1.50
☐ *Mystery Mile,* Manor 12280, 1975 . . .	1.35	1.85	1.50
☐ *Mystery Mile,* Penguin 761, 1963, fifth edition	2.00	3.00	2.50
☐ *Mystery Mile,* MacFadden 60-292, 1967, second edition	1.25	1.75	1.50
☐ *No Love Lost,* Penguin 1416, 1960, second edition	1.75	2.50	2.12
☐ *No Love Lost,* MacFadden 50-130, 1962	1.25	1.75	1.50

		Current Price Range		C/Y Avg.
☐	*No Love Lost,* MacFadden 60-245, 1966, second edition	3.00	4.00	3.50
☐	*No Love Lost,* Manor 12350, 1975 . . .	2.00	2.75	2.37
☐	*Pearls Before Swine,* Manor 12240, 1974, fourth edition	1.75	2.50	2.12
☐	*Police At The Funeral,* MacFadden 60-122, 1963	1.15	1.50	1.25
☐	*Police At The Funeral,* Manor 95233, 1973, third edition	1.50	2.00	1.75
☐	*Police At The Funeral,* Manor 15219, no date	1.75	2.50	2.12
☐	*Police At The Funeral,* Penguin 219, 1974, twelfth edition	1.35	1.85	1.50
☐	*Police At The Funeral,* Bestseller B51, no date	1.35	1.85	1.50
☐	*Sweet Danger,* Penguin 769, 1975, twelfth edition	2.00	2.75	2.37
☐	*Sweet Danger,* Penguin 769, 1956, fourth edition	3.00	3.75	3.37
☐	*Ten Were Missing,* Dell R102, 1961 . .	3.25	4.00	3.62
☐	*Tether's End,* MacFadden 75-314, 1970	1.35	1.85	1.50
☐	*Tiger In The Smoke,* Manor 95247, 1973, second edition	1.35	1.85	1.50
☐	*Tiger In The Smoke,* Dell 777, 1954 . .	2.00	3.00	2.50
☐	*The Tiger In The Smoke,* MacFadden 60-344, 1968	1.25	1.75	1.50
☐	*The Tiger In The Smoke,* Penguin 1216, 1959, second edition	3.50	4.50	4.00
☐	*The Tiger In The Smoke,* Penguin 1216, 1961, third edition	3.50	4.50	4.00
☐	*Traitor's Purse,* Manor 12340, 1975 . .	1.35	1.85	1.50
☐	*Traitor's Purse,* Manor 95263, 1973, second edition	1.35	1.85	1.50
☐	*Traitor's Purse,* Penguin 772, 1950 . .	8.00	11.00	8.00
☐	**Allison, Clyde,** *Million Dollar Mistress,* Midwood 64 (cover artwork by Raden)	4.00	5.00	4.50
☐	**Allport, Gordon W.,** *Nature of Prejudice,* Anchor 149	3.25	4.25	3.75
☐	**Ambler, Eric,** *A Coffin For Dimitrios,* Dell 1303, 1964, second edition	1.25	1.75	1.50

		Current Price Range		C/Y Avg.
☐	*Dirty Story,* Bantam S3812, 1968	1.25	1.75	1.50
☐	*Doctor Frigo,* Fontana 3996, 1975 ...	2.00	2.50	2.25
☐	*Epitaph For A Spy,* Ballantine 25915, 1978	1.50	2.00	1.75
☐	*Epitaph For A Spy,* Hodder 431, 1960	3.00	4.00	3.50
☐	*Epitaph For A Spy,* Pan 71, 1948	6.00	8.00	6.37
☐	*The Intercom Conspiracy,* Bantam N5594, second edition	1.25	1.75	1.50
☐	*The Intercom Conspiracy,* Fontana 2765, 1972, third edition	3.00	3.75	3.37
☐	*Journey Into Fear,* Pocket 193, 1944, fifth edition	6.00	8.00	6.00
☐	*Journey Into Fear,* Pocket 193, 1943	4.50	5.50	5.00
☐	*Journey Into Fear,* Dell D343, 1960 ..	2.00	2.75	2.37
☐	*Judgment On Deltchev,* Ballantine 25917, 1977	1.25	1.75	1.50
☐	*Judgment On Deltchev,* Pocket 887, 1952	3.50	4.75	3.50
☐	*Judgment On Deltchev,* Bantam F2781, 1964	1.75	2.50	2.12
☐	*A Kind Of Anger,* Fontana 1338, 1967, second edition	2.00	3.00	2.50
☐	*A Kind Of Anger,* Bantam S3056, 1965	2.00	2.75	2.37
☐	*The Levanter,* Bantam T7603, 1973 ..	1.25	1.75	1.50
☐	*The Levanter,* Fontana 3259, 1973 ..	2.50	3.25	2.87
☐	*The Light Of Day,* Bantam F2780, 1964	2.00	3.00	2.50
☐	*The Mask Of Dimitrios,* Pan 114, 1949	9.00	12.00	9.50
☐	*The Mask Of Dimitrios,* Fontana 2081, 1971, third edition	2.00	2.25	2.12
☐	*Night-Comers,* Pan G115, 1959, second edition	2.50	3.75	3.12
☐	*The Night-Comers,* Fontana 1554, 1967, second edition	2.00	3.00	2.50
☐	*Passage Of Arms,* Bantam H2970, 1965, second edition	1.75	2.50	2.12
☐	*Passage Of Arms,* Bantam F2246, 1961	2.50	3.50	3.00
☐	**Anders, Burt,** *The Perfumed World,* Beacon #8633F	1.50	2.00	1.75
☐	**Anderson, Edward,** *Your Red Wagon,* Bantam 350 (photo cover picturing Farley Granger)	4.00	5.50	4.50

	Current Price Range		C/Y Avg.
☐ **Anderson, Poul,** *After Doomsday,* Ballantine 579, 1962	2.75	3.50	3.12
☐ *Beyond The Beyond,* Signet T3947, 1969	1.75	2.25	2.00
☐ *Brain Wave,* Ballantine 393K, 1960 . .	2.00	3.00	2.50
☐ *Brain Wave,* Ballantine 80, 1954	7.00	10.00	7.00
☐ *The Broken Sword,* Sphere 1157, 1973	2.50	3.50	3.00
☐ *A Circus Of Hells,* Signet T4250, 1970	1.75	2.25	2.00
☐ *A Circus Of Hells,* Signet E9045, third edition	2.00	3.00	2.38
☐ *Cold Victory,* TOR 48-527, 1982	2.00	3.00	2.50
☐ *The Corridors Of Time,* Lancer 74742, 1969, second edition	2.00	2.75	2.50
☐ *The Dancer From Atlantis,* Signet Q4894, 1972	1.35	1.85	1.50
☐ *The Day Of Their Return,* Signet Y6371, 1975	1.35	1.85	1.50
☐ *The Day Of Their Return,* Signet W7941, third edition	1.75	2.50	2.12
☐ *The Devil's Game,* Pocket 83689, 1980	2.00	3.00	2.50
☐ *The Enemy Stars,* Berkley F1112, 1965	2.25	3.25	2.50
☐ *The Enemy Stars,* Berkley G289, 1959	3.00	4.00	3.50
☐ *Ensign Flandry,* Lancer 73-677, 1967	1.50	2.25	1.87
☐ *Ensign Flandry,* Ace 20724, 1979	1.50	2.25	1.87
☐ *Ensign Flandry,* Lancer 75347, no date	3.25	4.50	3.50
☐ *Fire Time,* Del Rey 28692, 1980, second edition	2.00	2.75	2.37
☐ *Fire Time,* Ballantine 24628, 1975 . . .	1.25	1.75	1.50
☐ *Guardians Of Time,* Ballantine 422K, 1960	3.25	4.50	3.87
☐ *The High Crusade,* Manor 95374, 1975	1.25	2.00	1.62
☐ *The High Crusade,* MacFadden 60-349, 1968, second edition	1.25	2.00	1.62
☐ *The Horn Of Time,* Signet P3349, 1968	1.85	2.50	2.12
☐ *The Horn Of Time,* Signet Q5480, 1973, third edition	1.85	2.50	2.12
☐ *Last Viking 1, The Golden Horn,* Zebra 597, 1980	2.00	3.00	2.37
☐ *The Long Way Home,* Ace 48922, 1978, second edition	2.00	3.00	2.37
☐ *A Midsummer Tempest,* Orbit 7857, 1975	2.00	3.00	2.50

		Current Price Range		C/Y Avg.
☐	(ED), *Nebula Award Stories Four,* Pocket 75646, 1970, second edition	2.00	3.00	2.37
☐	(ED), *Nebula Award Stories Four,* Pocket 5646, 1971	1.25	1.75	1.50
☐	*No World Of Their Own,* Ace D-550, no date	4.00	6.00	5.00
☐	*Orbit Unlimited,* Pyramid G615, 1961	1.75	2.50	2.12
☐	*Orbit Unlimited,* Pyramid F-818, 1963, second edition	2.00	3.00	2.50
☐	*Orbit Unlimited,* Pyramid G615, 1961	2.00	2.75	2.37
☐	*Orbit Unlimited,* Pyramid N3274, 1974, fourth edition	1.35	1.85	1.50
☐	*The People Of The Wind,* Signet Q5479, 1973	1.35	1.85	1.50
☐	*The Peregrine,* Ace 65949, 1978, second edition	1.35	1.85	1.50
☐	*Planet Of No Return,* Universal 5223, 1978, second edition	2.00	2.75	2.37
☐	*The Queen Of Air and Darkness,* Signet Q5713, 1973	1.25	1.75	1.50
☐	*The Rebel Worlds,* Signet Q5714, 1969	2.00	2.75	2.37
☐	*Satan's World,* Lancer 74698, no date	2.00	2.75	2.37
☐	*Shield,* Berkley F743, 1963	2.50	3.50	3.00
☐	*Shield,* Berkley S1862, 1970	1.75	2.25	2.00
☐	*Shield,* Berkley 04704, 1982	2.25	2.75	2.50
☐	Berkley N2673, third edition	2.00	2.50	2.25
☐	**Anderson, Poul, and Dickson,** *Earthman's Burden,* Avon Camelot ZS166 ..	2.00	3.00	2.50
☐	**Anderson, Poul, and Eklund, G.,** *Inheritors Of Earth,* Pyramid V4068, 1976 ...	1.50	2.00	1.75
☐	**Anderson, Robert,** *Tea and Sympathy,* Signet 1343 (painted cover picturing Deborah Kerr, John Kerr, Leif Erickson and Edward Andrews)	6.00	8.00	6.50
☐	**Andrade, E.N.,** *Rutherford and the Nature Of the Atom,* Anchor S35	3.00	4.00	3.25
☐	**Andriola, Alfred and Mel Casson,** *Ever Since Adam and Eve,* Signet 1361 (Alfred Andriola was creator of the comic strip Kerry Drake)	9.00	12.00	10.00
☐	**Anthony, Evelyn,** *Warrior's Mistress,* Hillman 134	3.85	4.75	4.00

	Current Price Range		C/Y Avg.
☐ **Anthony, Rock,** *With Eyes Wide Open,* Midwood F309, no date	1.85	2.50	2.12
☐ **Anthony, Rock,** *Fringe Benefits,* Midwood 278	3.75	4.75	4.00
☐ **Archer, Alma,** *Your Power as a Woman,* Western Printing (no serial number), 1957	6.00	8.00	6.75
☐ **Ard, William,** *Babe in the Woods,* Monarch 172	4.00	5.00	4.50
☐ **Armstrong, Charlotte,** *The Balloon Man,* Crest T1975, no date	2.00	2.75	2.37
☐ *The Balloon Man,* Crest T1255, 1969	2.00	2.75	2.37
☐ *The Better To Eat You,* Berkley S1844, 1970, second edition	3.00	4.00	3.50

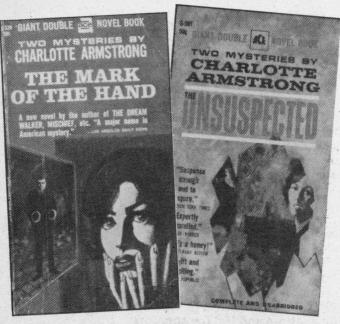

Left to Right: **The Mark of The Hand,** by Charlotte Armstrong, 1955, Ace, G526, **$1.75–$2.55;**
The Unsuspected, by Charlotte Armstrong, 1959, Ace, G501, **$2.75–$3.50.**

		Current Price Range		C/Y Avg.
☐	*The Black-Eyed Stranger,* Pocket 880, 1952	4.00	5.50	4.50
☐	*Case Of The Weird Sisters,* Mercury 85, no date	1.25	1.75	1.50
☐	*Case Of The Weird Sisters,* Berkley S1835, 1970	1.85	2.50	2.12
☐	*The Chocolate Cobweb,* Berkley X1402, 1968, second edition	2.50	3.50	2.37
☐	*The Chocolate Cobweb,* Pocket 575, 1949	2.00	2.75	2.37
☐	*A Dram Of Poison,* Crest 191, 1957	1.85	2.50	2.12
☐	*A Dram Of Poison,* Crest R1335, no date	2.00	2.50	2.25
☐	*A Dram Of Poison,* Crest 383, 1960, third edition	1.35	1.85	1.50
☐	*The Dream Walker,* Berkley S2168, 1972	1.25	1.75	1.50
☐	*The Gift Shop,* Crest M1611, no date	2.00	2.50	2.25
☐	*Girl With A Secret,* Berkley 2631, third edition	2.50	3.50	3.00
☐	*The Girl With A Secret,* Crest 383, fourth edition	1.00	1.50	1.25
☐	*The Girl With A Secret,* Crest R1370, 1970, fifth edition	1.35	1.85	1.50
☐	*The Innocent Flower,* Pocket 427, 1947	2.00	3.00	2.50
☐	*Lemon In The Basket,* Gold Medal R1198, 1969, second edition	1.50	2.00	1.75
☐	*Lemon In The Basket,* Crest T1491	1.50	2.00	1.75
☐	*A Little Less Than Kind,* Ace G-540, no date	2.00	2.50	2.25
☐	*Mischief,* Berkley X1501, 1968	1.75	2.25	2.00
☐	*Mischief,* Berkley S1985, 1970, fourth edition	1.25	1.75	1.50
☐	*Murder's Nest,* Pocket 1058, 1955	2.00	3.00	2.50
☐	*The One-Faced Girl,* Ace 62936, no date	1.75	2.25	2.00
☐	*The Protege,* Crest T1505, 1971	1.25	1.75	1.50
☐	*Something Blue,* Ace 77480, no date	2.00	3.00	2.37
☐	*The Turret Room,* Gold Medal T1317	1.25	1.75	1.50
☐	*The Turret Room,* Crest R1077, 1967	2.00	3.00	2.37
☐	*The Unsuspected,* Pocket 444, 1947	6.00	8.00	6.00

	Current Price Range		C/Y Avg.

☐ *The Unsuspected,* Pocket 444, 1947, fourth edition 2.50 3.50 **3.00**

☐ *Unsuspected,* Pocket 444, 1947, second edition 2.50 3.50 **3.00**

☐ *Walk Out On Death,* Pocket 1034, 1954 2.00 3.00 **2.50**

☐ *The Witch's House,* Crest T1445, no date 1.75 2.50 **2.12**

☐ **Arno, Peter,** *The New Peter Arno Pocket Book,* Pocket Books 1087 .... 7.00 10.00 **8.25**

☐ *The Peter Arno Pocket Book,* Pocket Books 417 .... 16.00 21.00 **17.75**

☐ **Arnold, Matthew,** *The Portable Matthew Arnold,* Viking 45, 1966 .... 2.75 3.50 **3.00**

☐ **Arquette, Cliff,** *Charley Weaver's Letters From Mama,* Dell D347 (photo cover picturing the author and Jack Paar) ... 6.00 8.00 **6.50**

☐ **Arthur, Burt,** *Boss Of The Far West,* MacFadden 40-163, 1965 .... 1.25 1.75 **1.50**

☐ *Bugles in the Night,* Signet 1873 ..... 3.75 4.75 **4.00**

☐ *Ride Out for Revenge,* Avon T198 (painted cover picturing Lloyd Bridges, Rory Calhoun and Gloria Grahame) 6.00 8.00 **6.75**

☐ **Asbury, Herbert,** *Chicago Underworld,* Ace K148 .... 3.50 4.50 **4.00**

☐ **Ascoli, Max,** *The Reporter Reader,* Doubleday (no serial number) 3.50 4.50 **4.00**

☐ **Asimov, Isaac,** *Asimov's Mysteries,* Crest 2-3223, first edition 1.65 2.25 **1.75**

☐ *Asimov's Mysteries,* Crest 0307, 1970, third edition 1.65 2.25 **1.75**

☐ (ED), *Before The Golden Age Book 3,* Crest Q2525, 1975 .... 1.25 1.75 **1.50**

☐ (ED), *Before The Golden Age Book 1,* Crest Q2410, 1975 .... 1.85 2.50 **2.12**

☐ *The Bicentennial Man,* Crest 2-3573, no date 2.00 3.00 **2.37**

☐ *Caves Of Steel,* Pyramid F-784, 1962 2.00 3.00 **2.50**

☐ *The Caves Of Steel,* Crest 2-0063, 1921 .... 2.25 3.25 **2.75**

☐ *The Caves Of Steel,* Crest Q2858, no date 1.25 1.75 **1.50**

The Martian Way, by Isaac Asimov,
Fawcett, 2–3783–4, **$2.25–$3.00.**

		Current Price Range		C/Y Avg.
☐	*The Currents Of Space,* Panther 00824, 1978, ninth edition	**2.00**	**3.00**	**2.50**
☐	*The Currents Of Space,* Lancer 72-104, 1966, second edition	**2.00**	**3.00**	**2.50**
☐	*Currents Of Space,* Lancer 74-816, 1963	**2.00**	**3.00**	**2.37**
☐	*Currents Of Space,* Crest T1541, 1971	**1.25**	**1.75**	**1.50**
☐	*Currents Of Space,* Crest M2193	**1.75**	**2.50**	**2.12**
☐	*The Currents Of Space,* Lancer 73-703, 1968, third edition	**2.25**	**3.25**	**2.62**
☐	*The Currents Of Space,* Signet 1082, 1953	**3.25**	**4.50**	**3.50**
☐	*David Starr Space Ranger,* Signet T4849, 1971	**1.50**	**2.50**	**2.00**
☐	*The Early Asimov Book One,* Crest P2087, 1974	**1.25**	**1.75**	**1.50**

		Current Price Range		C/Y Avg.
☐	*Earth Is Room Enough,* Bantam A1978, 1959	4.50	6.75	5.00
☐	*Earth Is Room Enough,* Crest T1401, 1970	1.75	2.50	2.12
☐	*The End Of Eternity,* Lancer 74-818, 1963	1.75	2.50	2.12
☐	*End Of Eternity,* Lancer 72-107, 1966	1.75	2.50	2.12
☐	*End Of Eternity,* Panther 881, 1959	3.50	5.00	4.25
☐	*End Of Eternity,* Signet S1493, 1958	3.50	5.00	4.25
☐	*End Of Eternity,* Crest T1619, 1971	1.25	1.75	1.50
☐	*The End Of Eternity,* Lancer 74-818, 1963	2.75	3.75	3.25
☐	*Fantastic Voyage,* Bantam 12655, 1930	2.00	2.75	2.37
☐	*Fantastic Voyage,* Bantam H3177, 1966	1.75	2.50	2.12
☐	*Fantastic Voyage,* Bantam, no #, twentieth edition	.75	1.00	.87
☐	*Fantastic Voyage,* Bantam Book Club edition	1.50	2.25	1.87
☐	*Foundation,* Avon V2248, 1968, fourth edition	1.85	2.65	2.12
☐	*Foundation,* Avon N304, 1970, ninth edition	1.85	2.65	2.12
☐	*Foundation,* Avon S224, 1966	1.85	2.65	2.12
☐	*Foundation and Empire,* Avon V2236, 1968, fourth edition	1.85	2.65	2.12
☐	*Foundation and Empire,* Panther 13555, 1971, tenth edition	1.85	2.65	2.12
☐	*Foundation and Empire,* Avon 42689, twenty-eighth edition	1.85	2.65	2.12
☐	*Foundation,* Avon N304, 1972, fourteenth edition	1.25	2.00	1.62
☐	*The Gods Themselves,* Crest X2883	1.75	2.50	2.12
☐	*The Gods Themselves,* Crest P1829, 1973	1.25	1.75	1.62
☐	*The Gods Themselves,* Crest P1829, 1973	1.85	2.50	2.12
☐	(ED), *The Great SF Stories 1 (1939),* DAW UE1454, 1979	1.85	2.50	2.12
☐	(ED), *Hugo Winners, Vol. 3, Book 1,* Crest 2-384, first edition	1.85	2.50	2.12

		Current Price Range		C/Y Avg.
☐	(ED), *Hugo Winners, Vol. 1,* Crest M1811, 1973	1.25	1.75	1.50
☐	(ED), *The Hugo Winners,* Avon S-127, no date	3.00	4.00	3.50
☐	*The Hugo Winners,* Avon S-127, no date	1.85	2.65	2.12
☐	(ED), *Hugo Winners, Vol. 3, Book 2,* Crest 2-4045, no date	1.85	2.65	2.12
☐	*I Robot,* Signet S1885, 1961, third edition	1.85	2.65	2.12
☐	*I Robot,* Signet D2458, 1964, fourth edition	1.85	2.65	2.12
☐	*I Robot,* Signet S1282, 1956	1.85	2.65	2.12
☐	*I Robot,* Crest T1453, no date	1.85	2.65	2.12
☐	*I Robot,* Signet P3540, 1968, third edition	1.85	2.65	2.12
☐	*I Robot, (SR),* Signet D2458, 1964 ...	1.85	2.65	2.12
☐	*I Robot,* Crest M1966, 1970	1.85	2.65	2.12
☐	*I Robot,* Crest Q2829, twenty-first edition	1.85	2.65	2.12
☐	*I Robot,* Crest P2355, 1970	1.25	1.75	1.50
☐	*L. Starr and Pirates Of Asteroids,* Signet T4850, 1971	1.25	1.75	1.50
☐	(ED), *Last Man On Earth,* Crest 2-4531, 1982	3.00	4.00	3.50
☐	*Lucky Starr and Big Sun Of Mercury,* Crest 2-3492, third edition	1.50	2.00	1.75
☐	*Lucky Starr and Big Sun Of Mercury,* Signet T4925, third edition	1.75	2.50	2.12
☐	*Lucky Starr and Moons Of Jupiter,* Signet T4975, 1972	1.50	2.00	1.75
☐	*Lucky Starr and The Rings Of Saturn,* Signet T4976, 1972	1.75	2.50	2.12
☐	*The Man Who Upset The Universe,* Ace F-216, no date	2.00	3.00	2.62
☐	*The Man Who Upset The Universe,* Ace D-125, no date	7.00	10.00	7.00
☐	*The Naked Sun,* Lancer 74-986, 1969, fourth edition	2.00	2.50	2.25
☐	*The Naked Sun,* Lancer 74644, 1970, fourth edition	2.25	3.00	2.62

	Current Price Range		C/Y Avg.
☐ (ED), *Nebula Award Stories 8,* Berkley Z2951, 1975	1.25	1.75	1.50
☐ *Nightfall,* Crest M1486, 1970	1.50	2.00	1.75
☐ *Nightfall,* Crest M1486, 1970	1.85	2.50	2.12
☐ *Nine Tomorrows,* Bantam A2121, 1960	1.85	2.50	2.12
☐ *Nine Tomorrows,* Crest T1344, no date	1.85	2.50	2.12
☐ *Nine Tomorrows,* Crest T1632, no date	1.25	1.75	1.50
☐ *The 1000 Year Plan,* Ace D-538, no date	3.50	5.00	4.12
☐ *The 1000-Year Plan,* Ace D-110, no date, special edition	5.50	7.50	6.00
☐ *Pebble In The Sky,* Sphere 1259, 1974, third edition	2.00	2.75	2.37
☐ *Pebble In The Sky,* Bantam FP47, fifth edition	2.00	2.75	2.37
☐ *Pebble In The Sky,* Galaxy SF Novel 14, 1953	8.00	11.00	8.50
☐ *Pebble In The Sky,* Crest T1567, 1971	1.50	2.00	1.75
☐ *Pebble In The Sky,* Crest M1855	1.75	2.50	2.12
☐ *Pebble In The Sky,* Bantam A1646, 1957	3.75	5.00	4.37
☐ **Asimov, Isaac, and Greenberg/ Olander** (ED), *Future I,* Crest 2-4366, 1981	2.00	4.00	3.00
☐ **Athens, Christopher,** *The Big Squeeze,* Chicago Paperback House 102	4.50	5.75	4.75
☐ **Atlee, Philip,** *The Death Bird Contract,* Gold Medal T2289	1.35	1.85	1.50
☐ *The Fer-De-Lance Contract,* Gold Medal 2370, 1971	1.35	1.85	1.50
☐ *The Green Wound Contract,* Gold Medal R2119, no date	1.35	1.85	1.50
☐ *The Green Wound Contract,* Gold Medal D1780, 1967, second edition	1.75	2.50	2.12
☐ *III Wind Contract,* Gold Medal R2087, 1969	1.25	1.75	1.50
☐ *Irish Beauty Contract,* Gold Medal D1694, no date	1.50	2.00	1.75
☐ *The Judah Lion Contract,* Gold Medal T2608, no date	1.35	1.85	1.50
☐ *The Kiwi Contract,* Gold Medal T2530, 1972	1.35	1.85	1.50

	Current Price Range		C/Y Avg.
☐ Kowloon Contract, Gold Medal M3028, 1974	1.75	2.50	2.12
☐ The Last Domino Contract, Gold Medal 1-3587, first edition	1.85	2.50	2.12
☐ The Last Domino Contract, Gold Medal 1-3587, second edition	1.25	1.75	1.50
☐ The Makassar Strait Contract, Gold Medal P3477, 1976	1.50	2.00	1.75
☐ The Paper Pistol Contract, Gold Medal T2477, no date	1.50	2.00	1.75
☐ The Shankill Road Contract, Gold Medal T2819, 1973	1.25	1.75	1.50
☐ Silken Baroness, Gold Medal K1489, no date	1.50	2.00	1.75
☐ The Spice Route Contract, Gold Medal T2697, 1973	1.25	1.75	1.50
☐ Star Ruby Contract, Gold Medal T2667, no date	2.25	3.00	2.37
☐ The Star Ruby Contract, Gold Medal D1770, 1967	1.50	2.00	1.75
☐ The Trembling Earth Contract, Gold Medal T2704, no date	1.35	1.85	1.50
☐ Trembling Earth Contract, Gold Medal R1281, no date	1.35	1.85	1.50
☐ The Trembling Earth Contract, Gold Medal R2181, no date	1.75	2.50	2.12
☐ The Trembling Earth Contract, Gold Medal T2704, no date	1.00	1.50	1.25
☐ The Trembling Earth Contract, Gold Medal R2181, 1969	1.50	2.00	1.75
☐ Underground Cities Contract, Gold Medal M2975, 1974	1.75	2.50	2.12
☐ The White Wolverine Contract, Gold Medal T2508, no date	2.00	3.00	2.50
☐ **Attaway, William,** Tough Kid, Lion LL-77, 1955, second edition	1.50	2.00	1.75
☐ **Auchincloss, Louis,** The House of Five Talents, Dell S14 (cover artwork by Hulings)	5.00	6.50	5.50
☐ **Auden, W.H.,** Romantic Poets, Viking 52	3.00	4.00	3.50
☐ **Austin, John,** Hollywood's Unsolved Mysteries, Ace 34249	4.25	5.25	4.50

	Current Price Range		C/Y Avg.

☐ **Avalonne, Mike,** *Never Love A Girl*, Midwood 205, 1962, first edition 4.50 6.00 5.20

☐ *The Little Black Book,* Midwood 135, cover artwork by Rader 6.00 8.00 6.75

☐ *The Man From Avon,* Avon G1307, no date 4.00 6.00 4.90

☐ **Baldwin, Faith,** *Enchanted Oasis,* Dell 255, no date........................ 3.00 3.75 3.37

☐ **Ballard, K.G.,** *The Coast of Fear,* Curtis 06039, no date 1.35 1.75 1.50

☐ **Ballard, P.D.,** *Brothers In Blood,* Gold Medal T2563, 1972 .... 1.35 1.75 1.50

☐ *The Death Brokers,* Gold Medal M2867, 1973 .... 1.50 2.00 1.75

☐ **Ballard, W.T.,** *Murder Can't Stop,* Graphic 26, 1950 .... 4.00 5.50 4.75

☐ *Murder Las Vegas Style,* Unibook, no date 1.00 1.50 1.25

☐ *Murder Las Vegas Style,* Tower 42-778, 1967 .... 1.75 2.50 2.12

☐ *Pretty Miss Murder, Perma M-4228, 1961* 2.75 3.75 3.25

☐ *Say Yes To Murder,* B.D.S., 9 1943 .. 5.50 7.50 6.12

☐ *The Seven Sisters,* Permabook M-4258, 1962 .... 2.25 3.25 2.75

☐ *Three For The Money,* Perma M-4297, 1963 .... 1.75 2.50 2.12

☐ **Ballem, John,** *The Dirty Scenario,* Paperbacks 7105, 1974 .... 1.25 1.75 1.50

☐ **Ballinger, Bill S.,** *The Body In The Bed,* Signet G2569, 1964, fifth edition 1.75 2.50 2.12

☐ *The Body In The Bed,* Signet G2569, 1964, third edition 2.25 3.25 2.75

☐ *Chinese Mask,* Signet D2715, 1965 .. 2.00 2.75 2.37

☐ *The Darkening Door,* Signet 1040, 1953 .... 3.25 4.50 3.50

☐ *Heist Me Higher,* Signet P3799, 1969 1.85 2.65 2.12

☐ *The Lopsided Man,* Pyramid X-1938, 1969 .... 1.85 2.65 2.12

☐ *Not I Said The Vixen,* Gold Medal K1529, 1965 .... 1.85 2.65 2.12

	Current Price Range		C/Y Avg.
☐ *Portrait In Smoke,* Signet D2650, 1965, fourth edition	1.85	2.65	2.12
☐ *Portrait In Smoke,* Signet 897, 1952 . .	3.25	4.50	3.50
☐ *Source Of Fear,* Signet P3655, 1968	1.75	2.50	2.12
☐ *Spy At Angkor Wat,* Signet D2899, 1966	2.00	2.75	2.37
☐ *Spy In The Java Sea,* Signet D2981, 1966	1.85	2.65	2.12
☐ *Spy In The Jungle,* Signet D2674, 1965	2.00	2.75	2.37
☐ *Wife Of Red-Haired Man,* Signet D2743, 1965, second edition	1.50	2.00	1.75
☐ *Wife Of Red-Haired Man,* Signet 1494, 1958	2.25	3.00	2.62
☐ *Beacon In the Night,* Signet 1794	3.25	4.25	3.50
☐ **Bancroft, Robert,** *Castillian Rose,* Pocket Books 6112 (cover artwork by Johnson)	4.00	5.10	4.50
☐ **Bankhead, T.,** *Tallulah,* Dell D132 (photo cover picturing the author)	3.00	3.75	3.25
☐ **Banks, Lynne R.,** *The L-Shaped Room,* Cardinal 433	4.00	5.00	4.50
☐ **Banks, Raymond,** *Computer Kill,* Popular Library G547 (cover artwork by McGinnis)	3.75	4.75	4.00
☐ **Bannon, Al,** *Old Girl Out,* Gold Medal S653, 1957, second edition	3.37	3.75	3.25
☐ **Bannon, Ann,** *The Marriage,* Gold Medal 1066	3.75	4.75	4.00
☐ **Barrett, Michael,** *The Golden Lure,* Crest 153, 1956	1.75	2.25	2.00
☐ **Barrett, William E.,** *Empty Shrine,* Cardinal 403	4.00	5.25	4.25
☐ *Irrational Man,* Anchor 321	3.50	4.50	4.00
☐ **Barron, Mike,** *A Professional Gambler Tells How To Win,* Belmont 544	4.00	5.00	4.50
☐ **Barry, Jerome,** *Murder Is No Accident,* Dell D369	3.75	4.75	4.00
☐ **Barry, Ken,** *The Love Itch,* Beacon #8536F	1.35	1.75	1.55
☐ **Barry, Phillip,** *The Philadelphia Story,* Pocket Books 102 (photo cover picturing Katharine Hepburn)	5.00	7.00	5.75

	Current Price Range		C/Y Avg.

☐ **Bartdorf, Steve,** *The Broads Make the Odds,* France 13 . . . .   4.25   5.50   4.50

☐ **Barzun, Jacques,** *Teacher in America,* Anchor 25 . . . .   3.50   4.50   3.75

☐ **Baum, L. Frank,** *The Wizard of Oz,* Crest 395 (interior artwork by W.W. Denslow)   6.00   8.00   6.75

☐ **Beach, Webb,** *No French Leave,* Gold Medal S1212, 1962 . . . .   1.25   1.75   1.50

☐ **Beaman, J. Frank,** *The Dotmakers,* Book Company of America 007 . . . .   4.00   5.00   4.25

☐ **Beaty, Betty,** *South To the Sun,* Harlequin 790 . . . .   3.25   4.25   3.50

☐ **Beauchamp, Loren,** *Sin on Wheels,* Midwood 276 (cover artwork by Raden) . . .   4.00   5.25   4.50

☐ **Beaumont, Charles,** *The Intruder,* Dell S32 . . . .   3.75   4.75   4.00

☐ **Beckett, Samuel,** *Molloy/Malone Dies/The Unnamable,* Grove 78 (three books in one) 4.75   6.00   5.00

☐ **Bell, Daniel,** *The Radical Right,* Anchor 376 . . . .   4.00   5.00   4.50

☐ **Bell, Josephine,** *The Upfold Witch,* Ballantine 2154 . . . .   3.75   4.75   4.00

☐ **Bellah, James W.,** *Ordeal At Blood River,* Ballantine 1054 . . . .   4.00   5.00   4.25

☐   *Reveille,* Gold Medal 1218 . . . .   4.00   5.00   4.25

☐ **Bellus, Jean,** *Clementine Cherie,* Crest 266 . . . .   7.00 10.00   8.00

☐ **Benet, Stephen Vincent,** *O'Halloran's Luck,* Penguin 546, no date 2.50   3.25   2.87

☐ **Bennett, Fletcher,** *Escape Into Vice,* Playtime 611 . . . .   4.00   5.00   4.25

☐ **Bensen, D.R.,** *The Unknown Five,* Pyramid 962 (cover artwork by Schoenherr)   4.50   5.50   5.00

☐ **Benson, Ezra T.,** *The Red Carpet,* Monarch 11 . . . .   3.75   4.75   4.00

☐ **Benson, O.G.,** *Cain's Woman,* Dell A200 (cover artwork by Darcy) 4.25   5.25   4.50

☐ **Bentley, Eric,** *In Search of Theater,* Vintage K6 . . . .   4.00   5.00   4.50

☐ **Bentley, Nicolas,** *The Floating Dutchman,* Penguin 975, 1954 . . . .   1.00   1.50   1.20

	Current Price Range		C/Y Avg.

☐ **Berenson, Bernard,** *Aesthetics and History,* Anchor 36 .... 2.75 3.50 3.00

☐ **Berenstain, Stanley and Janice Berenstain,** *Baby Book,* Bantam 1074 ...... 7.00 10.00 8.25

☐ **Berkeley, Anthony,** *Trial And Error,* Pocket 307, 1945, second edition 7.50 10.00 8.25

☐ *Trial And Error,* Dell 9096, 1967 ..... 1.25 1.75 1.50

☐ **Berkey, Ben,** *The Girl With the Golden G-String,* Kozy 148 .... 4.00 5.00 4.25

☐ **Berle, Milton,** *Out of My Trunk,* Bantam 550 .... 6.00 8.00 6.50

☐ **Berliner, Ross,** *The Manhood Ceremony,* Signet E8509, 1979 .... 2.00 2.75 2.37

☐ **Bernard, Judo,** *Inside Out (Telly Savalas Movie),* Tandem 16934, 1975 .... 2.25 3.00 2.62

☐ **Bernard, Trevor,** *Brightlight,* Manor 15278, 1977 .... 1.35 1.75 1.50

☐ **Bernhard, Robert,** *The Ullman Code,* Berkley K3137, 1976 .... 1.35 1.75 1.50

☐ **Bernkopf, Jeanne F.,** (ED), *The Cream Of Crime,* Dell 1571, 1972 .... 1.25 1.75 1.50

☐ (ED), *Menace Masters,* Dell 5537, 1971 .... 1.25 1.75 1.50

☐ **Berra, Lawrence,** *Behind the Plate,* Pratt 104 .... 4.00 5.00 4.50

☐ **Berrill, N.J.,** *Man's Emerging Mind,* Premier 159 .... 3.75 4.75 4.25

☐ **Berson, Fred,** *After The Big House,* Popular G122, 1953 .... 3.75 5.00 4.12

☐ **Beste, R. Vernon,** *Moonbeams,* Lancer 72-733, 1964 .... 1.75 2.50 2.12

☐ *Repeat The Instructions,* Corgi 08238, 1969 .... 2.25 3.00 2.62

☐ **Bertrande, Sister,** *A Woman Named Louise,* Macillac (no 5.20 serial number), 1956 .... 5.00 6.50 6.00

☐ **Beyer, William,** *Murder Secretary,* Bart House 24, 1946 .... 7.00 9.25 8.12

☐ **Bezzerides, A.I.,** *Tough Guy,* Lion 153, 1953 .... 4.50 6.00 5.25

☐ **Bickham, Jack,** *Gunmen Can't Hide,* Ace F120 .... 3.50 4.50 3.75

	Current Price Range		C/Y Avg.

☐ **Biggers, Earl D.,** *The Chinese Parrot,*
Popular Library 52-228 . . . .   3.75   4.75   4.00
☐   *7 Keys To Baldpate,* Popular 132, 1948   11.50   15.00   12.50
☐ **Billany, Dan,** *It Takes A Thief,* Black Cat
9, 1944 . . . .   8.00   11.00   8.87
☐ **Bingham, Carson,** *The Gang Girls,* Mon-
arch 372, 1963 . . . .   7.00   10.00   7.75
☐   *Run Tough Run Hard,* Monarch 194
(cover artwork by Johnson) 4.00   5.00   4.50
☐ **Bingham, John,** *Double Agent,* Panther
2905, 1970, second edition 2.00   2.75   2.37
☐   *Fragment Of Fear,* Bantam H4314,
1969 . . . .   1.75   2.50   2.37
☐   *Fragment Of Fear,* Panther 2321, 1967   2.00   2.75   2.37
☐   *Marion,* Pan G368, 1960 . . . .   3.00   3.75   3.37
☐   *Murder Off The Record,* Dell D351,
1960 . . . .   2.25   3.00   2.62
☐   *Murder Plan Six,* Penguin C1949, 1964   2.50   3.25   2.87
☐   *Murder Plan Six,* Dell R112, 1962 . . . .   1.75   2.50   2.12
☐   *Night's Black Agent,* Penguin C2241,
1965 . . . .   2.25   3.00   2.62
☐   *The Tender Poisoner,* Dell 873, 1955   2.50   3.25   2.87
☐ **Bird, Brandon,** *Dead And Gone,* Dell
857, 1955 . . . .   2.25   3.00   2.60
☐   *Death In Four Colors,* Dell Map 531,
1951 . . . .   3.25   4.00   3.62
☐ **Birkley, Dolan,** *The Blue Geranium,* Bart
House 8, 1944 . . . .   9.50   12.50   10.50
☐ **Birmingham, Stephen,** *Barbara Greer,*
Cardinal 407 . . . .   3.75   4.75   4.00
☐ **Bishop, Jim,** *The Murder Trial Of Judge
Peel,* Perma M-5068, 1963 . . . .   2.00   2.75   2.37
☐ **Black, Bryan,** *Eve Without Adam,* Bea-
con #8692X 1.65   2.15   1.75
☐ - *The Passionate Professor,* Beacon
#8660F 1.65   2.15   1.75
☐   *The Strangest Marriage,* Beacon
#8638F 1.60   2.15   1.75
☐ **Black, Gavin,** *The Cold Jungle,* Fontana
2216, 1970 . . . .   2.00   2.75   2.37
☐   *The Cold Jungle,* Popular Library
02538, no date 1.50   2.00   1.75

		Current Price Range		C/Y Avg.
☐	*A Dragon For Christmas,* Banner B60-102, 1967	1.85	2.50	2.12
☐	*A Dragon For Christmas,* Perennial P473, 1979	1.75	2.50	2.00
☐	*The Eyes Around Me,* Perennial Library P485, 1980	2.00	3.00	2.50
☐	*Suddenly At Singapore,* Fontana 4784, 1977, fourth edition	1.75	2.50	2.12
☐	*A Time For Pirates,* Fontana 3231, 1973	1.50	2.25	1.65
☐	*You Want To Die Johnny?,* Perennial P472, 1979	1.65	2.25	1.87
☐	*You Want To Die Johnny?,* Popular 02537, no date	1.65	2.25	1.87
☐	**Blacker, Irwin R.,** *Kilroy Gambit,* Signet 2063 (cover artwork by Hooks)	4.00	5.25	4.50
☐	**Blaine, Jud,** *The Fling,* Beacon 909 . . .	3.50	4.50	3.80
☐	**Blair, Joan,** *The Way To the Wedding,* Harlequin 811	3.00	3.75	3.25
☐	**Blair, Kathryn,** *Bewildered Heart,* Harlequin 861	4.00	5.00	4.35
☐	*The Man At Mulera,* Harlequin 920 . . .	4.00	5.00	4.25
☐	*This Kind of Love,* Harlequin 878	4.00	5.00	4.25
☐	**Blaisdell, Anne,** *Nightmare,* Crest 518	4.50	5.50	5.00
☐	**Blake, Andrew,** *Love Hostess,* Beacon #8664F	1.50	2.00	1.75
☐	**Blake, Michael,** *Hollywood Rapist,* Carousel 523	4.25	5.25	4.75
☐	**Blake, Nicholas,** *The Beast Must Die,* Dell D227, 1958	2.50	3.25	2.87
☐	*The Beast Must Die,* Black Cat Detective 7, 1943	9.00	12.00	9.50
☐	*Case Of Abominable Snowman,* White Circle 202, 1944	5.00	7.00	6.00
☐	*Catch and Kill,* Bestseller Mystery B193, no date	3.50	4.50	4.00
☐	*Corpse In The Snowman,* Perennial Library P427, 1977	1.50	2.00	1.75
☐	*The Corpse In The Snowman,* Popular 60, 1945	2.50	3.50	3.00
☐	*The Dreadful Hollow,* Perennial P493, 1979	1.75	2.50	2.12

	Current Price Range		C/Y Avg.
☐ End Of Chapter, Berkley X1647, 1969	2.00	3.00	2.50
☐ End Of Chapter, Perennial Library P397, 1978, third edition	1.25	1.75	1.50
☐ End Of Chapter, Berkley X1647, 1969	1.75	2.50	2.12
☐ Head Of A Traveler, Berkley F985, 1964	1.75	2.50	2.12
☐ Head Of A Traveler, Pocket 742, 1950	3.25	4.50	3.50
☐ Head Of A Traveler, Berkley F985, 1964	1.75	2.50	2.12
☐ Head Of A Traveler, Perennial P398, 1976	1.75	2.50	2.12
☐ Malice With Murder, Pyramid R1008, 1964	1.75	2.50	2.12
☐ Minute For Murder, Pocket 548, 1949	4.75	6.50	5.37
☐ A Penknife In My Heart, Perennial P521, 1980	1.75	2.50	2.12
☐ A Penknife In My Heart, Crest S388, 1960	2.00	2.75	2.37
☐ The Sad Variety, Avon V2424, 1972	1.25	1.75	1.50
☐ The Sad Variety, Perennial Library P4003A, 1965	1.75	2.50	2.12
☐ Smiler With The Knife, Berkley F970, 1964	2.00	3.00	2.50
☐ The Smiler With The Knife, Popular 41, no date	5.50	7.50	6.00
☐ The Smiler With The Knife, Popular 41, 1944	9.00	12.00	9.50
☐ There's Trouble Brewing, Pan 111, 1949	7.50	10.00	8.50
☐ There's Trouble Brewing, Popular 30, 1944	7.00	9.50	7.75
☐ Thou Shell Of Death, Perennial P428, 1977	1.75	2.50	2.12
☐ The Widow's Cruise, Fontana 495, 1961	1.75	2.50	2.12
☐ The Widow's Cruise, Perennial Library P399, 1978, third edition	1.50	2.00	1.75
☐ The Widow's Cruise, Dell 9538, 1963	2.00	2.75	2.37
☐ The Worm Of Death, Perennial Library P400, 1976	1.35	1.75	1.50
☐ **Blake, Steve,** *Sex and the Starlet,* Merit 7M813 [photo illustrated (adult)]	4.00	5.00	4.25

	Current Price Range		C/Y Avg.

☐ **Blake, Walker E.,** *Heartbreak Ridge,* Monarch 247 (cover artwork by Stanley)	4.25	5.25	4.50
☐ **Blake, William,** *The Portable Blake,* Viking 26, 1969	3.25	4.25	3.75
☐ **Blankfort, Michael,** *Juggler,* Dell 686, no date	2.50	3.25	2.87
☐ **Blatty, William P.,** *John Goldfarb Please Come Home,* Crest 763 (photo cover picturing Shirley MacLaine, Peter Ustinov and Richard Crenna—hard to believe that this zany comedy was authored by the man who wrote *The Exorcist*)	4.50	6.00	5.00
☐ **Bledsoe, Robert,** *Tropic of Scorpio,* Kozy 175	4.00	5.00	4.50
☐ **Bligh, Norman,** *The Sisters,* Beacon 363	3.50	4.50	3.75
☐ **Blish, James,** *Black Easter,* Dell 0653, 1969	1.85	2.50	2.12
☐ *A Case Of Conscience,* Del Rey 28023, 1979, fifth edition	1.85	2.50	2.12
☐ *A Case Of Conscience,* Ballantine U2251, 1966, second edition	2.00	2.75	2.37
☐ *A Case Of Conscience,* Arrow 906370, 1975	1.75	2.50	2.12
☐ *A Case Of Conscience,* Ballantine 02755, 1972, third edition	1.25	1.75	1.50
☐ *Earthman Come Home,* Arrow 908690, 1974, second edition	2.00	3.00	2.50
☐ *Earthman Come Home,* Avon S218, 1968, fifth edition	1.75	2.50	2.12
☐ *Earthman Come Home,* Avon T-225, 1958	2.25	3.25	2.75
☐ *Esper,* Avon T-268, 1958	2.25	3.25	2.75
☐ *The Frozen Year,* Ballantine 197, 1957	5.50	7.25	5.87
☐ *Galactic Cluster,* Signet D2790, 1965	2.00	3.00	2.50
☐ *Galactic Cluster,* Signet S1719, 1959	2.50	3.50	3.00
☐ *Jack Of Eagles,* Arrow 909710, 1977, second edition	2.00	3.00	2.37
☐ *Jack Of Eagles,* Avon S337, 1968, third edition	2.00	3.00	2.37
☐ *Life For The Stars,* Avon H-107, 1963	2.00	3.00	2.37
☐ *Life For The Stars,* Avon G1280, 1968, fifth edition	2.00	3.00	2.37

		Current Price Range		C/Y Avg.
☐	*Midsummer Century,* Arrow 909720, 1975	2.00	2.75	2.37
☐	*Mission To The Heart Stars,* Granada 04574, 1980	2.50	3.50	3.00
☐	*(ED), Nebula Award Stories Five,* Pocket 77423, 1971, second edition	1.25	2.00	1.62
☐	*(ED), New Dreams This Morning,* Ballantine U2331, 1966	1.25	2.00	1.62
☐	*The Night Shapes,* Ballantine F647, 1962	3.25	4.25	3.50
☐	*The Night Shapes,* Arrow 918400, 1978	2.25	3.25	2.75
☐	*The Quincunx Of Time,* Dell 7244, 1973	2.00	2.50	2.25
☐	*The Seedling Stars,* Signet D2549, 1964, second edition	2.00	2.50	2.25
☐	*The Seedling Stars,* Signet S1622, 1959	3.75	4.75	4.00
☐	*So Close To Home,* Ballantine 465K, 1961	2.50	3.50	3.00
☐	*The Star Dwellers,* Avon F-122, 1962	2.50	3.50	3.00
☐	*The Star Dwellers,* Avon G1268, 1965, third edition	2.25	3.25	2.75
☐	*The Star Dwellers,* Avon 57976, 1982	2.25	3.25	2.75
☐	*Star Dwellers,* Avon F-122, 1962	1.85	2.50	2.12
☐	*Star Dwellers,* Berkley S1922, 1970 ..	1.85	2.50	2.12
☐	*They Shall Have Stars,* Avon S210, 1966, third edition	1.85	2.50	2.12
☐	*They Shall Have Stars,* Arrow 908670, 1974, second edition	2.00	2.75	2.37
☐	*Titan's Daughter,* Berkley G507, 1961	2.00	2.75	2.37
☐	*Titan's Daughter,* Berkley F1163, 1966, second edition	2.25	3.00	2.62
☐	*Triumph Of Time,* Avon S221, 1966, third edition	1.75	2.50	2.12
☐	*Triumph Of Time,* Avon T-279, 1958	3.25	4.25	3.50
☐	*Vor.,* Avon T-238, 1958	2.25	2.75	2.50
☐	*Vor.,* Avon S313, 1967, second edition	1.75	2.50	2.12
☐	*The Warriors Of Day,* Galaxy SF Novel 16, 1953	6.00	8.00	5.87
☐	*Warriors Of Day,* Arrow 919910, 1979	2.75	3.75	3.25

	Current Price Range		C/Y Avg.
☐ *Year 2018!,* Avon T-193, 1957	2.75	3.75	3.25
☐ **Bloch, Robert,** *American Gothic,* Crest P2391, 1975	1.25	1.75	1.50
☐ *Atoms and Evil,* Corgi 10486, 1977 . .	2.75	3.50	3.12
☐ *Blood Runs Cold,* Popular 50-8013, 1962	4.25	6.00	5.00
☐ *The Cunning (Serpent In Eden),* General 8037, no date	2.00	3.00	2.50
☐ *The Dead Beat,* Popular Library 2299, no date	1.25	1.75	1.50
☐ *Firebug,* Corgi 10403, 1977	2.50	3.50	3.00
☐ *Night-World,* Crest M1845, 1973	1.25	1.75	1.50
☐ *Psycho,* Corgi 08272, 1969, seventh edition	3.00	4.25	3.62
☐ *Psycho,* Crest S385, 1960	2.75	3.75	3.25
☐ *Psycho II,* Warner 30-612, 1982	3.00	4.00	3.50
☐ *Psycho,* Bantam H3808, 1969	2.00	2.75	2.37
☐ *Scarf of Passion,* Avon 211, no date	9.00	12.00	10.25
☐ *The Scarf,* Gold Medal D1727, 1966	2.25	3.00	2.50
☐ *There Is A Serpent In Eden,* Zebra 514, 1979	2.25	3.00	2.50
☐ **Blochman, Lawrence G.,** *Bengal Fire,* Dell Map 311, 1949	3.00	4.00	3.50
☐ *Blow-Down,* Dell Map 740, 1953	4.25	5.50	4.62
☐ *Blow-Down,* Dell Map 740, no date . .	2.75	3.50	3.12
☐ *Bombay Mail,* Dell Map 488, 1951 . . .	4.00	5.50	4.75
☐ *Death Walks Marble Halls,* Dell 19, 1951	10.00	14.00	10.50
☐ *Midnight Sailing,* Dell Map 43, 1944 . .	8.00	11.00	8.00
☐ *Pursuit,* Handi-Book 128, 1951	5.50	7.50	5.75
☐ *Rather Cool For Mayhem,* Bestseller B140, no date	4.25	5.75	4.87
☐ *Recipe For Homicide,* Dell 833	2.50	3.25	2.87
☐ *See You At The Morgue,* Dell Map 638, no date	2.75	3.50	3.12
☐ *See You At The Morgue,* Collier AS478V, 1962	2.00	3.00	2.50
☐ **Block, Lawrence, and King, Harold,** *Code Of Arms,* Berkley 05493	2.50	3.25	2.87
☐ *Deadly Honeymoon,* Dell 1739, 1973	1.75	2.50	2.12
☐ *Deadly Honeymoon,* Dell 1739, 1969	2.00	3.00	2.50

	Current Price Range		C/Y Avg.

☐ *Here Comes A Hero,* Gold Medal R2008, 1968 .... **1.75** **2.50** **2.12**

☐ *In The Midst Of Death,* Dell 4037, 1976 **1.00** **1.50** **1.25**

☐ *Markham,* Belmont 236, 1961 .... **3.25** **4.50** **3.50**

☐ *The Specialists,* Gold Medal R2067, 1969 .... **1.50** **2.00** **1.75**

☐ *A Stab In The Dark,* Jove 06717, 1982 **2.00** **3.00** **2.50**

☐ *Tanner's Tiger,* Gold Medal 1940, 1968 **1.75** **2.50** **2.12**

☐ *Tanner's Twelve Swingers,* Gold Medal D1869, 1967 .... **1.50** **2.00** **1.75**

☐ *Two For Tanner,* Gold Medal D1896, 1968 .... **2.00** **3.00** **2.50**

☐ **Bluestone, George,** *The Private World of Curry Powers,* Ace K137 .... **4.25** **5.25** **4.50**

☐ **Boal, Sam,** *The Man From the Diner's Club,* Lancer 70-041 (photo cover picturing Danny Kaye and Kay Stevens) **4.50** **5.75** **5.00**

☐ **Bodenheim, Maxwell,** *Sixty Seconds,* Novel Library 38, no date **6.00** **8.00** **6.75**

☐ **Bohle, Edgar,** *The Man Who Disappeared,* Dell 1013 (cover artwork by Rose) **4.25** **5.25** **4.50**

☐ **Bolt, Robert,** *A Man For All Seasons,* Vintage V321 .... **4.00** **5.00** **4.50**

☐ **Bonham, Barbara,** *Diagnosis: Love,* Monarch 466 (cover artwork by Marchetti) **3.75** **4.50** **4.00**

☐ **Bonham, Frank,** *By Her Own Hand,* Monarch 361 (cover artwork by Johnson) .. **4.00** **5.00** **4.50**

☐ **Bonner, Parker,** *Tough In the Saddle,* Monarch 452 (cover artwork by Johnson) **3.75** **4.75** **4.00**

☐ **Bonner, Paul Hyde,** *Hotel Talleyrand,* MacFadden 75-354, 1970, second edition **1.75** **2.50** **2.12**

☐ *S.P.Q.R.,* Pyramid T-1352, 1966 ..... **2.00** **2.75** **2.37**

☐ **Bonney, Joseph L.,** *Death By Dynamite,* Black Knight 19, no date **7.00** **10.00** **7.00**

☐ **Boone, Pat,** *Twixt Twelve and Twenty,* Dell D312 (photo cover picturing the author) **3.25** **4.00** **3.50**

☐ **Booth, Edwin,** *The Troublemaker,* Ace F126 .... **3.75** **4.75** **4.00**

	Current Price Range		C/Y Avg.

☐ **Booth, Ernest** *With Sirens Screaming,* Pyramid 564, 1958 .... **1.75** **2.50** **2.12**

☐ **Borden, Lee,** *The Secret Of Sylvia,* Gold Medal 744, 1958 .... **3.00** **4.00** **3.50**

☐ **Borden, Mary,** *Action For Slander,* Pan 90, 1949 .... **6.50** **8.50** **7.00**

☐ **Boswell and Thompson,** *Advocates Of Murder* (non-fiction), Collier AS357, 1962 **2.25** **3.00** **2.62**

☐ **Boswell, Charles,** *They All Died Young,* Handi-Book 94, 1949 .... **6.00** **8.00** **6.25**

☐ **Bosworth, Jim,** *The Long Way North,* Ace F286 .... **3.50** **4.25** **3.75**

☐ **Botein, Bernard,** *The Prosecutor,* Cardinal C-279, 1957 .... **1.75** **2.50** **2.12**

☐ **Boucher, Anthony,** *Case Of The Seven Sneezes,* Dell Map 334, 1949 .... **7.00** **10.00** **7.00**

☐ *Case Of The Crumpled Knave,* Pyramid R-1585, 1967 .... **1.75** **2.50** **2.12**

☐ *Case Of The Seven Sneezes,* Pyramid R-1542, 1966 .... **1.50** **2.25** **1.87**

☐ *(ED), PB Of True Crime Stories,* Pocket 213, 1943 .... **12.00** **16.00** **12.50**

☐ *PB Of True Crime Stories,* Pocket 213, 1943, second edition **9.50** **12.00** **10.25**

☐ *(ED), Pocket Book Of True Crime,* Pocket 213, 1943 .... **4.25** **6.00** **5.00**

☐ *(ED), Quintessence Of Queen,* Avon G-1159 .... **2.25** **3.00** **2.62**

☐ *Rocket To The Morgue,* Dell 591, no date **7.50** **10.00** **8.00**

☐ *Rocket To The Morgue,* Pyramid X-1681, 1967 .... **2.00** **2.75** **2.37**

☐ **Boulle, Pierre,** *Noble Profession,* Bantam F2832, 1964 .... **1.75** **2.50** **2.12**

☐ *The Bridge Over the River Kwai,* Bantam 1677 (painted cover picturing William Holden and Alec Guinness) **3.75** **4.75** **4.00**

☐ **Bouma, J.L.,** *Never Say No,* Midwood 353 (cover artwork by Raden) **3.50** **4.50** **3.75**

☐ **Bourgeau, Art,** *A Lonely Way To Die,* Charter 49706, 1980 .... **1.60** **2.25** **1.87**

	Current Price Range		C/Y Avg.

☐ **Boutell, Anita,** *Death Has A Past,* Bantam 897, 1951 .... **2.50** **3.25** **2.87**

☐ *Death Has A Past,* Bantam 897, 1951 **2.25** **3.00** **2.62**

☐ **Bowen, Elizabeth,** *Death of the Heart,* Vintage V21 .... **3.50** **4.50** **4.00**

☐ **Bowen, Robert Sidney,** *Make Mine Murder,* Black Knight, No #, no date **2.50** **3.50** **2.87**

☐ *Silent Wings,* Monarch 430 (cover artwork by Schaare) **4.00** **5.00** **4.50**

☐ **Bowlen, Ruth,** *West Through the Wilderness,* Moody (no serial number) **3.75** **4.50** **3.88**

☐ **Box, Edgar,** *Death Before Bedtime,* Bantam N7573, 1973 .... **1.50** **2.25** **1.87**

☐ *Death In The Fifth Position,* Bantam S7586, 1972 .... **1.25** **1.75** **1.50**

☐ *Death In The Fifth Position,* Signet 1475, 1957, second edition **2.25** **3.00** **2.62**

☐ *Death In The Fifth Position,* Signet G2505, 1964, third edition **1.75** **2.50** **2.12**

☐ *Death In The Fifth Position,* Signet 1036, 1953 .... **3.00** **4.00** **3.50**

☐ *Death Likes It Hot,* Signet G2540, 1964, fourth edition **1.75** **2.50** **2.12**

☐ *Death Likes It Hot,* Vintage V-55, 1979 **1.50** **2.25** **1.87**

☐ *Death Likes It Hot,* Signet 1217, 1955 **2.75** **3.75** **3.25**

☐ **Boyd, Eunice Mays,** *Murder Wears Mukluks,* Dell Map 259, 1948 .... **7.00** **9.50** **7.62**

☐ **Boyd, Frank,** *Johnny Staccato,* Gold Medal 980, 1960 .... **2.25** **3.00** **2.37**

☐ **Boyd, John,** *Rocket To The Morgue,* Bantam N3567, 1975, second edition .. **2.25** **3.00** **2.37**

☐ **Boyd, T.S.,** *Kitty,* Beacon #8405 ..... **2.25** **3.00** **2.25**

☐ **Boyd, Thomas,** *Through the Wheat,* Award 120 .... **4.00** **5.00** **4.25**

☐ **Bracken, Peg,** *The I Hate to Cook Book,* Crest (no serial number) **3.00** **3.75** **3.25**

☐ **Bracken, Steve,** *Baby Moll,* Crest 206, 1958 .... **2.25** **3.00** **2.37**

☐ **Bradbury, Ray,** *The Autumn People,* Ballantine U2141, 1965 .... **1.75** **2.50** **2.12**

☐ *Dandelion Wine,* Bantam FP55, fourth edition **1.75** **2.50** **2.12**

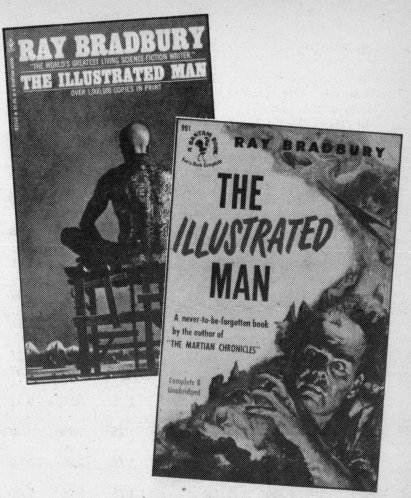

Left to Right: **The Illustrated Man,** by Ray Bradbury,
Bantam, Q2112, **$2.25–$3.00;**
The Illustrated Man, by Ray Bradbury,
1952, Bantam, 991, **$5.00–$7.00.**

	Current Price Range		C/Y Avg.
☐ *Dandelion Wine,* Corgi 08276, 1969, second edition	3.00	4.00	3.50
☐ *Dandelion Wine,* Bantam A1922, 1959	4.00	5.50	4.37
☐ *Dandelion Wine,* Bantam, NP8027, twenty-third edition	1.25	1.75	1.50
☐ *The Day It Rained Forever,* Penguin 1878, 1980, eighth edition	2.00	3.00	2.50
☐ *Fahrenheit 451,* Ballantine U5060, 1966, seventh edition	2.25	3.00	2.37
☐ *Fahrenheit 451,* Ballantine 01636, 1970, twenty-second edition	2.25	3.00	2.37
☐ *Fahrenheit 451,* Bal-Hi U2843, 1967, second edition	2.25	3.00	2.37
☐ *Fahrenheit 451, Bal-Hi 70002, 1969, seventh edition*	2.25	3.00	2.50
☐ *Fahrenheit 451,* Del Rey 29234, 1981, fifty-fourth edition	2.25	3.00	2.37
☐ *Fahrenheit 451,* Ballantine 25049, 1975, thirty-ninth edition	1.50	2.00	1.75
☐ *Fahrenheit 451,* Ballantine 02302, 1971, twenty-third edition	1.00	1.50	1.25
☐ *Fahrenheit 451,* Ballantine 41, 1953	5.00	7.00	5.37
☐ *Fahrenheit 451,* Ballantine 382K, no date	2.75	3.50	3.12
☐ *The Golden Apples Of The Sun,* Bantam H3357, 1967, third edition	1.25	1.75	1.50
☐ *Golden Apples Of The Sun,* Bantam J2306, 1961	1.75	2.25	2.00
☐ *Golden Apples Of The Sun,* Bantam S4867, eighth edition	1.75	2.25	2.00
☐ *The Golden Apples Of The Sun,* Bantam A1241, 1954	5.00	7.00	5.37
☐ *The Golden Apples Of The Sun,* Bantam Q2247, fifteenth edition	1.25	1.75	1.50
☐ *The Halloween Tree,* Bantam QP8470, 1974	2.00	2.75	2.37
☐ *I Sing The Body Electric,* Corgi 09706, 1975, third edition	2.25	3.00	2.62
☐ *I Sing The Body Electric,* Bantam 11942, tenth edition	1.75	2.25	2.00

	Current Price Range		C/Y Avg.
☐ *Illustrated Man*, Bantam 991, 1952 ...	5.00	7.00	3.62
☐ *Illustrated Man*, Bantam 1282, 1954, third edition	4.25	6.00	5.00
☐ *Illustrated Man*, Bantam 1282, 1954, third edition	3.50	5.00	4.00
☐ *Illustrated Man*, Bantam H3484, 1967, sixth edition	2.25	2.75	2.50
☐ *Illustrated Man*, Bantam S4482, 1969, eleventh edition	2.25	2.75	2.50
☐ *The Illustrated Man*, Bantam H3484, seventh edition	2.00	2.50	2.25
☐ *The Machineries Of Joy*, Bantam 23120, 1983, second edition	2.50	3.25	2.87
☐ *Machineries Of Joy*, Panther 4361, 1977	2.00	2.75	2.37
☐ *Machineries Of Joy*, Bantam H2988, 1965	2.00	2.75	2.37
☐ *The Machineries Of Joy*, Bantam S5258, eleventh edition	1.75	2.25	2.00
☐ *The Martian Chronicles*, Bantam N5613, 1970, twenty-first edition	1.75	2.25	2.00
☐ *Martian Chronicles*, Bantam 886, 1951	9.00	12.00	8.25
☐ *Martian Chronicles*, Bantam 1261, 1954, third edition	6.00	8.00	6.00
☐ *Martian Chronicles*, Bantam Special Edition, sixteenth edition	1.85	2.35	2.00
☐ *Martian Chronicles*, Bantam NP5613, thirty-sixth edition	1.85	2.35	2.00
☐ *The Martian Chronicles*, Scholastic 16109, no date	1.35	1.85	1.50
☐ *The Martian Chronicles*, Bantam F3243, tenth edition	1.35	1.85	1.50
☐ *Medicine For Melancholy*, Bantam A2069, 1960.....................	3.50	4.75	3.50
☐ *Medicine For Melancholy*, Bantam H3398, fifth edition	2.00	3.00	2.12
☐ *Medicine For Melancholy*, Bantam S5268, fifth edition	2.00	3.00	2.12
☐ *A Medicine For Melancholy*, Bantam N8098, fourteenth edition	2.00	3.00	2.00
☐ *October Country*, Ballantine F580, 1962, second edition	2.00	3.00	2.50

		Current Price Range		C/Y Avg.

☐	*October Country,* Ballantine U2139, 1964, third edition	2.50	3.50	2.62
☐	*The October Country,* Ballantine 1968, 72138, fifth edition	2.00	2.75	2.37
☐	*R Is For Rocket,* Bantam FP164, 1966	1.75	2.25	2.00
☐	*R Is For Rocket,* Bantam NP7988, 1974, fourteenth edition	1.25	1.75	1.50
☐	*S Is For Space,* Bantam S5621, 1970	1.75	2.50	2.12
☐	*Something Wicked This Way Comes,* Bantam H2630, 1963	3.50	4.75	3.50
☐	*Something Wicked This Way Comes,* Bantam S3408, eighth edition	2.00	2.75	2.37
☐	**Brady, Leo,** *Edge of Doom,* Popular Library 260 (painted cover picturing Dana Andrews and Farley Granger)	7.00	10.00	8.25
☐	**Braine, John,** *Room at the Top,* Signet 1569 (painted cover picturing Laurence Harvey)	5.00	7.00	5.75
☐	**Brand, Max,** *The King Bird Rides,* Warner 90-305, 1980	2.50	3.25	2.75
☐	**Brandon, Ralph,** *Joy Killer,* Vega V4 . . .	4.00	5.00	4.50
☐	**Brebner, John B.,** *Explorers of North America,* Anchor 44	2.75	3.50	3.00
☐	**Brecht, Bertold,** *The Good Woman of Setzuan,* Grove 117	4.00	5.25	4.50
☐	**Brennan, Alice,** *Snows Of Summer,* Midwood 136, 1961	3.00	4.00	3.50
☐	**Brennan, Dan,** *No Sense Of Shame,* Midwood F323, 1963	1.75	2.50	2.12
☐	*The President's Right Hand,* Tower 43-878, 1967	4.00	5.00	4.25
☐	**Brennan, Joseph P.,** *Nine Horrors,* Ballantine 587 (cover artwork by Powers)	4.25	5.25	4.75
☐	**Brennen, Alice,** *Circle of Fear,* Monarch 476 (cover artwork by Marchetti)	3.75	4.50	4.00
☐	**Brenner, Charles,** *An Elementary Textbook of Psychoanalysis,* Anchor 102 . .	2.50	3.25	2.75
☐	**Breslin, Howard,** *A Hundred Hills,* Perma 4204	3.50	4.50	3.75
☐	**Brett, Michael,** *Diecast,* Gold Medal K1360, 1963	1.50	2.25	1.87
☐	*Ear For Murder,* Pocket 50518, 1967	2.00	2.75	2.37

		Current Price Range		C/Y Avg.
☐	*Ear For Murder,* Pocket 50518, 1968, second edition	1.35	1.85	1.50
☐	*The Flight Of The Stiff,* Pocket 55092, 1969, second edition	1.35	1.85	1.50
☐	*The Flight Of The Stiff,* Pocket 50528, 1967	1.85	2.65	2.12
☐	*Kill Him Quickly It's Raining,* Pocket 50517, 1967, second edition	1.85	2.65	2.12
☐	*Kill Him Quickly It's Raining,* Pocket 50517, 1966	1.85	2.65	2.12
☐	*Lie A Little Die A Little,* Pocket 55003, 1969, second edition	1.25	1.75	1.50
☐	*Slit My Throat Gently,* Pocket 55091, 1969, second edition	1.85	2.65	2.12
☐	*Slit My Throat Gently,* Pocket 55093, 1969, second edition	1.85	2.65	2.12
☐	*Turn Blue You Murderers,* Pocket 55093, 1969, second edition	1.25	1.75	1.50
☐	*We The Killers,* Pocket 50561, 1967	1.75	2.50	2.12
☐	*We The Killers,* Pocket 55094, 1969, second edition	1.25	1.75	1.50
☐	**Brett, Rosalind,** *Spring at the Villa,* Harlequin 908	3.00	3.75	3.30
☐	**Brett, Simon,** *Cast In Order Of Disappearance,* Berkley 04134, 1979	1.50	2.25	1.87
☐	**Brewer, Gil,** *13 French Street,* Gold Medal 1326	3.00	3.75	3.30
☐	**Brickhill, Paul,** *The Dam Busters,* Ballantine 101 (photo cover picturing Richard Todd and Michael Redgrave)	4.00	5.50	4.50
☐	**Brickhill, Paul,** *Great Escape,* Crest S436, 1961	1.00	1.50	1.25
☐	**Brister, Richard,** *The Wolf Streak,* Avon T548	3.75	4.50	4.25
☐	**Bristow, Gwen,** *This Side of Glory,* Perma 5089	3.25	4.00	3.50
☐	**Brogan, D.W.,** *The American Character,* Vintage V37	2.75	3.50	3.00
☐	**Bronte, Emily,** *Wuthering Heights,* Dell LC169 (cover artwork by Pucci)	3.00	3.75	3.25
☐	**Brooks, Barbara,** *Just The Two Of Us,* Midwood F323, no date	1.75	2.50	2.12

	Current Price Range		C/Y Avg.
☐ **Brooks, Robert,** *Adultery in Suburbia,* Midwood 866, 1967	4.00	5.00	4.50
☐ **Brown, Carter,** *And The Undead Sing,* Signet T5864, 1973	1.25	1.75	1.50
☐ *Angel!,* Signet D3413, third edition ...	1.85	2.50	2.12
☐ *Angel!,* Signet D3413, 1968, second edition	1.85	2.50	2.12
☐ *Blonde On The Rocks,* Signet T4682, 1971	1.25	1.75	1.50
☐ *Blonde On A Broomstick,* Signet D2831, 1966	2.25	3.00	2.37
☐ *The Body,* Signet T4550, fifth edition	1.75	2.50	2.12
☐ *The Bombshell,* Signet 1767, 1960 ..	1.50	2.00	1.75
☐ *The Bombshell,* Signet D3097, 1967, second edition	1.85	2.50	2.12
☐ *The Bombshell,* Signet D3097, third edition	1.85	2.50	2.12
☐ *The Born Loser,* Signet T5496, 1973	1.50	2.00	1.75
☐ *The Brazen,* Signet S1836, 1960	2.25	3.00	2.37
☐ *The Brazen,* Signet P4298, 1970, second edition	1.85	2.50	2.12
☐ *The Brazen,* Signet P4298, third edition	1.85	2.50	2.12
☐ *The Bump and Grind Murders,* Signet G2451, 1964	2.00	2.75	2.37
☐ *Burden Of Guilt,* Signet Y7885, 1978	1.35	1.85	1.50
☐ *Burden Of Guilt,* Signet P4219, 1970	1.35	1.85	1.50
☐ *Catch Me A Phoenix!,* Signet Q5910, third edition	1.85	2.65	2.12
☐ *Charlie Sent Me!,* Signet T4775, third edition	1.85	2.65	2.12
☐ *The Coffin Bird,* Signet P4394, 1970	1.50	2.00	1.75
☐ *The Hang-Up Kid,* Signet P4159, 1970	1.75	2.50	2.12
☐ *The Hellcat,* Signet S2122, 1962	2.00	2.75	2.37
☐ *The Hong Kong Caper,* Signet S2180, 1962	1.85	2.65	2.12
☐ *House Of Sorcery,* Signet D3218, 1967	1.85	2.65	2.12
☐ *The Ice-Cold Nude,* Signet P3876, 1969, second edition	1.85	2.65	2.12
☐ *The Invisible Flamini,* Signet T4854, 1971	1.85	2.65	2.12
☐ *The Jade-Eyed Jungle,* Signet G2355, 1963	2.75	3.75	2.87

	Current Price Range		C/Y Avg.
☐ *Lament For A Lousy Lover,* Signet S1856, 1960	4.00	5.50	4.25
☐ *Lament For A Lousy Lover,* Signet 03162, 1967, second edition	2.00	3.00	2.12
☐ *Long Time No Leola,* Signet D3190, 1967	1.75	2.50	2.12
☐ *The Lover,* Signet 02741, third edition	1.75	2.50	2.12
☐ *Lover Don't Come Back!,* Signet P3963, third edition	1.50	2.00	1.75
☐ *The Loving and The Dead,* Signet 1654, 1959	2.25	3.00	2.50
☐ *The Loving and The Dead,* Signet D2808, third edition	2.25	2.50	2.50
☐ *The Master,* Signet T5363, 1973	1.25	1.75	1.50
☐ *The Million Dollar Babe,* Signet D3636, 1968, second edition	1.75	2.50	2.12
☐ *The Mini-Murders,* Signet D3585, 1968	2.00	2.75	2.37
☐ *Model For Murder,* Tower 51527, 1980	1.00	1.50	1.25
☐ *Murder In The Family Way,* Signet T4722, 1971	1.85	2.65	2.12
☐ *Murder Is The Message,* Signet P4105, 1969	1.85	2.65	2.12
☐ *Murder Is So Nostalgic!,* Signet T5064, 1972	1.75	2.50	2.37
☐ *Murder Is A Package Deal,* Signet G2530, 1964	2.00	2.75	2.37
☐ *Murder Is A Package Deal,* Signet T5532, third edition	1.75	2.50	2.12
☐ *Murder Wears A Mantilla,* Signet S2048, 1962	1.25	1.75	1.50
☐ *Murder Wears A Mantilla,* Signet T5275, third edition	1.75	2.50	2.12
☐ *A Murderer Among Us,* Signet P4081, third edition	1.50	2.00	1.75
☐ **Brown, Carter,** *The Plush-Lined Coffin,* Signet D3289, 1967	1.75	2.50	2.12
☐ *The Sad-Eyed Seductress,* Signet P4246, 1970, second edition	1.75	2.50	2.12
☐ *The Sad-Eyed Seductress,* Signet P4246, third edition	1.75	2.50	2.12
☐ *The Savage Salome,* Signet S1896, 1961	1.50	2.00	1.75

		Current Price Range		C/Y Avg.
☐	*The Seven Sirens,* Signet T4908, 1972	1.25	1.75	1.50
☐	*The Sex Clinic,* Signet T4658, 1971 ..	1.25	1.75	1.50
☐	*The Silken Nightmare,* Signet T5277, third edition	1.85	2.65	2.12
☐	*The Silken Nightmare,* Signet G2400, 1963	1.85	2.65	2.12
☐	*The Sometime Wife,* Signet D2757, 1965	1.85	2.65	2.12
☐	*The Streaked-Blonde Slave,* Signet P4042, 1969	1.90	2.40	2.15
☐	*Suddenly By Violence,* Signet 1722, 1959	1.85	2.65	2.12
☐	*The Temptress,* Signet D2898, third edition	1.85	2.65	2.12
☐	*Terror Comes Creeping,* Signet D2934, third edition	1.85	2.65	2.12
☐	*True Son Of The Beast!,* Signet P4268, 1970	2.00	2.75	2.37
☐	*Until Temptation Do Us Part,* Signet Y6840, third edition	1.75	2.50	2.12
☐	*The Up-Tight Blonde,* Signet P3955, 1969	1.75	2.50	2.12
☐	*The Victim,* Signet D2606, 1964, second edition	2.00	3.00	2.50
☐	*The Victim,* Signet D2606, third edition	1.75	2.50	2.12
☐	*The Wanton,* Signet D2962, 1966, second edition	1.75	2.50	2.12
☐	*The Wanton,* Signet D2962, third edition	1.75	2.50	2.12
☐	**Brown, Fredric,** *Death Has Many Doors,* Bantam 1567, 1957, third edition	6.00	8.00	6.00
☐	*Death Has Many Doors,* Bantam 1040, 1952	8.00	11.00	8.50
☐	*The Deep End,* Bantam 1215, 1954 ..	6.75	9.00	7.00
☐	*The Fabulous Clipjoint,* Bantam 1134, 1953, second edition	6.50	8.50	6.00
☐	*Here Comes A Candle,* Bantam 943, 1951	12.50	18.00	12.50
☐	*Knock Three-One-Two,* Bantam A2135, 1960	4.50	6.00	4.62
☐	*The Lenient Beast,* Bantam 1712, 1958	6.50	8.50	6.75

	Current Price Range		C/Y Avg.
☐ *Madball*, Gold Medal S1132, 1961 ...	4.50	6.00	5.00
☐ *Madball*, Bantam 2E, 1953	8.00	11.00	8.50
☐ *Mostly Murder*, Pennant P59, 1954 ..	5.50	7.25	6.12
☐ *The Murderers*, Bantam J2587, 1963	4.25	5.75	6.12
☐ *Nightmares and Geezenstacks*, Bantam J2296, 1961	6.75	8.75	7.00
☐ *Nightmares and Geezenstacks*, Bantam 12456, 1979	1.50	2.00	1.87
☐ *One For The Road*, Bantam 1990, 1959	6.00	8.00	6.62
☐ *The Screaming Mimi*, Bantam 831, 1950	8.25	11.00	8.75
☐ *The Screaming Mimi*, Bantam 1312, 1955, second edition	4.25	5.75	4.50
☐ *The Screaming Mimi*, Bantam 1757, 1958, third edition	3.75	4.75	4.00
☐ *The Wench Is Dead*, Bantam 1565, 1957	9.00	12.00	9.50
☐ **Brown, Helen G.,** *Sex and the Single Girl,* Pocket Books 75041 (photo cover picturing Natalie Wood and Tony Curtis)	7.00	10.00	8.25
☐ **Brown, Himan,** *Strange Tales From Mystery Theater,* Popular 08543, 1976	1.50	2.25	1.87
☐ **Brown, Joe David,** *Paper Moon,* Signet W6409, fifteenth edition	1.50	2.25	1.87
☐ **Brown, Joy,** *Night Of Terror,* Harlequin 72, 1950	5.00	7.00	5.12
☐ **Brown, MacKenzie,** *The White Umbrella,* University of California Press (no serial number), 1959	6.00	8.00	6.75
☐ **Brown, R.D.,** *Prime Suspect,* Tower 51685, 1981	1.50	2.25	1.87
☐ **Brown, Dr. Walter,** *The Single Girl,* Monarch 515	3.75	4.75	4.00
☐ **Brown, Wenzell,** *The Hoods Ride In,* Pyramid G439, 1959	2.25	3.00	2.62
☐ *The Murder Kick,* Gold Medal S1013, 1960	2.50	3.25	2.87
☐ *Run Chico Run,* Gold Medal S1042, 1960, third edition	2.25	3.00	2.62

		Current Price Range		C/Y Avg.
☐	*Sherry,* Monarch 403, 1964	3.75	4.75	4.00
☐	*The Wicked Streets,* Gold Medal 640, 1957	4.00	5.75	4.25
☐	**Browne, Gerald A.,** *11 Harrowhouse,* Dell 2315, 1973	1.25	1.75	1.50
☐	*Green Ice,* Dell 13224, 1979	2.25	3.00	2.62
☐	*Hazard,* Pocket 82387, fourth edition	1.65	2.35	1.87
☐	*Slide,* Dell 17701, 1977, second edition	1.65	2.35	1.87
☐	**Browne, Howard,** *Thin Air,* Dell 894, 1956	4.00	5.50	4.12
☐	**Bruce, Jean,** *The Last Quarter Hour,* Crest K795, 1965	3.50	4.50	3.62
☐	*Photo Finish,* Corgi GC7210, 1965 ...	2.50	3.25	2.87
☐	*Pole Reaction,* Corgi 08623, 1971, second edition	1.75	2.50	2.12
☐	*Shock Tactics,* Corgi GC7495, 1966	2.00	2.75	2.37
☐	*Soft Sell,* Corgi GC7138, 1965	2.75	3.50	3.12
☐	*Trouble In Tokyo,* Crest K806, 1965	2.25	3.00	2.62
☐	**Brucker, Margaretta,** *Murder At Lovers Lake,* Dagger House 20, 1943	7.00	10.00	7.12
☐	**Brunner, John,** *The Avengers of Carrig,* Dell 0356, 1969	2.25	3.00	2.37
☐	*The Avengers Of Carrig,* DAW UE1509, #369, 1980	2.25	3.00	2.37
☐	*Bedlam Planet,* Ace G-709, 1968	2.25	3.00	2.37
☐	*Black Is The Color,* Pyramid X1955, 1969	2.25	3.00	2.62
☐	*Blacklash,* Pyramid T-2107, 1969	1.75	2.50	2.12
☐	*Born Under Mars,* Ace 07161, 1973, second edition	1.25	1.75	1.50
☐	*Catch A Falling Star,* Ace G-761, 1968	1.25	1.75	1.50
☐	*Day Of The Star Cities,* Ace F-361, 1965	2.00	2.75	2.37
☐	*Double Double,* Del Rey 27964, 1979, second edition	2.00	2.75	2.25
☐	*Double Double,* Ballantine 72019, 1969	1.75	2.25	2.00
☐	*Double Double,* Ballantine 27694, 1979, second edition	1.50	2.00	1.75
☐	*Dramaturges Of Yan,* Ace 16668, 1972	2.00	2.75	2.37
☐	*The Dramaturges Of Yan,* Nel 018245, 1974	2.25	3.25	2.75

	Current Price Range		C/Y Avg.
☐ *The Dreaming Earth,* Pyramid N3456, 1975, fourth edition	1.50	2.00	1.75
☐ *The Dreaming Earth,* Pyramid F-829, 1963	2.00	3.00	2.50
☐ *The Dreaming Earth,* Pyramid T2325, 1970, second edition	1.85	2.65	2.12
☐ *From This Day Forward,* DAW UQ1072, #72, 1973	1.85	2.65	2.12
☐ *Give Warning To The World,* DAW UQ1122, #112, 1974	2.00	2.75	2.37
☐ *Good Men Do Nothing,* Pyramid T2443, 1971	1.25	2.75	1.50
☐ *Into The Slave Nebula,* Lancer 73-797, 1968	2.00	3.00	2.50
☐ *The Long Result,* Ballantine U2329, 1966	1.50	2.00	1.75
☐ *The Long Result,* Ballantine 01887, 1970, second edition	1.25	1.75	1.50
☐ *The Long Result,* Del Rey 29639, 1981, second edition	2.00	2.75	2.37
☐ *Meeting At Infinity,* Ace 52400, no date	1.75	2.50	2.12
☐ *Now Then!,* Avon S323, 1968	2.50	3.50	3.00
☐ *Out Of My Mind,* Ballantine U5064, 1967	2.00	2.75	2.37
☐ *Polymath,* DAW UY1217, third edition	1.50	2.00	1.75
☐ *The Productions Of Time,* DAW UW1329, #261, 1977	1.85	2.35	2.00
☐ *The Productions Of Time,* Signet P3113, 1967	1.85	2.35	2.00
☐ *Quicksand,* Bantam S4212, 1969	1.85	2.35	2.00
☐ *The Repairmen Of Cyclops,* DAW UE1638, #443, 1981	2.00	2.75	2.37
☐ *The Sheep Look Up,* Orbit, 1292, 1977	2.50	3.25	2.87
☐ *The Shockwave Rider,* Ballantine 24853, 1976	1.75	2.25	2.00
☐ *The Squares Of The City,* Ballantine 01886, 1970, second edition	2.00	2.75	2.37
☐ *The Squares Of The City,* Ballantine 23436, 1973, third edition	1.25	1.75	1.60
☐ *The Squares Of The City,* Del Rey 27739, 1978, fourth edition	1.50	2.00	1.75

	Current Price Range		C/Y Avg.
☐ *The Squares Of The City,* Ballantine 06035, 1965	2.50	3.50	3.00
☐ *The Stardroppers,* DAW UQ1023, #23, 1972	1.75	2.25	2.00
☐ *The Stone That Never Came Down,* DAW UY1150, #133, 1975	1.00	1.50	1.25
☐ *The Super Barbarians,* Ace D-547, 1962	4.00	5.50	4.37
☐ *Times Without Number,* Ace 81271, 1969	2.00	2.75	2.37
☐ **Bryan, George,** *Stronger Than Passion,* Monarch 1959	1.25	1.75	1.50
☐ *Timescoop,* Dell 8916, 1969	1.75	2.25	2.00
☐ *To Conquer Chaos,* Ace F-277, 1964	2.00	3.00	2.55
☐ *Total Eclipse,* DAW UY1993, #162, 1975	1.75	2.25	2.00
☐ *Total Eclipse,* DAW UW1398, third edition	1.50	2.00	1.75
☐ *The Traveler In Black,* Ace 82210, 1971	2.00	3.00	2.50
☐ *Wear The Butchers' Medal,* Pocket 50129, 1965	1.75	2.50	2.12
☐ *Web Of Everywhere,* Bantam Q8398, 1974	1.00	1.50	1.25
☐ *The Whole Man,* Ballantine 01885, 1970, second edition	2.00	2.75	2.37
☐ *The Whole Man,* Del Rey 17088, 1977, fourth edition	1.75	2.25	2.00
☐ *The Whole Man,* Ballantine U2219, 1964	2.50	3.50	2.62
☐ *The World Swappers,* Ace G-649, no date	1.25	1.75	1.50
☐ *The Wrong End Of Time,* DAW UQ1061, #61, 1973	1.75	2.50	2.12
☐ *The Wrong End Of Time,* Methuen 34580, 1976	2.00	3.00	2.50
☐ *The Wrong End Of Time,* DAW UE1598, fifth edition	1.50	2.00	1.75
☐ **Buchan, John,** *Greenmantle,* Penguin 1132, 1961, fourth edition	3.00	4.00	3.50
☐ *Greenmantle,* Pocket 94, 1945, eighth edition	5.00	7.00	5.00

	Current Price Range		C/Y Avg.
☐ *Mountain Meadow,* Bantam 71, 1946	5.00	7.00	5.00
☐ *The 39 Steps,* Pocket 69, 1941, seventh edition	4.50	6.00	4.62
☐ *The 39 Steps,* Pocket 69, 1940, second edition	6.00	8.00	6.00
☐ *The Thirty-Nine Steps,* Popular Library K58, 1963	3.00	4.00	3.50
☐ *The Thirty-Nine Steps,* Pan 14, 1955, sixth edition	2.00	2.75	2.37
☐ *The Thirty-Nine Steps,* Pan G218, 1964, fifteenth edition	1.75	2.50	2.12
☐ *The Thirty-Nine Steps,* Pan G218, 1967, eighteenth edition	2.25	3.00	2.62
☐ *The Thirty-Nine Steps,* Pan X696, 1967, nineteenth edition	2.25	3.00	2.62
☐ *The Thirty-Nine Steps,* Popular Library 08312, no date	1.75	2.50	2.12
☐ *The Three Hostages,* Bantam 31, 1946	2.50	3.50	3.00
☐ **Buck, Pearl S.,** *The Hidden Flower,* Pocket Books 78942, 1975	2.00	3.00	2.40
☐ *Fourteen Stories,* Cardinal GC163 ...	4.00	5.50	4.50
☐ *The Good Earth,* Reader's League (no serial number), 1943	5.00	6.50	5.50
☐ *Hidden Flower,* Cardinal 387 (cover artwork by Charles)	3.00	4.00	3.25
☐ *Satan Never Sleeps,* Cardinal C429 (photo cover picturing William Holden, Clifton Webb and France Nuyen)	5.00	7.00	5.75
☐ **Buell, John,** *The Pyx,* Crest 408 (cover artwork by Phillips)	3.50	4.25	3.75
☐ **Bueltmann, A.J.,** *White Queen of the Cannibals,* Moody 6, 1959	5.00	6.50	5.50
☐ **Buffalo Bill,** *Leap For Life,* Gold Star 33 (This was not the original Buffalo Bill—William S. Cody—but a modern novelist using the name)	3.00	3.75	3.50
☐ **Bullitt, Stimson,** *To Be A Politician,* Anchor 264	3.00	3.75	3.50
☐ **Bunch, Taylor G.,** *Behold the Man,* Southern Publishing (no serial number), 1946	5.00	7.00	5.75

Left to Right: **The Hidden Flower,** by Pearl S. Buck,
$2.00–$3.00; This Side of Innocence,
by Taylor Caldwell, 1974,
Fawcett Popular Library, **$2.00–$3.00.**

	Current Price Range		C/Y Avg.

☐ **Burke, John,** *A Hard Day's Night,* Dell 0489 (photo cover picturing The Beatles) — 8.00 / 11.00 / 9.00

☐ **Burroughs, Edgar Rice,** *A Fighting Man of Mars,* Ace F190 (cover artwork by Krenkel) .... — 3.00 / 4.00 / 3.25

☐ *At the Earth's Core,* Ace F156 (cover artwork by Krenkel) .... — 3.00 / 4.00 / 3.25

☐ *Back To the Stone Age,* Ace F245 (cover artwork by Frazetta) .... — 4.00 / 5.00 / 4.25

☐ *The Beasts of Tarzan,* Ace F203 (cover artwork by Frazetta) .... — 6.00 / 7.00 / 6.00

☐ *Beyond the Farthest Star,* Ace F282 (cover artwork by Frazetta) .... — 4.00 / 5.00 / 4.25

☐ *Carson of Venus,* Ace F247 (cover artwork by Frazetta) .... — 4.00 / 5.00 / 4.25

☐ *The Chessmen of Mars,* Ace F170 (cover artwork by Krenkel) .... — 6.00 / 7.00 / 6.50

☐ *Escape on Venus,* Ace 21560 (cover artwork by Krenkel) .... — 3.00 / 4.00 / 3.25

☐ *The Eternal Savage,* Ace 21801 (cover artwork by Krenkel) .... — 3.00 / 4.00 / 3.25

☐ *Land of Hidden Men,* Ace 47011 (cover artwork by Krenkel) .... — 3.00 / 4.00 / 3.25

☐ *Land of Terror,* Ace 46996 (cover artwork by Frazetta) .... — 3.00 / 4.00 / 3.25

☐ *The Land That Time Forgot,* Ace F213 (cover artwork by Krenkel) .... — 4.00 / 5.00 / 4.25

☐ *The Lost Continent,* Ace F235 (cover artwork by Frazetta) .... — 4.00 / 5.00 / 4.25

☐ *Lost on Venus,* Ace F221 (cover artwork by Frazetta) .... — 4.00 / 5.00 / 4.25

☐ *The Mad King,* Ace 51401 (cover artwork by Frazetta) .... — 3.00 / 4.00 / 3.25

☐ *The Mastermind of Mars,* Ace F181 (cover artwork by Krenkel) .... — 6.00 / 7.00 / 6.50

☐ *The Monster Men,* Ace F182 (cover artwork by Frazetta) .... — 5.00 / 6.00 / 5.25

☐ **Burstein, A. Joseph,** *The Sexually Neurotic Male,* Midwood 827, 1967 .... — 4.00 / 5.00 / 4.25

☐ **Busch, Niven,** *Duel in the Sun,* Popular Library 102 (photo cover picturing Gregory Peck and Jennifer Jones) .... — 6.00 / 8.00 / 6.50

	Current Price Range		C/Y Avg.

☐ *The Furies,* Bantam 777 (painted cover picturing Wendell Corey and Barbara Stanwyck) **3.50 4.50 3.75**

☐ **Butterworth, W.E.,** *The Love-Go-Round,* Berkley 619 (cover artwork by Phillips, 1962) **4.50 5.50 4.75**

☐ **Byrd, Richard E.,** *Alone,* Ace K102 .... **3.00 4.00 3.25**

☐ **Cadell, Elizabeth,** *I Love A Lass,* Berkley 686 .... **3.00 4.00 3.25**

☐ **Caesar, Gene,** *Rifle For Rent,* Monarch 338, 1963 .... **4.50 5.50 5.00**

☐ **Caille, Ward,** *Behold The Man,* Lumen 534, 1955 (A work by this same title, authored by Taylor Bunch, was published in 1946) **4.00 5.00 4.50**

☐ **Caldwell, Erskine,** *Claudelle Inglish,* Signet 1778 .... **4.00 5.25 4.50**

☐ *Jenny By Nature,* Signet 2121 .... **4.00 5.25 4.50**

☐ *This Very Earth,* Signet 2682 .... **4.00 5.25 4.50**

☐ *When You Think of Me,* Signet 1839 (artwork by Louis MacOuillard) **4.00 5.25 4.50**

☐ **Caldwell, Taylor,** *Your Sins and Mine,* Gold Medal 525, 1955 .... **2.75 3.75 2.87**

☐ **Calet, Henri,** *Paris My Love,* Berkley #G-20 .... **2.50 3.00 2.75**

☐ **Callahan, John,** *Come in Shooting,* Ace F120 .... **3.75 4.50 4.00**

☐ **Calvano, Tony,** *High Road to Shame,* Leisure 1121 .... **3.00 3.75 3.25**

☐ **Cameron, Lou,** *Angel's Flight,* Gold Medal 1047, 1960 .... **5.00 6.50 5.50**

☐ **Campbell, Alexander,** *Flesh of the Earth,* Monarch 511 (cover artwork by Kalin) **3.75 4.50 4.00**

☐ **Campbell, Jean,** *The Oldest Profession,* Belmont #210 .... **1.75 2.25 2.00**

☐ **Camus, Albert,** *The Fall,* Vintage V223 (The author's name is pronounced Al-bare Ca-moo) **3.00 4.00 3.25**

☐ **Canary, Glenn,** *The Sadist,* Monarch 280 (cover artwork by DeSoto, 1962) **4.00 5.25 4.50**

	Current Price Range		C/Y Avg.

		Current Price Range		C/Y Avg.
☐ **Canning, Victor,** *Bird Of Prey,* Berkley F810, 1963		2.75	3.75	2.87
☐ *Black Flamingo,* Berkley F1038, 1965		2.25	3.25	2.37
☐ *Black Flamingo,* Pan 23490, 1977, second edition		1.75	2.50	2.12
☐ *The Burning Eye,* Crest S484, 1961 . .		1.75	2.50	2.12
☐ *The Chasm,* Yellowjacket C75, 1952		5.75	7.75	6.12
☐ *The Chasm,* Berkley F802, 1963		2.50	3.25	2.87
☐ *The Chasm,* Bantam 313, 1949		4.50	6.00	4.75
☐ *A Delivery Of Furies,* Mayflower 12052, 1972		2.50	3.50	2.62
☐ *Doubled In Diamonds,* Pan 02125, 1968		2.50	3.50	2.62
☐ *A Forest Of Eyes,* Berkley F874, 1964		1.75	2.50	2.12
☐ *A Forest Of Eyes,* Harlequin 393, 1957		5.50	7.75	6.00
☐ *The Golden Salamander,* Berkley F758, 1963		1.75	2.50	2.12
☐ *A Handful Of Silver,* Berkley F889, 1964		1.75	2.50	2.12
☐ *House Of The Seven Flies,* Hodder C208, 1958, second edition		2.75	3.75	3.00
☐ *The House Of The 7 Flies,* Berkley F730, 1963		1.75	2.50	2.12
☐ *The House Of The 7 Flies,* Pan 23597, 1973		2.25	3.00	2.62
☐ *The House Of The Seven Flies,* Hodder C208, 1958, second edition		2.25	3.00	2.62
☐ *The House Of The Seven Flies,* Pan 23597, 1977, second edition		2.75	3.75	2.87
☐ *The Kingsford Mark,* Pan 25176, 1977		2.00	2.75	2.37
☐ *The Kingsford Mark,* Charter 44600, no date		1.75	2.50	2.12
☐ *The Limbo Line,* Berkley F1085, 1965		1.75	2.50	2.12
☐ *The Limbo Line,* Pan X423, 1965		2.75	3.75	2.87
☐ *The Limbo Line,* Pan 10423, 1966, third edition		2.00	2.75	2.37
☐ *The Man From The Turkish Slave,* Berkley F746, 1963		1.85	2.65	2.12
☐ *The Melting Man,* Pan 02538, 1970 . .		1.85	2.65	2.12
☐ *Mr. Finchley Discovers England,* Yellow Jacket 177, no date		4.00	5.50	4.00

		Current Price Range		C/Y Avg.

☐ *The Python Project,* Pan 02364, 1973, second edition **2.00** **2.75** **2.87**

☐ *Queen's Pawn,* Dell 7202, 1973 ..... **1.25** **1.75** **1.50**

☐ *The Rainbird Pattern,* Award AD1294, no date **1.25** **1.75** **1.50**

☐ *The Rainbird Pattern,* Pan 24298, 1974 **2.00** **2.75** **2.37**

☐ *The Scorpio Letters,* Pan X523, 1966 **2.25** **3.00** **2.62**

☐ *The Scorpio Letters,* Avon S204, 1966 **1.50** **2.25** **1.87**

☐ *Scorpio Letters,* Pan X523, 1967, second edition **2.25** **3.00** **2.37**

☐ *The Whip Hand,* Pan X674, 1967 .... **2.25** **3.00** **2.37**

☐ *The Whip Hand,* Signet P3004, 1966 **1.75** **2.50** **2.12**

☐ **Cannon, Brenda,** *Good Neighbors,* Moody 198 .... **3.50** **4.50** **3.75**

☐ **Cannon, Curt,** *Cannon For Hire,* Gold Medal 1325 .... **2.75** **3.50** **3.00**

☐ **Cantor, Hal,** *Ghosts and Things,* Berkley 666 (anthology) **3.75** **4.50** **4.00**

☐ **Cantwell, John,** *The Awakening,* Hillman 156 .... **3.00** **4.00** **3.25**

☐ **Capote, Truman,** *Breakfast at Tiffany's,* Signet 1727 (photo cover picturing Audrey Hepburn) **4.00** **5.50** **4.50**

☐ **Capp, Al,** *The World of Li'l Abner,* Ballantine 8 .... **17.00** **23.00** **19.00**

☐ **Cappelli, Mario,** *Scramble,* Ace F132 (cover artwork by Tossey) **3.50** **4.25** **4.00**

☐ **Carco, Francis,** *Only A Woman,* Berkley #337 .... **2.75** **3.50** **3.12**

☐ **Cargoe, Richard,** *The Back Of The Tiger,* Belmont #242 .... **1.00** **1.50** **1.25**

☐ **Carleton, Marjorie,** *One Night of Terror,* Berkley 411 .... **4.00** **5.00** **4.50**

☐ **Carlova, John,** *Song of Penang,* Berkley 2042 (cover artwork by Nappi) **4.00** **5.00** **4.50**

☐ **Carmichael, Stokely,** *Black Power,* Vintage V33 .... **5.00** **6.00** **5.75**

☐ **Carpenter, Margaret,** *Experiment Perilous,* Pyramid 961 .... **3.75** **4.50** **4.00**

	Current Price Range		C/Y Avg.

☐ **Carpozi, George,** *Marilyn Monroe: Her Own Story,* Belmont L508 (photo cover picturing Marilyn Monroe, and with interior photos) **10.00 15.00 11.50**

☐ **Carr, Jay,** *Vacation Girls,* Beacon #8675F **1.50 2.00 1.75**

☐ **Carr, John Dickson,** *4 False Weapons,* Detective Novel Classic 40, no date ... **9.00 12.00 9.50**

☐ *Arabian Nights Murder,* Collier 01835, 1978, eighth edition **1.50 2.00 1.75**

☐ *Below Suspicion,* Bantam A2120, 1960 **2.50 3.25 2.87**

☐ *Below Suspicion,* Bantam F3440, 1967, second edition **2.00 2.75 2.37**

☐ *Below Suspicion,* Bantam 1119, 1953 **4.50 6.00 4.62**

☐ *Below Suspicion,* Award AD1634, 1976 **1.50 2.00 1.75**

☐ *The Blind Barber,* Penguin 528, 1945, fourth edition **7.00 9.50 7.25**

☐ *The Blind Barber,* Collier 01839, 1970, fourth edition **1.75 2.50 2.12**

☐ *The Blind Barber,* Berkley G-80, no date **2.00 3.00 2.50**

☐ *The Blind Barber,* Penguin 528, 1945, third edition **1.75 2.50 2.12**

☐ *Burning Court* (Jones Cover), Award AN1199, no date **1.25 1.75 1.50**

☐ *Burning Court,* Bantam 1207, 1954 .. **6.00 8.00 6.12**

☐ *The Burning Court,* Bantam J2706, 1963, second edition **2.00 2.75 2.37**

☐ *Burning Court* (Jones Cover), Award A459X, 1969 .... **2.00 2.75 2.37**

☐ *The Burning Court* (Jones Cover), Award AN1199, no date **2.25 3.00 2.50**

☐ *Captain Cut-Throat,* Bantam F2708, 1963, second edition **2.50 3.25 2.87**

☐ *Captain Cut-Throat,* Award AD1645, 1976 .... **1.75 2.50 2.12**

☐ *Captain Cut-Throat,* Charter 09134, 1980 .... **1.35 1.85 1.50**

☐ *Case Of Constant Suicide,* Collier 01847, 1975, sixth edition **1.35 1.85 1.50**

☐ *Case Of Constant Suicides,* Collier 01847, 1972, fifth edition **1.75 2.50 2.12**

	Current Price Range		C/Y Avg.
☐ *Case Of Constant Suicides,* Berkley G-60, 1957	3.25	4.50	3.50
☐ *Case Of Constant Suicides,* Collier 01847, 1977, seventh edition	2.00	2.75	2.37
☐ *Case Of The Constant Suicides,* Dell Map 91, 1945	10.00	13.00	10.50
☐ *Castle Skull,* Pocket 448, 1947	6.60	8.50	7.00
☐ *Castle Skull,* Berkley F960, 1964, second edition	2.00	2.75	2.37
☐ *Castle Skull,* Berkley X1600, 1968, third edition	2.00	3.00	2.50
☐ *Castle Skull,* Berkley G412, 1960	2.50	3.25	2.87
☐ *Corpse In the Wax Works,* Dell 775, 1954	4.00	5.50	4.00
☐ *Corpse In The Wax Works,* Collier 01850, 1972, fourth edition	1.75	2.50	2.12
☐ *The Corpse In The Wax Works,* Avon 33, 1943, first edition	6.00	8.00	6.37
☐ *The Corpse In The Wax Works,* Dell 775, no date	4.00	5.00	4.50
☐ *The Crooked Hinge,* Popular 19, 1943	11.00	15.00	11.50
☐ *The Crooked Hinge,* Berkley G-157, 1958	2.00	2.75	2.37
☐ *The Crooked Hinge,* Dell 859, no date	3.00	4.00	3.50
☐ *Dark Of The Moon,* Berkley S1656, 1969	1.75	2.50	2.12
☐ *The Dead Man's Knock,* Bantam F3557, 1967, second edition	2.00	3.00	2.50
☐ *Death Turns The Tables,* Berkley F929, 1964	3.00	4.25	3.62
☐ *Death Watch,* Penguin 914, 1953	4.50	6.50	5.00
☐ *The Devil In Velvet,* Bantam S3637, 1968, second edition	2.00	3.00	2.50
☐ *Dodskortet (In Danish),* Martins Forlag, no date	4.50	6.50	5.00
☐ *The Emperor's Snuff Box,* Penguin C949, 1967, second edition	3.00	4.00	3.50
☐ *Emperor's Snuff Box,* Berkley F1027, 1964	2.75	3.50	3.12
☐ *Emperor's Snuff Box,* Berkley X1652, 1969, fourth edition	2.00	3.00	2.50

		Current Price Range		C/Y Avg.

☐	*Fire Burn,* Bantam S3638, 1968, second edition	1.85	2.35	2.00
☐	*Fire Burn!,* Award AD1483, 1975	1.85	2.35	2.00
☐	*Fire Burn,* Bantam A1847, 1959	3.50	4.25	3.87
☐	*The Four False Weapons,* Collier 01871, 1976, fourth edition	1.50	2.25	1.87
☐	*The Four False Weapons,* Collier 01871, 1979, fifth edition	1.25	1.75	1.50
☐	*The Four False Weapons,* Berkley G-91, no date	2.50	3.25	2.87
☐	*Hag's Nook,* Dell Map 537, 1951	4.00	6.00	5.00
☐	*Hag's Nook,* Berkley G-129, 1958 ...	2.00	2.75	2.37
☐	*Hag's Nook,* Collier 01879, 1970, fourth edition	1.75	2.50	2.12
☐	*Hag's Nook,* Collier 01879, 1966, third edition	2.00	2.75	2.37
☐	*He Who Whispers,* Award AD1518, 1976	1.25	1.75	1.50
☐	*He Who Whispers,* Bantam 896, 1951	6.50	8.50	7.00
☐	*He Who Whispers,* Bantam F3087, 1965, second edition	1.50	2.00	1.67
☐	*He Who Whispers,* Penguin 948, 1955, second edition	3.50	4.50	4.00
☐	*He Who Whispers,* Bantam 1684, 1957, second edition	3.00	4.00	3.50
☐	*The House At Satan's Elbow,* Charter 34372, no date	2.00	2.75	2.37
☐	*The House At Satan's Elbow,* Award AQ1353, 1974	2.00	2.75	2.37
☐	*It Walks By Night,* Pocket 101, 1941	13.00	18.00	14.00
☐	*It Walks By Night,* Avon 621, 1955 ...	8.00	11.00	8.50
☐	*It Walks By Night,* Avon PN283, 1970	1.50	2.00	1.75
☐	*The Lost Gallows,* Pocket 436, 1947	9.00	12.00	9.50
☐	*The Mad Hatter Mystery,* Collier 01881, 1978, sixth edition	1.25	1.75	1.50
☐	*The Mad Hatter Mystery,* Collier 01881, 1965	1.75	2.50	2.12
☐	*The Mad Hatter Mystery,* Berkley G-117, no date	3.00	4.00	3.50
☐	*The Man Who Could Not Shudder,* Bantam 365, 1949	7.50	10.00	8.00

	Current Price Range		C/Y Avg.
☐ *The Man Who Could Not Shudder,* Bantam 365, 1949	7.50	10.00	8.00
☐ *Man Who Could Not Shudder,* Bantam 1504, 1956, second edition	4.00	5.50	4.50
☐ *Man Who Could Not Shudder,* Bantam F2837, 1964, second edition	2.75	3.50	3.12
☐ *Men Who Explained Miracles,* Pyramid R-1083, 1964	3.00	4.00	3.50
☐ *Patrick Butler For The Defense,* Bantam 1682, 1957	4.00	5.25	4.62
☐ *Poison In Jest,* Berkley G-72, 1957 ..	2.75	3.50	3.12
☐ *Poison In Jest,* Collier 01880, 1974, fourth edition	2.00	2.75	2.37
☐ *Poison In Jest,* Collier, 01880, 1965 ..	1.75	2.50	2.12
☐ *Poison In Jest,* Collier 01880, 1968, second edition	2.00	3.00	2.50
☐ *Poison In Jest,* Popular 349, 1951 ...	9.00	12.00	9.50
☐ *Prob. Of Green Capsule,* Bantam 1501, 1956, second edition	4.00	5.50	4.75
☐ *Prob. Of Green Capsule,* Bantam F2751, 1964, second edition	1.75	2.50	2.12
☐ *Problem Of The Green Capsule,* Bantam 101, 1947	8.00	11.00	8.50
☐ *The Problem Of The Wire Cage,* Bantam 304, 1948	10.50	14.00	10.50
☐ *Problem Of The Wire Cage,* Bantam 1503, 1956, second edition	3.75	4.75	4.00
☐ *Problem Of Green Capsule,* Berkley S1890, 1970	1.75	2.50	2.12
☐ *Problem Of The Green Capsule,* Award AD1565, 1976	2.00	2.75	2.37
☐ *Problem Of Green Capsule,* Bantam 1505, 1956, second edition	1.75	2.50	2.12
☐ *Problem Of The Green Capsule,* Bantam 101, 1947	3.75	4.75	4.00
☐ *Problem Of The Wire Cage,* Berkley S1907, 1970	1.75	2.50	2.12
☐ *Problem Of The Wire Cage,* Bantam 304, 1948	3.50	4.50	4.00
☐ *Problem Of Green Capsule,* Award AD1565, 1976	2.00	2.75	2.37

		Current Price Range		C/Y Avg.

☐	*Problem Of The Wire Cage,* Bantam F2877, 1964, second edition	2.50	3.25	2.87
☐	*Scandal At High Chimneys,* Bantam A2155, 1960	2.75	3.75	3.25
☐	*The Sleeping Sphinx,* Bantam 996, 1952	7.00	8.00	7.50
☐	*The Third Bullet,* Bantam H4587, 1969, fourth edition	2.00	3.00	2.50
☐	*The Third Bullet,* Bantam 1447, 1956	5.00	6.50	5.75
☐	*The Third Bullet,* Bantam F2927, 1965, third edition	2.00	3.00	2.50
☐	*The Three Coffins,* Popular 174, 1949	7.00	10.00	7.12
☐	*The Three Coffins,* Bestseller Mystery B47, no date	3.00	4.25	3.25
☐	*The Three Coffins,* Award AQ1330, 1974	1.75	2.50	2.12
☐	*The Three Coffins,* Dell D323, 1960, second edition	3.25	4.00	3.62
☐	**Carroll, Lewis,** *Alice in Wonderland,* Best Seller Classics CL601 (Artwork by John Tenniel. The Tenniel illustrations appeared in the first edition and have traveled with this work through most of its numerous reprintings.)	3.00	4.00	3.50
☐	**Carse, Robert,** *End of Innocence,* Monarch 492	3.00	4.00	3.50
☐	**Carson, Rachel,** *Under The Sea Wind,* Mentor M128, 1955	1.25	1.75	1.50
☐	**Carter, Alex,** *Change Partners,* Beacon #8568F	1.50	2.00	1.75
☐	**Carter, Lin,** *As The Green Star Rises,* DAW UY1156, #138, third edition	1.50	2.00	1.75
☐	*The Barbarian Of World's End,* DAW UW1300, #243, 1977	1.85	2.65	2.12
☐	*Beyond The Gates Of Dream,* Belmont B60-1032, 1969	1.85	2.65	2.12
☐	*Beyond The Gates Of Dream,* Five Star, 1973	1.85	2.65	2.12
☐	*Beyond The Gates Of Dream,* Belmont B60-1032, 1969	1.85	2.65	2.12
☐	*Black Legion Of Callisto,* Dell 9025, 1972	1.25	1.75	1.50

		Current Price Range		C/Y Avg.
☐	The Black Star, Dell 9032, 1973	1.75	2.50	2.12
☐	By The Light Of The Green Star, DAW UQ1120, #110, 1974	2.00	2.75	2.37
☐	(ED), Discoveries In Fantasy, Ballantine 02546, 1972	5.00	7.00	5.37
☐	The Enchantress Of World's End, DAW UY1172, #150, 1975	1.25	1.75	1.50
☐	(ED), Flashing Swords! #2, Dell 3123, 1974	2.00	2.75	2.37
☐	(ED), Flashing Swords! #2, Mayflower 12419, 1975	2.50	3.25	2.87
☐	Hurok Of The Stone Age, DAW UE1597, #423, 1981	1.75	2.50	2.12
☐	In The Green Star's Glow, DAW UY1216, #180, 1976	1.50	2.00	1.75
☐	In The Green Star's Glow, DAW UW1399, fourth edition	2.00	2.75	2.37
☐	Jandar Of Callisto, Dell 4182, 1972 ..	1.25	1.75	1.50
☐	Jandar Of Callisto, Dell 14182, 1977, third edition	1.50	2.00	1.75
☐	Lankar Of Callisto, Dell 4648, 1975 ..	1.50	2.00	1.75
☐	Lost World Of Time, Dell P4068, 1969	2.00	3.00	2.37
☐	Lost Worlds, DAW UJ1556, #398, 1980	2.00	3.00	2.37
☐	The Man Who Loved Mars, Gold Medal T2690, 1973	1.25	1.75	1.50
☐	Mind Wizards Of Callisto, Dell 5600, 1975	1.25	1.75	1.50
☐	(ED), New Worlds For Old, Ballantine 02365, 1971	5.50	7.75	6.25
☐	The Pirate Of World's End, DAW UE1410, #310, 1978	1.75	2.25	2.00
☐	The Quest Of Kadju, Belmont B95-2146, 1971	1.75	2.25	2.00
☐	Sky Pirates Of Callisto, Orbit 7830, 1975	1.75	2.25	2.00
☐	Sky Pirates Of Callisto, Dell 8050, 1973	1.25	1.75	1.50
☐	Star Rogue, Lancer 74649, 1970	2.00	3.00	2.50
☐	Thongor Against The Gods, Paplib 52-586, 1967	3.50	4.75	3.62
☐	Thongor And The Dragon City, Berkley N3068, second edition	1.25	2.00	1.62

	Current Price Range		C/Y Avg.

☐ *Thongor And The Wizard Of Lemuria,* Berkley N3042, 1976	1.25	2.00	1.62
☐ *Thongor In The City Of Magicians,* Paplib 53-665, 1968	2.00	3.00	2.50
☐ *Thongor Of Lemuria,* Tandem 12394, 1973, second edition	2.00	2.75	2.37
☐ *Thongor Of Lemuria,* Ace F-383, 1966	3.25	4.50	3.50
☐ *Time War,* Dell 8625, 1974	2.00	2.75	2.37
☐ *Tower At Edge Of Time,* Tower 43-321, no date	1.25	1.75	1.50
☐ *Tower At Edge Of Time,* Belmont Tower 40126, 1972	1.50	2.00	1.75
☐ *Tower At Edge Of Time,* Belmont Tower 51224	2.50	3.25	2.87
☐ *Tower At The Edge Of Time,* Belmont B50-804, 1968	1.75	2.50	2.12
☐ *Under The Green Star,* DAW UQ1030, #30, 1972	1.25	1.75	1.50
☐ *The Valley Where Time Stood Still,* Popular 00344, 1976	1.65	2.15	1.75
☐ *The Warrior Of World's End,* DAW #25, UQ1140, 1974	1.25	1.75	1.50
☐ *When The Green Star Calls,* DAW UQ1062, #62, 1973	2.00	3.00	2.37
☐ *When The Green Star Calls,* DAW UY1267, #62, fifth edition	2.00	3.00	2.37
☐ *The Wizard Of Lemuria,* Ace F-326, 1965	2.50	3.50	3.00
☐ *(ED), Year's Best Fantasy 2,* DAW UY1248, #205, 1976	1.25	1.75	1.50
☐ *Ylana Of Callisto,* Dell 14244, 1977 ..	1.25	1.75	1.50
☐ *Zanthodon,* DAW UE1543, #391, 1980	1.75	2.50	2.12
☐ **Carter, Ralph,** *Shadows Of Lust,* Croydon 14, no date (cover artwork by L.B. Cole)	12.00	15.00	13.00
☐ **Cartey, Wilfred,** *African Reader,* Vintage V628	3.00	4.00	3.25
☐ **Caryl, Warren,** *Riot Night in Cedarville,* Monarch 496 (cover artwork by DeSoto)	3.00	4.00	3.25
☐ **Casanova, Jacques,** *The Many Loves of Casanova,* Holloway House (no serial number, artwork by Monte Rogers)	3.75	4.50	4.00

	Current Price Range		C/Y Avg.

□ **Cash, W.J.,** *The Mind of the South,* Vintage V98 .... 3.00 4.00 3.25

□ **Caspary, Vera,** *Bedelia,* Popular 111, 1947 .... 8.00 11.00 8.50

□ *Bedelia,* Pan 122, 1950 .... 6.00 8.00 6.25

□ *A Chosen Sparrow,* Dell 1269, 1965 2.25 3.25 2.75

□ *Evvie,* Dell 2416, 1966 .... 1.75 2.50 2.12

□ *The Husband,* Pyramid G400, 1959 .. 2.75 3.50 3.12

□ *Laura,* Great Mystery Library, Dell D188, 1957 .... 2.50 3.25 2.87

□ *Laura,* Dell 4704, 1966 .... 1.85 2.50 2.12

□ *Laura,* Dell F163, 1961 .... 1.85 2.50 2.12

□ *Laura,* Bestseller Mystery B74, no date 4.50 6.00 5.00

□ *Laura,* Avon Pe253, 1970 .... 1.75 2.50 2.12

□ *The Man Who Loved His Wife,* Dell 5292, 1967 .... 1.25 1.75 1.50

□ *Stranger Than Truth,* Reader's Choice II, 1946 .... 6.50 8.00 7.12

□ *Stranger Than Truth,* Reader's Choice II, 1946 .... 6.50 8.00 7.12

□ *Thelma,* Popular M2078, no date 1.75 2.75 2.25

□ *The Weeping And The Laughter,* Popular Library 373, 1951 .... 2.50 3.50 3.00

□ **Cassidy, Bruce,** *While Murder Waits,* Graphic 145, 1957 .... 3.75 5.00 4.12

□ *While Murder Waits,* Graphic 145, no date 1.25 1.75 1.50

□ **Cassil, R.V.,** *Dormitory Women,* Lion 216, no date...................... 5.00 7.00 5.65

□ **Castle, Frank,** *Hawaiian Eye* (from TV series), Dell K112, 1962, first edition .. 3.75 5.00 4.12

□ *Murder In Red,* Gold Medal 709, 1957 2.25 3.25 2.75

□ *The Violent Hours,* Gold Medal 554, 1956 .... 2.75 3.75 3.25

□ **Catto, Max,** *The Melody Of Sex,* Popular Library SP149, 1962 .... 2.00 2.75 2.37

□ *The Tiger In The Bed,* Pan X415, 1965 2.75 3.50 3.12

□ **Causey, James O.,** *Frenzy,* Eclipse, no date 1.75 2.50 2.12

□ *Killer Take All!,* Graphic 147, 1957 ... 2.50 3.25 2.87

□ **Causey, James,** *The Baby Doll Murders,* Gold Medal 698, 1957 .... 3.00 4.00 3.50

	Current Price Range		C/Y Avg.

☐ **Cavanna, Betty,** *The Black Spaniel Mystery,* SBS T61, 1965, seventh edition .. 2.25 2.75 2.37

☐ **Cave, Peter,** *Foxbat,* Jove Y4878, 1979 2.25 2.75 2.37

☐ *Seige,* Nelson 601437, 1980 .... 2.50 3.25 2.87

☐ **Cellini, Benvenuto,** *Autobiography of Benvenuto Cellini,* Bantam Bio 404 (cover artwork by Roberts) 3.00 4.00 3.50

☐ **Cerf, Bennett,** *The Pocket Book of Cartoons,* Pocket Books 233 .... 10.00 14.00 11.50

☐ *(ED), Stories From The Unexpected,* Bantam FP30, 1963 .... 2.25 3.00 2.87

☐ **Chaber, M.E.,** *Bonded Dead,* Paperback Library 64-684, 1971 .... 1.25 1.75 1.50

☐ *The Day It Rained Diamonds,* Paplib 63-231, 1970 .... 1.50 2.00 1.75

☐ *The Flaming Man,* Paperback Library 63-353, 1970 .... 1.35 1.85 1.50

☐ *The Gallows Garden,* Paplib 63-549, 1971 .... 1.35 1.85 1.50

☐ *Green Grow The Graves,* Paperback Library 63-568, 1971 .... 1.35 1.85 1.50

☐ *Hangman's Harvest,* Paplib 63-507, 1971 .... 1.50 2.00 1.75

☐ *Jade For A Lady,* Paperback Library 63-204, 1970 .... 1.25 1.75 1.50

☐ *A Lonely Walk,* Paplib 63-421, 1970 1.25 1.75 1.50

☐ *A Man In The Middle,* Paplib 63-203, 1970 .... 1.25 1.75 1.50

☐ *The Man Inside,* Paplib 63-213, 1970 1.50 2.00 1.75

☐ *The Man Inside,* Popular Library G282, 1958 .... 2.25 3.25 2.75

☐ *No Grave For March,* Paplib 63-440, 1970 .... 1.25 1.75 1.50

☐ *So Dead The Rose,* Pocket 1274, 1960 1.75 2.50 2.12

☐ *So Dead The Rose,* Paperback Library 63-396, 1970 .... 1.25 1.75 1.50

☐ *Softly In The Night,* Paplib 63-288, 1970 .... 1.50 2.00 1.75

☐ *The Splintered Man,* Paplib 63-308, 1970 .... 1.25 1.75 1.50

☐ *The Splintered Man,* Perma M-3080, 1957 .... 2.00 3.00 2.50

	Current Price Range		C/Y Avg.

☐ *Take One For Murder,* Bestseller B202, no date **3.75** **5.00** **4.00**

☐ *Uneasy Lies The Dead,* Paplib 63-328, 1970 .... **1.50** **2.00** **1.75**

☐ *Wanted Dead Men,* Paplib 63-460, 1970 .... **1.25** **1.75** **1.50**

☐ *Wild Midnight Falls,* Paplib 63-265, 1970 .... **1.00** **1.50** **1.25**

☐ **Chadwick, Joseph,** *Edge of the Badlands,* Hillman 176 .... **3.50** **4.50** **3.75**

☐ **Challis, George,** *The Bait and the Trap,* Ace G527 .... **3.75** **4.50** **4.00**

☐ **Chambers, Dana,** *The Blonde Died First,* Bestseller Mystery B89, no date **2.75** **3.50** **3.12**

☐ *Blood On The Blonde,* Jonathan Press J55, no date **3.75** **5.00** **4.00**

☐ *Darling This Is Death,* Handi-Book 51, 1946 .... **6.50** **8.75** **7.12**

☐ *Darling This Is Death,* Jonathan Press J43, no date **4.00** **5.50** **4.37**

☐ *Death Against Venus,* Handi-Book 57, 1946 .... **4.00** **5.50** **4.37**

☐ *Death Against Venus,* Jonathan Press J50, no date **2.75** **3.50** **3.12**

☐ *Death Against Venus,* Handi-Book 57, 1946 .... **7.00** **10.00** **7.50**

☐ *The Frightened Man,* Jonathan Press J38, no date **3.50** **4.50** **4.00**

☐ *The Last Secret,* Jonathan Press J46, no date **7.00** **10.00** **7.50**

☐ *Rope For An Ape,* Jonathan Press J63, no date **3.00** **4.00** **3.50**

☐ *Rope For An Ape,* Bestseller Mystery B103, no date **3.50** **4.50** **4.00**

☐ *She'll Be Dead By Morning,* Eagle EB5, 1953 .... **2.00** **3.00** **2.50**

☐ *She'll Be Dead By Morning,* Popular 238, 1950 .... **4.50** **6.00** **4.75**

☐ *Some Day I'll Kill You,* Popular (CDN) 177, 1949 .... **3.50** **4.50** **4.00**

☐ *Too Like The Dead,* Bestseller Mystery B133, no date **3.25** **4.25** **3.75**

	Current Price Range		C/Y Avg.

☐ **Chambers, Whitman,** *In Savage Surrender,* Monarch 416 (cover artwork by Barton, 1964) 4.00 5.00 4.25

☐ **Chandler, Raymond,** *The Big Sleep,* Pocket 696, 1950 .... 5.50 7.50 6.12

☐ *The Big Sleep,* Pocket 2696, 1958, fourth edition 4.50 6.00 4.75

☐ *The Big Sleep,* Avon 38, 1943, not first edition 35.00 45.00 33.75

☐ *The Big Sleep,* Penguin 652, 1955, seventh edition 2.50 3.25 2.87

☐ *The Big Sleep,* Penguin 652, 1949, second edition 2.75 3.50 3.12

☐ *The Big Sleep,* Pocket 50541, 1968, seventh edition 1.75 2.50 2.12

☐ *The Big Sleep,* Pocket 50541, 1967, sixth edition 1.50 2.25 1.87

☐ *The Big Sleep,* Vintage V-631, 1976 1.50 2.25 1.87

☐ *The Blue Dahlia,* S. Il. Univ. Press 766, 1976, second edition 8.00 11.00 8.50

☐ *Farewell My Lovely,* Pocket 212, 1943 5.50 7.50 5.87

☐ *Farewell My Lovely,* Penguin 701, 1959, sixth edition 2.25 3.00 2.62

☐ *Farewell My Lovely,* Pocket 4002, 1964, fourteenth edition 2.00 2.75 2.37

☐ *Farewell My Lovely,* Ballantine 02202, 1971 .... 1.00 1.50 1.25

☐ *Farewell My Lovely,* Pocket 212, 1945, tenth edition 3.50 4.50 4.00

☐ *Farewell My Lovely,* Pocket 55058, 1968, fifteenth edition 2.00 2.75 2.37

☐ *The High Window,* Pocket 320, 1945 5.75 7.50 6.12

☐ *The High Window,* Penguin 851, 1961, sixth edition 3.00 4.00 3.50

☐ *The High Window,* Pocket 2320, 1955, third edition 4.50 6.00 4.62

☐ *The High Window,* Penguin 851, 1956, fourth edition 2.50 3.50 3.00

☐ *The High Window,* Ballantine 02203, 1971 .... 1.35 2.00 1.62

☐ *Killer In The Rain,* Ballantine 02665, 1972 .... 1.35 2.00 1.62

		Current Price Range		C/Y Avg.
☐	Killer In The Rain, Pocket 75138, 1965	3.50	4.50	3.62
☐	Killer In The Rain, Penguin 2445, 1977, seventh edition	2.00	2.75	2.37
☐	The Lady In The Lake, Pocket 389, 1954, fifth edition	2.50	3.25	2.87
☐	The Lady In The Lake, Penguin 867, 1954, second edition	2.50	3.25	2.87
☐	The Lady In The Lake, Pocket 389, 1946, second edition	8.00	8.50	8.37
☐	The Lady In The Lake, Cardinal C-344, 1959	3.75	4.75	4.12
☐	The Lady In The Lake, Pocket 50230, 1966, eighth edition	1.50	2.25	1.87
☐	The Little Sister, Pocket 750, 1950 ..	15.00	20.00	16.00
☐	The Little Sister, Pocket 4001, 1963, fourth edition	3.75	4.75	4.12
☐	The Long Goodbye, Ballantine 22396, 1974, fifth edition	1.50	2.25	1.87
☐	Pick-Up On Noon Street, Pocket 50178, 1965, seventh edition	1.25	1.75	1.50
☐	Pick-Up On Noon Street, Pocket 2846, 956, fourth edition	3.75	4.75	4.12
☐	Playback, Penguin 1608, 1961	2.75	3.50	3.12
☐	Playback, Ballantine 25169, 1977	1.50	2.25	1.87
☐	The Simple Art Of Murder, Pocket 916, 1952	3.00	4.00	3.50
☐	Trouble Is My Business, Pocket 50127, 1965, fifth edition	2.00	2.75	2.37
☐	Trouble Is My Business, Penguin 741, 1957, fifth edition	2.50	3.25	2.87
☐	Trouble Is My Business, Ballantine 22450, 1973, second edition	1.25	1.75	1.62
☐	**Chandos, Fay,** Nurse Incognito, Harlequin 796	2.00	2.75	2.25
☐	**Charteris, Leslie,** Alias The Saint, Bonded 5, 1945	9.00	12.00	9.50
☐	Alias The Saint, Pan 254, 1953	3.00	4.00	3.50
☐	Alias The Saint, Avon 818, 1958	2.00	2.75	2.37
☐	Alias The Saint, Fiction K110, no date	2.00	2.75	2.37
☐	Arrest The Saint, Avon 708, no date	4.50	6.00	4.50
☐	The Avenging Saint, Coronet 19393, 1975, third edition	1.75	2.50	2.12

		Current Price Range		C/Y Avg.
☐	*The Avenging Saint,* Avon 147, 1948	7.50	10.00	7.50
☐	*The Avenging Saint,* Fiction K104 ...	1.75	2.50	2.12
☐	*The Avenging Saint,* Avon T518	2.50	3.25	2.87
☐	*The Brighter Buccaneer,* Fiction K112, no date	2.00	2.75	2.37
☐	*The Brighter Buccaneer,* Avon 756, 1957	2.50	3.50	3.00
☐	*The Brighter Buccaneer,* Hodder 143, 1962	3.75	5.00	4.37
☐	*The Brighter Buccaneer,* Pan 236, 1953	8.00	11.00	8.50
☐	*Call For The Saint,* Avon 526, 1953 ..	5.00	6.75	5.25
☐	*Call For The Saint,* Avon (CDN) C811, 1948	5.50	7.00	5.75
☐	*Call For The Saint,* MacFadden 60-273, 1967	1.25	1.75	1.50
☐	(ED), *Death Stops At Tourist,* St. Myst. Lib. 124, 1959	2.75	3.50	3.12
☐	(ED), *Death Walks In Marble,* St. Myst. Lib. 130, 1960	2.75	3.50	3.12
☐	*Enter The Saint,* Pocket 257, 1945, fourth edition	7.00	9.50	7.50
☐	*Enter The Saint,* Pocket 257, 1944 ...	3.75	5.00	4.37
☐	*Enter The Saint,* Pocket 257, 1945, fifth edition	3.00	3.75	3.37
☐	*Enter The Saint,* Hodder C43, 1951 ..	3.00	3.75	3.37
☐	*Enter The Saint,* Pocket 257, 1944, second edition	6.00	8.00	6.00
☐	*Featuring The Saint,* Hodder 00742, 1969, second edition	2.00	3.00	2.50
☐	*Featuring The Saint,* Charter 23155, no date	1.75	2.50	2.12
☐	*Featuring The Saint,* Fiction K109, no date	1.25	1.75	1.50
☐	*Follow The Saint,* Avon 533, no date	4.50	6.50	5.00
☐	(ED), *Frightened Millionaire,* St. Myst. Lib. 121, 1959	3.00	4.00	3.50
☐	*The Happy Highwayman,* Pocket 272, 1945, third edition	6.50	8.75	7.12
☐	(ED), *Innocent Bystander,* St. Myst. Lib. #129, 1960	2.75	3.75	3.25

		Current Price Range		C/Y Avg.
☐	(ED), *Murder Made In Moscow*, St. Myst. Lib. 122, 1959	2.25	3.00	2.62
☐	(ED), *Murder Seeks An Agent*, St. Myst. Lib. 127, 1960	1.75	2.50	2.12
☐	(ED), *Murder Set To Music*, St. Myst. Lib. 120, 1959	4.00	5.00	4.50
☐	*Paging The Saint*, Bonded 7, 1945 ...	7.00	10.00	7.50
☐	(ED), *Red Snow At Darjeeling*, St. Myst. Lib. 125, 1959	2.00	3.00	2.50
☐	*Saint and Last Hero*, Avon C813	3.50	4.50	4.00
☐	*Saint and Mr. Teal*, Fiction K114	3.00	4.00	3.50
☐	*The Saint Abroad*, Charter 74896, no date	1.75	2.50	2.12
☐	*The Saint Abroad*, Curtis 07137, no date	1.25	1.75	1.50
☐	*Saint and Hapsburg Necklace*, Charter 74898, no date	1.50	2.00	1.75
☐	*The Saint and Mr. Teal*, Pan 02527, 1970, fourth edition	2.50	3.25	2.87
☐	*The Saint and Mr. Teal*, Fiction K114, no date	2.00	3.00	2.50
☐	*Saint and The Last Hero*, Avon (CDN) C813, no date	3.00	4.00	3.50
☐	*The Saint and The Ace of Knaves*, Avon 663, no date	3.50	4.75	4.75
☐	*Saint and the Fiction Makers*, Curtis 07199, no date	1.25	1.75	1.50
☐	*Saint At The Thieves' Picnic*, Avon 440, 1952	2.75	3.50	3.12
☐	*The Saint At The Thieves' Picnic*, Avon 440, 1952	4.50	6.00	4.75
☐	*The Saint Cleans Up*, Avon 848, no date	3.00	4.00	3.50
☐	*The Saint Closes The Case*, Fiction K103, no date	2.25	3.25	2.75
☐	*The Saint Closes The Case*, Pan G358, 1960	4.50	5.75	4.62
☐	*The Saint Closes The Case*, Pan G358, 1962, third edition	3.00	4.00	3.50
☐	*The Saint Closes The Case*, Hodder 02347, 1970, fourth edition	2.00	3.00	2.50

	Current Price Range		C/Y Avg.

☐ *The Saint Goes On,* Avon 34, 1943, not first edition **12.00 16.00 13.00**

☐ *The Saint Goes West,* Avon (CDN), 130, 1948 . . . . **5.50 7.50 5.75**

☐ *The Saint Goes On,* Yellowjacket C183, 1955 . . . . **5.25 7.00 5.37**

☐ *The Saint Goes On,* Coronet 16227, 1972, second edition **2.00 2.75 2.37**

☐ *The Saint Goes West,* Avon 635, 1954 **3.00 4.00 3.50**

☐ *The Saint Goes West,* MacFadden, 60-246, 1966 . . . . **1.75 2.50 2.12**

☐ *The Saint Goes West,* Hodder 1712, 1968, second edition **2.00 2.75 2.37**

☐ *The Saint In Action,* Avon 118, 1947 **9.00 12.00 9.50**

☐ *The Saint In Action,* Avon 463, 1952 **7.00 10.00 7.37**

☐ *The Saint In Europe,* Avon 611, 1954 **2.75 3.50 3.12**

☐ *The Saint In Miami,* Pan 361, 1957, second edition **4.25 5.50 4.50**

☐ *The Saint In Miami,* Avon T-234, no date **3.00 4.25 3.62**

☐ *The Saint In New York,* Avon 321, 1951 **8.00 11.00 8.50**

☐ *The Saint In New York,* Curtis 07184, no date **1.00 1.50 1.25**

☐ *The Saint In New York,* Fiction K106, no date **1.50 2.00 1.75**

☐ *The Saint In New York,* Avon 44, 1944 **7.00 10.00 7.00**

☐ *The Saint Intervenes,* Avon (CDN), 72, 1945 . . . . **4.50 6.00 4.62**

☐ *The Saint Meets His Match,* Fiction K108, no date **1.25 1.75 1.50**

☐ *The Saint On The Spanish Main,* Charter 74889, 1981 . . . . **1.75 2.50 2.12**

☐ *Saint Overboard,* Avon 432, 1952 . . . **10.00 14.00 10.50**

☐ *The Saint Overboard,* Fiction K111, no date **2.00 3.00 2.37**

☐ *The Saint Overboard,* Charter 74895, no date **2.00 3.00 2.50**

☐ *The Saint Overboard,* Pan 348, 1956, second edition **2.25 3.25 2.75**

☐ *Saint Overboard,* Hodder C66, 1951 **3.00 4.00 3.50**

☐ *The Saint Sees It Through,* Avon 341, 951 . . . . **10.00 14.00 10.50**

	Current Price Range		C/Y Avg.
☐ *The Saint Sees It Through,* Avon 619, 1954, second edition	2.00	3.00	2.50
☐ *The Saint Sees It Through,* Avon T-619, 1954	3.00	4.00	3.50
☐ *Saint Sees It Through,* Avon 341, 1951	2.50	3.50	3.00
☐ *Saint Sees It Through,* Hodder C68 ..	3.00	4.00	3.50
☐ *Saint Sees It Through,* Pan G438, 1961	2.50	3.50	3.00
☐ *Saint Sees It Through,* Fiction K102 ..	1.25	1.75	1.50
☐ *Saint Sees It Through,* Curtis 7209, 1972	1.75	2.50	2.12
☐ *The Saint Steps In,* Avon 610, 1954 ..	2.50	3.25	2.87
☐ *The Saint Steps In,* Fiction 101, no date	1.25	1.75	1.50
☐ *The Saint Steps In,* Avon 610, no date	3.50	4.50	4.00
☐ *The Saint To The Rescue,* Perma M4196, 1961	2.25	3.00	2.67
☐ *The Saint To The Rescue,* Hodder 01729, 1970, third edition	1.85	2.65	2.12
☐ *Saint To The Rescue,* MacFadden 60-307, 1968	1.85	2.65	2.12
☐ **Chase, Borden,** *Lone Star,* Gold Medal 236 (painted cover picturing Clark Gable and Ava Gardner, by Phillips)	10.00	15.00	11.25
☐ **Chase, James Hadley,** *An Ace Up My Sleeve,* Corgi 09424, 1973	2.25	3.00	2.37
☐ *Believe This Believe Anything,* Corgi 11468, 1980, second edition	2.25	3.00	2.37
☐ *But A Short Time To Live,* Panther 1103, 1960	2.50	3.25	2.87
☐ *But A Short Time To Live,* Corgi 10477, 1977	2.00	3.00	2.50
☐ *Cade,* Panther 025383, 1968	1.75	2.25	2.00
☐ *Case Of Strangled Starlet,* Signet 1586, 1958	1.50	2.00	1.75
☐ *Consider Yourself Dead,* Corgi 11042, 1979	3.00	4.00	3.50
☐ *Dead Ringer,* Ace 14150, no date ...	1.25	1.75	1.50
☐ *The Dead Stay Dumb,* Harlequin 124, 1951	8.00	11.00	8.50
☐ *Dead Stay Dumb,* Panther 03444, 1973, third edition	2.25	3.25	2.75
☐ *The Dead Stay Dumb,* Pocket 75740, 1973	1.25	1.75	1.50

		Current Price Range		C/Y Avg.
☐	*The Doll's Bad News,* Corgi 10991, 1979	2.00	3.00	2.50
☐	*Double Shuffle,* Corgi 09550, 1974	2.00	3.00	2.50
☐	*Eve,* Panther 13423, 1968, sixth edition	2.00	2.75	2.50
☐	*Eve,* Panther 1342, 1966, fifth edition	2.00	2.75	2.37
☐	*Flesh Of The Orchid,* Pocket 75717, 1972	1.50	2.00	1.75
☐	*The Flesh Of The Orchid,* Corgi 10178, 1976	2.00	3.00	2.50
☐	*The Guilty Are Afraid,* Signet 1749, 1959	2.00	3.00	2.50
☐	*Have A Change Of Scene,* Corgi 09648, 1974	1.75	2.50	2.12
☐	*Have This One On Me,* Panther 02916, 1977, fifth edition	1.75	2.50	2.12
☐	*He Won't Need It Now,* Panther 03627, 1975	2.00	3.00	2.50
☐	*Hit and Run,* Corgi 10656, 1978	2.50	3.25	2.87
☐	*I Hold The Four Aces,* Corgi 10715, 1978	2.00	3.00	2.50
☐	**Chessman, Caryl,** *The Kid Was a Killer,* Gold Medal 1002 (Caryl Chessman authored a number of books during his long stay in prison. His pleas that he had reformed as a result of becoming a successful writer were ignored, and he was executed. Though he admitted to numerous crimes, Chessman denied being California's "red light bandit," the case which sent him to the gas chamber.)	5.00	6.50	5.50
☐	**Chesterton, G.K.,** *The Amazing Adventures of Father Brown,* Dell 0095	2.00	2.50	2.25
☐	**Chestnut, Robert,** *The Syndicate,* Newsstand Library 513	3.75	4.50	4.00
☐	**Crichton, Kyle,** *The Marx Brothers,* Popular Library 410 (painted cover picturing Harpo, Groucho, Chico, Zeppo and Gummo Marx)	30.00	40.00	30.00
☐	**Chidsey, Donald B.,** *Fancy Man,* Avon T432, 1960	5.00	6.25	5.25
☐	**Christian, Linda,** *Linda,* Dell 4840 (autobiography of actress)	5.00	6.25	5.25

Left to Right: **And Then There Were None,** by Agatha
Christie, 1959, Cardinal Edition, C–360, **$2.75–$3.50;**
A Pocket Full of Rye, by Agatha Christie,
Pocket Book, 1036, **$3.50–$4.75.**

	Current Price Range		C/Y Avg.

□ **Christie, Agatha,** *And Then There Were None,* Wash Sq 46250, 1968, fourth edition	2.00	3.00	2.12
□ *And Then There Were None,* Pocket 50437, 1964, fourteenth edition	2.00	3.00	2.12
□ *And Then There Were None,* Pocket 261, 1944	9.00	12.00	9.50
□ *And Then There Were None,* Pocket 77581, 1972, thirtieth edition	1.50	2.25	1.87
□ *And Then There Were None,* Pocket 261, 1944, third edition	3.00	4.00	3.12
□ *And Then There Were None,* Pocket 77581, 1973, thirty-second edition . . .	1.25	1.75	1.50
□ *And Then There Were None,* Pocket 261, 1944, second edition	3.75	5.00	3.62
□ *And Then There Were None,* Pocket 77581, 1973, thirty-first edition	1.25	1.75	1.50
□ *And Then There Were None,* Cardinal C-360, 1959, second edition	2.75	3.50	3.12
□ *Appointment With Death,* Bestseller B58, no date	6.00	8.00	5.75
□ *Appointment With Death,* Dell Map 105, 1946	8.50	11.00	8.75
□ *Appointment With Death,* Dell 10246, 1978	1.50	2.25	1.87
□ *Appointment With Death,* Dell 0246, 1975	1.25	1.75	1.50
□ *Appointment With Death,* Dell 0246, 1971	1.00	1.50	1.25
□ *At Bertram's Hotel,* Fontana 3487, 1979	2.00	2.75	2.37
□ *At Bertram's Hotel,* Fontana 1521, 1971, seventh edition	2.50	3.25	2.87
□ *At Bertram's Hotel,* Pocket 50452, 1967	1.75	2.50	2.12
□ *At Bertram's Hotel,* Pocket 75658, 1971, fifth edition	1.25	2.00	1.62
□ *The Big Four,* Penguin 1196, 1957 . . .	3.25	4.50	3.50
□ *The Big Four,* Dell 0562, 1972	1.50	2.25	1.87
□ *The Big Four,* Dell 0562, 1968	1.75	2.50	2.12
□ *The Body In The Library,* Pocket 341, 1945	10.00	14.00	10.50

		Current Price Range		C/Y Avg.

☐	*The Body In The Library,* Pocket 2341, 1958, fifth edition	3.00	4.00	3.50
☐	*The Body In The Library,* Pocket 2341, 1957, fourth edition	2.50	3.25	2.87
☐	*The Body In The Library,* Pocket 50453, 1967, eighth edition	1.75	2.50	2.12
☐	*The Body In The Library,* Scherz Phoenix 19, second edition	16.00	21.00	17.00
☐	*The Boomerang Clue,* Dell Map 46, 1944	4.70	6.50	5.25
☐	*The Boomerang Clue,* Dell Map 664, 1953	3.50	4.75	3.75
☐	*The Boomerang Clue,* Dell D340, 1960	3.00	4.00	3.12
☐	*The Boomerang Clue,* Dell 0704, 1975	1.25	1.75	1.50
☐	*The Boomerang Clue,* Dell 0704, 1971	1.25	1.75	1.50
☐	*The Boomerang Clue,* Bestseller B39, no date	5.00	7.00	5.25
☐	*The Burden,* (Westmacott), Dell 0863, 1967	2.00	2.75	2.37
☐	*By Pricking Of My Thumbs,* Fontana 2682, 1971, second edition	2.25	3.00	2.67
☐	*By The Pricking Of My Thumbs,* Pocket 78477, 1974, seventh edition	1.25	1.75	1.50
☐	*By The Pricking Of My Thumbs,* Pocket 75419, 1969	1.75	2.50	2.12
☐	*Cards On The Table,* Fontana 166, 1960, third edition	3.00	4.00	3.25
☐	*A Caribbean Mystery,* Pocket 50449, 1966	2.15	2.85	2.37
☐	*Cat Among The Pigeons,* Fontana 950, 1970, eleventh edition	2.15	2.85	2.37
☐	*Cat Among The Pigeons,* Fontana 950, 1964, third edition	2.25	3.00	2.62
☐	*Cat Among The Pigeons,* Pocket 55364, 1969, third edition	1.75	2.50	2.12
☐	*The Clocks,* Pocket 80595, 1976, eighth edition	1.65	2.35	1.87
☐	*The Clocks,* Pocket 50442, 1967, second edition	1.65	2.35	1.87
☐	*Crooked House,* Pocket 75438, 1970, fifth edition	1.25	1.75	1.50

	Current Price Range		C/Y Avg.
☐ *Curtain-Poirot's Last Case,* Fontana 4599, 1976	2.25	3.00	2.62
☐ *Curtain,* Pocket 80720, 1976, third edition	1.25	1.75	1.50
☐ *Dead Man's Folly,* Fontana 2305, 1970, second edition	2.25	3.00	2.62
☐ *Dead Man's Folly,* Cardinal C-420, 1961	3.25	4.50	3.50
☐ *Dead Man's Folly,* Pocket 75494, 1970, fourth edition	1.50	2.25	1.87
☐ *Dead Man's Mirror,* Dell 1699, 1966	1.75	2.50	2.12
☐ *Dead Man's Mirror,* Dell 1699, 1975	1.25	1.75	1.50
☐ *Death Comes As The End,* Pocket 465, 1947	7.00	10.00	7.00
☐ *Death Comes As The End,* Penguin 926, 1957, third edition	3.00	4.00	3.50
☐ *Death Comes As The End,* Penguin 926, 1954, second edition	4.75	6.50	5.12
☐ *Death Comes As The End,* Pocket 465, 1948, second edition	4.50	5.75	4.50
☐ *Death Comes As The End,* Cardinal C-335, 1959	2.00	3.00	2.50
☐ *Death Comes As The End,* Pocket 55357, 1969, eleventh edition	2.00	2.75	2.37
☐ *Death Comes As The End,* Pocket 77445, 1971, fourteenth edition	1.25	1.75	1.50
☐ *Death Comes As The End,* Pocket 77445, 1973, eighteenth edition	1.25	1.75	1.50
☐ *Death In The Air,* Popular K57, 1963	2.50	3.25	2.87
☐ *Death In The Air,* Avon 658, 1955	2.75	3.50	3.12
☐ *Death In The Air,* Avon 658, third edition	2.00	2.75	2.37
☐ *Death In The Air,* Popular 60-2135, no date	1.75	2.50	2.12
☐ *Death In The Air,* Jonathan Press J10, no date	3.75	5.00	4.12
☐ *Death On The Nile,* Penguin 927, 1958, fourth edition	5.50	7.00	5.87
☐ *Death On The Nile,* Penguin 927, 1955, second edition	7.00	10.00	7.12
☐ *Death On The Nile,* Bantam 12539, 1978	1.75	2.50	2.12

		Current Price Range		C/Y Avg.
☐	*Death On The Nile,* Bantam S5710, ninth edition	1.50	2.25	1.87
☐	*Death On The Nile,* Mercury 66, no date	5.00	7.25	5.37
☐	*Double Sin,* Dell 2144, 1964	2.25	3.00	2.62
☐	*Double Sin,* Dell 2144, 1970	1.00	1.50	1.25
☐	*Easy To Kill,* Cardinal C-397, 1960 ...	3.75	5.00	4.12
☐	*Easy To Kill,* Pocket 80524, 1976, twenty-second edition..............	1.25	1.75	1.50
☐	*Easy To Kill,* Pocket 50441, 1966, eighth edition	2.50	3.25	2.87
☐	*Easy To Kill,* Pocket 50441, 1965, seventh edition	1.75	2.50	2.12
☐	*Easy To Kill,* Pocket 2319, 1957, third edition	1.50	2.25	1.87
☐	*Easy To Kill,* Pocket 319, 1945	7.00	9.75	5.75
☐	*Easy To Kill,* Pocket 77447, 1971, fifteenth edition	1.25	1.75	1.50
☐	*Elephants Can Remember,* Dell 2329, 1974, third edition	1.25	1.75	1.50
☐	*Elephants Can Remember,* Dell 2329, 1973	1.00	1.50	1.25
☐	*Endless Night,* Pocket 55363, 1969 ..	1.25	1.75	1.50
☐	*Evil Under The Sun,* Pocket 2285, 1957, sixth edition	2.50	3.25	2.87
☐	*Evil Under The Sun,* Pocket 285, 1945	7.00	10.00	6.00
☐	*Evil Under The Sun,* Pocket 50454, 1967, tenth edition	1.75	2.50	2.12
☐	*Evil Under The Sun,* Pocket 82260, twenty-fourth edition	1.50	2.25	1.87
☐	*Funerals Are Fatal,* Pocket 1003, 1954	2.50	3.25	2.87
☐	*Funerals Are Fatal,* Pocket 50445, 1969, seventh edition	1.75	2.50	2.12
☐	*Funerals Are Fatal,* Pocket 50445, 1966, fifth edition	1.65	2.15	1.75
☐	*The Golden Ball,* Dell 3272, 1972	1.54	2.15	1.75
☐	*The Golden Ball,* Dell 13272, 1977, second edition	1.75	2.50	2.12
☐	*Hallowe'en Party,* Pocket 75636, 1971, third edition	1.00	1.50	1.25
☐	*Hickory Dickory Dock,* Fontana 2033, 1965, fourth edition	2.75	3.50	3.12
☐	*A Holiday For Murder,* Avon 443, 1952	5.00	7.25	6.12

		Current Price Range		C/Y Avg.

☐	*A Holiday For Murder,* Avon 124, 1947	6.00	8.00	4.12
☐	*A Holiday For Murder,* Bantam S5722, sixteenth edition	1.25	1.75	1.50
☐	*Mr. Parker Pyne: Detective,* Dell 961	9.00	12.00	10.00
☐	*Mr. Parker Pyne: Detective,* Dell	6.50	8.50	7.25
☐	*Mrs. McGinty's Dead,* Pocket Books	8.00	11.00	9.25
☐	*Murder in Retrospect,* Dell 871	6.00	8.00	6.75
☐	*Murder With Mirrors,* Pocket Books 1021	6.00	8.00	6.75
☐	*Sad Cypress,* Dell D217	6.50	8.50	7.10
☐	**Christopher, John,** *A Scent of White Poppies,* Avon T463	3.75	4.50	4.05
☐	**Christy, Helen,** *Mr. Ace,* Bart 101 (photo cover picturing George Raft and Sylvia Sydney)	6.00	8.00	6.80
☐	**Churchill, Allen,** *The Year the World Went Mad,* Hillman 199	3.50	4.25	3.85
☐	**Clagett, John,** *U.S. Navy in Action,* Monarch 350	2.00	2.50	2.15
☐	**Clark, Al,** *Trail of Vengeance,* Vega (no serial number)	3.75	4.50	4.10
☐	**Clark, Dorine,** *Lover's Tour,* Gaslight 123, 1964	4.00	5.25	4.50
☐	**Clark, Ford,** *The Open Square,* Gold Medal 1220, 1962	4.00	5.25	4.39
☐	**Clay, Manning,** *Wild Body,* Beacon 376	3.25	4.00	3.48
☐	**Clay, Matthew,** *Slum Doctor,* Bedside #BB817	2.50	3.00	2.75
☐	**Cleary, Jon,** *The Sundowners,* Pocket Books 6012 (photo cover picturing Deborah Kerr and Robert Mitchum)	6.00	8.00	6.70
☐	**Clements, Mark,** *Teacher's Pet,* Midwood F333, no date	1.75	2.50	2.12
☐	**Clinton, Jeff,** *Fighting Buckaroo,* Berkley 577, 1965	4.00	5.00	4.29
☐	**Clou, John,** *Golden Blade,* Graphic G209, 1955	3.00	4.00	3.50
☐	**Coburn, Walt,** *Invitation To a Hanging,* Avon F181, 1963	4.00	5.00	4.26
☐	**Cody, Al,** *Big Corral,* Pyramid 539 (cover artwork by Schaare)	3.75	4.50	4.10

	Current Price Range		C/Y Avg.
☐ *Powdersmoke Payoff,* Leisure 834, no date	2.25	3.00	2.50
☐ **Cohen, Lester,** *Sweepings,* Crest S190, 1957	2.50	3.25	2.87
☐ **Colby, Robert,** *Executive Wife,* Monarch 427 (cover artwork by Miller, 1964)	4.00	5.00	4.35
☐ *Kim,* Monarch 244, 1962	1.75	2.50	2.12
☐ *Lament For Julie,* Monarch 196 (cover artwork by Barton, 1961)	5.00	6.00	5.50
☐ *Star Trap,* Gold Medal 1043, 1960 ...	5.00	6.00	5.50
☐ **Cole, Jackson,** *Gunsmoke Trail,* Pyramid 666 (cover artwork by Leone)	4.00	5.00	4.32
☐ *Massacre Canyon,* Pyramid 638 (cover artwork by Doore)	4.00	5.00	4.32
☐ **Coles, Manning,** *Dangerous By Nature,* Berkley F1039, 1965	2.50	3.25	2.87
☐ *Drink To Yesterday,* Hodder C9, 1951	4.50	5.75	4.75
☐ *Drink To Yesterday,* Berkley F872, 1964	2.25	3.00	2.62
☐ *The Fifth Man,* Berkley F880, 1964 ..	2.25	3.00	2.62
☐ *Let The Tiger Die,* Hodder 185, 1960	3.50	4.50	3.75
☐ *The Man In The Green Hat,* Jonathan Press J90, no date	3.50	4.50	3.75
☐ *The Man In The Green Hat,* Dolphin C42, 1955	3.50	4.50	3.75
☐ *The Mystery Of The Stolen Plans,* Berkley G300, 1960	2.25	3.00	2.62
☐ *Night Train To Paris,* Pyramid R-847, 1962	2.50	3.25	2.87
☐ *Not Negotiable,* Berkley F926, 1964	2.25	3.00	2.62
☐ *Now Or Never,* Jonathan Press J62, no date	5.50	7.00	5.87
☐ *Operation Manhunt,* Jonathan Press J68, no date	5.50	7.00	5.87
☐ *They Tell No Tales,* Berkley F899, 1964	2.25	3.00	2.62
☐ *They Tell No Tales,* Berkley F899, 1964	2.00	2.75	2.37
☐ *A Toast To Tomorrow,* Berkley F873, 1964	2.25	3.00	2.62
☐ *A Toast To Tomorrow,* Bantam 118, 1947	7.00	10.00	7.00
☐ *The Vengeance Man,* Pyramid X-1631, 1967	2.00	2.75	2.37

	Current Price Range		C/Y Avg.

☐	*With Intent To Deceive,* Berkley F984, 1964	2.25	3.00	2.62
☐	**Colette (no last name),** *Gigi,* Signet 1525 (painted cover picturing Leslie Caron and Maurice Chevalier)	6.00	8.00	6.75
☐	**Collins, A.J.,** *Wail of the Lonely Wench,* Chicago Paperback House 111 (cover artwork by Nystrom, 1962)	5.00	6.25	5.65
☐	**Collins, Hunter,** *Tomorrow and Tomorrow,* Pyramid 654 (cover artwork by Mitchell)	4.00	5.00	4.40
☐	**Collins, Larry and Dominique Lapierre,** *5th Horseman,* Avon 54734, 1981	2.75	3.50	3.12
☐	**Collins, Mary,** *Dead Center,* Bantam 62, second edition	4.25	5.50	4.62
☐	*Dog Eat Dog,* Bantam 877, 1951	1.75	2.50	2.12
☐	*The Fog Comes,* Bantam 23, 1946	4.75	6.25	5.25
☐	*The Sister Of Cain,* Bantam 787, 1950	3.75	4.75	4.00
☐	**Collins, Max,** *Bait Money,* Pinnacle 41, 159, 1981	1.50	2.25	1.87
☐	*Blood Money,* Pinnacle 41-160, 1981	1.25	1.75	1.50
☐	*Blood Money,* Curtis 07277, 1973	1.25	1.75	1.50
☐	*The Broker's Wife,* Berkley D3187, 1976	1.25	1.75	1.50
☐	*Fly Paper,* Pinnacle 41-161, 1981	1.75	2.50	2.12
☐	*Hard Cash,* Pinnacle 41-163, 1982	1.50	2.25	1.87
☐	*The Slasher,* Berkley 03499, 1977	1.25	1.75	1.60
☐	**Collins, Michael,** *The Brass Rainbow,* Bantam H5328, 1970	1.75	2.50	2.12
☐	*The Brass Rainbow,* Playboy 16672, 1980	1.50	2.25	1.87
☐	*Night Of The Toads,* Bantam S6548, 1971	1.35	1.85	1.50
☐	*Shadow Of A Tiger,* Playboy 16506, 1978	1.35	1.85	1.50
☐	*The Silent Scream,* Playboy 16525, 1979	1.50	2.25	1.87
☐	*The Slasher,* Playboy 16855, 1981	1.50	2.25	1.87
☐	**Collins, Wilkie,** *The Moonstone,* Pyramid 19, 1950	5.25	7.00	6.12
☐	*The Yellow Mask,* Paperback Library 52-541, 1967	2.50	3.50	3.00

	Current Price Range		C/Y Avg.

- ☐ **Colombo, Pat,** *Throw Back the Little Ones,* Avon F171 .... 3.00 3.75 3.29
- ☐ **Colter, Eli,** *The Gulf Cove Murders,* Detective Novel Classic 41, no date 7.00 9.75 7.62
- ☐ **Comber, Leon,** *Strange Cases of Magistrate Pao,* Panther 03341, 1970 .... 2.25 3.00 2.62
- ☐ **Conant, James B.,** *Education and Liberty,* Vintage V506 .... 2.50 3.25 2.75
- ☐ **Conant, Paul,** *Dr. Gatskill's Blue Shoes,* Dell 741, 1953 .... 4.50 6.00 4.75
- ☐ *Dr. Gatskill's Blue Shoes,* Dell 741, no date 2.00 2.75 2.37
- ☐ **Condon, Richard,** *Winter Kills,* Dell 6007, 1975, second edition 1.50 2.25 1.87
- ☐ **Congdon, Don,** *Tales of Love and Horror,* Ballantine 522 .... 3.25 4.00 3.39
- ☐ **Conklin, Geoff** (ED), *12 Great Classics Of SF,* Gold Medal R2192 .... 1.75 2.50 2.12
- ☐ (ED), *12 Great Classics Of SF,* Gold Medal D1366, 1963 .... 2.50 3.50 2.62
- ☐ (ED), *Above The Night,* Dell 8741, 1965 2.50 3.50 2.62
- ☐ (ED), *13 Great Stories of SF,* Gold Medal T2174, no date 1.75 2.25 2.00
- ☐ (ED), *13 Great Stories Of SF,* Gold Medal D1444, no date 2.00 2.75 2.37
- ☐ (ED), *13 Great Stories Of SF,* Coronet 02481, 1973, third edition 2.25 3.00 2.62
- ☐ (ED), *13 Great Stories Of SF,* GMK1243, 1962, second edition 2.00 2.75 2.37
- ☐ (ED), *13 Great Stories Of SF,* Gold Medal T2601 .... 1.75 2.25 2.00
- ☐ (ED), *13 Great Stories Of SF,* Gold Medal D1444, no date 1.50 2.00 1.50
- ☐ (ED), *13 Great Stories Of SF,* Hodder Fawcett 2482, 1967 .... 2.25 3.25 2.75
- ☐ (ED), *13 Great Stories Of SF,* Gold Medal S997, 1960 .... 2.00 3.00 2.50
- ☐ (ED), *17 X Infinity,* Dell 7746, 1963 .. 2.00 3.00 2.50
- ☐ (ED), *4 For The Future,* Pyramid G434, 1959 .... 3.25 4.50 3.75
- ☐ (ED), *4 For The Future,* Pyramid F-743, 1962, second edition 2.25 3.25 2.75

	Current Price Range		C/Y Avg.
☐ (ED), *5 Unearthly Visions,* Gold Medal D1549, 1965	2.25	3.00	2.62
☐ (ED), *5 Unearthly Visions,* Gold Medal D1868, no date	1.75	2.25	2.00
☐ (ED), *6 Great Short Novels Of SF,* Dell D9, 1954, first edition	3.50	4.50	4.00
☐ (ED), *6 Great Short SF Novels,* Dellist C111, 1960, first edition	1.75	2.25	2.00
☐ (ED), *7 Trips Thru Time and Space,* Gold Medal R 1924	1.75	2.25	2.00
☐ (ED), *7 Trips Thru Time and Space,* Coronet 10866, 1976, third edition . .	2.00	2.75	2.37
☐ (ED), *Another Part Of Galaxy,* Gold Medal D 1628, 1966	1.50	2.00	1.50
☐ (ED), *The Big Book Of SF,* Berkley F975, 1957, second edition	3.00	4.00	3.50
☐ (ED), *Crossroads In Time,* Perma P254, 1953	6.50	8.75	7.25
☐ (ED), *Dimension 4,* Pyramid F-973, 1964	3.00	4.00	3.50
☐ (ED), *Five-Odd,* Pyramid R-1056, 1964	2.25	3.25	2.75
☐ (ED), *Five-Odd,* Pyramid T2450, 1971, second edition	1.25	1.75	1.50
☐ (ED), *Giants Unleashed,* Tempo T-111, 1966	1.75	2.25	2.00
☐ (ED), *Great SF About Doctors,* Collier AS518, 1963	2.50	3.50	3.00
☐ (ED), *Great SF By Scientists,* Collier AS 218, 1962	2.00	2.75	2.37
☐ (ED), *Great SF By Scientists,* Collier O 1903, 1966, third edition	2.00	2.75	2.00
☐ (ED), *Great Stories Space Travel,* Tempo T39, 1966, third edition	2.00	2.75	2.00
☐ (ED), *Great Stories Space Travel,* Tempo 5313, 1970, second edition . .	2.00	1.75	2.00
☐ (ED), *Invaders Of Earth,* Pocket 1074, 1955	2.00	2.75	2.37
☐ (ED), *Invaders Of Earth,* Tempo T6, 1962	3.00	4.00	3.50
☐ (ED), *Possible Worlds Of SF,* Berkley G-3, 1955	5.00	7.00	5.62

		Current Price Range		C/Y Avg.

		Current Price Range	C/Y Avg.
☐ (ED), *Possible Worlds Of SF*, Berkley G471, 1960	1.75	2.25	2.00
☐ **Connable, Alfred,** *Twelve Trains To Babylon*, Sphere 2471, 1975	1.75	2.50	2.12
☐ **Connell, Vivian,** *Man Of Parts*, Gold Medal 711, 1957, second edition	1.25	1.75	1.50
☐ **Conrad, Earl,** *Crane Eden*, Pyramid 803	3.00	3.75	3.30
☐ **Conrad, Harold,** *Battle at Apache Pass*, Avon 437 (painted cover picturing Jeff Chandler, Susan Cabot and John Lund)	6.00	8.00	6.85
☐ **Conroy, Albert,** *Mr. Lucky*, Dell B165 (cover artwork by Engle, 1960)	4.25	5.25	4.50
☐ **Conroy, Jim,** *Always Available*, Midwood 883, 1967	4.00	5.00	4.35
☐ **Constiner, Merle,** *Outrage at Bearskin Forks*, Ace F401, 1966	3.25	4.00	3.35
☐ *Top Gun From the Dakotas*, Ace G578, 1966	3.25	4.00	3.35
☐ **Conway, John** *A Sin in Time*, Monarch 222 (cover artwork by Barton, 1961)	4.50	5.75	4.95
☐ *The Apache Wars*, Monarch 309 (cover artwork by Stanley, 1961)	4.00	5.00	4.40
☐ *Hard Man From Texas*, Monarch 465 (cover artwork by Thurston, 1964)	4.00	5.00	4.40
☐ *The Valiant Breed*, Monarch 349 (cover artwork by Thurston, 1963)	4.00	5.00	4.40
☐ **Cooke, Alistair,** *Mencken*, Vintage V25	2.00	2.50	2.20
☐ **Cooke, Ronald J.,** *House On Craig Street*, Newstand Library 11A, 1949	2.50	3.50	3.00
☐ **Cooper, Morton,** *Innocent and The Willing*, Gold Medal 588, 1956	4.00	5.75	4.37
☐ **Cooper, Saul,** *It Started in Naples*, Gold Medal 1017 (photo cover picturing Clark Gable and Sophia Loren)	6.00	8.00	6.75
☐ **Coppel, Alfred,** *Night of Fire and Snow*, Crest S212, 1958	2.50	3.25	2.87
☐ **Corbin, Gary,** *The Last Time I Saw Mary*, Jade 209 (cover artwork by Caples)	4.00	5.00	4.37
☐ **Cord, Barry,** *Trail Boss From Texas*, Avon T545	3.00	4.00	3.25
☐ **Corgan, Frank,** *Swing Shift*, Midwood F384, no date	1.75	2.50	2.12

	Current Price Range		C/Y Avg.

☐ **Costain, Thomas B.,** *The Magnificent Century,* Popular Library W1148, no date — 3.00 / 3.75 / 3.25

☐ *Chord of Steel,* Perma 5055 .... — 2.50 / 3.00 / 2.70

☐ *The Moneyman,* Perma 7502 .... — 2.00 / 2.50 / 2.19

☐ *Son of a Hundred Kings,* Perma 5000 (cover artwork by Banberry) .... — 3.25 / 4.00 / 3.42

☐ **Cotton, Jerry,** *In the Lion's Den,* Three Star 101 (cover artwork by Seltzer) .... — 3.00 / 4.00 / 3.40

☐ **Coughlan, Robert,** *Private World of William Faulkner,* Avon G1144 .... — 3.00 / 4.00 / 3.40

☐ **Coulter, Adam,** *Four to Go-Go-Go,* Boudoir 1042 .... — 2.50 / 3.00 / 2.75

☐ **Cousteau, Jacques,** *The Silent World,* Cardinal GC119 .... — 2.00 / 2.50 / 2.25

☐ **Coward, Noel,** *Pomp and Circumstance,* Dell S37 (cover artwork by McGinnis) .. — 4.00 / 5.00 / 4.45

☐ **Cox, William R.,** *Death Comes Early,* Dell B191 (cover artwork by McGinnis, 1961) — 5.00 / 6.00 / 5.65

☐ **Coxe, George H.,** *Glass Triangle,* Dell 81, no date .... — 3.50 / 4.50 / 4.00

☐ **Craig, D.W.,** *None But The Wicked,* Midwood F249, 1963 .... — 2.00 / 2.75 / 2.37

☐ **Craig, Georgia,** *Nurse With Wings,* Avon F160 (cover artwork by Phillips) .... — 3.00 / 4.00 / 3.40

☐ **Craig, Jonathan,** *Case Of The Cold Coquette,* Gold Medal 645, 1957 .... — 3.00 / 3.75 / 3.37

☐ **Craig, Margaret M.,** *Trish,* Berkley #G-88 .... — 2.25 / 2.75 / 2.50

☐ **Crane, Milton,** *Fifty Great Short Stories,* Bantam C192 (anthology) .... — 2.00 / 2.50 / 2.20

☐ **Crankshaw, Edward,** *Gestapo,* Pyramid 632 (cover artwork by Schaare) .... — 3.00 / 3.75 / 3.35

☐ **Creasey, John,** *Accident For Inspector West,* Pan 10619, 1970, third edition .. — 2.00 / 2.75 / 2.37

☐ *Accuse The Toff,* John Long Services Edition, no date .... — 10.00 / 14.00 / 10.50

☐ *Alibi,* Award AQ 1342, 1974 .... — 1.50 / 2.00 / 1.75

☐ *Baron and Missing Old Masters,* Magnum 74701, no date .... — 1.75 / 2.50 / 2.12

☐ *Baron and Mogul Swords,* Avon S348, 1968 .... — 1.75 / 2.50 / 2.12

		Current Price Range		C/Y Avg.

☐	*Baron and The Missing Old Masters,* Lancer 74701, no date	1.50	2.00	1.75
☐	*Baron and The Chinese Puzzle,* Avon G1304, 1967	2.00	2.75	2.37
☐	*The Baron and The Stolen Legacy,* Avon S364, 1968	2.00	2.75	2.37
☐	*Baron and The Mogul Swords,* Avon V2350, 1970, third edition	1.75	2.25	2.00
☐	*Baron and The Chinese Puzzle,* Avon V2395, 1971, third edition	1.25	1.75	1.50
☐	*The Baron Branches Out,* Avon V2341, 1970	1.00	1.50	1.25
☐	*The Baron Goes East,* Coronet 16042, 1972, second edition	2.00	2.75	2.37
☐	*The Baron On Board,* Magnum 75193, no date	1.75	2.50	2.12
☐	*The Beauty Queen Killer,* Lancer 74757, no date	1.75	2.50	2.00
☐	*Beauty Queen Killer,* Berkley F1095, 1965	2.00	2.50	2.25
☐	*The Beauty Queen Killer,* Lancer 74757, no date	1.25	1.75	1.50
☐	*The Big Call,* Corgi GC7258, 1965 . . .	2.00	3.00	2.50
☐	*A Blast Of Trumpets,* Corgi 10253, 1976	1.85	2.50	2.12
☐	*The Blight,* Lancer 74623, no date . . .	1.85	2.50	2.12
☐	*A Bundle For The Toff,* Magnum 74711, no date	1.25	1.75	1.50
☐	*A Bundle For The Toff,* Lancer 74711, no date	1.75	2.50	2.12
☐	*Call The Toff,* Lancer 74622, 1970 . . .	1.50	2.00	1.75
☐	*Call The Toff,* Hodder C231, 1956 . . .	7.00	10.00	7.00
☐	*Carriers Of Death,* Arrow 055, 1968 . .	1.50	2.00	1.75
☐	*Carriers Of Death,* Popular Library 01550, no date	1.25	1.75	1.50
☐	*Death of a Racehorse,* Berkley 757 (cover artwork by Kalin)	3.00	4.00	3.35
☐	**Creighton, John,** *The Blonde Cried Murder,* Ace F115, 1961	3.50	4.50	3.90
☐	**Crichton, Robert,** *The Great Imposter,* Perma 5027 (photo cover picturing Tony Curtis)	5.00	7.00	5.85

	Current Price Range		C/Y Avg.

☐ **Cronin, Vincent,** *Wise Man From the West,* Image 44 (cover artwork by Wong, 1957) 5.00 6.50 5.60

☐ **Crosby, Bing,** *Call Me Lucky,* Cardinal C146 (photo cover picturing the author) 7.00 8.00 8.25

☐ **Croy, Homer,** *Family Honeymoon,* Bantam 413 (painted cover picturing Claudette Colbert and Fred MacMurray) ... 6.00 8.00 6.75

☐ **Culver, Edward,** *She Had To Be Loved,* Newstand Library U117, 1959 ...... 2.00 2.50 2.25

☐ **Cunningham, John,** *Wait Till Dark,* Gold Medal 1207, 1962 ...... 3.75 4.75 4.15

☐ **Cuppy, Will,** *The Decline and Fall of Practically Everybody,* Dell 1878 ...... 2.00 2.50 2.20

☐ **Curry, Tom and Wood Cowan,** *Famous Figures of the Old West,* Monarch 553 3.00 4.00 3.35

☐ **Curtis, Brad,** *Man Trap,* Midwood F313, no date 1.75 2.50 2.12

☐ **Curtiss, Ursula,** *Face of the Tiger,* Ace G503 ...... 2.75 3.50 3.10

☐ **Cushman, Dan,** *The Con Man,* Crest S381, 1960 ...... 1.75 2.25 2.00

☐ **Dahl, Ronald,** *Kiss Kiss,* Dell Great Mystery Library 4572, 1965 ...... 1.75 · 2.50 2.05

☐ **d'Allard, Hunter,** *Long Sword,* Avon G1099 ...... 3.00 3.75 3.15

☐ **Daniels, Frank,** *Mating Cry,* Gold Medal 449, 1954 ...... 4.25 5.75 4.62

☐ **Daniels, John S.,** *Smoke of the Gun,* Signet 2303 ...... 3.00 3.75 3.17

☐ **Daniels, Norman,** *Lover Let Me Live,* Avon T479, 1960 ...... 5.00 6.50 5.50

☐ **Dante,** *The Portable Dante,* Viking 32, 1958 ...... 3.00 4.00 3.35

☐ **Dare, Will,** *Web of Women,* Beacon 656 3.00 3.75 3.25

☐ **Darrow, Whitney,** *Hold It Florence,* Dell 786 ...... 9.00 12.00 10.15

☐ **Davenport, Marcia,** *Constant Image,* Cardinal GC104 ...... 2.75 3.50 3.15

☐ **Davidson, Bill,** *The Real and the Unreal,* Lancer 72-636 ...... 3.75 4.50 4.00

	Current Price Range		C/Y Avg.

☐ **Davis, Franklin,** *Bamboo Camp,* Monarch 236, no date .... | 5.00 | 7.00 | 5.75

☐ *A Medal For Frankie,* Pocket Books 6010 .... | 3.00 | 4.00 | 3.40

☐ *Breakthrough,* Monarch 306, 1961 ... | 4.75 | 6.00 | 5.15

☐ *Kiss the Tiger,* Pyramid 663 (cover artwork by Miller) .... | 4.00 | 5.00 | 4.40

☐ **Davis, Gil,** *Missile Island,* Pec An-07, 1967 .... | 2.50 | 3.25 | 2.87

☐ **Davis, Gordon,** *Counterfeit Kill,* Gold Medal K1348, 1963 .... | 1.75 | 2.50 | 2.12

☐ *House Dick,* Gold Medal S1103, 1961 | 2.75 | 3.50 | 3.12

☐ *Ring Around Rosy,* Gold Medal K1380, 1964 .... | 3.75 | 4.75 | 4.00

☐ *Where Murder Waits,* Gold Medal K1531, 1965 .... | 2.00 | 2.75 | 2.37

☐ **Davis, Maggie,** *Rommel's Gold,* Pyramid M3835, 1975, second edition .... | 1.85 | 2.50 | 2.12

☐ **Davis, Maxine,** *Sex and the Adolescent,* Perma 5028 .... | 3.00 | 4.00 | 3.37

☐ **Davis, Mildred,** *The Dark Place,* Ace G-751, no date........................ | 1.85 | 2.50 | 2.12

☐ *The Invisible Boarder,* Dell 13938, 1977 .... | 1.50 | 2.25 | 1.87

☐ *The Room Upstairs,* Pocket 638, 1949, second edition .... | 2.75 | 3.50 | 3.12

☐ *They Buried A Man,* Mercury Mystery 204, no date..................... | 3.75 | 4.75 | 4.12

☐ *They Buried A Man,* Pocket 80900, 1977 .... | 1.50 | 2.25 | 2.00

☐ *Voice On The Telephone,* MacFadden 75-288, 1969, second edition .... | 1.75 | 2.50 | 2.12

☐ **Davis, Norbert,** *Dead Little Rich Girl,* Handi-Book 40, 1945 .... | 10.00 | 13.00 | 10.50

☐ *Oh Murderer Mine,* Handi-Book 54, 1946 .... | 17.00 | 23.00 | 17.00

☐ **Day, Chon,** *Brother Sebastian,* Pocket Books 1224 (Brother Sebastian was a one-panel cartoon which appeared weekly in Look Magazine) .... | 7.00 | 10.00 | 8.15

☐ **Day, Clarence,** *Life With Father,* Pocket Books 2280 (cover artwork by Bacon) | 4.00 | 5.25 | 4.45

	Current Price Range		C/Y Avg.

☐ **Dean, Amber,** *Deadly Contract,* Popular Library SP327	3.50	4.25	3.90
☐ *Encounter With Evil,* Perma 4254	3.00	4.00	3.35
☐ **Dean, Anthony,** *What Floor Please?,* Wee Hours 501, 1966	4.00	5.25	4.40
☐ **Dean, Dudley,** *Lila My Lovely,* Gold Medal 1014, 1960	4.00	5.00	4.32
☐ **Dean, Nell M.,** *Fashions For Carol,* Ace F112	2.00	3.00	2.35
☐ **Dean, Spencer,** *Murder After a Fashion,* Pocket Books 6111 (cover artwork by Bennett)	3.75	4.50	4.15
☐ *Pricetag For Murder,* Pocket Books 6048	4.00	5.00	4.32
☐ **DeBekker, Jay,** *Keyhole Peeper,* Beacon B110, 1955	1.75	2.50	2.12
☐ **DeBorchgrve, Arnaud and Moss,** *The Spike,* Avon 54270, 1981	2.75	3.75	3.25
☐ **DeCapite, Raymond,** *The Coming of Fabrizze,* Popular Library G563	4.00	5.00	4.39
☐ **DeFoe, Daniel,** *Robinson Crusoe,* Washington Square Press RE112	2.00	2.50	2.20
☐ *Roxana,* Marvin Miller Enterprises 6002	5.00	6.50	5.62
☐ **Deford, Mirian Allen,** *Overbury Affair,* Avon F-125, 1960	2.50	3.25	2.87
☐ *Overbury Affair,* Avon F-125, 1960 . . .	1.75	2.50	2.12
☐ **Deighton, Len,** *Billion Dollar Brain,* Dell 0583, 1967, second edition	1.85	2.50	2.12
☐ *Billion Dollar Brain,* Penguin 2662, 1967, second edition	2.25	3.00	2.62
☐ *Catch A Falling Spy,* Pocket 81685, 1977	1.50	2.00	1.75
☐ *An Expensive Place To Die,* Berkley 04470, 1980	1.85	2.50	2.12
☐ *Funeral In Berlin,* Dell 2773, 1965 . . .	1.85	2.50	2.12
☐ *Funeral In Berlin,* Penguin 2461, 1966	2.25	3.00	2.62
☐ *Horse Under Water,* Dell 3724, 1967	1.75	2.50	2.12
☐ *Horse Under Water,* Penguin 2322, 1965, second edition	2.75	3.75	3.25
☐ *Ipcress File* (Movie Cover), Panther 1629, 1966, ninth edition	2.00	2.75	2.37

		Current Price Range		C/Y Avg.
☐	*The Ipcress File,* Crest R807, 1965, fourth edition	1.75	2.50	2.12
☐	*The Ipcress File,* Crest R807, 1968, fifth edition	1.25	1.75	1.50
☐	*Spy Story,* Pocket 82686, sixth edition	1.75	2.50	2.12
☐	*Spy Story,* Pocket 80058, 1975	1.50	2.25	1.87
☐	*SS-GB,* Panther 05002, 1979, second edition	2.25	3.00	2.62
☐	*Twinkle Twinkle Little Spy,* Panther 04500, 1977	2.00	2.75	2.37
☐	*Yesterday's Spy,* Panther 04347, 1976, second edition	2.00	2.75	2.37
☐	*Yesterday's Spy,* Warner 89-087, 1976	1.25	1.75	1.50
☐	**DeJohn, Peter,** *Make Me An Orgy,* Nite Time 110	2.50	3.25	2.69
☐	**DeLaCroix, Robert,** *They Flew the Atlantic,* Monarch 166	3.00	3.75	3.25
☐	**Delaney, Laurence,** *The Triton Ultimatum,* Dell 18744, 1979	2.00	2.75	2.37
☐	**Del Rey, Lester,** *And Some Were Human,* Ballantine 552, no date	3.75	4.75	4.12
☐	*Attack From Atlantis,* Tempo 5682, no date	1.25	1.75	1.50
☐	*Attack From Atlantis,* Tempo 5306, 1969	2.00	2.75	2.37
☐	(ED), *Best SF Stories Of Year,* Ace 05475, 1973, first edition	1.25	1.75	1.50
☐	*Day Of The Giants,* Airmont SF5, 1973	1.25	1.75	1.50
☐	*Day of The Giants,* Airmont SF5, 1964	2.50	3.25	2.87
☐	*The Early Del Rey,* Vol. 1, Ballantine 25063, 1976	1.75	2.50	2.12
☐	*Early Del Rey,* Vol. 2, Ballantine 25111, 1976	1.50	2.00	1.75
☐	*The Eleventh Commandment,* Regency RB 113, 1962	2.75	3.75	3.00
☐	*The Eleventh Commandment,* Ballantine 02068, 1970	2.00	2.75	2.37
☐	*The Eleventh Commandment,* Ballantine 23987, 1976, second edition	1.25	1.75	1.50
☐	*The Eleventh Commandment,* Del Rey 29641, 1981, third edition	2.25	3.00	2.62

		Current Price Range		C/Y Avg.
☐	*Gods and Golems,* Ballantine 03087, 1973	1.75	2.50	2.12
☐	*The Man Without A Planet,* Lancer 74-538, 1969	2.00	3.00	2.50
☐	*Marooned On Mars,* Paperback Library 52-415, 1967	2.00	3.00	2.50
☐	*Moon Of Mutiny,* Signet KP536, 1969	2.00	2.75	2.37
☐	*Moon Of Mutiny,* Signet Q5539, third edition	1.25	1.75	1.50
☐	*Mortals and Monsters,* Ballantine U2236, 1965	2.25	3.25	2.75
☐	*Nerves,* Ballantine 151, 1956	3.50	4.50	4.00
☐	*Nerves,* Ballantine 24995, 1976	1.25	2.00	1.62
☐	*Nerves,* Ballantine 02069, 1970, third edition	1.25	2.00	1.62
☐	*Nerves,* Del Rey 28912, 1979, seventh edition	1.50	2.25	1.87
☐	*Outpost Of Jupiter,* Del Rey 27120, 1978	1.75	2.50	2.12
☐	*Police Your Planet,* Del Rey 29858, 1981, second edition	2.00	2.75	2.37
☐	*Rocket Jockey,* Del Rey 27542, 1978	1.25	1.75	1.50
☐	*The Scheme Of Things,* Belmont B50-682, 1966	3.75	4.75	4.00
☐	*Siege Perilous,* Lancer 73-468, 1966	1.25	1.75	1.50
☐	*Step To The Stars,* Paperback Library 52-955, 1966	3.75	4.75	4.00
☐	*Tunnel Through Time,* Scholastic TX1065, 1967	1.75	2.50	2.12
☐	*Tunnel Through Time,* Scholastic TX1065, 1970, third edition	1.75	2.50	2.12
☐	*Tunnel Through Time,* Scholastic TX1065, 1973, fourth edition	1.35	1.85	1.50
☐	*Tunnel Through Time,* Scholastic TX1065, 1974, fifth edition	1.35	1.85	1.50
☐	*Tunnel Through Time,* Scholastic TX1065, sixth edition	2.00	2.75	2.37
☐	**DeMaris, Ovid,** *The Parasite,* Berkley 669, 1962	4.00	5.00	4.32
☐	**DeMars, George,** *Ruling Passion,* Crest S343, 1959	1.75	2.50	2.12

	Current Price Range		C/Y Avg.
☐ **DeMaupassant, Guy,** *A Woman's Life,* Lion LL-2, 1954	4.00	5.00	4.50
☐ *The Diary Of A Madman,* Pan 24849, 1976	2.50	3.25	2.87
☐ *The Private Affairs of Bel Ami,* Avon 87 (painted cover picturing George Sanders, Angela Lansbury and Ann Dvorak)	6.00	8.00	6.70
☐ **DeMexico, N.R.,** *Strange Pursuit,* Suspense #1, 1951	9.50	12.00	10.50
☐ **Deming, Richard,** *Dragnet: The Case of the Courteous Killer,* Pocket Books 1198 (photo cover picturing Jack Webb)	5.00	7.00	6.00
☐ *She'll Hate Me Tomorrow,* Monarch 365 (cover artwork by Marchetti, 1963)	5.00	6.50	5.80
☐ *This Game of Murder,* Monarch 439 (cover artwork by Barton, 1964)	5.00	6.00	5.32
☐ **Dennis, Patrick,** *Little Me: The Story of Belle Poitrine,* Crest 570 (Actually there was no such person as Belle Poitrine, but the model who posed for the cover photo and interior photos became known for the rest of her life as "Belle Poitrine.")	6.00	8.00	6.75
☐ **DePoinay, Peter,** *In Raymond's Wake,* Panther 02849, 1969	2.00	3.00	2.50
☐ **Dere, Will,** *Web of Women,* Beacon #8656F	1.50	2.00	1.75
☐ **DeRoo, Edward,** *The Little Caesars,* Ace D-486, 1961	2.00	3.00	2.37
☐ **DesLigneris, Francoise,** *Fort Frederick,* Avon T456, no date (domination cover—woman with whip)	18.00	23.00	20.00
☐ *Psyche 59,* Avon T482, no date	7.00	10.00	8.25
☐ **DeSteiguer, Walter,** *Jewels For A Shroud,* Dell 614, 1952	4.50	6.00	4.87
☐ **DeVilliers, Gerard,** *Checkpoint Charlie,* Pinnacle 220626, 1975	1.25	1.75	1.50
☐ **Devlin, Barry,** *Night Of The Lash,* Beacon #8283	3.00	4.00	3.12
☐ **DeVries, Robert,** *Of Sin and The Flesh,* Crest 5140, 1956	1.75	2.25	2.00

	Current Price Range		C/Y Avg.

☐ **Dewey, Thomas B.,** *Don't Cry For Long,* Pocket Books 50223 (This was not the Governor of New York, whose name was Thomas *E.* Dewey.) .... | 3.75 | 4.50 | 4.50

☐ **DeWohl, Louis,** *The Spear,* Popular Library R3 .... | 3.50 | 4.50 | 3.75

☐ **Dexter, John,** *Lust's Butterfly,* Candid Reader 980, 1969 .... | 3.50 | 4.50 | 3.80

☐ *Passion Tramp,* Midnight Reader 455 | 3.50 | 4.50 | 3.80

☐ *The Shame of Julie Watson,* Nightstand 1798, 1966 .... | 4.00 | 5.00 | 4.40

☐ **Dickens, Charles,** *A Tale of Two Cities,* Cardinal C35 (photo cover picturing Dirk Bogarde, Dorothy Tutin and Cecil Parker) | 6.00 | 8.00 | 6.70

☐ *A Tale of Two Cities,* Reader 119, no date .... | 9.00 | 12.00 | 10.35

☐ **Dickinson, Peter,** *The Glass-Sided Ants' Nest,* Penguin 5864, 1981 .... | 2.25 | 3.00 | 2.62

☐ *The Glass-Sided Ants' Nest,* Ace 28960, no date .... | 1.50 | 2.25 | 1.87

☐ *One Foot In The Grave,* Penguin 5779, 1981 .... | 2.00 | 3.00 | 2.50

☐ *The Sinful Stones,* Ace 76721, no date | 1.25 | 1.75 | 1.60

☐ *Skin Deep,* Panther 02904, 1973, third edition .... | 2.00 | 2.75 | 2.37

☐ **Dickson, Carter,** *Behind The Crimson Blind,* Dell 690, no date .... | 3.50 | 4.50 | 4.00

☐ *The Bowstring Murders,* Belmont Tower 50702, 1974 .... | 1.75 | 2.50 | 2.12

☐ *The Bowstring Murders,* Berkley G-214, 1959 .... | 2.75 | 3.75 | 3.25

☐ *The Bowstring Murders,* Jonathan Press J4, no date .... | 6.00 | 8.00 | 6.37

☐ *The Curse Of The Bronze Lamp,* Pocket 568, 1949 .... | 3.75 | 4.75 | 4.25

☐ *Death And The Gilded Man,* Pocket 478, 1947 .... | 8.00 | 11.00 | 8.50

☐ *Death In Five Boxes,* Dell Map 108, 1946 .... | 6.00 | 8.00 | 6.37

☐ *Death In Five Boxes,* Belmont Tower 50567, 1973 .... | 2.00 | 3.00 | 2.12

		Current Price Range		C/Y Avg.
☐	*Death In Five Boxes,* Bantam 20373, 1982	2.00	3.00	2.12
☐	*Death In Five Boxes,* Berkley F879, 1964	3.00	4.00	3.50
☐	*Death In Five Boxes,* Belmont Tower 51203, no date	1.75	2.50	2.12
☐	*A Graveyard To Let,* Dell Map 543, 1951	6.50	8.50	6.87
☐	*A Graveyard To Let,* Berkley X1502, 1968	2.50	3.50	3.00
☐	*A Graveyard To Let,* Belmont Tower 50580, 1973	1.50	2.25	1.87
☐	*My Late Wives,* Pocket 633, 1949 ...	7.00	8.50	7.62
☐	*My Late Wives,* Pocket 633, 1947, second edition	6.00	8.00	6.37
☐	*Night At The Mocking Widow,* Berkley X1574, 1969	2.00	3.00	2.50
☐	*Nine And Death Makes Ten,* Pocket 335, 1946, second edition	7.00	9.50	7.00
☐	*The Peacock Feather Murders,* Berkley F861, 1963	1.75	2.50	2.12
☐	*The Plague Court Murders,* Jonathan Press J19, no date	6.00	8.00	6.37
☐	*The Reader Is Warned,* Pocket 303, 1945	6.00	8.00	6.37
☐	*The Red Widow Murders,* Pocket 86, 1940	18.00	23.00	17.00
☐	*She Died A Lady,* Pocket 507, 1948	11.00	15.00	10.50
☐	*Skeleton In The Clock,* Belmont Tower 51194, no date	1.50	2.25	1.87
☐	*The Skeleton In The Clock,* Dell Map 481, 1951	5.00	7.00	5.00
☐	*The Skeleton In The Clock,* Bantam 20282, 1982	2.25	3.00	2.37
☐	*The Skeleton In The Clock,* Belmont Tower 50568, 1973	1.25	1.75	1.50
☐	*The Unicorn Murders,* Mercury Mystery 52, no date	5.75	7.50	6.12
☐	*The White Priory Murders,* Pocket 156, 1942	4.50	6.00	4.75
☐	*White Priory Murders,* Belmont Tower 50593, 1973	1.25	2.00	1.62

	Current Price Range		C/Y Avg.

- [ ] *The White Priory Murders,* Bantam 20572, 1982 .... | 1.75 | 2.50 | 2.12
- [ ] **Didelot, Francis,** *The Many Ways Of Death,* Belmont B50-645, 1966 .... | 1.75 | 2.50 | 2.12
- [ ] *Seventh Juror,* Belmont 90-272, 1963 | 2.00 | 2.75 | 2.37
- [ ] **Dietrich, Robert,** *Angel Eyes,* Dell, B203, 1961, first edition .... | 1.50 | 2.25 | 1.87
- [ ] *Angel Eyes,* Dell B203, 1961, first edition .... | 2.50 | 3.25 | 2.87
- [ ] *Calypso Caper,* Dell B182 (cover artwork by Miller, 1961) .... | 4.50 | 5.50 | 4.90
- [ ] *The House On Q Street,* Dell A175, 1959, first edition .... | 2.50 | 3.50 | 2.50
- [ ] *Mistress To Murder,* Dell B162, 1960, first edition .... | 3.50 | 4.50 | 3.62
- [ ] *Murder On Her Mind,* Dell B163, 1960, first edition .... | 1.50 | 2.25 | 1.87
- [ ] *My Body,* Lancer 70-010, 1962 ...... | 3.00 | 4.00 | 3.25
- [ ] *One For The Road,* Pyramid 235, 1957 | 2.00 | 3.00 | 2.50
- [ ] *Steve Bentley's Calypso Caper,* Dell B182, 1961, first edition .... | 3.25 | 4.00 | 3.62
- [ ] **Diment, Adam,** *The Bang Bang Birds,* Pan 02382, 1969 .... | 2.25 | 3.00 | 2.37
- [ ] *The Dolly Dolly Spy,* Pan 02150, 1968 | 2.25 | 3.00 | 2.37
- [ ] *The Dolly Dolly Spy,* Bantam S3888, 1968 .... | 1.50 | 2.25 | 1.87
- [ ] **Dimona, Joseph,** *Last Man At Arlington,* Dell 4652, 1974 .... | 1.50 | 2.25 | 1.87
- [ ] *To The Eagle's Nest,* Dell 18944, 1981 | 3.50 | 4.50 | 3.75
- [ ] **Dinesen, Isak,** *Winter's Tales,* Dell D191, 1957 .... | 3.50 | 4.50 | 3.75
- [ ] **Dinneen, Joseph F.,** *Anatomy Of A Crime,* Avon 701, 1956 .... | 3.75 | 4.75 | 4.00
- [ ] *The Anatomy Of A Crime,* Avon 701, 1956 .... | 3.25 | 4.25 | 3.37
- [ ] **Dipper, Alan,** *The Wave Hangs Dark,* Popular Library 02534, no date .... | 1.75 | 2.50 | 2.12
- [ ] **Dirksen, Joan,** *I'll Find My Love,* Berkley 682 .... | 2.50 | 3.50 | 2.85
- [ ] **Disney, Doris Miles,** *2 Little Children How They Grew,* Ace 83370, 1975 .... | 1.25 | 1.75 | 1.50

	Current Price Range		C/Y Avg.
☐ *Compound For Death,* Bestseller Mystery B65, no date	4.50	6.00	4.75
☐ *Dark Lady,* Popular SP249, 1964	1.25	1.75	1.50
☐ *Dark Road,* Popular 01465, no date ..	1.75	2.50	2.12
☐ *Day Miss Bessie Lewis Disappear,* Ace 13928, 1976	1.25	1.75	1.50
☐ *Dead Stop,* Dell 929, no date	3.25	4.50	3.50
☐ *Do Unto Others,* MacFadden 75-377, 1970	1.00	1.50	1.25
☐ *Don't Go Into Woods Today,* Signet Q6474, 1975	1.50	2.25	1.87
☐ *Family Skelton,* Mystery Novel Classic 98, no date	3.75	4.75	3.67
☐ *Find The Woman,* Popular 01464, no date	1.50	2.25	1.87
☐ *Find The Woman,* Popular SP264, 1964	2.00	3.00	2.50
☐ *Hospitality Of The House,* MacFadden 60-276, 1967	1.25	1.75	1.50
☐ *The Last Straw,* Popular SP363, no date	1.35	1.85	1.50
☐ *Look Back On Murder,* Ace 48990, 1976	1.35	1.85	1.50
☐ *The Magic Grandfather,* Manor 12305, 1975	1.35	1.85	1.50
☐ *The Magic Grandfather,* MacFadden 60-320, 1968	1.75	2.50	2.12
☐ *Shadow Of A Man,* MacFadden 60-358, 1968	1.75	2.50	2.12
☐ *Testimony By Silence,* Signet Q6110, 1974	1.50	2.25	1.87
☐ *Three's A Crowd,* Ace 80790, 1975 ..	1.25	1.75	1.50
☐ *Voice From The Grave,* MacFadden 75-324, 1970	1.25	1.75	1.50
☐ **Disney, Dorothy Cameron,** *The Balcony,* Pocket 152, 1942	9.00	12.00	9.50
☐ *Crimson Friday,* Dell Map 137, 1946	7.50	10.00	8.00
☐ *Death In The Back Seat,* Dell Map 76, no date	3.00	4.00	3.50
☐ *Death In The Back Seat,* Dell Map 76, 1945	7.50	10.00	8.00

		Current Price Range		C/Y Avg.

	Title	Low	High	Avg.
☐	*Death In The Back Seat,* Mercury Mys 71, no date	4.00	5.25	4.62
☐	*Explosion,* Bantam 761, 1950	6.00	8.00	6.25
☐	*Golden Swan Murder,* Dell Map 15, 1943	6.50	8.50	7.00
☐	*The Hangman's Tree,* Ace K-189, no date	1.25	1.75	1.50
☐	*The Strawstack Murders,* Dell Map 62, 1944	6.50	8.50	7.00
☐	**Dispaldo, A.R.,** *I Am Teresa,* Belmont #91-257	1.50	2.00	1.75
☐	**Dittami, Mario L.,** *I Thee Wed,* Lumen 524, 1956	4.00	5.00	4.40
☐	**Dixon, H.V.,** *The Pleasure Seekers,* Monarch 298 (cover artwork by Marchetti, 1963)	4.00	5.00	4.40
☐	**Donalds, Richard,** *Sign Here For Sin,* Midwood 270 (cover artwork by Raden, 1963)	4.25	5.25	4.55
☐	**Donovan, Robert J.,** *PT 109,* Crest 523	3.00	3.75	3.30
☐	**Dos Passos, John,** *Number One,* Lion LL-1, 1954	4.75	6.00	5.00
☐	**Doss, Helen,** *The Family Nobody Wanted,* Monarch 169	3.50	4.25	3.75
☐	**Dostoyevsky, Fyodor,** *Crime and Punishment,* Quick Reader 114, no date	9.00	12.00	10.35
☐	(The Quick Reader series comprised miniature-size paperbacks, not the ideal format for Crime and Punishment).			
☐	**Douglas, Jack,** *A Funny Thing Happened On My Way To The Grave,* Perma 5065 (interior photos)	4.00	5.00	4.42
☐	**Douglas, Lloyd,** *Doctor Hudson's Secret Journal,* Dell 304, no date	2.75	3.50	3.12
☐	*Magnificent Obsession,* Reader's League (no serial number), (cover artwork by Hoffman, 1944)	5.00	6.25	5.50
☐	**Douglas, Malcolm,** *Pure Sweet Hell,* Gold Medal 972	3.50	4.50	3.90

	Current Price Range		C/Y Avg.

☐ **Douglass, Donald M.,** *Many Brave Hearts,* Pocket Books 1273 (cover artwork by Bennett) 3.75 4.50 4.10

☐ **Doyle, Sir Arthur C.,** *The Lost World,* Pyramid 514 (painted cover picturing Jill St. John and Claude Rains, by Beecham) 6.00 8.00 6.70

☐ **Drago, Harry,** *The Lone Trail North,* Pocket Books 6081, 1961 .... 4.50 5.50 4.95

☐ *Montana Road,* Popular Library G489 (cover artwork by Ross) 4.50 5.50 4.87

☐ *Sun in Their Eyes,* Pocket Books 6131 4.00 5.00 4.39

☐ *Wild Grass,* Perma 3085 (cover artwork by Ryan) 4.00 5.00 4.32

☐ **Dratler, Jay,** *Dr. Paradise,* Popular Library G529 .... 3.50 4.50 3.87

☐ **DuBois, Rene,** *Mirage of Health,* Anchor 258 .... 2.00 2.50 2.21

☐ **Dubrevil, Linda,** *Pandora Descending,* Midwood 125–27, 1970 .... 3.00 4.00 3.33

☐ **Duff, James** *Some Die Young,* Graphic 139, 1956 .... 2.75 3.50 3.12

☐ *Who Dies There?,* Graphic 134, 1956 2.00 3.00 2.50

☐ **Duggan, Alfred,** *Children of the Wolf,* Ace K118 .... 3.00 3.75 3.28

☐ **Duhart, William H.,** *Deadly Pay-Off,* Gold Medal 805, 1958 .... 1.75 2.50 2.12

☐ **Duke, Madelaine,** *The Bormann Receipt,* Charter 07095, 1977 .... 1.75 2.50 2.12

☐ **Duke, Will,** *Fair Prey,* Graphic 142, 1956 2.75 3.50 3.12

☐ *Fair Prey,* Graphic 142, 1956 .... 2.00 2.75 2.37

☐ **Dumont, Jessie,** *I Prefer Girls,* Monarch 381 (cover artwork by McGuire, 1963) 4.00 5.00 4.37

☐ **Duncan, Peter,** *The Telltale Tart,* Gold Medal S1127, 1961 .... 2.75 3.50 3.12

☐ **Duncan, Robert L.,** *Brimstone,* Tor 48-025, 1981 .... 2.00 2.75 2.37

☐ *Dragons At The Gate,* Signet J6984, 1976 .... 1.25 1.75 1.50

☐ *Fire Storm,* Ballantine 28174, 1979 .. 2.00 2.75 2.37

☐ *Temple Dogs,* Ballantine 27166, 1978 1.75 2.50 2.12

☐ **Dundee, Robert,** *Pandora's Box,* Signet 1980 (cover artwork by Phillips) 3.75 4.50 4.10

	Current Price Range		C/Y Avg.

☐ *Restless Lovers,* Signet 1768 (cover artwork by Phillips)	4.00	5.00	4.30
☐ **Dunham, Donald,** *Zone of Violence,* Belmont L92-532, 1962	2.00	3.00	2.50
☐ **Dunn, Dorothy,** *Murder's Web,* Pocket 806, 1951	4.50	6.00	4.62
☐ **Dunne, John Gregory,** *True Confessions,* Pocket 81988, 1978	2.25	3.00	2.37
☐ **Dunning, Lawrence,** *Taking Liberty,* Avon 77297, 1981	2.25	3.00	2.37
☐ **Durand, Robert,** *Lady In A Cage* (Movie Tie-In), Popular PC1034, no date	1.75	2.50	2.12
☐ **Durbin, Charles,** *Vendetta,* Dell 9381, 1971	1.25	1.75	1.50
☐ **Durbridge, Francis,** *The World Of Tim Frazer,* Hodder 544, 1962	2.75	3.75	3.25
☐ **Durrant, Theo,** *The Big Fear,* Popular 507, 1953	3.00	4.00	3.50
☐ **Durrell, Lawrence,** *Balthazar,* Cardinal GC99	2.00	2.75	2.30
☐ *Clea,* Cardinal GC767	2.00	2.75	2.30
☐ *Mountolive,* Cardinal GC766	2.00	2.75	2.30
☐ **Dutourd, Jean,** *A Dog's Head,* Avon H102	3.00	3.75	3.35
☐ **Dwyer, K.R.,** *Dragonfly,* (Dean Koontz), Ballantine 25140, 1976	1.75	2.50	2.12
☐ **Dyer, Walter,** *TV Tramps,* Midwood 186, 1962	3.00	3.75	3.35
☐ **Eberhardt, Walter F.,** *A Dagger In The Dark,* Green 11, no date	9.50	12.00	10.50
☐ **Eberhart, Mignon G.,** *5 Passengers From Lisbon,* Collins, no #, no date ...	3.00	4.25	3.62
☐ *5 Passengers From Lisbon,* Popular 60-2454, no date	1.25	1.75	1.50
☐ *Another Man's Murder,* Dell D259, 1959	2.50	3.50	3.00
☐ *Another Man's Murder,* Dell D259, 1959	1.50	2.25	1.87
☐ *Another Woman's House,* Bantam 849, 1950	3.50	4.50	3.62
☐ *Another Woman's House,* Collins 236C, no date	2.00	3.00	2.50

		Current Price Range		C/Y Avg.
☐	*Call After Midnight,* Popular 60-2455, no date	1.75	2.50	2.12
☐	*Call After Midnight,* Popular Library 00446, 1977	1.25	1.75	1.50
☐	*Call After Midnight,* Popular 50-436, no date	1.25	1.75	1.50
☐	*Cases Of Susan Dare,* Popular 00324, no date	1.50	2.25	1.87
☐	*Cases Of Susan Dare,* Popular 60-2197, no date	1.50	2.25	1.50
☐	*The Chiffon Scarf,* Popular 01481, no date	1.50	2.25	1.50
☐	*The Chiffon Scarf,* Popular Library 60-2150, no date	1.75	2.50	1.87
☐	*Chiffon Scarf,* Popular Library 00679	1.75	2.50	1.87
☐	*Cup The Blade Or The Gun,* Popular 60-2304, no date	1.25	1.75	1.50
☐	*Danger In The Dark,* Popular 2, 1943	11.00	14.00	11.00
☐	*Danger In The Dark,* MacFadden 50-186, 1963	2.25	3.00	2.62
☐	*Danger In The Dark,* MacFadden 60-271, 1966, second edition	1.75	2.50	2.12
☐	*Danger Money,* Popular 00343, no date	1.25	1.75	1.50
☐	*The Dark Garden,* Bestseller Mystery B49, no date	3.75	4.75	4.00
☐	*The Dark Garden,* MacFadden 60-241, 1966, second edition	1.75	2.50	2.12
☐	*The Dark Garden,* Popular 00480, no date	1.25	1.75	1.50
☐	*The Dark Garden,* Bestseller Mystery B49, no date	3.75	4.75	4.00
☐	*Dead Men's Plans,* Popular 00549, no date	1.25	1.75	1.50
☐	*Dead Men's Plans,* Popular 60-2360, no date	1.75	2.50	2.12
☐	*Dead Men's Plans,* Dell 767, 1954 ...	4.50	6.00	4.75
☐	*Dead Men's Plans,* Popular Library K47, 1963	2.50	3.25	2.87
☐	*Deadly Is The Diamond,* Dell 10, #7, no date	8.00	11.00	9.25
☐	*Deadly Is The Diamond,* Popular 60-2372, no date	2.00	2.75	2.37

		Current Price Range		C/Y Avg.
☐	*Enemy In The House,* Popular K53, 1963	2.00	3.00	2.50
☐	*Enemy In The House,* Popular Library 01604, no date	1.25	1.75	1.50
☐	*Escape The Night,* Bantam 46, third edition	4.00	5.75	4.00
☐	*Escape The Night,* Bantam 46, 1946, second edition	6.00	8.00	6.25
☐	*Escape The Night,* Collins 281C, no date	2.75	3.75	3.00
☐	*Escape The Night,* Popular 00615, no date	1.50	2.00	1.50
☐	*Fair Warning,* Mystery Novel Classic 47, 1943	7.50	10.00	8.12
☐	*Fair Warning,* Popular Library 00648	1.75	2.50	1.87
☐	*Fair Warning,* Popular 60-2148, no date	2.00	3.00	2.12
☐	*Five Passengers From Lisbon,* Popular SP407, no date	2.00	2.75	2.37
☐	*Five Passengers From Lisbon,* Popular 00415, 1976	1.75	2.50	1.87
☐	*From This Dark Stairway,* Popular 27, 1944	7.50	10.00	8.25
☐	*The Glass Slipper,* Popular 60-2182, no date	2.00	3.00	2.12
☐	*The Glass Slipper,* Popular 01482, no date	1.50	2.00	1.50
☐	*The Hangman's Whip,* Popular 60-2204, no date	1.50	2.00	1.50
☐	*The Hangman's Whip,* Popular 293, 1950	7.50	10.00	8.25
☐	*Hangman's Whip,* Bestseller Mystery B60, no date	5.00	7.00	5.12
☐	*Hasty Wedding,* Popular Library 73, 1946	5.00	7.00	5.12
☐	*Hasty Wedding,* Mercury Mystery 51, no date	6.00	8.00	5.75
☐	*Hasty Wedding,* Popular 60-2327, no date	1.50	2.00	1.50
☐	*House of Storm,* Popular Library 00563, no date	1.50	2.00	1.50
☐	*House Of Storm,* Popular Library 60-2370, no date	1.50	2.00	1.50

		Current Price Range		C/Y Avg.
☐	*The House On The Roof,* Popular Library 17, 1943	9.00	12.00	8.75
☐	*Hunt With Hounds,* Popular Library K39, 1963	2.50	3.25	2.87
☐	*Hunt With The Hounds,* Dell Map 546, 1951	3.25	4.25	3.75
☐	*Jury Of One,* Popular Library 00544, no date	1.35	1.85	1.50
☐	*Jury Of One,* Popular Library 60-2320, no date	1.35	1.85	1.50
☐	*Jury Of One,* Popular G553, 1961	1.75	2.50	2.12
☐	*Man Missing,* Dell 877, 1955	2.00	2.75	2.37
☐	*Man Next Door,* Dell Map 161, 1947	3.50	4.75	4.12
☐	*The Man Next Door,* Dell Map 161, 1947	6.75	8.75	6.87
☐	*The Man Next Door,* Popular Library 60-2116, no date	1.25	2.00	1.20
☐	*Message From Hong Kong,* Popular 02488, no date	1.75	2.50	2.12
☐	*Message From Hong Kong,* Popular 04032, no date	1.25	1.75	1.50
☐	*Mystery Of Hunting's End,* Popular 35, 1944	7.50	10.00	7.75
☐	*Mystery of Hunting's End,* Popular 60-2298, no date	1.75	2.50	2.12
☐	*Never Look Back,* Dell 669, 1953	3.75	4.75	4.00
☐	*Never Look Back,* Popular K16, 1962	2.00	2.75	2.37
☐	*The Pattern,* Bestseller Mystery B55, no date	5.00	7.00	5.25
☐	*The Pattern,* Popular 00637, no date	1.50	2.25	1.87
☐	*Postmark Murder,* Dell 955, 1957	2.25	3.00	2.62
☐	*The Promise Of Murder,* Dell 7154, 1966	2.00	2.75	2.37
☐	*R.S.V.P. Murder,* Popular 00471, no date	1.50	2.25	1.87
☐	*Run Scared,* Popular 60-2423, no date	1.75	2.50	2.12
☐	*Run Scared,* Popular Library SP328 . .	1.25	1.75	1.50
☐	*Run Scared,* Popular Library 00596, no date	1.25	1.75	1.50
☐	*Speak No Evil,* Dell Map 25, 1943 . . .	7.00	10.00	7.62
☐	*Speak No Evil,* Dell Map 628, 1952 . .	4.00	5.50	4.37

		Current Price Range		C/Y Avg.
☐	*Unidentified Woman,* Dell Map 213, 1948	5.00	6.75	5.12
☐	*Unidentified Woman,* Popular Library SP368	1.75	2.50	2.12
☐	*Unidentified Woman,* Popular 60-2452, no date	1.75	2.50	2.12
☐	*Unknown Quantity,* Dell 811, 1954	3.50	4.75	3.25
☐	*Unknown Quantity,* Popular Library K60, 1963	2.75	3.75	3.25
☐	*While Patient Slept,* MacFadden 60-244, 1966, second edition	1.75	2.50	2.12
☐	*While The Patient Slept,* MacFadden 50-167, 1963	1.75	2.50	2.12
☐	*While The Patient Slept,* Pocket 64, 1941, seventh edition	3.00	4.25	3.62
☐	*The White Cockatoo,* Mercury Mystery 88, no date	3.75	4.75	4.00
☐	*White Cockatoo,* Popular Library 01529, no date	1.50	2.25	1.87
☐	*The White Dress,* Popular 02533, no date	2.00	2.75	2.37
☐	*The White Dress,* Popular Library SP 418, no date	1.25	1.75	1.50
☐	*The White Dress,* Bantam 739, 1949	2.00	3.00	2.50
☐	*With This Ring,* Popular 02509, no date	1.75	2.50	2.12
☐	*With This Ring,* Dell Map 83, 1945	6.00	8.00	5.87
☐	*With This Ring,* Popular Library 60-2128, no date	1.65	2.25	1.87
☐	*Witness At Large,* Popular 60-2277, no date	1.65	2.25	1.87
☐	*Wolf In Man's Clothing,* Popular 60-2426, no date	1.65	2.25	1.87
☐	*Wolf In Man's Clothing,* Dell Map 136, 1946	7.00	9.50	7.62
☐	**Eby, Lois and J.C. Fleming,** *Velvet Fleece,* Dell Map 272, 1949	5.00	6.75	5.75
☐	**Edd, Karl,** *Teen Tramp,* Beacon 399 (Not to be confused with the Carl Edd who drew the comic strip Harold Teen.)	3.00	4.00	3.36
☐	**Eddy, Roger,** *The Worldly Adventures of a Teenage Tycoon,* Scholastic T656	4.00	5.00	4.40

	Current Price Range		C/Y Avg.

☐ **Edelman, Maurice,** *A Dream Of Treason,* Beacon Books, 1957 .... 4.00 5.25 4.62

☐ **Edgar, Keith,** *Honduras Double Cross,* Howard, 1944 .... 13.00 16.00 12.50

☐ *I Hate You To Death,* Howard, 1944 12.00 16.00 12.50

☐ **Edgley, Leslie,** *False Face,* Harlequin 132, 1951 .... 4.50 6.00 5.12

☐ *Fear No More,* Bestseller B104, no date 4.25 5.50 4.75

☐ *One Blonde Died,* Bestseller B171, no date 4.25 5.50 4.75

☐ **Edmonds, Walter,** *The Wedding Journey,* Dell 10 #6, no date 8.00 11.00 9.35

☐ **Edmondson, Paul,** *Little Revolution,* Crest S335, 1959 .... 2.50 3.25 2.87

☐ **Edmonson, G.C.,** *The Ship That Sailed the Time Stream,* Ace M109, 1965 .... 5.00 6.50 5.39

☐ **Edwards, Frank,** *Stranger Than Science,* Ace K117 .... 3.00 4.00 3.40

☐ **Edwards, Samuel,** *Devil's Prize,* Crest S259, 1959 .... 1.75 2.50 2.12

☐ **Eggleston, E.,** *The Hoosier Schoolmaster,* Books Inc. 66, 1943 .... 1.25 1.75 1.40

☐ **Ehrlich, Jack,** *Cry Baby,* Dell B227 (cover artwork by Abbett, 1962) 5.00 6.00 5.35

☐ *Slow Burn, Slow Burn,* Dell B220 (cover artwork by Abbett, 1961) 5.00 6.00 5.35

☐ **Eiseley, Loren,** *The Immense Journey,* Vintage V157 .... 3.00 3.75 3.39

☐ **Elder, Philip,** *Sex Plan,* Midwood 245, 1963 .... 3.50 4.25 3.85

☐ **Eliot, T.S.,** *The Wasteland and Other Poems,* Harvest 1 .... 3.50 4.25 3.85

☐ **Elliot, Ben,** *Contract in Cartridges,* Ace F264 .... 3.00 4.00 3.30

☐ *Weekend Wife,* Beacon 931 .... 3.00 4.00 3.30

☐ **Elliott, Don,** *Sin Club,* Nightstand 1574, 1961 .... 3.00 4.00 3.30

☐ **Ellis, Joan,** *Campus Jungle,* Midwood 182, 1962 .... 4.00 5.00 4.35

☐ *Day In, Day Out,* Midwood F332, no date 1.75 2.50 2.12

	Current Price Range		C/Y Avg.

☐ *Everything Nice,* Midwood 826, 1967	3.00	4.00	3.35
☐ **Ellsworth, Henry,** *The College Male,* Monarch 548	3.00	4.00	3.35
☐ *21 Sunset Drive,* Monarch 397 (cover artwork by Miller, 1963)	4.00	5.00	4.37
☐ **Elston, Allan V.,** *Montana Masquerade,* Pocket Books 6037 (cover artwork by Sticker)	2.00	2.50	2.20
☐ *Roundup On The Picketwire,* Dell 810, no date	1.25	1.75	1.50
☐ *Wyoming Manhunt,* Pocket Books 1278	4.00	5.00	4.32
☐ **English, Arnold,** *Resort Secretary,* Midwood F227, 1962	2.50	3.25	2.87
☐ **Engstrand, Stuart,** *Son Of The Giant,* Crest 5129, 1956	1.75	2.25	2.00
☐ **Erdman, Paul,** *The Silver Bears,* Arrow 910350, 1979, fourth edition	2.00	3.00	2.50
☐ **Erikson, Nancy Watson,** *Splinters Of Fear,* Avon T-471, 1960	2.00	3.00	2.50
☐ **Ernenwein, Leslie,** *The Faro Kid,* Pyramid 505 (cover artwork by Leone)	3.00	3.75	3.29
☐ *Warrior Basin,* Avon T478	4.00	5.25	4.40
☐ **Ernst, Paul,** *The Bronze Mermaid,* Pennant P41, 1954	3.00	4.00	3.50
☐ *Hangman's Hat,* Pocket 923, 1953 ...	2.00	2.75	2.37
☐ *Short Of Murder,* Airmont M2, 1962 ..	2.00	3.00	2.50
☐ **Eshleman, John M.,** *Death Of A Cheat,* Mercury Mystery 206, no date	3.25	4.25	3.75
☐ **Esslin, Martin,** *Brecht: The Man and His Work,* Anchor 244	2.00	2.50	2.18
☐ **Estes, Carroll Cox,** *Embrace Of Death,* Bestseller Mystery B183, no date	3.50	4.75	4.12
☐ **Ethan, John B.,** *The Black Gold Murders,* Pocket 6013, 1960	2.00	2.75	2.37
☐ *Murder On Wall Street,* Pocket 6094, 1961	2.50	3.25	2.87
☐ *Murder On Wall Street,* Pocket 6094, 1961	1.75	2.50	2.12
☐ **Eustis, Helen,** *The Fool Killer,* Popular SP261, 1964	1.50	2.25	1.87

		Current Price Range		C/Y Avg.
☐	*The Horizontal Man,* Pocket 557, 1949, second edition	4.50	6.00	4.75
☐	**Evans, Dean,** *This Kill Is Mine,* Graphic 131, 1956	2.00	3.00	2.50
☐	**Evans, Jean,** *Three Men,* Grove 40	5.00	6.25	5.50
☐	**Evans, John,** *Halo For Satan,* Bantam 800, 1950	2.00	3.00	2.12
☐	*Halo In Blood,* Bantam 74, 1946	2.00	2.75	2.37
☐	*Halo In Brass,* Pocket 709, 1950, second edition	2.25	3.00	2.62
☐	*Halo In Brass,* Bantam 1727, 1958 ...	2.50	3.25	2.87
☐	*Weep Not Fair Lady,* Harlequin 49, 1950	7.00	10.00	7.62
☐	**Evans, Jonathan,** *Misfire,* Tor 48-032, 1982	3.00	4.00	3.50
☐	*Takeover,* Tor 48-044, 1982	3.00	4.00	3.50
☐	**Fairman, Paul W.,** *Coffy,* Lancer 75487, 1973	1.50	2.25	1.87
☐	*Pattern For Destruction,* MacFadden 75-308, 1970	1.25	1.75	1.50
☐	*To Catch A Crooked Girl,* Pinnacle P020-N, 1971	2.50	3.25	2.62
☐	**Falstein, Louis,** *Slaughter Street,* Lion LB172, 1957, second edition	3.00	4.00	3.30
☐	*Slaughter Street,* Lion 151, 1953	2.75	3.50	3.12
☐	*Slaughter Street,* Pyramid G437, 1959	2.50	3.25	2.87
☐	*Sole Survivor,* Dell 29, first edition, 1954	4.00	5.50	4.75
☐	**Fantoni, Barry,** *Mike Dime,* Sphere 3433, 1982	3.00	4.00	3.50
☐	**Farago, Ladislas,** *After-Math,* Avon 25387, fourth edition	1.50	2.25	1.87
☐	**Farjeon, J.J.,** *The Judge Sums Up,* Collins Rime Club 169C, no date	3.00	4.25	3.62
☐	**Farjeon, Jefferson,** *Greenmask,* Dell Map 111, 1946	9.00	12.00	9.25
☐	*Greenmask,* White Circle 250, 1946 ..	5.50	7.50	5.62
☐	*The House Of Shadows,* White Circle 284, 1946	7.00	9.50	7.00
☐	*The Judge Sums Up,* White Circle 87, 1944	7.75	10.25	7.75

		Current Price Range		C/Y Avg.
☐	*Prelude To Crime,* Crime Club 199C, no date	8.00	11.00	7.75
☐	*Room No. 6,* White Circle 239, 1945	5.00	7.00	5.25
☐	*The Third Victim,* White Circle 311, 1947	6.00	8.00	6.37
☐	**Farley, Ralph Milne,** *The Radio Beasts,* Ace F304	3.00	3.75	3.30
☐	**Farmer, Philip Jose,** *Fabulous Riverboat,* Panther 03989, 1979, third edition	3.25	4.50	3.37
☐	*The Fabulous Riverboat,* Berkley 02329, 1973	2.36	3.00	2.50
☐	*Father To The Stars,* Tor 48-504, 1981	2.25	3.00	2.50
☐	*A Feast Unknown,* Playboy 16586, 1980	2.25	3.00	2.37
☐	*Flesh,* Signet T3861, 1969	2.25	3.00	2.37
☐	*Flesh,* Signet Q5097, third edition	2.25	3.00	2.37
☐	*The Gate Of Time,* Belmont B75-2016, 1970	2.25	3.00	2.50
☐	*The Gate Of Time,* Belmont B50-717, 1966	1.75	2.50	2.12
☐	*The Gates Of Creation,* Ace 27389, 1981	2.00	2.75	2.37
☐	*The Gates Of Creation,* Ace F-412, 1966	3.75	4.75	4.00
☐	*The Green Odyssey,* Ballantine 210, 1957	3.75	4.75	4.00
☐	*The Green Odyssey,* Ballantine U2345, 1966, second edition	3.75	5.00	4.37
☐	*Hadon Of Ancient Opar,* DAW UY1107, 1100, 1974	1.50	2.00	1.75
☐	*Hadon Of Ancient Opar,* DAW UE1637, 1442, sixth edition	2.25	3.25	2.50
☐	*Hadon Of Ancient Opar,* DAW UY1107, #100, 1974	2.00	3.00	2.50
☐	*Inside Outside,* Berkley 04041, 1979	5.50	7.75	5.75
☐	*Inside Outside,* Ballantine U2192, 1964	3.00	4.25	3.62
☐	**Farmer, Philip Jose,** *Jesus On Mars,* Pinnacle 40-184, 1979	2.00	2.75	2.37
☐	*Lord Tyger,* Signet 05096, third edition	1.50	2.00	1.75
☐	*Lord Tyger,* Signet W7577, fourth edition	1.75	2.50	2.12

	Current Price Range		C/Y Avg.
☐ Lord Tyger, Panther 03958, 1974	3.00	4.00	3.50
☐ The Lovers, Ballantine 02762, 1972, second edition	1.75	2.50	2.12
☐ The Magic Labyrinth, Berkley 04854, 1981	2.25	3.25	2.75
☐ The Maker Of Universes, Ace F-367, 1965	3.00	4.00	3.50
☐ Night Of Light, Berkley S2249, third edition	1.75	2.25	2.00
☐ Night Of Light, Berkley F1248, 1966	4.75	6.25	5.12
☐ A Private Cosmos, Sphere 3442, 1975, third edition	2.50	3.25	2.87
☐ A Private Cosmos, Ace G-724, 1968	3.00	4.00	3.50
☐ A Private Cosmos, Ace 67952, no date	1.75	2.25	2.00
☐ The Stone God Awakens, Ace 78651, 1973, second edition	2.25	3.00	2.62
☐ Stone God Awakens, Panther 04226, 1979, second edition	2.25	3.00	2.62
☐ The Stone God Awakens, Ace 78654, 1980	2.00	2.75	2.37
☐ The Stone God Awakens, Ace 78650, 1970	2.50	3.25	2.87
☐ Strange Relations, Avon 41418, third edition	1.25	1.75	1.50
☐ Strange Relations, Ballantine 391K, 1960	6.00	8.00	5.75
☐ Tarzan Alive, Popular 00427, no date	2.50	3.50	3.00
☐ Time's Last Gift, Del Rey 25843, 1977	1.75	2.50	2.12
☐ To Scattered Bodies Go, Panther 3939, 1978, third edition	2.50	3.50	3.00
☐ To Your Scattered Bodies Go, Berkley 02333, fifth edition	1.75	2.50	2.12
☐ To Your Scattered Bodies Go, Berkley 03744, eleventh edition	1.75	2.50	2.12
☐ To Your Scattered Bodies Go, Berkley S2057, 1971	3.00	4.00	3.50
☐ Tongues Of The Moon, Pyramid R-1055, 1964	4.50	6.50	5.00
☐ Tongues Of The Moon, Jove A4595, 1978	2.25	3.25	2.75
☐ Tongues Of The Moon, Pyramid T2260, 1970, second edition	1.50	2.00	1.75

	Current Price Range		C/Y Avg.

☐	*Traitor To The Living,* Panther 04200, 1978, second edition	2.50	3.50	3.00
☐	*Traitor To The Living,* Del Rey 27446, 1978, second edition	2.00	2.75	2.37
☐	*Traitor To The Living,* Ballantine 23613, 1973	2.25	3.00	2.62
☐	*Two Hawks From Earth,* Ace 83365, 1979	1.75	2.50	2.12
☐	*Wind Whales Of Ishmael,* Ace 89237	1.50	2.00	1.75
☐	*Wind Whales Of Ishmael,* Ace 89238	2.25	3.00	2.62
☐	*The Wind Whales of Ishmael,* Ace 89240, fourth edition	1.75	2.50	2.12
☐	**Farmer, Philip Jose, and Rosny, J.H.,** *Ironcastle,* DAW UJ1545, third edition	1.75	2.50	2.90
☐	*Ironcastle,* DAW UY1225, #187, 1976	2.50	3.25	2.87
☐	**Farr, John,** *Naked Fear,* Jonathan Press J82, no date	3.50	4.75	3.62
☐	**Farrell, Henry,** *Death On The 6th Day,* Avon G-1157	1.85	2.50	2.12
☐	*The Hostage,* Avon G1189	1.85	2.50	2.12
☐	*How Awful About Allan,* Avon G1275, 1965	2.25	3.00	2.62
☐	*What Ever Happened To Baby Jane?,* Avon PN282, 1970, eighth edition ...	1.75	2.50	2.12
☐	*What Ever Happened To Baby Jane?* Avon G-1146, no date	1.25	1.75	1.50
☐	**Farrell, James T.,** *Boarding House Blue,* Paperback Library S103, 1961	3.00	4.00	3.30
☐	*It Has Come To Pass,* Paperback Library 52-141, no date	2.50	3.50	2.90
☐	*Side Street and Other Stories,* Paperback Library 52-113, 1961	3.00	4.00	3.30
☐	**Farrer, Katherine,** *The Cretan Counterfeit,* Penguin 1103, 1955	2.25	3.00	2.45
☐	**Farrere, Claude,** *Black Opium,* Berkley G120, no date (cover artwork by Maguire)	45.00	60.00	51.75
☐	**Farrington, Fielden,** *A Little Game,* Popular Library 60-2428, no date	1.75	2.50	2.05
☐	*Street of Brass,* Hillman 203	4.00	5.00	4.32
☐	**Farris, John,** *Shatter,* Popular Library 0-4693, 1982	2.50	3.25	2.87

	Current Price Range		C/Y Avg.

☐ **Fast, Julius,** *And Then Murder,* Hillman 126, 1959 . . . . 3.25 4.50 3.87

☐   *Bright Face Of Danger,* Black Cat Detective 27, 1947 . . . . 5.50 7.00 5.87

☐   *Down Through The Night,* Crest 136, 1956 . . . . 2.25 3.00 2.62

☐ **Faulkner, John,** *Uncle Good's Girls,* Gold Medal 729, 1958, third edition . . . 1.25 1.75 1.50

☐ **Faulkner, William,** *Mosquitos,* Dell 708, no date 3.00 3.75 3.37

☐   *Pylon,* Signet 1485 (photo cover picturing Rock Hudson and Dorothy Malone) 5.00 7.00 5.75

☐   *Sanctuary,* Signet 1900 (photo cover picturing Lee Remick) 5.00 7.00 5.75

☐ **Fehrenbach, T.R.,** *The Battle of Anzio,* Monarch 317 (cover artwork by Stanley, 1962) 2.50 3.00 2.75

☐   *U.S. Marines in Action,* Monarch 319, 1962 . . . . 2.50 3.00 2.75

☐ **Feiffer, Jules,** *The Explainers,* Signet 2422 (cover artwork by the author) 9.00 12.00 10.00

☐ **Feldstein, Albert B.,** *Greasy Mad Stuff,* Signet 2343 . . . . 7.00 10.00 8.00

☐   *The Voodoo Mad,* Signet 2276 (cover artwork by Freas; selections from Mad Magazine) 7.00 10.00 8.00

☐ **Fenisong, Ruth,** *But Not Forgotten,* Ace G508 . . . . 2.50 3.00 2.75

☐ **Ferber, Edna,** *They Brought Their Women,* Avon Modern Short Story 19, no date 3.00 4.00 3.40

☐ **Ferber, Richard,** *Doctor With a Gun,* Dell A198 (cover artwork by Leone, 1960) . . 4.00 5.00 4.50

☐ **Fergusson, Francis,** *The Idea of a Theater,* Anchor 3.00 3.75 3.50

☐ **Ferrari, Ivy,** *Nurse at Ryeminsley,* Harlequin 874 . . . . 2.00 2.50 2.25

☐ **Fielding, Henry,** *Tom Jones,* Vintage V130 . . . . 2.00 2.75 2.25

☐ **Finney, Jack,** *Assault on a Queen,* Dell D377, 1960 . . . . 2.00 3.00 2.50

	Current Price Range		C/Y Avg.

(The queen in question was an ocean liner named in honor of a British queen.)

☐ **Fischer, Bruno,** *Murder in the Raw,* Gold Medal 1011 . . . . **2.50** · **3.00** · **2.75**

☐ **Fischer, Marjorie,** *Mrs. Sherman's Summer,* Popular Library G509 (cover artwork by Zuckerberg) . . . . **3.00** · **3.75** · **3.35**

☐ **Fischer, Markoosha,** *The Right To Love,* Crest 165, 1957 . . . . **2.00** · **2.75** · **2.37**

☐ **Fisher, Clay,** *Blood Alley,* Gold Medal 499 (painted cover picturing John Wayne and Lauren Bacall) . . . . **6.00** · **8.00** · **6.75**

☐ *Yellowstone Kelly,* Pocket Books 1209 (photo cover picturing Clint Walker and Edward Byrnes) . . . . **5.00** · **7.00** · **5.75**

☐ **Fitzpatrick, William,** *Tokyo After Dark,* MacFadden 50-326, 1967, third edition **1.25** · **1.75** · **1.50**

☐ **Fleishman, A.S.,** *Shanghai Flame,* Gold Medal 514, 1955, third edition . . . . **4.00** · **5.50** · **4.37**

☐ **Fleming, Ian,** *Casino Royale,* Signet 1997 (cover artwork by Phillipps) . . . . . . **7.00** · **10.00** · **7.90**

☐ *The Diamond Smugglers,* Dell 1921 (cover artwork by Crowley) . . . . **8.00** · **11.00** · **9.10**

☐ *Diamonds Are Forever,* Signet D2029, 1961 . . . . **6.00** · **8.00** · **6.50**

☐ *Doctor No,* Signet 2036 (cover artwork by Phillips) . . . . **7.00** · **10.00** · **8.20**

☐ *From Russia With Love,* Signet 2030 **7.00** · **10.00** · **8.20**

☐ *Goldfinger,* Signet 2729 (cover artwork by Phillips) . . . . **3.00** · **4.00** · **3.35**

☐ *Live and Let Die,* Signet 2051 (cover artwork by Phillips) . . . . **7.00** · **10.00** · **8.10**

☐ *Moonraker,* Signet 2053 (cover artwork by Phillips) . . . . **7.00** · **10.00** · **8.10**

☐ *Moonraker,* Signet 2731 (cover artwork by Phillips) . . . . **3.00** · **4.00** · **3.35**

☐ *On Her Majesty's Secret Service,* Signet 2732 . . . . **3.00** · **4.00** · **3.35**

☐ *The Spy Who Loved Me,* Signet 2280 (cover artwork by Phillips) . . . . **6.00** · **8.00** · **6.55**

☐ *Thunderball,* Signet 2126 (cover artwork by Phillips) . . . . **7.00** · **10.00** · **8.35**

Diamonds Are Forever, by Ian Fleming, Signet Book, D2029, 1961, **$6.00–$8.00.**

		Current Price Range		C/Y Avg.
☐	*You Only Live Twice,* Signet 2712 ...	3.00	4.00	3.35
☐	**Flemming, Tom,** *Call Me Liz,* Boudoir 1046, 1963	4.00	5.00	4.40
☐	**Flew, Anthony,** *Logic and Language,* Anchor 449	3.00	3.75	3.30
☐	**Flint, Homer,** *The Lord of Death and the Queen of Life,* Ace F345 (cover artwork by Gaughan)	5.00	6.00	5.60
☐	**Flint, John B.,** *Lover Boy,* Belmont 1240	1.00	1.50	1.25
☐	*Lover Boy,* Stanley SL71, 1959	4.00	5.00	4.40
☐	**Flora, Fletcher,** *Take Me Home,* Monarch 120, 1959	1.25	1.75	1.50
☐	**Floren, Lee,** *High Thunder,* Ace F103 ..	2.50	3.25	2.70
☐	*John Wesley Hardin: Texas Gunfighter,* MacFadden 35-114, 1962. Though Jesse James garnered more headlines (and far more sympathy), John Wesley Hardin was by far the most feared of all gunfighters.	3.00	4.00	3.40

	Current Price Range		C/Y Avg.
☐ **Flynn, Errol,** *Showdown,* Dell 351 (painted cover picturing the author)	6.00	8.00	6.75
☐ *My Wicked Wicked Ways,* Dell S11 (photo cover picturing the author) ...	6.00	8.00	6.75
☐ **Flynn, Jay,** *Five Faces of Murder,* Avon F156	2.50	3.25	2.80
☐ **Fontenay, Charles,** *The Day the Oceans Overflowed,* Monarch 443 (cover artwork by Brillhart)	4.00	5.00	4.35
☐ **Foote, Horton,** *Baby the Rain Must Fall,* Popular Library SP325 (photo cover picturing Steve McQueen and Lee Remick)	4.00	5.50	4.60
☐ **Forbes, Kathryn,** *Mama's Bank Account,* Bantam 135 (photo cover picturing Irene Dunne). When this novel was made into a TV series it was retitled "I Remember Mama," and Peggy Wood played the Irene Dunne role.	6.00	8.00	6.70
☐ **Ford, F. Madox,** *The Good Soldier,* Vintage V45	2.00	2.50	2.25
☐ **Ford, Leslie,** *Old Lover's Ghost,* Popular 60-2411, no date	1.75	2.50	2.12
☐ *Old Lover's Ghost,* popular 1963	2.00	2.75	2.37
☐ *The Philadelphia Murder Story,* Dell Map 354, 1949	2.25	3.00	2.62
☐ *The Philadelphia Murder Story,* Popular SP408, no date	1.75	2.50	2.12
☐ *Reno Rendezvous,* Popular 24, 1944	5.00	7.00	6.00
☐ *Road To Folly,* Popular Library 60-2158, no date	1.25	1.75	1.50
☐ *Road To Folly,* Bantam 42, fourth edition	3.50	4.25	3.87
☐ *Road To Folly,* Bantam 42, third edition	3.75	4.75	4.25
☐ *Road To Folly,* Bantam 42, 1946	6.50	8.50	7.12
☐ *The Simple Way of Poison,* Pocket 122, 1941	11.00	15.00	11.50
☐ *The Simple Way Of Poison,* Popular SP321, no date	1.75	2.50	2.12
☐ *Siren In The Night,* Bantam 303, 1948	7.00	9.50	7.87
☐ *Siren In The Night,* Popular 60-2442, no date	1.75	2.50	2.12

		Current Price Range		C/Y Avg.

☐ *Siren In The Night,* Popular Library K68, 1964 .... 2.75 3.75 3.25

☐ *Three Bright Pebbles,* Popular 6, 1943 6.00 8.00 6.62

☐ *Trial By Ambush,* Popular K37, 1963 2.50 3.25 2.87

☐ *Trial By Ambush,* Popular 60-2409, no date 1.75 2.50 2.12

☐ *Washington Whispers Murder,* Popular Library 01405, no date 1.75 2.50 2.12

☐ *Washington Whispers Murder,* Dell 908, no date 3.25 4.50 3.50

☐ *The Woman In Black,* Dell Map 447, 1950 .... 4.50 6.50 5.00

☐ *The Woman In Black,* Popular Library K63, 1963 .... 2.50 3.25 2.87

☐ *The Woman In Black,* Popular 60-2443, 1963 .... 1.85 2.50 2.12

☐ **Ford, Marcia,** *Island Nurse,* Monarch 251 (cover artwork by Miller) 2.25 3.00 2.50

☐ **Forester, C.S.,** *The African Queen,* Bantam 2111 .... 3.00 4.00 3.35

☐ *Captain Horatio Hornblower,* Bantam 912, (painted cover picturing Gregory Peck and Virginia Mayo) 4.00 5.50 4.60

☐ **Foster, Bennett,** *Kid From Dodge City,* Lion LL-43, 1955, second edition 1.85 2.50 2.12

☐ **Foster, Charles,** *First Steps,* Moody 23 2.00 2.50 2.00

☐ **Foster, Jack,** *Adventures at Timberline,* Monitor (no serial number) 4.00 5.00 4.50

☐ **Foster, John,** *Return to Vista,* Fabian Z138, 1960 .... 4.00 5.00 4.50

☐ **Foster, Joseph,** *Stephana,* Monarch 138, no date (cover artwork by Maguire) 3.00 4.00 3.35

☐ **Fowler, Gene,** *Beau James,* Bantam 1626 (painted cover picturing Bob Hope, Vera Miles and Paul Douglas) 4.00 5.00 4.50

☐ *Schnozzola,* Perma 210 (photo cover picturing Jimmy Durante) 5.00 6.00 5.50

☐ *Skyline,* MacFadden 60-104. The MacFadden Publishing Co. was founded by bodybuilder/nutritionist Bernard MacFadden for the purpose of publishing Physical Culture Magazine in 1898.

	Current Price Range		C/Y Avg.

Later, various other magazines and books were added to the line and eventually it became a general publishing house. 3.00 4.00 3.45

☐ **Fox, Clayton,** *End of a Big Wheel,* Ace F143 .... 2.00 2.50 2.25

☐ *Never Forget,* Ace F102, 1961 ...... 4.00 5.00 4.40

☐ **Fox, James M.,** *Code Three,* Pennant P79, 955 .... 2.25 3.00 2.62

☐ *Death Commits Bigamy,* Dell 845, 1955 3.50 4.50 4.00

☐ *Fatal In Furs,* Dell 623, 1952 .... 3.00 4.00 3.50

☐ *Free Ride,* Eagle E882, 1957 .... 2.25 3.25 2.50

☐ *The Gentle Hangman,* Dell Map 526, 1951 .... 2.25 3.25 2.50

☐ *The Inconvenient Bride,* Dell Map 463, 1950 .... 3.50 4.50 3.50

☐ *The Iron Virgin,* Dell 719, 1953 ...... 4.75 6.00 5.12

☐ *The Lady Regrets,* Dell Map 338, 1949 4.00 5.50 4.00

☐ *The Scarlet Slippers,* Dell 685, 1953 3.50 4.50 3.50

☐ *The Wheel Is Fixed,* Dell Map 573, 1952 .... 3.00 3.75 3.12

☐ **Foxx, Gardner, F.,** *The Conquering Prince,* Crest 166, 1957 .... 3.75 4.75 4.00

☐ **Francis, Connie,** *For Every Young Heart,* Monarch 435 (interior photographs) ... 6.00 8.00 6.90

☐ **Frank, Anne,** *The Diary of Anne Frank,* Cardinal C317 (photo cover picturing Millie Perkins) 5.00 7.00 5.75

☐ **Frank, Pat,** *Mr. Adam,* Pocket Books 2498 (cover artwork by Phillips) 4.00 5.00 4.40

☐ **Franklin, Frieda K.,** *Combat Nurse,* Pocket Books 6056 .... 3.00 3.50 3.25

☐ **Frazee, Steve,** *A Day to Die,* Avon T458, 1964 .... 3.75 4.75 3.95

☐ *The Alamo,* Avon T446 (photo cover picturing John Wayne, Richard Widmark, Laurence Harvey) 6.00 8.00 6.70

☐ **Frazer, Robert Caine,** *Hollywood Hoax,* Pocket Books 6064 (cover artwork by Bennett) 4.00 5.00 4.40

		Current Price Range		C/Y Avg.

☐ *Mark Kilby and the Secret Syndicate,* Pocket Books 6000 (cover artwork by Abbett) **4.00** **5.00** **4.40**

☐ *Mark Kilby Takes a Risk,* Pocket Books 6104 .... **3.75** **4.75** **3.95**

☐ **Fredericks, Diana,** *Diana,* Berkley G-11 **2.00** **2.50** **2.25**

☐ **Freeling, Nicolas,** *Because Of The Cats,* Ballantine U2131, 1965 .... **2.00** **3.00** **2.50**

☐ *Criminal Conversation,* Ballantine U551, 1967 .... **2.00** **3.00** **2.12**

☐ *Death In Amsterdam,* Ballantine U2130, 1964 .... **2.00** **3.00** **2.50**

☐ *Double Barrel,* Ballantine U2133, 1966 **2.00** **3.00** **2.12**

☐ *Double Barrell,* Penguin 2585, 1975, second edition **1.75** **2.50** **1.87**

☐ *The Dresden Green,* Ballantine 71107, 1968 .... **1.75** **2.50** **1.87**

☐ *Gadget,* Penguin 4898, 1979 .... **1.75** **2.50** **1.87**

☐ *Gun Before Butter,* Penguin C2280, 1965 .... **4.00** **5.50** **4.00**

☐ *King Of The Rainy Country,* Penguin 2853, 1975, second edition **2.00** **3.00** **2.12**

☐ *Love In Amsterdam,* Penguin 2281, 1975, third edition **2.00** **3.00** **2.12**

☐ *Question Of Loyalty,* Ballantine U2132, 1965 .... **2.00** **3.00** **2.50**

☐ *Tsing-Boum,* Penguin 3298, 1971 .... **2.00** **3.00** **2.12**

☐ **Freuchen, Peter,** *Eskimo,* Ace K124. The author, a highly distinguished arctic explorer, was somehow persuaded to become a contestant on the TV quiz show "$64,000 Question" in the 1950s. **3.00** **4.00** **3.40**

☐ **Freud, Sigmund,** *The Future of an Illusion,* Anchor 381. It is said that total sales on all of Freud's books have surpassed those of virtually all modern novelists, despite the fact that they were intended for specialized readership. **2.00** **2.50** **2.25**

☐ *Moses and Monotheism,* Vintage K14 Monotheism is the belief that only one true religion exists. **2.00** **2.50** **2.20**

	Current Price Range		C/Y Avg.

☐ **Friedman, Stanley,** *The Magnificent Kennedy Women,* Monarch 25, (interior photographs) 4.00 5.00 4.45

☐ **Friedman, Stuart,** *Damned Are the Meek,* Monarch 407 (cover artwork by DeSoto, 1964) 3.25 4.00 4.50

☐ *The Fly Girls,* Monarch 201 (cover artwork by Maguire, 1961) 4.00 5.00 4.50

☐ *Luscious Puritan,* Monarch 437, (cover artwork by Olson) 3.00 3.75 3.35

☐ *Nikki Revisited,* Monarch 377 (cover artwork by Miller, 1963) 4.00 4.75 4.32

☐ *Ravaged,* Monarch 257 (cover artwork by Johnson, 1962) 4.25 5.25 4.50

☐ *Revolt of Jill Braddock,* Monarch 378 (cover artwork by Barton) 4.00 4.75 4.35

☐ *The Surgeons,* Monarch 272 (cover artwork by Schaare, 1962) 4.50 5.75 5.00

☐ *The Trouble With Ava,* Monarch 181 4.75 6.00 5.55

☐ *The Troubles of Dr. Cortland,* Monarch 552 .... 3.00 3.75 3.25

☐ *The Way We Loved,* Monarch 170 (cover artwork by Barton, 1960) 5.00 6.50 5.50

☐ **Frizell, Bernard,** *Ten Days in August,* Popular Library SP82. Perfect example of the way book titles tend to repeat themselves: "Seven Days in May" was a best seller in the early 1960s. 2.75 3.50 3.00

☐ **Froscher, Wingate,** *Comforts of the Damned,* Hillman 201 .... 3.00 3.75 3.20

☐ **Fulbright, J.W.,** *Old Myths and New Realities,* Vintage V264. The author, a U.S. Senator, was an outspoken critic of the Vietnam War. 2.75 3.50 3.10

☐ **Fullbrook, Gladys,** *Nurse Prue in Ceylon,* Harlequin 771 .... 2.00 2.50 2.15

☐ **Fuller, Roger,** *The Facts of Life,* Perma 4207 (photo cover picturing Bob Hope and Lucille Ball) 5.00 7.00 5.75

☐ *On the Double,* Cardinal C427 (photo cover picturing Danny Kaye, Dana Wynter and Margaret Rutherford) ... 6.00 8.00 6.90

	Current Price Range		C/Y Avg.

☐ *Who Killed Beau Sparrow?*, Perma 4310 (photo cover picturing Gene Barry) **5.00** **7.00** **5.75**

☐ **Fuller, William,** *Local Talent*, Dell B153 (cover artwork by Hooks) **2.50** **3.00** **2.70**

☐ **Furlough, John,** *Half Girl, Half Woman*, Beacon 18467F **1.65** **2.15** **1.75**

☐ **Gaddis, Peggy,** *Women Of The Evening*, Belmont 191–260 .... **1.65** **2.15** **1.75**

☐ **Gaines, William M.,** *The Brothers Mad*, Ballantine 267 .... **4.00** **6.00** **4.65**

☐ *Inside Mad*, Ballantine 265 .... **4.00** **6.00** **4.65**

☐ *Like Mad*, Signet 1838 (cover artwork by Freas) **7.00** **10.00** **8.25**

☐ *Mad Strikes Back*, Ballantine 207 .... **7.00** **10.00** **8.25**

☐ *Son of Mad*, Signet 1701 (cover artwork by Freas) **7.00** **10.00** **8.25**

☐ *Utterly Mad*, Ballantine 178 .... **6.00** **8.00** **7.00**

☐ **Gainier, Christine,** *Fetish*, Dell 731, no date **3.00** **3.75** **3.37**

☐ **Galambos, Robert,** *Nerves and Muscles*, Anchor S25 .... **2.75** **3.50** **2.95**

☐ **Gallagher, Richard F.,** *Women Without Morals*, Avon G1190, no date, first edition **4.00** **6.00** **4.75**

☐ **Gallun, Raymond Z.,** *Planet Strappers*, Pyramid 658 (cover artwork by Schoenherr) **4.00** **5.00** **4.40**

☐ **Gallup, George H.,** *The 1955 Pocket Almanac*, Cardinal GC1955. The compiler was a well-known director of a public opinion survey company. **3.00** **4.00** **3.35**

☐ **Galus, Henry S.,** *The Impact of Women*, Monarch 549 .... **2.00** **2.75** **2.35**

☐ *Teenage Brides*, Monarch 517 (cover artwork by Maguire) **2.50** **3.00** **2.75**

☐ *Unwed Mothers*, Monarch 524 (cover artwork by Maguire, 1962) **2.50** **3.00** **2.75**

☐ **Gann, Ernest K.,** *Trouble With Lazy Ethel*, Perma Books, M4159, 1960 .... **1.25** **1.75** **1.50**

☐ **Gardner, Earl Stanley,** *The Case of the Dangerous Dowager*, Pocket Books 252 **8.00** **11.00** **8.85**

Left to Right: **The Case of The Mythical Monkeys,** by Erle
Stanley Gardner, Pocket Book, 6082, **$4.50–$5.75;**
Gold Comes in Bricks, by A.A. Fair,
Dell, D406, **$3.75–$5.00.**

	Current Price Range		C/Y Avg.
☐ The Case of the Fan-Dancer's Horse, Pocket Books 886	9.00	12.00	10.00
☐ The Case of the Lazy Lover, Pocket Books 909	7.00	10.00	8.15
☐ The Case of the Negligent Nymph, Pocket Books 1029	7.00	10.00	8.15
☐ The Case of the Sulky Girl, Cardinal C309	5.00	6.00	5.60
☐ The Case of the Turning Tide, Pocket Books 544	8.00	11.00	9.15
☐ The Case of the Vagabond Virgin, Pocket Books 965	7.00	10.00	8.00
☐ Case Of Perjured Parrot, Pocket 378, 1952, ninth edition	2.25	3.25	2.50
☐ Case Of The Perjured Parrot, Cardinal C-379, 1959	2.00	3.00	2.50
☐ Case Of The Perjured Parrot, Pocket 378, 1950, eighth edition	2.00	3.00	2.50
☐ Case Of The Restless Redhead, Pocket 6107, 1961, second edition ..	1.75	2.50	2.12
☐ Case Of the Restless Redhead, Cardinal C-1170, 1957	3.00	4.00	2.87
☐ Case Of The Rolling Bones, Pocket 50315, 1967, eighteenth edition	1.25	1.75	1.50
☐ Case Of The Rolling Bones, Pocket 50315, 1965, sixteenth edition	1.50	2.00	1.75
☐ Case Of The Rolling Bones, Pocket 6005, 1960, fourteenth edition	2.00	3.00	2.50
☐ Case Of The Rolling Bones, Pocket 50315, 1965, seventeenth edition ...	1.50	2.00	1.75
☐ Case Of The Runaway Corpse, Cardinal C-281, 1957	4.00	5.50	4.00
☐ Case Of Screaming Woman, Pocket 4523, 1963, fourth edition	2.00	3.00	2.50
☐ Case Of The Shapely Shadow, Pocket 4507, 1962	2.00	3.00	2.50
☐ Case Of The Shapely Shadow, Pocket 4507, 1963, third edition	1.75	2.50	2.12
☐ Case Of Shoplifter's Shoe, Pocket 50313, 1965, fourteenth edition	2.00	2.75	2.37
☐ Case Of Shoplifter's Shoe, Pocket 212, 1945, first edition	4.00	5.50	4.00

	Current Price Range		C/Y Avg.
☐ *Case Of The Shoplifters Shoe,* Pocket 312, 1945, second edition	2.00	2.75	2.37
☐ *Case Of The Silent Partner,* Pocket 4506, 1962, seventeenth edition	2.25	3.00	2.62
☐ *Case Of The Silent Partner,* Pocket 4506, 1963, twentieth edition	3.50	4.75	3.62
☐ *Case Of The Silent Partner,* Pocket 2468, 1956, fifteenth edition	2.00	2.75	2.37
☐ *The Case of the Singing Skirt,* Pocket Books 6089	5.00	6.50	5.45
☐ *Case Of Sleepwalker's Niece,* Pocket 50308, 1967, twenty-first edition	1.85	2.50	2.12
☐ *Case Of Sleepwalker's Niece,* Pocket 50308, 1965, eighteenth edition	1.85	2.50	2.12
☐ *Case Of Sleepwalker's Niece,* Pocket 277, 1949, twelfth edition	3.50	4.75	3.50
☐ *Case Of The Sleepwalker's Niece,* Pocket 277, 1944	4.75	6.50	4.62
☐ **Gardner, Gerald,** *The Quotable Mr. Kennedy,* Popular Library K44	3.00	4.00	3.35
☐ **Gardner, Jeffrey K.,** *Cleopatra,* Pyramid 787 (cover artwork by Abbett)	2.00	2.50	2.20
☐ **Gardner, Martin,** *Fads and Fallacies,* Ballantine 446	2.00	2.50	2.35
☐ **Garis, Roger,** *Never Take Candy From a Stranger,* Dell B206, 1961	4.00	5.00	4.40
☐ **Garland, Bennett,** *Seven Brave Men,* Monarch 292 (cover artwork by Stanley, 1962)	4.00	5.00	4.40
☐ **Garon, Jay,** *Erotica Exotica,* Belmont L691-68	2.75	3.50	3.12
☐ **Garrity (no first name),** *Cry Me a Killer,* Gold Medal 1170, 1961. Title inspired by the Julie London hit record of several years earlier, "Cry Me a River."	3.75	4.75	3.95
☐ **Garson, Barbara,** *MacBird,* Grove 132 (artwork by Lisa Lyons) This book, made into a successful play, was a satire on then-president Lyndon Johnson.	9.00	12.00	10.00
☐ **Garson, Noel,** *Cumberland Rifles,* Dell 736, no date	2.00	2.75	2.37

	Current Price Range		C/Y Avg.

☐ **Garve, Andrew,** *The Ascent of D-13,* Popular Library 02515, no date .... | 1.25 | 1.75 | 1.50

☐ *The Ashes Of Loda,* Pan 10698, 1971, second edition .... | 2.00 | 3.00 | 2.50

☐ *The Ashes Of Loda,* Popular 02562, no date .... | 1.85 | 2.50 | 2.12

☐ *Boomerang,* Popular 01445, no date | 1.85 | 2.50 | 2.12

☐ *By-Line For Murder,* Lancer 72-715, 1964 .... | 2.50 | 3.25 | 2.87

☐ *By-Line For Murder,* Dell 765, no date | 2.00 | 3.00 | 2.50

☐ *The Cuckoo Line Affair,* Lancer 72-677, 1963 .... | 2.50 | 3.25 | 2.87

☐ *The End Of The Track,* Lancer 72-699, 1963 .... | 2.25 | 3.00 | 2.50

☐ *The Far Sands,* Lancer 72-693, 1963 | 2.25 | 3.00 | 2.50

☐ *The Galloway Case,* Lancer 72-716, 1964 .... | 2.50 | 3.25 | 2.87

☐ *The Golden Deed,* Lancer 73-602, 1967 .... | 1.75 | 2.50 | 2.12

☐ *A Hero For Leanda,* Lancer 72-783, 1965 .... | 2.00 | 2.75 | 2.37

☐ *The House Of Soldiers,* Lancer 72-674, 1963 .... | 2.00 | 3.00 | 2.50

☐ *The House Of Soldiers,* Pan 10623, 1971, second edition .... | 1.75 | 2.50 | 2.12

☐ *The Long Short Cut,* Dell 4993, 1972 | 1.50 | 2.00 | 1.75

☐ *The Megstone Plot,* Pyramid G360, 1958 .... | 3.50 | 4.50 | 4.00

☐ *Murder Through The Looking Glass,* Lancer 72-987, 1965 .... | 2.25 | 3.25 | 2.50

☐ *Murder Through The Looking Glass,* Dell 827, 1955 .... | 2.25 | 3.25 | 2.50

☐ *Murder Through The Looking Glass,* Dell 827, no date .... | 1.50 | 2.00 | 1.75

☐ **Gary, Romain,** *A European Education,* Cardinal GC106 (Romain Gary might hold the record for most appearances by a novelist on TV talk shows, closely followed by Norman Mailer) .... | 3.00 | 4.00 | 3.35

☐ **Gaulden, Ray,** *High Country Showdown,* Monarch 489 (cover artwork by Ross, 1965) .... | 3.00 | 4.00 | 3.35

	Current Price Range		C/Y Avg.

☐ **Gault, William C.,** *Million Dollar Tramp,* Crest 61, 1960 . . . . | 1.75 | 2.50 | 2.12

☐ **Gazzo, Michael V.,** *A Hatful of Rain,* Signet 1412 (photo cover picturing Anthony Franciosa, Eva Marie Saint, Don Murray and Lloyd Nolan) . . . . | 7.00 | 10.00 | 8.10

☐ **Gehman, Richard,** *Humphrey Bogart,* Gold Medal 1572 (photo cover picturing Humphrey Bogart; Richard Gehman was known for many years as the dean of Hollywood writers, both in magazines and books.) . . . . | 6.00 | 8.00 | 6.75

☐ **Gellhorn, Martha,** *His Own Man,* Mac-Fadden 40-104, 1962 . . . . | 3.50 | 4.50 | 3.90

☐ **Gerber, Albert B.,** *Life of Adolf Hitler,* Mercury MB-101, 1961 (Several hundred biographies of Adolf Hitler have been published, including one by himself.) . . . | 3.25 | 4.00 | 3.45

☐ **Gibbon, Edward,** *The Portable Gibbon,* Viking 60, 1969 (Historian Edward Gibbon compiled *The Decline and Fall of the Roman Empire.*) . . . . | 2.50 | 3.00 | 2.70

☐ **Gibbs, Carlton,** *Behind Respectable Doors,* Beacon I8461F . . . . | 2.00 | 2.50 | 2.25

☐ *The Night Lovers,* Beacon I8681X . . . | 1.50 | 2.00 | 1.75

☐ **Gibson, Walter,** (ED), *The Fine Art Of Spying,* Tempo T-149, 1967 . . . . | 2.00 | 2.75 | 2.37

☐ **Gibbs, Willa,** *The Dedicated,* Hillman 191 | 2.50 | 3.00 | 2.75

☐ **Gide, Andre,** *The Immoralist,* Vintage V8 | 2.00 | 2.50 | 2.25

☐ *Lafcadio's Adventures,* Vintage V96 | 3.00 | 3.50 | 3.35

☐ **Gielgud, Val-Cat,** *Fontana* 439, 1960 . . | 2.50 | 3.25 | 2.87

☐ **Gifford, Thomas,** *The Cavanaugh Quest,* Ballantine 25653, 1977 . . . . | 1.50 | 2.00 | 1.87

☐ *The Glendower Legacy,* Pocket 82678, 1979 . . . . | 2.00 | 2.75 | 2.37

☐ *Hollywood Gothic,* Ballantine 29009, 1980 . . . . | 2.00 | 2.75 | 2.37

☐ *The Wind Chill Factor,* Ballantine 24800, 1976 . . . . | 1.25 | 1.75 | 1.50

☐ **Gilbert, Anthony,** *After the Verdict,* Pyramid 1041 (cover artwork by Bacon) . . . | 3.00 | 3.75 | 3.35

	Current Price Range		C/Y Avg.
☐ *And Death Came Too,* Pyramid 1107 (cover artwork by Bacon)	3.00	3.75	3.35
☐ *The Black Stage,* Penguin 1105, 1955	4.50	6.50	5.00
☐ *Dark Death,* Pyramid R-906, 1963 ...	2.25	3.00	2.62
☐ *Death Casts A Long Shadow,* Pyramid R-1292, 1966	1.75	2.50	2.12
☐ *The Looking Glass Murder,* Pyramid X-1874, 1968	1.75	2.50	2.12
☐ *Missing From Her Home,* Beagle 95137, 1971	1.50	2.00	1.50
☐ *Mr. Crook Lifts The Mask,* Beagle 95172, 1971	1.50	2.00	1.50
☐ *Murder Cheats The Bride,* Bantam 138, 1948	3.25	4.50	3.62
☐ *Murder Comes Home,* Pyramid R-1150, 1965	2.25	3.25	2.75
☐ *Murder Comes Home,* Mercury Mystery 168, no date	2.75	3.50	3.12
☐ *Murder Comes Home,* Pyramid T2373, 1970, second edition	1.50	2.25	1.87
☐ *Out For The Kill,* Pyramid R-1269, 1965	2.50	3.25	2.87
☐ *A Question Of Murder,* Pyramid R-1258, 1965	2.50	3.25	2.87
☐ *The Wrong Body,* Mercury Mystery 193, no date	4.00	5.50	4.00
☐ **Gilbert, Elliott,** *Too Much Woman,* Beacon 419	2.00	2.75	2.35
☐ **Gilbert, Michael,** *After The Fine Weather,* Lancer 72-771, 1964	2.75	3.50	3.12
☐ *Blood And Judgment,* Lancer 72-790, 1965	3.25	4.50	3.37
☐ *Blood And Judgement,* Hodder 522, 1962, second edition	2.00	2.75	2.37
☐ *Death Has Deep Roots,* Dell 744, 1953	4.00	5.75	4.12
☐ *Death Has Deep Roots,* Lancer 72-738, 1964	2.25	3.00	2.50
☐ *Death Has Deep Roots,* Dell 744, no date	2.25	3.00	2.50
☐ *The Empty House,* Penguin 5142, 1980	2.25	3.00	2.37
☐ *The Family Tomb,* Popular 01458, no date	1.50	2.25	1.87
☐ *Fear To Tread,* Lancer 72-736, 1964	2.50	3.50	3.00

		Current Price Range		C/Y Avg.

		Current Price Range		C/Y Avg.
☐	*Fear To Tread*, Hodder C283, 1957 ..	4.00	5.50	4.75
☐	*The Night Of The Twelfth*, Penguin 4615, 1978	2.00	2.75	2.37
☐	*Smallbone Deceased*, Lancer 72-737, 1964	2.75	3.50	3.12
☐	**Giles, Guy Elwyn,** *3 Died Variously*, Black Cat Detective 1, 1943	13.00	17.00	13.50
☐	*Target For Murder*, Big Green 5, no date	5.00	7.00	5.25
☐	*Target For Murder*, Big Green Detective 5, no date	8.50	11.00	8.25
☐	**Gill, Josephine,** *Dead Of Summer*, Popular SP288, no date	1.50	2.25	1.87
☐	**Gillespie, Susan,** *Himalayan View*, Albatross 537, no date	4.00	6.00	4.85
☐	**Gillian, Michael,** *Warrant For A Wanton*, Pennant P12, 1953	2.00	2.75	2.37
☐	*Warrant For A Wanton*, Pennant P12, 1953	1.50	2.25	1.87
☐	**Gilman, Dorothy,** *The Clairvoyant Countess*, Crest 2-2965, no date	1.25	1.75	1.50
☐	*Mrs. Pollifax On Safari*, Crest 2-3414, second edition	2.00	2.75	2.37
☐	*Mrs. Pollifax On Safari*, Crest 2-3414, no date	1.35	1.85	1.50
☐	*A Palm For Mrs. Pollifax*, Crest M2225, 1974	1.35	1.85	1.50
☐	*A Palm For Mrs. Pollifax*, Crest 2-3446, ninth edition	1.35	1.85	1.50
☐	*The Unexpected Mrs. Pollifax*, Crest T1485, 1970	1.50	2.25	1.87
☐	**Gilmore, Cecile,** *Man in the Moonlight*, Berkley 678	3.00	4.00	3.35
☐	**Gingrich, Arnold,** *The Armchair Esquire*, Popular Library W1100 (anthology)	3.00	4.00	3.55
☐	**Ginsberg, Allen,** *Howl and Other Poems*, City Lights 4, 1974 (This publishing company derived its name from the title of a Charles Chaplin movie. The film "City Lights" became a favorite of the intelli-			

	Current Price Range		C/Y Avg.

gensia of the 1920s as it was one of the first efforts to present a movie as an artwork.) **3.00** **4.00** **3.25**

☐ **Gipson, Fred,** *Hound Dog Man*, Perma Books M4168, 1959 .... **1.35** **1.85** **1.50**

☐ **Gladdis, Peggy,** *Big City Nurse*, MacFadden 40-117 .... **2.00** **2.50** **2.25**

☐ *Clinic Nurse*, MacFadden 40-134 .... **2.00** **2.50** **2.25**

☐ *Future Nurse*, MacFadden 40-119 ... **2.00** **2.50** **2.25**

☐ *Meredith Blake, M.D.,* Avon F155. The central characters in Peggy Gladdis' novels were almost always nurses or female physicians **2.00** **2.50** **2.25**

☐ *Nurse Christine,* MacFadden 40-115 **2.00** **2.50** **2.25**

☐ **Godey, John,** *The Blue Hour*, Berkley 02515, 1974 .... **1.35** **1.85** **1.50**

☐ *The Clay Assassin,* Berkley 02411, 1973 .... **1.35** **1.85** **1.50**

☐ *The Fifth House,* Berkley 02399, 1973 **1.35** **1.85** **1.50**

☐ *The Gun And Mr. Smith,* Berkley 02376, 1973 .... **1.35** **1.85** **1.50**

☐ *The Gun And Mr. Smith,* Berkley 02376, 1973, second edition **1.35** **1.85** **1.50**

☐ *Nella,* Dell 16111, 1982 .... **2.00** **2.75** **2.37**

☐ *The Taking Of Pelham One Two Three,* Dell 8495, 1974 .... **1.50** **2.00** **1.75**

☐ *The Talisman,* Berkley 03492, 1977 .. **1.50** **2.00** **1.75**

☐ *This Year's Death,* Bestseller Mystery B174, no date **2.75** **3.50** **3.12**

☐ *A Thrill A Minute With Jack Albany,* Gold Medal D1956, 1967 .... **2.00** **2.75** **2.37**

☐ *A Thrill A Minute With Jack Albany,* GM M2801, 1973 .... **1.50** **2.00** **1.75**

☐ **Goffman, Erving,** *The Presentation of Self in Everyday Life,* Anchor 174 ..... **2.75** **3.50** **3.50**

☐ **Golden, Francis L.,** *Jest: What the Doctor Ordered,* Pocket Books 872 (cover artwork by Jones) **7.00** **10.00** **8.00**

☐ **Golden, Harry,** *For 2¢ Plain,* Perma 5021 This was a recollection of boyhood memories of growing up in a Jewish section of New York City. The title refers to plain

	Current Price Range		C/Y Avg.

sodas (soda water with no flavoring) served in drugstores of the early 1900s. **2.00 2.50 2.20**

☐ **Golding, William,** *Lord of the Flies,* Capricorn 14, 1959 (This very offbeat novel, attacked as barbaric by some critics when it first appeared, is now firmly entrenched as an American classic.) **7.00 10.00 8.00**

☐ **Goldman, Eric,** *Crucial Decade,* Vintage V183 . . . . **2.50 3.00 2.60**

☐ *Rendezvous with Destiny,* Vintage V31 **2.50 3.00 2.60**

☐ **Goldsmith, Oliver,** *She Stoops to Conquer,* Crofts Classics (no serial number), 1951 (Scottish dramatist and wit Oliver Goldsmith was a member of Samuel Johnson's literary circle and a leading character in Boswell's biography of Johnson.) **3.50 4.50 4.00**

☐ **Golightly, Bonnie,** *A Breath of Scandal,* Avon T474 (photo cover picturing Sophia Loren, Maurice Chevalier and John Gavin) **6.00 8.00 6.70**

☐ *The Integration Of Maybelle Brown,* Belmont L521 . . . . **1.35 1.85 1.50**

☐ **Gonzales, John,** *Death For Mr.* Bigm Gold Medal 1100 (cover artwork by Phillipps) **3.00 4.00 3.50**

☐ **Gooch, Mary S.,** *Tainted Rosary,* Fabian Z-139, no date **1.35 1.85 1.50**

☐ **Goodis, David,** *Moon In The Gutter,* Gold Medal 348, 1953 . . . . **3.75 4.75 4.25**

☐ *Nightfall,* Lion Library 131 (painted cover picturing Anne Bancroft and Aldo Ray) **5.00 7.00 6.00**

☐ **Goodman, Irv,** *Stan the Man,* Bart 2, biography of baseball player Stan Musial. **6.00 8.00 6.90**

☐ **Gordon, Anthony,** *Doctor Of Lesbos,* Beacon I8671X **1.50 2.00 1.75**

☐ **Gordon, Gary,** *Anatomy of Adultery,* Monarch 448 . . . . **3.00 3.75 3.30**

☐ *Robert F. Kennedy,* Monarch 66 . . . . . **4.00 5.00 4.35**

☐ **Goscinny, Rene,** *French and Frisky,* Lion Library 99 . . . . **6.00 8.00 6.75**

	Current Price Range		C/Y Avg.
☐ **Gosling, John and Douglas Warner,** *City of Vice,* Hillman 184	2.50	3.00	2.60
☐ **Goudge, Elizabeth,** *The Dean's Watch,* Cardinal GC114	2.75	3.50	3.00
☐ **Graham, Billy,** *The Secret of Happiness,* Perma 4274	2.00	2.50	2.20
☐ **Graves, Charles,** *A Pipe Smoker's Guide,* Icon 15, 1969	6.00	8.00	6.75
☐ **Graves, Robert,** *Goodbye to All That,* Anchor 123	3.00	4.00	3.35
☐ **Gray, Berkeley,** *6 Feet Of Dynamite,* White Circle 60, 1943	6.00	8.00	6.00
☐ *Blonde For Danger,* White Circle 227, 1945	5.00	6.75	5.37
☐ *Calamity Conquest,* Five Star, No. 1, 1973	2.00	3.00	2.50
☐ *Cavalier Conquest,* Fontana 835, 1963	1.85	2.50	2.12
☐ *Conquest In Scotland,* Fontana 687, 1962	1.85	2.50	2.12
☐ *Conquest On The Run,* Four Square 825, 1963	2.00	2.75	2.37
☐ *The Conquest Touch,* Collins 368M, no date	3.50	4.75	3.50
☐ *Dare-Devil Conquest,* White Circle 486, 1951	5.75	7.50	6.00
☐ *Duel Murder,* Collins 395M, no date . .	3.00	4.00	3.50
☐ *Duel Murder,* White Circle CD 442, 1950	5.00	7.00	5.25
☐ *Gay Desperado,* White Circle 244, 1945	6.00	8.00	5.75
☐ *Killer Conquest,* White Circle CD 383, 1949	6.50	8.50	6.50
☐ *Meet The Don,* White Circle 344, 1948	3.00	4.00	3.50
☐ *Miss Dynamite,* White Circle 85, 1944	6.00	8.00	6.00
☐ *Mr. Ball Of Fire,* White Circle 360, 1948	3.50	4.75	3.87
☐ *Operation Conquest,* White Circle 527, 1952	5.25	6.50	4.12
☐ *Seven Dawns To Death,* White Circle CD 512, 1951	7.00	10.00	6.87
☐ *The Spot Marked X,* White Circle CD 465, 1950	3.75	4.75	4.00

	Current Price Range		C/Y Avg.

☐ *The Spot Marked X,* Collins 342M, no date .... — 2.00 | 3.00 | 2.50

☐ **Green, Abel and Joe Laurie Jr.,** *Show Biz,* Perma 217 (painted cover picturing Groucho Marx, Fred Allen and Jimmy Durante. Abel Green was the publisher of "Variety," the show business newspaper.) .... — 4.00 | 5.50 | 4.45

☐ **Green, F.L.** *Odd Man Out,* Pocket Books 472 (photo cover picturing James Mason) .... — 6.00 | 8.00 | 6.70

☐ **Green, Gerald,** *The Lotus Eaters,* Cardinal GC761 .... — 3.50 | 4.25 | 3.75

☐ **Greene, Graham,** *Brighton Rock,* Bantam 315, 1949 .... — 4.00 | 5.75 | 4.00

☐ *The Confidential Agent,* Bantam 971, 1952 .... — 6.00 | 7.75 | 5.62

☐ *The End Of The Affair,* Bantam A1306, 1955 .... — 2.00 | 3.00 | 2.50

☐ *A Gun For Sale,* Penguin 1896, 1972, fifth edition .... — 2.25 | 3.25 | 2.75

☐ *The Human Factor,* Penguin 4956, 1978 .... — 2.00 | 3.00 | 2.50

☐ *The Man Within,* Bantam F2680, 1964 — 1.75 | 2.50 | 2.12

☐ *The Man Within,* Penguin 3283, 1971 — 2.25 | 3.00 | 2.62

☐ *The Man Within,* Bantam 355, 1948 .. — 4.00 | 5.75 | 4.87

☐ *The Ministry Of Fear,* Bantam F2615, 1963 .... — 2.00 | 3.00 | 2.50

☐ *The Ministry Of Fear,* Penguin 530, 1946, second edition .... — 3.00 | 4.00 | 3.50

☐ *Nineteen Stories,* Lion L131, 1955 ... — 2.00 | 3.00 | 2.50

☐ *Our Man In Havana,* Penguin 1790, 1968, fourth edition .... — 2.00 | 3.00 | 2.50

☐ *The Portable Graham Greene,* Viking 75, 1973 .... — 2.50 | 3.00 | 2.70

☐ *The Quiet American,* Bantam A1669, 1957 .... — 2.75 | 3.75 | 3.25

☐ *The Quiet American,* Bantam F2209, sixth edition .... — 1.75 | 2.50 | 2.12

☐ *The Third Man,* Bantam 797, 1950 ... — 3.50 | 4.75 | 3.50

☐ *The Third Man,* Bantam 797, 1950, second edition .... — 2.75 | 3.50 | 3.12

Left to Right: **The Human Factor,** by Graham Greene,
February 1979, Avon Books, 4149, **$2.75–$3.75;**
Laramie Nelson, by Romer Zane Grey,
Belmont Tower, 51458, **$2.50–$3.50.**

	Current Price Range		C/Y Avg.

☐ *The Third Man,* Bantam J2427, 1962 — 1.75 / 2.50 / 2.12

☐ *This Gun For Hire,* Bantam 1316, 1955 — 2.75 / 3.50 / 3.12

☐ *This Gun For Hire,* Bantam A2045, 1960 .... — 2.25 / 3.00 / 2.62

☐ *This Gun For Hire,* Superior M652, 1945 .... — 4.50 / 6.00 / 5.00

☐ **Gregor, Manfred,** *Town Without Pity,* Dell F164 (painted cover picturing Kirk Douglas) .... — 5.00 / 6.50 / 5.75

☐ **Gregory, Dick,** *From the Back of the Bus,* Avon S129 (interior photos). The author, a nightclub comedian, was a leading Civil Rights activist in the 1960s. ...... — 4.00 / 5.00 / 4.50

☐ **Gressley, Edward,** *Funny Stories,* Pocket Books Junior 45 .... — 4.00 / 6.00 / 4.75

☐ **Gregory, Paul,** *The Casting Couch,* Beacon I8524F .... — 1.35 / 1.75 / 1.50

☐ **Grey, Romer Z.,** *Laramie Nelson,* Belmont Tower 0-505, no date .... — 2.50 / 3.50 / 2.85

☐ **Grey, Zane,** *Black Mesa,* Cardinal 402 — 2.00 / 2.50 / 2.25

☐ **Grider, George and Lydel Sim,** *War Fish,* Pyramid 640 .... — 2.00 / 2.50 / 2.25

☐ **Griffin, Gwyn,** *By the North Gate,* Popular Library G465 (cover artwork by Hooks)............................ — 3.00 / 4.00 / 3.30

☐ **Gronowicz, Antoni,** *Hitler's Woman,* Belmont I219 .... — 2.50 / 3.00 / 2.75

☐ **Grove, Fred,** *Sun Dance,* Ballantine 671 (cover artwork by Crair, 1958) .... — 4.00 / 5.00 / 4.50

☐ **Grove, Walt,** *Man Who Said No,* Gold Medal S801, 1958, third edition .... — 1.00 / 1.50 / 1.25

☐ *Wings Of Eagles,* Gold Medal 649, 1957 .... — 3.75 / 4.50 / 4.12

☐ **Gruber, Frank,** *Bridge Of Sand,* Bantam S3926, 1969 .... — 1.25 / 1.75 / 1.50

☐ *Brothers Of Silence,* Bantam F2903, 1965 .... — 1.50 / 2.00 / 1.75

☐ *Brothers Of Silence,* Belmont Tower 50616, 1973 .... — 1.50 / 2.00 / 1.75

☐ *The Buffalo Box,* Bantam 50, 1946 .. — 4.50 / 6.25 / 5.00

☐ *The Corpse Moved Upstairs,* Belmont 92-607, 1964 .... — 2.00 / 3.00 / 2.50

	Current Price Range		C/Y Avg.
☐ *The French Key Mystery,* Murder Myst Monthly 4, 1942	14.00	19.00	15.00
☐ *The French Key,* Dell B75-2040, 1970	1.50	2.25	1.87
☐ *The Gift Horse,* Bantam 2, 1945	8.00	11.00	8.50
☐ *The Gold Gap,* Pyramid N2558, 1971	2.00	2.75	2.37
☐ *The Honest Dealer,* Belmont Tower 50255, 1972	1.25	1.75	1.50
☐ *The Hungry Dog Murders,* Murder Myst Monthly 12, 1943	15.00	20.00	17.50
☐ *The Laughing Fox,* Penguin 538, 1946, second edition	2.25	3.00	2.50
☐ *The Limping Goose,* Bantam 1488, 1956	2.25	3.00	2.50
☐ *The Lock and the Key,* Readers Choice 15, 1948	8.00	11.00	8.50
☐ *The Long Arm Of Murder,* Jonathan Press J85, no date	7.00	10.00	7.75
☐ *Market For Murder,* Flamingo, no date	1.50	2.00	1.75
☐ *Market For Murder,* Penguin 651, 1947	6.00	8.00	6.50
☐ *The Mighty Blockhead,* Superior M655, 1945	4.50	6.25	5.00
☐ *Mood For Murder (Lonesome Badger),* Graphic 119, 1956	2.75	3.50	3.12
☐ *Murder 97,* Readers Choice 16, no date	10.00	14.00	10.50
☐ *Murder One,* Belmont Tower 50590, 1973	1.50	2.00	1.75
☐ *The Navy Colt,* Superior MY49, 1945	4.50	6.25	5.00
☐ *Once Over Deadly,* Jonathan Press J89, 1980	4.00	5.50	4.50
☐ *The Silver Jackass,* Belmont Tower 50570, 1973	1.35	1.85	1.50
☐ *Tales of Wells Fargo,* Bantam 1726, (painted cover picturing Dale Robertson)	6.00	8.00	6.90
☐ **Guild, Leo,** *Bachelor's Joke Book,* Avon 513	10.00	14.00	12.20
☐ **Guild, Les,** *What Are The Odds?,* Crest 369, 1960	1.35	1.85	1.50
☐ **Guild, Nicholas,** *Old Acquaintance,* Jove K5229, 1980	2.00	2.75	2.37
☐ **Guinn, William,** *Death Lies Deep,* Gold Medal 503, 1955	1.75	2.50	2.12

	Current Price Range		C/Y Avg.

☐ **Gunn, James,** *Deadlier Than The Male,* Signet 709, 1949 . . . .   5.00   6.50   5.25

☐ **Gunn, Victor,** *The Dead Man Laughs,* White Circle 271, 1946 . . . .   3.75   4.75   4.00

☐ *Dead Man's Warning,* Collins 385M, no date 3.75   4.75   4.00

☐ *Death At Traitors' Gate,* Five Star No. 1, 1973 . . . .   2.00   2.75   2.37

☐ *Footsteps Of Death,* White Circle 61, 1943 . . . .   6.00   8.00   6.12

☐ *Mad Hatter's Rock,* Collins 389M, no date 4.50   5.75   4.62

☐ *Madhatter's Rock,* White Circle CD 436, 1950 . . . .   7.00   10.00   7.50

☐ *Murder At The Motel,* Five Star, 1973   2.00   2.75   2.37

☐ **Gurr, David,** *Troika,* Bantam Seal 01599, 1980 . . . .   2.00   2.75   2.37

☐ **Guthrie, A.B.,** *These Thousand Hills,* Cardinal C267 (photo cover picturing Don Murray, Richard Egan and Lee Remick) 5.00   6.50   5.50

☐ **Gutteridge, Lindsay,** *Fratricide Is A Gas,* Futura 8047, 1979 . . . .   2.75   3.75   3.25

☐ **Guttmacher, Manfred,** *Mind Of Murderer,* Black Cat BB-16, 1962 . . . .   1.85   2.50   2.12

☐ **Haas, Joseph L.,** *Vendetta,* Pyramid M4057, 1976 . . . .   1.25   1.75   1.50

☐ **Hackelmann, Charles,** *River Queen,* second edition 1.75   2.50   2.12

☐ **Hadas, Moses,** *Old Wine,* Cardinal GC778 . . . .   2.50   3.00   2.70

☐ **Hadley, Franklin,** *Planet Big Zero,* Monarch 431 (cover artwork by Brillhart, 1964) 4.00   5.00   4.50

☐ **Hagedorn, Hermann,** *The Free Citizen,* Theodore Roosevelt Association (no serial number), 1956 . . . .   3.00   4.00   3.35

☐ **Haggard, H. Rider,** *Cleopatra,* Pocket Books 7025. More novelists than you would want to count took a fling at fictionalized biographies of Cleopatra. H. Rider

	Current Price Range		C/Y Avg.

Haggard, who usually specialized in westerns, turned out one of the better ones.

	Current Price Range		C/Y Avg.
Haggard, who usually specialized in westerns, turned out one of the better ones.	2.00	2.50	2.25
☐ *King Solomon's Mines,* Dell 433 (photo cover picturing Deborah Kerr and Stewart Granger)	5.00	6.00	5.75
☐ **Hahn, Emily,** *House in Shanghai,* Crest S203, 1958	2.00	2.75	2.37
☐ **Hailey, Arthur,** *Airport,* Bantam T3982, 1971 (photo cover)	2.00	3.00	2.50
☐ **Halacy, D.S.,** *America's Major Air Disasters,* Monarch 316, 1961	4.00	5.00	4.50
☐ **Haley, J. Evetts,** *A Texan Looks at Lyndon,* Palo Duro (no serial number), 1964	4.00	5.00	4.50
☐ **Hall, Austin,** *The Spot of Life,* Ace F318, 1964. This was not the Austin Hall convicted of kidnapping Bobby Greenlease.	6.00	8.00	6.75
☐ **Hall, Bennie C.,** *Redheaded Nurse,* Dell D413 (cover artwork by Riswold)	3.00	4.00	3.35
☐ **Hall, Manly P.,** *Magic,* Philosophical Research (no serial number)	3.50	4.50	4.00
☐ **Hall, Radclyffe,** *Well of Loneliness,* Perma M4024, tenth edition, 1956	2.00	3.00	2.35
☐ **Halliday, Brett,** *A Taste for Cognac,* Dell 10-115, no date	8.00	11.00	9.35
☐ *Before I Wake,* Dell 829, 1955	1.75	2.50	2.12
☐ *Blood On Biscayne Bay,* Dell Map 268, 1949	3.75	4.75	4.00
☐ *Bodies Are Where You Find Them,* Popular 192, 1949	3.25	4.25	3.50
☐ *The Corpse Came Calling,* Dell Map 168, 1947	3.75	4.75	4.00
☐ *The Corpse Came Calling,* Dell D401, 1961	1.75	2.50	2.15
☐ *Counterfeit Wife,* Dell Map 280, 1949	3.75	4.75	4.00
☐ *Dead Man's Diary and Dinner Dupres,* Dell Map 427, 1950	4.50	6.00	4.50
☐ *Death Has Three Lives,* Dell 865, 1955	3.25	4.50	3.50
☐ *Dividend On Death,* Popular 98, 1946	5.00	7.00	5.25
☐ *Dolls Are Deadly,* Dell D424, 1961	1.50	2.00	1.75
☐ *Fourth Down To Death,* Dell 2699, 1970	1.25	1.75	1.50

Left to Right: **She Woke to Darkness,** *by Brett Halliday,*
1954, Dell, 867, **$4.00–$5.50;**
Airport, *by Arthur Hailey,*
Bantam, T3982, 1971, **$2.00–$3.00.**

		Current Price Range		C/Y Avg.
☐	*In A Deadly Vein,* Dell 905, 1956	3.00	4.00	3.50
☐	*Marked For Murder,* Dell Map 222, 1948	4.50	6.25	5.00
☐	*Michael Shayne's Long Chance,* Dell Map 112, 1946	4.50	6.25	5.00
☐	*Murder and the Married Virgin,* Dell Map 323, 1949	2.75	3.50	3.12
☐	*Murder Is My Business,* Dell Map 184, 1947	4.00	5.50	4.37
☐	*Murder Is My Business,* Dell Map 326, 1949	4.00	5.50	4.37
☐	*Murder Spins The Wheel,* Dell 6123, 1970	1.35	1.85	1.50
☐	*Murder Takes No Holiday,* Dell 6126, 1967	1.50	2.00	1.75
☐	*Pay-Off In Blood,* Dell 6858, 1972 ...	1.00	1.50	1.25
☐	*Six Seconds To Kill,* Dell 8001, 1970	1.50	2.00	1.75
☐	*Stranger In Town,* Dell D425, 1961 ..	1.75	2.50	2.12
☐	**Halsey, Margaret,** *This Demi-Paradise,* Avon F101	2.00	2.50	2.25
☐	**Hamill, Ethel,** *Golden Image,* Hillman 204..............................	3.00	4.00	3.35
☐	**Hamilton, Donald,** *Death of a Citizen,* Gold Medal 957, 1960	4.00	5.00	4.00
☐	*Death of a Citizen,* Gold Medal 1334	3.00	3.75	3.50
☐	*Murders Row,* Gold Medal R2102, no date	2.00	2.75	2.37
☐	*Night Walker,* Dell 27, 1954, first edition	3.25	4.50	3.50
☐	*Night Walker,* Dell 27, 1954, first edition	2.25	3.00	2.62
☐	*Night Walker,* Gold Medal K1472, 1964	1.75	2.50	2.12
☐	*The Poisoners,* Gold Medal T2392, 1971	1.50	2.25	1.87
☐	*The Poisoners,* Coronet 15472, 1971	2.00	2.75	2.37
☐	*The Ravagers,* Gold Medal K1452, no date	1.50	2.25	1.87
☐	*The Ravagers,* Gold Medal R2072, no date	1.25	1.75	1.50
☐	*The Ravagers,* Gold Medal D1673, 1966, fifth edition	1.75	2.50	2.12
☐	*The Removers,* Gold Medal S1082, 1961	2.75	3.75	3.25

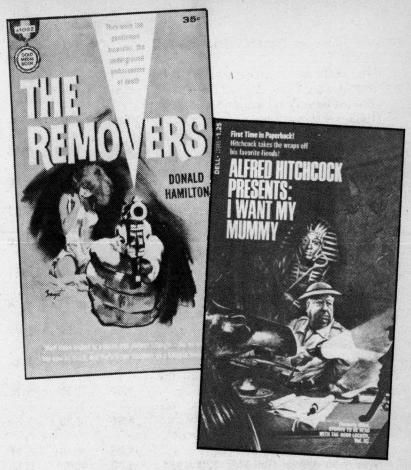

Left to Right: **The Removers,** by Donald Hamilton,
1961, Gold Medal Book, S1082, **$2.75–$3.75;**
I Want My Mummy, Alfred Hitchcock (editor),
Dell, 13985, 1977, **$1.00–$1.50.**

	Current Price Range		C/Y Avg.
☐ *The Removers,* Gold Medal K1336, no date	1.85	2.65	2.12
☐ *The Removers,* Gold Medal R2057, third edition	1.85	2.65	2.12
☐ *The Removers,* Gold Medal K1336, 1963, second edition	1.85	2.65	2.12
☐ *The Retaliators,* Gold Medal 1-3567, 1976	1.25	1.75	1.50
☐ *The Retaliators,* Gold Medal 1-3984, third edition	1.25	1.75	1.50
☐ *The Revengers,* Gold Medal 14487, 1982	2.50	3.25	2.87
☐ *The Shadowers,* Gold Medal K1386, no date	1.50	2.00	1.50
☐ *The Shadowers,* Gold Medal D1602, no date	2.00	2.75	2.37
☐ *The Shadowers,* Gold Medal R2085, 1969, seventh edition	1.85	2.65	2.12
☐ *The Shadowers,* Gold Medal 1-4006, fifteenth edition	1.85	2.65	2.12
☐ *The Silencers,* Gold Medal K1392, no date	1.85	2.65	2.12
☐ *The Silencers,* Gold Medal R2133, no date	1.00	1.50	1.25
☐ *The Silencers,* Gold Medal D1641, no date	1.50	2.25	1.87
☐ *The Silencers,* Gold Medal D1641, 1966, seventh edition	1.25	1.75	1.50
☐ *The Steel Mirror,* Dell Map 473, 1951	3.00	4.00	3.50
☐ *The Steel Mirror,* Gold Medal D1617, no date	1.75	2.50	2.12
☐ *The Terminators,* Gold Medal 3665, fifth edition	2.00	2.75	2.37
☐ *The Terrorizers,* Gold Medal 1-3865, second edition	1.85	2.65	2.12
☐ *The Wrecking Crew,* Gold Medal K1335, 1963, second edition	1.85	2.65	2.12
☐ *The Wrecking Crew,* Gold Medal 1025, no date	1.85	2.65	2.12
☐ *The Wrecking Crew,* Gold Medal R2020, no date	1.50	2.25	1.87

	Current Price Range		C/Y Avg.

☐ **Hamilton, Greg,** *Monica,* Midwood F314, no date **1.75 2.50 2.12**

☐ **Hamlin, Ken,** *Guns of Revenge,* Monarch 555 (cover artwork by Ross, 1960 ..... **4.00 5.00 4.40**

☐ **Hammett, Dashiell,** *Blood Money,* Dell 53, no date **22.00 26.00 24.00**

☐ **Hancock, Lucy A.,** *Special Nurse,* Pocket Books 6054 (cover artwork by Dawson) **3.00 4.00 3.45**

☐ **Handlin, Oscar,** *Race and Nationality in American Life,* Anchor 110 .... **3.00 4.00 3.35**

☐ **Hano, Arnold,** *Willie Mays,* Bart (no serial number). Arnold Hano specialized in fictional sports books for teenagers, but this was a non-fiction biography. **6.00 8.00 6.70**

☐ **Hardin, Clement,** *Colt Wages,* Ace 11530 .... **2.50 3.25 2.70**

☐ **Harding, Matt,** *Motel Iraq,* Beacon 8549F **1.50 2.25 1.87**

☐ *Near Nude,* Beacon 572 .... **3.00 3.75 3.45**

☐ **Hardy, William,** *Case of the Missing Coed,* Dell D360 (cover artwork by Coconos) **3.75 4.50 4.15**

☐ **Harmon, Jackson,** *Night Spot,* Midwood 699, 1966 .... **4.00 5.00 4.50**

☐ **Harris, A.M.** *The Tall Man,* Pocket Books 1267 (cover artwork by Dunn). Made into a motion picture starring Jane Russell. **4.00 5.00 4.50**

☐ **Harris, Amy,** *The Janitor's Daughter,* Midwood 807, 1967 .... **3.25 4.25 3.65**

☐ **Harris, Eleanor,** *The Real Story of Lucille Ball,* Ballantine 78 (photo cover picturing Lucille Ball, Desi Arnaz, Vivian Vance and William Frawley) **11.00 16.00 11.00**

☐ **Harris, Frank G.,** *Love Toy,* Midwood F380, no date **1.25 1.75 1.50**

☐ **Harris, Sara,** *Skid Row, U.S.A.,* Belmont 223 .... **2.00 2.50 2.25**

☐ **Harris, John D.,** *Junkie Priest,* Pocket Books 50116, 1964 .... **3.00 4.00 3.35**

☐ **Harrison, Timothy,** *Hot Summer,* Beacon 8485 .... **1.75 2.25 2.00**

	Current Price Range		C/Y Avg.

☐ **Harsh, James,** *Riptide,* Newstand Library U110, 1959 .... | 2.00 | 2.50 | 2.25

☐ **Hart, Moss,** *Act One,* Signet 1849. Autobiography of noted playwright, husband of actress Kitty Carlisle. .... | 3.00 | 4.00 | 3.30

☐ **Harte, Bret,** *Selected Short Stories,* Pyramid PR36 (cover artwork by Bernstein). Nineteenth century novelist Bret Hart was the first successful writer of western fiction, leading the way for Zane Grey and others. .... | 3.00 | 4.00 | 3.30

☐ **Harvey, James,** *Stag Model,* Midwood Y138, 1961 .... | 2.75 | 3.50 | 3.00

☐ **Haskill, Frank,** *Hotel Doctor,* Belmont 192–245 .... | 2.00 | 2.50 | 2.25

☐ **Hastings, March,** *Savage Surrenders,* Midwood F201, 1962 .... | 1.75 | 2.50 | 2.12

☐ **Hatch, Gerald,** *The Day the Earth Froze,* Monarch 534 (cover artwork by Brillhart) | 4.00 | 5.00 | 4.40

☐ **Hatlo, Jimmy,** *Another New Jimmy Hatlo Book,* Avon 826. Jimmy Hatlo was the creator of the comic strips "Li'l Iodine" and "They'll Do it Every Time". .... | 7.00 | 10.00 | 8.15

☐ **Haunt, Tom,** *Hotrod Babe,* Gaslight 124, 1964 .... | 4.00 | 5.00 | 4.45

☐ **Haupt, Enid,** *The Seventeen Book of Young Living,* Popular Library G522 ... | 3.00 | 4.00 | 3.35

☐ **Haviland, Monica,** *Lana,* Monarch 373, 1963 .... | 1.25 | 1.75 | 1.50

☐ **Hawthorne, Nathaniel,** *The Portable Hawthorne,* Viking 38, 1966 .... | 2.50 | 3.00 | 2.70

☐ *Short Stories,* Vintage V15 .... | 2.50 | 3.00 | 2.70

☐ **Haycox, Ernest,** *Deep West,* Pocket Books 2594 (cover artwork by Ryan) .. | 3.00 | 4.00 | 3.40

☐ **Haycox, Ernest,** *Man in the Saddle,* Dell 120, no date .... | 4.50 | 6.00 | 4.62

☐ *Rim of the Desert,* Pocket Books 2466, (cover artwork by Miller) .... | 3.00 | 4.00 | 3.40

☐ **Haydn, Hiram,** *The Hands of Esau,* Cardinal GC957 .... | 3.00 | 4.00 | 3.35

	Current Price Range		C/Y Avg.

- ☐ **Hayes, Joseph,** *The Third Day,* Crest 816 (photo cover picturing George Peppard and Elizabeth Ashley) .... — 4.50 — 6.00 — 5.25
- ☐ **Heinrich, Willi,** *Lonely Conqueror,* Perma 5067 (cover artwork by Abbett) — 3.75 — 4.50 — 4.00
- ☐ **Heller, David,** *The Berlin Crisis,* Monarch 2, 1961 .... — 4.00 — 5.00 — 4.35
- ☐ *The Cold War,* Monarch 8, 1962 ..... — 4.00 — 5.00 — 4.35
- ☐ *Jacqueline Kennedy,* Monarch 54 ... — 6.50 — 5.50 — 5.50
- ☐ **Helser, Albert,** *The Glory of the Impossible,* Evangelical Press (no serial number), 1943 .... — 5.00 — 6.50 — 5.00
- ☐ **Helseth, Henry, E.,** *The Chair for Martin Rome,* Pocket Books 484 (photo cover picturing Victor Mature and Richard Conte) .... — 5.00 — 6.50 — 5.75
- ☐ **Hely, Elizabeth,** *I'll Be Judge,* Dell R108 (cover artwork by Kalin) .... — 3.75 — 4.50 — 4.10
- ☐ **Hemingway, Ernest,** *Green Hills Of Africa,* Perma Books M3056, 1956, second edition .... — 1.00 — 1.50 — 1.25
- ☐ **Henderson, Ernest,** *The World of Mr. Sheraton,* Popular Library PC1013 ..... — 3.75 — 4.50 — 3.95
- ☐ **Herbert, Frank,** *21st Century Sub,* Avon G-1092, no date .... — 3.00 — 4.00 — 3.50
- ☐ *21st Century Sub,* Avon T-146, 1956 — 7.00 — 10.00 — 7.00
- ☐ *21st Century Sub,* Avon T-146, no date — 3.00 — 4.00 — 3.50
- ☐ *Children Of Dune,* Berkley 03310, 1977 — 1.25 — 1.75 — 1.50
- ☐ *Destination Void,* Berkley S1864, 1970, third edition .... — 1.25 — 1.75 — 1.50
- ☐ *The Dosadi Experiment,* Berkley 03834, third edition .... — 2.00 — 2.75 — 2.37
- ☐ *The Dragon In The Sea,* Avon S290, 1967, fourth edition .... — 1.85 — 2.50 — 2.12
- ☐ *The Dragon In The Sea,* Avon V2330, 1970, sixth edition .... — 1.85 — 2.50 — 2.12
- ☐ *Dune,* Ace 17261, no date .... — 1.50 — 2.00 — 1.75
- ☐ *Dune,* Ace 17263, no date .... — 1.25 — 1.75 — 1.50
- ☐ *Dune,* Ace 17265, no date .... — 1.75 — 2.50 — 2.12
- ☐ *Dune,* Berkley T2706, fourth edition .. — 1.50 — 2.00 — 1.75
- ☐ *The Eyes of Heisenberg,* Berkley S1865, 1970, third edition .... — 2.00 — 2.75 — 2.37

		Current Price Range		C/Y Avg.

☐	*The Eyes Of Heisenberg,* Berkley 04237, twelfth edition	1.75	2.50	2.12
☐	*The Godmakers,* Berkley 02344, fifth edition	2.00	3.00	2.37
☐	*The Green Brain,* Ace-F-379, 1966 . .	2.00	3.00	2.50
☐	*The Green Brain,* Ace 30261, no date	1.25	1.75	1.50
☐	*The Green Brain,* Ace 30264, 1979 . .	1.50	2.00	1.75
☐	*The Green Brain,* Ace 30265, third edition	1.85	2.65	2.12
☐	*The Heaven Makers,* Avon S319, 1968	1.85	2.65	2.12
☐	*The Heaven Makers,* Del Rey 25304, 1977	1.86	2.65	2.12
☐	*Hellstrom's Hive,* Bantam T8276, 1974	1.85	2.65	2.12
☐	*The Santaroga Barrier,* Berkley S1615, sixth edition	2.00	2.75	2.37
☐	*Soul Catcher,* Berkley 04250, 1979 . .	1.85	2.65	2.12
☐	*Whipping Star,* Berkley S1909, third edition	1.85	2.65	2.12
☐	*Whipping Star,* Berkley 03504, sixth edition	1.85	2.65	2.12
☐	*The Worlds Of Frank Herbert,* Ace 90925, no date	1.75	2.50	2.12
☐	*The Worlds of Frank Herbert,* Ace 90926, no date	1.00	1.50	1.25
☐	**Herbert, Gil,** *Ginny,* Midwood 805, 1967	4.25	5.25	4.85
☐	**Herlin, Hans,** *Commemorations,* Ballantine 25223, 1976	1.50	2.25	1.87
☐	**Herr, Dann and Joel Wells,** (Ed), *Bodies and Souls,* Dell 0656, 1963	1.50	2.25	1.87
☐	**Herries, Norman,** *Death Has 2 Faces,* Ace S-97, 1955	4.00	5.50	4.25
☐	**Herrington, Lee,** *Carry My Coffin Slowly,* Dell 641, 1952	3.25	4.50	3.50
☐	**Hersey, John,** *The Marmot Drive,* Popular Library G475	3.00	3.75	3.45
☐	**Hershatter, Richard L.,** *Spy Who Hated Licorice,* Signet D3059, 1966	1.85	2.50	2.12
☐	**Hershfield, Harry,** *The Sin of Harold Diddlebock,* Bart 102 (photo cover picturing Harold Lloyd)	7.00	10.00	8.25
☐	**Hershman, Morris,** *Guilty Witness,* Belmont 90-306, 1964	2.00	2.75	2.37

	Current Price Range		C/Y Avg.

Guilty Witness, Belmont 90-306, 1964	1.85	2.50	2.12
Target For Terror, Belmont B50-748, 1967	1.85	2.50	2.12
Hesky, Olga, The Serpent's Smile, Arrow 078, 1968	2.25	3.00	2.62
Time For Treason, Arrow 161, 1969	2.25	3.00	2.62
Hess, Dean, Battle Hymn, Popular Library SP 137	3.00	4.00	3.50
Heth, Edward Harris, The Big Bet, Bantam 553, 1948	5.00	6.50	5.75
The Big Bet, Bantam 553, 1948	2.75	3.75	3.25
Heuman, William, Mulvane's War, Avon T386, 1960	3.75	4.75	4.25
Hewes, Henry, Famous American Plays of the 1940s, Dell 2490	3.00	4.00	3.50
Heyer, Georgette, A Blunt Instrument, Bantam F3101, 1966	1.25	1.75	1.50
A Blunt Instrument, Bantam F3101, 1966	2.00	3.00	2.12
Death In The Stocks, Panther 1495, 1967, fifth edition	2.00	2.75	2.37
Death In The Stocks, Panther 02694, 1972, seventh edition	1.75	2.50	2.12
Death In the Stocks, Panther 02694, 1975, ninth edition	1.75	2.50	2.12
Detection Unlimited, Bantam S5709	1.25	1.75	1.50
Duplicate Death, Bantam S5543, 1970	1.35	1.85	1.50
Envious Casca, Bantam N7118, fourth edition	1.35	1.85	1.50
Penhallow, Bantam N7284, 1972	1.35	1.85	1.50
They Found Him Dead, Bantam S4764, 1970, fourth edition	1.35	1.85	1.50
The Unfinished Clue, Bantam N5792, 1971	1.50	2.25	1.87
Heyerdahl, Thor, Aku-Aku, Cardinal GC758. The author is a noted explorer of the South Sea Islands.	5.00	7.00	6.00
Heyes, Douglas, The Kiss-Off, Signet 949, 1952	2.00	2.75	2.37
The Kiss-Off, Signet 1329, 1956	2.50	3.50	3.00
Heyman, Evan Lee, Miami Undercover, Popular Library G554, 1961	1.50	2.25	1.87

	Current Price Range		C/Y Avg.
☐ *The Thomas Crown Affair,* Avon S354, 1968	1.35	1.85	1.50
☐ **Higgins, George V.,** *The Digger's Game,* Popular Library 08256, no date	1.25	1.75	1.35
☐ *The Friends Of Eddie Coyle,* Bantam T7504, 1973	1.35	1.85	1.50
☐ *Judgment Of Deke Hunter,* Ballantine 25862, 1978	1.35	1.85	1.50
☐ *A Year Or So With Edgar,* Berkley 04584, 1980	2.00	2.75	2.37
☐ **Higgins, Jack,** *The Dark Side Of The Island,* Coronet 22960, 1978	2.50	3.50	3.00
☐ *Day Of Judgment,* Pan 25851, 1979	2.00	2.75	2.37
☐ *Day Of Judgment,* Bantam 13202, 1980	2.25	3.00	2.50
☐ *The Eagle Has Landed,* Pan 24630, 1976, fourth edition	2.25	3.00	2.37
☐ *In The Hour Before Midnight,* Coronet 12795, 1978, fifth edition	2.25	3.00	2.50
☐ *In The Hour Before Midnight,* Gold Medal P3355, 1975	1.00	1.50	1.25
☐ *The Iron Tiger,* Gold Medal 1-3753, fourth edition	1.85	2.50	2.12
☐ *The Iron Tiger,* Coronet 17852, 1976, third edition	1.85	2.50	2.12
☐ *The Keys Of Hell,* Coronet 12774, 1976, fourth edition	2.00	3.00	2.37
☐ *The Last Place God Made,* Pan 25329, 1977	2.00	3.00	2.50
☐ *A Prayer For The Dying,* Coronet 19896, 1978, third edition	2.00	3.00	2.50
☐ *The Savage Day,* Pan 25328, 1977 ..	2.00	3.00	2.37
☐ *Solo,* Dell 18165, 1981	2.50	3.25	2.87
☐ *Storm Warning,* Pan 25035, 1977	2.00	2.75	2.37
☐ *Storm Warning,* Bantam 10700, 1977	1.50	2.25	1.87
☐ *Toll For The Brave,* Arrow 914000, 1978, fourth edition	2.00	2.75	2.37
☐ **High, Philip E.,** *No Truce With Terra,* Ace F275	3.00	4.00	3.50
☐ **Highet, Gilbert,** *The Art of Teaching,* Vintage K1	2.00	2.50	2.25

	Current Price Range		C/Y Avg.

☐ **Highsmith, David,** *Step Down To Darkness,* Midwood 90, 1961 .... 4.50 5.75 4.65
☐ **Highsmith, Patricia,** *Deep Water,* Penguin 58, 1979, second edition 2.50 3.25 2.87
☐ *Deep Water,* Penguin 3858, 1974 .... 2.00 2.75 2.37
☐ *A Dog's Ransom,* Penguin 3944, 1980, third edition 3.00 4.00 3.55
☐ *The Glass Cell,* Penguin 3603, 1980, second edition 2.00 2.75 2.37
☐ *Ripley's Game,* Pyramid M3744, 1976 1.75 2.50 2.12
☐ *The Story-Teller,* Manor 12364, 1976 1.35 1.75 1.50
☐ *The Story-Teller,* MacFadden 75-230, 1969 .... 1.35 1.75 1.50
☐ *Strangers On A Train,* Penguin 3796, 1974 .... 2.00 3.00 2.50
☐ *The Talented Mr. Ripley,* Dell D282, 1959 .... 3.75 5.00 4.12
☐ *The Talented Mr. Ripley,* Penguin 4020, 1981, fourth edition 2.25 3.25 2.75
☐ *This Sweet Sickness,* Perennial P4009, 1965 .... 2.00 3.00 2.50
☐ **Hildick, E.W.,** *A Cat Called Amnesia,* Pocket 29839, 1977 .... 1.50 2.75 1.87
☐ **Hill, Douglas,** (ED), *The Devil His Due,* Avon S389, 1969 .... 1.75 2.50 2.12
☐ **Hill, Marjorie,** *Look For the Stars,* Berkley 685 .... 3.00 4.00 3.50
☐ **Hill, Patti,** *One Thing I Know,* Avon H105 2.75 3.50 3.00
☐ **Hilliard, Dr. Marion,** *Women and Fatigue,* Perma 5038 .... 2.50 3.00 2.75
☐ **Hilton, James,** *Random Harvest,* Cardinal 418. He was the author of *Lost Horizon.* 5.00 6.50 5.75
☐ *Without Armor,* Pyramid 956 .... 4.00 5.25 4.65
☐ **Hirsh, Phil,** *Kidding Around,* Pyramid 1852 (cover artwork by Hageman) 6.00 8.00 7.00
☐ **Hitchcock, Alfred** (Ed), *I Want My Mummy,* Dell 13985, 1977 .... 1.25 1.50 1.35
☐ *Rope,* Dell 262 (photo cover picturing James Stewart) 10.00 14.00 12.00
☐ **Hitchens, Bert,** *The Man Who Followed Women,* Perma 4220 .... 3.00 4.00 3.50

	Current Price Range		C/Y Avg.

☐ **Hitchens, Dolores,** *The Watcher,* Perma
4205 .... 3.00 4.00 3.50

☐ **Hitt, Orrie,** *As Bad As They Come,* Midwood 23, 1959 .... 7.00 10.00 8.50

☐   *Dirt Farm,* Beacon 836 .... 4.00 5.00 4.40

☐   *Easy Women,* Novel Books 5065 .... 6.00 8.00 6.75

☐   *Ex-Virgin,* Beacon 8668F 1.35 1.75 1.55

☐   *Mail Order Sex,* Midwood 150 .... 6.00 8.00 7.00

☐   *Never Cheat Alone,* Beacon 338 .... 4.50 5.75 4.95

☐   *Summer Romance,* Midwood 16, 1959 7.00 10.00 8.50

☐   *Unfaithful Wives,* Deacon 378 .... 4.75 6.00 5.25

☐ **Hodge, Marshall,** *Your Fear of Love,*
Dolphin 483, 1967 .... 3.00 4.00 3.50

☐ **Hodgins, Eric,** *Mr. Blandings Builds His
Dream House,* Pocket Books 505 (cartoon cover picturing Cary Grant, Myrna
Loy, Melvyn Douglas, as drawn by William Steig) 5.00 6.50 5.75

☐ **Hofstadter, Richard,** *The American Political Tradition,* Vintage V9 .... 3.00 4.00 3.50

☐ **Hogan, Ray,** *A Marshall For Lawless,*
Ace F126 .... 2.50 3.00 2.75

☐   *The Life and Death of Johnny Ringo,*
Signet 2311. Johnny Ringo became
much better known when Lorne
Greene, star of "Bonanza," made a recording about him. It reached the #1
spot on the charts and sold over a million copies. 3.00 4.00 3.50

☐ **Hogan, Robert J.,** *Feud at Sundown,*
Manor 12447, 1976 .... 1.75 2.50 2.05

☐ **Holding, Elisabeth,** *The Blank Wall,* Ace
G512 .... 2.00 2.50 2.25

☐   *The Innocent Mrs. Duff,* Ace G509 ... 2.00 2.50 2.25

☐   *Kill Joy,* Ace G534 .... 2.00 2.50 2.25

☐   *Net of Cobwebs,* Ace G530 .... 2.00 2.50 2.25

☐   *The Obstinate Murderer,* Ace G519 .. 2.00 2.50 2.25

☐ **Holland, Dell,** *The Far Out Ones,* Playtime 650 .... 4.00 5.00 4.45

☐ **Holland, Ken,** *The Strange Young Wife,*
Beacon 18682X 1.35 1.75 1.55

	Current Price Range		C/Y Avg.
☐ **Holles, Robert,** *Spawn,* Sphere 4616, 1979	2.50	3.25	2.87
☐ **Holley, Helen,** *Blood On the Beach,* Red Dagger 29, 1947	8.00	11.00	8.62
☐ **Holliday, Don,** *Flesh Adjuster,* Leisure 1188	4.00	5.00	4.50
☐ **Hollis, Jim,** *The Case Of The Bludgeoned Teacher,* Avon 725, no date ...	3.50	4.50	4.00
☐ **Hollister, Paul and Robert Strunsky,** *From D Day Through Victory in Europe,* C.B.S. (no serial number), 1945	4.00	5.00	4.50
☐ **Holloway, Elizabeth Hughes,** *Cobweb House,* Dell Map 133, 1946	6.00	8.25	7.12
☐ **Holloway, Teresa,** *Lynn Daly: Newspaper Girl,* Berkley, 583 (cover artwork by Miller)	4.00	5.00	4.50
☐ **Holly, J. Hunter,** *Encounter,* Monarch 240 (cover artwork by Schoenherr)	4.00	5.00	4.50
☐ *The Flying Eyes,* Monarch 260 (cover artwork by Schoenherr)	4.00	5.00	4.50
☐ *The Green Planet,* Monarch 213 (cover artwork by Schoenherr)	4.00	5.00	4.50
☐ *The Running Man,* Monarch 342 (cover artwork by Brillhart)	4.00	5.00	4.50
☐ **Holman, Hugh,** *Death Like Thunder,* Hangman's House 8, no date	5.25	6.75	6.00
☐ **Holmes, David C.,** *The Velvet Ape,* Perma M3122, 1958	2.00	3.00	2.50
☐ **Holmes, H.H.,** *Nine Times Nine,* Penguin 553, 1945	11.00	14.00	12.25
☐ **Holmes, Paul,** *Retrial Murder and Dr. Sam Sheppard,* Bantam SZ3472, 1966	1.75	2.50	2.12
☐ **Holmes, Rick,** *Love Under Capricorn,* Monarch 346 (cover artwork by Maguire, 1963)	3.00	4.00	3.50
☐ *New Widow,* Beacon 620	3.00	4.00	3.50
☐ **Holt, Allison,** *Death For A Hussy,* Red Dagger 21, 1946	6.00	8.00	6.25
☐ **Holt, Gavin,** *Ivory Ladies,* Yellowjacket C17, 1951	5.50	7.00	5.75

	Current Price Range		C/Y Avg.
☐ *Ladies In Ermine,* Hodder 91, 1952 ..	3.00	4.00	3.50
☐ **Holt, Henry,** *The Mayfair Mystery,* Mellifont 443, no date	6.50	8.50	7.00
☐ **Holton, Leonard,** *Deliver Us From Wolves,* Dell 1887, 1966	1.75	2.50	2.12
☐ *The Saint Maker,* Dell R104, 1961 ...	2.00	3.00	2.50
☐ *Secret Of The Doubting Saint,* Dell 7713, 1965	2.00	2.75	2.37
☐ **Homer,** *Odyssey,* Mentor M92, 1953, sixth edition	1.00	1.50	1.25
☐ *The Odyssey translated by Robert Fitzgerald,* Anchor 333	3.00	3.75	3.50
☐ **Honig, Donald,** *Blue and Gray,* Avon T512	2.00	2.50	2.25
☐ **Hope, Bob,** *I Owe Russia $1200,* Cardinal 50008 (photo cover picturing the author, also interior photos)	5.00	6.50	5.75
☐ **Horowitz, Robert S.,** *The Ramparts We Watch,* Monarch 484	2.50	3.00	2.75
☐ **Hough, Emerson,** *Covered Wagon,* Pocket Books 6028	3.00	3.75	3.35
☐ **Howard, Bob,** *Sin Lottery,* Brandon 603	3.00	3.75	3.35
☐ **Howard, David,** *We Die Alone,* Ace G569 (cover artwork by Tossey)	4.00	5.25	4.75
☐ **Howard, Leigh,** *Chance Meeting,* Avon T404 (photo cover picturing Hardy Kruger)	4.50	6.00	5.25
☐ **Howard, Vince,** *Countdown for Lisa,* Jade 212.........................	4.00	5.00	4.50
☐ *Rendezvous in Rio,* Onsco (no serial number)	4.00	5.00	4.50
☐ **Hsueh-Chin,** *Dream of the Red Chamber,* Anchor 159 (cover artwork by Seong-Moy)	4.00	5.00	4.50
☐ **Hudson, Dean,** *Sin Street,* Nightstand 1642	3.00	3.75	3.35
☐ **Hudson, W.H.,** *Green Mansions,* Bantam C182 (interior artwork by Sheilah Beckett)	3.00	4.00	3.50
☐ **Hudson, Jan,** *The Virtuous Harlots,* Playtime 644	3.25	4.00	3.45

	Current Price Range		C/Y Avg.

☐ **Huffaker, Clair,** *Cowboy,* Gold Medal 736 (photo cover picturing Glenn Ford, Brian Donlevy and Jack Lemmon) 6.00 8.00 7.00

☐ *Flaming Lance,* Crest 421 .... 2.50 3.25 2.75

☐ **Hughes, H. Stuart,** *Consciousness and Society,* Vintage V201 .... 2.50 3.25 2.70

☐ **Hughs, Ludwell,** *Spring Fever,* Midwood F327, no date 1.75 2.50 2.12

☐ **Hugo, Victor,** *The Hunchback of Notre Dame,* Avon T190 (photo cover picturing Gina Lollobrigida and Anthony Quinn, also interior illustrations) 10.00 14.00 11.30

☐ **Huie, William B.,** *The Americanization of Emily,* Signet 1825 (cover artwork by Phillips) 3.00 4.00 3.35

☐ **Huizinga, J.,** *The Waning of the Middle Ages,* Anchor 3.00 3.75 3.25

☐ **Hull, E.M.,** *Sheik,* Dell 174, no date 6.50 8.50 6.50

☐ **Hulme, Kathryn,** *The Wild Place,* Cardinal 394 .... 2.50 3.00 2.70

☐ **Humphrey, William,** *Home From the Hill,* Perma 4128 (photo cover picturing Robert Mitchum, Eleanor Parker and George Hamilton) 6.00 8.00 7.00

☐ **Hunter, Evan,** *A Matter of Conviction,* Cardinal GC94 (photo cover picturing Burt Lancaster, Dina Merrill and Shelley Winters) 6.00 8.00 7.00

☐ **Hunter, Floyd,** *Community Power Structure,* Anchor 379 .... 2.50 3.00 2.75

☐ **Hunter, Sam,** *Modern French Painting,* Dell 5762 .... 2.75 3.50 3.10

☐ **Hurst, Fannie,** *Family,* Perma 4244 (cover artwork by Bennett) 2.75 3.50 3.10

☐ *God Must Be Sad,* Perma 5059 (cover artwork by Bennett) 2.50 3.25 2.85

☐ *Imitation of Life,* Perma 4124 (photo cover picturing Lana Turner and John Gavin) 6.00 8.00 7.00

☐ **Hutchins, Maude,** *Hands of Love,* Pyramid 782 (cover artwork by Miller) 3.00 4.00 3.50

	Current Price Range		C/Y Avg.

☐ **Hutchinson, A.S.,** *If Winter Comes,* Pocket Books 486 (photo cover picturing Walter Pidgeon, Deborah Kerr and Angela Lansbury) 6.00 8.00 7.00

☐ **Huxley, Aldous,** *After Many a Summer Dies the Swan,* Avon G2001 .... 3.00 4.00 3.50

☐ **Huxley, Julian,** *Living Thoughts of Darwin,* Premier 215 .... 3.25 4.25 3.75

☐ **Hytes, Jason,** *Secret Session,* Midwood 527 .... 3.00 4.00 3.50

☐ **Idell, Albert,** *This Woman,* Gold Medal 953 (cover artwork by Phillips) 3.50 4.50 4.00

☐ **Iverson, Andrina,** *Gifts of Love,* Hillman 172 .... 2.00 2.50 2.25

☐ **Jackson, Charles,** *Fall of Valor,* Lion LL-35, 1955 .... 3.25 4.50 3.50

☐ *Thread Of Evil,* Lion LL-143, 1957 ... 4.00 5.50 4.12

☐ **Jaffe, Rona,** *The Best of Everything,* Cardinal GC68 (photo cover picturing Joan Crawford and Hope Lange) 4.00 5.25 4.60

☐ **James, Al,** *Potent Stuff,* Novel Books 5048 .... 3.00 4.00 3.35

☐ **James, Don,** *Dark Hunger,* Monarch 343 (cover artwork by Johnson) 3.00 4.00 3.35

☐ *The Pitchmen,* Monarch 358 (cover artwork by Miller, 1963) 3.00 4.00 3.35

☐ **James, Henry,** *Turn of the Screw/Daisy Miller* (double), Dell 800, no date 1.25 1.75 1.50

☐ **James, Neal,** *Her Student Lover,* Beacon 8677X 1.25 1.75 1.45

☐ **James, Stuart,** *Frisco Flat,* Monarch 481 3.75 4.50 3.95

☐ **James, Terry,** *Women's Doctor,* Beacon 8553F 1.50 2.00 1.75

☐ **Janifer, Laurence,** *Wonder War,* Pyramid 963 .... 5.00 6.00 5.50

☐ **Janson, Hank,** *A Nice Way To Die,* Gold Star 14 .... 4.00 5.00 4.50

☐ *Becky,* Gold Star 70 .... 4.00 5.00 4.50

☐ *Brazen Seductress,* Gold Star 13 .... 4.00 5.00 4.50

☐ *Cold Dead Coed,* Gold Star 22 ...... 4.00 5.00 4.50

☐ *Hell's Angels,* Gold Star 16 .... 6.00 8.00 7.00

	Current Price Range		C/Y Avg.

☐ *Hot House*, Gold Star 17 .... **4.00** **5.00** **4.50**

☐ *Passionate Playmates*, Gold Star 18 **4.00** **5.00** **4.50**

☐ **Jaspers, Karl,** *Man in the Modern Age*, Anchor 101 .... **3.00** **3.75** **3.30**

☐ **Jerome, E.D.,** *Love Hungry*, Croydon 12, no date (L.B. Cole cover) **20.00** **25.00** **21.75**

☐ **Jessup, Richard,** *Young Don't Cry*, Gold Medal S660, 1957, second edition. **1.25** **1.75** **1.50**

☐ **Johnson, Annabel,** *The Hungry Years*, Crest S201, 1958 .... **1.50** **2.00** **1.75**

☐ **Johnson, George,** *Eleanor Roosevelt*, Monarch 61, 1963 .... **2.50** **3.00** **2.75**

☐ *The Washington Waste Makers*, Monarch 20 .... **2.50** **3.00** **2.75**

☐ **Johnson, George C. and Jack G. Russell,** *Ocean's Eleven*, Cardinal C412, (photo cover picturing Frank Sinatra, Dean Martin, Sammy Davis Jr., Peter Lawford and Angie Dickinson) **6.00** **8.00** **6.75**

☐ **Johnson, Robert S.,** *Thunderbolt*, Ballantine 514 .... **3.00** **4.00** **3.50**

☐ **Johnson, Ryerson,** *Lady in Dread*, Gold Medal 459, 1955 .... **1.75** **2.50** **2.12**

☐ **Johnson, Victor H.,** *Cry Torment*, Graphic 101, 1955 .... **3.00** **3.75** **3.37**

☐ **Johnston, William, Dr.** *Starr in Crisis*, Monarch 442 (cover artwork by Miller) **3.25** **4.25** **3.75**

☐ **Jones, Ernest,** *Hamlet and Oedipus*, Anchor 31 .... **3.00** **4.00** **3.45**

☐ **Jones, Guy,** *Peabody's Mermaid*, Pocket Books 503 (photo cover picturing Ann Blyth and William Powell) **6.00** **8.00** **6.75**

☐ **Jones, Robert P.,** *The Heisters*, Monarch 396 (cover artwork by Marchetti, 1963) **5.00** **6.50** **5.75**

☐ **Judson, Jeannie,** *Barbara Ames*, Ace F112 .... **2.00** **2.50** **2.25**

☐ **Kane, Frank,** *Bare Trap*, Dell D333 (cover artwork by Bennett) **4.00** **5.25** **4.65**

☐ *The Conspirators*, Dell C127 (cover artwork by Engle, 1962) **4.00** **5.25** **4.65**

		Current Price Range		C/Y Avg.

☐ *Due or Die,* Dell B174 (cover artwork by Bennett, 1961) **5.00   6.50   5.75**

☐ *Final Curtain,* Dell 2522 (cover artwork by Lesser) **4.00   5.00   4.50**

☐ *Grave Danger,* Dell D335 (cover artwork by Bennett) **4.00   5.00   4.45**

☐ *Key Witness,* Dell B173 (cover artwork by Greene, 1960) **5.00   6.50   5.75**

☐ *Mourning After,* Dell B226 (cover artwork by Bennett) **4.50   5.75   5.10**

☐ *Poisons Unknown,* Dell D334 (cover artwork by Bennett) **4.25   5.25   4.65**

☐ *Time To Prey,* Dell B159 (cover artwork by Bennett, 1960) **5.00   6.50   5.75**

☐ **Kane, Henry,** *Peter Gunn,* Dell B155 (photo cover picturing Craig Stevens) The first private eye series to make a hit on TV. Each episode opened with a view of Peter Gunn's secretary seated at her desk—but you never saw her face, only her legs. The legs belonged to the then-unknown Mary Tyler Moore. **4.50   6.00   5.25**

☐ **Kane, Joseph N.,** *Facts About the Presidents,* Pocket Books 75001 . . . .   **2.00   2.50   2.25**

☐ **Kane, Sid,** *Naked Obsession,* Headline 102 . . . .   **3.00   3.75   3.45**

☐ **Kanin, Garson,** *The Rat Race,* Cardinal C401 (photo cover picturing Tony Curtis and Debbie Reynolds) **6.00   8.00   6.85**

☐ **Kantor, Mackinlay,** *One Wild Oat,* Gold Medal 675, 1957, third edition **1.50   2.50   1.25**

☐ **Karmel, Alex,** *Something Wild,* Belmont 212 (painted cover picturing Carroll Baker) **4.00   6.00   5.00**

☐ **Karney, Louis,** *Devil's Lash,* Newstand Library 506, 1959 . . . .   **1.50   2.00   1.75**

☐ **Karson, Arlene,** *Walk Out of Darkness,* Monarch 376 (cover artwork by Schaare, 1963) **4.00   5.00   4.50**

☐ **Katcher, Leo,** *The Money People,* Pocket Books 7021 . . . .   **2.75   3.50   3.50**

	Current Price Range		C/Y Avg.

☐ **Katzman, Lawrence,** *Calling Nurse Nellie,* Dell B190 .... **8.00** **11.00** **9.50**

☐ *Nellie's Cartoons To Get Well By,* Dell 6282, 1964 .... **6.00** **8.00** **7.00**

☐ **Kaufman, George S. and Moss Hart,** *The Man Who Came to Dinner,* Pocket Books 143 (photo cover picturing Bette Davis and Monty Woolley) **12.00** **16.00** **13.00**

☐ **Kaufman, Walter,** *The Faith of a Heretic,* Anchor 336 .... **3.00** **3.75** **3.35**

☐ *The Portable Nietzsche,* Viking 62 ... **2.50** **3.25** **2.65**

☐ **Kazantzakis, Nikos,** *Zorba the Greek,* Ballantine U6020 (painted cover picturing Anthony Quinn and Irene Papas) .. **4.50** **6.00** **4.95**

☐ **Kazin, Alfred,** *On Native Grounds,* Anchor 69 .... **3.00** **3.75** **3.30**

☐ **Keane, Bill,** *Family Circus,* Pocket Books 6110, 1961 .... **7.00** **10.00** **8.10**

☐ **Keefe, Lynn,** *How Did A Nice Girl Like You Get Into This Business?,* Paperback Library S2-272, 1964 .... **2.25** **3.00** **2.62**

☐ **Keene, Day,** *Payola,* Pyramid 529 (cover artwork by Schaare) **4.00** **5.00** **4.50**

☐ **Keene, Day and Dwight Vincent,** *Chautauqua,* Dell X5 (cover artwork by Hooks) **4.00** **5.00** **4.50**

☐ **Keller, James,** *Three Minutes a Day,* Christopher (no serial number), 1949 .. **1.50** **2.00** **1.75**

☐ **Kelley, K.P.,** *The Plot,* Flagship 701, 1967 .... **4.00** **5.00** **4.50**

☐ **Kelly, Amy,** *Eleanor of Aquataine,* Vintage V50 .... **3.00** **4.00** **3.50**

☐ **Kemeny, Tony,** *A Puppet No More,* Thomas Lithograph Co. (no serial number), interior artwork by Rex Grillo **5.00** **6.00** **5.40**

☐ **Kendricks, James,** *She Wouldn't Surrender,* Monarch 301 (cover artwork by Kendricks, 1960) **4.00** **5.00** **4.40**

☐ *Sword Of Casanova,* Monarch 111, 1959 .... **1.00** **1.50** **1.25**

☐ **Kennedy, Burt,** *Seven Men From Now,* Berkley 361 (painted cover picturing Lee Marvin, Randolph Scott and Gail Russell) **3.00** **4.00** **3.45**

	Current Price Range		C/Y Avg.

☐ **Kennedy, John F.,** *Profiles in Courage,* Cardinal GC238. The hardcover edition of this book made a total of more than 100 appearances on the *New York Times* best seller list, but at various times. Its longest run was when first published; it became a best seller again when Kennedy was running for President; and finally made the list for the third time when he was assassinated. . . . . . . | 2.00 | 2.50 | 2.25 |

☐ **Kennery, Berne,** *Lust Show,* Spartan SL163, 1967. Good example of "sixties sleaze." . . . . | 4.00 | 5.00 | 4.50 |

☐ **Kent, Nial,** *The Divided Path,* Pyramid 32, no date . . . . | 6.00 | 8.00 | 6.75 |

☐ **Kent, Simon,** *Fire Down Below,* Popular Library W500 (painted cover picturing Rita Hayworth and Robert Mitchum) . . . | 4.00 | 5.50 | 4.75 |

☐ **Keon, Michael,** *The Durian Tree,* Perma 4225 (cover by Johnson) . . . . | 2.50 | 3.25 | 2.85 |

☐ **Kerman, Joseph,** *Opera As Drama,* Vintage V88 . . . . | 3.75 | 4.75 | 4.10 |

☐ **Kern, Seymour,** *Golden Scalpel,* Dell F136 (cover artwork by Abbett) . . . . | 3.00 | 4.00 | 3.45 |

☐ **Kerouac, Jack,** *Maggie Cassidy,* Avon G1035, no date, first edition . . . . | 18.00 | 23.00 | 20.50 |

☐ *On The Road,* Signet 1619, no date | 12.00 | 16.00 | 14.00 |

☐ *The Dharma Bums,* Signet 1718, no date . . . . | 10.00 | 14.00 | 12.00 |

☐ *The Subterraneans,* Avon T390, no date. A classic "beat generation" literature of the 1950s. Kerouac was so poor at the start of his career that he couldn't afford a box of typing paper; he typed an entire novel on a roll of paper towels and submitted it in that form to a publisher. . . . . | 10.00 | 15.00 | 12.50 |

☐ **Kerr, Geoffrey,** *Under the Influence,* Berkley 518 (cover artwork by Powers) | 3.25 | 4.25 | 3.75 |

	Current Price Range		C/Y Avg.

☐ **Kerr, Jean,** *Please Don't Eat the Daisies,* Crest 263. If your edition has a higher serial number it will be worth somewhat less. 3.00 4.00 3.35

☐ *The Snake Has All the Lines,* Crest 514 (interior artwork by Whitney Darrow) 6.00 8.00 6.75

☐ **Kersh, Gerald,** *Night and the City,* Dell 374 (photo cover picturing Richard Widmark and Gene Tierney) 5.00 6.50 5.65

☐ **Ketcham, Hank,** *Dennis the Menace: Household Hurricane,* Pocket Books 1217 . . . . 7.00 10.00 8.35

☐ *More Dennis the Menace,* Avon 600 7.00 10.00 8.35

☐ *Teacher's Threat,* Crest 378 . . . . 7.00 10.00 8.35

☐ **Ketchum, Phil,** *Harsh Reckoning,* Ballantine 585 . . . . 2.50 3.25 2.70

☐ *Renegade Range,* Monarch 256 . . . . . 4.00 5.00 4.40

☐ **Key, Ted,** *Hazel,* Bantam 1404 . . . . 7.00 10.00 8.50

☐ **Keyes, Francis P.,** *Dinner At Antoine's,* Dell 443, no date 2.00 2.75 2.40

☐ **King, Don,** *Bitter Love,* Newstand Library U124, 1959. . . . . 1.50 2.00 1.75

☐ **Kinsella, Leo J.,** *The Man For Her,* Valiant (no serial number), 1957 . . . . 5.00 6.50 5.80

☐ **Kirby, Mark,** *Harling College,* Beacon 18384 . . . . 2.00 2.75 2.50

☐ **Kirkbridge, Ronald,** *Tamiko,* Monarch 146, no date, cover artwork by Maguire 5.00 7.00 5.85

☐ **Kitto, H.D.F.,** *Greek Tragedy,* Anchor 38 (cover artwork by Ascherl) 2.75 3.50 3.18

☐ **Klein, Alexander,** *Magnificent Scoundrels,* Ballantine 427 . . . . 3.00 4.00 3.50

☐ **Kling, Samuel G.,** *Legal Encyclopedia,* Perma 5012 . . . . 3.00 4.00 3.50

☐ **Klinger, Henry,** *Murder Off Broadway,* Perma 4255 (cover artwork by Bennett) 3.00 3.75 3.30

☐ **Kluckhorn, Frank L.,** *America Listen,* Monarch 4.00 5.00 4.50

☐ *The Inside of LBJ,* Monarch 457 . . . . . 3.00 4.00 3.55

☐ *What's Wrong With U.S. Foreign Policy?,* Monarch 18 . . . . 4.00 5.00 4.35

	Current Price Range		C/Y Avg.
☐ **Knerr, Michael,** *The Violent Lady,* Monarch 395 (cover artwork by Barton, 1963)	4.25	5.25	4.75
☐ **Knight, Damon,** *Mind Switch,* Berkley F1160, 1965	1.75	2.25	2.00
☐ *Natural State and Other Stories,* Pan 24442, 1975	2.75	3.75	3.25
☐ *The People Maker,* Zenith ZB-14, 1959	5.00	7.00	5.15
☐ *The Rithian Terror,* Award AS 1008, no date	1.75	2.25	2.00
☐ *Rule Golden and Other Stories,* Avon 43646, 1979	2.00	2.75	2.50
☐ *Three Novels,* Berkley X1706, 1969 . .	1.85	2.50	2.25
☐ *Turning On,* Ace G-677, 1967	1.85	2.50	2.25
☐ *Two Damon Knight SF Novels,* Lancer 74-601, 1970	1.50	2.00	1.75
☐ *The World and Thorinn,* Berkley 05193, 1981	2.25	3.00	2.75
☐ (ED), *13 French SF Stories,* Bantam F2817, 1965	2.50	3.50	3.00
☐ *Beyond Tomorrow,* Gold Medal T2081, no date	1.75	2.50	2.00
☐ (ED), *A Century of Science Fiction,* Dell 1157, 1963	3.00	4.00	3.00
☐ (ED), *A Century Of Science Fiction,* Pan T19, 1966	3.00	4.00	3.00
☐ (ED), *Century Of Great Short SF Novels,* Dell 1158, 1965	2.00	2.75	2.50
☐ (ED), *Cities Of Wonder,* MacFadden 75-183, 1967	2.00	2.75	2.50
☐ (ED), *Dimension X,* Coronet 16787, 1974	3.75	4.75	4.00
☐ (ED), *Elsewhere X 3,* Coronet 18616, 1974	2.75	3.50	3.00
☐ (ED), *First Contact,* Pinnacle P062N, 1971	1.50	2.00	1.75
☐ (ED), *First Flight,* Lancer 72-672, 1963	2.50	3.50	3.00
☐ (ED), *First Flight,* Lancer 72-145, 1966	2.50	3.50	3.00
☐ (ED), *The Metal Smile,* Belmont B60-082, 1968	2.00	2.75	2.50
☐ (ED), *The Metal Smile,* Belmont Tower 50722, 1974	1.25	1.75	1.50

		Current Price Range		C/Y Avg.
☐	(ED), *Nebula Award Stories*, Pocket 75275, 1967	1.75	2.25	2.00
☐	(ED), *Nebula Award Stories*, Pocket 75275, 1969	1.25	1.75	1.50
☐	(ED), *Now Begins Tomorrow*, Lancer 74-585, 1969, third edition	2.00	3.00	2.50
☐	(ED), *Orbit 10*, Berkley N2236, 1972	1.35	1.85	1.50
☐	(ED), *Orbit 13*, Berkley N2698, 1974.	1.35	1.85	1.50
☐	(ED), *Orbit 3*, Berkley S1608, 1968 . .	1.75	2.25	2.00
☐	(ED), *Orbit 5*, Berkley S1778, 1969 . .	1.00	1.50	1.25
☐	(ED), *Orbit 9*, Berkley N2116, 1972 . .	1.50	2.25	2.00
☐	(ED), *Science Fiction Inventions*, Lancer 73-691, 1967	2.75	3.75	3.25
☐	(ED), *The Shape Of Things*, Popular SP352, 1965	1.75	2.50	2.00
☐	(ED), *A Shocking Thing*, Pocket 77775, 1974, second edition	1.25	1.75	1.50
☐	(ED), *Tomorrow X 4*, Gold Medal D1428, 1964	3.00	4.00	3.50
☐	(ED), *Worlds To Come*, Gold Medal R1942, no date	2.00	2.75	2.50
☐	(ED), *Worlds To Come*, Gold Medal T2271, no date	2.00	2.75	2.50
☐	**Knight, Dorcas,** *Flesh Is Willing*, Midwood F156, 1962	1.75	2.50	2.00
☐	**Knowlton, Bill,** *Classroom Capers*, Berkley 681	6.00	8.00	6.75
☐	**Koestler, Arthur,** *Gladiators*, Graphic S213, 1956, second edition	2.25	3.00	2.75
☐	**Komroff, Manuel,** *Gods and Demons*, Lion LL-8, 1954	2.25	3.00	2.75
☐	**Korr, Jerry,** *The Raising of the Queen*, Perma 5057	3.00	4.00	3.45
☐	**Koslow, Jules,** *The Bohemian*, Pyramid 83, 1953	9.00	12.00	10.00
☐	**Kramer, Karl,** *A Flame Too Hot*, Monarch 490 (cover artwork by Barton, 1965) . . .	3.25	4.00	3.65
☐	*Common Law Wife*, Midwood 75, 1961	2.50	3.25	2.87
☐	*The Deadly September*, Monarch 159 (cover artwork by Maguire, 1960) . . .	4.00	5.00	4.50
☐	*Kiss Me Quick*, Monarch 433 (cover artwork by Maguire)	3.25	4.00	3.65

	Current Price Range		C/Y Avg.

☐ **Krauss, Bob,** *Here's Hawaii,* Perma 4215 — 2.75 3.50 3.10

☐ **Krepps, Robert,** *El Cid,* Gold Medal 1169 (painted cover picturing Charlton Heston and Sophia Loren) .... — 6.00 8.00 6.90

☐ **Krim, Seymour,** *The Beats,* Gold Medal 1328 .... — 4.00 5.00 4.50

☐ **Kruger, Paul,** *Message From Marise,* Gold Medal 1323 (cover artwork by Zuckerburg, 1963) .... — 4.00 5.00 4.50

☐ **Kurpin, Alexandre,** *Yama the Pit,* Pyramid 541 (cover artwork by Zeil) .... — 5.00 6.00 5.50

☐ **Kurtzman, Harvey,** *Jungle Book,* Ballantine 93 (Harvey Kurtzman was a frequent contributor to Mad Magazine as well as the creator of Little Annie Fanny, a cartoon which appeared in Playboy Magazine.) .... — 12.00 16.00 14.00

☐ *Second Helping,* Gold Medal 1225, 962 — 7.00 10.00 8.50

☐ **Labhey, Richard,** *Alters of the Heart,* Berkley G-279 .... — 1.25 1.75 1.25

☐ **Lacy, Ed.,** *Harlem Underground,* Pyramid R 1220, no date .... — 3.00 4.00 3.35

☐ *South Pacific Affair,* Belmont 1220 ... — 1.50 2.00 1.75

☐ **Lafarre, Joel,** *Shameless Game,* Spartan SL162, 1967 .... — 4.00 5.25 4.25

☐ **Lagerkvist, Par,** *Barabbas,* Bantam 2417 (painted cover picturing Anthony Quinn) .... — 6.00 8.00 7.00

☐ **Lake, Stuart N.,** *Wyatt Earp,* Bantam 2015 .... — 3.00 4.00 3.45

☐ **l'Amour, Louis,** *The High Graders,* Bantam 2902 .... — 3.00 4.00 3.35

☐ *Tall Stranger,* Gold Medal 1430 ..... — 3.00 4.00 3.35

☐ **Lancaster, Evelyn,** *The Final Face of Eve,* Hillman 161. Sequel to *"Three Faces of Eve,"* which was made into a successful motion picture. .... — 3.00 3.75 3.45

☐ **Landon, Margaret,** *Anna and the King of Siam,* Cardinal C222. (photo cover picturing Yul Brynner and Deborah Kerr). Better known as "The King and I." .... — 5.00 6.50 5.50

	Current Price Range		C/Y Avg.

☐ **Lansky, Bernard,** *Seventeen,* Pocket Books 1253 ...... 6.00 8.00 6.85

☐ **Larrick, Nancy,** *A Parent's Guide to Children's Reading,* Cardinal GC218 ...... 2.00 2.50 2.15

☐ **Larrimore, Lida,** *Stars Still Shine,* Dell 249, no date 2.00 2.75 2.37

☐ **Laurence, Will,** *For Value Received,* Midwood 117, 1961 ...... 5.25 6.50 5.75

☐ **Lawrence, David,** *Imparient,* Midwood F374, no date 1.75 2.50 2.12

☐ **Lawrence, D.H.,** *The Captain's Doll,* Berkley G-43, 1948 ...... 4.00 5.50 4.12

☐ *Lady Chatterley's Lover,* Penguin 610, third edition 1.25 1.75 1.50

☐ *The Man Who Died,* Vintage V71 .... 3.00 4.00 3.50

☐ *The Portable D.H. Lawrence,* Viking 28, 1959 ...... 3.00 3.75 3.45

☐ *Sea and Sardinia,* Anchor 39 (cover artwork by Ascherl) 3.50 4.25 3.90

☐ *Sons and Lovers,* Signet 1829 (painted cover picturing Trevor Howard, Dean Stockwell, Wendy Hiller, Heather Sears and Mary Ure) 6.00 8.00 6.75

☐ *Studies in Classic American Literature,* Anchor 5 (D.H. Lawrence was one of very few celebrated British novelists to acknowledge the significance of American literature.) 3.00 4.00 3.45

☐ **Lawrence, Gil,** *Fury With Legs,* Pyramid 802 ...... 3.75 4.50 4.10

☐ **Lawrence, Steven,** *A Noose For Slattery,* Ace F138, 1962 ...... 4.25 5.50 4.50

☐ **Lawrence, William,** *Abortion,* Tower 42-820, 1967 ...... 6.00 8.00 7.00

☐ *After Hours,* Belmont 190-300 ...... 1.50 2.00 1.75

☐ **Lawson, Joan,** *Registered Nurse,* Monarch M8520, 1962 ...... 1.35 1.85 1.37

☐ **Layne, Jim,** *The Fire in a Woman,* Beacon 697 ...... 3.00 4.00 3.45

☐ **LeCarre, John,** *A Murder of Quality,* Signet 2529 ...... 3.00 4.00 3.45

Left to Right: **Aaron's Rod,** by D.H. Lawrence,
1950, Avon Books, G1039, **$3.50–$4.50;**
Elmer Gantry, by Sinclair Lewis,
Signet Book, Q3090, **$2.00–$3.00.**

	Current Price Range		C/Y Avg.

☐ **Lederer, William J.,** *A Nation of Sheep,*
545 (This work, a national bestseller, is
credited by some for sparking the anti-
establishment movement of the 1960s.)   4.00   5.00   4.50

☐ **Lee, C.Y.,** *Flower Drum Song,* Dell F175
(painted cover picturing Nancy Kwan,
James Shigeta and Miyoshi Umeki) 5.00   6.50   5.75

☐ **Lee, James,** *Career,* Dell B148 (photo
cover picturing Dean Martin, Shirley Mac-
Laine, Carolyn Jones and Anthony Fran-
ciosa) 6.00   8.00   6.45

☐ **Lee, Marjorie,** *The Lion House,* Crest
S413, 1960 . . . .   1.35   1.85   1.37

☐ **Lefebvre, Georges,** *The Coming of the
French Revolution,* Vintage V43 . . . .   2.00   2.50   2.19

☐ **Leguin, Ursula K.,** *City Of Illusions,* Ace
G-626, 1967 . . . .   1.75   2.50   2.12

☐   *City of Illusions,* Ace 10701, no date   2.00   2.75   2.37

☐   *City Of Illusions,* Ace 10702, no date   1.85   2.65   2.12

☐   *The Dispossessed,* Avon 24885, 1975   1.85   2.65   2.00

☐   *The Left Hand Of Darkness,* Ace
47803, 1974, seventh edition 1.85   2.65   2.12

☐   *The Left Hand Of Darkness,* Ace
47806, 1982 . . . .   2.00   2.75   2.37

☐   *The Left Hand Of Darkness,* Ace
47805, 1977, fourteenth edition 1.35   1.85   1.50

☐   *The Left Hand Of Darkness,* Ace
47805, 1976, twelfth edition 1.35   1.85   1.50

☐   *The Left Hand Of Darkness,* Ace
47802, 1974, seventh edition 1.35   1.85   1.50

☐   *The Left Hand Of Darkness,* Ace
47800, 1969 . . . .   1.50   2.00   1.75

☐   (ED), *Nebula Award Stories,* 11, Ban-
tam 11742, 1978 . . . .   1.50   2.00   1.75

☐   *Planet Of Exile,* Ace 66957, 1982, sixth
edition 1.85   2.75   2.12

☐   *Planet Of Exile,* Tandem 6429, 1972   1.85   2.75   2.12

☐   *Planet Of Exile,* Ace 66951, no date   1.85   2.75   2.12

☐   *Planet Of Exile,* Ace 66953, 1974,
fourth edition 1.25   1.75   1.50

☐   *Planet Of Exile,* Ace 66952, 1973, third
edition 2.00   2.75   2.37

	Current Price Range		C/Y Avg.

☐ *Rocannon's World,* Ace 73294, 1980, eighth edition **1.85** **2.65** **2.12**

☐ *Rocannon's World,* Ace 73291, no date **1.85** **2.65** **2.12**

☐ *Rocannon's World,* Ace 73292, no date **1.85** **2.65** **2.12**

☐ *Rocannon's World,* Ace 73293, no date **1.25** **1.75** **1.50**

☐ *The Tombs Of Atuan,* Bantam 11600, 1977, eighth edition **1.50** **2.00** **1.75**

☐ *A Wizard Of Earthsea,* Puffin 0477, 1976, seventh edition **2.25** **3.25** **2.75**

☐ *A Wizard Of Earthsea,* Puffin 0477, 1976, eighth edition **2.75** **3.75** **3.25**

☐ *A Wizard Of Earthsea,* Bantam 11609, 1977, eighth edition **1.25** **1.75** **1.50**

☐ *The Word För World Is Forest,* Berkley 03279, fourth edition **2.00** **2.75** **2.37**

☐ *Word For World Is Forest,* Berkley 05185, 1981, fifth edition **2.00** **2.75** **2.37**

☐ **Lehman, Ernest,** *Sweet Smell of Success,* Signet 1413 (photo cover picturing Burt Lancaster, Tony Curtis and Susan Hayward, also interior illustrations) **7.00** **10.00** **8.10**

☐ **Lehman, Paul Evan,** *Poverty Range,* Avon T547 .... **3.00** **3.75** **3.35**

☐ *Range Justice,* Pyramid 512 (cover artwork by Stanley **3.00** **3.75** **3.35**

☐ *Smoke of the Texan,* Hillman 150 ... **3.00** **3.75** **3.35**

☐ **Leigh, Michael,** *Velvet Underground,* MacFadden 60-142, 1963 .... **4.00** **6.00** **4.85**

☐ **Leighton, Lee,** *Gut Shot,* Ballantine 578, 1962 .... **4.00** **5.00** **4.50**

☐ *Tomahawk,* Ballantine 672 (cover artwork by Crair) **3.75** **4.75** **4.25**

☐ **Leinster, Murray,** *The Aliens,* Berkley G410, 1960 .... **2.50** **3.50** **3.00**

☐ *Checkpoint Lambda,* Berkley F1263, 1966 .... **2.25** **3.00** **2.62**

☐ *Creatures Of The Abyss,* Berkley G549, 1961 .... **2.00** **3.00** **2.50**

	Current Price Range		C/Y Avg.

☐ *Doctor To The Stars,* Pyramid T2367, 1971, second edition	1.25	1.75	1.50
☐ *The Forgotten Planet,* Ace D25 18, no date	4.50	6.25	5.50
☐ *Four From Planet 5,* Gold Medal K 1397, 1964, second edition	2.25	3.00	2.75
☐ *Four From Planet 5, Gold Medal S937, 1959*	2.75	3.50	3.00
☐ *Get Off My World!,* Belmont B50-676, 1966	2.50	3.50	3.00
☐ *The Greeks Bring Gifts,* MacFadden 50-224, 1964	2.50	3.50	3.00
☐ *The Greeks Bring Gifts,* MacFadden 50-418, 1968, second edition	1.75	2.50	2.00
☐ *The Greeks Bring Gifts,* Manor 95400, 1975	1.25	1.75	1.50
☐ *Invaders Of Space,* Berkley F1022, 1964	2.25	3.00	2.75
☐ *Invaders Of Space,* Tandem T201, 1968	3.50	4.75	4.00
☐ *The Last Space Ship,* Cherry Tree 404, 1950	10.00	13.00	11.50
☐ *Men Into Space,* Berkley G461, 1960	3.00	4.00	3.50
☐ *Miners In The Sky,* Avon G1310, 1967	1.75	2.50	2.00
☐ *Monsters And Such,* Avon T-345, 1959	4.50	6.25	5.00
☐ *Operation Outer Space,* Signet S1346, 1957	2.25	3.00	2.75
☐ *Operation Terror,* Berkley F694, 1962	3.00	4.00	3.50
☐ *The Other Side Of Nowhere,* Berkley F918, 1964	2.25	3.25	2.75
☐ **Leopold, Jules,** *Check Your Wits,* Popular Library 315	20.00	27.50	23.45
☐ **Lerner, Alan Jay,** *My Fair Lady,* Signet 2536 (painted cover picturing Rex Harrison, Audrey Hepburn and Stanley Holloway)	5.00	6.50	5.50
☐ **Levine, Irving,** *Main Street U.S.S.R.,* Signet 1803 (interior photographs)	4.00	5.25	4.45
☐ **Levine, Rex,** *The Insect Warriors,* Ace F334	5.00	6.00	5.30
☐ **Lewis, Anthony,** *Gideon's Trumpet,* Vintage V315	3.00	4.00	3.40

	Current Price Range		C/Y Avg.

☐ **Lewis, C. Day,** *The Aeneid of Virgil,* Anchor 20 . . . . 2.00 2.50 2.25

☐ **Lewis, Jack,** *Blood Money,* Headline 108 4.00 5.00 4.50

☐ *Of Guns and Glory,* Challenge VP313, 1968 (anthology) 4.00 5.25 4.75

☐ **Lewis, Sinclair,** *Babbit,* Tauchnitz 4590, 1922 . . . . 3.00 4.00 3.35

☐ *Elmer Gantry,* Signet Q3090, no date 2.00 3.00 2.50

☐ *Elmer Gantry,* Dell 2266 (photo cover picturing Burt Lancaster and Jean Simmons. Burt Lancaster produced this film himself.) 6.00 8.00 7.00

☐ **Lewis, W.H.,** *The Splendid Century,* Anchor 122 . . . . 3.00 4.00 3.50

☐ **Lieberman, Jerry,** *Off the Cuff,* Pocket Books 1100 (cover artwork by Bacon) 7.00 10.00 8.50

☐ **Lindbergh, Anne Morrow,** *Gift From the Sea,* Vintage V329 . . . . 2.50 3.00 2.70

☐ **Lindsay, Rachel,** *Leslie Forrest M.D.,* Berkley 653 . . . . 2.00 2.50 2.20

☐ **Linton, Adelin,** *The Tree of Culture,* Vintage V76 . . . . 2.50 3.25 2.80

☐ **Lipset, Seymour,** *Political Man,* Anchor 330 . . . . 3.00 3.75 3.45

☐ **Lipsky, Eleazar,** *Kiss of Death,* Penguin 642 (painted cover picturing Victor Mature, Brian Donlevy and Colleen Grey) 4.00 5.50 4.45

☐ **Lisitzky, Gene,** *Thomas Jefferson,* Pyramid E15 . . . . 2.00 2.50 2.25

☐ **Liston, Jack,** *Man Bait,* Dell B158 (cover artwork by McGuire) 4.50 5.75 5.10

☐ **Little, Charles,** *And Love So Wild,* Monarch 191 (cover artwork by DeSoto, 1961) 4.75 6.00 5.19

☐ *The Sound of Trumpets,* Monarch 493 (cover artwork by Greene) 3.00 3.75 3.45

☐ **Llewellyn, Richard,** *Up Into the Mountain,* Cardinal GC108 . . . . 3.00 3.75 3.25

☐ **Locke, Douglas,** *Customer's Woman,* Beacon 726 . . . . 2.75 3.50 2.90

☐ **Lockridge, Frances,** *Death Has a Small Voice,* Avon T422 . . . . 2.25 3.00 2.45

	Current Price Range		C/Y Avg.

☐ *The Lone Skeleton*, Pyramid 824 (cover artwork by Bacon)	2.25	3.00	2.45
☐ *Voyage Into Violence*, Pyramid 884, (cover artwork by Bacon)	2.25	3.00	2.45
☐ **Logan, Ford,** *Fire in the Desert*, Ballantine 666	3.00	3.75	3.45
☐ **Lomax, Bliss,** *Stranger With a Gun*, Dell 18344, 1977	2.50	3.50	3.00
☐ **London, Jack,** *The Call Of the Wild*, Pocket Books 2593 (cover artwork by Allison)	2.00	2.75	2.35
☐ *Martin Eden*, Penguin 587, no date ..	3.50	4.50	4.00
☐ **Loomis, Frederick,** *Consultation Roon*, Pocket Books 2654, (cover artwork by Meltzoff)	4.00	5.00	4.50
☐ **Loomis, Noel,** *Ferguson's Ferry*, Avon F119	3.00	3.75	3.40
☐ **Loos, Anita,** *Gentlemen Prefer Blondes*, Avon F109	2.00	2.50	2.35
☐ *Gentlemen Prefer Blondes*, Tauchnitz 4749, 1930	3.00	4.00	3.40
☐ **Lorca, Federico,** *Selected Poems*, Noonday 114	3.00	3.75	3.45
☐ **Lord, James,** *The Loving and the Lost*, Crest S175, 1957	2.50	3.25	2.87
☐ **Lord, Sheldon,** *Born to be Bad*, Midwood 14, 1959	5.00	6.75	5.00
☐ *The Bedroom Route*, Beacon 18603F	1.35	1.75	1.55
☐ *Older Women*, Beacon 18552F	1.75	2.25	2.00
☐ *Pads are for Passions*, Beacon 18387	1.50	2.00	1.75
☐ *The Rivals*, Beacon 680	3.00	3.75	3.45
☐ **Lord, Walter,** *A Time To Stand*, Pocket Books 7023	3.25	4.00	3.55
☐ **Loren, Francis,** *Bachelor Girl*, Beacon 18583F	1.75	2.25	2.00
☐ **Lorraine, Louis,** *Blonde Dynamite*, Beacon 18458F	1.35	1.75	1.55
☐ **Lorrys, Pierre,** *Aphrodite*, Berkley 1G-46	3.25	4.00	3.62
☐ **Lowell, Juliet,** *Dear Sir*, Avon 318	8.00	11.00	8.95
☐ **Lowenkopf, Shelley,** *The Love of the Lion*, Kozy 149	3.50	4.25	3.85

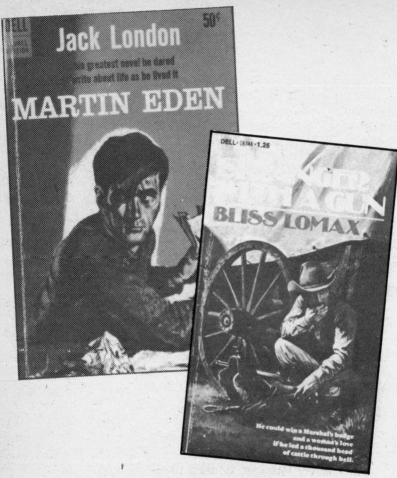

Left to Right: **Martin Eden,** by Jack London,
1958, Dell, LC114, **$4.00–$4.50;**
Stranger With A Gun, by Bliss Lomax,
Dell, 18344, 1977, **$2.50–$3.50.**

	Current Price Range		C/Y Avg.
☐ **Lowrey, Walter B.,** *Summer Boy,* Pyramid 864 (cover artwork by Kokinos) ...	3.00	3.75	3.39
☐ **Lowry, Robert,** *That Kind of Woman,* Pyramid 430 (photo cover picturing Sophia Loren and Tab Hunter)	9.00	12.00	10.40
☐ **Lucchesi, Aldo,** *The Tour,* Tower T1251 (cover artwork by Alvora, 1969)	4.00	5.00	4.45
☐ **Lynne, David,** *Games Women Play,* Tower T0751, 1969	2.00	2.50	2.25
☐ **Lyon, Dana,** *The Frightened Child,* Ace G535 (cover artwork by Nappi)	2.50	3.25	2.75
☐ *Spin the Web Tight,* Ace G525	2.50	3.25	2.75
☐ **MacBrian, James,** *The Revolt of Abbe Lee,* Monarch 429 (cover artwork by Miller, 1964)	4.00	5.00	4.45
☐ *Roz,* Monarch 382 (cover artwork by Borack, 1963)	4.00	5.00	4.45
☐ **MacDonald, John D.,** *Bright Orange For the Shroud,* Gold Medal 1573	2.50	3.25	2.80
☐ *Judge Me Not,* Gold Medal 1394 (cover artwork by Phillips), later reissued with serial number 1580, value slightly lower.	3.00	4.00	3.35
☐ *Moving Target,* Pocket Books 2680, (cover artwork by Allison)	3.00	4.00	3.45
☐ *The Only Girl in the Game,* Gold Medal 1015, 1960	4.75	5.75	4.95
☐ **MacDonald, John D.,** *The Price of Murder,* Dell A152, 1958, second edition ..	2.00	3.00	2.50
☐ *Slam the Big Door,* Gold Medal 961, 1960	4.75	5.75	5.10
☐ **MacDonald, John Ross,** *The Drowning Pool,* Pocket Books 2821 (cover artwork by Meese)............................	2.75	3.50	3.10
☐ *The Way Some People Die,* Pocket Books 6021	2.00	2.50	2.25
☐ **MacDonald, Phillip,** *The List of Adrian Messenger,* Bantam A2186, 1961	2.50	3.50	3.00
☐ **MacLean, Alistair,** *Fear is the Key,* Perma 4260 (cover artwork by Abbett)	2.50	3.25	2.75

	Current Price Range		C/Y Avg.

☐ *Guns of Navarone,* Perma 4089 (photo cover picturing Gregory Peck, David Niven and Anthony Quinn) 6.00   8.00   6.90

☐ **MacLeod, Jean S.,** *My Heart's in the Highlands,* Harlequin 711 . . . .   2.00   2.50   2.18

☐   *The Valley of Palms,* Harlequin 748 . .   2.00   2.50   2.25

☐ **MacLeod, Kevin,** *The Sweet Pain,* Beacon 669 . . . .   3.00   3.75   3.35

☐ **MacNeil, Neil,** *Mexican Slay Ride,* Gold Medal 1182 (cover artwork by Hooks, 1962) 3.00   4.00   3.40

☐ **Madel, George,** *Borderline Cases,* Signet 2232 (cover artwork by the author, 1962) 6.00   8.00   6.75

☐ **Madigan, Kip,** *Rene,* Fabian Z-107, no date 1.50   2.00   1.75

☐ **Malcolm, Margaret,** *Fortune Goes Begging,* Harlequin 723 . . . .   2.25   3.00   2.55

☐   *Dr. Sandy,* Harlequin 945 . . . .   2.25   3.00   2.45

☐ **Malinowski, Dr. Bronislaw,** *Magic, Science and Religion,* Anchor 23 . . . .   2.00   2.50   2.25

☐ **Malley, Louis,** *Shakedown Strip,* Avon T394 . . . .   3.00   4.00   3.45

☐ **Maltz, Dr. Maxwell,** *The Magic Scalpel,* Avon T475 . . . .   2.00   2.75   2.30

☐ **Manford, Frederick,** *Conquering Horse,* Cardinal GC90 . . . .   3.25   4.25   3.75

☐ **Mankowitz, Wolf,** *Cockatrice,* Perma 5096 . . . .   2.00   2.75   2.30

☐ **Mann, Thomas,** *Death in Venice,* Vintage V3. This novel became the basis for an opera. 2.00   2.50   2.25

☐ **Mannix, Edward,** *An End to Fury,* Cardinal GC80 (cover artwork by Maguire) . .   3.00   3.75   3.35

☐ **Mansfield, Katherine,** *Stories by Katherine Mansfield,* Vintage V36 . . . .   2.00   2.50   2.25

☐ **Mantley, John,** *Woman Obsessed,* Perma 4146 (photo cover picturing Susan Hayward) 6.00   8.00   6.75

☐ **Marchel, Lucie,** *The Mesh,* Bantam 862, no date 4.00   6.00   4.70

	Current Price Range		C/Y Avg.
☐ **Markham, Virgil,** *The Devil Drives,* Bart House 10, no date	5.00	7.00	5.80
☐ **Marlett, Melba,** *Death is in the Garden,* Popular Library SP383, no date	4.00	5.50	4.50
☐ **Marlowe, Dan,** *The Name of the Game is Death,* Gold Medal 1184 (cover artwork by Phillips, 1962)	4.00	5.25	4.50
☐ **Marmor, Arnold,** *The Ninth Virgin,* Nite-Time 103	4.00	5.00	4.45
☐ **Marquand, John P.,** *Ming Yellow,* Pyramid 873 (cover artwork by Bacon)	3.00	3.75	3.35
☐ *Your Turn Mr. Moto,* Berkley 756 (cover artwork by Phillips)	3.00	3.75	3.50
☐ **Marr, Reed,** *Catch A Falling Star,* Gold Medal 576, 1956	1.75	2.50	2.12
☐ **Marric, J.J.,** *Gideon's Fire,* Berkley 663 (cover artwork by Kalin)	4.00	5.25	4.55
☐ *Gideon's Night,* Pyramid 872 (cover artwork by Bacon)	4.00	5.25	4.55
☐ **Marsden, Martha,** *Intimate,* Midwood Y128, 1961	2.00	2.75	2.37
☐ **Marshall, Alan,** *Backstage Love,* Midwood 17, 1959	6.00	8.00	6.75
☐ **Marshall, Alan,** *Man Hungry,* Midwood 20, 1959	3.00	3.75	3.37
☐ *Passion's Playthings,* Bedside BB1208.	2.50	3.00	3.75
☐ **Marshall, Edison,** *Upstart,* Dell 233, no date	4.50	6.00	4.62
☐ **Marshall, Joseph R.,** *Carla,* Gold Medal 1173, 1961	4.25	5.25	4.60
☐ **Marshall, Rosamond,** *Rib of the Hawk,* Popular Library G528	3.00	3.75	3.35
☐ **Martel, David,** *Old Enough,* Midwood F339, no date	1.75	2.50	2.12
☐ **Martin, George V.,** *The Bells of St. Mary's,* Bantam 103 (photo cover picturing Bing Crosby and Ingrid Bergman)	6.00	8.00	6.80
☐ **Martin, Jerome,** *Pen Pals,* Unique 123, 1967	4.00	5.00	4.50
☐ **Martin, Kay,** *Payment in Sin,* Hillman 190	2.50	3.25	2.87

	Current Price Range		C/Y Avg.

☐ **Martin, Pete,** *Hollywood Without Makeup,* Bantam 721 (photo cover picturing Ava Gardner) 6.00 8.00 6.70

☐ **Martin, Thom,** *Serenade To Seduction,* Newstand Library 508, 1980 .... 1.65 2.25 1.75

☐ **Marvin, Ron,** *Mr. Ballerina,* Regency RB 103, no date 5.00 7.00 5.75

☐ **Marx, Groucho,** *Groucho and Me,* Dell F112 (photo cover picturing the four Marx Brothers) 6.00 8.00 6.85

☐ **Mason, Ernst,** *Tiberius,* Ballantine 361, 1960 .... 3.00 3.75 3.25

☐ **Mason, Raymond,** *Long After Five,* Gold Medal 589, 1956 .... 3.25 4.00 3.62

☐ **Masterson, Whit,** *A Showod in the Wild,* Bantam 2090 .... 3.00 3.75 3.50

☐ **Masur, Harold Q.,** *So Rich, So Lovely and So Dead,* Pocket Books 998 ...... 6.00 8.00 6.70

☐ *You Can't Live Forever,* Pocket Books 860 .... 7.00 10.00 8.35

☐ **Matheson, Richard,** *Shock,* Dell B195 (cover artwork by Powers) 4.00 5.00 4.40

☐ **Matthews, Clayton,** *The Corrupter,* Monarch 461 (cover artwork by Borack, 1964) 3.75 4.50 4.15

☐ *Discontented Wives,* Beacon 440 .... 3.50 4.25 3.90

☐ *Faithless,* Monarch 289 (cover artwork by Johnson, 1962) 4.00 5.00 4.55

☐ **Matthews, Kelvin,** *The Devil Sword,* Hillman 140 .... 3.00 3.75 3.35

☐ **Matthews, William H.,** *Invitation to Geology,* American Museum B22 .... 2.00 2.50 2.20

☐ **Mattingly, Harold,** *Roman Imperial Civilization,* Anchor 60 .... 2.00 2.50 2.20

☐ **Maugham, W. Somerset,** *Cosmopolitans,* Berkley IG-268 .... 2.00 2.50 2.25

☐ **Mauldin, Bill,** *A Sort of a Saga,* Bantam 855 .... 6.00 8.00 6.70

☐ *Back Home,* Bantam 461 .... 4.00 5.25 4.55

☐ *Bill Mauldin's Army,* Paperback Library 52-138, 1962 .... 4.00 6.00 4.85

	Current Price Range		C/Y Avg.
☐ *Up Front*, Bantam 83	7.00	10.00	8.10
☐ **Maurette, Marcelle,** *Anastasia*, Signet 1356 (photo cover picturing Ingrid Bergman and Yul Brynner). This novel was based on the legend that one of the czar's daughters escaped the Russian Revolution of 1918–19 and fled to a foreign country. In actual fact, quite a few "Anastasias" surfaced over the years, but none could convincingly prove that they were the exiled empress.	5.00	6.50	5.65
☐ **Maxwell, Bob,** *Forbidden Nectar*, Playtime 648, 1963	3.75	4.50	4.05
☐ **Mayer, Martin,** *The Schools,* Anchor 331 (cover artwork by Osborn)	2.00	2.50	2.20
☐ **Mayo, Dallas,** *Pretty Puppet,* Midwood F371, no date	1.75	2.50	2.12
☐ **McBain, Ed,** *Cop Hater,* Perma 4268 ..	2.25	3.00	2.60
☐ *Give the Boys a Great Big Hand,* Perma 4187	2.25	3.00	2.55
☐ *Killer's Payoff,* Perma 4265	2.25	3.00	2.55
☐ *Lady I Did It,* Perma 4253	2.25	3.00	2.55
☐ **McCarthy, Justin,** *Inside Brother Juniper,* Pocket Books 6182, 1963	6.00	8.00	7.00
☐ **McCloy, Helen,** *The Man in The Moonlight,* Dell 72, no date	3.50	3.80	4.50
☐ **McClusky, Thorp,** *Your Health and Chiropractic,* Pyramid RR39	3.00	4.00	3.45
☐ **McCool, Grace,** *Gunsmoke: The True Story of Old Tombstone,* Gateway (no serial number)	4.00	5.00	4.55
☐ **McCoy, Dean,** *The Night it Happened,* Beacon 634	2.00	2.50	2.15
☐ *No Empty Bed For Her,* Beacon 550	2.50	3.25	2.87
☐ **McCoy, Owen,** *No Empty Bed For Her,* Beacon 8550F	1.65	2.10	1.75
☐ **McDonald, N.C.,** *Song of the Axe,* Ballantine 499	3.00	3.75	3.35
☐ **McElfresh, Adeline,** *Dr. Jane Comes Home,* Bantam 2158	3.00	3.75	3.55

	Current Price Range		C/Y Avg.
☐ *Dr. Jane's Mission,* Bantam 2053	3.00	3.75	3.35
☐ *Hospital Hill,* Dell B201 (cover artwork by Abbett, 1961)	4.00	5.00	4.40
☐ *Night Call,* Dell B177 (cover artwork by Abbett, 1961)	4.00	5.00	4.40
☐ *Wings For Nurse Bennett,* Dell A206 (cover artwork by Shoemaker, 1960)	4.25	5.25	4.70
☐ **McFeatters, Dale,** *Strictly Business,* Berkley 349	3.00	4.00	3.50
☐ **McGivern, William,** *Odds Against Tomorrow,* Cardinal C316 (photo cover picturing Harry Belafonte and Robert Ryan)	4.00	5.50	4.65
☐ *Rogue Cop,* Pocket Books 1030 (photo cover picturing Robert Taylor)	4.00	5.50	4.70
☐ *Seven Lies South,* Crest 499 (cover artwork by Bennett)	4.00	5.00	4.45
☐ **McGovern, James,** *Love Among the Damned,* Hillman 160	2.50	3.25	2.80
☐ **McGuide, Shelagh,** *A Room At Polly's Place,* Beacon 8691X	1.65	2.10	1.75
☐ **McKenney, Ruth,** *My Sister Eileen,* Berkley 1045	2.50	3.00	2.70
☐ **McKimmey, James,** *The Wrong Ones,* Dell B192 (cover artwork by McGinnis, 1961)	4.00	5.00	4.40
☐ **McKnight, Bob,** *A Stone Around Her Neck,* Ace F143, 1962	3.50	4.25	3.83
☐ *The Flying Eye,* Ace F102	4.00	5.00	4.39
☐ **McKown, Robin,** *Foreign Service Girl,* Berkley 524	4.25	5.25	4.79
☐ **McLane, Ben V.,** *Chasm Of Lust,* Newstand Library U161, 1961	1.65	2.10	1.75
☐ **McLaughlin, Dean,** *Dome World,* Pyramid 763	5.00	6.50	5.60
☐ **Mead, S.,** *How To Succeed in Business Without Really Trying,* Ballantine 127 ..	4.00	6.00	4.87
☐ **Meade, Richard,** *Resident Physician,* Medical Fiction 203	2.50	3.00	2.72
☐ **Medearis, Mary,** *Big Doc's Girl,* Pyramid PG28 (cover artwork by Marchetti)	4.00	5.00	4.39
☐ **Meeker, Richard,** *Torment,* Uni-Books 13, no date	5.00	7.00	5.70

	Current Price Range		C/Y Avg.

☐ **Mehling, Harold,** *Scandalous Scamps,* Ace K125 .... | 3.00 | 3.75 | 3.31

☐ **Melville, Herman,** *Moby Dick,* Riverside A9, 1956 .... | 2.00 | 3.00 | 2.40

☐ **Memmi, Albert,** *Strangers,* Avon F153 (cover artwork by Powers) .... | 4.00 | 5.00 | 4.50

☐ **Menke, Frank,** *Encyclopedia of Sports,* Barnes (no serial number), 1955 ...... | 5.00 | 6.50 | 5.72

☐ **Merimee, Prosper,** *The Loves of Carmen,* Pocket Books 559 (painted cover picturing Rita Hayworth and Glenn Ford) | 5.00 | 6.50 | 5.61

☐ **Metalious, Grace,** *Tight White Collar,* Dell S25 (cover artwork by Hulings) ... | 4.25 | 5.25 | 4.72

☐ **Meyer, Jerome S.,** *Great Inventions,* Perma 6003 .... | 2.00 | 2.50 | 2.19

☐ **Meyerhoff, Hans,** *The Philosophy of History in Our Time,* Anchor 163 .... | 3.00 | 3.75 | 3.29

☐ **Meyers, C.L.,** *Sex and The Caged Woman,* Edka EK-114, 1966 (cover artwork by Maguire) .... | 5.00 | 7.00 | 5.80

☐ **Michaud, Don,** *The Beckoning Flame,* Newsstand Library 509 .... | 3.00 | 3.75 | 3.32

☐ **Miles, William E.,** *The College Female,* Monarch 540 .... | 3.00 | 3.75 | 3.36

☐ **Mill, John Stuart,** *On Liberty,* Crofts (no serial number), 1947 .... | 3.00 | 3.75 | 3.36

☐ **Millard, Joseph,** *Mansion of Evil,* Gold Medal 129, no date .... | 60.00 | 80.00 | 60.00

☐ **Miller, Henry,** *The Air Conditioned Nightmare,* Avon V2038 .... | 2.00 | 2.50 | 2.23

☐ *Quiet Days in Clichy,* Grove 98 ...... | 4.00 | 5.25 | 4.60

☐ *Tropic of Cancer,* Grove 10 .... | 5.00 | 6.50 | 5.70

☐ **Miller, John J.,** *New Doctor at Tower General,* Monarch 454 (cover artwork by Stanley, 1964) .... | 3.00 | 3.75 | 3.29

☐ **Miller, Nolan,** *Why Am I So Beat,* Ace D398 .... | 5.00 | 6.80 | 5.67

☐ **Miller, Percy,** *American Puritans,* Anchor 80 (cover artwork by Gorey) .... | 3.50 | 4.25 | 3.80

☐ **Miller, Wade,** *Deadly Weapon,* Signet 1805 .... | 2.50 | 3.00 | 2.71

	Current Price Range		C/Y Avg.

☐ *South of the Sun*, Gold Medal 1001 (cover artwork by Phillips) 3.00 3.75 3.34

☐ *Stolen Woman*, Gold Medal 1128 .... 2.75 3.50 3.09

☐ **Miller, Warren**, *The Cool World*, Crest 386................................. 3.00 3.50 3.21

☐ **Mills, C. Wright**, *The Causes of World War Three*, Ballantine 568 .... 2.50 3.00 2.72

☐ **Milosz, Czeslaw**, *Captive Mind*, Vintage V19 .... 4.00 5.00 4.47

☐ **Mitchell, Anthea**, *Naked Sword*, Popular Library G470 .... 3.00 3.75 3.27

☐ **Mitgang, Herbert**, *The Return*, Hillman 174.................................. 3.00 3.75 3.27

☐ **Moll, Elick**, *Seidman and Son*, Signet 1763. This was made into a very successful Broadway play. 3.00 3.75 3.27

☐ **Montheriant, Henri de**, *Desert Love*, Berkley G-277 .... 1.25 1.65 1.32

☐ **Mooney, Booth**, *Here Is My Body*, Gold Medal 781, 1958, second edition 1.25 1.65 1.32

☐ **Moore, Brian**, *The Luck of Ginger Coffey*, Dell F147 (cover artwork by Liebman) 3.75 4.50 4.00

☐ **Moore, Shirley**, *Science Projects Handbook*, Ballantine 445, 1960 .... 2.75 3.50 3.07

☐ **Moorehouse, Henry**, *The Prodigal*, Moody 48 .... 4.00 5.00 4.42

☐ **Morgan, Millicent**, *Mollie Sloan Special Nurse*, Perma 4270, 1962 .... 3.75 4.75 4.11

☐ **Morgan, Murry**, *Doctors to the World*, Pyramid E36 .... 3.00 3.75 3.26

☐ **Morningside, Mae**, *Strange But True*, Gold Medal 450. This was done along the lines of Robert Ripley's Believe It Or Not. 6.00 8.00 6.80

☐ **Morris, Donald**, *All Hands on Deck*, Perma 4132 (photo cover picturing Pat Boone, Buddy Hackett and Barbara Eden) 4.00 5.50 4.69

☐ **Morton, Bowie**, *Water Witch*, Kozy 154 4.00 5.00 4.39

☐ **Moyse, Alphonse**, *150 Ways to Play Solitaire*, Whitman (no serial number), 1950 4.00 5.00 4.40

☐ **Mozes, Eugene**, *Crime and Passion*, Monarch 505 (cover artwork by Maguire) 4.00 5.00 4.40

	Current Price Range		C/Y Avg.

☐ **Munn, H. Warner,** *Ship From Atlantis,*
Ace G618 (cover artwork by Gaughan) — 4.25 · 5.50 · 4.80

☐ **Munson, Donn,** *Zacapa,* Challenge 205,
1967 .... — 4.75 · 6.00 · 5.37

☐ **Murasaki, Lady,** *The Sacred Tree,* Anchor 176 (cover artwork by Seong Moy) — 3.00 · 3.75 · 3.36

☐ *The Tale of Genji,* Anchor 55 (cover artwork by Seong Moy) .... — 3.50 · 4.25 · 3.87

☐ **Myers, John,** *The Alamo,* Bantam 2089 — 3.00 · 3.75 · 3.30

☐ **Mykle, Agnar,** *Lasso Round the Moon,*
Dell S12 (cover artwork by Abbett) .... — 3.75 · 4.50 · 4.14

☐ **Myrdal, Gunnar,** *Challenge to Affluence,*
Vintage V274 .... — 2.50 · 3.00 · 2.75

☐ **Nathan, Robert,** *Portrait of Jennie,* Popular Library G572 (cover artwork by Zuckerberg) .... — 3.00 · 3.75 · 3.31

☐ **Naughton, Edmund,** *McCabe,* Berkley
482................................ — 3.00 · 3.75 · 3.31

☐ **Neal, Hilary,** *Factory Nurse,* Harlequin
812................................ — 2.00 · 2.50 · 2.21

☐ **Nehru, Jawaharlal,** *The Discovery of India,* Anchor 200 .... — 2.50 · 3.00 · 2.69

☐ **Nelkin, Sandy,** *Cartoons For Men Only,*
Pyramid 346 .... — 6.00 · 8.00 · 6.85

☐ **Nemec, John,** *War at Blue Stem Basin,*
Vega (no serial number) .... — 2.00 · 2.50 · 2.18

☐ **Newbury, Will,** *Call Boy,* Monarch 226
(cover artwork by Marchetti, 1961) .... — 4.00 · 5.00 · 4.40

☐ **Newman, Ernest,** *Great Operas,* Vintage
V118 .... — 2.00 · 2.50 · 2.17

☐ **Niall, Michael,** *Bad Day at Black Rock,*
Gold Medal 451 (painted cover picturing Spencer Tracy and Ann Francis) ...... — 6.00 · 8.00 · 6.85

☐ *Run Like a Thief,* Monarch 421 (cover artwork by Borack) .... — 3.00 · 3.75 · 3.27

☐ **Nichols, Fan,** *Love Me Now,* Monarch
348 (cover artwork by DeSoto) .... — 3.00 · 3.75 · 3.27

☐ **Nickson, Hilda,** *Operation Love,* Harlequin 670 .... — 2.00 · 2.50 · 2.17

☐ *Surgeon's Return,* Harlequin 794 .... — 2.00 · 2.50 · 2.13

☐ *The World of Nurse Mitchell,* Harlequin
820 .... — 2.00 · 2.50 · 2.20

	Current Price Range		C/Y Avg.
☐ **Nietzsche, Friedrich,** *The Birth of Tragedy,* Anchor 81	1.75	2.25	2.00
☐ **Nininger, H.H.,** *A Comet Strikes the Earth,* American Meteorite Museum (no serial number), 1953	3.50	4.25	3.80
☐ **Nixon, Henry L.,** *Confessions of a Psychiatrist,* Beacon 837	3.00	3.75	3.30
☐ **Noel, Sterling,** *Empire of Evil,* Avon F112	2.50	3.25	2.72
☐ **Nordhoff, Charles and James N. Hall,** *Mutiny on the Bounty,* Cardinal C456 (photo cover picturing Marlon Brando)	5.00	6.50	5.55
☐ **Norton, Andre,** *The Beast Master,* Ace G-690, no date	2.25	3.50	2.50
☐ *The Beast Master,* Ace F-315, no date	2.25	3.50	2.50
☐ *The Book Of Andre Norton,* DAW UY1198, #165, 1975	1.25	1.75	1.50
☐ *Breed To Come,* Ace 07895, 1973 . . .	1.75	2.50	2.12
☐ *Catseye,* Ace F-167, 1962	2.00	3.00	2.50
☐ *Catseye,* Ace G-654, 1967	1.75	2.25	2.00
☐ *The Crossroads Of Time,* Ace 12313, 1978, fourth edition	1.75	2.25	2.00
☐ *The Crossroads Of Time,* Ace F-391, 1966	2.00	3.00	2.50
☐ *The Crossroads of Time,* Ace 12311, no date	1.25	1.75	1.50
☐ *The Crystal Gryphon,* DAW UY1187, #75, fourth edition	1.85	2.50	2.12
☐ *The Crystal Gryphon,* DAW UQ1076, 1973	1.85	2.50	2.12
☐ *The Crystal Gryphon,* DAW UQ1076, #75, third edition	2.25	3.00	2.37
☐ *The Crystal Gryphon,* DAW UE1701, eleventh edition	2.25	3.00	2.37
☐ *Dark Piper* (signed), Crest 2-4328, 1980	2.50	3.50	2.87
☐ *Dark Piper,* Ace 13795, no date	1.75	2.50	2.12
☐ *Daybreak, 2250 A.D.,* Ace D-534, no date	2.25	3.00	2.37
☐ *Daybreak, 2250 A.D.,* Ace G-717, no date	2.00	3.00	2.50
☐ *Daybreak, 2250 A.D.,* Ace F-323, no date	2.25	3.00	2.50

	Current Price Range		C/Y Avg.

☐ *Daybreak, 2250 A.D.,* Ace F-323, no date	2.25	3.00	2.50
☐ *Daybreak, 2250 A.D.,* Ace 13994, no date	1.25	1.75	1.50
☐ *Daybreak, 2250 A.D.,* Ace, no #, no date	1.00	1.50	1.25
☐ *The Defiant Agents,* Ace F-183, no date	2.00	3.00	2.37
☐ *The Defiant Agents,* Ace 14236, 1980, seventh edition	1.75	2.50	2.12
☐ *The Defiant Agents,* Ace 14235, 1978, eighth edition	1.75	2.50	2.12
☐ *The Defiant Agents,* Ace M-150, no date.	2.50	3.25	2.87
☐ *The Defiant Agents,* Ace F-183, no date	3.00	3.75	3.12
☐ *Dragon Magic,* Ace 16644, 1980, second edition	1.75	2.50	2.12
☐ *Dread Companion,* Ace 16669, no date	1.50	2.00	1.75
☐ *Dread Companion,* Ace 16671, no date	1.50	2.00	1.75
☐ *Dread Companion,* Ace 16670, no date	1.85	2.65	2.00
☐ *Eye Of The Monster,* Ace 22375, no date	1.85	2.65	2.00
☐ *Forerunner Foray,* Ace 24622, 1980	1.85	2.50	2.00
☐ *Forerunner Foray,* Ace 24620, no date	1.25	1.75	1.50
☐ *Galactic Derelict,* Ace, F-310, no date	2.00	2.75	2.37
☐ *Galactic Derelict,* Ace D-498, no date	2.25	3.00	2.62
☐ *Garan The Eternal,* DAW UQ1045, #45, 1973	1.50	2.00	1.75
☐ *Gryphon In Glory,* Del Rey 30950, 1983	2.75	3.50	3.12
☐ *Here Abide Monsters,* DAW UY1134, #121, 1974	1.25	1.75	1.50
☐ *High Sorcery,* Ace 33704, 1979, fifth edition	1.75	2.50	2.12
☐ *High Sorcery,* Ace 33700, 1970	1.25	1.75	1.50
☐ *Horn Crown,* DAW UE1635, #440, 1981	2.25	3.25	2.75
☐ *Huon Of The Horn,* Ace F-226, no date	2.00	3.00	2.50
☐ *Huon Of The Horn,* Ace 35421, 1969, second edition	1.85	2.50	2.12
☐ *Ice Crown,* Ace 35842, no date	2.00	2.75	2.37
☐ *Ice Crown,* Ace 35840, no date	1.25	1.75	1.50

		Current Price Range		C/Y Avg.
☐	*Ice Crown,* Ace 35843, sixth edition ..	2.00	2.75	2.37
☐	*Iron Butterflies,* Crest 2-4309, 1980 ..	1.85	2.50	2.12
☐	*Iron Cage,* Ace 37290, no date	2.00	2.75	2.37
☐	*Judgment On Janus,* Ace F-308, no date	2.00	3.00	2.50
☐	*Judgment On Janus,* Ace F-308, 1964	1.75	2.50	2.12
☐	*Judgment On Janus,* Ace 41551, no date	1.25	1.75	1.50
☐	*Judgment On Janus,* Ace 41550, no date	1.75	2.50	2.12
☐	*Key Out Of Time,* Ace 43672, no date	2.00	2.75	2.37
☐	*Key Out Of Time,* Ace M-156, no date	1.75	2.50	2.12
☐	*Key Out Of Time,* Ace F-287, no date	1.50	2.25	1.87
☐	*Key Out Of Time,* Ace F-287, 1964 ..	1.35	1.85	1.50
☐	*Knave Of Dreams,* Ace 45000, no date	1.35	1.85	1.50
☐	*Knave Of Dreams,* Ace 45001, 1980	1.75	2.25	2.00
☐	*The Last Planet,* Ace F-366, no date	2.00	3.00	2.50
☐	*The Last Planet,* Ace D-542, no date	2.00	3.00	2.50
☐	*The Last Planet,* Ace M-151, no date	1.75	2.50	2.12
☐	*The Last Planet,* Ace D-96, special edition, no date	5.00	7.00	4.62
☐	*The Last Planet,* Ace 47163, no date	2.00	2.75	2.37
☐	*The Last Planet,* Ace 47161, no date	1.75	2.25	2.00
☐	*Lord Of Thunder,* Ace G-691, no date	2.00	3.00	2.50
☐	*Lord Of Thunder,* Ace 49237, no date	1.75	2.25	2.00
☐	*Lord Of Thunder,* Ace F-243, 1963 ...	2.25	3.25	2.75
☐	*Lord Of Thunder,* Ace 49236, no date	1.25	1.75	1.50
☐	*Merlin's Mirror,* DAW UY1175, #152, third edition	1.50	2.00	1.75
☐	*Merlin's Mirror,* DAW UW1340, #152, sixth edition	1.75	2.50	2.12
☐	*Merlin's Mirror,* DAW UY1175, #152, 1975	1.25	1.75	1.50
☐	*Moon Of Three Rings,* Ace H-33, no date	2.00	3.00	2.50
☐	*Moon Of Three Rings,* Ace 54102, no date	2.00	2.75	2.00
☐	*Moon Of Three Rings,* Ace 54105, no date	2.00	2.75	2.00
☐	*Moon Of Three Rings,* Ace H-33, no date	2.00	2.75	2.00

		Current Price Range		C/Y Avg.
☐	*Night Of Masks,* Ace F-365, 1965 ...	2.00	3.00	2.55
☐	*Night Of Masks,* Ace 57751, no date	1.50	2.00	1.50
☐	*Night Of Masks,* Ace 57752, 1973, third edition	1.50	2.00	1.50
☐	*No Night Without Stars,* Crest 2-3264, sixth edition	2.00	2.75	2.00
☐	*Operation Time Search,* Ace 63410, no date	2.00	2.75	2.00
☐	*Ordeal In Otherwhere,* Ace F-325, 1965	2.00	2.75	2.37
☐	*Ordeal In Otherwhere,* Ace 63821, no date	1.25	1.75	1.50
☐	*Ordeal In Otherwhere,* Ace F-325, no date	1.50	2.00	1.75
☐	*Outside,* Avon Camelot 26211, 1976	2.00	3.00	2.50
☐	*Perilous Dreams,* DAW UY1237, #196, 1976	1.25	1.75	1.50
☐	*Perilous Dreams,* DAW UE 1405, fourth edition	1.75	2.50	2.12
☐	*Plague Ship,* Ace F-291, no date	2.00	3.00	2.50
☐	*Plague Ship,* Ace 66832, 1973, third edition	1.25	1.75	1.50
☐	*Plague Ship,* Magnet 88280, 1979 ...	2.00	3.00	2.50
☐	*Plague Ship,* Ace 66836, no date	1.75	2.50	2.12
☐	*Postmarked The Stars,* Ace 67555, no date	1.50	2.00	1.76
☐	*Quest Crosstime,* Ace 69683, no date	2.00	2.75	2.37
☐	*Quest Crosstime,* Ace 69684, 1981 ..	2.00	3.00	2.50
☐	*Quest Crosstime,* Ace G-595, 1966 ..	1.75	2.50	2.12
☐	*Sargasso Of Space,* Magnet 88290, 1979	2.35	3.25	2.50
☐	*Sargasso Of Space,* Ace 74985, 1981	2.25	3.25	2.50
☐	*Sargasso Of Space,* Ace F-279, no date	1.35	1.85	1.50
☐	*Sea Siege,* Ace 75695, no date	1.35	1.85	1.50
☐	*Sea Siege,* Crest 204293, 1980	1.35	1.85	1.50
☐	*Secret Of The Lost Race,* Ace 75830, no date	1.75	2.25	2.00
☐	*Shadow Hawk,* Ace G-538, no date ..	2.00	3.00	2.50
☐	*The Sioux Spaceman,* Ace F-408, 1966	2.00	3.00	2.50
☐	*The Sioux Spaceman,* Ace 76802, no date	2.00	2.75	2.00

		Current Price Range		C/Y Avg.
☐	*The Sioux Spaceman*, Ace 76801, no date	2.00	2.75	2.00
☐	*Sorceress Of The Witch World*, Ace 77551, no date	2.00	2.75	2.00
☐	*Sorceress Of The Witch World*, Ace 77556, 1978	2.00	2.75	2.00
☐	*Sorceress Of The Witch World*, Tandem 5055, 1970	2.25	3.25	2.50
☐	*Sorceress Of The Witch World*, Ace H-84, 1968	2.25	3.25	2.50
☐	*Spell Of The Witch World*, DAW UQ1001, #1, 1972	1.85	2.35	2.00
☐	*Spell Of The Witch World*, DAW UY1179, #1, fifth edition	1.85	2.35	2.00
☐	*Star Born*, Ace 78016, ninth edition	1.85	2.35	2.00
☐	*Star Gate*, Ace F-231, no date	2.00	3.00	2.50
☐	*Star Gate*, Ace F-231, 1963	1.75	2.25	2.00
☐	*Star Gate*, Ace 78072, no date	1.25	1.75	1.50
☐	*Star Gate*, Ace M-157, no date	2.00	3.00	2.50
☐	*Star Guard*, Ace D-527, no date	3.50	4.75	4.12
☐	*Star Guard*, Ace G-599, 1966	2.00	2.75	2.37
☐	*Warlock Of The Witch World*, Ace 87319, no date	1.75	2.50	2.12
☐	*Warlock Of The Witch World*, Ace G-30, 1967	1.75	2.50	2.12
☐	*Web Of The Witch World*, Ace F-263, 1964	2.00	3.00	2.50
☐	*Web Of The Witch World*, Ace 87875, eighth edition	12.75	2.50	2.12
☐	*Web Of The Witch World*, Ace G-716, no date	2.00	3.00	2.50
☐	*Witch World*, Ace 89703, no date	1.75	2.50	2.12
☐	*Witch World*, Ace 89701, no date	2.00	2.75	2.37
☐	*Witch World*, Ace F-197, 1963	3.00	3.75	3.25
☐	*Wraiths Of Time*, Crest 2-3532, no date	1.75	2.50	2.12
☐	*Wraiths Of Time*, Crest 2-3532, second edition	1.50	2.00	1.75
☐	*Wraiths Of Time*, Crest 2-3532, second edition	1.75	2.50	2.12
☐	*The X Factor*, Ace G-646, 1967	1.75	2.50	2.00
☐	*The X Factor*, Ace 92551, no date	1.50	2.00	1.75

		Current Price Range		C/Y Avg.
☐	*The X Factor,* Ace 92553, no date ...	1.75	2.25	2.00
☐	*Year Of The Unicorn,* Ace F-357, 1965	1.50	2.00	1.75
☐	*Year Of The Unicorn,* Ace 94252, no date	1.75	2.50	2.12
☐	*Year Of The Unicorn,* Tandem 5063, 1970	2.00	2.75	2.37
☐	*Year Of The Unicorn,* Ace 94255, 1981, sixth edition	2.00	3.00	2.50
☐	*Year Of The Unicorn,* Ace F-357, 1965	2.50	3.25	2.75
☐	*Year Of The Unicorn,* Ace 94251, no date	1.75	2.50	2.12
☐	*Year Of The Unicorn,* Ace 94255, 1979, fifth edition	1.75	2.25	2.00
☐	*Yurth Burden,* DAW UE1400, #304, 1978	1.50	2.00	1.75
☐	*Zarsthor's Bane,* Ace 95490, 1978 ...	1.85	2.35	2.00
☐	*The Zero Stone,* Ace 95961, no date	1.85	2.35	2.00
☐	**Nyn, Nelson C.,** *Gunfight at the O.K. Corral,* Hillman 164 (painted cover picturing Burt Lancaster). This was the fictionalized account of the famous encounter between Doc Holliday and the Earp Brothers with a band of desperados. It did not occur in a corral, but in a street alley, and at the subsequent hearings some interesting facts were learned: Doc Holliday was carrying a rifle, contrary to local law; one of the Earps was shooting at an unarmed man; and several of the Earps were shooting at a man who lay on the sidewalk.	6.00	8.00	6.70
☐	**O'Bannon, Brian,** *Instant Love,* Beacon 652	2.20	3.00	2.47
☐	**O'Brien, John A.,** *Winning Converts,* Notre Dame University Press (no serial number), 1957	2.00	2.50	2.21
☐	**O'Connor, Frank,** *Stories by Frank O'Connor,* Vintage V29	2.00	2.50	2.23
☐	**O'Connor, Richard,** *Bat Masterson,* Bantam 1968 (painted cover picturing Gene Barry). There really was a Bat Masterson. After gaining a reputation as			

	Current Price Range		C/Y Avg.

a sheriff in Arizona, he opened a gambling house, became a sports writer, and finally retired to New York City. He turned down an offer to go back into law enforcement because, as he put it, "a lot of people would want to shoot me just so they could say they shot Bat Masterson." **5.00 6.50 5.75**

☐ **O'Connor, Richard,** *Down To Eternity,* Gold Medal S550, 1956 . . . . **2.75 3.75 3.12**

☐ **O'Hara, Ralph C.,** *The Divorcee,* Monarch 519 (cover artwork by Maguire, 1962) **4.00 5.00 4.50**

☐ **Oliver, Douglas L.,** *Invitation to Anthropology,* American Museum Science Books B9 . . . . **2.00 2.50 2.20**

☐ **Omarr, Sydney,** *My Bed Has Echoes,* Fabian Z-113, no date **1.75 2.50 2.12**

☐ **O'Neal, Cothburn,** *Gods of Our Time,* Crest 443 . . . . **3.00 3.75 3.31**

☐ **O'Neill, Eugene,** *Desire Under the Elms,* Signet 1502 (photo cover picturing Sophia Loren, Tony Perkins and Burl Ives) **9.00 12.00 10.50**

☐ **O'Rourke, Frank,** *Bandoleer Crossing,* Ballantime 496, 1961 . . . . **4.00 5.00 4.30**

☐ **Orwell, George,** *A Collection of Essays,* Anchor 29 . . . . **2.00 2.50 2.20**

☐ **Osborne, O. O.,** *The Rise and Fall of Dr. Carey,* Gold Medal 1174 . . . . **2.50 3.25 2.81**

☐ *Rise and Fall of Dr. Carey,* Gold Medal 576A, 1958 . . . . **1.00 1.50 1.25**

☐ **O'Shea, Sean,** *Operation Boudoir,* Belmont #850-760 . . . . **1.50 2.00 1.75**

☐ **Otha, T.,** *The Golden Wind,* Boni Books, no serial number, 1929 (Boni Books was the paperback division of Boni and Liveright, one of the major publishers of that era.) **4.00 6.00 4.00**

☐ **Otis, James,** *Toby Tyler,* Books Inc. 64, 1939 . . . . **1.00 1.50 1.15**

☐ **Oursler, Will and Laurence D. Smith,** *Hooked: Narcotics, America's Peril,* Popular Library 528 . . . . **15.00 20.00 16.25**

	Current Price Range		C/Y Avg.

☐ **Overholser, Wayne,** *Hearn's Valley,* Dell D400 (cover artwork by Stanley) **3.50 4.25 3.77**

☐ *Violent Land,* Dell 875, no date **3.00 4.00 3.37**

☐ **Owen, Dean,** *The End of the World,* Ace D548 (photo cover picturing Ray Milland, Jean Hagen and Frankie Avalon. Jean Hagen played Danny Thomas' wife on "Make Room for Daddy.") **4.00 5.50 4.65**

☐ *Pistol Belt,* Monarch 204 (cover artwork by Stanley, 1961) **3.75 4.50 4.07**

☐ *Rawhider From Texas,* Monarch 401 (cover artwork by Thurston) **3.00 3.75 3.30**

☐ *Rebel of the Broken Wheel,* Monarch 218, 1961 .... **1.75 2.50 2.12**

☐ *The Sam Houston Story,* Monarch 308 (cover artwork by Ross) **3.50 4.25 3.80**

☐ **Owen, Ralph,** *One Kind Of Women,* Beacon #8657F **1.00 1.50 1.25**

☐ **Ozaki, Milton,** *Inquest,* Gold Medal 981 (cover artwork by Phillips, 1960) **4.00 5.00 4.40**

☐ **Packard, Vance,** *The Status Seekers,* Cardinal GC601. In both hardcover and paperback this was one of the best selling novels of the 1960s. **1.50 2.00 1.75**

☐ **Packer, Peter,** *Dark Surrender,* Popular Library G444 .... **2.75 3.50 3.07**

☐ **Packer, Vin,** *The Girl on the Best Seller,* Gold Medal 976 (cover artwork by McGinnis, 1960) **4.00 5.00 4.42**

☐ **Page, Patti,** *Once Upon a Dream,* Popular Library G496 .... **4.00 5.25 4.51**

☐ **Palmer, Bernard,** *The Orlis Twins,* Moody 43 .... **2.50 3.00 2.70**

☐ **Palmer, Bruce,** *Shattered Affair,* Avon T442 .... **2.25 3.00 2.45**

☐ **Palmer, Stuart,** *Cold Poison,* Pyramid 1040 (cover artwork by Bacon) **3.25 4.00 3.50**

☐ **Paris, John,** *Kimono,* Continental Books, no serial number, 1932 .... **2.00 2.50 2.20**

☐ **Parkes, Henry B.,** *The American Experience,* Vintage V84 .... **2.50 3.25 2.80**

	Current Price Range		C/Y Avg.

☐ **Parkhurst, Helen,** *Undertow,* Monarch
494 . . . . 2.00 2.50 2.21
☐ **Parrington, Vernon L.,** *The Colonial Mind,* Harvest 4 . . . . 2.00 3.00 2.75
☐ *The Romantic Revolution,* Harvest 5 2.50 3.00 2.75
☐ **Partch, Virgil,** *Vip Tosses a Party,* Crest 394. Virgil Partch died in an auto crash in 1984. . . . . 7.00 10.00 8.50
☐ **Patrick, Q.,** *The Grindle Nightmare,* Ballantine F722, 1963 . . . . 3.00 4.00 3.50
☐ *Murder At Cambridge,* Popular, 263, no date 2.00 2.50 2.12
☐ *Return To The Scene,* Popular 47, no date 8.00 11.00 8.00
☐ **Patten, Lewis B.,** *Angry Horseman,* Hillman 144 . . . . 3.00 3.75 3.29
☐ **Patterson, Harry,** *To Catch A King,* Crest 2-4323, 1980 . . . . 2.00 3.00 2.50
☐ *The Valhalla Exchange,* Arrow 915910, 1977 . . . . 1.75 2.75 2.25
☐ **Patterson, James,** *The Jericho Commandment,* Ballantine 29241, 1981 . . . . 2.00 3.00 2.50
☐ **Patterson, Robert,** *Gold Is The Color Of Blood,* Ballantine 371K, 1960 . . . . 3.00 4.25 3.62
☐ **Pattinson, James,** *Contact Mr. Delgado,* Corgi SN823, 1960 . . . . 5.50 7.25 5.75
☐ *Feast Of The Scorpion,* Fleetway Thriller 3, 1977 . . . . 2.00 2.75 2.37
☐ **Paul, Elliot,** *Hugger-Mugger In The Louvre,* Pocket 151, 1942 . . . . 8.00 11.00 8.00
☐ *Hugger-Mugger In The Louvre,* Ballantine F624, no date 2.25 3.00 2.50
☐ *Mayhem In B Flat,* Bantam 850, 1950 2.25 3.00 2.50
☐ *Mayhem In B Flat,* Collier AS245V, 1962 . . . . 1.75 2.50 2.12
☐ *Mysterious Mickey Finn,* Murder Of The Month 2, 1942 . . . . 15.00 20.00 15.50
☐ **Paul, Gene,** *The Big Make,* Lion LL 158, 1957, second edition 3.00 4.00 3.50
☐ **Paul, Hugo,** *The Smashers,* Lancer 72936, 1965 . . . . 2.00 2.75 2.12

	Current Price Range		C/Y Avg.
☐ **Paul, Jessyca**, *Passport To Danger*, Award A303X, 1968	1.35	1.85	1.50
☐ *Rendezvous With Death*, Award A489X, 1969	2.00	2.75	2.12
☐ **Payne, Laurence**, *The First Body*, Avon G1225, no date	2.00	3.00	2.50
☐ *The Nose On My Face*, Penguin C2111, 1964	3.00	4.00	3.25
☐ **Payne, Robert**, *The Barbarian and the Geisha*, Signet 1513 (painted cover picturing John Wayne)	4.50	6.00	5.21
☐ **Pearl, Jack**, *Battleground World War I*, Monarch 24, 1964. This was not the Jack Pearl who starred as "Baron Munchausen" on radio.	3.25	4.25	3.63
☐ *Blood and Guts Patton*, Monarch 305, 1961	2.00	2.50	2.20
☐ *The Crucifixion Of Peter McCabe*, Pocket 75277, 1968	1.75	2.50	2.12
☐ *Our Man Flint*, Pocket 50243, 1965 . .	2.00	3.00	2.50
☐ *Robin And The 7 Hoods*, Pocket 50033, 1964	2.25	3.25	2.70
☐ *A Time To Kill. . . .A Time To Die*, Manor 95-206, 1972	1.35	1.85	1.50
☐ *Victims*, Pocket 77639, 1973	1.35	1.85	1.50
☐ **Pearson, William**, *The Beautiful Frame*, Pocket 1039, 1954	2.75	3.50	3.12
☐ *Hunt The Man Down*, Pocket 1141, 1956	2.50	3.25	2.87
☐ **Pease, Howard**, *The Tattooed Man*, Comet 10, 1948, second edition	7.00	10.00	7.50
☐ **Peck, David W.**, *The Greer Case*, Penguin C1889, 1963	2.00	3.00	2.50
☐ **Peebles, Niles N.**, *See The Red Blood Run*, Pyramid R-1772, 1968	1.75	2.50	2.12
☐ **Pendower, Jacques**, *Betrayed*, Paperback Library 53-481, 1967	1.75	2.50	2.12
☐ *Mission Tunis*, Paperback Library 53496, no copy	1.25	1.75	1.50
☐ **Pentecost, Hugh**, *The 24th Horse*, Popular 82, 1946	8.00	11.00	8.75

		Current Price Range		C/Y Avg.
☐	*Birthday Deathday*, Pyramid T3115, 1973	1.25	1.75	1.50
☐	*Dead Woman Of The Year*, Zebra 0027, 1974	1.75	2.50	2.12
☐	*Death After Breakfast*, Dell 11687, 1980	1.75	2.50	2.00
☐	*The Girl With Six Fingers*, Zebra 0031, 1974	1.36	1.85	1.50
☐	*Hide Her From Every Eye*, Zebra 0014, 1974	1.35	1.85	1.50
☐	*I'll Sing At Your Funeral*, Popular 109, 1947	7.50	10.00	8.25
☐	*A Plague Of Violence*, Pinnacle 22–451, 1974	1.85	2.75	2.12
☐	*Random Killer*, Dell 17210, 1981	1.75	2.75	2.12
☐	*Sniper*, Zebra 0012, 1974	1.85	2.75	2.12
☐	*The Tarnished Angel*, Avon G 1276, 1965	2.50	3.50	3.00
☐	**Pepis, Betty,** *Be Your Own Decorator*, Pyramid XRL8	2.00	2.50	2.18
☐	**Perdue, Lewis,** *The Delphi Betrayal*, Pinnacle 41-139, 1981	2.00	2.75	2.25
☐	**Perdue, Virginia,** *The Singing Clock*, Mercury Mystery 1961, no date	4.25	5.75	4.62
☐	**Perowne, Barry,** *10 Words Of Poison*, Green Dragon 13, no date	10.00	14.00	10.65
☐	**Persico, Joseph,** *The Spiderweb*, Bantam 14334, 1981	2.00	2.50	2.12
☐	**Perutz, Leo,** *Master Of The Day Of Judgment*, Collier AS528V, 1963	2.00	2.50	2.12
☐	**Petaja, Emil,** *The Caves of Mars*, Ace M133, 1965	3.50	4.25	3.75
☐	*The Stolen Sun*, Ace G618 (cover artwork by Gaughan, 1966)	3.25	4.00	3.39
☐	**Peters, Bryan,** *Hong Kong Kill*, Belmont 209, 1960	2.50	3.25	2.87
☐	**Peters, Ellis,** *Death And The Joyful Woman*, Avon G-1180, 1964, second edition	1.50	2.00	1.75
☐	*Death And The Joyful Woman*, Avon G-1180, 1963	2.00	3.00	2.50

	Current Price Range		C/Y Avg.
☐ *The Knocker On Death's Door,* Dell 4595, 1972	1.25	1.75	1.50
☐ *The Piper On The Mountain,* Lancer 73-648, 1968	1.25	1.75	1.50
☐ **Peters, Ron,** *Stash Spots A Murder,* Curtis 07292, 1973	1.25	1.75	1.50
☐ **Petersen, Herman,** *The D.A.'s Daughter,* Harlequin 17, 1949	7.25	9.50	7.50
☐ *Old Bones,* Dell Map 127, 1946	7.75	10.50	8.25
☐ **Pettit, Mike,** *The Axmann Agenda,* Dell 10152, 1980	2.25	3.25	2.70
☐ **Phelps, William Lyon,** (ED), *PB Of Mystery Stories,* Pocket 117, 1942, eighth edition	2.00	2.75	2.37
☐ (ED), *PB Of Mystery Stories,* Pocket 117, 1941	3.00	4.00	3.50
☐ *(ED), PB of Mystery Stories,* Pocket 117, 1941, third edition	3.00	4.00	3.50
☐ *(ED), PB Of Mystery Stories,* Pocket 117, 1943, ninth edition	2.75	3.75	3.26
☐ (ED), *PB Of Mystery Stories,* Pocket 117, 1944, tenth edition	5.50	7.00	5.75
☐ (ED), *PB Of Mystery Stories,* Pocket 117, 1945, eleventh edition	5.00	6.50	5.00
☐ **Philips, Judson,** *Murder Clear Track Fast,* Perma M-4273, 1962	1.75	2.50	2.12
☐ **Phillips, Clyde B.,** *The Driver,* DAW 27295, 1978	1.50	2.00	1.75
☐ **Phillips, David Atlee,** *The Carlos Contract,* Ballantine 28370, 1980	1.25	1.75	1.50
☐ **Phillips, James Atlee,** *The Deadly Mermaid,* Dell 26, 1954, first edition	3.50	4.50	4.00
☐ *Suitable For Framing,* Pocket 725, 1950	4.00	5.00	4.50
☐ **Phillips, Leon,** *The Hothead,* Pocket Books 6034, 1960	3.75	4.50	4.13
☐ **Phillips, Mark,** *Brain Twister,* Pyramid 783, cover artwork by Schoenherr	2.75	3.50	2.89
☐ **Pia, Pascal,** *Baudelaire,* Grove P22	3.25	4.00	3.42
☐ **Pierce, John R.,** *Electrons and Waves,* Anchor S38	3.00	3.75	3.36

	Current Price Range		C/Y Avg.

☐ **Piper, H. Beam,** *The Cosmic Computer,* Ace F274 .... | 3.25 | 4.00 | 3.41

☐ **Plantz, Donald,** *Marked For Death,* Monarch 449 (cover artwork by DeSoto, 1964) .... | 3.50 | 4.25 | 3.80

☐ **Potter, Charles F.,** *Faiths Men Live By,* Ace K101 .... | 1.75 | 2.25 | 2.00

☐ **Potter, J.L.,** *Murder For Free,* Chicago Paperback House 104 (cover artwork by Cloutier, 1962) .... | 3.75 | 4.50 | 4.11

☐ **Potts, Jean,** *Lightning Strikes Twice,* Dell R120 (cover artwork by Teason) ...... | 3.00 | 3.75 | 3.29

☐ **Powell, Talmadge,** *Start Screaming Murder,* Perma 4251 .... | 2.00 | 2.50 | 2.18

☐ **Praskins, Leonard,** *Three Violent People,* Gold Medal 615 (photo cover picturing Charlton Heston, Anne Baxter and Gilbert Roland) .... | 5.50 | 7.00 | 6.15

☐ **Prather, Richard S.,** *Dagger of Flesh,* Gold Medal 1157 .... | 2.00 | 2.50 | 2.19

☐ *Bodies In Bedlam,* Gold Medal 496, 1957, fifth edition .... | 1.85 | 2.65 | 2.12

☐ *Dance With the Dead,* Gold Medal 990, 1960 .... | 2.75 | 3.50 | 2.98

☐ *Dead Heat,* Pocket Books 4801 (cover artwork by Phillips) .... | 5.00 | 6.50 | 5.62

☐ *Dead Man's Walk,* Pocket Books 50177 (cover artwork by Phillips, 1965) | 3.00 | 4.00 | 3.50

☐ *Dig That Crazy Grave,* Gold Medal 1144 (cover artwork by Phillips, 1961) | 3.00 | 3.75 | 3.25

☐ *Dig That Crazy Grave,* Gold Medal 1298 .... | 2.25 | 3.00 | 2.41

☐ *Everybody Had a Gun,* Gold Medal 1402 (cover artwork by Phillips) ..... | 2.00 | 2.75 | 2.26

☐ *Joker in the Deck,* Gold Medal 1376 (cover artwork by Phillips, 1964) .... | 2.00 | 2.75 | 2.25

☐ *Kill the Clown,* Gold Medal 1208 (cover artwork by Hooks, 1962) .... | 2.50 | 3.25 | 2.80

☐ *The Kubla Khan Caper,* Pocket Books 50535 .... | 2.00 | 2.50 | 2.15

☐ *Lie Down Killer,* Gold Medal 1166 (cover artwork by Phillips) .... | 2.50 | 3.25 | 2.69

		Current Price Range		C/Y Avg.

☐ *Pattern For Panic,* Gold Medal 1092 (cover artwork by Phillips) **2.50** **3.25** **2.84**

☐ *Shell Scott's Seven Slaughters,* Gold Medal 1287 .... **2.00** **2.50** **2.19**

☐ *Take a Murder,* Gold Medal 1129 (cover artwork by Phillips) **2.50** **3.25** **2.89**

☐ *Three's A Shroud,* Gold Medal 1060 **2.75** **3.50** **2.95**

☐ *The Trojan Hearse,* Pocket Books 45020 (cover artwork by Phillips, 1964) **2.75** **3.50** **2.95**

☐ *Way of a Wanton,* Gold Medal 1032 **2.75** **3.50** **2.91**

☐ **Pratt, Fletcher,** *Alien Planet,* Ace F257 **3.25** **4.00** **3.49**

☐ **Pratt, Theodore,** *Escape To Eden* Gold Medal S339, 1953 .... **1.85** **2.65** **2.12**

☐ *Handsome,* Gold Medal 1518 .... **2.50** **3.25** **2.90**

☐ **Pressley, Hilda,** *There Came a Surgeon,* Harlequin 900 .... **2.00** **2.50** **2.12**

☐ **Preston, Charles,** *Office Laffs,* Crest 159 **6.00** **8.00** **6.70**

☐ **Preston, Lillian,** *Sex Habits of Single Women,* Beacon 748 .... **3.00** **3.75** **3.31**

☐ **Priest, J.C.,** *Private School,* Beacon 8269 .... **1.85** **2.65** **2.12**

☐ **Proctor, Maurice,** *The Devil Was Handsome,* Pyramid R-1191, 1965 .... **2.25** **3.00** **2.50**

☐ *Devil's Due,* Collier ASS66Y, 1961 ... **1.85** **2.65** **2.12**

☐ *The Graveyard Rolls,* Popular 02506, no date **1.85** **2.65** **2.12**

☐ *His Weight In Gold,* Popular 02557, no date **1.85** **2.65** **2.12**

☐ *Murder Somewhere In This City,* Avon 696, 1956 .... **3.00** **4.00** **3.50**

☐ *The Pub Crawler,* Pyramid R-1138, 1965 .... **2.00** **2.75** **2.37**

☐ *Rogue Running,* Popular 02558, no date **1.75** **2.50** **2.12**

☐ *Three At The Angel,* Popular 02505, no date **1.75** **2.50** **2.12**

☐ *Somewhere in This City,* Pyramid 1082 (cover artwork by Bacon) **2.00** **2.50** **2.25**

☐ **Pronzini, Bill and Halzberg,** *Acts Of Mercy,* Tower 51617, no date **1.50** **2.25** **1.87**

☐ *Blowback,* Dale 01154, no date **1.25** **1.75** **1.50**

☐ *Night Screams,* Playboy 16788, 1981 **2.00** **3.00** **2.50**

	Current Price Range		C/Y Avg.

☐ *Panic!* Pocket 77676, 1976, fourth edition **1.35** **1.85** **1.50**

☐ *The Snatch,* Pocket 77663, 1973, second edition **1.35** **1.85** **1.50**

☐ *Snowbound,* Crest Q2408, 1975 ..... **1.35** **1.85** **1.50**

☐ *The Stalker,* Pocket 77635, 1974, fourth edition **1.35** **1.85** **1.50**

☐ *The Vanished,* Pocket 77714, 1974 .. **1.35** **1.85** **1.50**

☐ *The Vanished,* Pocket 77714, 1974, second edition **1.35** **1.85** **1.50**

☐ **Propper, Milton,** *Case Of The Cheating Bride,* Black Cat 5, 1943 .... **7.00** **9.75** **7.50**

☐ *The Great Insurance Murders,* Prize Mystery 7, 1943 .... **5.85** **7.50** **6.00**

☐ **Pruitt, Alan,** *The Restless Corpse,* Handi-Book 104, 1950 .... **5.85** **7.50** **6.00**

☐ **Pugh, John J.,** *High Carnival,* Ace K170 **2.50** **3.25** **2.79**

☐ **Punshon, E.R.,** *Information Received,* Penguin 1084, 1955 .... **2.50** **3.50** **3.00**

☐ **Purdy, James,** *Malcolm,* Avon T465 (cover artwork by Powers) **3.00** **3.75** **3.32**

☐ **Purvis, Melvin H.,** *The Violent Years,* Hillman 157 .... **2.25** **3.00** **2.42**

☐ **Puzo, Mario,** *The Godfather,* Crest 01388, 1970 .... **1.75** **2.50** **2.12**

☐ **Quandt, Albert L.,** *Zip-Gun Angels,* Original 1952 .... **5.50** **7.00** **5.62**

☐ **Quarry, Nick,** *The Don Is Dead,* Gold Medal T2527, 1972 .... **1.25** **1.75** **1.50**

☐ *The Hoods Come Calling,* Gold Medal 747, 1958 .... **2.50** **3.50** **3.00**

☐ *No Chance In Hell,* Gold Medal 1033, 1960 .... **1.75** **2.50** **2.12**

☐ *Some Die Hard,* Gold Medal S1150, 1961 .... **2.50** **3.25** **2.87**

☐ *Till It Hurts,* Gold Medal 1053, 1960 .. **1.50** **2.25** **1.87**

☐ *Trail Of A Tramp,* Gold Medal 824, 1958 .... **2.00** **2.75** **2.37**

☐ **Queen, Ellery,** *Adventures Of Ellery Queen,* Readers' League, no date **8.00** **11.00** **8.00**

☐ *Adventures Of Ellery Queen,* Signet T4488, 1971 .... **1.75** **2.50** **2.12**

Left to Right: **The Siamese Twin Mystery**, by Ellery
Queen, Pocket Book, 6135, **$3.25–$4.50**;
The Roman Hat Mystery, by Ellery Queen,
Pocket Book, 6134, **$2.50–$3.25**.

		Current Price Range		C/Y Avg.
☐	American Gun Mystery, Mercury Mystery 42, no date	5.00	7.00	5.25
☐	The American Gun Mystery, Mercury Mystery 164, no date	4.50	6.00	4.62
☐	American Gun Mystery, Dell Map 4, 1943	10.00	14.00	10.50
☐	American Gun Mystery, Dell Map 4, 1943	8.00	11.00	8.00
☐	The American Gun Mystery, Avon 523, 1953	6.00	8.00	6.25
☐	American Gun Mystery, Ballantine 25334, 1976, second edition	1.25	1.75	1.50
☐	And On The Eighth Day, Pocket 50209, 1967, second edition	1.75	2.50	2.12

		Current Price Range		C/Y Avg.
☐	*And On The Eighth Day,* Pocket 50209, 1966	2.00	2.75	2.37
☐	*And On The Eighth Day,* Ballantine 28291, 1979, third edition	1.50	2.25	1.87
☐	*Beware The Young Stranger,* Pocket 50489, 1965	2.00	3.00	2.50
☐	*The Black Hearts Murder,* Magnum 74640, no date	1.25	1.75	1.50
☐	*The Black Hearts Murder,* Lancer 74640, no date	1.75	2.50	2.12
☐	*Blow Hot Blow Cold,* Pocket 45007, 1964	2.00	2.75	2.37
☐	*Calendar Of Crime,* Signet Q5166, 1972	1.50	2.25	1.87
☐	*Calendar Of Crime,* Pocket 960, 1957, second edition	2.50	3.50	3.00
☐	*Cat Of Many Tails,* Cardinal C-357, 1959	2.00	3.00	2.50
☐	*Cat Of Many Tails,* Pocket 822, 1952, second edition	3.00	4.00	3.12
☐	*Cat Of Many Tails,* Bantam F3026, 1965	1.50	2.25	1.87
☐	*The Chinese Orange Mystery,* Pocket 17, 1943, twentieth edition	4.50	6.00	4.75
☐	*Cop Out,* Signet T4196, 1970	2.00	2.75	2.37
☐	*Cop Out,* Signet Y6996, 1970	1.25	1.75	1.50
☐	*The Copper Frame,* Pocket 50490, 1965	2.50	3.25	2.87
☐	*Dead Man's Tale,* Pocket 6117, 1961	2.00	2.75	2.37
☐	*Death Spins The Platter,* Signet T5507, 1973	1.50	2.25	1.87
☐	*Death Spins The Platter,* Pocket 6126, 1962	1.75	2.50	2.12
☐	*The Devil To Pay,* Pocket 270, 1945, fifth edition	4.00	5.50	4.00
☐	*The Devil To Pay,* Signet T4657, 1971	1.25	1.75	1.50
☐	*The Door Between,* Pocket 45014, 1964, fifth edition	2.25	3.00	2.62
☐	*The Door Between,* American Mercury 32, no date	7.00	10.00	7.37
☐	*The Door Between,* Pocket 471, 1952, third edition	3.00	4.00	3.50

	Current Price Range		C/Y Avg.
☐ *Double Double,* Pocket 874, 1953, second edition	2.50	3.25	2.87
☐ *The Dragon's Teeth,* Mercury Mystery 57, no date	5.00	6.50	5.25
☐ *The Dragon's Teeth,* Pocket 459, 1947	5.00	6.50	5.25
☐ *The Dutch Shoe Mystery,* Pocket 202, 1952, tenth edition	2.00	3.00	2.50
☐ *The Egyptian Cross Mystery,* Bestseller B17, no date	4.50	6.00	5.00
☐ *The Egyptian Cross Mystery,* Penguin C1842, 1964, second edition	2.25	3.00	2.62
☐ *The Egyptian Cross Mystery,* Pocket 227, 1945, fifth edition	4.00	5.50	4.25
☐ *The Egyptian Cross Mystery,* Pocket 6017, 1960, tenth edition	1.75	2.50	2.12
☐ *The Finishing Stroke,* Signet P3142, 1967	2.00	2.75	2.37
☐ *The Finishing Stroke,* Pocket 4702, 1963, third edition	1.75	2.50	2.12
☐ *The Finishing Stroke,* Cardinal C-343, 1959	2.00	1.75	2.37
☐ *The Four Of Hearts,* Signet T4422, 1970	1.75	2.50	2.12
☐ *The Four Of Hearts,* Pocket 245, 1943	6.00	8.00	6.12
☐ *Four Of Hearts,* Mercury Mystery 47, no date	3.00	4.00	3.50
☐ *The Four Of Hearts,* Avon T-242, 1958	1.50	2.25	1.87
☐ *Fourth Side Of The Triangle,* Pocket 50508, 1967	1.50	2.25	1.87
☐ *Fourth Side Of Triangle,* Ballantine 28288, 1979, third edition	1.45	1.85	1.50
☐ **Quentin, Patrick,** *Suspicious Circumstances,* Dell D394, no date (cover artwork by Maguire)	2.00	3.00	2.35
☐ **Quinn, Vernon,** *Fifty Card Games for Children,* Whitman (no serial number) 1946	3.00	4.00	3.29
☐ **Rabe, Peter,** *Murder Me For Nickels,* Gold Medal 996, 1960	3.00	3.75	3.36
☐ **Rackham, John,** *Time to Live,* Ace G606 (cover artwork by Gaughan)	3.75	4.50	4.14

	Current Price Range		C/Y Avg.

☐ **Rainwater, Coleman,** *Workingman's Wife,* MacFadden 75–101 . . . . — 2.50 — 3.25 — 2.76

☐ **Rand, Matt,** *Gun-Hell at Big Bend,* Belmont 267 . . . . — 2.50 — 3.25 — 2.81

☐ **Rand, Steve,** *All Her Vices,* Monarch 193, 1961 . . . . — 1.35 — 1.85 — 1.50

☐ *All Her Vices,* Monarch 193 (cover artwork by Marchetti, 1961) . . . . — 4.00 — 5.00 — 4.50

☐ **Randolph, Terry,** *Registered Nurse,* Berkley 513 . . . . — 2.00 — 2.50 — 2.21

☐ **Raspail, Jean,** *Welcome Honorable Visitors,* Crest 430 (cover artwork by Hooks) — 2.56 — 3.25 — 2.81

☐ **Rattigan, Terence,** *The Prince and the Showgirl,* Signet 1409 (photo cover picturing Marilyn Monroe and Laurence Olivier) . . . . — 10.00 — 14.00 — 12.00

☐ **Rawson, Tabor,** *I Want To Love,* Signet 1567 (photo cover picturing Susan Hayward) . . . . — 5.00 — 6.50 — 5.37

☐ **Reagan, Thomas,** *The Caper,* Berkley X1836, 1970 . . . . — 1.85 — 2.65 — 2.12

☐ **Redgate, John,** *The Killing Season,* Pocket 75270, 1969, second edition . . . — 1.85 — 2.65 — 2.12

☐ *The Last Decathlon,* Dell 14643, 1980 — 1.85 — 2.65 — 2.12

☐ **Redlich, Fritz and June Bingham,** *The Inside Story,* Vintage V99 . . . . — 2.00 — 2.50 — 2.19

☐ **Reed, Blair,** *Pass Key To Murder,* Harlequin 40, 1950 . . . . — 8.50 — 11.00 — 9.37

☐ **Reed, David V.,** *I thought I'd Die,* Green Dragon 23, no date . . . . — 8.50 — 11.00 — 9.37

☐ **Reed, Ellot,** *The Maras Affair,* Perma M-3025, 1956, second edition . . . . — 1.75 — 2.50 — 2.12

☐ *Tender To Danger,* Perma M-3005, 1955 . . . . — 2.00 — 3.00 — 2.50

☐ **Reeder, Red,** *The MacKenzie Raid,* Ballantine 460 . . . . — 2.00 — 2.50 — 2.16

☐ **Reese, John,** *Pity Us All,* Ace 66650, no date . . . . — 1.75 — 2.50 — 2.12

☐ *The Sharpshooter,* Leisure 433ZK, 1974 . . . . — 1.25 — 1.75 — 1.50

☐ **Reeves, Robert,** *Cellini Smith Detective,* Pony 54, 1946 . . . . — 8.50 — 11.00 — 9.37

	Current Price Range		C/Y Avg.

□ **Reid, Desmond,** *Frenzy In The Flesh,* MacFadden 60–353, 1968 . . . . | 2.00 | 2.75 | 2.37

□ **Reid, Ed,** *Mafia* (Non-Fiction), Signet 1151, 1954 . . . . | 5.50 | 7.00 | 5.75

□ **Reilly, Helen,** *All Concerned Notified,* Century 29, no date . . . . | 9.75 | 13.00 | 10.12

□ *The Canvas Dagger,* Manor 15259, no date . . . . | 1.25 | 1.75 | 1.50

□ *The Canvas Dagger,* Bantam 1858, 1959 . . . . | 2.00 | 3.00 | 2.50

□ *The Canvas Dagger,* MacFadden 75–349, 1970 . . . . | 1.75 | 2.50 | 2.12

□ *Certain Sleep,* Manor 95331, 1974, second edition . . . . | 1.25 | 1.75 | 1.50

□ *Compartment K,* MacFadden 75-445, 1971 . . . . | 1.50 | 2.25 | 1.87

□ *The Day She Died,* Ace G-536, no date | 1.75 | 2.50 | 2.12

□ *Dead Man Control,* American Library 5, no date . . . . | 9.00 | 12.00 | 10.50

□ *Death Demands An Audience,* Popular, 1943 . . . . | 11.00 | 15.00 | 11.50

□ *Death Demands An Audience,* Manor 95365, 1974 . . . . | 1.25 | 1.75 | 1.50

□ *Death Demands An Audience,* MacFadden 95-170, 1971, fourth edition | 1.50 | 2.25 | 1.87

□ *Death Demands An Audience,* MacFadden 60-284, 1967 . . . . | 1.75 | 2.50 | 2.12

□ *Death Demands An Audience,* MacFadden 60-413, 1969, third edition . . | 1.25 | 1.75 | 1.40

□ *Death Demands An Audience,* Popular 7, no date . . . . | 7.00 | 10.00 | 6.62

□ *The Double Man,* Dell 732, 1953 . . . . | 3.00 | 4.00 | 3.50

□ *The Line-Up,* MacFadden 60-293, 1967 . . . . | 1.75 | 2.50 | 2.12

□ *Mourned On Sunday,* Dell Map 63, no date . . . . | 3.00 | 4.00 | 3.25

□ *Mr. Smith's Hat,* MacFadden 60-312, 1968 . . . . | 1.75 | 2.50 | 2.12

□ *Mr. Smith's Hat,* Popular 48, 1945 . . . | 3.75 | 4.75 | 4.00

□ *Mr. Smith's Hat,* MacFadden 60-312, 1968 . . . . | 1.25 | 1.75 | 1.50

		Current Price Range		C/Y Avg.
☐	*Murder At Arroways,* Dell Map 576, 1952	3.75	4.75	4.00
☐	*Murder In Shinbone Alley,* MacFadden 60-328, 1968, second edition	1.50	2.25	1.87
☐	*Murder In Shinbone Alley,* Popular 20, 1943	5.00	7.00	4.87
☐	*Murder In Shinbone Alley,* Popular 20, 1943	10.00	14.00	10.50
☐	*Murder In Shinbone Alley,* MacFadden 50-209, 1964	1.75	2.25	2.00
☐	*Murder In The Mews,* MacFadden 60-266, 1966	1.75	2.25	2.00
☐	*The Opening Door,* Dell Map 200, 1947	7.00	10.00	7.00
☐	*The Opening Door,* Dell 917, 1956	3.75	4.75	4.25
☐	*The Silver Leopard,* Dell Map 287, 1949	8.50	11100	8.75
☐	*Staircase 4,* Dell Map 498, 1950	5.00	6.50	5.12
☐	*Tell Her It's Murder,* Bestseller Mystery B201, no date	4.00	5.00	4.50
☐	*Three Women In Black,* Dell Map 114, 1946	10.00	14.00	10.50
☐	**Reisner, Mary,** *Black Hazard,* Belmont B50-693, 1966	2.00	2.75	2.37
☐	*The House Of Cobwebs,* Armed Services Q-22, 1944	7.00	10.00	7.50
☐	**Remarque, E.M.,** *All Quiet On The Western Front,* Lion LL-81, 1956, second edition	1.75	2.50	2.12
☐	**Renault, Mary,** *The King Must Die,* Cardinal GC78 (cover artwork by Hill)	2.00	2.50	2.19
☐	*Return To Night,* Dell 394, no date	2.00	2.75	2.37
☐	**Reynolds, Mack,** *Episode on the Riviera,* Monarch 205 (cover artwork by Schaare)	4.00	5.00	4.37
☐	*The Jet Set,* Monarch 405 (cover artwork by Miller)	3.50	4.25	3.87
☐	**Reynolds, Quentin,** *70,000 To One,* Pyramid 545	3.00	3.75	3.28
☐	**Rhodes, Frank,** *Geology,* Golden Press 24349	2.00	2.50	2.18
☐	**Richard, Louis,** *Artist's Woman,* Beacon #8678X	1.50	2.00	1.75

	Current Price Range		C/Y Avg.

☐ **Richards, Lee,** *The Eager Beavers,* Beacon 628 .... 2.50 3.25 2.71

☐ **Richards, Rick,** *Motel Hostess,* Midwood 124, 1961 .... 3.50 4.75 3.62

☐ **Richelfelder, William,** *A Seed Upon The Wind,* Berkley #G-7 .... 1.50 2.00 1.75

☐ **Richmond, Roe,** *The Hard Men,* Pyramid 755 (cover artwork by Leone) 3.00 3.75 3.32

☐ **Richmond, Walter and Leigh Richmond,** *Gallagher's Glacier,* Ace 27235 (cover artwork by Freas). Frank K. Freas, the cover artist, was a frequent contributor to Mad Magazine. 4.00 5.00 4.50

☐ **Richter, Conrad,** *The Sea of Grass,* Pocket Books 413 (painted cover picturing Spencer Tracy and Katharine Hepburn) 4.50 6.00 5.25

☐ **Richter, Hans W.,** *Beyond Defeat,* Crest S188, 1957 .... 3.50 4.75 3.50

☐ **Reisman, David,** *The Lonely Crowd,* Anchor 16 .... 4.50 6.00 5.17

☐ *Selected Essays From Individualism Reconsidered,* Anchor 58 .... 4.25 5.50 4.87

☐ **Rigby, Ray,** *The Hill,* Dell 3599 (photo cover picturing Sean Connery) 5.00 6.50 5.62

☐ **Rinehart, Mary R.,** *The Bat,* Dell 652, no date 3.00 4.00 3.12

☐ **Ripley, Robert,** *Believe It Or Not,* Seventh Series, Pocket Books 6023 ...... 1.50 2.00 1.75

☐ *Believe It Or Not,* Ninth Series, Pocket Books 6202 .... 1.50 2.00 1.75

☐ **Ripley, Thomas,** *They Died With Their Boots On,* Pocket Books 6165 (The title was used for a motion picture starring Errol Flynn. However the movie bore little resemblance to the book. The book consisted of biographies of various Old West characters who went down shooting, while the movie dealt exclusively with General George A. Custer.) 3.25 4.00 3.59

☐ **Ritow, Ira,** *Capsule Calculus,* Dolphin 336 .... 3.25 4.00 3.42

	Current Price Range		C/Y Avg.

☐ **Robbins, Harold,** *79 Park Avenue,* Cardinal GC130 (cover artwork by Phillips) .. | 3.00 | 3.75 | 3.26

☐ *Stiletto,* Dell 8284 (cover artwork by Abbett) .... | 2.00 | 2.50 | 2.15

☐ *Where Love Has Gone,* Cardinal GC784 .... | 2.00 | 2.50 | 2.21

☐ **Roberts, Herb,** *Strange Wife,* Beacon 75146 .... | 2.00 | 2.50 | 2.23

☐ **Roberts, Lee,** *If the Shoe Fits,* Crest 415 (cover artwork by McGinnis) .... | 3.00 | 3.75 | 3.31

☐ **Roberts, Lowell,** *This Climate of Love,* Monarch 367 (cover artwork by Engel, 1963) .... | 4.00 | 5.00 | 4.50

☐ **Roberts, Luke,** *Harlem Doctor,* Uni-Books 75, no date .... | 11.00 | 15.00 | 12.50

☐ **Roberts, Richard E.,** *Second Time Around,* Perma 4246 (photo cover picturing Debbie Reynolds, Steve Forrest and Andy Griffith) .... | 5.00 | 6.50 | 5.60

☐ **Robertson, Don,** *The Three Days,* Ace K108 .... | 2.00 | 2.50 | 2.14

☐ **Robertson, Terence,** *The Hurricane,* Ballantine 410 .... | 2.00 | 2.50 | 2.17

☐ *The Ship With Two Captains,* Berkley 402 .... | 2.00 | 2.50 | 2.19

☐ **Robins, Patricia,** *Lady Chatterley's Daughter,* Ace K150, no date (The character Lady Chatterley was created by D.H. Lawrence.) .... | 2.50 | 3.50 | 2.85

☐ **Robinson, Henry M.,** *The Cardinal,* Cardinal GC782 .... | 2.50 | 3.25 | 2.72

☐ **Robison, Harold,** *Rat Alley,* Monarch 559 .... | 2.00 | 2.50 | 2.16

☐ **Rogan, James,** *The Plot at Nicaragua,* Mission Press (no serial number), 1952 | 4.00 | 5.25 | 4.37

☐ **Rogers, Joel,** *Red Right Hand,* Pyramid 1026 (cover artwork by Bacon) .... | 3.00 | 3.75 | 3.32

☐ **Rohmer, Elizabeth Sax,** *Bianca In Black,* Airmont M3, 1972 .... | 1.50 | 2.25 | 1.75

☐ *Bianca In Black,* Airmont M3, 1976 .. | 1.25 | 1.75 | 1.40

☐ **Rohmer, Sax,** *The Bride Of Fu Manchu,* Pyramid X-2113, 1969, second edition | 1.25 | 1.75 | 1.40

		Current Price Range		C/Y Avg.
☐	*Daughter Of Fu Manchu,* Pyramid R-1032, 1964	2.50	3.25	2.75
☐	*The Daughter Of Fu Manchu,* WDL M913, 1960	7.50	9.75	8.50
☐	*Daughter Of Fu Manchu,* Pyramid X-2149, 1970, second edition	1.75	2.50	2.00
☐	*The Day The World Ended,* Ace F-283, no date	3.00	4.00	3.30
☐	*The Dream Detective,* Pyramid R-1316, 1966	2.75	3.50	3.00
☐	*The Drums Of Fu Manchu,* Pyramid R-1307, 1966, second edition	2.00	2.75	2.30
☐	*The Drums Of Fu Manchu,* Pyramid F-804, 1962	2.25	3.00	2.50
☐	*Emperor Fu Manchu,* Gold Medal S929, 1959	8.00	11.00	9.15
☐	*Emperor Fu Manchu,* Pyramid R-1310, 1966	1.75	2.50	1.95
☐	*Emperor Fu Manchu,* Pyramid V3946, 1976, second edition	1.25	1.75	1.40
☐	*The Hand Of Fu Manchu,* Pyramid R-1306, 1966, second edition	2.00	3.00	2.30
☐	*The Hand Of Fu Manchu,* Pyramid S-2342, 1971, third edition	1.75	2.50	2.00
☐	*The Hand Of Fu-Manchu,* Pyramid F-688, 1962	2.50	3.25	2.75
☐	*The Insidious Doctor Fu Manchu,* Pyramid F-908, 1963, second edition	2.50	3.25	2.75
☐	*The Insidious Doctor Fu Manchu,* Pyramid R-1301, 1965, third edition	2.25	3.00	2.50
☐	*The Insidious Dr. Fu Manchu,* Pyramid X-2166, 1970, fourth edition	1.75	2.50	2.00
☐	*The Island Of Fu Manchu,* Pyramid X1481, 1971, third edition	1.25	1.75	1.40
☐	*The Island Of Fu Manchu,* Pyramid F-858, 1963	2.00	2.75	2.25
☐	*Mask Of Fu Manchu,* Pyramid R-1303, 1967, third edition	1.75	2.50	2.05
☐	*The Mask Of Fu Manchu,* Pyramid R-1303, 1966, third edition	1.25	1.75	1.40
☐	*The Mask Of Fu Manchu,* Pyramid X2248, 1970, fifth edition	2.00	2.75	2.25

		Current Price Range		C/Y Avg.

☐ *The Mask Of Fu Manchu,* Pyramid R-1303, 1966, second edition **2.00 2.75 2.25**

☐ *The Mystery Of Dr. Fu Manchu,* Star 30115, 1977 .... **2.00 3.00 2.35**

☐ *President Fu Manchu,* Pyramid F-946, 1963 .... **3.00 4.25 3.50**

☐ *President Fu Manchu,* Pyramid X-2135, 1969, second edition **1.75 2.50 2.00**

☐ *President Fu Manchu,* Pyramid F-946, 1963 .... **1.75 2.50 2.00**

☐ *Re-Enter Fu Manchu,* Gold Medal K1458, no date **3.00 4.00 3.30**

☐ *Re-Enter Fu Manchu,* Gold Medal S684, 1957 .... **4.75 6.50 5.20**

☐ *Re-Enter Fu Manchu,* Gold Medal K1458, no date **2.00 2.75 2.30**

☐ *The Return Of Dr. Fu Manchu,* Pyramid X-2225, 1970, third edition **1.50 2.25 1.70**

☐ *The Return Of Dr. Fu Manchu,* Pyramid G641, 1961 .... **2.00 2.75 2.20**

☐ *The Return Of Dr. Fu Manchu,* Pyramid R-1302, 1965, second edition **1.75 2.50 2.00**

☐ *Return Of Sumuru,* Gold Medal 868, 1959, second edition **9.00 12.00 10.00**

☐ *Shadow Of Fu Manchu,* Pyramid F-837, 1963 .... **3.00 4.00 3.30**

☐ *The Shadow Of Fu Manchu,* Pyramid X2294, 1970, third edition **1.50 2.25 1.25**

☐ *The Shadow Of Fu Manchu,* Pyramid R-1304, 1966, second edition **1.75 2.50 1.95**

☐ *Sumuru,* Gold Medal 199, 1951 ..... **11.00 15.00 12.75**

☐ *Tales of Chinatown,* Popular 217, 1950 **16.00 20.00 17.75**

☐ *The Trail Of Fu Manchu,* Pyramid R-1003, 1964 .... **2.25 3.00 2.50**

☐ *The Trail Of Fu Manchu,* Pyramid R-1308, 1966, second edition **2.25 3.00 2.50**

☐ *The Trail Of Fu Manchu,* Pyramid X-2192, 1970, third edition **1.50 2.25 1.75**

☐ **Roleine, Roberta** *Deadly Triangle,* Mystique 73038, 1979 .... **1.25 1.75 1.40**

☐ **Rolfe, Edwin and Lester Fuller,** *The Glass Room,* Bantam, 310, 1948 ...... **6.00 8.25 6.85**

	Current Price Range		C/Y Avg.

☐ **Rollins, Alfred,** *Franklin D. Roosevelt and the Age of Action,* Dell LC157 .... — 2.00 — 2.50 — 2.11

☐ **Romer, Alfred,** *The Restless Atom,* Anchor S12 — 2.00 — 2.50 — 2.11

☐ **Ronald, James,** *Murder In The Family,* Belmont 90-393, 1964 — 1.75 — 2.50 — 1.95

☐ *They Can't Hang Me,* Popular 64, no date — 5.25 — 7.25 — 6.00

☐ *They Can't Hang Me,* Popular Library 64, 1945 — 5.25 — 7.25 — 6.00

☐ **Ronns, Edward,** *But Not For Me,* Pyramid 445 (cartoon cover picturing Clark Gable and Carroll Baker, artwork by Engle) — 6.00 — 8.00 — 6.70

☐ *The Lady Takes a Flyer,* Avon T228 (photo cover picturing Jeff Chandler and Lana Turner) — 7.00 — 10.00 — 8.50

☐ **Roripaugh, Robert A.,** *A Fever For Living,* Dell S34 (cover artwork by Hulings) — 2.00 — 2.50 — 2.23

☐ **Rose, Thomas,** *Violence in America,* Vintage V559 — 3.00 — 3.70 — 3.29

☐ **Rosen, Harry and David Rosen,** *But Not Next Door,* Avon G1150 — 2.00 — 2.75 — 2.31

☐ **Ross, James B.,** *The Portable Renaissance Reader,* Viking 61 (cover artwork by Hoffman) — 2.50 — 3.00 — 2.18

☐ **Rossiter, F.M.,** *Bride and Groom,* Banner (no serial number) — 3.00 — 3.75 — 3.27

☐ **Rostand, Edmond,** *Cyrano deBergerac,* Bantam 859 (painted cover picturing Jose Ferrer) — 5.00 — 6.50 — 5.65

☐ **Rosten, Leo,** *Captain Newman M.D.,* Crest 604 (photo cover picturing Gregory Peck, Tony Curtis, Angie Dickinson and Bobby Darin) — 5.00 — 6.50 — 5.61

☐ **Rourke, Constance,** *American Humor,* Anchor 12 — 2.00 — 2.50 — 2.11

☐ **Royal, O.,** *She Couldn't Say No,* Belmont #875-206 — 1.50 — 2.00 — 1.65

☐ **Royce, Patrick M.,** *Sailing Illustrated,* Royce 3, 1963 — 3.50 — 4.25 — 3.80

	Current Price Range		C/Y Avg.
☐ **Ruark, Robert,** *Grenadine Etching,* Ace K121	3.00	3.75	3.30
☐ **Rubel, James L.,** *Fraudulent Broad,* Newstand Library 102, 1958	4.00	5.00	4.40
☐ **Rudel, Hans U.,** *Stuka Pilot,* Ballantine 459	3.00	3.75	3.29
☐ **Rukeyser, Merryle,** *The Attack on our Free Choice,* Monarch 22	3.00	3.75	3.27
☐ **Runbeck, Margaret,** *Three Secrets,* Gold Medal 128 (painted cover picturing Eleanor Parker, Patricia Neal and Ruth Roman)	6.00	8.00	6.90
☐ **Runyon, Damon,** *Guys and Dolls,* Pocket Books 241 (photo cover picturing Frank Sinatra, Marlon Brando, Jean Simmons and Vivian Blaine)	5.00	6.50	5.71
☐ **Russell, William,** *A Wind Is Rising,* Belmont #222	1.50	2.00	1.65
☐ **Russo, Paul V.,** *Image Of Evil,* Midwood F329, no date	1.75	2.25	2.00
☐ **Ryan, Don,** *Devil's Brigade,* Berkley #G-8	2.00	2.40	2.20
☐ **Ryan, Steve,** *The Fortune Hunter,* Playtime 651	3.25	4.00	3.40
☐ **Sabatini, Rafael,** *The Fortunes of Captain Blood,* Popular Library 241 (painted cover picturing Patricia Medina)	6.00	8.00	6.80
☐ **Sackville-West, Virginia,** *No Signposts in the Sea,* Popular Library K2 (cover artwork by Hooks)	4.00	5.00	4.37
☐ **Sagan, Francois,** *Bonjour Tristesse,* Dell S29	3.00	3.75	3.29
☐ **Salamanca, J.R.,** *Lilith,* Bantam 2421 ..	4.00	5.00	4.39
☐ **Salem, Randy,** *Man Among Women,* Beacon #8348	1.00	1.50	1.65
☐ **Sambrot, William,** *Island of Fear,* Perma 4278	2.00	2.50	2.22
☐ **Sancton, Thomas,** *Magnificent Rascal,* Crest S208, 1958	2.00	2.75	2.30
☐ **Sanderson, Nora,** *The Two Faces of Nurse Roberts,* Harlequin 787	2.00	2.50	2.17

	Current Price Range		C/Y Avg.
☐ **Santayana, George,** *Character and Opinion in the U.S.,* Anchor 73	2.00	2.50	2.15
☐ **Sarban (no first name),** *Ringstones,* Ballantine 498, 1961	3.50	4.25	3.80
☐ *The Sound of His Horn,* Ballantine 377, 1960	3.50	4.25	3.81
☐ **Sarrazin, Albertine,** *Astragal,* Grove 221	2.50	3.25	2.75
☐ **Sartre, Jean-Paul,** *No Exit,* Vintage K16	2.00	2.50	2.21
☐ *The Reprieve,* Bantam 2774	2.00	2.50	2.21
☐ **Sarver, Steve,** *The Wild Weekend,* Beacon 1029	2.50	3.25	2.76
☐ **Savage, George,** *The Affairs of Laura,* Beacon 972	2.50	3.00	2.62
☐ **Savage, George,** *The Deal Makers,* Beacon #8521F	1.50	2.00	1.65
☐ *Runaway Wife,* Beacon 955	2.50	3.01	2.65
☐ *Toni,* Beacon #8686X	1.50	2.00	1.65
☐ **Savage, James,** *Girl In A Jam,* Avon T-356, 1959	5.00	6.50	5.35
☐ **Savage, John,** *A Shady Place To Die,* Dell A137, 1957, first edition	2.00	3.00	2.20
☐ **Savage, Les,** *The Royal City,* Ace K112	2.50	3.25	2.84
☐ **Saxby, C. and L. Molnar,** *Death Over Hollywood,* Detec Nov Classic 29, no date	7.00	9.00	7.75
☐ **Saxby, Charles,** *Death In The Sun,* Green Publishing 10, 1940	7.00	9.00	7.75
☐ *Murder At The Mike,* Prize Mystery 2, 1943	3.50	4.50	3.80
☐ **Saxon, Alex,** *A Run In Diamonds,* Pocket 77657, 1973	1.25	1.85	1.50
☐ **Sayers, Dorothy** (ED), *Stories of Supernatural,* Manor 95313, 1974, third edition	1.35	1.85	1.50
☐ *Busman's Honeymoon,* Avon 29595, sixth edition	2.00	3.00	2.12
☐ *Busman's Honeymoon,* Avon 50344, eighth edition	2.00	3.00	2.12
☐ *Clouds Of Witness,* 4 Square 761, 1962	3.00	3.75	3.12
☐ *Clouds Of Witness,* Avon S198, 1966	1.75	2.50	2.12
☐ *Clouds Of Witness,* Avon V2287, 1969, second edition	2.25	2.50	2.12

	Current Price Range		C/Y Avg.
☐ *Clouds Of Witness*, New English Library 29565, 1976	2.25	3.25	2.62
☐ *Clouds Of Witness*, Nel 013332, 1974, third edition	1.85	2.65	2.12
☐ *Clouds Of Witness*, Avon 41954, tenth edition	1.85	2.65	2.12
☐ *The Documents In The Case*, Avon 35204, seventh edition	1.25	1.75	1.50
☐ *The Documents In The Case*, Nel 05341, 1981, sixth edition	2.00	3.00	2.50
☐ *Five Red Herrings*, Avon N451, 1972, third edition	1.25	1.75	1.50
☐ *Five Red Herrings*, Nel 26671, 1975, fourth edition	1.85	2.65	2.12
☐ *Gaudy Night*, Nel 021548, 1974, third edition	1.85	2.65	2.12
☐ *Hangman's Holiday*, Penguin 1780, 1963, second edition	3.00	4.00	3.50
☐ *Hangman's Holiday*, Bestseller B38, no date	3.00	4.00	3.50
☐ *In The Teeth Of The Evidence*, Four Square 221, 1960	5.00	7.00	5.25
☐ *In The Teeth Of The Evidence*, Four Square 221, 1960	2.00	3.00	2.50
☐ *Lord Peter Views The Body*, Avon V2289, 1969	1.75	2.50	2.12
☐ *Lord Peter Views The Body*, Penguin 1779, 1963, second edition	2.00	3.00	2.50
☐ *Murder Must Advertise*, Avon 21634, fifth edition	2.00	3.00	2.37
☐ *Murder Must Advertise*, Signet T3369, 1968, second edition	1.25	1.75	1.50
☐ *Murder Must Advertise*, Avon 42036, tenth edition	1.25	1.75	1.50
☐ *Murder Must Advertise*, Nel 015556, 1974, third edition	1.75	2.50	2.12
☐ *The Nine Tailors*, Pocket 185, 1942 ..	8.00	11.00	9.50
☐ *(ED), Stories Of Supernatural*, Mac-Fadden 50-170, no date	2.00	3.00	2.50
☐ *Strong Poison*, New English Library 31373, 1977, fifth edition	2.00	2.75	2.37
☐ *Strong Poison*, Four Square 196, 1960	3.00	4.00	3.55

	Current Price Range		C/Y Avg.

☐ *Strong Poison,* Nel Four Square P3264, 1967	1.85	2.65	2.12
☐ *Strong Poison,* Nel 23923, 1975, third edition	1.85	2.65	2.12
☐ *Strong Poison,* Avon 22616, seventh edition	1.85	2.65	2.12
☐ *Strong Poison,* Avon 40543, eighth edition	2.00	3.00	2.37
☐ *(ED), Tales Detect And Mystery,* Mac-Fadden 50-143, 1962	1.75	2.50	2.12
☐ *Unnatural Death,* Four Square 978, 1964	2.25	3.25	2.75
☐ *Unnatural Death,* Nel 020983, 1974, fourth edition	1.85	2.65	2.12
☐ *Unpleasantness At Bellona Club,* Nel 016307, 1974, sixth edition	1.85	2.65	2.12
☐ *Unpleasantness At The Bellona Club,* Avon G1184, no date	3.00	4.25	2.50
☐ *Unpleasantness At Bellona Club,* Nel 016307, 1973, third edition	2.00	3.00	2.12
☐ *Unpleasantness At Bellona Club,* Four Square 807, 1963	3.00	4.25	3.00
☐ *Whose Body?,* Avon S189, 1965, second edition	2.00	3.00	2.50
☐ *Whose Body?,* Signet P3295, 1967 ..	2.00	3.00	2.37
☐ *Whose Body?* Four Square 775, 1963	3.00	4.00	3.50
☐ *Whose Body?,* Nel 015114, 1973, third edition	1.75	2.50	2.12
☐ **Sayers, Dorothy and Eustace, R.,** *Documents In The Case,* Nel 26663, 1975	1.75	2.50	2.12
☐ **Schaefer, Kermit,** *Super Bloopers,* Crest 1829 (interior artwork by Howard Schneider, 1963)	6.00	8.00	6.85
☐ **Scherf, Margaret,** *The Banker's Bones,* Popular 60-2402, no date	2.00	3.00	2.37
☐ *Diplomat And The Gold Piano,* Popular SP345, no date	2.00	3.00	2.50
☐ **Schmitz, James H.,** *A Tale Of Two Clocks,* Belmont B-50-643, 1965	3.00	4.00	3.50
☐ **Schoenfeld, Howard,** *Let Them Eat Bullets,* Gold Medal 586, 1957, second edition	2.00	3.00	2.50

	Current Price Range		C/Y Avg.

☐ **Scholefield, Alan,** *Venom,* Popular Library 04378, first edition 1.75 2.50 2.12

☐ **Schulberg, Budd,** *What Makes Sammy Run?,* Bantam 18, 1945 .... 7.00 9.00 8.00

☐ **Schulman, Arthur,** *A Hole in the Head,* Gold Medal 891 (photo cover picturing Frank Sinatra, Edward G. Robinson, Eleanor Parker and Carolyn Jones) 5.00 6.50 5.64

☐ **Schultz, Charles M.,** *Good Grief Charlie Brown,* Crest 619 .... 4.00 5.50 4.60

☐ **Schwartz, Alan,** *The Wandering Tellurian,* Ace H20 (cover artwork by Powell) 3.00 3.75 3.30

☐ **Schweitzer, Gertrude,** *Obsessed,* Gold-Medal 754, 1958, second edition 1.00 1.50 1.25

☐ **Scotland, Jay,** *Traitor's Legion,* Ace G532, 1963 .... 3.00 3.75 3.28

☐ **Scott, Bradford,** *The Desert Killers,* Pyramid 684 (cover artwork by Podwil) ... 3.00 3.75 3.28

☐ *Gundown,* Pyramid 831 (cover artwork by Crair) 2.75 3.50 3.07

☐ *Gun Justice,* Pyramid 854 (cover artwork by Crair) 2.75 3.50 3.11

☐ *Guns of Bangtown,* Pyramid 714 (cover artwork by Bates) 3.00 3.75 3.28

☐ *Horseman of the Shadows,* Pyramid 992 (cover artwork by Ryan) 2.75 3.50 3.12

☐ *Valley of Hunted Men,* Pyramid 573 (cover artwork by Stanley) 3.75 4.00 3.40

☐ **Scott, Geoffrey,** *Architecture of Humanism,* Anchor 33 .... 2.00 2.50 2.19

☐ **Scott, J.M.,** *Seawife,* Crest 162 (photo cover picturing Richard Burton and Joan Collins) 6.00 8.00 6.50

☐ **Scott, Robert L.,** *God is my Co-pilot,* Ballantine 694 .... 2.50 3.25 2.83

☐ **Scott, Sir Walter,** *Ivanhoe,* Cardinal C79 (photo cover picturing Robert Taylor) ... 5.00 6.50 5.52

☐ **Scott, Tarn,** *Sex Marks the Spot,* Hillman 152.................................. 2.00 2.50 2.23

☐ **Seager, Allan,** *Death of Anger,* Avon G1097, no date 4.00 6.00 4.90

	Current Price Range		C/Y Avg.

☐ **Seagrave, Gordon,** *The Life of a Burma Surgeon,* Ballantine 374	2.00	2.50	2.21
☐ **Seale, Sara,** *These Delights,* Harlequin 918	2.00	2.50	2.21
☐ **Sebreng, Lupo,** *She Pawn,* Lantern 106	2.50	3.25	2.68
☐ **Seeley, Mabel,** *The Crying Sisters,* Pyramid 823 (cover artwork by Bacon)	3.00	3.75	3.29
☐ *The Listening House,* Pyramid 1009 (cover artwork by Bacon)	2.75	3.50	3.08
☐ *The Whistling Shadow,* Pyramid 1054 (cover artwork by Bacon)	2.75	3.50	3.08
☐ **Seifert, Elizabeth,** *Doctor at the Crossroads,* Dell D436 (cover artwork by Abbett)	2.50	3.00	2.69
☐ *The Doctor's Bride,* Dell D443 (cover artwork by Miller)	2.50	3.00	2.62
☐ *Doctor of Mercy,* Perma 4179 (cover artwork by Abbett)	2.50	3.00	2.59
☐ *The Doctor Takes a Wife,* Perma 4219	2.25	2.75	2.42
☐ *The Honor of Dr. Shelton,* Dell 3702 (cover artwork by App)	2.50	3.25	2.81
☐ *The Strange Loyalty of Dr. Carlisle,* Perma 4193	2.00	2.75	2.30
☐ *When Doctors Marry,* Dell D428 (cover artwork by Miller)	2.00	2.75	2.30
☐ **Seltzer, Nadine,** *More Sweetie Pie,* Berkley 381	5.00	6.00	5.75
☐ *Sweetie Pie,* Berkley 567	3.75	4.50	4.14
☐ **Semple, Gordon,** *Bad Company,* Price 60, 1945	4.00	6.00	4.75
☐ **Sewell, Anna,** *Black Beauty,* Best Seller Classics CL602	2.00	2.50	2.15
☐ **Shadegg, Stephen,** *Barry Goldwater: Freedom is his Flight Plan,* MacFadden 60-123	4.00	5.25	4.38
☐ **Shakespeare, William,** *Julius Caesar,* Washington Square Press W112	1.50	2.00	1.75
☐ *King Lear,* Washington Square Press W113	1.50	2.00	1.75
☐ *Much Ado About Nothing,* Crofts (no serial number), 1948	2.50	3.00	2.70
☐ *The Taming of the Shrew,* Dell 8480	1.50	2.00	1.69

	Current Price Range		C/Y Avg.

☐ **Shane, Ted,** *Bar Guide,* Gold Medal 135 (interior artwork by Virgil Partch) 6.00   8.00   6.95

☐ **Shapiro, Lionel,** *Sealed Verdict,* Bantam 357 (painted cover picturing Ray Milland)   6.00   8.00   6.70

☐ **Shaw, Andrew,** *But Loving None,* Leisure 1155, 1966 ....   3.50   4.00   3.29

☐ **Shaw, Bob,** *Night Walk,* Banner 110 (cover artwork by Frazetta, 1967) 6.00   8.00   6.59

☐ **Shaw, George B.,** *Back to Methselah,* Tauchnitz 4578, no date 3.00   4.00   3.50

☐ *Saint Joan,* Penguin 3, 1951 ....   3.75   4.75   4.25

☐ *Three Plays for Puritans,* Tauchnitz 4531, no date 3.00   4.00   3.50

☐ **Sheers, James,** *Counterfeit Courier,* Dell B186 (cover artwork by Abbett, 1961)   4.00   5.00   4.48

☐ **Sheinwold, Alfred,** *Five Weeks to Winning Bridge,* Perma 5015 ....   2.00   2.50   2.19

☐ **Sheldon, Walt,** *House of Happy Mayhem,* Banner 106, 1967 ....   3.00   3.75   3.29

☐ **Shepard, Fern,** *Night Nurse,* Avon F186   2.00   2.50   2.15

☐ **Shirer, William L.,** *Midcentury Journey,* Signet 1968 ....   2.00   2.50   2.19

☐ **Shirreffs, Gordon,** *The Border Guidon,* Signet 2233 ....   2.50   3.00   2.59

☐ **Short, Luke,** *Station West,* Bantam 139 (photo cover picturing Dick Powell and Jane Greer) 6.00   8.00   6.80

☐ *Sunset Graze,* Bantam 22890-0, 1982   1.25   1.75   1.50

☐ *Trumpets West!* Dell 10m #1, no date   10.00   15.00   11.60

☐ **Shubin, Seymour,** *Wellville, U.S.A.,* Beacon #8588F 1.65   2.25   1.75

☐ **Shulman, Alix,** *Red Emma Speaks,* Vintage V172 ....   3.00   3.75   3.32

☐ **Shulman, Irving,** *Children of the Dark,* Popular Library G175 (painted cover picturing James Dean) 6.00   8.00   7.00

☐ *College Confidential,* Gold Medal 1005 (photo cover picturing Steve Allen, Mamie van Doren and Jayne Meadows) 6.00   8.00   7.00

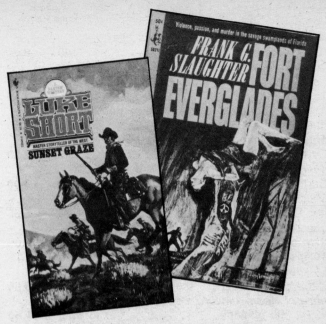

Left to Right: **Sunset Graze,** by Luke Short,
Bantam, 22890–0, 1982, **$1.25–$1.75;**
Fort Everglades, by Frank G. Slaughter,
Pocket Books, 50211, 1966, **$3.00–$4.00.**

	Current Price Range		C/Y Avg.
☐ **Shulman, Max,** *Barefoot Boy With Cheek,* Bantam 1939 (cover artwork by Dedini)	6.00	8.00	7.00
☐ *The Feather Merchants,* Bantam 1940 (cover artwork by Dedini)	6.00	8.00	7.00
☐ *The Zebra Derby,* Pocket Books 840 (cover artwork by Jones)	6.00	8.00	7.00
☐ **Shute, Nevil,** *No Highway,* Dell 516 (photo cover picturing James Stewart and Marlene Dietrich)	4.00	5.50	4.65
☐ *On the Beach,* Signet 1562 (photo cover picturing Gregory Peck, Ava Gardner, Fred Astaire, Tony Perkins and Donna Anderson)	7.00	10.00	8.15

	Current Price Range		C/Y Avg.

☐ **Silverstein, Shel,** *Grab Your Socks,* Ballantine 163 . . . . **6.00 8.00 6.85**

☐ **Simenon, Georges,** *Maigret Goes Home,* Penguin 1901, 1970, second edition **1.75 2.50 2.12**

☐ *Maigret Hesitates,* Curtis 07160, no date **1.50 2.00 1.75**

☐ *Maigret In New York's Underworld,* Curtis 06117, no date **1.75 2.50 2.12**

☐ *Maigret In New York's Underworld,* Curtis 09197, no date **2.00 3.00 2.50**

☐ *Maigret In New York's Underworld,* Signet 1338, 1956 . . . . **4.25 5.50 4.50**

☐ *Maigret In Vichy,* Avon 25239, 1975, third edition **1.50 2.00 1.75**

☐ *Maigret In Vichy,* Avon PN330, 1970 **2.00 2.75 2.37**

☐ *Maigret Meets A Milord,* Penguin C2027, 1963 . . . . **2.50 3.50 3.00**

☐ *Maigret Meets A Milord,* Penguin 2027, 1974, fifth edition **1.75 2.50 2.12**

☐ *Maigret Mystified,* Penguin C2024, 1964 . . . . **2.00 2.75 2.37**

☐ *Maigret Mystified,* Penguin 2024, 1979, eighth edition **2.50 3.25 2.87**

☐ *Maigret Mystified,* Penguin 2024, 1975, sixth edition **1.75 2.50 2.12**

☐ *Maigret Sets A Trap,* Curtis 09191, no date **1.25 1.75 1.50**

☐ *Maigret Stonewalled,* Penguin 2026, 1970, third edition **2.00 3.00 2.50**

☐ *Maigret Stonewalled,* Penguin 2026, 1972, fourth edition **2.00 3.00 2.50**

☐ *Maigret's Boyhood Friend,* Curtis 07158, no date **1.25 1.75 1.50**

☐ *Maigret's Boyhood Friend,* Curtis 07158, 1971 . . . . **1.25 1.75 1.50**

☐ *Maigret's Failure,* Popular Library 00369, 1976 . . . . **1.25 1.75 1.50**

☐ *Maigret's Mistake,* Penguin 1222, 1960, second edition **3.50 4.50 4.00**

☐ *Man From Everywhere/Newhaven,* Penguin 855, 1942 . . . . **6.75 9.00 7.50**

	Current Price Range		C/Y Avg.

☐	*The Mouse,* Penguin C2378, 1966 ...	**2.25**	**3.00**	**2.50**
☐	*The Murderer,* Penguin 1223, 1958 ..	**3.00**	**3.75**	**3.50**
☐	*The Patience Of Maigret,* Bestseller B69, no date	**3.25**	**4.00**	**3.60**
☐	*Poisoned Relations,* Penguin 1224, 1962, third edition	**3.25**	**4.00**	**3.62**
☐	*The Sailors' Rendezvous,* Penguin 3136, 1975, third edition	**1.75**	**2.50**	**2.12**
☐	*The Saint-Fiacre Affair,* Pocket 141, 1941	**7.00**	**10.00**	**7.87**
☐	*Short Cases Of Inspector Maigret,* Ace F-198, no date	**2.00**	**3.00**	**2.50**
☐	**Simmons, Kenneth,** *Kriegie,* Hillman 165	**2.00**	**2.50**	**2.17**
☐	**Simpson, Ronald,** *End of a Diplomat,* Monarch 413 (cover artwork by Barton, 1964)	**3.00**	**3.75**	**3.25**
☐	*Eve's Apple,* Monarch 185 (cover artwork by Barton, 1961)	**3.25**	**4.00**	**3.40**
☐	*The Return of Colonel Pho,* Monarch 562	**3.00**	**3.75**	**3.30**
☐	**Sinclair, Upton,** *World's End,* Perma 5017	**2.00**	**2.50**	**2.18**
☐	**Singer, Kurt,** *Spies Who Changed History,* Ace K122	**2.00**	**2.50**	**2.18**
☐	**Singh, K.,** *Train to Pakistan,* Grove BA1	**4.00**	**5.00**	**4.50**
☐	**Sire, Glen,** *Something Foolish,* Berkley 791	**4.00**	**5.00**	**4.50**
☐	**Sjoman, Vilgot,** *I Am Curious/Yellow,* Grove 184 (interior photos, 1968)	**5.00**	**6.50**	**5.60**
☐	**Skinner, Cornelia O.,** *Excuse It Please,* Pocket Books 963 (cover artwork by Otto Soglow). Otto Soglow was creator of the comic strip The Little King.	**4.00**	**5.25**	**4.42**
☐	**Slaughter, Frank G.,** *A Touch of Glory,* Perma 5093 (cover artwork by Cuffari)	**2.00**	**2.75**	**2.31**
☐	*Battle Surgeon,* Perma 5092 (cover artwork by Phillips)	**2.00**	**2.75**	**2.31**
☐	*Buccaneer Surgeon,* Perma 5070	**2.00**	**2.75**	**2.31**
☐	*The Crown and the Cross,* Perma 5019	**2.00**	**2.75**	**2.31**
☐	*The Curse of Jezebel,* Perma 5052 (cover artwork by Bennett)	**2.00**	**2.75**	**2.31**

		Current Price Range		C/Y Avg.

☐	*Darien Venture*, Perma 4249	2.25	3.00	2.36
☐	*Daybreak*, Perma 5058	2.00	2.75	2.28
☐	*Deadly Lady of Madagascar*, Perma 5086	2.00	2.75	2.28
☐	*Devil's Harvest*, Perma 5085	2.00	2.75	2.28
☐	*Fort Everglades*, Pocket Books 50211, 1966 (cover artwork by Harry Bennett)	3.00	4.00	3.35
☐	*The Golden Ones*, Perma 5078	2.00	2.75	2.28
☐	*The Healer*, Perma 5039	2.00	2.75	2.28
☐	*In a Dark Garden*, Perma 5025	2.00	2.75	2.28
☐	*Lorena*, Perma 5064 (cover artwork by Garrido)	2.00	2.75	2.28
☐	**Small, Marvin,** *The World's Best Recipes,* Pocket Books 7008	3.00	3.75	3.30
☐	**Smith, Ben,** *Peril of the Peloncillos,* Monarch 440 (cover artwork by Stanley) ...	3.00	3.75	3.27
☐	**Smith, Edward,** *Skylard of Valeron,* Pyramid 948	3.00	3.75	3.32
☐	**Smith, George,** *Strange Harem,* France 1024 (gatefold photo cover)	4.00	5.00	4.51
☐	**Smith, H. Allen,** *Don't Get Personal With A Chicken,* Perma Books M4177, 1960	1.00	1.50	1.25
☐	*Low Man on a Totem Pole*, Popular Library G493	1.00	1.50	1.25
☐	**Smith, Lillian,** *The Journey,* Hillman 180	2.50	3.25	2.75
☐	**Smith, Mary,** *Wildmen I Have Known,* Brandon 628	3.00	3.75	3.33
☐	**Smith, Pauline,** *Nothing But Blood,* Chicago Paperback House 110 (cover artwork by Nystrom, 1962)	4.00	5.00	4.30
☐	**Sneider, Vernon,** *A Long Way From Home,* Signet 1870 (cover artwork by Phillips)	3.00	3.75	3.31
☐	*Teahouse of the August Moon*, Signet 1348 (painted cover picturing Marlon Brando, Glenn Ford and Machiko Kyo)	5.00	6.50	5.62
☐	**Snelling, O.F.,** *007 James Bond*, Signet 2652. This was not a James Bond novel (none have been written by anyone except Ian Fleming), but an overview of the			

	Current Price Range		C/Y Avg.
impact made by James Bond in movies, books, etc. Incidentally Signet is also the publisher of Ian Fleming's works.......	5.25	6.50	5.75
☐ **Snow, C.P.,** *The Masters,* Anchor 162 (cover artwork by Gorey)	2.75	3.50	3.00
☐ **Sollers, Philippe,** *Concha,* Belmont #216................................	3.50	4.50	4.00
☐ **Southern, Terry,** *Flash and Filigree,* Berkley #G-409	2.00	2.50	2.25
☐ **Spillane, Mickey,** *The Big Kill,* Signet S1700	6.00	8.00	7.00
☐ *Bloody Sunrise,* Signet D2718, 1965	2.00	2.75	2.37
☐ *The Body Lovers,* Signet P3221, 1967	1.75	2.50	2.12
☐ *The By-Pass Control,* Signet P3077, 1967	2.00	2.75	2.37

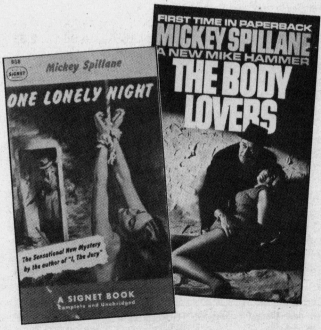

Left to Right: **One Lonely Night,** *by Mickey Spillane, 1952, Signet, 888,* **$2.75–$3.50;**
The Body Lovers, *by Mickey Spillane, 1965, Signet, P3221,* **$2.00–$2.75.**

		Current Price Range		C/Y Avg.
☐	*Day Of The Guns,* Signet T5037, fifth edition	1.85	2.65	2.12
☐	*Day Of The Guns,* Signet D2643, 1965	1.85	2.65	2.12
☐	*The Death Dealers,* Signet D2886, 1966	1.85	2.65	2.12
☐	*The By-Pass Control,* Signet P3077, 1967	2.00	2.75	2.37
☐	*Day Of The Guns,* Signet T5037, fifth edition	1.85	2.65	2.12
☐	*Day Of The Guns,* Signet D2643, 1965	1.85	2.65	2.12
☐	*The Death Dealers,* Signet D2886, 1966	1.85	2.65	2.12
☐	*The Deep,* Signet D2044, 1962, fourth edition	1.85	2.65	2.12
☐	*The Deep,* Signet E8688, eleventh edition	1.85	2.65	2.12
☐	*The Delta Factor,* Signet T4659, sixth edition	1.85	2.65	2.12
☐	*The Delta Factor,* Signet P3377, 1968	1.85	2.65	2.12
☐	*The Delta Factor,* Signet Y7592, eighth edition	2.00	2.75	2.37
☐	*The Girl Hunters,* Signet D2266, 1963	1.75	2.50	2.12
☐	*I The Jury,* White Circle CD384, 1949, second edition	5.50	7.50	6.00
☐	*I The Jury,* White Circle CD 385, 1949, second edition	5.00	6.50	5.37
☐	*I The Jury,* Signet 699, 1952, second edition	2.50	3.50	3.00
☐	*I The Jury,* Signet 699, 1954, fifth edition	3.50	4.75	3.87
☐	*Interdit Aux Moins De 16 Ans,* Presses 1001, 1973	1.50	2.25	1.87
☐	*Killer Mine,* Signet P3483, 1968	1.25	1.75	1.50
☐	*Kiss Me Deadly,* Signet 1000, 1958, nineteenth edition	2.25	3.00	2.62
☐	*Kiss Me Deadly,* Signet 1000, 1955, eleventh edition	2.00	2.75	2.37
☐	*Kiss Me Deadly,* Signet 1000, 1954, tenth edition	2.00	2.75	2.37
☐	*Kiss Me Deadly,* Signet 1000, 1953 ..	3.00	4.50	3.75
☐	**Stagg, DeLang,** *Glory Jumpers,* Monarch 140, 1959	1.25	1.75	1.50

	Current Price Range		C/Y Avg.

☐ **Stark, John,** *Vice Dolls,* Midwood F334, no date **1.75** **2.50** **2.12**

☐ **Steinbeck, John,** *Moon Is Down,* Penguin S219, 1943 . . . . **3.50** **4.25** **3.87**

☐ **Stark, Richard,** *The Black Ice Score,* Gold Medal D1949, 1968 . . . . **1.75** **2.50** **2.12**

☐ *The Black Ice Score,* Berkley 02356, second edition **2.00** **2.75** **2.37**

☐ *The Black Ice Score,* Berkley 02356, 1973 . . . . **1.25** **1.75** **1.50**

☐ *The Damsel,* Signet P3874, 1969 . . . . **1.50** **2.00** **1.75**

☐ *Deadly Edge,* Berkley 02502, 1974 . . **1.75** **2.50** **2.12**

☐ *The Green Eagle Score,* Gold Medal D1861, 1967 . . . . **3.00** **4.00** **3.50**

☐ *The Handle,* Pocket 50220, 1966 . . . . **3.50** **4.50** **4.00**

☐ *The Hunter,* Perma M-4272, 1962 . . . **4.50** **6.00** **4.50**

☐ *The Outfit,* Berkley 02418, 1973 . . . . . **1.75** **2.50** **2.12**

☐ *Point Blank!,* Gold Medal D1856, no date **2.25** **3.25** **2.75**

☐ *Point Blank!,* Berkley 02354, 1973 . . . **1.25** **1.75** **1.50**

☐ *Point Blank!,* (*The Hunter*), Gold Medal D1856, no date **1.50** **2.00** **1.75**

☐ *Point Blank!,* Gold Medal D1856, no date **2.00** **3.00** **2.50**

☐ *Run Lethal,* Berkley 02479, 1973 . . . . **1.75** **2.50** **2.12**

☐ *Slay-Ground,* Berkley 02355, 1973 . . . **1.50** **2.00** **1.75**

☐ *The Sour Lemon Score,* Gold Medal R2037, 1969 . . . . **2.25** **3.25** **2.50**

☐ *The Split,* Gold Medal D1997, no date **2.25** **3.25** **2.50**

☐ **St. John, Burton,** *Maureen,* Beacon 18592F **1.40** **1.85** **1.62**

☐ *Smoldering Women,* Beacon 18585F **1.50** **2.00** **1.75**

☐ **Steinbeck, John,** *The Red Pony,* Bantam 402 (photo cover picturing Myrna Loy, Robert Mitchum and Peter Miles) **6.00** **8.00** **6.72**

☐ **Stoker, Bram,** *Dracula,* Perma Books M4088, 1957 . . . . **2.75** **3.50** **3.12**

☐ **Stone, Hampton,** *The Babe With The Twistable Arm,* Popular K54, 1963 . . . . **2.50** **3.25** **2.87**

☐ *The Corpse in the Corner Saloon,* Dell Map 464, 1950 . . . . **3.00** **4.00** **3.50**

		Current Price Range		C/Y Avg.
☐	*The Corpse That Refused To Stay Dead,* Dell 790, 1954	3.00	4.00	3.50
☐	*Corpse Who Had Too Many Friends,* Paplib 64-588, 1971	1.25	1.75	1.50
☐	*Corpse Who Had Too Many Friends,* Bestseller 173, no date	4.00	5.50	4.62
☐	*The Funniest Killer In Town,* Paplib 64-503, 1971	1.25	1.75	1.50
☐	*Girl Who Kept Knocking Them Dead,* Dell D278, 1959	2.75	3.50	3.12
☐	*Kid Was Last Seen Hanging Ten,* Pablib 64-506, 1971	1.25	2.00	1.62
☐	*Man Who Looked Death In Eye,* Paplib 64-652, 1971	1.25	2.00	1.62
☐	*Murder That Wouldn't Stay Solved,* Dell 883, 1956	3.00	4.00	3.50
☐	*Murder That Wouldn't Stay Solved,* Pablib 64-526, 1971	1.25	2.00	1.62
☐	*Needle That Wouldn't Hold Still,* Pablib 64-735, 1971	1.35	2.00	1.62
☐	*The Real Serendipitous Kill,* Paplib 64-504, 1971	1.35	2.00	1.62
☐	*Swinger Who Swung By The Neck,* Paplib 64-763, 1971	1.35	2.00	1.62
☐	**Stone, Irving,** *They Also Ran,* Signet Y5192, 1968	2.00	3.00	2.50
☐	**Stratton, Ted,** *Wild Breed,* Gold Medal 443, 1954	4.00	5.25	4.62
☐	**Storm, Christopher,** *The Young Duke,* Beacon 8683X	1.35	1.75	1.55
☐	**Stout, Rex,** *Bad For Business,* Century 28, no date	8.00	11.00	8.50
☐	*Bad For Business,* Dell Map 299, no date	8.00	11.00	8.50
☐	*Bad For Business,* Dell Map 299, 1949	5.50	7.50	6.00
☐	*Bad For Business,* Pyramid R-1166, 1965	3.00	4.00	3.12
☐	*Before Midnight,* Bantam F2704, 1963, third edition	1.75	2.50	2.12
☐	*Before Midnight,* Fontana 2329, 1970, second edition	2.00	3.00	2.50

They Also Ran, by Irving Stone, Signet Books, Y5192, 1968, *$2.00–$3.00*.

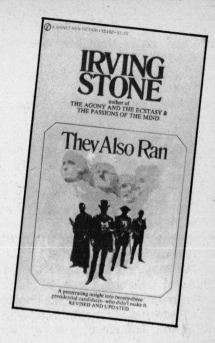

	Current Price Range		C/Y Avg.
☐ *Black Orchids,* Mercury Mystery, 1972, no date	3.25	4.25	3.62
☐ *Black Orchids,* Pyramid V4027, 1976, ninth edition	1.20	1.70	1.45
☐ *The Broken Vase,* Jonathan Press J9, no date	4.50	6.00	5.12
☐ *The Broken Vase,* Dell Map 674, 1953	3.50	4.50	4.00
☐ *The Broken Vase,* Pyramid R-1149, 1965	4.25	5.50	4.50
☐ *The Broken Vase,* Pyramid V4065, 1976, eighth edition	1.25	1.75	1.50
☐ *The Case of the Black Orchids,* Avon 714, 1956, fourth edition	3.25	4.50	3.50
☐ *The Case of the Black Orchids,* Avon 256, 1950	2.25	3.00	2.62

	Current Price Range		C/Y Avg.

☐ *Case of the Red Box,* Avon T-216, 1958	4.00	5.50	4.37
☐ *Champagne For One,* Bantam A2023, 1960	3.00	4.00	3.50
☐ *Cordially Invited To Meet Death,* Jonathan J15, no date	4.25	5.50	4.62
☐ *Death of a Doxy,* Bantam F3476, 1967	1.75	2.50	2.12
☐ *Double For Death,* Dell Map 9, no date	5.00	7.00	5.25
☐ *Double For Death,* Pyramid R-1025, 1964	2.75	3.50	3.12
☐ *Double For Death,* Dell Map 495, 1951	4.50	6.00	5.00
☐ *Double For Death,* Pyramid N3119, 1973, fourth edition	1.25	1.75	1.50
☐ *Double For Death,* Crime Club C359, 1946 (services edit.)	8.00	11.00	8.50
☐ *The Father Hunt,* Bantam H4467, 1969	1.25	1.75	1.50
☐ **Streeter, Edward,** *Father of the Bride,* Hillman 48 (photo cover picturing Spencer Tracy and Elizabeth Taylor)	6.00	8.00	6.45
☐ **Sturgeon, Theodore,** *Aliens 4,* Avon T-304, 1959	4.75	6.25	5.00
☐ *Beyond,* Avon T-439, 1960	2.00	2.75	2.37
☐ *The Cosmic Rape,* Dell 1512, 1968 ..	1.25	1.75	1.50
☐ *The Cosmic Rape,* Dell B 120, 1958, first edition	3.75	4.75	4.00
☐ *The Dreaming Jewels,* Corgi 09749, 1975, second edition	2.75	3.75	3.25
☐ *E Pluribus Unicorn,* Ballantine U2247, 1965, second edition	2.50	3.25	2.37
☐ *E Pluribus Unicorn,* Pocket 83149, second edition	1.85	2.50	2.12
☐ *The Golden Helix,* Dell 12885, 1980	1.25	1.75	1.50
☐ *More Than Human,* Ballantine 46, 1953	2.25	3.00	2.62
☐ *More Than Human,* Ballantine 24389, 1975, ninth edition	1.25	1.75	1.50
☐ *More Than Human,* Ballantine 462K, 1960, second edition	3.25	4.25	3.75
☐ *More Than Human,* Ballantine U2231, 1965, third edition	2.25	3.00	2.62
☐ *More Than Human,* Ballantine 02199, 1971, sixth edition	1.75	2.25	2.00

		Current Price Range		C/Y Avg.

☐	*(ED), New Soviet SF,* Collier 22650, 1980	4.50	6.00	4.87
☐	*Starshine,* Pyramid T2658, 1972, third edition	1.25	1.75	1.50
☐	*Starshine,* Pyramid X-1977, 1969, second edition	2.00	2.75	2.37
☐	*The Synthetic Man,* Pyramid 533, 1957	3.25	4.25	3.62
☐	*The Synthetic Man,* Pyramid X-1691, 1967, fourth edition	1.75	2.25	2.00
☐	*The Synthetic Man,* Pyramid G636, 1961, second edition	2.50	3.50	2.62
☐	*The Synthetic Man,* Pyramid R-1126, 1965, third edition	2.50	3.50	2.62
☐	*The Synthetic Man,* Pyramid X-2007, 1969, fifth edition	1.75	2.25	2.00
☐	*A Touch Of Strange,* Berkley F1058, 1965	2.50	3.50	3.00
☐	*Venus Plus X,* Pyramid G544, 1960	3.00	4.00	3.50
☐	**Suyin, Han,** *A Many Splendored Thing,* Signet 1183 (photo cover picturing William Holden)	6.00	8.00	6.80
☐	**Swados, Felice,** *House of Fury,* Avon 430, no date. (This work became much better known under another title, *Reform School Girl.*)	20.00	30.00	23.70
☐	**Swarthout, Glendon,** *They Came to Cordura,* Signet 1679 (photo cover picturing Gary Cooper, Tab Hunter, Richard Conte and Michael Callan)	5.00	6.50	5.49
☐	**Tabori, George,** *The Journey,* Bantam 1868 (painted cover picturing Deborah Kerr and Yul Brynner)	5.00	6.50	5.49
☐	**Taylor, Valerie,** *Whisper Their Love,* Crest 187, 1957	3.25	4.00	3.62
☐	**Terry, C. V.,** *The Deadly Lady of Madagascar,* Perma M4165, 1960	2.00	3.00	2.30
☐	**Tessitore, John,** *For Love or Money,* Gold Medal 1341 (photo cover picturing Kirk Douglas and Mitzi Gaynor)	5.00	6.50	5.53
☐	*Nero's Mistress,* Gold Medal 952, 1960	1.35	1.85	1.50
☐	**Tey, Josephine,** *Brat Farrar,* Berkley F613, 1963, fourth edition	3.00	4.00	3.50

	Current Price Range		C/Y Avg.
☐ *Brat Farrar,* Pan 280, 1957 second edition	2.50	3.25	2.87
☐ *Brat Farrar,* Pan G237, 1961, fourth edition	2.25	3.00	2.62
☐ *The Daughter Of Time,* Dell 1672, 1969, fifth edition	1.75	2.50	2.12
☐ *The Daughter Of Time,* Penguin 990, 1960, fourth edition	2.00	3.00	2.50
☐ *The Daughter Of Time,* Penguin 990, 1954	4.00	5.50	4.75
☐ *The Franchise Affair,* Penguin 841, 1959, third edition	3.00	4.00	3.25
☐ *The Franchise Affair,* Penguin C841, 1964, sixth edition	2.25	3.25	2.70
☐ *The Franchise Affair,* Pocket 671, 1950	6.00	10.00	7.75
☐ *Killer in the Crowd,* Mercury 200, no date	3.00	4.00	3.50
☐ *The Man in the Queue,* Dell D255, 1959	2.25	3.00	2.62
☐ *The Man in the Queue,* Pan G134, 1964, fourth edition	2.00	2.75	2.37
☐ *Miss Pym Disposes,* Berkley F596, 1961, second edition	1.85	2.50	2.12
☐ *A Shilling For Candles,* Pan G170, 1960, third edition	1.85	2.50	2.12
☐ *A Shilling For Candles,* Pan G170, 1964, fourth edition	2.00	2.75	2.37
☐ *A Shilling For Candles,* Dell 7823, 1964	2.25	3.00	2.62
☐ **Thomas, Kenneth,** *Devil's Mistress,* Gold Medal S802, 1958, second edition	1.00	1.50	1.25
☐ **Thomas, Lee,** *A Woman's Game,* Beacon 18554F	1.65	2.25	1.75
☐ *Mazie,* Beacon 18684F	1.65	2.25	1.75
☐ **Thompson, John B.,** *Half Caste,* Beacon 18224	2.75	3.50	3.12
☐ *Hot Blood,* Beacon 18265	3.00	3.75	3.37
☐ **Thurber, James,** *The Beast In Me,* Avon T437	6.00	8.00	6.70
☐ **Thurman, Steve,** *Gun Fighting,* Graphic 96, 1955	4.00	5.50	4.25
☐ **Tilsley, Frank,** *H.M.S. Defiant,* Ballantine 596 (photo cover picturing Alec Guinness)	4.00	5.25	4.40

	Current Price Range		C/Y Avg.

☐ **Tolstoy, Leo,** *Anna Karenina,* Pocket Books 515 (photo cover picturing Vivien Leigh and Ralph Richardson) **6.00 8.00 6.39**

☐ **Torres, Tereska,** *Dangerous Games,* Crest S243, 1958 . . . . **2.50 3.25 2.87**

☐ *The Golden Cage,* Avon T448, no date **4.00 6.00 4.70**

☐ **Trainer, Russell,** *The Warden's Wife,* Beacon 18510F **1.85 2.50 2.00**

☐ **Traven, B.,** *Treasure of the Sierra Madre,* Pocket Books 455 (painted cover picturing Humphrey Bogart). Though not pictured on the cover, Walter Houston also appeared in this film. It was the only movie in which both he and his son, John Houston, appeared together. John preferred directing. **6.00 8.00 6.28**

☐ **Tucker, William,** *Long Loud Silence,* Dell 791, no date **6.00 8.00 6.50**

☐ **Turner, Robert,** *Chester,* Beacon 18432 **2.00 2.50 2.25**

☐ *Wagonmaster,* Pocket Books 1196 (painted cover picturing Ward Bond) When this one got to television it was retitled "Wagon Train." **6.00 8.00 6.41**

☐ **Twain, Mark,** *Life on the Mississippi,* Bantam 1, no date **9.00 12.00 10.20**

☐ (billed as Samuel L. Clemens), *The Prince and the Pauper,* Books Inc. 77, no date **1.75 2.50 2.05**

☐ **Ullman, Allen,** *Sorry Wrong Number,* Bantam 356 (painted cover picturing Barbara Stanwyck and Burt Lancaster) . . . **5.00 6.50 5.39**

☐ **Ullman, James R.,** *Third Man on the Mountain,* Cardinal C391 (painted cover picturing Michael Rennie. The movie version was produced by Disney.) **6.00 8.00 6.69**

☐ **Vail, John,** *Hold Back The Sun,* Gold Medal 556, 1956 . . . . **3.00 3.75 3.37**

☐ **Vail, Thomas,** *Blackmail and Old Lace,* Newstand Library U172, 1961 . . . . **2.00 2.75 2.37**

☐ **Vance, Ethel,** *Winter Meeting,* Bantam 400 (photo cover picturing Bette Davis) **6.00 8.00 6.82**

		Current Price Range		C/Y Avg.

☐ **Vance, Jack,** *The Anome,* Dell 0441, 1973		2.25	3.00	2.62
☐ *The Asutra,* Dell 3157, 1974		1.25	2.00	1.62
☐ *The Best Of Jack Vance,* Pocket 80510, 1976		1.85	2.50	2.00
☐ *Big Planet,* Ace G-661, no date		1.85	2.50	2.00
☐ *The Blue World,* Del Rey (CDN), 15784, 1977, second edition		1.85	2.55	2.00
☐ *The Blue World,* Mayflower 12497, 1977		2.00	2.75	2.37
☐ *The Blue World,* Ballantine U2 169, 1966		1.75	2.50	2.12
☐ *The Book Of Dreams,* DAW 1UE1587, 1416, 1981		2.00	2.75	2.37
☐ *The Brave Free Men,* Coronet 19828, 1975		2.25	3.00	2.62
☐ *The Brave Free Men,* Dell 1708, 1973		2.00	2.75	2.37
☐ *The Brave Free Men,* Ace 07200, 1978		1.75	2.50	2.12
☐ *City Of The Chasch,* Ace G-688, 1968		2.75	3.50	3.12
☐ *City Of The Chasch,* Mayflower 12340, 1974		2.00	2.75	2.37
☐ *City Of The Chasch,* DAW UE1461, 339, third edition		1.85	2.65	2.12
☐ *The Dirdir,* DAW UE1478, 1347, 1979		1.85	2.65	2.12
☐ *The Dirdir,* Ace 66901, 1969		2.50	3.50	3.00
☐ *The Dragon Masters,* Ace 16648, 1973, third edition		1.75	2.25	2.00
☐ *The Dragonmasters,* Ace 16651, 1981		1.50	2.00	1.75
☐ *Dust Of Far Suns,* DAW UE1588, 1417, 1981		2.00	2.75	2.37
☐ *The Dying Earth,* Lancer 75373, 1972, third edition		2.50	3.25	2.87
☐ *The Dying Earth,* Lancer 74-547, 1969		2.75	3.75	3.25
☐ *The Dying Earth,* Mayflower 12091, 1972, second edition		2.00	2.75	2.37
☐ *The Dying Earth,* Lancer 74-807, no date		1.50	2.00	1.75
☐ *Emphyrio,* Dell 2345, 1970		2.50	3.00	2.62
☐ *Emphyrio,* DAW UE1504, 1365, 1979		2.50	3.00	2.62
☐ *The Eyes Of The Overworld,* Pocket 80904, 1977		1.50	2.00	1.75

	Current Price Range		C/Y Avg.

☐ *The Eyes Of The Overworld*, Ace M-149, 1966 .... **3.50** **4.50** **4.00**

☐ *Fantasms and Magics*, Mayflower 12498, 1978 .... **2.25** **3.00** **2.62**

☐ *The Five Gold Bands*, DAW UG1518, 1374, 1980 .... **1.75** **2.50** **2.12**

☐ *Future Tense*, Ballantine U2214, 1964 **1.85** **2.65** **2.12**

☐ *The Gray Prince*, Avon 26799, 1975 **1.75** **2.50** **2.12**

☐ *The Killing Machine*, DAW UE1409, 1309, third edition **1.75** **2.50** **2.12**

☐ *The Killing Machine*, Berkley F1003, 1964 .... — **4.00** **6.00** **5.00**

☐ *The Languages Of Pao*, Mayflower 12307, 1974 .... **3.00** **4.00** **3.50**

☐ *The Languages Of Pao*, Ace 47401, no date **1.85** **2.50** **2.00**

☐ *The Languages Of Pao*, DAW UE1541, 1389, 1980 .... **1.75** **2.25** **1.85**

☐ *The Languages Of Pao*, Ace F-390, 1966 .... **3.00** **4.00** **3.50**

☐ *The Last Castle*, Ace 47073, 1982 ... **1.75** **2.50** **2.12**

☐ *The Last Castle*, Ace 47072, no date **2.00** **2.75** **2.37**

☐ **Van Druten, John,** *Bell, Book and Candle*, Bantam 1842 (photo cover picturing James Stewart and Kim Novak) **6.00** **8.00** **6.70**

☐ **Verne, Jules,** *Around The World in 80 Days*, Lion LL-90, 1956 .... **2.00** **2.75** **2.37**

☐ *A Journey To the Center of the Earth*, Perma 4161 (photo cover picturing Pat Boone, James Mason, Arlene Dahl and Diane Baker) **6.00** **8.00** **6.62**

☐ *Around the World in 80 Days*, Avon T148 (photo cover picturing David Niven, Frank Sinatra, Red Skelton, Peter Lorre, Ronald Colman, Shirley MacLaine, Robert Newton and others) **6.00** **8.00** **6.62**

☐ *The Master of the World*, Ace D504 (photo cover picturing Vincent Price) **5.00** **6.00** **5.41**

☐ **Vidal, Gore,** *The Best Man*, Signet 2423 (photo cover picturing Henry Fonda and Cliff Robertson) **5.00** **6.50** **5.39**

	Current Price Range		C/Y Avg.

☐ **Vonnegut, Kurt,** *The Sirens of Titan,* Dell B 138, no date 8.00 11.00 9.20

☐ **Walker, David,** *Harry Black,* Bantam 1828 (painted cover picturing Stewart Granger) 6.00 8.00 6.65

☐ **Wallace, Edgar,** *Again the Three,* Hodder C114, 1957 .... 5.00 6.50 5.75

☐ *The Angel Of Terror,* Pan G270, 1962, second edition 3.00 4.00 3.50

☐ *The Angel Of Terror,* Pan G270, 1959 3.50 4.50 4.00

☐ *The Avenger* Arrow 906870, 1973 ... 2.25 3.00 2.50

☐ *Big Foot,* Arrow 907080, 1973 ...... 2.25 3.00 2.50

☐ *Clue of the Silver Key,* Harlequin 361, 1956 .... 10.00 14.00 10.37

☐ *The Clue of the Twisted Candle,* Pan GG40, 1963, third edition 3.00 4.00 3.12

☐ *Clue of the Silver Key,* Harlequin 361, 1956 .... 5.00 7.00 5.25

☐ *The Crimson Circle,* Hodder C202, 1955 .... 5.00 7.75 6.00

☐ *The Devil Man,* White Circle 255, 1946 8.00 11.00 8.00

☐ *The Door With Seven Locks,* Pan G378, 1960 .... 3.00 4.00 3.50

☐ *The Door With Seven Locks,* Avon 125, 1947 .... 4.00 5.50 4.75

☐ *The Door With Seven Locks,* Hodder C61, 1951 .... 8.00 11.00 8.50

☐ *Double Dan,* Harlequin 444, 1958 .... 8.00 11.00 8.50

☐ *The Feathered Serpent,* Dell Map 49, 1944 .... 5.00 7.00 6.00

☐ *The Feathered Serpent,* Harlequin 418, 1958 .... 8.00 11.00 8.50

☐ **Wallace, Lew,** *Ben-Hur,* Cardinal GC75 (painted cover picturing Charlton Heston. Lew Wallace served as a General in the Civil War before settling down to a literary career.) 6.00 8.00 7.00

☐ **Wallach, Ira,** *Muscle Beach,* Dell D357, 1960 .... 3.00 4.00 3.50

☐ **Wallop, Douglas,** *Damn Yankees,* Cardinal C328 (photo cover picturing Gwen Verdon) 6.00 8.00 7.00

	Current Price Range		C/Y Avg.

☐ **Ward, Della,** *On The Make,* Newstand Library U149, 1960 .... **1.25 1.75 1.50**

☐ **Ward, Don,** *Gunsmoke,* Ballantine 236. (photo picturing James Arness). This was later reissued with serial number 364 and a new picture of James Arness. It has about the same value. **3.00 3.75 3.28**

☐ **Ward, Mary J.,** *The Snake Pit,* Signet 696. (painted cover picturing Olivia deHavilland). Undoubtedly Olivia deHavilland's most famous screen role, though far from her most glamorous. **6.00 8.00 6.59**

☐ **Watkins, Glenn,** *The Shame of Vanna Gilbert,* Croydon, 20, no date **6.00 11.00 8.90**

☐ **Watson, E. L. Grant,** *The Nun and the Bandit,* Albatross 286, undated **10.00 14.00 11.00**

☐ **Webb, Jack,** *The Damned Lovely,* Signet 1233, no date (cover artwork by Maguire) **4.00 5.50 4.70**

☐ *The Badge,* Crest 341 (photo cover picturing the author and Ben Alexander) **6.00 8.00 7.00**

☐ **Webb, Mary,** *Gone to Earth,* Dell 436 (painted cover picturing Jennifer Jones) **4.50 6.00 4.97**

☐ **Weidman, Jerome,** *I Can Get it For You Wholesale,* Avon 356 (painted cover picturing Susan Hayward and George Sanders) An unknown 19-year-old actress named Barbra Streisand was in this production when it was on Broadway. **6.00 8.00 6.83**

☐ **Wellman, Paul,** *Fiery Flower,* Perma Books M4192, 1961 .... **1.00 1.50 1.25**

☐ **Wells, Charles,** *Let the Night Cry,* Signet 1167, no date **4.00 6.00 4.65**

☐ **West, Edwin,** *Young and Innocent,* Monarch 165, 1960 .... **1.25 1.75 1.50**

☐ **Westcott, Jan,** *Captain for Elizabeth,* Perma Book M4171, 1960 .... **2.00 2.75 2.37**

☐ **White, James,** *The Aliens Among Us,* Ballantine 01545, 1969 .... **1.00 1.50 1.25**

☐ *All Judgment Fled,* Ballantine 02016, 1970 .... **1.25 2.00 1.62**

☐ *All Judgment Fled,* Del Ray 28025, 1979, second edition **1.00 1.75 1.37**

	Current Price Range		C/Y Avg.

☐ **Whitney, Phillis A.,** *Step to the Music,* Berkley, IG-294 .... | 2.25 | 2.75 | 2.50

☐ **Whittington, Harry,** *A Woman of the Place,* Ace S143, no date .... | 5.00 | 7.00 | 5.80

☐ *Die Lover,* Avon T450, no date ...... | 3.25 | 4.50 | 3.50

☐ *Doomsday Mission,* Banner B60-106, no date (Vietnam War theme) ...... | 3.25 | 4.50 | 3.60

☐ *Love Cult,* Lancer 71-315, no date ... | 3.25 | 4.50 | 3.50

☐ *69 Babylon Place,* Avon F146, 1962 | 2.50 | 3.00 | 3.50

☐ *Strange Bargain,* Avon T347, no date | 4.50 | 6.50 | 5.00

☐ *The Naked Jungle,* Ace S95, no date | 2.50 | 3.50 | 3.00

☐ **Wilder, Thornton,** *The Bridge of San Luis Rey,* Boni Books, no serial number, 1929 .... | 5.00 | 7.00 | 6.00

☐ **Wilheim, Gale,** *We Too Are Drifting,* Berkley 327 .... | 3.75 | 4.50 | 4.12

☐ **Williams, Charles,** *Aground,* Pocket 77394, 1971 .... | 1.35 | 1.85 | 1.50

☐ *Aground,* Crest S471, 1961 .... | 2.00 | 2.75 | 2.12

☐ *And The Deep Blue Sea,* Signet Q4515, 1971 .... | 1.50 | 2.00 | 1.75

☐ *The Big Bite,* Pocket 77506, 1973, second edition .... | 1.50 | 2.00 | 1.55

☐ *The Big Bite,* Dell A114, 1956 .... | 1.75 | 2.50 | 2.12

☐ *Dead Calm,* Pocket 77365, 1971 .... | 2.00 | 2.75 | 2.37

☐ *Dead Calm,* Avon G1255, 1965 ..... | 2.00 | 2.65 | 2.25

☐ *Go Home Stranger,* Gold Medal K1344, 1963, third edition .... | 2.00 | 2.65 | 2.25

☐ *Go Home Stranger,* Gold Medal 625, 1956, second edition .... | 3.00 | 4.00 | 3.12

☐ *Go Home Stranger,* Gold Medal 371, 1954 .... | 4.50 | 6.00 | 4.75

☐ **Williams, Jay,** *Solomon and Sheba,* Bantam 1958 (painted cover picturing Yul Brynner and Gina Lollobrigida) .... | 5.00 | 6.50 | 5.41

☐ **Williams, Tennessee,** *The Fugitive Kind,* Signet 1745 (painted cover picturing Marlon Brando, Anna Magnani, Joanne Woodward, Maureen Stapleton) .... | 6.00 | 8.00 | 6.82

	Current Price Range		C/Y Avg.

☐ *The Night of the Iguana,* Signet 2481 (painted cover picturing Richard Burton, Ava Gardner, Deborah Kerr and Sue Lyon) **6.00 8.00 6.82**

☐ *Period of Adjustment,* Signet 2210 (photo cover picturing Anthony Franciosa, Jane Fonda and James Hutton) **7.00 10.00 8.10**

☐ *Suddenly Last Summer,* Signet 1757 (photo cover picturing Elizabeth Taylor, Montgomery Clift and Katharine Hepburn) **6.00 8.00 6.82**

☐ *Summer and Smoke,* Signet 2019 (photo cover picturing Laurence Harvey and Geraldine Page) **6.00 8.00 6.82**

☐ **Williams, Wirt,** *Ada Dallas,* Dell S16 (painted cover picturing Susan Hayward) **6.00 8.00 6.82**

☐ **Wilson, Meredith,** *The Music Man,* Pyramid 736 (photo cover picturing Robert Preston and Shirley Jones) **7.00 10.00 8.21**

☐ **Winwar, Frances,** *Joan of Arc,* Bantam 459 (photo cover picturing Ingrid Bergman) **5.00 6.50 5.50**

☐ **Wouk, Herman,** *Marjorie Morningstar,* Signet 1454 (photo cover picturing Natalie Wood) **6.00 8.00 7.00**

☐ **Yates, Bill,** *Too Funny For Words,* Dell First Edition 39 .... **8.00 11.00 9.20**

☐ **Yordan, Philip,** *Anna Lucasta,* Dell 331 (photo cover picturing Paulette Goddard) **5.00 6.50 5.78**

☐ **Zola, Emile,** *Theresa,* Bantam 1020 ... **3.00 3.75 3.35**

Magazines

HISTORY OF MAGAZINES

The history of magazines bears very little resemblance to the history of books. Books were being written by the Greeks and Romans more than a thousand years before the invention of the printing press. They were produced one at a time, by handwriting. Tons of books came out in that fashion and circulated far and wide. But there were no magazines in the time of the Greek philosophers or the Twelve Caesars. Periodicals depend on speed of publication and equal speed of distribution. And there was no way, writing out copies individually by hand, to achieve anything better than a snail's pace.

Even when the printing press came to the world, around 1450 A.D., magazines did not immediately start up. There was another serious strike against magazines: most people were illiterate. Book publishing could be lucrative, 500 and more years ago. A publisher could run off an edition of a few hundred copies and sell each for a princely sum to the connoisseurs of the time. Success in periodical publishing demanded large-scale readership, since each sale would not bring in too much profit. There was no way to get large-scale readership if the general public couldn't read. In fifteenth century England the literacy rate was only about 10 percent. In most other countries it was even lower.

Things improved gradually in the succeeding years, and occasional stabs were made at periodical publications and newspapers, too. The earliest magazines all failed after short trials, however, and this discouraged others from making attempts. Mostly they were in the nature of highly opinionated discussions of current political and religious topics. They were not entertaining and not even newsworthy, and undoubtedly that was one reason for their lack of success. Anyone who wanted long-winded monologues could get them daily at the local coffeehouse.

It was not until the eighteenth century that magazines made any real strides in sales and popularity. The times had something to do with the fact that they finally clicked: eighteenth-century folk loved to read, loved gossip, wit, and anecdotes. Of course the magazine publishers had stiff competition from book publishers. Magazine publishers tried to give the public equally good reading matter, just as good as could be found in books, and at a much lower price. To accomplish this they cut corners wherever possible. They used no covers on their magazines. The page size was usually very small, no more than 5½" x 8", and the pages were simply sewn together with thread at the back to keep them together. Issues ran from just a few pages up to a hundred or more, but the average was around 20 or 30. Of course there were no photographic illustrations, since photography had not yet been developed. When illustrations appeared they were either in wood or copper engraving, but their use was held to a bare minimum to reduce costs. Some eighteenth century magazines carried advertisements, but these were in the nature of small classified ads, either unillustrated or with *stock* illustrations such as pointing hands. By today's standards they were extremely dull-looking, but so were the majority of books. They rank as collector's items nevertheless, and can be rare and valuable.

The first really popular, best-selling magazine was *The Spectator,* from early eighteenth century England. This classic of classics became one of the most talked-about, influential publications of all times. It was only a small pamphlet, issued twice a week, but the brains behind it were brains indeed: *The Spectator* was composed and published by Joseph Addison and Richard Steele, a pair of bright devilish wits who left an indelible mark on literature. Both had numerous books and other writings, including plays, to their credit. They were poets, humorists, satirists, and general critics of everything from A to Z in London society. Nothing escaped their attention and nobody was sacred to them. Luckily for Addison and Steele, it was a rollicking age with an *anything goes* mood—at another time they might have gone to the gallows for some of the things they wrote. Though it was highly successful, *The Spectator* did not have a really long run. Addison and Steele abandoned it in favor of other projects.

After *The Spectator,* the next popular magazine was Samuel Johnson's *The Rambler.* Johnson used *The Spectator* as a model for his *Rambler.* In fact it was almost identical in format and style. Johnson wrote almost all of the issues single-handedly. *The Rambler* dates to the early part of his career, long before he won universal fame as an oracle of literature. In fact he was unknown at the time, and struggled to raise the money to publish each issue.

Prompted by the success of *The Spectator* and *The Rambler,* a number of publishers brought out similar magazines. It seemed obvious that if a one-man effort such as *The Rambler* could make a hit, a magazine backed by a publishing house and staff of editors should do even better. At first these larger magazines had a mixed acceptance—they were just not as good literarily as the small ones, even though they were better looking and gave the reader more for his money. The first to achieve a large circulation was *The Gentleman's Magazine,* published in England in the mid 1700s. It was a monthly and established the monthly publication schedule for most magazines which followed. *The Gentleman's Magazine* carried writings of all sorts, relating to art, the theater, new books, people in the news and anything of current interest to the upper crusts of society. As the years passed its circulation greatly increased and it carried on into the 1900s, having been published for a full century and a half. Assembling a complete run of *The Gentleman's Magazine* is an almost impossible task for collectors—but a very inviting challenge.

After *The Gentleman's Magazine,* magazines started coming out by the score, in various parts of the world. They were not sold by subscription or on newsstands (newsstands did not exist until much, much later). Mostly the publishers worked out arrangements with bookshops, taverns and coffee houses to sell them. Also, copies were *hawked* in the street by vendors who sold them from pouches.

The nineteenth century saw the rise of mass-distribution magazines, aimed at a far larger audience. By the mid-nineteenth century, magazine publishing had become a major industry. It was doing so well that book publishers were worrying about the competition, and many of them starting putting out magazines of their own. *Scribner's Monthly* was one of the best-known magazines from a book publisher. The *Atlantic Monthly* was also issued by a book publisher. But undoubtedly the most historic magazine put out by a book publisher was *Harper's Weekly* (not to be confused with *Harper's Monthly*). It used full-page engraved illustrations and attempted to provide a pictorial—as well as written—record of everything of importance in the world. Issues of *Harper's Weekly* from the Civil War years are highly prized for their engravings of battlefield action. In many ways, *Harper's Weekly* was far ahead of its time. It was a picture magazine before the era of photography in magazines. The camera existed by then, but reproducing and printing photo-images was a tricky, costly process. So *Harper's* chose to stay with engravings.

The nineteenth century also ushered in the specialized magazine, aimed to one segment of the reading population rather than to general readers. Children's magazines started up in that century, and periodicals for women. Of the latter, the best seller was *Godey's Lady's Book,* which went on for many years. Like *Harper's,* it's highly valued for its vintage illustrations, which were also produced by the engraving process. *Godey's* presents a matchless record of the fashions of Victorian days.

The Saturday Evening Post, the longest-publishing American magazine, had foundations in the eighteenth century but did not reach a large audience until well into the nineteenth century. For most years between about 1890 and 1950 it had the largest circulation of any American weekly magazine, and was usually looked upon by the competition as the industry's style-setter. The number of top artists and writers whose work appeared in the *Post* was unmatched by any other periodical. Included among the writers was almost every best-selling American novelist of the early twentieth century.

In 1880, *National Geographic* was founded. It was considered, at the time, a daring concept for a magazine to focus upon the natural and scientific wonders of the world. Not too many copies of the first issue were printed (the exact number is unknown), and they've become very scarce. This is now one of the most valuable of all magazines. As the subscription rolls grew, issues were printed in larger and larger quantities, so the later issues are not nearly as hard to get.

Eight years later, in 1886, E.P. Collier, a New York publisher, founded *Collier's Weekly*. It had basically the same style and format as *Saturday Evening Post,* except that, in later years, it made more use of photographic illustrations than did the *Post.* It was an extremely popular title, achieving a high in circulation of around six million copies per week.

Though general-interest magazines did very well in the early years of the twentieth century, their sales and advertising declined after World War II. They were being hurt not by a lack of interest in magazines, but by competition from the smaller specialized titles. During the 1950s and 1960s most of the gigantic general interest magazines went out of business, though two of them *(Post and Life)* later returned.

Publishers reasoned this way: if some people were buying general-interest magazines because of the fiction, why not give them a fiction magazine? So they brought out *The Literary Digest* and *The New Yorker,* which were not strictly fiction in content but leaned heavily in that direction. The twentieth century also ushered in sports magazines on a large scale. There had been some earlier, mostly in England and mostly relating to horseracing. In 1922, Nat Fleischer started up his *Ring Magazine* on boxing. Even before that time, *Baseball Magazine* was being issued.

Some men's magazines were published before World War II, but they were generally of very low quality. The belief was, apparently, that anyone buying a *pin-up* magazine was only interested in the clarity of the photos and that nothing else counted. *The Police Gazette* was the leading men's magazine in the years from about 1900 to 1945. The revolution in men's magazines was sparked by Hugh Hefner's *Playboy,* founded in 1953, which featured a reproduction of the famous Marilyn Monroe calendar photo in its first issue. The photo was already four years old, but Hefner, starting on a shoestring, was in no position to hire models. When *Playboy* made it big, dozens of competitors hit the newstands, the most successful of which has been *Penthouse.*

HOW DO MAGAZINES BECOME VALUABLE?

The first thing to realize about values is that they aren't arbitrary. They are not arrived at by guesswork or estimates. Magazines bring the prices they bring because buyers are willing to pay those prices. If a magazine has a value of $1, this means buyers are not willing to pay more for it—at least not at the moment. A magazine selling for $50 or $75 has attained that level because collectors see it as ultra-desirable and do not object to "reaching" for it. But what makes a magazine desirable in the first place?

Several factors are involved. Some titles such as *Life, National Geographic* and *TV Guide* are very valuable, issue by issue, in relation to their scarcity. Huge quantities were printed, as these magazines enjoyed a very large circulation. Yet they have still become valuable—much MORE valuable than many magazines which had less circulation. This is mostly due to the popularity among SET collectors within the backdate magazine hobby. Many collectors are attempting to build up complete sets of these titles, which creates a great demand for *all* the issues—even those which did not carry particularly enticing content. Of course, the better issues sell higher than the ordinary ones, but even the so-so issues of (say) *TV Guide* from the 1960s bring more than issues of most other 1960s magazines.

Scarcity is another factor which can enter into price. The word *can* is important. Scarcity is sometimes no factor at all—a circumstance which often strikes beginning collectors as peculiar. They assume that a highly valuable collector's item, whether it's a magazine or mechanical bank or whatever, must have a certain degree of scarcity behind it to boost the price. Scarcity in itself will not do too much for the value of a magazine, if the title is obscure and not really pursued by collectors. But when scarcity is coupled with a popular title, the result can be a strong price. The classic example is the first issue of *National Geographic,* which has attained a very high price level. Though *National Geographics* on the whole are common, even going back many years, the first issue is anything but *common*. There were no big subscription rolls in those days, close to 100 years ago. Only a small batch was printed and of these, of course, an even smaller number managed to survive. The first issue of *National Geographic* has been reported to have sold for more than $1,000 in private transactions between dealers and collectors. In analyzing this price, it would have to be concluded that most of the value is for popularity and only a minor portion for scarcity. Why? Because there are certainly many other magazines just as scarce as the first *National Geographic,* which can be bought for a few dollars or even less. If *National Geographic* did not become successful, that first issue could never have attained anything close to a $1,000 pricetag. More likely it would now be unknown to most collectors, and unwanted, too.

The first issue of any popular magazine (popular with hobbyists, that is) will inevitably carry a premium value. This is borne out in the listings in this book. The first issue is not automatically the *most* valuable, however. If a subsequent issue carried some kind of really noteworthy content, it could be more valuable than Volume 1, Number 1.

One reason for first issues being valuable is that some backdate magazine enthusiasts collect *nothing but* first issues. They try to accumulate as many first issues as possible of many different magazines. This creates an additional market for first issues or "premier issues" as collectors often call them. It is not at all unusual for a first issue to sell for twice as much as issue No. 2, or even more.

Content is another important factor in the value of a backdate magazine.

Good content can lend super value to a magazine which would otherwise be lucky to sell for $1 or $2. This is thanks to purchases made by collectors whose principal hobby is something other than backdate magazines. An Elvis collector will very seldom concentrate strictly on backdate magazines, but will buy just about anything relating to Elvis in the way of memorabilia. The magazines he buys are very carefully selected for their coverage on Elvis, especially the photos. A serious Elvis collector wants (and is willing to pay the appropriate premiums for) *early* magazines with cover photos and/or articles, the earlier the better. Those from 1956—the year in which Elvis burst upon the national scene—are the most in demand, but others from the late fifties and sixties are also very collectible. Just as there are Elvis collectors seeking out good magazine items, there are collectors of the Beatles and other stars doing the same. Chiefly, the value will depend on the number of active collectors to which the *content* appeals. In the case of Elvis and the Beatles there are tens of thousands of collectors, so the values can go soaring. With celebrities of somewhat less fame and popularity, there will usually be fewer active collectors and lower prices. The same is true for politicians, sports figures, and anyone who attracts a fan following.

But "fans" are not the only specialist collectors who buy backdate magazines. Many specialist buyers come from the ranks of space-flight collectors who want "moon walk" issues and other pertinent issues. History-minded collectors account for the premium prices on issues of *Life* with important World War II coverage.

You will note in the listings for *Life* and *TV Guide* that certain special issues—designed to *be* special at the time of publication—carry premium prices. With *TV Guide,* the annual Fall Preview issue always becomes a collector's item and usually ends up selling for three times as much as a regular issue from that same year.

Yet another contributing factor in the value of a backdate magazine, especially a *very* old one, can be the advertisements.

Old ads have become very popular in themselves, as a facet of the "advertising collectibles" hobby. When offering an early magazine for sale, a dealer will sometimes call attention to the type of ads it contains and even the manufacturers whose products are advertised. Full-color ads are, of course, of more appeal to collectors than black and whites. While colored ads were used in magazine advertising before 1900, they did not come into really widespread use until after World War I, which ended in 1918. Early auto ads are especially sought after; also desirable are full-page color ads for soft drinks, beer, Shirley Temple dolls (from the 1930s), motorcycles, and cigarettes. The most valuable ads are those in which a "collectible" celebrity, such as Ronald Reagan, is endorsing a product. Since his election in 1980, hobbyists and dealers have been combing through magazines of the 1940s and 1950s for "Reagan ads."

COLLECTING MAGAZINES

Collectors have been coming into the field of magazines in droves within recent years. Compared to paperback collecting, magazine collecting is definitely not a new hobby. Titles like *National Geographic* and some of the other oldies were being actively pursued by collectors more than a half a century ago. However, in terms of large-scale, all-out fervent collecting, this has been a phenomenon of the 1970s and 1980s. The result? Higher prices, for one thing. And windfalls for many individuals who just "saved" their old magazines, without having the least intention of actually collecting. Many magazines that were bought in the 1950s for 25¢ or 35¢ each can now be sold for $5, $10 or even more—and when you have a whole carton or two of them, it adds up pretty fast.

Magazine collecting often begins as an offshoot of some other hobby. An avid sports fan might develop an interest in the historic side of his favorite sport and start buying books, memorabilia, and old magazines relating to it. The camera buff goes after photography magazines, and so on. This kind of a magazine collection is called *topical*—it pertains to a single specific topic, and the hobbyist collects any and all magazines on that theme. Since so many specialized magazines exist, a topical collection can be built around just about any subject that interests you. Of course, the broader the subject, the more latitude you'll have. By the same token, if the subject is of recent origin—such as space flight—you won't have the fun of digging for magazines published ages and ages ago.

There can be other aspects to a topical collection, too.

And that's where the fun really begins.

Suppose your topical interest is African big game. You won't find an entire magazine on that subject, but articles on African big game (hunting it, photographing it, preserving it, carting it off to zoos) have appeared in hundreds of magazines all over the world going back to very early times. The search for these articles, and for copies of the magazines carrying them, can be a real treasure hunt. And that is precisely how many magazine collectors choose to approach the hobby. First, you must track down the articles. This means trips to the library and some sessions with reference books such as *Reader's Guide to Periodical Literature.* References to articles will also show up in many other books. You can never "complete" this kind of collection, as there will always be articles you're not aware of, in some magazine or other. But with some work and a lot of persistence in contacting dealers, it can be built up to impressive proportions.

As the magazine hobby stands today, in the 1980s, content of a magazine sets the price more than anything else. A Beatles cover or a Marilyn Monroe cover or article results in a much higher price for that issue than the magazine's other issues bring. So there is obviously no doubt that many, many hobbyists are collecting in that fashion: pursuing their favorite stars or subjects in backdate magazines, and not really caring *what* magazine they find them in. This represents a big change of pace from the traditional approach to magazine collecting, which concentrated on sets and runs of popular titles.

In set collecting, the object is to assemble a full set of the magazine from its first issue to the present day—or until the termination issue, if it no longer publishes. Set collecting has its definite appeal for many people. By working on a set, there is a tangible goal and you know—at all times—just how far you are from reaching that goal, both in terms of the number of additional issues needed and the approximate cost. When the set is finally completed you know you have it all—that nothing needs to be added. This in itself is rather satisfying. And of course a complete set or run will always carry somewhat more value than the individual issues.

The problem with set collecting is that it just isn't possible to build complete sets of many of the long-running magazines, due to the scarcity of many of their pioneer issues. In Britain the favorite magazine of set collectors is *Punch,* the humor weekly which has been publishing

52 issues per year since its inception in 1841. A little arithmetic shows that 52 issues times the 140-odd years from 1841 until today yields over 7,000 issues. Even if none of these issues were particularly scarce, it would be a colossal achievement to locate all of them. In the case of *National Geographic,* the first few issues are rare and very costly, the first issue sometimes selling for a thousand dollars or even more. Of course, a set collection can be rewarding even if it never reaches completion. If you're willing to live with some empty spaces in your collection, there should be no real obstacle to becoming a set collector.

BUYING MAGAZINES

There are many sources for backdate magazines. A beginning collector might want to buy where the prices are lowest, such as a flea market. This would be suitable if his chosen target is, say, building a set of *Life.* He could probably pick up dozens of issues of *Life* by visiting a few flea markets, and the prices are apt to be less than full market value. After getting the nucleus of a collection together, however, sources such as flea markets, garage sales and charity bazaars are no longer as lucrative. By then the quest will be for specific issues and it is usually difficult, or impossible, to find them at such locations.

As you get more advanced, you will undoubtedly be buying from backdate magazine shops (some of which also sell used paperbacks and hardcovered books, too) and from the lists of dealers who operate by mail.

The general backdate magazine shop is an American institution with a long history. These establishments have been with us since well before World War II. Some of them are really gigantic in terms of the number of issues stocked, with 500,000 or even one million magazines under one roof. Before the current age of hot-and-heavy magazine collecting, backdate magazine shops had a somewhat different level of clientele. Instead of the hobbyists, they mainly catered to libraries and people doing research, who needed certain articles on certain subjects. The amount of business done with pure collectors was very limited. Today it's just the reverse, as collectors account for the majority of sales made by backdate magazine shops.

You will find that some backdate magazine shops are more collector-oriented than others, and you will run across some still doing business as they (or their predecessors) did in the 1950s, seemingly unaware that the nature of the clientele has changed. In a collector-oriented shop, you will find displays of the scarce, more desirable magazines and those with collectible covers. These will be in vinyl protective bags, usually on the walls or hanging from strings on the ceiling. Prices will not be marked on the magazine itself but written in crayon on the vinyl bag. This technique of retailing backdate magazines was adapted from dealers in old comic books, and of course it works equally well for magazines. In a collector-oriented shop, you will find a preponderance of titles on subjects with definite collector appeal, such as show business, men's magazines, the outdoors, and various kinds of hobbies. These books will be "up front" where you can't miss them, and there will probably be more just like them scattered throughout the shop's stock. In a non-collector-oriented shop, you may find huge batches of magazines that have very little current collector interest, such as those on religion or farming.

When a backdate magazine shop tries to stock a little of everything (no shop can stock a lot of everything, when it comes to magazines), it won't present very much for the collector. Still, such shops ought to be thoroughly investigated, as you never know what may turn up. In some cases, browsing will not be allowed, as the files of magazines are all arranged carefully by issue number or date and the proprietor wants to prevent people from shuffling them around. Browsers are notorious for not putting things back where they came from, so you have to sympathize with the shop owner. In a no-browsing shop, you can use a want list. Just give the proprietor your list (prepared in advance), and he'll pull all the available items from his stock. If the magazines you want are not too old, and are popular titles, he may succeed in filling the entire want list. Don't expect the average backdate shop to score too many hits on a want list of magazines from the 1920s and 1930s, however. No shop has a comprehensive stock of the oldies. It would mean tying up too much capital in stock that just doesn't move fast enough.

If you intend to buy a scarce magazine in a sealed vinyl bag, take it out and examine it first. Ask the proprietor's permission before doing this.

Even when buying low-value backdate magazines, they should be carefully inspected. With hundreds of magazines coming and going constantly, the shopkeepers simply don't have the time to check each one thoroughly. If the magazine *appears* to be in good condition, it goes into their stock; but a magazine can be quite presentable looking from the outside and still have defects inside, such as staining, clippings missing, or whole pages gone. This (as you can imagine) is more of a problem with the men's magazines. You will often find copies that look pristine, but have the centerfold missing. A missing centerfold will reduce the value by around 50 percent, even though the centerfold in itself isn't worth very much. Some backdate dealers sell loose centerfolds and the price is usually a standard $1 each. If you happen to have a scarce *Playboy* or *Penthouse* lacking the centerfold, you could get lucky and find the right one in these mixed batches.

Most backdate magazine shops have a bargain counter or bargain boxes, where magazines are selling for discounted prices. These, of course, are "reading" copies, for customers who just want something to read—or for topical collectors interested in one article rather than the whole issue. Bargain copies are sure to have something wrong with them. The constant handling they receive from browsers in the shop reduces their condition even further. Usually, the shop has better-grade copies of the same issues in its regular stock, if any of them appeal to you. These are simply its rejects which it wants to move along quickly.

Another way of buying backdate magazines is by mail. You will find advertisements for backdate magazines in most of the hobbyist newspapers, some of which are sure to be available at your local public library. Lists of magazines are issued by numerous dealers, usually of a specialty nature—confined to issues of a single magazine, or magazines on a certain topic. You will find some dealers selling nothing but old *Lifes,* others dealing in *National Geographic* or *TV Guide* or *Playboy.* These specialist dealers carry very comprehensive stocks, sometimes, in fact, stocking a full run of the magazine from its first issue onward. They are certainly the best source for an advanced, serious collector who knows exactly what he wants and doesn't care to waste too much time searching for it. They can fill just about any gap in your collection, if you collect the specific magazines they deal in. Of course, in buying from specialist dealers you pay "top of the market" prices. These dealers are not only in close touch with the market, they *make* the market to some extent by their pricing policies. When a famous, beloved celebrity dies, the dealer will raise his prices for issues carrying cover photos or articles on that celebrity, knowing there will be an increased demand. And there always is! In recent years, magazines with features on John Lennon, Elvis Presley, Natalie Wood, John Wayne, Henry Fonda, and Princess Grace have all climbed dramatically in price, most of them doubling or tripling in value during the first year after the celebrity's death. As these issues are likely to go even higher in the future, it's usually a good bet to get them as early as possible.

A typical dealer's list will mention the condition of each magazine. Failing that, there will be a note at the beginning of the list, to the effect that all magazines are in Very Good condition unless stated otherwise. If there is no statement of condition, approach with caution!

Any time something is bought sight-unseen, you take a mild risk. The objective is to make the risk as mild as possible! Of course, you should check the dealer's terms of sale to see whether he accepts returns, and, if so, whether he issues a cash refund or a credit slip. Some dealers will take returns only against a credit on a future purchase, and this is really of no value if you have no intention of buying anything further from that dealer.

You will usually be required to pay the postage on magazines bought through the mail. First class delivery is available if you care to pay the extra cost, but this is really an unnecessary expense. A shipment of valuable magazines should always be insured.

MAGAZINES IN BINDINGS

All prices listed in *The Official Price Guide to Paperbacks and Magazines* are for loose issues of magazines, unbound, just as they were issued. However, on the market you will sometimes find bound volumes of magazines, especially of the older magazines. Usually, a bound volume comprises a whole year's worth of the magazine, but in the case of a weekly or a large monthly it may be only six months.

There is mixed opinion about magazines in bindings. If the binding is attractive, such as buckram covers with a morocco spine and neat gold gilding, it will certainly look better on your bookshelf than the unbound magazines. Still, the preference of most collectors is for loose issues, and you will discover that in the majority of cases a bound volume is worth *less* than the loose issues would be. The early years of *National Geographic,* for example, invariably sell at discount prices in bound volumes as compared to the prices of loose individual issues. While that may seem hard to comprehend—since the binding represents an expense in itself—collectors are very much addicted to "original state." If a publication was issued in a hard binding, they want it that way. If it came in soft covers, most collectors believe it should remain in soft covers for the rest of its existence.

Thus, our advice is *not* to have any of your magazines bound into hard covers. You will be incurring an extra cost, while possibly reducing their resale value at the same time.

GRADING MAGAZINES

Notes on the condition grade now appear in virtually all dealers' lists and advertisements. While in some instances dealers use nonstandard terminology of their own creation ("a really nice copy"), the trend within the market is toward standardized grading. Unless a seller actually takes the trouble and space to describe a magazine's faults in graphic detail, standard terminology is the only means of clearly expressing its condition. By the use of letter symbols a very clear understanding of a magazine's physical condition is conveyed to the potential customer. The most frequently used symbols are *VF, F, VG* and *G* (see explanations below). If you do not find one of these symbols in a dealer's description of a magazine, and nothing is mentioned about its condition, read the introductory notes appearing above his listings. He may state that all his magazines are F unless otherwise indicated, or VF, or some other standard grade.

A magazine, regardless of its age or other factors, is expected to be complete even if it falls into a low condition grade. There are no provisions in the condition grades for missing covers or missing pages. When a dealer is offering a magazine with missing covers or missing pages, he is obliged to mention this fact along with the condition grade. It is entirely possible that a magazine can grade VF and still have a cover or page missing, just as it is possible for one to be in very poor condition and be complete. Missing covers and pages were seldom detached through excessive handling: they were purposely cut or torn away.

M (Mint). Newsstand condition, bright and fresh with no evidence of having been handled. Few backdate magazines qualify for this designation. The collector who seeks M specimens of magazines published in the 1930s or 1940s will be disappointed.

VF (Very Fine). The magazine shows some slight evidence of being handled and minor deterioration as the result of age, but it has suffered no injury nor has been carelessly handled. The covers are not creased or stained. The page corners are not turned down. There are no markings on the pages. There may be a subscription label on the front cover and evidence of an old "subscription fold" running the entire length of the magazine (vertically), as the result of having been folded for mailing. This does not detract from a VF grading, though some ultra purist collectors object to such copies.

F (Fine). A magazine graded F falls somewhat short of the VF grading but is entirely sound with nothing that can be termed damage. It is simply a copy that has seen more handling and there is a vague look of fatigue about it, but no tears, stains, heavy creases or repairs. The cover gloss, if any existed originally, is likely to be gone. The cover may likewise be somewhat faded as the result of display in a dealer's shop window. F graded magazines are entirely satisfactory to the great majority of collectors, and in the case of very old magazines this is often the highest obtainable grade.

VG (Very Good). Some creasing will be apparent on the covers. There may be chips missing from the corners of the covers, as well as from some pages. Some page corners will likely be turned down and there may be a bit of light pencil scribbling on the insides of the covers or possibly elsewhere. The front cover may be more faded than one would expect of a copy graded F. Still the magazine should be intact, it should not show any water staining, and there should be no tape repairs either on the covers or pages. If the magazine is loose in its covers—that is, fully detached from them—it should not be graded VG.

G (Good). In this grade one finds some light moisture staining, heavier cover and page creasing than in the VG grade, and possibly minor repairs made with cellophane tape. If repairs have been made with nontransparent tape, such as masking or electrical tape, the magazine should not be graded G. There should be no clippings or pages missing. Pieces may be missing from one or both covers.

FR (Fair). This is basically a reading or "cutting" copy. The term cutting copy is used in reference to magazines with valuable ads or other content, whose overall condition is so low that there is no hesitation to extract material for framing. Dealers are more than content when they can salvage a few good ads from a damaged magazine and this is probably the smartest philosophy for collectors as well. FR graded magazines are rather badly moisture stained, with covers and/or pages torn, but as previously stated there should be no pages or covers actually missing. In many instances the covers will be held in place with tape.

P (Poor). A specimen that no collector would want, though it should be complete and readable.

INVESTING OFF THE NEWSSTAND

The listings in this book include numerous magazines now selling for $50, $100 and more. Everyone had a chance to buy these issues at their original cover price and save them as investments. The fact that few persons did this was, of course, a contributing factor in their present scarcity and high market values.

There is no reason why some magazines currently available at newsstands should fail to rank just as highly as investments. Using a certain degree of strategy it should be possible to build up an "investment portfolio" of magazines purchased for no more than their cover prices. Some would probably become salable at a profit within a year or two of publication date. Others may take longer to increase in value. By holding for an extended period, say 10 years or more, there is a potential for a very considerable value increase.

The investment buyer should concentrate on certain types of magazines and positively avoid all others. There is no real profit potential in ordinary issues of heavily distributed national magazines. Such magazines should be considered for investment only if the issue is special in some respect: major news coverage (royal wedding, royal baby, assassination, etc.) or a cover photo and article on a celebrity in whom there is great collector interest (the major rock idols would all fall into this category). Issues with very controversial content are also a possibility for investment.

But even better than these, for investment buying, are the "one shots" dealing exclusively with a given celebrity. They have more collector appeal and will not be as readily obtainable on the backdate magazine market. Some ability to guess the future is required, as one needs to predict which celebrities will continue to be fan and collector favorites in the next decade.

In buying magazines for investment off the newsstand, they should always be purchased in multiple copies. If you own enough copies you can virtually "corner the market" and become a supplier for the dealers, when the price gets high enough. The alternative is to become a dealer yourself and advertise your magazines to the public in one of the collector's periodicals. If you choose this course, do not mention the number of duplicate copies you have on hand, as the availability of duplicates will dampen a collector's enthusiasm.

PRESERVING YOUR MAGAZINES

As a general rule, magazines should not be stored on bookcase shelves *unless* they've been bound into hard covers (which is not recommended, as it usually reduces the value). Loose magazines do not belong on shelving. They will suffer a great deal of needless wear and tear this way, not to mention the fact that it's exasperating trying to keep a shelf of magazines from toppling over whenever you remove some of them. The best approach is to use acid-free storage boxes with lids. If your magazines are of more than modest value, they should be placed in individual vinyl or mylar bags before going into the boxes. Special acid-free boxes, which are sold under various trade names, are available from some dealers in backdate magazines and comic books. If you cannot get them locally, they're readily obtained by mail. Just check the advertisements appearing regularly in the pages of hobbyist magazines.

When repairs are necessary they should be made with white glue, using just enough to do the job. Avoid all kinds of tape. Always realize that repairs will do nothing more than enhance the appearance of a damaged magazine and possibly retard further damage (such as a tear becoming longer or a cover falling off). They will not add to the cash value. If you have really valuable magazines you might want to consider using the services of a professional paper restorer rather than attempting a do-it-yourself operation.

SELLING BACKDATE MAGAZINES

Selling backdate magazines is not really very different than selling any other kind of collector's item. If you have worthwhile in-demand material, in a good state of physical condition, there will be no trouble at all finding potential buyers for it. On the other hand, if your magazines are very recent, or titles which have not scored much popularity with collectors, or if the condition is somewhat less than presentable, they may be difficult to sell.

The established backdate magazine dealers want to buy good magazines! They have to buy in order to replenish their stock, and they would much prefer buying from the public than anywhere else. The public is their biggest supplier, as they cannot phone a wholesaler and ask for ten copies of *Playboy* No. 11 to be sent over. The constant turnover of backdate magazines, going from the hands of the public to dealers and then to collectors, keeps the dealers in business. If everyone wanted to buy, and nobody wanted to sell, the backdate magazine trade would soon come to a grinding halt.

Just like many collectors, quite a few of the dealers have "want lists." These are printed lists detailing the type of magazines, and in some cases the specific magazine and issue number, that the dealer is especially anxious to buy. These are the magazines for which the dealer has the strongest demand from his customers; without circulating a want list he might have difficulty keeping them in sufficient supply. Some dealer want lists have prices and some do not. If prices are not indicated, it will most likely be the dealer's practice not to discuss price until he has the magazines in his hands and can examine their condition.

Whether or not a dealer issues a want list, you are still at liberty to offer him *any* magazines that you want to sell, in person or by mail. If you contact the dealer by mail, enclose a complete list of all your magazines. Give the title of each along with the date and issue number. Also state the condition (and be objective about it!). You can set prices if you wish, but this really depends on how anxious you are to make a sale. When a dealer receives a list with prices, it is treated just like a price list from another dealer—as if you were a professional. If your prices are really attractive he will buy, of course. But most dealers do prefer making offers or at least negotiating the price with the owner.

When writing to a dealer, be sure to state whether you want to sell your magazines as a collection, or if you would be willing to sell just some issues if he cares to pick and choose.

You can bring your magazines to a backdate shop for an on-the-spot offer. If any scarce issues are included, they should be enclosed in protective vinyl bags.

What sort of price will you get?

On popular magazines worth $10 or more apiece, the buying price will average around 40 percent of the selling price. Occasionally you may find dealers who pay more than this, but 40 percent seems the general average within the trade. For magazines with a retail value under $10, the buying offer will be somewhat less. On the occasional scarce, much-in-demand magazine worth $75, $100 or more, the buying offers could vary quite a bit, so you might want to contact several dealers before reaching a decision. Of course, magazines should always be sold to dealers who specialize in that particular kind of magazine, whenever possible.

MAGAZINE LISTINGS

	Current Price Range		C/Y Avg.

AINSLEE'S
☐ December 1906 ("The Chariot of Fate" by Joseph C. Lincoln; "Compliments of the Season" by O. Henry) 8.00   10.00   9.00

AL CAPONE ON THE SPOT
☐ No. 1, 1931 (One Issue Only; Portrait of Al Capone, on cover) 40.00   50.00   45.00

ANTIQUE AUTOMOBILE
☐ Summer 1954 (Published by Antique Automobile Club of America) 6.00   8.00   7.00

THE AMERICAN MAGAZINE
☐ December 1950 ("Christmas Dinner with Santa Claus" by Don Eddy) 5.00   7.00   6.00
☐ June 1951 ("Going to Work With God on Monday" by Wallace C. Speers) 5.00   7.00   6.00
☐ January 1952 ("My Brother Bob Taft" by Helen Taft Manning) 5.00   7.00   6.00
☐ July 1952 ("At Last Your Dollar is Getting Bigger" by Roger W. Babson) 5.00   7.00   6.00
☐ August 1952 ("The Cross-Eyed Cupid" by Marjorie Carleton) 5.00   7.00   6.00
☐ December 1952 ("Murder by Moonlight" by Lew Dietz) 5.00   7.00   6.00
☐ October 1954 (J. Edgar Hoover tells How Communists Try to Control Our Thinking) 4.00   6.00   5.00
☐ August 1955 (The Amazing Secret of Walt Disney) 10.00   12.00   11.00
☐ September 1955 (Jayne and Audrey Meadows: Sisters With a Secret) 3.00   5.00   4.00
☐ February 1956 ("Maid in Manhattan" by Jerrold Beim) 3.00   5.00   4.00
☐ April 1956 ("I Disarmed the A-Bomb" by Dr. John C. Clark) 3.00   5.00   4.00

The American Magazine, January 1952, $5.00–$7.00.

	Current Price Range		C/Y Avg.
THE AMERICAN MONTHLY REVIEW OF REVIEWS			
☐ September 1900 (Can China Be Saved?; The Prohibition Party of 1900)	9.00	11.00	10.00
☐ September 1904 (A Chinaman on the "Yellow Peril")	9.00	11.00	10.00
☐ November 1904 (Canada In 1904; An Epidemic of Railroad Accidents)	14.00	16.00	15.00
☐ December 1904 (The Sweeping Approval of President Roosevelt; Electric Versus Steam Locomotives)	14.00	16.00	15.00
☐ February 1905 (The Panama Canal—Problems for the Chief Engineer)	10.00	12.00	11.00
☐ April 1905 (Portland and the Lewis and Clark Centennial)	9.00	11.00	10.00
☐ July 1905 (Theodore Roosevelt, Peacemaker)	9.00	11.00	10.00

	Current Price Range		C/Y Avg.

☐ March 1906 (Sane Restrictions on Immigration) **8.00 10.00 9.00**

☐ April 1906 (Is the Russian Revolution Constructive?; The Life-Work of Susan B. Anthony) **9.00 11.00 10.00**

☐ May 1906 (San Francisco Earthquake) **20.00 25.00 22.50**

☐ July 1906 (Frontispiece: The Formal Opening of the Olympic Games of 1906) **17.00 19.00 18.00**

AMERICAN WOMAN
☐ November 1916 (McMein artwork, on cover) **8.00 10.00 9.00**

ANTIQUE AUTOMOBILE
☐ Summer 1954 (Published by Antique Automobile Club of America) **6.00 8.00 7,00**

ART NEWS
☐ October 14, 1942 (Charles D. Gibson artwork, on cover) **20.00 25.00 22.50**

ASIA
☐ January 1929 (Assamese Dancer, Painting by Frank McIntosh, on cover) **25.00 30.00 27.50**

ASSOCIATION MEN

This was a publication of the YMCA.

☐ February 1917 (W. Louderback illustration, on cover) **5.00 7.00 6.00**

THE ATLANTIC MONTHLY
☐ June 1887 ("Our Hundred Days In Europe IV" by Oliver Wendell Holmes) ... **14.00 16.00 15.00**

BANDLEADERS
☐ June 1946 (Stan Kenton on cover) **11.00 13.00 12.00**

BEATLES' MONTHLY BOOK
☐ March 1965 (Ringo Star on cover) **20.00 25.00 22.50**

BEHIND THE SCENES
☐ December 1954 .... **1.00 3.00 2.00**
☐ February 1955 .... **1.00 3.00 2.00**
☐ March 1955 .... **1.00 3.00 2.00**

	Current Price Range		C/Y Avg.
☐ April 1955	1.00	3.00	2.00
☐ May 1955	1.00	3.00	2.00
☐ June 1955	1.00	3.00	2.00

BELFORD'S MAGAZINE

☐ December 1888 ("Dead-shot Dan" by W. J. Florence; "Joe: A Story of Frontier Life" by Rosalie Kaufman)	8.00	10.00	9.00

BLACK MASK

Some of the best work of writers Dashiell Hammett and Erle Stanley Gardner appeared in *Black Mask* in the 1920s and 1930s. Gardner went on to create the Perry Mason series.

☐ November 1921 ("The Emperor of Blunderland")	200.00	250.00	225.00
☐ March 1925 ("The Continental Detective" by Dashiell Hammett)	70.00	80.00	75.00
☐ February 1926 ("Bob Larkin" by E. S. Gardner; "The Assistant Murderer" by Dashiell Hammett)	70.00	80.00	75.00
☐ February 1927 ("The Big Knockover" by Dashiell Hammett; "Cat Woman" by E.S. Gardner)	70.00	80.00	75.00
☐ April 1927 (A Race Williams Story)	130.00	155.00	142.50
☐ August 1928 (Old West Issue)	130.00	155.00	142.50
☐ January 1930 ("The Maltese Falcon" by Dashiell Hammett—"The Maltese Falcon" was the most famous of all of Hammett's stories. It became an equally famous motion picture)	130.00	155.00	142.40
☐ March 1930 ("The Glass Key" by Dashiell Hammett)	35.00	40.00	37.50
☐ January 1935 ("Killer in the Rain" by Raymond Chandler)	60.00	70.00	65.00
☐ May 1936 (Stories by E.S. Gardner and G.H. Coxe)	70.00	80.00	75.00

BOLD

☐ June 1954	1.00	3.00	2.00
☐ September 1954	1.00	3.00	2.00
☐ October 1954	1.00	3.00	2.00

	Current Price Range		C/Y Avg.
☐ November 1954	1.00	3.00	2.00
☐ December 1954	1.00	3.00	2.00
☐ February 1955	1.00	3.00	2.00
☐ April 1955	1.00	3.00	2.00
☐ May 1955	1.00	3.00	2.00
☐ June 1955	1.00	3.00	2.00
☐ August 1955	1.00	3.00	2.00
☐ September 1955	1.00	3.00	2.00
☐ June 1956	1.00	3.00	2.00

THE BOYS' MAGAZINE

☐ May 1913 ("No Man a 'Tall" by Charles Askins)	4.00	6.00	5.00

BOYS' LIFE

Norman Rockwell first established himself as a national illustrator of note via the covers of *Boys' Life*. Even after he moved on to the *Saturday Evening Post* after World War II, Rockwell continued infrequently gracing the covers of the national Boy Scouts monthly with his artwork.

☐ February 1948 (Norman Rockwell artwork on cover).....................	18.00	20.00	19.00
☐ February 1959 (Norman Rockwell artwork on cover).....................	12.00	14.00	13.00

BRIGITTE BARDOT

☐ 1958 (one issue only)	35.00	40.00	37.50

BROWN BOOK OF BOSTON

☐ May 1903 ("The Moor of Purley Horton" by A.J. Dawson)	9.00	11.00	10.00
☐ June 1903 ("A Chance for the Children" by Isabel Brown)	9.00	11.00	10.00
☐ July 1903 ("At the Sign of the Tea-Cup" by Temple Bailey)	9.00	11.00	10.00
☐ August 1903 ("Gwendolen's Stockings" by Laura Leonard)	9.00	11.00	10.00
☐ September 1903 ("La Juliette" by Kathryn Jarboe)	9.00	11.00	10.00
☐ October 1903 ("The 'Round-Up' " by R. Farrington Elwell)	9.00	11.00	10.00
☐ November 1903 ("The Girls and I, A Chat Page" by Helen C. Candee)	9.00	11.00	10.00

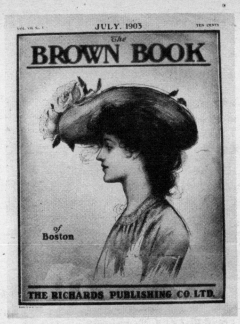

The Brown Book of Boston, July 1903, $9.00–$11.00.

	Current Price Range		C/Y Avg.
☐ January 1904 ("Mrs. Dash's Dilemma" by J.J. Bell)	8.00	10.00	9.00
☐ March 1904 ("The Dower-Chest of Ann Ponsford" by V. L. Siberrad)	8.00	10.00	9.00
☐ April 1904 ("Jobina's Jewels" by Kathryn Jarboe)	8.00	10.00	9.00
☐ May 1904 ("The Mutiny of the 'Laughing Mary'" by W. H. Durham)	8.00	10.00	9.00
☐ July 1904 ("The Last Word" by Eben E. Rexford)	8.00	10.00	9.00
☐ August 1904 ("Cindy's Widowhood" by Charles McIlvaine)	8.00	10.00	9.00
☐ September 1904 ("A Visit to the Old Farm" by Mary Minerva Barrows)	8.00	10.00	9.00
☐ October 1904 ("The Quest of a Cow" by Edward Mumford)	8.00	10.00	9.00
☐ December 1904 ("The Christmas Wayfarers" by Temple Bailey)	8.00	10.00	9.00

	Current Price Range		C/Y Avg.
☐ January 1905 ("Cecily—Emergency Cook" by Emily Wright)	7.00	9.00	8.00
☐ March 1905 ("The Fruit of the Tree" by Temple Bailey)	7.00	9.00	8.00
☐ April 1905 ("Sherlock Holmes' Daughter" by H.H. Ballard)	17.00	19.00	18.00
☐ May 1905 ("The Girl Who Wondered" by Carroll Watson Rankin)	7.00	9.00	8.00

CALLING ALL GIRLS
☐ July 1948 (Elizabeth Taylor on cover) ..	12.00	14.00	13.00

CAMEO
☐ October 1953 (first issue)	3.50	5.50	4.50
☐ November 1953	1.50	3.50	2.50
☐ December 1, 1953	1.50	3.50	2.50

CAPT. BILLY'S WHIZ BANG
☐ November 1919 ("Savage Love")	35.00	40.00	37.50

Capt. Billy's Whiz Bang was the brain-child of W.H. Fawcett, founder of Fawcett Publications. He was, in fact, the "Capt. Billy" of the magazine's title. It was essentially a sophisticated risque humor publication, with contributions by many famous names.

☐ January 1922 (Explosion of Pedigreed Bunk)	30.00	35.00	32.50

CAPTAIN FUTURE

Captain Future Magazine was an experiment to see if adults would be interested in the kind of superhero stories published in comic books.

☐ Spring 1940 ("Calling Captain Future: A Complete Book-Length Novel of Solar Doom" by Edmund Hamilton)	25.00	30.00	27.50
☐ Fall 1940 ("The Triumph of Captain Future" by Edmund Hamilton)	15.00	20.00	17.50
☐ Winter 1940	25.00	30.00	27.50
☐ Winter 1942 (Captain Future Penetrates the Very Core of the Universe in "Quest Beyond the Stars")	15.00	20.00	17.50

	Current Price Range		C/Y Avg.

CARNIVAL
☐ December 1953	1.75	2.25	2.00
☐ February 1954	1.75	2.25	2.00

CARTOON COMEDY PARADE
☐ January 1963 (Bill Ward art)	5.00	7.00	6.00
☐ March 1963	1.00	1.50	1.25
☐ July 1963	1.00	1.50	1.25
☐ September 1963	1.00	1.50	1.25

CARTOON PARADE
☐ January 1, 1962 (Wolverton)	5.00	7.00	6.00
☐ March 1962 (Wolverton, plus Ward cover)	7.00	9.00	8.00
☐ May 1962 (Wolverton)	7.00	9.00	8.00
☐ November 1962	1.00	1.50	1.20
☐ January 1963	1.00	1.50	1.20
☐ August 1967	1.00	1.50	1.20
☐ December 1967	1.00	1.50	1.20
☐ February 1968	1.00	1.50	1.20
☐ August 1968	.90	1.25	1.00

CARTOONS
☐ August 1918 (Waging Peace in Europe; Women Will Win the War)	40.00	45.00	42.50

CAVALIER
☐ January 1963 (Changing Hollywood, Elizabeth Taylor, Carl Sandburg's Marilyn Monroe, Edward R. Murrow)	4.00	6.00	5.00
☐ April 1963 (Brigitte Bardot, fiction by Eugene Burdick, centerfold model photographed by Peter Gowland)	4.00	6.00	5.00

THE CENTURY MAGAZINE
☐ October 1887 (Mrs. Stowe's Uncle Tom at Home In Kentucky)	14.00	16.00	15.00
☐ February 1892 (The Jews In New York)	8.00	10.00	9.00

CHIC
☐ February 1955	1.75	2.50	2.00
☐ April 1955	1.75	2.50	2.00
☐ May 1955	1.75	2.50	2.00
☐ June 1955	1.75	2.50	2.00

	Current Price Range		C/Y Avg.

CHICKS AND CHUCKLES

☐ June 1955	2.75	3.50	3.00
☐ June 1956	2.75	3.50	3.00
☐ October 1956	2.75	3.50	3.00
☐ December 1956	2.75	3.50	3.00
☐ February 1957	2.75	3.50	3.00
☐ June 1957	2.75	3.50	3.00

THE CHRISTIAN ENDEAVOR WORLD

☐ January 28, 1909 ("The Servant of the Isle" by Alice Lee)	4.00	6.00	5.00
☐ February 4, 1909 (The Taj Mahal on cover)	4.00	6.00	5.00
☐ February 11, 1909 (Abraham Lincoln on cover)	9.00	11.00	10.00
☐ February 13, 1909 ("A Happy Home, Young Folks!" by Caroline Mason)	4.00	6.00	5.00
☐ February 18, 1909 ("Gambling on 'Change" by the Hon. J. Thomas Heflin)	4.00	6.00	5.00
☐ February 25, 1909 (President Taft and His Family on cover)	13.00	15.00	14.00
☐ March 4, 1909 (Boston's Glorious Awakening)	4.00	6.00	5.00
☐ March 11, 1909 (Mr. Horace Fletcher, A Better Way to Live, on cover)	4.00	6.00	5.00
☐ March 18, 1909 (Fanny Crosby, Hymn-Writer, on cover)	4.00	6.00	5.00
☐ April 8, 1909 (Easter Issue; "The Room with the Portiere" by Sophie Swett)	4.00	6.00	5.00
☐ October 7, 1909 (Walbridge Park, Toledo and Genesee Valley Parkway, Rochester on cover)	4.00	6.00	5.00

CLICK, THE NATION'S PICTURE MONTHLY

☐ August 1938 (Mail-Order Love, Inside Sing Sing, Nazis in U.S.)	5.00	7.00	6.00
☐ December 1939 (Keeping Us Out of War, How Roosevelt is Handling the World's Toughest Job, An Interview with Stalin and Hitler, The Fight for Free Ham and Eggs in California)	5.00	7.00	6.00

	Current Price Range		C/Y Avg.

☐ August 1940 (Victor Moore and William Gaxton on cover, article on The Vanderbilts) **4.00** **6.00** **5.00**

COLLIER'S
☐ June 7, 1902 (artwork by Howard C. Christy) **8.00** **10.00** **9.00**

☐ July 12, 1902 (photos of Theodore Roosevelt) **8.00** **10.00** **9.00**

☐ December 3, 1910 (News-Stand Edition)

☐ February 5, 1916 ("The Redemption Handicap" by Charles E. Van Loan) ... **5.00** **7.00** **6.00**

☐ February 12, 1916 ("All For Russia" by Richard Washburn Child) **5.00** **7.00** **6.00**

☐ March 4, 1916 ("The House with the Hidden Door" by Wadsworth Camp) **5.00** **7.00** **6.00**

☐ March 11, 1916 ("The Homeless Hordes of Russia" by Richard Washburn Child) **5.00** **7.00** **6.00**

☐ March 18, 1916 ("The War's Lesson to Us" by Frederick Palmer) **5.00** **7.00** **6.00**

☐ March 25, 1916 ("The Madness of May" by Meredith Nicholson) **5.00** **7.00** **6.00**

☐ December 16, 1916 (With the Russians West of Minsk) **5.00** **7.00** **6.00**

☐ November 6, 1937 (illustration of Mickey Mouse, Pluto and Donald Duck, on cover) **40.00** **50.00** **45.00**

☐ February 17, 1951 (Herbert Hoover—"The Personal Memoirs of Herbert Hoover," on cover) **11.00** **13.00** **12.00**

☐ April 14, 1951 ("What Truman Would Do to Congress" by Jonathan Daniels) **2.00** **4.00** **3.00**

☐ May 5, 1951 ("Secret 'Mr. Big' of Florida" by Lester Velie) **2.00** **4.00** **3.00**

☐ January 4, 1957 (Princess Grace of Monaco on cover) **3.00** **5.00** **4.00**

THE COLUMBIAN
☐ December 1910 ("Yah! Yah! Yah!" by Jack London; American Aviation—Sidelights on its Present Status) **14.00** **16.00** **15.00**

	Current Price Range		C/Y Avg.

COMEDY

☐ January 1956	1.00	1.50	1.25
☐ May 1956	1.00	1.50	1.25
☐ July 1956	1.00	1.50	1.25
☐ September 1956	1.00	1.50	1.25
☐ November 1956	1.00	1.50	1.25
☐ January 1957	1.00	1.50	1.25
☐ May 1957	1.00	1.50	1.25
☐ January 1959	1.00	1.50	1.25
☐ July 1959 (Ward cover)	1.00	1.50	1.25
☐ November 1959	1.00	1.50	1.25
☐ January 1960	1.00	1.50	1.25

COMMENTATOR

☐ August 1938 (Lou Gehrig on cover)	20.00	25.00	22.50

COMPLETE DETECTIVE

☐ May 1938 (first issue; cover artwork by Saunders of woman dancing with skeleton)	45.00	55.00	50.00

COMPLETE PHOTOGRAPHER

☐ September 20, 1941 (first issue)	11.00	13.00	12.00
☐ September 30, 1941	6.00	8.00	7.00
☐ October 10, 1941	6.00	8.00	7.00

CONFIDENTIAL

☐ May 1957 (Marilyn Monroe on cover) ..	50.00	60.00	55.00

CONNECTICUT CIRCLE

☐ May–June 1962 (21st Annual Issue) ...	1.00	2.00	1.50

COSMIC SCIENCE FICTION

☐ May 1941 (artwork by Morris Dollens and David A. Kyle)	40.00	45.00	42.50
☐ July 1941 ("The Red Death" by David H. Keller)	40.00	45.00	42.50

THE COSMOPOLITAN

☐ May 1891 (Cleopatras of the Stage) ...	11.00	13.00	12.00
☐ May 1894 (A Review of the Theatrical Year; England's Latest Conquest in Africa)	11.00	13.00	12.00

	Current Price Range		C/Y Avg.

☐ November 1898 (A Dangerous Mission To Spain; "Jimmy Goggles the God" by H. G. Wells) **10.00 12.00 11.00**

☐ February 1899 (Fiction and Travel Number; After the Capture of Manila) **10.00 12.00 11.00**

☐ June 1899 (Ideal and Practical Organization of a Home; Progress in Air-Ships) **10.00 12.00 11.00**

☐ September 1901 (Souvenir Number of the Buffalo Exposition) **19.00 21.00 20.00**

☐ October 1902 (Alexander Hamilton by John Fiske; The Coronation and Its Significance) **8.00 10.00 9.00**

☐ November 1902 ("Mankind in the Making III" by Herbert George Wells) **8.00 10.00 9.00**

☐ January 1907 ("The Moonlit Road" by Ambrose Bierce) **6.00 8.00 7.00**

☐ May 1910 (The Man-Bird and His Wings) **19.00 21.00 20.00**

☐ December 1918 (artwork by Howard C. Christy, photos of actress Marion Davies) **8.00 10.00 9.00**

☐ November 1932 (story by Pearl S. Buck) **5.00 7.00 6.00**

☐ October 1940 (cover artwork by Bradshaw Crandall) **4.00 6.00 5.00**

CORONET
☐ July 1951 .... **2.00 4.00 3.00**
☐ May 1952 .... **1.00 3.00 2.00**
☐ February 1953 .... **1.00 3.00 2.00**

CRYSTAL PALACE
☐ November 26, 1888 ("The Frozen Stream," First Page Illustration) **12.00 14.00 13.00**

DARE
☐ November 1952 (first issue) **4.00 6.00 5.00**
☐ January 1953 .... **1.50 3.50 2.50**
☐ March 1953 .... **1.50 3.50 2.50**
☐ April 1953 .... **1.50 3.50 2.50**
☐ May 1953 .... **1.50 3.50 2.50**
☐ June 1953 .... **1.50 3.50 2.50**
☐ July 1953 .... **1.50 3.50 2.50**
☐ August 1953 .... **1.50 3.50 2.50**

DOC SAVAGE
☐ September 1933 (The Lost Oasis) **175.00 200.00 187.50**

	Current Price Range		C/Y Avg.
☐ January 1935 ("The Mystic Mullah" by Kenneth Robeson)	60.00	70.00	65.00
☐ January 1939 (Mad Mesa)	50.00	60.00	55.00
☐ October 1939 (The Stone Man)	35.00	45.00	40.00
☐ September 1940 (The Purple Dragon) ..	30.00	45.00	35.00
☐ December 1944 (color cover with Uncle Sam, President Franklin Roosevelt, Winston Churchill, General Tojo, Josef Stalin)	70.00	80.00	75.00
☐ March–April 1948 (cover artwork by Cartier)	20.00	30.00	25.00

DOCTOR DEATH

☐ February 1935 (first issue)	150.00	175.00	162.50
☐ March 1935 (Gray Creatures)	100.00	125.00	112.50

DOUBLE DETECTIVE

☐ November 1937 (first issue)	60.00	70.00	65.00
☐ June 1940 (first appearance of "Green Lama")	50.00	60.00	55.00

DYNAMIC SCIENCE STORIES

☐ April–May 1939 (stories by L. Sprague de-Camp, Manley Wade Wellman, Eando Binder; artwork by Norman Saunders)	30.00	35.00	32.50

ESQUIRE

☐ October 1944	14.00	16.00	15.00
☐ September 1951 (Color print of Marilyn Monroe)	45.00	55.00	50.00
☐ February 1952 (Mauro Scali painting) ..	14.00	16.00	15.00
☐ June 1952 (Pete Lawley painting)	14.00	16.00	15.00
☐ October 1952 (Pete Lawley painting) ...	14.00	16.00	15.00
☐ November 1952 (Eddie Chan painting)	14.00	16.00	15.00
☐ July 1953 (Peggy Carr)	14.00	16.00	15.00
☐ January 1954 (holiday issue)	20.00	25.00	22.50
☐ March 1954	14.00	16.00	15.00
☐ July 1954 (Sylvana Mangano)	17.00	19.00	18.00
☐ March 1955 (Mike Ludlow painting)	14.00	16.00	15.00
☐ September 1955 (Kim Novak)	14.00	16.00	15.00
☐ October 1955 (Mike Ludlow painting) ..	14.00	16.00	15.00
☐ November 1955 (George Petty drawing)	20.00	25.00	22.50
☐ October 1966	2.00	4.00	3.00
☐ June 1970	1.50	3.50	2.50

	Current Price Range		C/Y Avg.
☐ July 1970	1.50	3.50	2.50
☐ October 1970	1.50	3.50	2.50
☐ August 1971	1.50	3.50	2.50
☐ August 1972	1.50	3.50	2.50

EUROPE'S TOP PIN-UPS

☐ No. 3 (undated, c. 1956, Gina Lollobrigida on cover)	18.00	20.00	19.00

EVERYBODY'S MAGAZINE

☐ July 1900 ("Fifty Years' Memories" by Stuart Robson)	6.00	8.00	7.00

EXCLUSIVE

☐ November 1960	1.75	2.25	2.00

EYE

☐ November 1952 (Marilyn Monroe)	7.00	9.00	8.00

FAMILY CIRCLE

☐ June 1960 (Ten Golden Rules for Parents)	1.00	1.50	1.25

FAMOUS DETECTIVE CASES

A short-lived puplication by the McFadden group in the 1930s.

☐ January 1936 (Huey Long's story)	8.00	12.00	10.00
☐ March 1936 (Huey Long, T. Todd story)	8.00	12.00	10.00
☐ April 1936	8.00	12.00	10.00
☐ May 1936 (Leopold-Loeb case)	8.00	12.00	10.00
☐ June 1936 (Jack McGurn story)	8.00	12.00	10.00
☐ August 1936 (Anna Sage's own story) ..	8.00	12.00	10.00

FAMOUS SPY STORIES

☐ January–February 1940 (first issues, all stories by Max Brand)	50.00	60.00	55.00

FANTASTIC ADVENTURES

☐ May 1939 (First issue)	30.00	35.00	32.50

THE FARMER'S WIFE

☐ November 1928 (A Cross-Atlantic Correspondence; Chronicles of Dad)	3.00	5.00	4.00
☐ December 1928 ("Meeker'n Moses" by Ernest Elwood Stanford)	3.00	5.00	4.00

The Farmer's Wife, June 1930, $2.00–$4.00.

	Current Price Range		C/Y Avg.
☐ March 1929 (A Daughter of Cain; The Call of the Farm)	3.00	5.00	4.00
☐ April 1929 ("New Channel" by C. M. Mc-Millan)	3.00	5.00	4.00
☐ February 1930 (The Story of American Farming; Back on the Farm)	2.00	4.00	3.00
☐ May 1930 (The Sere and Yellow Leaf; Where Rainbows Begin)	2.00	4.00	3.00
☐ June 1930 (What Manner of Man is This?; Doctor Dave Troubleshooter)	2.00	4.00	3.00
☐ July 1930 (If You Can't Whip'em Fine'em; Four Thousand Peaceful Years)	2.00	4.00	3.00
☐ November 1930 (Danny—A Sure Enough Champion; Some Women Succeed by Going to Congress)	2.00	4.00	3.00
☐ October 1931 (Crowing Hens; The Black and White Kitten)	2.00	4.00	3.00

	Current Price Range		C/Y Avg.

FAVORITE WESTERNS OF FILMLAND
☐ May 1960 (first issue), Richard Boone on cover, articles on Rory Calhoun, Steve McQueen, Don Durant, "Wagon Train," "Rawhide") 20.00   25.00   22.50

FAWCETT FIGURE PHOTOGRAPHY
☐ 1954 (nudes by Peter Gowland; one issue only) 8.00   10.00   9.00

THE FLAPPER
☐ May 1923 ("Underneath the Skin" by Eve Woodburn Leary) 25.00   30.00   27.50

FLASH
☐ January 1951 .... 1.75   2.25   2.00

FILMLAND
☐ August 1951 (Jane Russell on cover) .. 22.00   27.00   24.50

The Flapper, May 1923, $25.00–$30.00.

	Current Price Range		C/Y Avg.
☐ December 1951 (Curtis and Leigh cover)	18.00	22.00	20.00
☐ December 1952 (Doris Day on cover; articles on Marilyn Monroe, Farley Granger, Tyrone Power, Rock Hudson, Ronald Reagan)	20.00	25.00	22.50
☐ February 1953 (Janet Leigh cover)	12.50	17.50	15.00
☐ March 1953 (Susan Hayward on cover; articles on Doris Day, Betty Hutton, Tony Curtis, Kirk Douglas, "Peter Pan")	18.00	20.00	19.00
☐ August 1953 (Elizabeth Taylor cover) ..	18.00	22.00	20.00
☐ May 1955 (Ava Gardner cover)	16.00	20.00	18.00
☐ February 1957 (Natalie Wood on cover; articles on Rod Steiger, Marilyn Monroe, Sal Mineo, Rita Hayworth, Terry Moore)	10.00	12.00	11.00

FILM PICTORIAL

☐ April 1938 (Sabu on cover; features on Shirley Temple, Cary Grant)	20.00	25.00	22.50

FILMS AND FILMING

☐ Christmas 1954 (Judy Garland on cover)	20.00	25.00	22.50

FM AND TELEVISION

☐ October 1946	8.00	10.00	9.00

FILM STARS

☐ Winter 1953 (Marilyn Monroe cover) ...	45.00	55.00	50.00

FILM WEEKLY

☐ November 21, 1931 (Greta Garbo and Ramon Novarro on cover; articles on Mickey Mouse)	35.00	40.00	37.50
☐ December 7, 1934 (montage cover with small portraits of various stars; articles on Greta Garbo, Robert Donat, Cecil B. DeMille, Myrna Loy, Loretta Young, Marx Brothers, W.C. Fields) .... :	30.00	35.00	32.50
☐ July 7, 1937 (Claudette Colbert on cover, articles on Dick Powell, Myrna Loy) ...	25.00	30.00	27.50

FOCUS

☐ April 1938 (Birth of a Dummy)	5.00	7.00	6.00
☐ August 1951	1.75	2.25	2.00
☐ October 1951	1.75	2.25	2.00

	Current Price Range		C/Y Avg.
☐ November 1951	1.75	2.25	2.00
☐ January 1952	1.75	2.25	2.00
☐ February 1952	1.75	2.25	2.00
☐ March 1952	1.75	2.25	2.00
☐ April 1952	1.75	2.25	2.00
☐ May 1952	1.75	2.25	2.00
☐ June 1952	1.75	2.25	2.00
☐ July 1952	1.75	2.25	2.00
☐ August 1952	1.75	2.25	2.00
☐ October 1952	1.75	2.25	2.00
☐ November 1952	1.75	2.25	2.00
☐ December 1952	1.75	2.25	2.00
☐ January 1953	1.75	2.25	2.00
☐ February 1953	1.75	2.25	2.00
☐ May 1953 (Marilyn Monroe on cover)	20.00	25.00	22.50

FOTORAMA

☐ August 1955	1.75	2.25	2.00
☐ November 1955	1.75	2.25	2.00
☐ July 1959 (photos of Elvis)	3.50	4.50	4.00
☐ February 1961	1.75	2.25	2.00

FRONT PAGE DETECTIVE

☐ October 1936	8.00	12.00	10.00
☐ September 1938 (great 31 page story of Chicago gangs)	12.50	17.50	15.00
☐ March 1939 (Philip Musica)	8.00	12.00	10.00
☐ November 1954	4.00	8.00	6.00
☐ May 1956 (Abbott case)	4.00	8.00	6.00
☐ January 1958 (Rhonda Martin death house interview)	2.00	6.00	4.00
☐ May 1958 (Starkweather case)	2.00	6.00	4.00
☐ July 1969 (Walter Winchell)	1.00	2.00	2.50

FUN HOUSE COMEDY

☐ March 1964	1.00	1.50	1.25
☐ July 1964	1.00	1.50	1.25
☐ September 1964	1.00	1.50	1.25

GANG WORLD

☐ June 1932 ("The Phantom Killer" by William Stueber; "Squealer's Pay" by Arthur Burks; cover artwork by Reusswig)	80.00	90.00	85.00

	Current Price Range		C/Y Avg.

GENE AUTRY'S CHAMPIONS MAGAZINE
☐ December 1950 (Gene Gets There First; photo of Gene with boxing champion Jack Dempsey) **45.00** **50.00** **47.50**

GLAMOUR OF HOLLYWOOD
☐ April 1939 (Ann Sheridan on cover) **25.00** **30.00** **27.50**

GOLD SEAL DETECTIVE
☐ March 1935 (cover artwork by DeSoto) **15.00** **20.00** **17.50**

GOOD HOUSEKEEPING
☐ August 1902 (Twins) **7.00** **9.00** **8.00**
☐ June 1926 ("Born to the Purple" by Mabel Potter Daggett) **5.00** **7.00** **6.00**
☐ December 1926 (A New Novel by Wm. J. Locke Begins in This Issue) **5.00** **7.00** **6.00**
☐ February 1929 ("The Incredible Year" by Faith Baldwin) **4.00** **6.00** **5.00**
☐ March 1929 ("Bird Girl" by Vivien R. Bretherton) **4.00** **6.00** **5.00**
☐ April 1929 (Beginning a New Serial by George Weston) **4.00** **6.00** **5.00**
☐ June 1929 ("The Missionary" by Edison Marshall) **4.00** **6.00** **5.00**
☐ July 1929 ("A Job For Every Woman" by Elizabeth Frazer) **4.00** **6.00** **5.00**
☐ August 1929 ("The White House Gang" by Earle Looker) **7.00** **9.00** **8.00**
☐ September 1929 (Beginning of a New Mystery Novel by Frederic Van De Water) **4.00** **6.00** **5.00**
☐ October 1929 ("Castles in Spain" by Frances Parkinson Keys) **4.00** **6.00** **5.00**
☐ November 1929 ("The Sea Was Waiting" by Elizabeth Petersen) **4.00** **6.00** **5.00**
☐ December 1929 ("Wallflowers" by Temple Bailey) **4.00** **6.00** **5.00**
☐ February 1930 ("Stars and Scissors" by Mary Lawton) **4.00** **6.00** **5.00**
☐ May 1930 ("The American Marquis" by George Weston) **4.00** **6.00** **5.00**

	Current Price Range		C/Y Avg.

□ November 1934 (Vernon Thomas art-
work on cover) **4.00** **6.00** **5.00**
□ December 1948 (Alexander Ross artwork
on cover) **3.00** **4.00** **3.50**
□ March 1954 .... **1.50** **2.00** **1.75**
□ August 1954 .... **1.50** **2.00** **1.75**
□ September 1954 .... **1.50** **2.00** **1.75**
□ October 1954 .... **1.50** **2.00** **1.75**
□ December 1954 .... **1.50** **2.00** **1.75**
□ August 1961 (painting of Caroline Ken-
nedy on cover. My Happy Life with 17
Kennedy Babies) **4.00** **6.00** **5.00**

GOOD LITERATURE
□ January 1907 ("Wrecked and Rescued"
by Mrs. Jane G. Austin) **2.00** **4.00** **3.00**
□ March 1907 ("The Schoolteacher at
Botle Flat" by John Habberton) **2.00** **4.00** **3.00**
□ April 1907 ("Mollie's Ghost" by Effie Ade-
laide Rowlands) **2.00** **4.00** **3.00**
□ May 1907 ("The Overseer" by Dr. R.B.
Hill) **2.00** **4.00** **3.00**
□ June 1907 ("Jessie Reeves' Portrait" by
Virginia Townsend) **2.00** **4.00** **3.00**
□ July 1907 ("The Copper King" by Agnes
Louise Provost) **2.00** **4.00** **3.00**
□ August 1907 ("Sir Rupert's Wife" by
Charlotte M. Braeme) **2.00** **4.00** **3.00**
□ December 1907 ("The Glyndon Conspir-
acy" by Mrs. Hariet Lewis) **2.00** **4.00** **3.00**

GOOD NEWS
□ June 26, 1890 (contains poster with
sketches of various baseball players including Connie Mack, Cap Anson,
Charles Comiskey) **125.00** **150.00** **137.50**

GROOVE

Groove was published by RCA Victor and contained news of its recording artists and their latest records.

□ November 1947 (Louis Prima on cover) **10.00** **12.00** **11.00**
□ March 1948 (Tommy Dorsey on cover) **10.00** **12.00** **11.00**

	Current Price Range		C/Y Avg.
☐ February 1949 (Spike Jones on cover, final issue)	10.00	12.00	11.00

HARPER'S NEW MONTHLY MAGAZINE

☐ August 1897 ("A Sergeant of the Orphan Troop" by Frederic Remington)	8.00	10.00	9.00

HARPER'S WEEKLY

☐ November 18, 1865 (includes 5″ x 14″ woodcut entitled "Baseball Match Between the Athletics of Philadelphia and the Atlantics of Brooklyn, Played at Philadelphia")	50.00	70.00	65.00
☐ November 25, 1865 (includes woodcut entitled "Champion Nine of the Atlantic Baseball Club of Brooklyn")	50.00	70.00	65.00

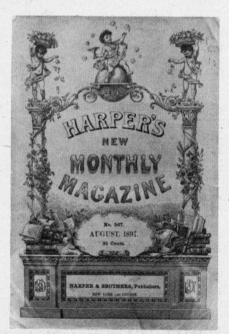

Harper's New Monthly Magazine, August 1897, $8.00–$10.00.

	Current Price Range		C/Y Avg.
☐ October 26, 1867 (includes woodcut entitled "The Champion Nine of the Union Baseball Club of Morrisania, New York") Morrisania, then a town in itself, subsequently became part of The Bronx.	40.00	50.00	45.00
☐ October 13, 1883 (woodcut entitled "The Boston Baseball Club")	35.00	40.00	37.50
☐ May 15, 1886 (contains coverage of "The New Grounds of the Metropolitan Baseball Club on Staten Island")	35.00	40.00	37.50

HIGH SOCIETY

☐ June 1976	18.00	22.00	20.00
☐ July 1976	14.00	16.00	15.00
☐ August 1976	14.00	16.00	15.00
☐ September 1976 (Greta Garbo on cover)	14.00	16.00	20.00
☐ October 1976	12.00	14.00	13.00
☐ January 1977	14.00	16.00	15.00
☐ February 1977	12.00	14.00	13.00
☐ March 1977	12.00	14.00	13.00
☐ May 1977	9.00	11.00	10.00
☐ June 1977	8.00	10.00	9.00
☐ July 1977	8.00	10.00	9.00
☐ August 1977	8.00	10.00	9.00
☐ September 1977	8.00	10.00	9.00
☐ October 1977	8.00	10.00	9.00
☐ December 1977	12.00	14.00	13.00
☐ April 1978 (Marilyn Monroe on cover) ..	17.00	19.00	18.00
☐ July 1978 (Suzanne Somers on cover)	14.00	16.00	15.00
☐ August 1978	7.00	9.00	8.00
☐ April 1979	7.00	9.00	8.00
☐ May 1979 (Lindsay Wagner on cover) ..	9.00	11.00	10.00
☐ June 1979 (Princes Caroline on cover)	11.00	13.00	12.00
☐ October 1979 (Connie Stevens on cover)	9.00	11.00	10.00
☐ December 1979 (Suzanne Somers on cover)	9.00	11.00	10.00
☐ January 1980 (Margot Kidder on cover)	8.00	10.00	9.00
☐ February 1980 (Laura Antonelli on cover)	8.00	10.00	9.00
☐ June 1980	7.00	9.00	8.00
☐ September 1980 (Diane Keaton on cover)	8.00	10.00	9.00

	Current Price Range		C/Y Avg.
☐ November 1980 (Angie Dickinson on cover)	8.00	10.00	9.00
☐ December 1980 (Ali MacGraw on cover)	8.00	10.00	9.00
☐ January 1981 (Farrah Fawcett on cover)	9.00	11.00	10.00
☐ February 1981 (Bo Derek on cover)	9.00	11.00	10.00
☐ April 1981 (Britt Eklund on cover)	7.00	9.00	8.00
☐ July 1981 (Nastassja Kinski on cover) ..	14.00	16.00	15.00
☐ October 1981	6.00	8.00	7.00

HIGH TIMES

☐ No. 1, 1974 (no month indicated, "Leary's Ultimate Trip," "A Lady Dealer Talks")	80.00	100.00	90.00

HOLIDAY

☐ May 1950 (baseball issue)	35.00	40.00	37.50
☐ February 1954	3.00	5.00	4.00
☐ October 1955	3.00	5.00	4.00

Hollywood, February 1943, $13.00–$15.00.

	Current Price Range		C/Y Avg.

HOLLYWOOD

☐ June 1934 (Constance Bennett on cover; articles on Claudette Colbert, Mae West, Norma Shearer)	20.00	25.00	22.50
☐ March 1936 (Jeanette MacDonald on cover)	20.00	25.00	22.50
☐ April 1936 (Gloria Stewart on cover) ...	20.00	25.00	22.50
☐ June 1936 (Shirley Temple on cover) ..	45.00	55.00	50.00
☐ February 1937 (Shirley Temple on cover)	45.00	55.00	50.00
☐ October 1937 (Dorothy Lamour on cover, articles on Gary Cooper, Lionel Barrymore, George Raft, Louis B. Mayer) ...	18.00	20.00	19.00
☐ November 1937 (Gail Patrick on cover; articles on George Burns and Gracie Allen, Gene Autry, W.C. Fields, Marx Brothers)	18.00	20.00	19.00
☐ January 1938 (Robert Taylor on cover; articles on Jimmy Durante, George Sanders, Judy Garland, Rosalind Russell, Ray Bolger)	17.00	19.00	18.00
☐ March 1940 (Tyrone Power on cover; articles on Carmen Miranda, Mae West, Basil Rathbone, James Cagney)	15.00	17.00	16.00
☐ January 1941 (Gary Cooper on cover; articles on Charles Laughton, Joan Crawford, Gary Cooper, Cary Grant, Ronald Reagan)	20.00	25.00	22.50
☐ August 1942 (Rita Hayworth on cover; articles on John Wayne, Joan Crawford, Nelson Eddy, Joe E. Brown)	15.00	17.00	16.00
☐ February 1943 (Janet Blair on cover) ...	13.00	15.00	14.00

HOLLYWOOD FAMILY ALBUM

☐ 1951 (annual publication—June Allyson on cover, articles on Judy Garland and Alan Ladd)	10.00	12.00	11.00

HOLLYWOOD LIFE STORIES

☐ 1952 (annual publication—June Allyson on cover, articles on Clark Gable and Judy Garland)	10.00	12.00	11.00

	Current Price Range		C/Y Avg.

☐ 1953 (annual publication—Audie Murphy on cover, articles on Esther Williams and Leslie Caron) **8.00 10.00 9.00**

☐ 1958 (annual publication—Elizabeth Taylor on cover, articles on Elvis Presley and Yves Montand) **20.00 25.00 22.50**

HOLLYWOOD PICTORIAL
☐ September 1950 (Roy Rogers on cover, special western issue with articles on "Broken Arrow," "Beyond the Purple Hills," "Copper Canyon," "The Showdown," "Hills of Oklahoma," "Gunfighter") **65.00 75.00 70.00**

HOLLYWOOD PIN-UPS
☐ 1953, No. 1 (3-D, value stated is for copy with glasses) **70.00 90.00 80.00**

HOLLYWOOD ROMANCES
☐ 1954 (annual publication—Audrey Hepburn on cover, articles on Ava Gardner and Frank Sinatra) **25.00 35.00 30.00**

HOLLYWOOD SCREEN PARADE
☐ March 1959 (Marilyn Monroe on cover) **35.00 45.00 40.00**

HOLLYWOOD SECRETS ANNUAL
☐ 1956 (No. 2, James Dean on cover; articles on Marilyn Monroe, Kim Novak, Jean Harlow, Montgomery Clift, Susan Hayward, Ingrid Bergman, Tab Hunter, Eddie Fisher) **25.00 30.00 27.50**

HOUSE BEAUTIFUL
☐ December 1919 (Christmas issue, L.K. Carroll watercolor on cover) **8.00 10.00 9.00**
☐ September 1926 (Fall building number) **7.00 9.00 8.00**
☐ May 1959 (Floors That Make a Room) **2.00 3.00 2.50**
☐ February 1960 (1960 Pace Setter) **2.00 3.00 2.50**

HUE
☐ November 1953 (first issue) **5.00 7.00 6.00**
☐ January 1954 .... **1.75 2.25 2.00**
☐ June 2, 1954 .... **1.75 2.25 2.00**

	Current Price Range		C/Y Avg.
☐ June 30, 1954	1.75	2.25	2.00
☐ July 14, 1954	1.75	2.25	2.00
☐ July 28, 1954	1.75	2.25	2.00
☐ September 1954	1.75	2.25	2.00
☐ October 1954	1.75	2.25	2.00
☐ November 1954	1.75	2.25	2.00

HUMAN LIFE

☐ January 1908 (Emperor Wilhelm of Germany on cover)	17.00	19.00	18.00

HUSTLER

☐ July 1974 (first issue)	85.00	105.00	95.00

ILLUSTRATED AMERICAN

☐ May 3, 1890 (photo of Brooklyn baseball club) This was the same team that later became known as Dodgers; at first they were called Bees, then Robins.	50.00	60.00	55.00

Human Life, January 1908, $17.00–$19.00.

The Illustrated Blue Book, November 1928, $30.00–$35.00.

	Current Price Range		C/Y Avg.

THE ILLUSTRATED BLUE BOOK

☐ October 1926 (Lemuel DeBra, H. Bedford-Jones, Calvin Ball and Others)	25.00	30.00	27.50
☐ October 1927 (A New Oriental Adventure Series by Culpeper Zandtt)	25.00	30.00	27.50
☐ August 1928 ("Lost Wings," the first of a series of Mysteries of Today)	25.00	30.00	27.50
☐ October 1928 ("Tarzan," A New Story of Tarzan, on cover)	30.00	35.00	32.50
☐ November 1928 ("Tarzan," Tarzan and the Lost Empire, on cover)	30.00	35.00	32.50
☐ August 1929 (Jonathan Brooks, Bertran Atkey, Captain Dingle, Clarence Herbert and others)	25.00	30.00	27.50

	Current Price Range		C/Y Avg.

ILLUSTRATED LOVE
☐ November 1931 (Warner Fabian. Author of "Flaming Youth." Begins his Thrilling New Novel of Today, "Week-End Girl") — 7.00 | 9.00 | 8.00

INSIDE
☐ May 1956 (James Dean on cover) ..... 7.00 | 9.00 | 8.00
☐ February 1957 (Anita Ekberg on cover) 2.50 | 3.50 | 3.00

INSIDE DETECTIVE
☐ April 1936 (Thelma Todd mystery) ..... 11.00 | 13.00 | 12.00
☐ January 1938 (Brady gang, Folsom riot) 11.00 | 13.00 | 12.00
☐ October 1957 (Bugs Moran) .... 7.00 | 9.00 | 8.00
☐ July 1958 (Stompanate killing, Birdman of Alcatraz) .... 9.00 | 11.00 | 10.00
☐ March 1970 (Charles Manson case) ... 9.00 | 11.00 | 10.00

JACK AND JILL
☐ December 1974 (cover artwork by Norman Rockwell) .... 10.00 | 12.00 | 11.00

JAMES BOND 007
☐ 1964 (one issue only) .... 50.00 | 70.00 | 60.00

JEST
☐ November 1951 .... 2.50 | 4.50 | 3.50
☐ March 1952 .... 2.50 | 4.50 | 3.50
☐ July 1953 .... 2.50 | 4.50 | 3.50
☐ May 1954 .... 2.50 | 4.50 | 3.50
☐ September 1956 (Ward art) .... 2.50 | 4.50 | 3.50
☐ November 1956 (Ward cover) .... 2.50 | 4.50 | 3.50
☐ May 1957 .... 2.50 | 4.50 | 3.50
☐ July 1959 (Ward cover) .... 2.50 | 4.50 | 3.50

JET
☐ April 1, 1954 .... 3.00 | 5.00 | 4.00
☐ April 8, 1954 .... 3.00 | 5.00 | 4.00
☐ April 15, 1954 .... 3.00 | 5.00 | 4.00
☐ April 22, 1954 .... 3.00 | 5.00 | 4.00
☐ April 29, 1954 .... 3.00 | 5.00 | 4.00
☐ May 6, 1954 .... 3.00 | 5.00 | 4.00
☐ May 13, 1954 .... 3.00 | 5.00 | 4.00
☐ June 3, 1954 .... 3.00 | 5.00 | 4.00
☐ June 10, 1954 .... 3.00 | 5.00 | 4.00

JUNGLE STORIES

Published by Fiction House, this was really an adult version of its Jungle Comics. *Jungle Stories* carried a few illustrations but was not in comic book format. However the settings, plots and characters were very similar.

	Current Price Range		C/Y Avg.
☐ Summer 1947 (Warrior Queen of Attila's Lost Legion)	25.00	30.00	27.50

KEN

☐ April 7, 1938 (The Coming Moroccan Revolt)	22.50	27.50	25.00

LADIES' HOME JOURNAL

Ladies' Home Journal was noted at the turn-of-the century for its attractive fashion covers, often the work of noted illustrator Harrison Fisher.

☐ February 1896 (cover artwork by Frank O'Small; interior artwork by Charles D. Gibson)	15.00	17.00	16.00
☐ March 1897 (cover artwork by Frank V. DuMond)	15.00	17.00	16.00
☐ October 1901 ("How The Leopard Got His Spots" by Rudyard Kipling)	15.00	17.00	16.00
☐ June 1902 ("The President's Mother" by Emma Hamilton Bulloch)	15.00	17.00	16.00
☐ July 1902 (Painting of Martha Washington Knitting for the Soldiers at Valley Forge)	13.00	15.00	14.00
☐ August 1902 ("The Green Hat" by Frances Lyman Howard)	13.00	15.00	14.00
☐ June 1903 ("The Girlishness of Ethel Barrymore" by Gustav Kobbe)	17.00	19.00	18.00
☐ March 1905 ("What I Expect to Find at the North Pole" by Commander Robert E. Peary, U.S. Navy)	10.00	12.00	11.00
☐ September 1905 (cover artwork by Harrison Fisher)	15.00	17.00	16.00
☐ March 1906 (Rudyard Kipling's Third Children's Story)	15.00	17.00	16.00

The Ladies' Home Journal, June 1903, $17.00–$19.00.

	Current Price Range		C/Y Avg.
☐ May 1906 ("What Music Means to Me" by Jan Kubelic)	12.00	14.00	13.00
☐ August 1906 ("The Princess Virginia" by C. N. and A. M. Williamson)	10.00	12.00	11.00
☐ March 1908 (The Spring Issue with 100 Fashion Pictures)	17.00	19.00	18.00
☐ May 15, 1911 (cover artwork by Harrison Fisher)	10.00	12.00	11.00
☐ July 1932 (cover artwork by C.E. Chambers)	5.00	7.00	6.00
☐ January 1933 (Anne O'Hare McCormick, Alice Roosevelt Longworth, cover artwork by George Rapp)	3.00	5.00	4.00
☐ December 1940	3.00	5.00	4.00

	Current Price Range		C/Y Avg.

THE LADIES' WORLD

☐ March 1915 (Have You Seen Our Ready-Made Girl?, painting by Clarence F. Underwood on cover) 7.00 9.00 8.00

☐ April 1908 (cover artwork by Marlatt) ... 10.00 12.00 11.00

LIBERTY

One of the great American magazines of the twentieth century, *Liberty* reached its peak in popularity during World War II.

☐ February 15, 1936 (The Most Melancholy Funny Man on the Screen: W.C. Fields) 10.00 12.00 11.00

☐ January 13, 1940 .... 5.00 7.00 6.00

☐ July 3, 1943 ("What the Nazis Leave Behind" by Maurice Hindus) 5.00 7.00 6.00

☐ June 6, 1944 .... 4.00 6.00 5.00

Liberty, July 1943, $5.00–$7.00.

LIFE

Life Magazine made its debut in November 1936 and soon was recognized as the leading photo-journalism magazine in America. The works of every major photographer appeared in *Life*. From a collecting standpoint, the subjects of the photos and articles contained in each issue determine the value. Naturally the earlier issues would be more scarce as they were not printed in large numbers, and were not being saved. This, too, is a factor in price.

If *Life* magazines were bought only by collectors building sets of them, the values would be much more uniform from one issue to another. However, collectors of *Life* are only one group of customers. They are also bought by collectors in other hobbies who want specific issues with certain content, such as a Jean Harlow collector buying an early *Life* with a Harlow cover.

All in all there is heavy demand for the better issues. When offered at auction (for example) they sometimes sell higher than the normal values. Of course the condition counts. Values given here are for complete issues with covers intact and no ads or photos clipped out, but showing ordinary signs of use. Absolutely mint specimens are almost impossible to obtain.

Complete Years. Sets of the full 52 issues for any of the *early* years—up to and including World War II—will sell for a slight premium, over and above their value as individual issues. This is not the case with later years, as it's relatively easy to assemble these sets.

Bound Volumes. Most collectors want their *Life* magazines unbound, just the way they were issued. Consequently, runs or full volumes in bindings tend to sell at a small discount.

Full Sets. Full sets of *Life* from No. 1 onward are owned by a number of collectors. Thus, the premium for a full set would not be high. Note that either the person or the subject of each cover story of *Life* is provided after the publication date for identification purposes.

	Current Price Range		C/Y Avg.
1936			
☐ November 23, 1936 (Fort Peck Dam) ..	90.00	110.00	100.00
☐ November 30, 1936 (West Point cadet)	40.00	45.00	42.50
☐ December 7, 1936 (Ski scene)	20.00	25.00	22.50
☐ December 14, 1936 (Archbishop of Canterbury on cover)	20.00	25.00	22.50

	Current Price Range		C/Y Avg.

1937

☐ January 4, 1937 (President Franklin Roosevelt on cover) **22.50** **27.50** **25.00**

☐ January 11, 1937 (Japanese soldiers on cover) **8.00** **10.00** **9.00**

☐ April 19, 1937 (British oceanliner Queen Mary on cover) **8.00** **10.00** **9.00**

☐ May 3, 1937 (Jean Harlow on cover) ... **27.50** **32.50** **30.00**

☐ May 17, 1937 (Dionne Quintuplets on cover) **40.00** **45.00** **42.50**

☐ May 31, 1937 (Golden Gate Bridge on cover) **8.00** **10.00** **9.00**

☐ September 6, 1937 (Harpo Marx on cover) **19.00** **21.00** **20.00**

☐ September 27, 1937 (Nelson Eddy on cover) **14.00** **16.00** **15.00**

☐ November 8, 1937 (Greta Garbo on cover) **32.50** **37.50** **35.00**

☐ December 3, 1937 (Railroad on cover) **14.00** **16.00** **15.00**

1938

☐ February 7, 1938 (Gary Cooper on cover) **20.00** **25.00** **22.50**

☐ February 21, 1938 (Carl Sandburg on cover) **8.00** **10.00** **9.00**

☐ April 4, 1938 (Anthony Eden on cover) **7.00** **9.00** **8.00**

☐ April 25, 1938 (John Thomas Winsett of Brooklyn Dodgers on cover) **14.00** **16.00** **15.00**

☐ May 2, 1938 (John Nance Garner on cover) **8.00** **10.00** **9.00**

☐ May 23, 1938 (Errol Flynn on cover) ... **20.00** **25.00** **22.50**

☐ June 6, 1938 (Youth Problem: 1938) ... **7.00** **9.00** **8.00**

☐ June 13, 1938 (Gertrude Lawrence on cover) **12.00** **14.00** **13.00**

☐ June 20, 1938 (Rudolph Valentino on cover) **25.00** **30.00** **27.50**

☐ July 11, 1938 (Shirley Temple on cover) **32.50** **37.50** **35.00**

☐ August 22, 1938 (Fred Astaire and Ginger Rogers on cover) **25.00** **30.00** **27.50**

☐ October 17, 1938 (Carole Lombard on cover) **20.00** **25.00** **22.50**

☐ October 31, 1938 (Raymond Massey on cover) **11.00** **13.00** **12.00**

	Current Price Range		C/Y Avg.
☐ December 19, 1938 (Mary Martin on cover)	11.00	13.00	12.00
1939			
☐ March 6, 1939 (Tallulah Bankhead on cover)	10.00	12.00	11.00
☐ March 13, 1939 (World's Fair)	25.00	30.00	27.50
☐ April 24, 1939 (British Prime Minister Neville Chamberlain on cover)	10.00	12.00	11.00
☐ May 15, 1939 (Anne Morrow Lindberg on cover)	7.00	9.00	8.00
☐ May 29, 1939 (Eleanor Roosevelt on cover)	14.00	16.00	15.00
☐ June 12, 1939 (Annapolis graduates on cover)	6.00	8.00	7.00
☐ July 10, 1939 (Japanese Home Guard on cover)	6.00	8.00	7.00
☐ July 24, 1939 (Anne Sheridan on cover)	12.00	14.00	13.00

Life, *May 1939, $14.00–$16.00.*

	Current Price Range		C/Y Avg.
☐ September 4, 1939 (Rosalind Russell on cover)	11.00	13.00	12.00
☐ September 11, 1939 (Benito Mussolini)	19.00	21.00	20.00
☐ October 23, 1939 (War & Fashions)	10.00	12.00	11.00
☐ November 6, 1939 (Planes over England)	6.00	8.00	7.00
☐ November 27, 1939 (Arturo Toscanini on cover)	6.00	8.00	7.00
☐ December 4, 1939 (Dancing California Co-Ed)	5.00	7.00	6.00
☐ December 11, 1939 (Betty Grable on cover)	14.00	16.00	15.00
☐ December 25, 1939 (Young women getting ready to throw a snowball)	5.00	7.00	6.00
1940			
☐ January 1, 1940 (Queen Elizabeth on cover)	8.00	10.00	9.00
☐ January 8, 1940 (Bowdoin Houseparty)	5.00	7.00	6.00
☐ January 29, 1940 (Lana Turner on cover)	12.00	14.00	13.00
☐ February 19, 1940 (King of Rumania and Hein on cover)	5.00	7.00	6.00
☐ March 4, 1940 (Woman wearing "sailor" hat on cover)	5.00	7.00	6.00
☐ May 6, 1940 (Aerial gunner on cover) ..	5.00	7.00	6.00
☐ June 10, 1940 (Italy's Army Chief on cover)	5.00	7.00	6.00
☐ July 8, 1940 (Chief of Naval Operations on cover)	5.00	7.00	6.00
☐ July 15, 1940 (Rita Hayworth on cover)	13.00	15.00	14.00
☐ September 30, 1940 (Wendell Willkie on cover)	13.00	15.00	14.00
☐ November 11, 1940 (Tom Harmon on cover)	13.00	15.00	14.00
☐ November 25, 1940 (Woman wearing wolverine coat on cover)	5.00	7.00	6.00
☐ December 9, 1940 (Ginger Rogers on cover)	13.00	15.00	14.00
1941			
☐ January 6, 1941 (Katharine Hepburn on cover)	10.00	12.00	11.00
☐ January 13, 1941 (Woman in bathing suit on cover)	4.00	6.00	5.00

Life, October 1941, $18.00–$20.00.

	Current Price Range		C/Y Avg.
☐ January 27, 1941 (Churchill on cover) ..	10.00	12.00	11.00
☐ February 13, 1941 (War News From Inside Germany)	4.00	6.00	5.00
☐ March 2, 1941 (Ginger Rogers on cover)	8.00	10.00	9.00
☐ March 17, 1941 (Panama Defense)	4.00	6.00	5.00
☐ May 5, 1941 (Harvard University)	4.00	6.00	5.00
☐ June 9, 1941 (Duke and Duchess of Windsor on cover)..................	8.00	10.00	9.00
☐ July 21, 1941 (Singapore's Commander in Chief on cover)	4.00	6.00	5.00
☐ September 1, 1941 (Rita Hayworth on cover)	10.00	12.00	11.00
☐ October 13, 1941 (Lana Turner and Clark Gable on cover)	18.00	20.00	19.00
☐ December 8, 1941 (General Douglas MacArthur on cover).................	22.50	27.50	25.00

	Current Price Range		C/Y Avg.

☐ December 22, 1941 (American Flag on cover) **22.50** **27.50** **25.00**

1942

☐ March 16, 1942 (Profile of Private Charles Edward Teed of U.S. Infantry) **4.00** **6.00** **5.00**

☐ March 30, 1942 (Shirley Temple Grows Up) **12.00** **14.00** **13.00**

☐ April 27, 1942 (Nelson Rockefeller on cover) **8.00** **10.00** **9.00**

☐ June 1, 1942 (Hedy Lamarr on cover) .. **8.00** **10.00** **9.00**

☐ July 6, 1942 (American Flag in color on cover) **7.00** **9.00** **8.00**

☐ July 20, 1942 (Woman wearing "Short Coat" on cover).................... **4.00** **6.00** **5.00**

☐ August 10, 1942 (General Chennault in China on cover).................... **4.00** **6.00** **5.00**

☐ September 28, 1942 (Admiral William Daniel Leahy on cover) **4.00** **6.00** **5.00**

☐ October 5, 1942 (Woman wearing unusual hat) **4.00** **6.00** **5.00**

☐ October 26, 1942 (Joan Leslie) **4.00** **6.00** **5.00**

☐ November 2, 1942 (Chaplain credited with saying "Praise the Lord and Pass the Ammunition") **4.00** **6.00** **5.00**

☐ December 7, 1942 (Marine Ace John Lucian Smith on cover) **4.00** **6.00** **5.00**

☐ December 14, 1942 (Coast Guard Skipper on cover) **4.00** **6.00** **5.00**

☐ December 28, 1942 (Raphael's Madonna on cover) **4.00** **6.00** **5.00**

1943

☐ January 11, 1943 (Kid's Uniforms) **4.00** **6.00** **5.00**

☐ January 25, 1943 (Eddie Rickenbacker Tells His Own Story) **4.00** **6.00** **5.00**

☐ February 8, 1943 (Plane Spotter) **4.00** **6.00** **5.00**

☐ March 29, 1943 (Joseph Stalin on cover) **8.00** **10.00** **9.00**

☐ May 31, 1943 (King Ibn Saud of Saudi Arabia on cover) **4.00** **6.00** **5.00**

☐ July 12, 1943 (Roy Rogers on cover) ... **37.50** **42.50** **40.00**

☐ August 30, 1943 (Anthony Eden on cover) **4.00** **6.00** **5.00**

	Current Price Range		C/Y Avg.
☐ September 6, 1943 (Jap Hunters)	4.00	6.00	5.00
☐ October 18, 1943 (Picture Romance) ..	4.00	6.00	5.00
☐ October 25, 1943 (Mary Martin on cover)	6.00	8.00	7.00

1944

☐ January 10, 1944 (Bob Hope on cover)	8.00	10.00	9.00
☐ February 7, 1944 (George Bernard Shaw on cover)	6.00	8.00	7.00
☐ March 27, 1944 (Infantry and Landing Craft on cover)	4.00	6.00	5.00
☐ April 17, 1944 (Esther Williams on cover)	8.00	10.00	9.00
☐ June 12, 1944 (Invasion by Air)	4.00	6.00	5.00
☐ July 10, 1944 (Admiral Chester Nimitz on cover)	4.00	6.00	5.00
☐ July 17, 1944 (Woman wearing "Peasant Clothes" on cover)	4.00	6.00	5.00
☐ August 7, 1944 (Geraldine Fitzgerald on cover)	4.00	6.00	5.00
☐ August 14, 1944 (In Normandy)	4.00	6.00	5.00
☐ August 21, 1944 (Landing Alligators) ...	4.00	6.00	5.00
☐ October 16, 1944 (Lauren Bacall on cover)	8.00	10.00	9.00
☐ October 30, 1944 (USS Iowa)	4.00	6.00	5.00
☐ November 13, 1944 (Charles De Gaulle on cover)	7.00	9.00	8.00
☐ December 11, 1944 (Judy Garland on cover)	13.00	15.00	14.00

1945

☐ January 15, 1945 (General George Patton on cover)	7.00	9.00	8.00
☐ February 12, 1945 (Soviet Soldier on cover)	4.00	6.00	5.00
☐ March 5, 1945 (The Pacific)	4.00	6.00	5.00
☐ March 19, 1945 (Dutch Girl on cover) ..	4.00	6.00	5.00
☐ March 26, 1945 (Carol Lynne on cover)	4.00	6.00	5.00
☐ April 2, 1945 (Sub-Deb Clubs)	4.00	6.00	5.00
☐ April 16, 1945 (General Dwight David Eisenhower on cover)	17.00	19.00	18.00
☐ April 23, 1945 (President Harry S. Truman on cover)	22.50	27.50	25.00
☐ April 30, 1945 (Life's War Artists)	11.00	13.00	12.00
☐ May 14, 1945 (Victorious Yank on cover)	12.00	14.00	13.00

Life, April 1945, $17.00–$19.00.

	Current Price Range		C/Y Avg.
☐ May 28, 1945 (Barbara Bates on cover)	5.00	7.00	6.00
☐ July 9, 1945 (Woman wearing bathing suit on cover)	4.00	6.00	5.00
☐ July 16, 1945 (Audie Murphy on cover)	8.00	10.00	9.00
☐ September 3, 1945 (General Douglas MacArthur on cover)	22.50	27.50	25.00
☐ September 17, 1945 (Jimmy Stewart on cover)	9.00	11.00	10.00
☐ October 1, 1945 (June Allyson on cover)	8.00	10.00	9.00
☐ October 15, 1945 (Fall Jewelry)	4.00	6.00	5.00
☐ November 5, 1945 (The Fleet's In)	8.00	10.00	9.00
☐ November 12, 1945 (Ingrid Bergman on cover)	12.00	14.00	13.00
☐ December 3, 1945 (Spencer Tracy on cover)	11.00	13.00	10.00
☐ December 17, 1945 (Paulette Goddard on cover)	10.00	12.00	11.00

Life, *November 1945,* **$12.00–$14.00.**

	Current Price Range		C/Y Avg.

1946

☐ January 21, 1946 (Cardinal Spellman on cover)	4.00	6.00	5.00
☐ January 28, 1946 (Jan Clayton on cover)	5.00	7.00	6.00
☐ February 4, 1946 (Bing Crosby and Bob Hope on cover)	11.00	13.00	12.00
☐ February 18, 1946 (Dorothy McGuire on cover)	5.00	7.00	6.00
☐ February 25, 1946 (Bird dog on cover)	3.00	5.00	4.00
☐ March 4, 1946 (Figure skater Gretchen Van Zandt on cover)	3.00	5.00	4.00
☐ March 11, 1946 (Michigan Senator Vanderberg on cover)	3.00	5.00	4.00
☐ March 18, 1946 (Paris: 1946)	3.00	5.00	4.00
☐ April 1, 1946 (Cardinals Pitcher Charles "Red" Barrett on cover)	13.00	15.00	14.00

	Current Price Range		C/Y Avg.

☐ April 8, 1946 (Clown and giraffe from Ringling Brothers and Barnum & Bailey circus on cover) **13.00 15.00 14.00**

☐ April 15, 1946 (Spring Fashions) **3.00 5.00 4.00**

☐ April 22, 1946 (Denver High School) ... **3.00 5.00 4.00**

☐ May 20, 1946 (Ice Show) **3.00 5.00 4.00**

☐ May 27, 1946 (Ozark farmer on cover) **3.00 5.00 4.00**

☐ June 3, 1946 (Children's Church) **3.00 5.00 4.00**

☐ June 10, 1946 (Donna Reed on cover) **7.00 9.00 8.00**

☐ June 17, 1946 (Woman wearing "Play Dress" on cover) **3.00 5.00 4.00**

☐ June 24, 1946 (Chief Justice of the United States) **3.00 5.00 4.00**

☐ July 1, 1946 (Sailboats) **3.00 5.00 4.00**

☐ July 8, 1946 (Woman wearing "Basque Shirt") **3.00 5.00 4.00**

☐ July 15, 1946 (Welded Water Gadgets) **3.00 5.00 4.00**

☐ July 22, 1946 (Mrs. Cornelius Vanderbilt Whitney and coachman on cover) **3.00 5.00 4.00**

☐ July 29, 1946 (Vivien Leigh on cover) .. **9.00 11.00 10.00**

☐ August 12, 1945 (Loretta Young on cover) **7.00 9.00 8.00**

☐ August 19, 1946 (Old Faithful on cover) **3.00 5.00 4.00**

☐ August 26, 1946 (Fall College Fashions) **3.00 5.00 4.00**

☐ September 9, 1946 (Jane Powell on cover) **5.00 7.00 6.00**

☐ September 30, 1946 (Jeanne Crain on cover) **5.00 7.00 6.00**

☐ October 7, 1946 (Bing Crosby and Joan Caulfield on cover) **8.00 10.00 9.00**

☐ November 4, 1946 (Palestinian and camel on cover) **3.00 5.00 4.00**

1947

☐ January 27, 1947 (Lighthouse) **3.00 5.00 4.00**

☐ February 3, 1947 (Three young Broadway actresses, including Patricia Neal, on cover) **4.00 6.00 5.00**

☐ March 24, 1947 (Beyond the Arctic Circle) **3.00 5.00 4.00**

☐ March 31, 1947 (Spring hats on cover) **3.00 5.00 4.00**

☐ May 19, 1947 (Teenager eating a "Super Sundae" on cover) **3.00 5.00 4.00**

	Current Price Range		C/Y Avg.
☐ June 2, 1947 (Jane Greer on cover) ...	4.00	6.00	5.00
☐ June 9, 1947 (Young Ballerina on cover)	3.00	5.00	4.00
☐ June 16, 1947 (Cape Hatteras Bay on cover)	3.00	5.00	4.00
☐ June 23, 1947 (Bathing Suits on cover)	3.00	5.00	4.00
☐ July 14, 1947 (Elizabeth Taylor on cover)	11.00	13.00	12.00
☐ July 28, 1947 (Princess Elizabeth on cover)	5.00	7.00	6.00
☐ September 29, 1947 (Quarterback Johnny Lujack on cover)	6.00	8.00	7.00
☐ October 6, 1947 (FDR at 13 on cover)	5.00	7.00	6.00
☐ October 20, 1947 (Child listening to folk songs on cover)	3.00	5.00	4.00
☐ November 10, 1947 (Rita Hayworth on cover)	8.00	10.00	9.00
☐ November 17, 1947 (Boxer dogs on cover)	3.00	5.00	4.00
☐ December 1, 1947 (Gregory Peck on cover)	6.00	8.00	7.00
☐ December 15, 1947 (Night Club Girls on cover)	3.00	5.00	4.00
☐ December 22, 1947 (Woman in bathing suit on cover)	3.00	5.00	4.00

1948

☐ February 9, 1948 (Robert A. Taft on cover)	4.00	6.00	5.00
☐ March 1, 1948 (Harold E. Stassen on cover)	4.00	6.00	5.00
☐ March 22, 1948 (Thomas E. Dewey on cover)	5.00	7.00	6.00
☐ April 12, 1948 (Barbara Bel Geddes on cover)	4.00	6.00	5.00
☐ May 10, 1947 (Earl Warren on cover) ..	4.00	6.00	5.00
☐ May 17, 1948 (Mrs. David Niven on cover)	4.00	6.00	5.00
☐ June 7, 1948 (Woman wearing "Hooded T-Shirt")	3.00	5.00	4.00
☐ June 14, 1948 (Phyllis Calvert on cover)	3.00	5.00	4.00
☐ June 28, 1948 (Kent School student) ...	3.00	5.00	4.00
☐ July 5, 1948 (F-84 Thunderjets)	3.00	5.00	4.00
☐ July 12, 1948 (Small-Town Girl on cover)	3.00	5.00	4.00

	Current Price Range		C/Y Avg.
☐ July 19, 1948 (Fun on the Beach)	3.00	5.00	4.00
☐ July 26, 1948 (Children's Ballet School on cover)	3.00	5.00	4.00
☐ August 2, 1948 (Olympic Sprinter Mel Patton on cover)	6.00	8.00	7.00
☐ August 9, 1948 (Marlene Dietrich on cover)	6.00	8.00	7.00
☐ August 16, 1948 (Child fisherman on cover)	3.00	5.00	4.00
☐ August 23, 1948 (Woman and pet deer on cover)	3.00	5.00	4.00
☐ August 30, 1948 (Colleen Townsend on cover)	3.00	5.00	4.00
☐ September 13, 1948 (Marshal Tito on cover)	4.00	6.00	5.00
☐ September 20, 1948 (Women in Broadway rehearsal on cover)	3.00	5.00	4.00
☐ September 27, 1948 (Football player Doak Walker of Southern Methodist on cover) ....:	8.00	10.00	9.00
☐ October 4, 1948 (Du Pont Chemical plant on cover)	3.00	5.00	4.00
☐ October 11, 1948 (Television star Rita Colton on cover)	5.00	7.00	6.00
☐ October 18, 1948 (Women wearing fur jackets on cover)	3.00	5.00	4.00
☐ October 25, 1948 (Students cheering at University of California on cover)	3.00	5.00	4.00
☐ November 1, 1948 (Lieut. Gen. Lauris Norsted on cover)	3.00	5.00	4.00
☐ November 8, 1948 (Helena Carter on cover)	3.00	5.00	4.00
☐ November 15, 1948 (Ingrid Bergman as Joan of Arc on cover)	8.00	10.00	9.00
☐ November 22, 1948 (President Harry Truman on cover)	9.00	11.00	10.00
☐ November 29, 1948 (Woman wearing "Dinner Hat" on cover)	3.00	5.00	4.00
☐ December 6, 1948 (Montgomery Clift on cover)	7.00	9.00	8.00
☐ December 13, 1948 (Dwight Eisenhower on cover)	9.00	11.00	10.00

	Current Price Range		C/Y Avg.
☐ December 20, 1948 (Teenagers playing "Passing the Ring" on cover)	3.00	5.00	4.00
☐ December 27, 1948 (Giotto painting of Christ child on cover)	3.00	5.00	4.00

1949

☐ January 3, 1949 (Famous babies of the year—infant Dwight D. Eisenhower II shown on cover)	4.00	6.00	5.00
☐ January 10, 1949 (Debutante Joanne Connelley on cover)	3.00	5.00	4.00
☐ January 17, 1949 (Resort Fashions) ...	3.00	5.00	4.00
☐ January 24, 1949 (French skier Emile Allais on cover)	3.00	5.00	4.00
☐ January 31, 1949 (Cocker spaniel on cover)	3.00	5.00	4.00
☐ February 7, 1949 (Winston Churchill's War Memoirs)	4.00	6.00	5.00
☐ February 28, 1949 (Children's "Costume Clothes" on cover)	3.00	5.00	4.00
☐ March 7, 1949 (Marge and Gower Champion on cover)	4.00	6.00	5.00
☐ April 4, 1949 (Paul G. Hoffman of the Economic Cooperative Administration on cover)	3.00	5.00	4.00
☐ April 18, 1949 (Mary Martin on cover) ..	4.00	6.00	5.00
☐ April 25, 1949 (Paris Fashion)	3.00	5.00	4.00
☐ May 2, 1949 (West Point ballplayer on cover)	4.00	6.00	5.00
☐ May 16, 1949 (Five-year-old boxer on cover)	3.00	5.00	4.00
☐ June 6, 1949 (Summer Playclothes)	3.00	5.00	4.00
☐ June 20, 1949 (High school graduate on cover)	3.00	5.00	4.00
☐ June 27, 1949 (Inland Sailing)	3.00	5.00	4.00
☐ July 11, 1949 (Athlete Bob Mathias on cover)	6.00	8.00	7.00
☐ August 1, 1949 (Joe DiMaggio on cover)	11.00	13.00	12.00
☐ August 8, 1949 (How to Dress for Hollywood)	3.00	5.00	4.00
☐ September 5, 1949 (Ben Turpin on cover)	8.00	10.00	9.00

	Current Price Range		C/Y Avg.
☐ September 12, 1949 (Marshal Tito on cover)	5.00	7.00	6.00
☐ September 19, 1949 (Arlene Dahl on cover)	4.00	6.00	5.00
☐ September 26, 1949 (How to Make Two Outfits Out of One)	3.00	6.00	5.00
☐ October 10, 1949 (Dr. J. Robert Oppenheimer on cover)	5.00	7.00	6.00
☐ October 17, 1949 (Jeanne Crain on cover)	4.00	6.00	5.00
☐ October 24, 1949 (Swedish girl in Sweden on cover)	3.00	5.00	4.00
☐ October 31, 1949 (Princes Margaret on cover)	4.00	6.00	5.00
☐ November 7, 1949 (Alfred Lunt and Lynne Fontanne on cover)	4.00	6.00	5.00
☐ November 14, 1949 (Woman wearing pearls on cover)	3.00	5.00	4.00
☐ November 21, 1949 (Ricardo Montalban on cover)	4.00	6.00	5.00
☐ November 28, 1949 (Movie dancer Nita Bieber on cover)	3.00	5.00	4.00
☐ December 5, 1949 (General Hoyt Vandenburg on cover)	3.00	5.00	4.00
☐ December 12, 1949 (Beauty on Fifth Avenue)	3.00	5.00	4.00
☐ December 26, 1949 (Michelangelo painting of God on cover)	3.00	5.00	4.00
1950			
☐ January 2, 1950 (American Life and Times 1900–1950, Special Issue)	11.00	13.00	12.00
☐ January 9, 1950 (Norma De Landa on cover)	3.00	5.00	4.00
☐ January 16, 1950 (Three-year-old skater on cover)	3.00	5.00	4.00
☐ January 23, 1950 (Woman wearing "Man-Tailored Suit" on cover)	3.00	5.00	4.00
☐ January 30, 1950 (Childbirth without fear)	3.00	5.00	4.00
☐ February 6, 1950 (Eva Gabor on cover)	4.00	6.00	5.00
☐ February 13, 1950 (Indonesian woman on cover)	3.00	5.00	4.00

	Current Price Range		C/Y Avg.

	Current Price Range		C/Y Avg.
☐ February 20, 1950 (Atomic explosion on cover)	5.00	7.00	6.00
☐ February 27, 1950 (Gregory Peck on cover)	4.00	6.00	5.00
☐ March 6, 1950 (Marsha Hunt on cover)	3.00	5.00	4.00
☐ March 13, 1950 (A Guided Tour of Spring Fashions)	3.00	5.00	4.00
☐ March 20, 1950 (Artist Edward John Stevens Jr. on cover)	3.00	5.00	4.00
☐ March 27, 1950 (Anne Bromley on cover)	3.00	5.00	4.00
☐ April 3, 1950 (Iris Mann and David Cole on cover)	3.00	5.00	4.00
☐ April 10, 1950 (Young horsewoman on cover)	3.00	5.00	4.00
☐ April 17, 1950 (General Dwight Eisenhower on cover)	8.00	10.00	9.00
☐ April 24, 1950 (Woman wearing checkered blouse on cover)	3.00	5.00	4.00
☐ May 1, 1950 (Ruth Roman on cover) ...	3.00	5.00	4.00
☐ May 8, 1950 (Jackie Robinson on cover)	9.00	11.00	10.00
☐ May 22, 1950 (Duke and Duchess of Windsor on cover)	7.00	9.00	8.00
☐ May 29, 1950 (Mrs. William O'Dwyer on cover)	3.00	5.00	4.00
☐ June 5, 1950 (Stasia Kos on cover)	3.00	5.00	4.00
☐ June 12, 1950 (Bill Boyd on cover)	18.00	20.00	19.00
☐ June 19, 1950 (Children's Sand Styles on cover)	3.00	5.00	4.00
☐ June 26, 1950 (Cecile Aubry on cover)	3.00	5.00	4.00
☐ July 3, 1950 (Thomas Sully painting of George Washington at Trenton on cover)	3.00	5.00	4.00
☐ July 10, 1950 (Miroslava on cover)	3.00	5.00	4.00
☐ July 17, 1950 (U.S. Jet Pilot After Shooting Down a YAK)	5.00	7.00	6.00
☐ July 24, 1950 (Boy Scout on cover)	5.00	7.00	6.00
☐ August 7, 1950 (Peggy Dow on cover)	3.00	5.00	4.00
☐ August 28, 1950 (General Douglas MacArthur on cover)	7.00	9.00	8.00
☐ September 18, 1950 (Ezio Pinza on cover)	4.00	6.00	5.00
☐ September 25, 1950 (Swedish Red Cross Girl on cover)	2.00	4.00	3.00

	Current Price Range		C/Y Avg.
☐ October 2, 1950 (Stuart Symington on cover)	2.00	4.00	3.00
☐ October 16, 1950 (U.S. Schools, Special Issue)	2.00	4.00	3.00
☐ December 4, 1950 (Berlin girl on cover)	2.00	4.00	3.00
☐ December 11, 1950 (Lilly Palmer and Rex Harrison on cover)	4.00	6.00	5.00
☐ December 18, 1950 (George C. Marshall on cover)	4.00	6.00	5.00
☐ December 25, 1950 (Artist John Koch on cover)	2.00	4.00	3.00

1951

☐ January 1, 1951 (War production boss Charles E. Wilson on cover)	2.00	4.00	3.00
☐ January 8, 1951 (Janice Rule on cover)	2.00	4.00	3.00
☐ January 15, 1951 (Grand Marshal of Rose Parade on cover)	2.00	4.00	3.00
☐ January 29, 1951 (Betsy Von Furstenberg on cover)	2.00	4.00	3.00
☐ February 5, 1951 (Police Commissioner Tom Murphy on cover)	2.00	4.00	3.00
☐ February 12, 1951 (Woman wearing veil-hat on cover)	2.00	4.00	3.00
☐ February 19, 1951 (The Adoption of Linda Joy)	2.00	4.00	3.00
☐ February 26, 1951 (Debbie Reynolds on cover)	5.00	7.00	6.00
☐ March 5, 1951 (Christian Dior fashions)	2.00	4.00	3.00
☐ March 12, 1951 (Paul Douglas on cover)	2.00	4.00	3.00
☐ March 19, 1951 (Navy Couple on cover)	2.00	4.00	3.00
☐ April 9, 1951 (General Omar Bradley on cover)	4.00	6.00	5.00
☐ April 16, 1951 (Esther Williams on cover)	3.00	5.00	4.00
☐ June 11, 1951 (Vivian Blaine of "Guys and Dolls" on cover)	3.00	5.00	4.00
☐ June 18, 1951 (Iran's Royal Crown on cover)	2.00	4.00	3.00
☐ June 25, 1951 (Janet Leigh on cover) ..	3.00	5.00	4.00
☐ July 30, 1951 (Gary Crosby on cover) ..	4.00	6.00	5.00
☐ August 13, 1951 (Dean Martin and Jerry Lewis on cover)	4.00	6.00	5.00

	Current Price Range		C/Y Avg.
☐ October 1, 1951 (Princess Elizabeth on cover)	4.00	6.00	5.00
☐ October 8, 1951 (The Lazy Life of a Slow Loris)	2.00	4.00	3.00
☐ October 15, 1951 (Zsa Zsa Gabor on cover)	4.00	6.00	5.00
☐ September 5, 1951 (Ginger Rogers on cover)	4.00	6.00	5.00
☐ November 5, 1951 (Ginger Rogers on cover)	4.00	6.00	5.00
☐ November 19, 1951 (Anthony Eden on cover)	2.00	4.00	3.00
☐ December 10, 1951 (President Harry Truman on cover)	8.00	10.00	9.00
☐ December 17, 1951 (Laurence Olivier and Vivian Leigh on cover)	7.00	9.00	8.00
1952			
☐ January 21, 1952 (Dwight D. Eisenhower on cover)	8.00	10.00	9.00
☐ March 31, 1952 (Li'l Abner on cover) ...	7.00	9.00	8.00
☐ April 7, 1952 (Marilyn Monroe on cover)	27.50	32.50	30.00
☐ April 28, 1952 (Dwight and Mamie Eisenhower on cover)	8.00	10.00	9.00
☐ May 5, 1952 (Diana Lynn on cover)	2.00	4.00	3.00
☐ June 23, 1952 (Mail-order fashions)	2.00	4.00	3.00
☐ July 7, 1952 (Arlene Dahl on cover)	3.00	5.00	4.00
☐ August 4, 1952 (Adlai Stevenson on cover)	4.00	6.00	5.00
☐ August 18, 1952 (Marlene Dietrich on cover)	5.00	7.00	6.00
☐ September 15, 1952 (Rita Gam on cover)	2.00	4.00	3.00
☐ October 20, 1952 (Mamie Eisenhower on cover)	5.00	7.00	6.00
☐ November 3, 1952 (United Nations on cover)	2.00	4.00	3.00
☐ November 17, 1952 (Dwight and Mamie Eisenhower on cover)	6.00	8.00	7.00
☐ December 29, 1952 (Salzburg marionettes on cover)	2.00	4.00	3.00
1953			
☐ January 12, 1953 (Resort clothes)	2.00	4.00	3.00

	Current Price Range		C/Y Avg.
☐ January 26, 1953 (Fashions)	2.00	4.00	3.00
☐ March 9, 1953 (Vanessa Brown on cover)	2.00	4.00	3.00
☐ April 6, 1953 (Lucille Ball on cover)	9.00	11.00	10.00
☐ April 20, 1953 (Marlon Brando on cover)	8.00	10.00	9.00
☐ April 27, 1953 (Queen Elizabeth on cover)	8.00	10.00	9.00
☐ May 25, 1953 (Marilyn Monroe and Jane Russell on cover)	25.00	30.00	27.50
☐ June 8, 1953 (Roy Campanella of Brooklyn Dodgers on cover)	19.00	21.00	20.00
☐ July 6, 1953 (Terry Moore on cover) ...	8.00	10.00	9.00
☐ July 20, 1953 (John F. and Jacqueline Kennedy on cover)	22.50	27.50	25.00
☐ August 31, 1953 (Donna Reed on cover)	9.00	11.00	10.00
☐ September 7, 1953 (Dinosaurs on cover)	6.00	8.00	7.00
☐ September 14, 1953 (Casey Stengel on cover)	5.00	7.00	6.00
☐ September 21, 1953 (Juanita Smith on cover)	2.00	4.00	3.00
☐ November 2, 1953 (Winston Churchill on cover)	4.00	6.00	5.00
☐ December 14, 1953 (Richard Nixon on cover)	6.00	8.00	7.00

1954

	Current Price Range		C/Y Avg.
☐ January 18, 1954 (Dwight Eisenhower and Richard Nixon on cover)	7.00	9.00	8.00
☐ February 1, 1954 (Bathing suits on cover)	2.00	4.00	3.00
☐ March 1, 1954 (Rita Moreno on cover)	2.00	4.00	3.00
☐ April 26, 1954 (Grace Kelly on cover) ..	9.00	11.00	10.00
☐ May 17, 1954 (Dawn Addams on cover)	2.00	4.00	3.00
☐ May 24, 1954 (Kaye Ballard on cover) ..	2.00	4.00	3.00
☐ May 31, 1954 (William Holden on cover)	3.00	5.00	4.00
☐ July 12, 1954 (Pier Angeli on cover) ...	2.00	4.00	3.00
☐ August 23, 1954 (Prince Philip on cover)	4.00	6.00	5.00
☐ September 13, 1954 (Judy Garland on cover)	9.00	11.00	10.00
☐ November 1, 1954 (Dorothy Dandridge on cover)	2.00	4.00	3.00
☐ November 22, 1954 (Gina Lollobrigida on cover)	4.00	6.00	5.00
☐ November 22, 1954 (Judy Holliday on cover)	3.00	5.00	4.00

	Current Price Range		C/Y Avg.

☐ December 27, 1954 (Pieter Bruegel painting on cover) .... | 2.00 | 4.00 | 3.00

1955
☐ January 10, 1955 (Greta Garbo on cover) | 6.00 | 8.00 | 7.00
☐ January 31, 1955 (Spencer Tracy on cover) .... | 6.00 | 8.00 | 7.00
☐ February 14, 1955 (Princess Margaret on cover) .... | 3.00 | 5.00 | 4.00
☐ February 28, 1955 (Shelley Winters on cover) .... | 3.00 | 5.00 | 4.00
☐ March 21, 1955 (Sheree North on cover) | 2.00 | 4.00 | 3.00
☐ April 11, 1955 (Grace Kelly on cover) .. | 8.00 | 10.00 | 9.00
☐ April 25, 1955 (Anthony Eden on cover) | 2.00 | 4.00 | 3.00
☐ May 23, 1955 (Leslie Caron on cover) .. | 3.00 | 5.00 | 4.00
☐ June 6, 1955 (Henry Fonda on cover) .. | 4.00 | 6.00 | 5.00
☐ July 11, 1955 (Susan Strasberg on cover) | 2.00 | 4.00 | 3.00
☐ July 18, 1955 (Audrey Hepburn on cover) | 3.00 | 5.00 | 4.00
☐ July 25, 1955 (Cathy Crosby on cover) | 3.00 | 5.00 | 4.00
☐ August 8, 1955 (Ben Hogan on cover) | 3.00 | 5.00 | 4.00
☐ August 15, 1955 (General Douglas MacArthur on cover) .... | 4.00 | 6.00 | 5.00
☐ August 22, 1955 (Sophia Loren on cover) | 5.00 | 7.00 | 6.00
☐ September 12, 1955 (Joan Collins on cover) .... | 8.00 | 10.00 | 9.00
☐ September 26, 1955 (Harry S. and Bess Truman on cover) .... | 8.00 | 10.00 | 9.00
☐ October 3, 1955 (Rock Hudson on cover) | 10.00 | 12.00 | 11.00
☐ October 10, 1955 (Princess Margaret on cover) .... | 6.00 | 8.00 | 7.00
☐ November 14, 1955 (Dwight Eisenhower on cover) .... | 8.00 | 10.00 | 9.00
☐ November 28, 1955 (Carol Channing on cover) .... | 3.00 | 5.00 | 4.00

1956
☐ January 16, 1956 (Anita Ekberg on cover) | 2.00 | 4.00 | 3.00
☐ February 6, 1956 (Shirley Jones on cover) | 3.00 | 5.00 | 4.00
☐ February 13, 1956 (Harry Truman and Douglas MacArthur on cover) .... | 7.00 | 9.00 | 8.00
☐ February 20, 1956 (Claire Bloom on cover) .... | 2.00 | 4.00 | 3.00

	Current Price Range		C/Y Avg.
☐ March 5, 1956 (Kim Novak on cover) ..	3.00	5.00	4.00
☐ March 12, 1956 (Dwight Eisenhower on cover)	6.00	8.00	7.00
☐ March 26, 1956 (Julie Andrews on cover)	3.00	5.00	4.00
☐ April 9, 1956 (Grace Kelly on cover) ...	7.00	9.00	8.00
☐ April 23, 1956 (Jayne Mansfield on cover)	6.00	8.00	7.00
☐ May 28, 1956 (Yul Brynner on cover) ..	5.00	7.00	6.00
☐ June 11, 1956 (Carroll Baker on cover)	2.00	4.00	3.00
☐ June 25, 1956 (Mickey Mantle on cover)	14.00	16.00	15.00
☐ July 16, 1956 (Gary Cooper on cover) ..	7.00	9.00	8.00
☐ August 20, 1956 (Audrey Hepburn on cover)	4.00	6.00	5.00
☐ August 27, 1956 (Adlai Stevenson and Eleanor Roosevelt on cover)	3.00	5.00	4.00
☐ September 24, 1956 (Janet Blair on cover)	3.00	5.00	4.00
☐ October 15, 1956 (Elizabeth Taylor on cover)	6.00	8.00	7.00
☐ November 5, 1956 (President Dwight Eisenhower on cover)	6.00	8.00	7.00
☐ November 12, 1956 (Rosalind Russell on cover)	3.00	5.00	4.00
☐ November 26, 1956 (Ingrid Bergman on cover)	4.00	6.00	5.00

1957

	Current Price Range		C/Y Avg.
☐ January 7, 1957 (Richard Nixon on cover)	7.00	9.00	8.00
☐ February 4, 1957 (Audrey Hepburn on cover)	4.00	6.00	5.00
☐ February 18, 1957 (Julie London on cover)	3.00	5.00	4.00
☐ March 4, 1957 (Queen Elizabeth and Prince Philip on cover)	3.00	5.00	4.00
☐ March 11, 1957 (John F. Kennedy on cover)	14.00	16.00	15.00
☐ March 18, 1957 (Bea Lillie on cover) ...	2.00	4.00	3.00
☐ March 25, 1957 (Princess Caroline of Monaco as infant on cover)	4.00	6.00	5.00
☐ April 15, 1957 (Ernie Kovacs on cover)	4.00	6.00	5.00
☐ May 6, 1957 (Sophia Loren on cover) ..	4.00	6.00	5.00
☐ May 13, 1957 (Bert Lahr on cover)	3.00	5.00	4.00

	Current Price Range		C/Y Avg.
☐ June 24, 1957 (Juan Carlos of Spain on cover)	2.00	4.00	3.00
☐ July 1, 1957 (Billy Graham on cover)	2.00	4.00	3.00
☐ August 12, 1957 (May Britt on cover)	2.00	4.00	3.00
☐ September 30, 1957 (Rex Harrison on cover)	2.00	4.00	3.00
☐ October 28, 1957 (Queen Elizabeth on cover)	3.00	5.00	4.00
☐ December 2, 1957 (Nikita Khushchev on cover)	3.00	5.00	4.00
☐ December 9, 1957 (Richard Nixon and James Hagerty on cover)	4.00	6.00	5.00

1958

	Current Price Range		C/Y Avg.
☐ January 6, 1958 (Astronaut on cover)	8.00	10.00	9.00
☐ January 20, 1958 (Lyndon Johnson on cover)	4.00	6.00	5.00
☐ February 3, 1958 (Shirley Temple on cover)	8.00	10.00	9.00
☐ February 10, 1958 (Ralph Bellamy on cover)	3.00	5.00	4.00
☐ March 10, 1958 (Yul Brynner on cover)	3.00	5.00	4.00
☐ March 17, 1958 (McGuire sisters on cover)	2.00	4.00	3.00
☐ March 24, 1958 (Moscow and Chicago students on cover)	2.00	4.00	3.00
☐ April 7, 1958 (Ray Robinson vs. Carmine Basilio on cover)	2.00	4.00	3.00
☐ April 14, 1958 (Gwen Verdon on cover)	2.00	4.00	3.00
☐ April 21, 1958 (John F. and Jacqueline Kennedy on cover)	14.00	16.00	15.00
☐ April 28, 1958 (Willie Mays on cover)	11.00	13.00	12.00
☐ May 26, 1958 (Richard Nixon on cover)	6.00	8.00	7.00
☐ June 2, 1958 (Charles DeGaulle on cover)	2.00	4.00	3.00
☐ June 30, 1958 (D. Eisenhower and Sherman Adams on cover)	4.00	6.00	5.00
☐ September 15, 1958 (Bing Crosby's sons on cover)	3.00	5.00	4.00
☐ September 22, 1958 (George Burns and Gracie Allen on cover)	3.00	5.00	4.00

	Current Price Range		C/Y Avg.
☐ November 17, 1958 (Mr. and Mrs. Nelson Rockefeller on cover)	2.00	4.00	3.00
☐ December 1, 1958 (Ricky Nelson on cover)	11.00	13.00	12.00

1959

	Current Price Range		C/Y Avg.
☐ January 12, 1959 (Hubert Humphrey on cover)	3.00	5.00	4.00
☐ February 2, 1959 (Pat Boone on cover)	2.00	4.00	3.00
☐ February 9, 1959 (Shirley MacLaine on cover)	2.00	4.00	3.00
☐ February 23, 1959 (Gwen Verdon on cover)	2.00	4.00	3.00
☐ March 9, 1959 (Jack Paar on cover) ...	2.00	4.00	3.00
☐ March 30, 1959 (Debbie Reynolds on cover)	2.00	4.00	3.00
☐ April 20, 1959 (Marilyn Monroe on cover)	19.00	21.00	20.00
☐ May 18, 1959 (Jimmy Hoffa on cover) ..	2.00	4.00	3.00
☐ June 8, 1959 (Audrey Hepburn on cover)	2.00	4.00	3.00
☐ June 29, 1959 (Zsa Zsa Gabor on cover)	2.00	4.00	3.00
☐ July 20, 1959 (Ingemar Johansson on cover)	2.00	4.00	3.00
☐ July 27, 1959 (Great White Fleet on cover)	2.00	4.00	3.00
☐ August 3, 1959 (Kingston Trio on cover)	2.00	4.00	3.00
☐ August 10, 1959 (Russian Women on cover)	2.00	4.00	3.00
☐ August 17, 1959 (May Britt on cover) ..	2.00	4.00	3.00
☐ August 24, 1959 (Jacqueline Kennedy on cover)	11.00	13.00	12.00
☐ August 31, 1959 (Rip Van Winkle on cover)	2.00	4.00	3.00
☐ September 7, 1959 (Bat Masterson on cover)	2.00	4.00	3.00
☐ September 14, 1959 (Astronauts on cover)	3.00	5.00	4.00
☐ September 21, 1959 (Astronauts' wives on cover)	3.00	5.00	4.00
☐ September 28, 1959 (Ducks on cover)	2.00	4.00	3.00
☐ October 5, 1959 (Nikita Khruschev on cover)	2.00	4.00	3.00

	Current Price Range		C/Y Avg.
☐ October 19, 1959 (Demonstrating in Peking on cover)	2.00	4.00	3.00
☐ November 2, 1959 (Jackie Gleason on cover)	2.00	4.00	3.00
☐ November 9, 1959 (Marilyn Monroe on cover)	18.00	20.00	19.00
☐ November 23, 1959 (Mary Martin on cover)	2.00	4.00	3.00
☐ November 30, 1959 (Postage stamps on cover)	3.00	5.00	4.00
☐ December 21, 1959 (Dwight Eisenhower on cover)	4.00	6.00	5.00
☐ December 28, 1959 (Good Life)	2.00	4.00	3.00

1960

☐ January 11, 1960 (Dina Merrill on cover)	2.00	4.00	3.00
☐ January 25, 1960 (Colonial Folklore) ...	2.00	4.00	3.00
☐ February 1, 1960 (Dinah Shore on cover)	2.00	4.00	3.00
☐ February 8, 1960 (U.S. ski team on cover)	2.00	4.00	3.00
☐ February 15, 1960 (Submarine Trieste on cover)	2.00	4.00	3.00
☐ February 22, 1960 (Henry and Jane Fonda on cover)	3.00	5.00	4.00
☐ February 29, 1960 (Winter Olympic skier on cover)	3.00	5.00	4.00
☐ March 7, 1960 (Hypnosis)	1.00	3.00	2.00
☐ March 14, 1960 (Princess Margaret and Lord Snowdon on cover)	2.00	4.00	3.00
☐ March 28, 1960 (John F. Kennedy and Harry S. Truman on cover)	4.00	6.00	5.00
☐ April 4, 1960 (Marlon Brando on cover)	2.00	4.00	3.00
☐ April 11, 1960 (Silvana Mangano on cover)	1.00	3.00	2.00
☐ May 9, 1960 (Actress Yvette Mimieux on cover)	1.00	3.00	2.00
☐ May 16, 1960 (Royal Wedding of Princess Margaret and Lord Snowdon on cover)	1.00	3.00	2.00
☐ May 23, 1960 (Minuteman statue on cover)	1.00	3.00	2.00
☐ May 30, 1960 (Nikita Krushchev on cover)	1.00	3.00	2.00

	Current Price Range		C/Y Avg.
☐ June 6, 1960 (Lee Remick on cover) ...	1.00	3.00	2.00
☐ June 13, 1960 (Hayley Mills on cover) ..	1.00	3.00	2.00
☐ June 20, 1960 (Los Angeles Freeway on cover)	1.00	3.00	2.00
☐ June 27, 1960 (Walrus on cover)	1.00	3.00	2.00
☐ July 11, 1960 (Nelson Rockefeller on cover)	1.00	3.00	2.00
☐ July 18, 1960 (Ina Balin)	1.00	3.00	2.00
☐ July 25, 1960 (Demonstration for John F. Kennedy)	3.00	5.00	4.00
☐ August 1, 1960 (Fun Safari)	1.00	3.00	2.00
☐ August 8, 1960 (Richard Nixon on cover)	3.00	5.00	4.00
☐ August 15, 1960 (Marilyn Monroe and Yves Montand on cover)	8.00	10.00	9.00
☐ August 22, 1960 (Olympic Swimmers on cover)	3.00	5.00	4.00
☐ August 29, 1960 (Record breaking Olympic jump on cover)	3.00	5.00	4.00
☐ September 5, 1960 (Ernest Hemingway on cover)	3.00	5.00	4.00
☐ September 12, 1960 (USA Gymnasts on cover)	3.00	5.00	4.00
☐ September 19, 1960 (Grandma Moses on cover)	3.00	5.00	4.00
☐ October 3, 1960 (Eisenhower addressing the United Nations on cover)	3.00	5.00	4.00
☐ October 10, 1960 (Doris Day on cover)	1.00	3.00	2.00
☐ October 24, 1960 (Nancy Kwan on cover)	1.00	3.00	2.00
☐ October 31, 1960 (Halloween)	1.00	3.00	2.00
☐ November 7, 1960 (Earth as viewed from a satellite on cover)	2.00	4.00	3.00
☐ November 14, 1960 (Sophia Loren on cover)	2.00	4.00	3.00
☐ November 21, 1960 (John F. and Jacqueline Kennedy on cover)	5.00	7.00	6.00
☐ November 28, 1960 (Carroll Baker on cover)	1.00	3.00	2.00
☐ December 5, 1960 (Baltimore Colts football kickoff on cover)	1.00	3.00	2.00
☐ December 12, 1960 (Jill Haworth and Sal Mineo on cover)	1.00	3.00	2.00

	Current Price Range		C/Y Avg.

☐ December 19, 1960 (John and Jacqueline Kennedy and John Jr. on cover) .. | 5.00 | 7.00 | 6.00

☐ December 26, 1960 (25 Years of Life—Special Double Issue) .... | 19.00 | 21.00 | 20.00

1961

☐ January 6, 1961 (The Civil War) .... | 2.00 | 4.00 | 3.00
☐ January 13, 1961 (Clark Gable on cover) | 4.00 | 6.00 | 5.00
☐ January 20, 1961 (Surgeon on cover) .. | 1.00 | 3.00 | 2.00
☐ January 27, 1961 (The Kennedy Inauguration on cover) .... | 5.00 | 7.00 | 6.00
☐ February 3, 1961 (Queen Elizabeth in India on cover) .... | 1.00 | 3.00 | 2.00
☐ February 10, 1961 (Chimpanzee in Space on cover) .... | 1.00 | 3.00 | 2.00
☐ February 17, 1961 (Shirley MacLaine on cover) .... | 1.00 | 3.00 | 2.00
☐ February 24, 1961 (Dag Hammarskjold on cover) .... | 1.00 | 3.00 | 2.00
☐ March 3, 1961 (John Glenn, Gus Grissom and Alan Shepard on cover) .... | 4.00 | 6.00 | 5.00
☐ March 10, 1961 (Bing Crosby and Maurice Chevalier on cover) .... | 2.00 | 4.00 | 3.00
☐ March 17, 1961 (Sheila Finn on cover) | 1.00 | 3.00 | 2.00
☐ March 24, 1961 (Jack Paar and Ed Sullivan on cover) .... | 1.00 | 3.00 | 2.00
☐ March 31, 1961 (Cherub on cover) ..... | 1.00 | 3.00 | 2.00
☐ April 7, 1961 (Sea fishing) .... | 1.00 | 3.00 | 2.00
☐ April 14, 1961 (Mrs. Clark Gable on cover) | 1.00 | 3.00 | 2.00
☐ April 21, 1961 (Soviet cosmonaut Yuri Gagarin on cover) .... | 2.00 | 4.00 | 3.00
☐ April 28, 1961 (Elizabeth Taylor on cover) | 2.00 | 4.00 | 3.00
☐ May 5, 1961 (Anna Maria Alberghetti on cover) .... | 1.00 | 3.00 | 2.00
☐ May 12, 1961 (Astronaut Alan Shepard on cover) .... | 2.00 | 4.00 | 3.00
☐ May 19, 1961 (Astronaut Alan Shepard on cover) .... | 2.00 | 4.00 | 3.00
☐ May 26, 1961 (Kennedys visiting Canada on cover) .... | 2.00 | 4.00 | 3.00

	Current Price Range		C/Y Avg.
☐ June 2, 1961 (Fidel Castro on cover) ...	1.00	3.00	2.00
☐ June 9, 1961 (John F. Kennedy visiting Paris on cover)	2.00	4.00	3.00
☐ June 16, 1961 (June weddings)	1.00	3.00	2.00
☐ June 23, 1961 (Princess Grace of Monaco on cover)	2.00	4.00	3.00
☐ June 30, 1961 (Leslie Caron on cover)	1.00	3.00	2.00
☐ July 7, 1961 (Dwight Eisenhower on cover)	2.00	4.00	3.00
☐ July 14, 1961 (Ernest Hemingway on cover)	2.00	4.00	3.00
☐ July 21, 1961 (Flavio rescued on cover)	1.00	3.00	2.00
☐ July 28, 1961 (Brigitte Bardot on cover)	2.00	4.00	3.00
☐ August 4, 1961 (John F. Kennedy on cover)	3.00	5.00	4.00
☐ August 11, 1961 (Sophia Loren on cover)	2.00	4.00	3.00
☐ August 18, 1961 (Mickey Mantle and Roger Maris on cover)	3.00	5.00	4.00
☐ September 8, 1961 (American tank on cover)	1.00	3.00	2.00
☐ September 15, 1961 (Civilian fallout suit on cover)	1.00	3.00	2.00
☐ September 22, 1961 (Hurricane Carla on cover)	1.00	3.00	2.00
☐ September 29, 1961 (Death of Dag Hammarskjold)	1.00	3.00	2.00
☐ October 6, 1961 (Elizabeth Taylor as Cleopatra on cover)	2.00	4.00	3.00
☐ October 13, 1961 (African tribal warrior on cover)	1.00	3.00	2.00
☐ October 20, 1961 (Communist leaders on cover)	1.00	3.00	2.00
☐ October 27, 1961 (Guerrilla warfare) ...	1.00	3.00	2.00
☐ November 3, 1961 (Girl kissing G.I. farewell on cover)	1.00	3.00	2.00
☐ November 10, 1961 (Nikita Krushchev on cover)	1.00	3.00	2.00
☐ November 17, 1961 (Minnesota Vikings football team on cover)	2.00	4.00	3.00
☐ November 24, 1961 (John Kennedy Jr. on cover)	2.00	4.00	3.00

	Current Price Range		C/Y Avg.

☐ December 1, 1961 (Italian fashions) ...	1.00	3.00	2.00
☐ December 8, 1961 (Plum pudding on cover)	1.00	3.00	2.00
☐ December 15, 1961 (Chartres Cathedral on cover)	1.00	3.00	2.00
☐ December 22, 1961, (Our Splendid Outdoors; Special Issue)	1.00	3.00	2.00

1962

☐ January 5, 1962 (Lucille Ball on cover)	2.00	4.00	3.00
☐ January 12, 1962 (Bomb shelter on cover)	2.00	4.00	3.00
☐ January 19, 1962 (Ice sailing on cover)	1.00	3.00	2.00
☐ January 26, 1962 (Robert Kennedy on cover)	2.00	4.00	3.00
☐ February 2, 1962 (John Glenn on cover)	2.00	4.00	3.00
☐ February 9, 1962 (Seattle World's Fair on cover)	2.00	4.00	3.00
☐ February 16, 1962 (Rock Hudson on cover)	3.00	5.00	2.00
☐ February 23, 1962 (Shirley MacLaine on cover)	2.00	4.00	3.00
☐ March 2, 1962 (John Glenn on cover) ..	2.00	4.00	3.00
☐ March 9, 1962 (Tickertape parade for John Glenn on cover)	2.00	4.00	3.00
☐ March 16, 1962 (Richard Nixon on cover)	3.00	5.00	4.00
☐ March 23, 1962 (Desert living)	1.00	3.00	2.00
☐ March 30, 1962 (Robert Frost on cover)	2.00	4.00	3.00
☐ April 13, 1962 (Elizabeth Taylor and Richard Burton on cover)	2.00	4.00	3.00
☐ April 20, 1962 (Audrey Hepburn on cover)	1.00	3.00	2.00
☐ April 27, 1962 (Astronauts' moon suit on cover)	2.00	4.00	3.00
☐ May 4, 1962 (Seattle World's Fair on cover)	2.00	4.00	3.00
☐ May 11, 1962 (Bob Hope on cover)	2.00	4.00	3.00
☐ May 18, 1962 (Astronaut Scott Carpenter on cover)	2.00	4.00	3.00
☐ May 25, 1962 (Juan Carlos)	1.00	3.00	2.00
☐ June 1, 1962 (Rene Carpenter, wife of astronaut Scott Carpenter on cover)	1.00	3.00	2.00

	Current Price Range		C/Y Avg.
☐ June 8, 1962 (Stock market flurry)	1.00	3.00	2.00
☐ June 15, 1962 (Natalie Wood on cover)	2.00	4.00	3.00
☐ June 22, 1962 (Marilyn Monroe on cover)	13.00	15.00	14.00
☐ June 29, 1962 (Ted Kennedy on cover)	2.00	4.00	3.00
☐ July 6, 1962 (Aerial balloon on cover) . .	1.00	3.00	2.00
☐ July 13, 1962 (John F. Kennedy visiting Mexico on cover)	2.00	4.00	3.00
☐ July 20, 1962 (Hydrogen bomb exploding on cover)	1.00	3.00	2.00
☐ July 27, 1962 (Elsa Martinelli on cover)	1.00	3.00	2.00
☐ August 3, 1962 (Astronaut Robert White on cover)	1.00	3.00	2.00
☐ August 10, 1962 (Janet Leigh on cover)	1.00	3.00	2.00
☐ August 17, 1962 (Marilyn Monroe on cover)	7.00	9.00	8.00
☐ August 24, 1962 (Russian space capsules on cover)	1.00	3.00	2.00
☐ August 31, 1962 (Mail robbery)	1.00	3.00	2.00
☐ September 7, 1962 (Caroline Kennedy on cover)	6.00	8.00	7.00
☐ September 14, 1962 (Special Issue on "Take-Over Generation")	1.00	3.00	2.00
☐ September 21, 1962 (Victims of Iranian Earthquake on cover)	1.00	3.00	2.00
☐ September 28, 1962 (Los Angeles Dodgers pitcher Don Drysdale on cover)	7.00	9.00	8.00
☐ October 5, 1962 (Jackie Gleason on cover)	1.00	3.00	2.00
☐ October 12, 1962 (Pope John XXIII on cover)	1.00	3.00	2.00
☐ October 19, 1962 (Yosemite on cover)	1.00	3.00	2.00
☐ November 2, 1962 (Cuban missile crisis)	4.00	6.00	5.00
☐ November 9, 1962 (Secretary General U. Thant on cover)	1.00	3.00	2.00
☐ November 16, 1962 (India/China war) . .	1.00	3.00	2.00
☐ November 30, 1962 (Sid Caesar on cover)	1.00	3.00	2.00
☐ December 7, 1962 (Boy running on cover)	1.00	3.00	2.00
☐ December 14, 1962 (Marlon Brando on cover)	2.00	4.00	3.00
☐ December 21, 1962 (Year-end double issue devoted to the sea)	1.00	3.00	2.00

	Current Price Range		C/Y Avg.

1963

☐ January 4, 1963 (Greek miracle)	1.00	3.00	2.00
☐ January 11, 1963 (Ann-Margaret on cover)	2.00	4.00	3.00
☐ January 18, 1963 (Trojan horse on cover)	1.00	3.00	2.00
☐ January 25, 1963 (Vietnamese prisoners of war on cover)	2.00	4.00	3.00
☐ February 1, 1963 (Alfred Hitchcock's motion picture "The Birds" on cover)	3.00	5.00	4.00
☐ February 8, 1963 (Grecian sculpture on cover)	1.00	3.00	2.00
☐ February 15, 1963 (Abraham Lincoln's casket on cover)	3.00	5.00	4.00
☐ February 22, 1963 (Kessler twins on cover)	1.00	3.00	2.00
☐ March 1, 1963 (Snakes on cover)	1.00	3.00	2.00
☐ March 15, 1963 (Fidel Castro on cover)	1.00	3.00	2.00
☐ March 22, 1963 (Polaris submarine on cover)	1.00	3.00	2.00
☐ March 29, 1963 (Crowd in Costa Rica on cover)	1.00	3.00	2.00
☐ April 5, 1963 (Greek wars)	1.00	3.00	2.00
☐ April 12, 1963 (Yukon ordeal)	1.00	3.00	2.00
☐ April 19, 1963 (Elizabeth Taylor and Richard Burton on cover)	2.00	4.00	3.00
☐ April 26, 1963 (Jacqueline Kennedy at age ten on cover)	2.00	4.00	3.00
☐ May 3, 1963 (Alexander The Great on cover)	1.00	3.00	2.00
☐ May 17, 1963 (Nelson Rockefeller and Happy Rockefeller on cover)	1.00	3.00	2.00
☐ May 24, 1963 (Astronaut Gordon Cooper on cover)	2.00	4.00	3.00
☐ May 31, 1963 (Mr. and Mrs. Gordon Cooper on cover)	2.00	4.00	3.00
☐ June 7, 1963 (Pope John XXIII on cover)	1.00	3.00	2.00
☐ June 14, 1963 (St. Peter's Basilica in Vatican City on cover)	1.00	3.00	2.00
☐ June 21, 1963 (Shirley MacLaine on cover)	2.00	4.00	3.00
☐ June 28, 1963 (Funeral of civil rights advocate Medgar Evers on cover)	1.00	3.00	2.00

	Current Price Range		C/Y Avg.
☐ July 5, 1963 (Pope Paul VI on cover) ...	1.00	3.00	2.00
☐ July 12, 1963 (Steve McQueen on cover)	2.00	4.00	3.00
☐ July 19, 1963 (Greek art on cover)	1.00	3.00	2.00
☐ July 26, 1963 (Tuesday Weld on cover)	1.00	3.00	2.00
☐ August 2, 1963 (Baseball pitcher Sandy Koufax on cover)	6.00	8.00	7.00
☐ August 9, 1963 (Nikita Krushchev and Averill Harriman on cover)	1.00	3.00	2.00
☐ August 16, 1963 (Kennedy's baby vigil on cover)	3.00	5.00	4.00
☐ August 23, 1963 (Frank Sinatra and Frank Sinatra Jr. on cover)	2.00	4.00	3.00
☐ August 30, 1963 (Elsa Martinelli on cover)	1.00	3.00	2.00
☐ September 6, 1963 (Civil rights leaders Bayard Rustin and Philip Randolph on cover)	1.00	3.00	2.00
☐ September 13, 1963 (Russian woman on cover)	1.00	3.00	2.00
☐ September 20, 1963 (Mount Everest on cover)	1.00	3.00	2.00
☐ September 27, 1963 (Team of newly selected astronauts on cover)	2.00	4.00	3.00
☐ October 4, 1963 (DNA molecule on cover)	1.00	3.00	2.00
☐ October 11, 1963 (Mme. Nhu, Vietnam's first lady on cover)	1.00	3.00	2.00
☐ October 18, 1963 (Scene from "Anastasia" on cover)	1.00	3.00	2.00
☐ October 25, 1963 (Yvette Mimieux on cover)	1.00	3.00	2.00
☐ November 1, 1963 (Senator Barry Goldwater on cover)	1.00	3.00	2.00
☐ November 8, 1963 (Bobby Baker on cover)	1.00	3.00	2.00
☐ November 15, 1963 (Vietnam coup on cover)	1.00	3.00	2.00
☐ November 22, 1963 (Elizabeth Ashley on cover)	4.00	6.00	5.00
☐ November 29, 1963 (Assassination of John F. Kennedy on cover)	19.00	21.00	20.00
☐ December 6, 1963 (Kennedy family on cover)	8.00	10.00	9.00

	Current Price Range		C/Y Avg.
☐ December 13, 1963 (Lyndon Johnson on cover)	6.00	8.00	7.00
☐ December 13, 1963 (Same date as regular issue, but this was a special issue sold only on stands, not sent to subscribers; "John F. Kennedy Memorial Edition," biography of Kennedy with summary of all news surrounding assassination and funeral.)	9.00	11.00	10.00
☐ December 20, 1963 (Special double issue on the movies)	4.00	6.00	5.00

1964

	Current Price Range		C/Y Avg.
☐ January 3, 1964 (Laconia fire on cover)	1.00	3.00	2.00
☐ January 10, 1964 (General Douglas MacArthur on cover)	1.00	3.00	2.00
☐ January 17, 1964 (Pilgrimage of Pope Paul VI on cover)	1.00	3.00	2.00

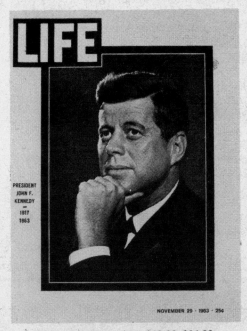

Life, November 1963, $19.00–$21.00.

	Current Price Range		C/Y Avg.

☐ January 24, 1964 (Rioting in Panama on cover)	1.00	3.00	2.00
☐ January 31, 1964 (Geraldin Chaplin on cover)	1.00	3.00	2.00
☐ February 7, 1964 (War in Tanganika) ...	1.00	3.00	2.00
☐ February 14, 1964 (Winter Olympics on cover)	2.00	4.00	3.00
☐ February 21, 1964 (Lee Harvey Oswald on cover)	6.00	8.00	7.00
☐ February 28, 1964 (War in Cyprus)	1.00	3.00	2.00
☐ March 6, 1964 (Muhammad Ali)	2.00	4.00	3.00
☐ March 13, 1964 (Western front of World War I on cover)	1.00	3.00	2.00
☐ March 20, 1964 (American ambassador Henry Cabot Lodge visiting Vietnam on cover)	1.00	3.00	2.00
☐ March 27, 1964 (Charles DeGaulle visiting Mexico on cover)	1.00	3.00	2.00
☐ April 3, 1964 (Carol Channing as "Dolly" on cover)	1.00	3.00	2.00
☐ April 10, 1964 (Earthquake in Alaska on cover)	1.00	3.00	2.00
☐ April 17, 1964 (General MacArthur's hat on cover)	1.00	3.00	2.00
☐ April 24, 1964 (Richard Burton as "Hamlet" on cover)	2.00	4.00	3.00
☐ May 1, 1964 (New York World's Fair on cover)	6.00	8.00	7.00
☐ May 8, 1964 (Lyndon Johnson and prospective running mates on cover)	5.00	7.00	6.00
☐ May 15, 1964 (Luci Baines Johnson on cover)	2.00	4.00	3.00
☐ May 22, 1964 (Barbara Streisand on cover)	2.00	4.00	3.00
☐ May 29, 1964 (Jacqueline Kennedy on cover)	2.00	4.00	3.00
☐ June 5, 1964 (Cremation of Indian leader Nehru)	1.00	2.00	1.50
☐ June 19, 1964 (Presidential hopeful William Scranton with his family on cover)	1.00	2.00	1.50
☐ July 3, 1964 (Robert Kennedy and his children on cover)	4.00	6.00	5.00

	Current Price Range		C/Y Avg.

☐ July 10, 1964 (Lee Harvey Oswald's diary on cover) **5.00** **7.00** **6.00**

☐ July 17, 1964 (Carroll Baker on cover) **1.00** **2.00** **1.50**

☐ July 24, 1964 (Republican National Convention on cover) **1.00** **2.00** **1.50**

☐ July 31, 1964 (Summer Olympics on cover) **2.00** **4.00** **3.00**

☐ August 7, 1964 (Marilyn Monroe on cover) **4.00** **6.00** **5.00**

☐ August 14, 1964 (Lyndon Johnson on cover) **4.00** **6.00** **5.00**

☐ August 21, 1964 (Lyndon Johnson on cover) **4.00** **6.00** **5.00**

☐ August 28, 1964 (The Beatles on cover) **20.00** **25.00** **22.50**

☐ September 4, 1964 (Lyndon Johnson on cover) **4.00** **6.00** **5.00**

☐ September 11, 1964 (Japan) **1.00** **2.00** **1.50**

☐ September 18, 1964 (Sophia Loren on cover) **1.00** **3.00** **2.00**

☐ September 25, 1964 (American space race) **1.00** **3.00** **2.00**

☐ October 2, 1964 (Warren Report on the assassination of John F. Kennedy on cover) **4.00** **6.00** **5.00**

☐ October 9, 1964 (Olympic swimmer on cover) **1.00** **3.00** **2.00**

☐ October 16, 1964 (Berlin tunnel on cover) **1.00** **2.00** **1.50**

☐ October 23, 1964 (New Soviet leader Leonid Brezhnev on cover) **1.00** **2.00** **1.50**

☐ October 30, 1964 (American Olympic medal winning swimmer Don Schollander on cover) **1.00** **3.00** **2.00**

☐ November 6, 1964 (Scene from the motion picture "Goldfinger" on cover) **5.00** **7.00** **6.00**

☐ November 13, 1964 (Lyndon Johnson and his running mate Hubert Humphrey on cover) **4.00** **6.00** **5.00**

☐ November 20, 1964 (Moscow parade on cover) **1.00** **2.00** **1.50**

☐ November 27, 1964 (Vietnam war) **1.00** **2.00** **1.50**

☐ December 4, 1964 (Dr. Paul Carlson on cover) **1.00** **2.00** **1.50**

	Current Price Range		C/Y Avg.

☐ December 11, 1964 (New York Radio City Music Hall Rockettes on cover) 1.00   2.00   1.50

☐ December 18, 1964 (Elizabeth Taylor on cover) 1.00   3.00   2.00

LIPPINCOTT'S
☐ September 1895 ("A Case in Equity" by Francis Lynde) 6.00   8.00   7.00

THE LITERARY DIGEST
☐ April 5, 1924 (American Food for German Children; Japan and the Recognition of Russia) 3.00   5.00   4.00

☐ May 31, 1924 (When France Swings Leftward; South Africa in Turmoil) 3.00   5.00   4.00

☐ June 7, 1924 (Hard Times in the Cotton-Mills; Italy's Place in Europe) 3.00   5.00   4.00

☐ June 21, 1924 (Canada to Help Dry Up the Border; An Argentinian View of All America) 3.00   5.00   4.00

☐ June 25, 1924 (Charles A. Lindberg on cover) 9.00   11.00   10.00

☐ July 19, 1924 (The Significance of La Follette; Growth of Socialism in Oxford) . .   3.00   5.00   4.00

☐ August 31, 1924 (Bringing Up Reserves on cover) 3.00   5.00   4.00

LONE RANGER
☐ July 1937 . . . .   35.00   45.00   40.00

LONE WOLF DETECTIVE
☐ December 1940 (cover artwork by Saunders) 35.00   45.00   40.00

LOOK

Following closely on the heels of *Life, Look* magazine took two decades to find its own identity. Early on, it was an unusual grab bag of press photos of film stars and "girlie" pictures mixed in with national and international news photos.

	Current Price Range		C/Y Avg.

☐ January 3, 1939 (Duke and Duchess of Windsor on cover) 11.00   13.00   12.00

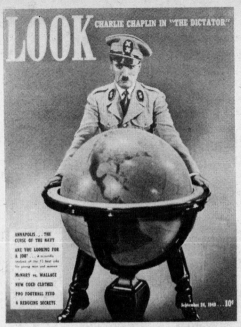

Look, September 1940, $18.00–$22.00.

	Current Price Range		C/Y Avg.
☐ December 19, 1939 ("The Coming Revolution in Germany," "Will 1940 Stop Joe Louis?," "America's Winter Paradise: Is it Florida or California?," "Inside Story of Graft in Massachusetts")	7.00	9.00	8.00
☐ March 26, 1940 ("Dewey: The Glamour Boy" by Harold L. Ickes)	7.00	9.00	8.00
☐ September 24, 1940 (Charlie Chaplin in "The Dictator" on cover)	18.00	22.00	20.00
☐ November 19, 1940 ("Hitler and Stalin in 1941" by Wythe Williams)	7.00	9.00	8.00
☐ March 25, 1941 ("An Open Letter to Anne Lindberg" by Dorothy Thompson)	6.00	8.00	7.00
☐ April 8, 1941 (Rep. Costello of California and Deanna Durbin on cover)	6.00	8.00	7.00
☐ April 22, 1941 ("The New Roosevelt" by Dorothy Thompson)	6.00	8.00	7.00

	Current Price Range		C/Y Avg.

☐ June 3, 1941 ("America's Ally Against Japan" by Edgar Show) 6.00   8.00   7.00

☐ June 17, 1941 (On What Terms Will England Make Peace?) 6.00   8.00   7.00

☐ July 15, 1941 ("What's Wrong With the Draft" by Mrs. Franklin D. Roosevelt) . .   6.00   8.00   7.00

☐ July 1, 1941 ("An Open Letter to Mr. Big" by Dorothy Thompson) 6.00   8.00   7.00

☐ October 7, 1941 (What Bob Hope Thinks of Bob Hope) 8.00   10.00   9.00

☐ November 4, 1941 ("To Keep the Record Straight" by Wendell L. Wilkie) 6.00   8.00   7.00

☐ December 16, 1941 ("Anti-Semitism in the U.S." by Lewis Browne) 8.00   10.00   9.00

☐ January 13, 1942 ("Our War with Japan" by Major George Fielding Eliot) 8.00   10.00   9.00

☐ January 11, 1944 (An article on predictions for 1944 carries forecasts by Vice President Henry Wallace, Walt Disney, Helen Hayes, Edward R. Murrow and others) 5.00   7.00   6.00

☐ March 20, 1945 (cover painting of General MacArthur by Harold von Schmidt. "We'll Be Fighting the Germans for Years" by Major George Fielding Eliot. Do We Know There's a War On?) 5.00   7.00   6.00

☐ January 13, 1953 . . . .   5.00   7.00   6.00

☐ April 7, 1953 (Debbie Reynolds on cover)   6.00   8.00   7.00

☐ December 28, 1954 (Lucille Ball and Desi Arnaz with their two children on cover)   9.00   11.00   10.00

☐ June 28, 1955 . . . .   3.00   5.00   4.00

☐ July 12, 1955 (John Wayne and Marx Brothers) 3.00   5.00   4.00

☐ September 4, 1956 . . . .   3.00   5.00   4.00

☐ May 1, 1956 . . . .   3.00   5.00   4.00

☐ January 8, 1957 (*Look's* 20th Anniversary Story. Four Diets You Can Trust. Annual TV Award Winners, montage cover photos of Queen Elizabeth, Jack Benny and Rochester, Franklin Roosevelt, Bishop Fulton Sheen, Elizabeth Taylor, others)   8.00   10.00   9.00

Look, *December 1954, $9.00–$11.00.*

	Current Price Range		C/Y Avg.
☐ February 19, 1957	2.00	3.00	2.50
☐ July 23, 1957	2.00	3.00	2.50
☐ July 22, 1958	2.00	3.00	2.50
☐ October 28, 1958	2.00	3.00	2.50
☐ February 3, 1959	2.00	3.00	2.50
☐ June 21, 1959	2.00	3.00	2.50
☐ August 4, 1959	2.00	3.00	2.50
☐ November 10, 1959 (Fred Astaire)	2.00	3.00	2.50
☐ December 22, 1959	2.00	3.00	2.50
☐ March 1, 1960	1.50	2.50	2.00
☐ November 22, 1960	1.50	2.50	2.00
☐ January 2, 1960	1.50	2.50	2.00
☐ February 27, 1962	1.50	2.50	2.00
☐ March 27, 1962	1.50	2.50	2.00
☐ April 24, 1962	1.50	2.50	2.00
☐ May 8, 1962	1.50	2.50	2.00
☐ June 19, 1962	1.50	2.50	2.00
☐ July 17, 1962	1.50	2.50	2.00

	Current Price Range		C/Y Avg.
☐ July 31, 1962	1.50	2.50	2.00
☐ October 9, 1962	1.50	2.50	2.00
☐ December 18, 1962	1.50	2.50	2.00
☐ February 26, 1963	1.00	2.00	1.50
☐ April 9, 1963	1.00	2.00	1.50
☐ April 23, 1963	1.00	2.00	1.50
☐ June 18, 1963	1.00	2.00	1.50
☐ August 13, 1963	1.00	2.00	1.50
☐ November 19, 1963	1.00	2.00	1.50
☐ December 3, 1963	1.00	2.00	1.50
☐ December 13, 1963	1.00	2.00	1.50
☐ January 28, 1964	1.00	2.00	1.50
☐ February 25, 1964 (Pope Paul visits U.S.)	1.00	2.00	1.50
☐ July 14, 1964	1.00	2.00	1.50
☐ October 20, 1964	1.00	2.00	1.50
☐ November 17, 1964	1.00	2.00	1.50

LOVE MIRROR

☐ March 1930 (Gone Wrong; My Last Party; Teacher's Temptation)	10.00	12.00	11.00

LOWDOWN

☐ January 1957 ("How Elvis Presley Got That Way," "James Dean's Torrid Love Letters," "What Billie Holliday Forgot to Remember," "The Ekberg Nude: Why She Did It," montage cover with photos of James Dean, Elvis Presley and Diana Dors)	20.00	25.00	22.50

MADEMOISELLE

☐ December 1941 (Special Christmas Issue, skiing cover)	5.00	7.00	6.00

MAFIA AT WAR

☐ 1972 (one issue only)	10.00	12.00	11.00

MAJOR BOWES' AMATEUR MAGAZINE

Major Bowes was moderator of the radio program "Amateur Hour," later hosted by Ted Mack.

☐ March 1936 (articles on David Sarnoff, Amelia Earhart, Fred Astaire, 96 pages, 8½ x 11½")	25.00	35.00	30.00

	Current Price Range		C/Y Avg.

MALE LIFE

☐ May 1956	1.50	2.50	2.00
☐ October 1956	1.50	2.50	2.00
☐ November 1956	1.50	2.50	2.00
☐ January 1957	1.50	2.50	2.00

MAN'S WAY

☐ May 1956	1.50	2.50	2.00
☐ July 1956	1.50	2.50	2.00
☐ August 1956	1.50	2.50	2.00
☐ October 1956	1.50	2.50	2.00
☐ November 1956	1.50	2.50	2.00
☐ December 1956	1.50	2.50	2.00
☐ February 1957	1.50	2.50	2.00

MARILYN MONROE PIN-UPS

☐ 1953 (one issue only, photos in color and black/white, cover photo shows her in swimsuit)	32.50	37.50	35.00

MARILYN'S LIFE STORY

☐ 1962 (one issue only)	25.00	30.00	27.50

MASTER DETECTIVE

Many of the stories were authored by police officials who participated in cases appearing in this magazine until the early 1940s.

☐ December 1929 (Chester Gillette story)	11.00	13.00	12.00
☐ April 1930 (Women murderers)	11.00	13.00	12.00
☐ October 1931 (Eva Dugan hanging)	11.00	13.00	12.00
☐ February 1934 (Hamm kidnapping)	11.00	13.00	12.00
☐ April 1934 (Dillinger gang)	14.00	16.00	15.00
☐ May 1935 (21-page story on Ma Barker)	14.00	16.00	15.00
☐ June 1936 (Baby-Face Nelson story)	14.00	16.00	15.00
☐ May 1939 (Pretty-Boy Floyd)	14.00	16.00	15.00

MAYFAIR

☐ June 1981	3.00	4.00	3.50
☐ July 1981	3.00	4.00	3.50
☐ October 1981	3.00	4.00	3.50
☐ January 1982	2.50	3.50	3.00
☐ February 1982	2.50	3.50	3.00
☐ March 1982	2.50	3.50	3.00
☐ April 1982	2.50	3.50	3.00
☐ May 1982	2.50	3.50	3.00

	Current Price Range		C/Y Avg.

McCALLS
☐ March 1945 .... 3.00   5.00   4.00
☐ May 1953 (New Diet, New Hairdos, New Make-Up, New Clothes, Complete Guide to a Prettier You) 2.00   4.00   3.00
☐ June 1974 .... 1.00   1.50   1.25

McCLURE'S MAGAZINE
☐ April 1899 ("Sketches In Egypt" by Charles Dana Gibson; "Stalky and Co., V" by Rudyard Kipling) 10.00   12.00   11.00
☐ August 1901 (Midsummer Fiction Number; "Kim" by Rudyard Kipling, Chapter XII continued and Chapter XIII) 12.00   14.00   13.00
☐ August 1918 (Long May It Wave—"The Flag of His Country" by Arthur Train) .. 4.00   6.00   5.00

MICKEY MOUSE ANNUAL
☐ 1950 (annual publication issued in Great Britain, stories featuring various Disney characters with artwork by Disney staff artists, 7½ x 10") 30.00   35.00   32.50

MODERN MOVIES
☐ December 1937 (Deanna Durbin on cover) 20.00   25.00   22.50
☐ August 1938 (Ginger Rogers on cover) 22.50   27.50   25.00
☐ October 1938 (Claire Trevor on cover) 20.00   25.00   22.50

MODERN PRISCILLA
☐ March 1913 .... 4.00   6.00   5.00
☐ September 1915 (cover artwork by Preeler) 4.00   6.00   5.00
☐ May 1916 (cover artwork by Emerson) 3.50   5.50   4.50
☐ January 1925 (cover artwork by Marland Stone) 3.00   5.00   4.00

MODERN ROMANCES
☐ November 1937 (The Man I Let Down) 8.00   10.00   9.00
☐ February 1939 (Thrill Hungry, Fatal Week-End, Frame-Up Marriage) 7.00   9.00   8.00

	Current Price Range		C/Y Avg.

MODERN SCREEN

☐ January 1931 (Joan Crawford on cover)	40.00	45.00	42.50
☐ September 1931 (Nancy Carroll on cover)	40.00	45.00	42.50
☐ June 1934 (Norma Shearer on cover) ..	37.50	42.50	40.00
☐ December 1935 (Claudette Colbert on cover)	37.50	42.50	40.00
☐ April 1936 (Dionne Quintuplets on cover)	42.50	47.50	45.00
☐ March 1937 (Clark Gable and Carole Lombard on cover)	37.50	42.50	40.00
☐ October 1938 (Irene Dunne on cover) ..	27.50	32.50	30.00
☐ May 1939 (Ginger Rogers on cover) ...	25.00	30.00	27.50
☐ May 1940 (Ginger Rogers on cover) ...	25.00	30.00	27.50
☐ June 1940 (Vivien Leigh on cover)	25.00	30.00	27.50
☐ November 1940 (Marlene Dietrich on cover)	25.00	30.00	27.50
☐ July 1941 (Paulette Goddard on cover)	25.00	30.00	27.50
☐ January 1943 (Ronald Reagan and wife Jane Wyman on cover)	70.00	80.00	75.00
☐ May 1944 (Deanna Durbin on cover) ...	22.50	27.50	25.00
☐ June 1944 (Hedy Lamarr on cover)	22.50	27.50	25.00
☐ March 1945 (Alan Ladd on cover)	22.50	27.50	25.00
☐ November 1945 (Ingrid Bergman on cover)	22.50	27.50	25.00
☐ January 1947 (Frank Sinatra on cover)	20.00	25.00	22.50
☐ March 1947 (Clark Gable on cover)	20.00	25.00	22.50
☐ May 1947 (Ingrid Bergman on cover) ...	20.00	25.00	22.50
☐ December 1947 (Tyrone Power on cover)	20.00	25.00	22.50
☐ February 1948 (Shirley Temple on cover)	27.50	32.50	30.00
☐ May 1948 (Ingrid Bergman on cover) ...	17.00	19.00	18.00
☐ August 1948 (Shirley Temple on cover)	27.50	32.50	30.00
☐ October 1948 (Judy Garland on cover)	25.50	30.00	27.50
☐ December 1948 (Betty Grable on cover)	17.00	19.00	18.00
☐ September 1949 (Betty Grable on cover)	15.00	17.00	16.00
☐ October 1950 (Ava Gardner on cover)	15.00	17.00	16.00
☐ December 1952 (Betty Grable on cover)	14.00	16.00	15.00
☐ October 1953 (Marilyn Monroe on cover)	45.00	55.00	50.00
☐ October 1954 (Elizabeth Taylor on cover)	15.00	17.00	16.00
☐ December 1954 (Grace Kelly on cover)	20.00	25.00	22.50
☐ October 1955 (Marilyn Monroe on cover)	37.50	42.50	40.00
☐ December 1955 (Janet Leigh on cover)	8.00	10.00	9.00

	Current Price Range		C/Y Avg.

☐ December 1956 (Elizabeth Taylor on cover)	8.00	10.00	9.00
☐ June 1959 (Rock Hudson on cover)	20.00	25.00	22.50
☐ November 1962 (Marilyn Monroe on cover)	25.00	30.00	27.50
☐ May 1963 (Taylor/Burton on cover)	6.00	8.00	7.00
☐ July 1963 (Elizabeth Taylor on cover) ..	6.00	8.00	7.00
☐ March 1964 (Elizabeth Taylor on cover)	5.00	7.00	6.00
☐ December 1964 (JFK & Jackie on cover)	25.00	30.00	27.50
☐ February 1965 (Taylor/Burton on cover)	2.00	4.00	3.00
☐ October 1967 (Jackie Kennedy on cover)	2.00	4.00	3.00
☐ June 1968 (Elizabeth Taylor on cover)	2.00	4.00	3.00
☐ October 1968 (Taylor/Burton on cover)	2.00	4.00	3.00
☐ June 1969 (Elizabeth Taylor on cover)	1.00	2.00	1.50
☐ October 1972 (Jackie Onassis on cover)	1.00	2.00	1.50
☐ June 1974 (Robert Redford on cover) ..	1.00	2.00	1.50
☐ June 1975 (Redford/Dunaway on cover)	1.00	2.00	1.50
☐ April 1976 (Burt Reynolds on cover) ...	1.00	2.00	1.50
☐ August 1977 (Farrah Fawcett on cover)	1.00	2.00	1.50
☐ June 1979 (Elvis Presley on cover)	8.00	10.00	9.00

MODERN SEX

☐ August 1964 (first issue)	3.00	5.00	4.00
☐ September 1964	1.00	2.00	1.50
☐ November 1964	1.00	2.00	1.50

MOTION PICTURE

☐ September 1921 (Douglas Fairbanks Sr. on cover)	60.00	70.00	65.00
☐ June 1929 (Mary Duncan on cover)	42.50	47.50	45.00
☐ September 1929 (Fay Wray on cover) ..	42.50	47.50	45.00
☐ August 1930 (Catherine Owen on cover)	42.50	47.50	45.00
☐ July 1937 (Marlene Dietrich on cover) ..	35.00	40.00	37.50
☐ August 1938 (Deanna Durbin on cover)	30.00	35.00	32.50
☐ September 1938 (Clark Gable on cover)	30.00	35.00	32.50
☐ December 1938 (Sonja Henie on cover)	27.50	32.50	30.00
☐ June 1939 (Myrna Loy on cover)	25.00	30.00	27.50
☐ October 1941 (Rita Hayworth on cover)	25.00	30.00	27.50
☐ January 1942 (Olivia de Haviland on cover)	22.50	27.50	25.00
☐ September 1942 (Veronica Lake on cover)	22.50	27.50	25.00

	Current Price Range		C/Y Avg.
☐ October 1942 (Janet Blair on cover) . . .	22.50	27.50	25.00
☐ August 1943 (Dolores Moran on cover)	22.50	27.50	25.00
☐ October 1945 (Joan Leslie on cover) . . .	22.50	27.50	25.00
☐ January 1948 (Barbara Stanwyck on cover)	17.00	19.00	18.00
☐ February 1948 (Joan Crawford on cover)	17.00	19.00	18.00
☐ May 1949 (Jane Russell on cover)	15.00	17.00	16.00
☐ July 1949 (Shirley Temple on cover) . . .	27.50	32.50	30.00
☐ January 1950 (Ava Gardner on cover) . .	15.00	17.00	16.00
☐ April 1950 (Elizabeth Taylor on cover) . .	15.00	17.00	16.00
☐ November 1950 (Shirley Temple on cover)	15.00	17.00	16.00
☐ February 1951 (Elizabeth Taylor on cover)	15.00	17.00	16.00
☐ March 1954 (Elizabeth Taylor on cover)	15.00	17.00	16.00
☐ February 1956 (Elizabeth Taylor on cover)	8.00	10.00	9.00
☐ October 1957 (Natalie Wood on cover)	8.00	10.00	9.00
☐ February 1958 (Elizabeth Taylor on cover)	8.00	10.00	9.00
☐ October 1958 (Kim Novak on cover) . . .	8.00	10.00	9.00
☐ September 1964 (Elizabeth Taylor on cover)	5.00	7.00	6.00
☐ March 1972 (Elizabeth Taylor on cover)	1.00	2.00	1.50
☐ September 1975 (Raquel Welch on cover)	1.00	1.50	1.25

MOTION PICTURE CLASSIC

☐ March 1926 (Greta Nissen on cover) . . .	45.00	50.00	42.50

MOTION PICTURE AND TELEVISION

☐ April 1952 (Elizabeth Taylor on cover) . .	10.00	12.00	11.00
☐ October 1953 (Janet Leigh on cover) . .	9.00	11.00	10.00

MOVIE CLASSIC

☐ April 1933 (Joan Bennett on cover)	40.00	45.00	42.50
☐ July 1934 (Jean Harlow on cover)	40.00	45.00	42.50
☐ March 1935 (Ginger Rogers on cover)	37.50	42.50	40.00
☐ May 1935 (Carole Lombard on cover) . .	40.00	45.00	42.50
☐ June 1935 (Joan Crawford on cover) . . .	37.50	42.50	40.00
☐ October 1935 (Miriam Hopkins on cover)	37.50	42.50	40.00
☐ January 1936 (Ginger Rogers on cover)	37.50	42.50	40.00

	Current Price Range		C/Y Avg.
☐ April 1936 (Myrna Loy on cover)	37.50	42.50	40.00
☐ January 1942 (Judy Garland and Mickey Rooney on cover)	30.00	35.00	32.50
☐ February 1942 (Betty Grable on cover)	22.50	27.50	25.00
☐ June 1942 (Lucille Ball and Desi Arnaz on cover)	30.00	35.00	32.50
☐ August 1942 (Hedy Lamarr on cover) ..	22.50	27.50	25.00
☐ October 1942 (Gary Cooper on cover)	22.50	27.50	25.00
☐ February 1943 (Linda Darnell on cover)	22.50	27.50	25.00
☐ March 1943 (Eleanor Powell on cover)	22.50	27.50	25.00
☐ May 1943 (Veronica Lake on cover) ...	22.50	27.50	25.00
☐ October 1943 (Betty Hutton on cover) ..	22.50	27.50	25.00
☐ February 1944 (Paulette Goddard on cover)	22.50	27.50	25.00
☐ May 1944 (Maureen O'Hara on cover)	22.50	27.50	25.00
☐ July 1944 (Jennifer Jones on cover) ...	22.50	27.50	25.00
☐ November 1944 (Dorothy Lamour on cover)	22.50	27.50	25.00
☐ February 1945 (Lana Turner on cover)	22.50	27.50	25.00
☐ September 1945 (Jeanne Crain on cover)	22.50	27.50	25.00

MOVIE FAN

☐ March–April 1951 (Linda Darnell on cover)	10.00	12.00	11.00

MOVIELAND

Title becomes *Movieland and TV Time* in 1960s.

☐ October 1947 (Lizabeth Scott on cover)	20.00	25.00	22.50
☐ June 1948 (Ava Gardner on cover)	17.00	19.00	18.00
☐ April 1949 (Rita Hayworth on cover) ...	17.00	19.00	18.00
☐ October 1952 (Marilyn Monroe on cover)	45.00	55.00	50.00
☐ October 1953 (Marilyn Monroe on cover)	45.00	55.00	50.00
☐ February 1954 (Marilyn Monroe on cover)	45.00	55.00	50.00
☐ June 1956 (Mr. and Mrs. Rock Hudson on cover)	30.00	35.00	32.50

MOVIE LIFE

☐ April 1939 (Ginger Rogers on cover) ...	25.00	30.00	27.50
☐ January 1940 (Judge Hardy and Family on cover)	25.00	30.00	27.50
☐ December 1941 (Abbott and Costello on cover)	25.00	30.00	27.50

	Current Price Range		C/Y Avg.

☐ May 1946 (Peter Lawford on cover) **20.00 25.00 22.50**
☐ January 1947 (Gregory Peck on cover) **20.00 25.00 22.50**
☐ June 1947 (Shirley Temple on cover) .. **20.00 25.00 22.50**
☐ July 1947 (Esther Williams on cover) ... **20.00 25.00 22.50**
☐ September 1947 (Jane Powell on cover) **20.00 25.00 22.50**
☐ October 1947 (Elizabeth Taylor on cover) **20.00 25.00 22.50**
☐ February 1948 (Shirley Temple on cover) **20.00 25.00 22.50**
☐ June 1948 (Ingrid Bergman on cover) .. **20.00 25.00 22.50**
☐ September 1948 (Gregory Peck on cover) **20.00 25.00 22.50**
☐ November 1948 (Roy Rogers and Dale Evans on cover) **35.00 40.00 37.50**
☐ September 1949 (Elizabeth Taylor on cover) **17.00 19.00 18.00**
☐ July 1950 (Elizabeth Taylor and Nicky Hilton on cover) **17.00 19.00 18.00**
☐ September 1950 (June Haver on cover) **17.00 19.00 18.00**
☐ January 1951 (Alan Ladd on cover) **17.00 19.00 18.00**
☐ June 1951 (Elizabeth Taylor on cover) **17.00 19.00 18.00**
☐ February 1952 (Doris Day on cover) ... **17.00 19.00 18.00**
☐ November 1952 (Marilyn Monroe on cover) **45.00 55.00 50.00**
☐ June 1953 (Elizabeth Taylor on cover) **15.00 17.00 16.00**
☐ January 1954 (Debbie Reynolds on cover) **14.00 16.00 15.00**
☐ September 1954 (Debbie Reynolds on cover) **14.00 16.00 15.00**
☐ November 1954 (Janet Leigh on cover) **14.00 16.00 15.00**
☐ April 1955 (Marilyn Monroe on cover) .. **40.00 45.00 42.50**
☐ July 1958 (Natalie Wood on cover) **25.00 30.00 27.50**

MOVIE LIFE YEARBOOK
☐ 1946 (annual publication, "Life Stories of 16 Stars, Nearly 1,000 Pictures," montage cover with portraits of Frank Sinatra, Gregory Peck, Roy Rogers and others) **25.00 30.00 27.50**
☐ 1966, No. 39 .... **8.00 10.00 9.00**

MOVIE MIRROR
☐ January 1934 (Jean Harlow on cover) .. **45.00 50.00 47.50**
☐ May 1934 (Irene Dunne on cover) **37.50 42.50 40.00**
☐ August 1934 (Carole Lombard on cover) **37.50 42.50 40.00**

	Current Price Range		C/Y Avg.
☐ April 1935 (Mae West on cover)	45.00	50.00	47.50
☐ June 1935 (Jean Harlow on cover)	45.00	50.00	47.50
☐ October 1935 (Shirley Temple on cover)	45.00	50.00	47.50
☐ December 1935 (Jeanette MacDonald on cover)	37.50	42.50	40.00
☐ March 1937 (Myrna Loy on cover)	30.00	35.00	32.50
☐ August 1937 (Jean Arthur on cover) . . .	30.00	35.00	32.50
☐ November 1937 (Claudette Colbert on cover)	30.00	35.00	32.50
☐ April 1939 (Lamarr/Tracy on cover)	25.00	30.00	27.50
☐ May 1939 (Priscilla Lane on cover) . / . .	25.00	30.00	27.50
☐ June 1939 (Tyrone Power on cover) . . .	25.00	30.00	27.50
☐ July 1939 (Ginger Rogers on cover) . . .	25.00	30.00	27.50

MOVIE PEOPLE

☐ May 1954 (3-D, value stated is for copy with glasses)	60.00	70.00	65.00

MOVIE PIX

☐ October 1952 (Marilyn Monroe on cover)	45.00	55.00	50.00
☐ April 1953 (Marilyn Monroe on cover) . .	45.00	55.00	50.00

MOVIE PLAY

☐ May 1954 (Elizabeth Taylor on cover) . .	14.00	16.00	15.00

MOVIES

☐ September 1935 (Norma Shearer on cover)	37.50	42.50	40.00
☐ February 1940 (Vivien Leigh on cover)	37.50	42.50	40.00
☐ November 1943 (Alexis Smith on cover)	22.50	27.50	25.00
☐ February 1944 (Clark Gable on cover) . .	30.00	35.00	32.50
☐ October 1944 (Ginny Simms on cover)	22.50	27.50	25.00
☐ September 1945 (Gene Tierney on cover)	22.50	27.50	25.00
☐ May 1947 (Rita Hayworth on cover)	22.50	27.50	25.00
☐ March 1948 (Betty Grable on cover) . . .	22.50	27.50	25.00

MOVIE SPOTLIGHT

☐ October 1949 (Roy Rogers/Trigger on cover)	55.00	65.00	60.00
☐ October 1952 (Marilyn Monroe on cover)	45.00	55.00	50.00

MOVIE SHOW

☐ May 1946 (Lana Turner on cover)	20.00	25.00	22.50

	Current Price Range		C/Y Avg.

☐ July 1946 (Joan Leslie on cover) **20.00 25.00 22.50**
☐ August 1946 (Betty Grable on cover) . . . **20.00 25.00 22.50**
☐ September 1946 (Ginger Rogers on cover) **20.00 25.00 22.50**
☐ August 1948 (Gary Cooper on cover) . . **20.00 25.00 22.50**

MOVIE STARS PARADE

Becomes *Movie Stars Magazine* in 1960s.

☐ July 1944 (Janet Blair on cover) **22.50 27.50 25.00**
☐ June 1946 (Lana Turner on cover) **20.00 25.00 22.50**
☐ October 1946 (Jennifer Jones on cover) **20.00 25.00 22.50**
☐ June 1947 (Peter Lawford on cover) . . . **20.00 25.00 22.50**
☐ November 1947 (Alan Ladd on cover) . . **20.00 25.00 22.50**
☐ July 1948 (Esther Williams on cover) . . . **20.00 25.00 22.50**
☐ August 1948 (Shirley Temple and John Agar on cover) **30.00 35.00 32.50**
☐ October 1948 (Rita Hayworth on cover) **17.00 19.00 18.00**
☐ December 1948 (Ava Gardner on cover) **17.00 19.00 18.00**
☐ May 1953 (Elizabeth Taylor on cover) . . **17.00 19.00 18.00**
☐ October 1953 (Marilyn Monroe on cover) **45.00 55.00 50.00**
☐ December 1953 (Janet Leigh on cover) **15.00 17.00 16.00**
☐ June 1956 (Kim Novak on cover) **13.00 15.00 14.00**
☐ October 1964 (Jacqueline Kennedy on cover) **20.00 25.00 22.50**

MOVIE STORY

☐ September 1937 (Jeanette MacDonald on cover) **30.00 35.00 32.50**
☐ September 1939 (Joan Crawford on cover) **25.00 30.00 27.50**
☐ June 1940 (Bing Crosby on cover) **30.00 35.00 32.50**
☐ October 1942 (Rosalind Russell on cover) **22.50 27.50 25.00**
☐ October 1949 (Ingrid Bergman on cover) **20.00 25.00 22.50**
☐ November 1949 (Linda Darnell on cover) **20.00 25.00 22.50**
☐ December 1949 (Errol Flynn and Greer Garson on cover) **17.00 19.00 18.00**
☐ January 1950 (Bob Hope and Rhonda Fleming on cover) **17.00 19.00 18.00**
☐ February 1950 (Hedy Lamarr and Victor Mature on cover) **17.00 19.00 18.00**

	Current Price Range		C/Y Avg.
☐ August 1950 (Kirk Douglas on cover) ..	17.00	19.00	18.00
☐ September 1950 (Tyrone Power on cover)	17.00	19.00	18.00
☐ November 1950 (Clark Gable and Barbara Stanwyck on cover) .,...........	17.00	19.00	18.00
☐ February 1951 (Esther Williams on cover)	17.00	19.00	18.00

MOVIE WEEKLY
☐ July 2, 1927 (Large picture of Katherine MacDonald inside)	42.50	47.50	45.00

MOVIE STORY YEARBOOK

Movie Story was different than most Hollywood magazines in that it carried stories about the movies rather than the stars themselves.

☐ 1948 Annual Publication (Ingrid Bergman on cover)	22.50	27.50	25.00

MOVIE TEEN
☐ May 1952 (Debbie Reynolds and Carleton Carpenter on cover)	15.00	17.00	16.00

MOVIE THRILLS

Though the title made no such indication, this was an all-western magazine.

☐ July 1950 (William Boyd on cover)	40.00	45.00	42.50

MOVIE WORLD
☐ September 1952 (Doris Day on cover)	15.00	17.00	16.00
☐ July 1953 (Esther Williams on cover) ...	15.00	17.00	16.00
☐ September 1953 (Marilyn Monroe on cover)	45.00	55.00	50.00
☐ August 1954 (Jane Russell on cover) ..	14.00	16.00	15.00

MOVING PICTURE STORIES
☐ February 4, 1930 (Mae Murray on cover)	25.00	30.00	27.50

MUNSEY
☐ September 1895 (The Kaiser As a Sportsman)	7.00	9.00	8.00
☐ December 1895 (The Heroes of the Icy North)	7.00	9.00	8.00
☐ June 1896 (Outing Number; Sarah Bernhardt at home)	7.00	9.00	8.00

NATIONAL GEOGRAPHIC

National Geographic, the monthly journal of the National Geographic Society of Washington, D.C., was the first magazine to draw active collector interest. *National Geographics* were being saved as long ago as the 1940s. Even then, the magazine was more than half-a-century old! Their top-quality articles and photography place them a cut above most commercial magazines, and of course they have a timeless appeal that makes them readable regardless of their age.

Even today, with magazine collecting expanding rapidly, there are probably more active collectors of *National Geographic* than any other title.

Some *National Geographic* enthusiasts collect them topically, going after issues with articles on special subjects (mountain climbing, seafaring, rare butterflies, etc.). Most, however, are intent on working toward a complete set. This is a tough challenge. There have been over 1000 issues published since the magazine began in 1888, and the very early ones are not only scarce but expensive. For some collectors there may also be a housing problem. A complete set of *National Geographic* weighs approximately a quarter of a ton!

Values stated are for issues in the original soft covers. Sometimes you'll run across bound volumes containing six issues. Values on bound volumes run lower (which surprises most people). If a volume contains six issues worth $10 each, it is not worth $60 but more likely $40 or $45. This is because less demand exists for the bound volumes, even though they look more impressive on a bookshelf. Why? Easy: if a collector is building up a set, he will likely have one or two of the issues contained and doesn't want to pay for duplicates.

An exception to this rule would be an occasional "deluxe" bound volume in full calf, rather than a standard library binding, which will sell at a premium over the value of the issues it contains.

	Current Price Range		C/Y Avg.
☐ January 1899	25.00	33.00	28.00
☐ February 1899	25.00	33.00	28.00
☐ March 1899	45.00	60.00	51.00
☐ April 1899	50.00	65.00	57.00
☐ May 1899	47.00	62.00	52.00
☐ June 1899	35.00	45.00	39.00
☐ July 1899	50.00	65.00	57.00
☐ August 1899	25.00	33.00	28.00
☐ September 1899	25.00	33.00	28.00
☐ October 1899	29.00	36.00	32.00

	Current Price Range		C/Y Avg.
☐ November 1899	25.00	33.00	28.00
☐ December 1899	29.00	36.00	32.00
☐ January 1900	25.00	33.00	28.00
☐ February 1900	22.00	28.00	24.50
☐ March 1900	22.00	28.00	24.50
☐ April 1900	22.00	28.00	24.50
☐ May 1900	22.00	28.00	24.50
☐ June 1900	30.00	38.00	33.00
☐ July 1900	30.00	38.00	33.00
☐ August 1900	22.00	28.00	24.50
☐ September 1900	30.00	38.00	33.00
☐ October 1900	22.00	28.00	24.50
☐ November 1900	22.00	28.00	24.50
☐ December 1900	22.00	28.00	24.50
☐ January 1901	24.00	31.00	27.00
☐ February 1901	30.00	38.00	33.00
☐ March, April, May, June, July, August, September, 1901	22.00	28.00	24.50
☐ January 1902	35.00	45.00	39.00
☐ February, March, April, May, June, 1902	22.00	28.00	24.50
☐ July 1902	23.00	29.00	25.00
☐ August 1902	28.00	35.00	31.00
☐ September, October, November, December, 1902	22.00	28.00	24.50
☐ January 1903	24.00	31.00	27.00
☐ February 1903	35.00	45.00	39.00
☐ March, April, 1903	22.00	28.00	24.50
☐ June, July, 1903	24.00	31.00	27.00
☐ August 1903	22.00	28.00	24.50
☐ September 1903	24.00	31.00	27.00
☐ October 1903	22.00	28.00	24.50
☐ November 1903	28.00	35.00	31.00
☐ December 1903	30.00	38.00	33.00
☐ January, February, March, 1904	35.00	45.00	39.00
☐ April 1904	24.00	31.00	27.00
☐ May 1904	35.00	45.00	39.00
☐ June, July, August, September, 1904 ...	24.00	31.00	27.00
☐ November 1904	32.00	41.00	36.00
☐ December 1904	24.00	31.00	27.00
☐ January, February, March, 1905	40.00	53.00	45.00
☐ April 1905	17.00	22.00	19.50
☐ May 1905	16.00	21.00	18.00

	Current Price Range		C/Y Avg.
☐ June 1905	11.00	15.00	12.50
☐ July, August, September, October, November, December, 1905	9.00	12.00	10.50
☐ January 1906	10.00	13.00	11.50
☐ February 1906	9.00	12.00	10.50
☐ March 1906	10.00	13.00	11.50
☐ June 1906 (San Francisco earthquake)	11.00	15.00	13.00
☐ July 1906	9.00	12.00	10.50
☐ August 1906	10.00	13.00	11.50
☐ September 1906	9.00	12.00	10.50
☐ October 1906	10.00	13.00	11.50
☐ November, December, 1906	9.00	12.00	10.50
☐ January 1907	10.00	13.00	11.50
☐ February, March, 1907	9.00	12.00	10.50
☐ April, May, June, 1907	8.00	11.00	9.50
☐ July 1907	9.00	12.00	10.50
☐ August, September 1907	8.00	11.00	9.50
☐ October 1907	9.00	12.00	10.50
☐ November, December, 1907	8.00	11.00	9.50
☐ January 1908	14.00	19.00	16.00
☐ February 1908	10.00	13.00	11.50
☐ March 1908	9.00	12.00	10.50
☐ April 1908	14.00	19.00	16.50
☐ May, June, July, August, 1908	9.00	12.00	10.50
☐ December 1908	8.00	11.00	9.50
☐ January 1909	18.00	25.00	21.00
☐ February 1909	10.00	13.00	11.50
☐ March 1909	9.00	12.00	10.50
☐ April 1909	7.50	10.00	8.50
☐ May 1909	8.00	11.00	9.50
☐ June 1909	7.50	10.00	8.50
☐ July 1909	9.00	12.00	10.50
☐ August 1909	7.50	10.00	8.50
☐ October 1909	10.00	13.00	11.50
☐ January 1910	7.50	10.00	8.50
☐ February, March, 1910	8.00	11.00	9.50
☐ July, August, September, October, November, December, 1910	7.50	10.00	8.50
☐ January, February, March, April, 1911 ..	7.00	9.50	8.00
☐ May 1911	7.50	10.00	8.50
☐ December 1911	7.00	9.50	8.00
☐ January, February, 1912	7.00	9.50	8.00

	Current Price Range		C/Y Avg.
☐ May, June, July, August, 1912	6.00	8.00	7.00
☐ September 1912 (Head Hunters)	7.00	9.50	8.00
☐ December 1912	6.00	8.00	7.00
☐ January 1913	7.00	9.50	8.00
☐ February 1913	6.00	8.00	7.00
☐ May, June, July, August, 1913	5.50	7.50	6.50
☐ September 1913 (Egyptian relics)	8.00	11.00	9.50
☐ January 1914 (North Africa)	5.00	7.00	6.00
☐ February, March, April, 1914	4.25	5.75	5.00
☐ May 1914 (birds)	5.00	7.00	6.00
☐ June 1914	4.25	5.75	5.00
☐ August 1914 (Grand Canyon)	5.00	7.00	6.00
☐ September 1914	4.25	5.75	5.00
☐ January, February, March, April, 1915 ..	4.00	5.50	4.75
☐ May 1915 (flowers)	4.25	5.75	5.00
☐ July 1915	4.00	5.50	4.75
☐ September 1915	3.25	4.50	3.75
☐ October, November, December, 1915 ..	4.00	5.50	4.75
☐ January, February, March, April, May, 1916	3.25	4.50	3.75
☐ June 1916 (flowers)	4.00	5.50	4.75
☐ July, August, September, October, 1916	3.25	4.50	3.75
☐ November 1916	4.25	5.75	5.00
☐ December 1916	3.25	4.50	3.75
☐ January, February, March, April, May, June, 1917	3.25	4.50	3.75
☐ October 1917 (American flag)	6.00	8.50	7.00
☐ November, December, 1917	3.25	4.50	3.75
☐ January 1918 (war coverage)	3.25	4.50	3.75
☐ May 1918 (animals)	4.25	5.75	5.00
☐ June, July, August, September, October, November, December, 1918	3.25	4.50	3.75
☐ January, February, 1919	3.25	4.50	3.75
☐ March 1919	7.00	10.00	8.50
☐ April, May, June, July, August, September, October, 1919	3.25	4.50	3.75
☐ December 1919 (military insignia)	7.00	10.00	8.50
☐ January, February, March, April, 1920 ..	3.25	4.50	3.75
☐ May 1920 (mushrooms)	4.25	5.75	5.00
☐ August, September, October, 1920	3.25	4.50	3.75
☐ December 1920 (birds)	4.00	5.50	4.75
☐ January 1921	2.50	3.50	3.00

	Current Price Range		C/Y Avg.

	Current Price Range		C/Y Avg.
☐ February, March, April, May, 1921	2.25	3.00	2.50
☐ June 1921 (grass)	3.25	4.50	3.75
☐ July, August, September, October, November, December, 1921	2.25	3.00	2.50
☐ January, February, March, April, May, June, 1922	2.25	3.00	2.50
☐ July 1922 (cathedrals)	2.50	3.50	3.00
☐ August, September, October, November, December, 1922	2.25	3.00	2.50
☐ January, February, March, April, 1923 ..	2.25	3.00	2.50
☐ May, 1923 (Howard Carter and Lord Carnarvan open King Tut's tomb)	10.00	14.00	12.00
☐ June, July, August, September, October, 1923	2.25	3.00	2.50
☐ November 1923 (horses)	4.00	5.50	4.75
☐ December 1923	2.25	3.00	2.50
☐ January, February, March, April, May, June, July, August, September, 1924 ..	2.25	3.00	2.50
☐ October 1924 (goldfish)	4.00	5.50	4.75
☐ November, December, 1924	2.25	3.00	2.50
☐ January, February, March, April, 1925 ..	2.25	3.00	2.50
☐ May 1925 (ferns)	2.75	3.75	3.15
☐ June, July, August, September, October, November, 1925	2.25	3.00	2.50
☐ December 1925 (cattle)	4.00	5.50	4.75
☐ January 1926 (pigeons)	3.25	4.50	3.75
☐ February, March, 1926	2.25	3.00	2.50
☐ April 1926 (one-cell life)	2.75	3.75	3.15
☐ May, June, July, 1926	2.25	3.00	2.50
☐ August 1926 (jellyfish)	2.75	3.75	3.15
☐ September, October, November, December, 1926	2.25	3.00	2.50
☐ January, February, March, 1927	2.25	3.00	2.50
☐ April 1927 (birds)	3.25	4.50	3.75
☐ May 1927 (flowers)	2.75	3.75	3.15
☐ June 1927	2.25	3.00	2.50
☐ July 1927 (butterflies)	5.00	7.00	6.00
☐ August, September, October, November, December, 1927	2.25	3.00	2.50
☐ January through December, 1928	2.25	3.00	2.50
☐ January, February, March, April, May, June, 1929	2.25	3.00	2.50

	Current Price Range		C/Y Avg.
☐ July 1929 (insects)	3.25	4.50	3.75
☐ August, September, October, November, December, 1929	2.25	3.00	2.50
☐ January through December, 1930	1.50	2.25	1.85
☐ January, February, 1931	1.50	2.25	1.85
☐ March 1931 (fish)	3.25	4.50	3.75
☐ April, May, June, July, August, 1931	1.50	2.25	1.85
☐ October 1931 (circus)	3.25	4.50	3.75
☐ November, December, 1931	1.50	2.25	1.85
☐ January through December, 1932	1.50	2.25	1.85
☐ January, February, March, April, May, June, 1933	1.50	2.25	1.85
☐ July 1933 (birds)	2.00	2.75	2.25
☐ August, September, October, November, December, 1933	1.50	2.25	1.85
☐ January 1934 (goldfish)	3.00	4.00	3.25
☐ February, March, April, 1934	1.50	2.25	1.85
☐ May 1934 (birds)	3.00	4.00	3.25
☐ June, July, August, 1934	1.50	2.25	1.85
☐ September, October, 1934	3.00	4.00	3.25
☐ November, December, 1934	1.50	2.25	1.85
☐ January through December, 1935	1.50	2.25	2.90
☐ January 1936	2.50	3.50	2.79
☐ February, March, April, May, June, July, August, 1936	1.50	2.25	1.85
☐ November 1936 (railroading)	2.00	2.75	2.25
☐ December 1936	1.50	2.25	1.85
☐ January 1937 (dogs)	2.00	3.00	2.35
☐ February, March, 1937	1.50	2.25	1.85
☐ April 1937 (Colonial Williamsburg)	1.75	2.50	2.15
☐ May 1937 (butterflies)	3.00	4.00	3.25
☐ June 1937	1.50	2.25	1.85
☐ July 1937 (insects)	1.75	2.50	2.15
☐ August, September, October, November, December, 1937	1.50	2.25	1.85
☐ January, February, March, April, May, June, July, 1938	1.50	2.25	1.85
☐ November 1938 (cats)	4.25	5.75	4.75
☐ December 1938 (birds)	4.00	5.50	4.60
☐ January through November, 1939	1.50	2.25	1.85
☐ December 1939	1.75	2.50	2.15

	Current Price Range		C/Y Avg.
☐ January 1940 (whales)	1.75	2.50	2.15
☐ February, March, April, May, June, July, August, 1940	1.25	1.75	1.35
☐ October 1941 (relics of ancient Egypt)	2.00	3.00	2.50
☐ December 1941 (working dogs)	1.50	2.00	1.65
☐ February 1942 (prehistoric reptiles)	2.00	3.00	2.50
☐ April 1942 (wildflowers of California) ...	1.50	2.00	1.60
☐ February 1943 (lions and tigers)	1.75	2.50	2.05
☐ June 1943 (military insignia)	3.00	4.50	3.60
☐ October 1943 (military service award) ..	3.00	4.50	3.60
☐ March 1944 (ancient Greece)	1.75	2.50	2.05
☐ July 1944 (Indians)	2.00	3.00	2.50
☐ January 1945 (Indians of the Northern Pacific)	2.00	3.00	2.50
☐ July 1946 (state seals)	1.00	1.50	1.20
☐ November 1946 (ancient Rome)	1.50	2.00	1.75
☐ July 1947 (gardening)	1.50	2.00	1.75
☐ September 1947 (hunting dogs)	2.00	3.00	2.50
☐ October 1947 (the Antarctic)	1.50	2.00	1.75
☐ February 1948 (Indians of the Far West)	2.00	3.00	2.50
☐ March 1948 (circus issue)	2.00	3.00	2.50

NATIONAL MONTHLY

	Current Price Range		C/Y Avg.
☐ November 1913 ("Big Business"—Hon. Joseph E. Davies, U.S. Commissioner of Corporations on cover)	4.00	6.00	5.00
☐ December 1915 (San Francisco's Farewell to the Liberty Bell)	4.00	6.00	5.00
☐ January 1916 (The Sixty-Fourth Congress)	4.00	6.00	5.00
☐ March 1916 (Industrial Future of South America)	4.00	6.00	5.00
☐ April 1916 (The Wilson Administration)	4.00	6.00	5.00
☐ June 1916 ("The Convention at St. Louis" by Frank B. Lord)	4.00	6.00	5.00
☐ July 1916 (President Woodrow Wilson, Renominated by the Democratic Party, at St. Louis, June 16, 1916—on cover) ...	4.00	6.00	5.00

NATURE

	Current Price Range		C/Y Avg.
☐ November 1945	1.50	2.00	1.75
☐ February 1946	1.50	2.00	1.75

	Current Price Range		C/Y Avg.

NEW MOVIE

☐ May 1930 (Joan Crawford on cover) ...	35.00	40.00	37.50
☐ September 1930 (Gloria Swanson on cover)	35.00	40.00	37.50
☐ May 1932 (Billie Dove on cover)	30.00	35.00	32.50
☐ October 1932 (Kay Francis on cover) ..	30.00	35.00	32.50
☐ December 1933 (Norma Shearer on cover)	30.00	35.00	32.50

NEW MOVIE ALBUM

☐ 1930 (Annual Publication; Greta Garbo on cover)	45.00	55.00	50.00

NEW MOVIE COVER

☐ October 1930 (Loretta Young on cover)	35.00	40.00	37.50

NEWS TEMPO

☐ August 9, 1954	2.50	3.50	3.00
☐ August 16, 1954	2.50	3.50	3.00
☐ August 23, 1954	2.50	3.50	3.00
☐ August 30, 1954	2.50	3.50	3.00

NEW YORKER

☐ January 27, 1951	2.00	4.00	3.00
☐ February 3, 1951	2.00	4.00	3.00
☐ February 10, 1951	2.00	4.00	3.00
☐ February 17, 1951	2.00	4.00	3.00

NICKELL MAGAZINE

☐ April 1897 (Some Old California Indians)	10.00	12.00	11.00

NOW

☐ November 1953	3.50	4.50	4.00

OFFICIAL DETECTIVE

All oversized 13" x 10½" issues.

☐ October 1937 (Brady gang)	9.00	11.00	10.00
☐ November 1942 (Fleagle gang)	7.00	9.00	8.00
☐ November 1948 (Caryl Chessman case)	9.00	11.00	8.00
☐ November 1951 (Lucky Luciano story)...	9.00	11.00	8.00
☐ August 1953 (Barbara Graham case) ...	9.00	11.00	10.00
☐ December 1953 (Greenlease kidnapping, Guard Young massacre)	9.00	11.00	10.00

	Current Price Range		C/Y Avg.

☐ November 1956 (Weinberger kidnapping) 6.00 8.00 7.00

OFFICIAL POLICE CASES
☐ April 1956 . . . . 1.50 2.50 2.00

OLD NICK'S ANNUAL T.N.T.
☐ No. 1 (undated, c.1930, early men's magazine with jokes, cartoons and a few photos; includes artwork by Carl Barks, who later rose to fame as Disney's chief artist for Donald Duck and Uncle Scrooge) .. 100.00 125.00 112.50

ORIENTAL STORIES
☐ October 1930 . . . . 110.00 135.00 122.50

ORIGINAL BEATLES BOOK
☐ 1964 (one issue only, "Delicious Insanity, Where Will it End ... Latest Scoop, Newest Photos," portraits of all four Beatles on cover) 20.00 25.00 22.50

OUI
☐ October 1972 (first issue) 20.00 25.00 22.50
☐ April 1973 . . . . 2.50 3.50 3.00
☐ June 1973 . . . . 2.50 3.50 3.00
☐ August 1973 . . . . 2.50 3.50 3.00
☐ September 1973 . . . . 2.50 3.50 3.00
☐ October 1973 . . . . 2.50 3.50 3.00
☐ December 1973 . . . . 2.50 3.50 3.00
☐ January 1974 . . . . 2.50 3.50 3.00
☐ February 1974 . . . . 2.50 3.50 3.00
☐ March 1974 . . . . 2.50 3.50 3.00

OUTDOOR LIFE
☐ March 1915 . . . . 7.00 9.00 8.00
☐ December 1916 . . . . 7.00 9.00 8.00

THE PACIFIC MONTHLY
☐ June 1905 (Portland and Oregon Number) 10.00 12.00 11.00

PAGEANT
☐ March 1953 ("Al Capp's America, A Special Comic Book for Adults Only") 20.00 25.00 22.50

	Current Price Range		C/Y Avg.

PATHFINDER DIGEST OF WORLD AFFAIRS

☐ May 23, 1951 (Herbert Hoover on cover)	10.00	12.00	11.00

PENTHOUSE

☐ March 1972	6.00	8.00	7.00
☐ April 1972	6.00	8.00	7.00
☐ February 1973	5.00	7.00	6.00
☐ November 1973	5.00	7.00	6.00
☐ June 1974	4.00	6.00	5.00
☐ September 1974	4.00	6.00	5.00
☐ October 1974	4.00	6.00	5.00

PEOPLE

Not related to the *People Magazine* currently being published.

☐ December 3, 1952 ("Exclusive, Marilyn Monroe off guard," "How to Handle Women," portrait of Marilyn on cover)	30.00	35.00	32.50

THE PEOPLE'S HOME JOURNAL

☐ January 1902 ("A Glint of Sunshine" by Patience Stapleton)	3.00	5.00	4.00
☐ March 1902 ("The Durand Legacy" by Mrs. Jennie Burton)	3.00	5.00	4.00
☐ April 1902 ("Flushman's Run" by Hero Strong)	3.00	5.00	4.00
☐ May 1902 ("Marion Apleigh's Penance" by Charlotte M. Braeme)	3.00	5.00	4.00
☐ June 1902 ("Judge Benson's Romance" by Clarence M. Boutelle)	3.00	5.00	4.00
☐ July 1902 ("A Match-Making Scheme" by Christian Reid)	3.00	5.00	4.00
☐ August 1902 ("Jasmine; Or, The Serpent Ring" by M.T. Caldor)	3.00	5.00	4.00

PEOPLE TODAY

☐ March 10, 1954	1.50	2.50	2.00
☐ March 24, 1954	1.50	2.50	2.00
☐ April 7, 1954	1.50	2.50	2.00
☐ April 21, 1954	1.50	2.50	2.00
☐ May 5, 1954	1.50	2.50	2.00
☐ May 19, 1954	1.50	2.50	2.00
☐ June 2, 1954	1.50	2.50	2.00

	Current Price Range		C/Y Avg.
☐ June 16, 1954	1.50	2.50	2.00
☐ June 28, 1954	1.50	2.50	2.00
☐ August 25, 1954	1.50	2.50	2.00
☐ September 22, 1954	1.50	2.50	2.00
☐ October 10, 1954	1.50	2.50	2.00
☐ November 3, 1954	1.50	2.50	2.00
☐ November 17, 1954	1.50	2.50	2.00

PETER MAX MAGAZINE

☐ No. 1, Vol.1, 1969	40.00	45.00	42.50

PHOTO

☐ June 1952 (first issue)	3.50	4.50	3.00
☐ July 1954	1.75	2.25	2.00
☐ February 1955	1.75	2.25	2.00
☐ July 1955	1.75	2.25	2.00

PHOTO LIFE

☐ October 1958	3.50	4.50	4.00
☐ February 1961	1.75	2.25	2.00

Peter Max Magazine, No. 1, Vol. 1, 1969, $40.00–45.00.

	Current Price Range		C/Y Avg.

PHOTOPLAY

	Current Price Range		C/Y Avg.
☐ November 1919 (Lillian Gish on cover)	65.00	70.00	67.50
☐ August 1920 (Mae Murray on cover) ...	60.00	65.00	62.50
☐ March 1921 (Priscilla Dean on cover) ..	55.00	60.00	57.50
☐ April 1921 (Mary MacLaren on cover) ..	55.00	60.00	57.50
☐ November 1923 (Mary Allison on cover)	55.00	60.00	57.50
☐ January 1924 (Barbara LaMarr on cover)	55.00	60.00	57.50
☐ February 1924 (Corinne Griffith on cover)	55.00	60.00	57.50
☐ July 1926 (Dorothy Mackaill on cover) ..	50.00	55.00	52.50
☐ May 1928 (Greta Garbo on cover)	45.00	55.00	50.00
☐ July 1931 (Claudette Colbert on cover)	35.00	40.00	37.50
☐ April 1935 (Lillian Harvey on cover)	35.00	40.00	37.50
☐ May 1935 (Jean Harlow on cover)	35.00	40.00	37.50
☐ July 1935 (Joan Bennett on cover)	30.00	35.00	32.50
☐ April 1936 (Joan Crawford on cover) ...	30.00	35.00	32.50
☐ April 1937 (Ginger Rogers on cover) ...	30.00	35.00	32.50
☐ May 1937 (Jean Harlow on cover)	35.00	40.00	37.50
☐ July 1937 (Jeanette MacDonald on cover)	27.50	32.50	30.00
☐ December 1937 (Loretta Young on cover)	27.50	32.50	30.00
☐ January 1938 (Irene Dunne on cover) ..	27.50	32.50	30.00
☐ December 1938 (Tyrone Power on cover)	27.50	32.50	30.00
☐ March 1939 (Sonja Henie on cover) ...	27.50	32.50	30.00
☐ June 1939 (Bette Davis on cover)	27.50	32.50	30.00
☐ July 1939 (Priscilla Lane on cover)	27.50	32.50	30.00
☐ October 1939 (Gary Cooper on cover)	27.50	32.50	30.00
☐ November 1939 (Hedy Lamarr on cover)	27.50	32.50	30.00
☐ February 1940 (Clark Gable as Rhett Butler on cover)	45.00	55.00	50.00
☐ August 1940 (Bette Davis on cover) ...	25.00	30.00	27.50
☐ December 1940 (Judy Garland on cover)	27.50	32.50	30.00
☐ October 1942 (Deanna Durbin on cover)	22.50	27.50	25.00
☐ March 1943 (Lana Turner on cover) ...	22.50	27.50	25.00
☐ April 1943 (Gene Tierney on cover)	22.50	27.50	25.00
☐ May 1943 (Veronica Lake on cover) ...	22.50	27.50	25.00
☐ June 1943 (Betty Grable on cover)	27.50	32.50	30.00
☐ April 1944 (Ginger Rogers on cover) ...	20.00	25.00	22.50
☐ May 1944 (Jennifer Jones on cover) ...	20.00	25.00	22.50
☐ September 1946 (Cornel Wilde on cover)	16.00	18.00	17.00

	Current Price Range		C/Y Avg.
☐ October 1946 (Lana Turner on cover) ..	16.00	18.00	17.00
☐ April 1947 (Jeanne Crain on cover)	15.00	17.00	16.00
☐ July 1947 (Esther Williams on cover) ...	15.00	17.00	16.00
☐ August 1947 (Lana Turner on cover) ...	15.00	17.00	16.00
☐ December 1947 (Joan Caulfield on cover)	15.00	17.00	16.00
☐ February 1948 (Ingrid Bergman on cover)	18.00	20.00	19.00
☐ August 1948 (Shirley Temple on cover)	25.00	30.00	27.50
☐ October 1948 (Jeanne Crain on cover)	15.00	17.00	16.00
☐ November 1948 (Rita Hayworth on cover)	15.00	17.00	16.00
☐ April 1949 (Betty Grable on cover)	15.00	17.00	16.00
☐ March 1950 (Jane Wyman and James Stewart on cover)	15.00	17.00	16.00
☐ October 1950 (Elizabeth Taylor on cover)	18.00	20.00	19.00
☐ November 1950 (Shirley Temple on cover)	22.50	27.50	25.00

PIC

☐ February 20, 1940 (Carole Landis on cover)	6.00	8.00	7.00
☐ April 16, 1940 (Carole Landis on cover)	6.00	8.00	7.00
☐ December 5, 1944 (Joy Skylar on cover)	4.00	6.00	5.00
☐ November 1945 ("The Disabled American Veteran" by Senator Claude Pepper)	3.00	5.00	4.00

PICTORIAL REVIEW

☐ February 1938 (features by Leslie Ford, Nella Gardner White, Faith Baldwin, Ted Malone, Elizabeth Dunn)	2.00	3.00	2.50

PICTURE

☐ February 1955	2.00	3.00	2.50

PICTURE DIGEST

☐ June 1956	1.00	1.50	1.25
☐ August 1957	1.00	1.50	1.25
☐ October 1957	1.00	1.50	1.25

PICTUREGOER

☐ February 22, 1936 (Jean Harlow on cover)	30.00	35.00	32.50
☐ August 28, 1948 (Ingrid Bergman on cover)	15.00	17.00	16.00

	Current Price Range		C/Y Avg.

PICTURE LIFE

☐ February 1954 (first issue)	3.00	5.00	4.00
☐ March 1954	1.50	2.50	2.00
☐ June 1954...........................	1.50	2.50	2.00
☐ July 1954	1.50	2.50	2.00
☐ September 1954	1.50	2.50	2.00
☐ December 1954	1.50	2.50	2.00

PICTURE PLAY

☐ January 1930 (Joan Crawford on cover)	35.00	40.00	37.50
☐ November 1932 (Marlene Dietrich on cover)	40.00	45.00	42.50
☐ July 1934 (Myrna Loy on cover)	25.00	30.00	27.50
☐ December 1934 (Pat Patterson on cover)	25.00	30.00	27.50
☐ October 1935 (Katharine Hepburn on cover)	25.00	30.00	27.50
☐ January 1937 (Carole Lombard on cover)	20.00	25.00	22.50
☐ April 1937 (Myrna Loy on cover)	20.00	25.00	22.50
☐ August 1937 (Luise Rainer on cover) ...	20.00	25.00	22.50
☐ November 1937 (Kay Francis on cover)	20.00	25.00	22.50
☐ December 1937 (Bette Davis on cover)	20.00	25.00	22.50
☐ February 1938 (Myrna Loy on cover) ...	20.00	25.00	22.50

PICTURE SHOW

☐ December 15, 1945 (Gary Cooper and Loretta Young on cover)	18.00	20.00	19.00
☐ December 28, 1946 (Robert Taylor and Katharine Hepburn on cover)	16.00	18.00	17.00
☐ January 25, 1947 (Bette Davis and Glenn Ford on cover)	16.00	18.00	17.00
☐ October 18, 1947 (Gregory Peck and Jennifer Jones on cover)	16.00	18.00	17.00
☐ December 27, 1947 (Judy Garland and Gene Kelly on cover)	20.00	22.00	21.00
☐ October 2, 1948 (Cornell Wilde and Linda Darnell on cover)	15.00	17.00	16.00
☐ October 16, 1948 (Stewart Granger on cover)	15.00	17.00	16.00
☐ December 25, 1948 (Ingrid Bergman on cover)	18.00	20.00	19.00
☐ February 19, 1949 (Tyrone Power and Anne Baxter on cover)	13.00	15.00	14.00
☐ April 2, 1949 (Danny Kaye on cover) ...	13.00	15.00	14.00

	Current Price Range		C/Y Avg.

PICTURE SPOTLIGHT
☐ April 1959 (first issue) 3.50   4.50   4.00

PICTURE WEEK
☐ May 2, 1957 . . . .   1.75   2.25   2.00

PLAY
☐ February 1954 . . . .   3.50   4.50   4.00

PLAYBOY

The story has become almost legend about Hugh Hefner starting *Playboy* on a shoestring—$600 and a kitchen table as his office. That was in 1953, and nothing quite like *Playboy* was on the newsstands. A number of publications, such as *Police Gazette,* carried pin-up photos, but they were not considered classy or sophisticated. Hefner's concept was of a top-quality magazine that would feature (a) models who looked much too "nice" to be posing for pin-ups, and (b) good articles and fiction. He did not have his own centerfold model for the first issue, so he ran a reprint of the famous Marilyn Monroe calendar photo instead, which by then was several years old.

Playboy has become one of the most avidly collected modern magazines. As with all pin-up magazines, buyers are cautioned to make a careful examination for possible clip-outs. In the early years it was intended for the centerfold to be removed and "posted," and most readers apparently did just that. This is one reason why early issues are rather expensive when intact.

Issue	Low	High	C/Y Avg.
☐ December 1953	90.00	110.00	100.00
☐ January 1954	90.00	110.00	100.00
☐ May 1954	55.00	65.00	60.00
☐ July 1954	55.00	65.00	60.00
☐ August 1954	32.50	37.50	35.00
☐ September 1954	32.50	37.50	35.00
☐ November 1954	32.50	37.50	35.00
☐ January 1955	80.00	90.00	85.00
☐ September 1955	32.50	37.50	35.00
☐ October 1955	30.00	35.00	32.50
☐ November 1955	30.00	35.00	32.50
☐ December 1955	35.00	40.00	37.50
☐ January 1956	20.00	25.00	22.50
☐ February 1956 (Jayne Mansfield on cover)	18.00	20.00	19.00

	Current Price Range		C/Y Avg.
☐ March 1956	18.00	20.00	19.00
☐ April 1956	18.00	20.00	19.00
☐ May 1956	18.00	20.00	19.00
☐ June 1976 (Lillian Muller on cover)	5.00	7.00	6.00
☐ July 1976 (Sarah Miles, Kris Kristofferson on cover)	4.00	6.00	5.00
☐ August 1976 (interview: Robert Altman)	3.00	5.00	4.00
☐ September 1976 (interview: David Bowie)	4.00	6.00	5.00
☐ October 1976	3.00	4.00	3.50
☐ November 1976 (interview: Jimmy Carter)	6.00	8.00	7.00
☐ December 1976	4.00	6.00	5.00
☐ January 1977	5.00	7.00	6.00
☐ February 1977	4.00	6.00	5.00
☐ March 1977	3.00	4.00	3.50
☐ April 1977	3.00	4.00	3.50
☐ May 1977	3.00	4.00	3.50
☐ June 1977 (Barbara Bach)	4.50	6.50	5.50
☐ July 1977	4.00	6.00	5.00
☐ August 1977	3.00	4.00	3.50
☐ September 1977	3.00	4.00	3.50
☐ October 1977 (interview: Barbara Streisand)	4.00	6.00	5.00
☐ November 1977 (interview: Billy Carter)	4.00	6.00	5.00
☐ December 1977 (interview: John Denver)	4.50	6.50	5.50
☐ January 1978	3.00	4.00	3.50
☐ February 1978	3.00	4.00	3.50
☐ March 1978 (interview: Bob Dylan)	3.00	4.00	3.50
☐ April 1978	3.00	4.00	3.50
☐ May 1978	3.00	4.00	3.50
☐ June 1978 (interview: George Burns) ...	4.00	6.00	5.00
☐ July 1978 (poster of Elvis Presley)	6.00	8.00	7.00
☐ August 1978	3.00	4.00	3.50
☐ September 1978 (interview: Sylvester Stallone)	3.00	4.00	3.50
☐ October 1978 (Dolly Parton on cover) ..	5.00	7.00	6.00
☐ November, 1978	4.00	6.00	5.00
☐ December 1978 (interview: John Travolta)	4.00	6.00	5.00
☐ January, 1979 (*Playboy's* silver anniversary issue)	6.00	8.00	7.00

	Current Price Range		C/Y Avg.
☐ February 1979	2.75	3.25	3.00
☐ March 1979	2.75	3.25	3.00
☐ April 1979	2.75	3.25	3.00
☐ May 1979	2.75	3.25	3.00
☐ June 1979	4.50	6.50	5.50
☐ July 1979 (Patti McGuire on cover)	4.00	6.00	5.00
☐ August 1979 (this issue had Dorothy Stratton as centerfold model, who was murdered shortly thereafter)	12.00	14.00	13.00
☐ September 1979 (interview: Pete Rose)	6.00	8.00	7.00
☐ October 1979	2.75	3.25	3.00
☐ November 1979	2.75	3.25	3.00
☐ December 1979 (Raquel Welch on cover)	5.00	7.00	6.00
☐ December 1983 (Joan Collins on cover)	7.00	9.00	8.00

POINT

☐ March 1954 (first issue)	3.50	5.50	4.50
☐ May/June 1954	1.50	2.50	2.00
☐ July 1954	1.50	2.50	2.00
☐ August 1954	1.50	2.50	2.00
☐ September 1954	1.50	2.50	2.00
☐ October 1954	1.50	2.50	2.00
☐ November 1954	1.50	2.50	2.00
☐ January 1955	1.50	2.50	2.00

POPULAR MECHANICS

☐ August 1951 (How Owners Rate the '51 Cadillac, How to Install Attic Ventilating Fans)	2.00	3.00	2.50
☐ April 1953 (What Owners Say About the Ford Six, Guard Your Car From Thieves, Build Your Own Camp Trailer, Twin Outboards, They Outsmart Death in the Air)	2.00	3.00	2.50

POPULAR SCIENCE

☐ January 1930 (Monster Electric Plant Run by Wind on cover)	16.00	18.00	17.00
☐ May 1930 (Lindberg Goes Gliding)	16.00	18.00	17.00

POSE

☐ August 1956	1.50	2.50	2.00
☐ September 1956	1.50	2.50	2.00
☐ November 1956	1.50	2.50	2.00

Popular Science, May 1930, $16.00–$18.00.

	Current Price Range		C/Y Avg.

PREVENTIVE MAINTENANCE MONTHLY

☐ August 1951 (cover artwork by Will Eisner, creator of "The Spirit") 80.00 90.00 85.00

PREVUE

This was a pocket size magazine measuring 4" x 6".

☐ May 1952 (first issue) 3.50 4.50 4.00
☐ October 1952 .... 1.50 2.50 2.00
☐ November 1952 .... 1.50 2.50 2.00
☐ December 1952 .... 1.50 2.50 2.00

PRO

☐ September 1955 .... 3.50 4.50 4.00
☐ October 1955 .... 1.75 2.25 2.00

PULSE

☐ October 1954 (first issue) 3.50 4.50 4.00

	Current Price Range		C/Y Avg.
☐ January 1955	1.50	2.50	2.00
☐ February 1955	1.50	2.50	2.00
☐ May 1955	1.50	2.50	2.00
☐ June 1955	1.50	2.50	2.00
☐ August 1955	1.50	2.50	2.00

QUICK

☐ February 20, 1950 (Roy Rogers, King of the Cowboys)	18.00	20.00	19.00

QUICK DIGEST

☐ February 1955	1.50	2.50	2.00
☐ April 1955	1.50	2.50	2.00

RADIO AND APPLIANCE JOURNAL

☐ January 1949	2.00	3.00	2.50

RADIO BROADCAST

☐ April 1929	5.00	7.00	6.00
☐ June 1929	5.00	7.00	6.00
☐ August 1929	5.00	7.00	6.00

RADIO AND DISTRIBUTION MAINTENANCE

☐ August 1949	2.00	3.00	2.50
☐ December 1949	2.00	3.00	2.50

RADIO AND TV MIRROR

☐ November 1939 (Artie Shaw, Tommy Dorsey, Charles Boyer)	30.00	35.00	32.50

RADIO CRAFT

☐ October 1929 (first issue)	10.00	12.00	11.00
☐ November 1929	4.00	6.00	5.00
☐ December 1929	4.00	6.00	5.00
☐ February 1930	3.50	5.50	4.00
☐ March 1930	3.50	5.50	4.00
☐ April 1930	3.50	5.50	4.00
☐ May 1930	3.50	5.50	4.00
☐ June 1930	3.50	5.50	4.00
☐ July 1933	3.00	5.00	4.00
☐ August 1933	3.00	5.00	4.00
☐ November 1939	2.50	3.50	3.00
☐ December 1939	2.50	3.50	3.00
☐ January 1940	2.50	3.50	3.00

	Current Price Range		C/Y Avg.

RADIO ELECTRONICS

☐ August 1949	2.50	3.50	3.00
☐ January 1950	2.50	3.50	3.00
☐ June 1952	2.50	3.50	3.00
☐ July 1952	2.50	3.50	3.00
☐ August 1952	2.50	3.50	3.00

RADIO GUIDE

☐ November 6, 1937 ("How to Live Like a Human Being," features on Fred Astaire, Tyrone Power, George Bernard Shaw, W.C. Fields)	15.00	17.00	16.00

RAVE

☐ June 1954	1.75	2.25	2.00

REAL DICK CLARK

☐ 1959, #1	27.50	32.50	30.00

REDBOOK

☐ August 1957	2.00	4.00	3.00
☐ September 1957	2.00	4.00	3.00
☐ October 1957 (Ernie Kovacks on cover)	5.00	7.00	6.00
☐ November 1957 (J.F. Kennedy on cover)	8.00	10.00	9.00
☐ December 1957 (Dr. Seuss)	4.00	6.00	5.00
☐ February 1958 (Marilyn Monroe on cover)	8.00	10.00	9.00

THE REVIEW OF REVIEWS

☐ March 1893 (America In Hawaii; Pasteur and His Work)	13.00	15.00	14.00

THE SATURDAY EVENING POST

☐ March 28, 1908 ("The Simple Case of Susan" by Jacques Futrelle)	8.00	10.00	9.00
☐ April 4, 1908 (Easter Issue; "Through Japanese Eyes" by I. K. Friedman)	8.00	10.00	9.00
☐ May 2, 1908 ("His Father's Business" by George Chester)	8.00	10.00	9.00
☐ May 16, 1908 ("The Firing Line" by Robert W. Chambers)	8.00	10.00	9.00
☐ May 23, 1908 ("The Tiger God" by W. A. Fraser)	8.00	10.00	9.00
☐ May 30, 1908 (Out-of-Doors Issue; "The Big Strike at Siwash" by George Fitch)	8.00	10.00	9.00

	Current Price Range		C/Y Avg.
☐ August 29, 1908 ("Tourists and Tourines" by Samuel G. Blythe)	8.00	10.00	9.00
☐ October 3, 1908 ("Our President Factories" by Samuel G. Blythe)	8.00	10.00	9.00
☐ November 21, 1908 ("Little Gorky" by Edward Hungerford)	8.00	10.00	9.00
☐ November 28, 1908 ("Fears of Reason and Flows of Soul" by Samuel G. Blythe)	8.00	10.00	9.00
☐ December 19, 1908 (More Than a Million a Week Circulation; "The King of Diamonds" by Jacques Futrelle)	8.00	10.00	9.00
☐ January 16, 1909 ("The Twisted Foot" by Henry Milner Rideout)	8.00	10.00	9.00
☐ December 1916 ("The Spreading Dawn" by Basil King)	4.00	6.00	5.00
☐ March 10, 1917 ("The Man-Killer" by Holworthy Hall)			
☐ April 28, 1917 ("Democracy is a Bad War Maker" by Lord Northcliffe)	4.00	6.00	5.00
☐ May 26, 1917 ("The High Heart" by Basil King)	4.00	6.00	5.00
☐ July 28, 1917 ("Tish Does Her Part" by Mary Roberts Reinhart)	4.00	6.00	5.00
☐ March 11, 1922 ("The Hooving of Hoover" by Kenneth L. Roberts)	3.00	5.00	4.00
☐ April 1, 1922 ("The Covered Wagon" by Emerson Hough)	3.00	5.00	4.00
☐ April 15, 1922 (Easter Issue; "Rita Coventry" by Julian Street)	3.00	5.00	4.00
☐ April 22, 1922 ("The Return to Normalcy" by Alice Duer Miller)	3.00	5.00	4.00
☐ April 12, 1924 ("That Pain in Our Northwest" by Garet Garrett)	3.00	5.00	4.00
☐ May 10, 1924 (The Making of a Stockbroker)	3.00	5.00	4.00
☐ May 24, 1924 ("Bill The Conqueror" by P. G. Wodehouse)	3.00	5.00	4.00
☐ July 26, 1924 ("Balisand" by Joseph Hergesheimer)	3.00	5.00	4.00
☐ August 9, 1924 ("A Speaking Likeness" by Julian Street)	3.00	5.00	4.00

	Current Price Range		C/Y Avg.

☐ August 16, 1924 ("Professor, How Could You!" by Harry Leon Wilson)	3.00	5.00	4.00
☐ September 6, 1924 ("East of the Setting Sun" by George Barr McCutcheon)	3.00	5.00	4.00
☐ October 11, 1924 ("Bringing Up the Northwest" by Garet Garrett)	3.00	5.00	4.00
☐ November 1, 1924 ("Our American Diplomat" by Richard Washburn Child)	3.00	5.00	4.00
☐ November 29, 1924 (Thanksgiving Issue; "The Custody of the Pumpkin" by P. G. Wodehouse)	3.00	5.00	4.00
☐ December 16, 1933 (Norman Rockwell cover)	25.00	30.00	27.50
☐ June 30, 1934 (Norman Rockwell cover)	25.00	30.00	27.50
☐ April 27, 1935 (Norman Rockwell cover)	25.00	30.00	27.50
☐ July 13, 1935 (Norman Rockwell cover)	25.00	30.00	27.50
☐ April 25, 1936 (Norman Rockwell cover)	20.00	25.00	22.50
☐ May 30, 1936 (Norman Rockwell cover)	20.00	25.00	22.50
☐ November 21, 1936 (Norman Rockwell cover)	20.00	25.00	22.50
☐ December 25, 1937 (Norman Rockwell cover)	18.00	20.00	19.00
☐ August 6, 1938 (Howard Fast, Irving Stone, P.G. Wodehouse, J.P. Marquand, Joe DiMaggio ad on back cover)	3.00	5.00	4.00
☐ November 25, 1939 (Beautiful J.C. Leyendecker cover; MacKinlay Kantor)	8.00	10.00	9.00
☐ May 10, 1942 ("The Body in the Library" by Agatha Christie)	3.00	5.00	4.00
☐ January 3, 1942 (J. C. Leyendecker cover; Katharine Hepburn story)	7.00	9.00	8.00
☐ August 1, 1942 ("Specialists in Sudden Death" by Davenport Steward)	3.00	5.00	4.00
☐ February 13, 1943 (Norman Rockwell life story, 12 of his *Post* covers are reproduced in color; Branch Rickey; William Faulkner)	22.50	27.50	25.00
☐ February 20, 1943 (Freedom of Speech; painting by Norman Rockwell)	18.00	20.00	19.00
☐ February 27, 1943 (Freedom of Worship; painting by Norman Rockwell)	18.00	20.00	19.00

	Current Price Range		C/Y Avg.
☐ March 6, 1943 (Freedom from Want; painting by Norman Rockwell)	14.00	16.00	15.00
☐ March 13, 1943 (Freedom from Fear; painting by Norman Rockwell)	*18.00	20.00	19.00
☐ May 8, 1943 (Norman Rockwell sketches American soldiers)	11.00	13.00	12.00
☐ March 25, 1944 (The War to Get War News; C. S. Forester; H. E. Bates)	14.00	16.00	15.00
☐ August 5, 1944 (Agatha Christie; Harold Lamb)	11.00	13.00	12.00
☐ November 4, 1944 (Norman Rockwell cover; He Shook Patton Loose)	19.00	21.00	20.00
☐ December 16, 1944 (Home Coming Isn't Easy; Post Cameraman in the Pacific)	14.00	16.00	15.00
☐ January 27, 1945 (The Common Cold—sketches by Norman Rockwell; Edgar Snow)	11.00	13.00	12.00
☐ February 10, 1945 (Lincoln's Birthday—painting by Norman Rockwell) ...	11.00	13.00	12.00
☐ May 19, 1945 (Booth Tarkington; Pete Martin in Hollywood)	14.00	16.00	15.00
☐ August 11, 1945 (Norman Rockwell cover; Behind Russian Lines in Austria)	24.00	26.00	25.00
☐ July 13, 1946 (Norman Rockwell painting; The Atom Bomb)	11.00	13.00	12.00
☐ October 5, 1946 (Willie Gillis picture by Norman Rockwell on cover)	22.00	24.00	23.00
☐ October 19, 1946 ("Why Air Passengers Get Mad" by Wesley Price)	8.00	10.00	9.00
☐ November 2, 1946 (Norman Rockwell painting)	11.00	13.00	12.00
☐ November 16, 1946 (Norman Rockwell cover)	27.50	32.50	30.00
☐ April 12, 1947 (Norman Rockwell painting and sketches)	11.00	13.00	12.00
☐ February 14, 1948 (Babe Ruth tells his own story)	11.00	13.00	12.00
☐ July 24, 1948 (Norman Rockwell painting and sketches; 12 Years with FDR)	14.00	16.00	15.00
☐ December 3, 1949 ("Falsehood: Russia's Sharpest Weapon" by Lt. Gen. Walter Bedell Smith)	7.00	9.00	8.00

The Saturday Evening Post, *October 1946, $22.00–$24.00.*

	Current Price Range		C/Y Avg.
☐ December 17, 1949 ("Dick Tracy's Boss" by Robert M. Yoder)	7.00	9.00	8.00
☐ May 19, 1956 (Norman Rockwell cover; "Marilyn Monroe" by Pete Martin)	22.50	27.50	25.00
☐ October 6, 1956 (Adlai Stevenson cover by Norman Rockwell; Kim Novak)	14.00	16.00	15.00
☐ October 13, 1956 (Eisenhower cover by Norman Rockwell; Rocky Marciano) . . .	19.00	21.00	20.00
☐ December 29, 1956 (Norman Rockwell cover)	32.50	37.50	35.00
☐ April 20, 1957 ("Milwaukee Will Win the Pennant" by Warren Spahn)	32.50	37.50	35.00
☐ May 25, 1957 (Norman Rockwell cover; "Groucho Marx" by Pete Martin)	14.00	16.00	15.00
☐ June 29, 1957 (Norman Rockwell cover; "I Was Always Hungry" by Kirk Douglas)	14.00	16.00	15.00
☐ June 28, 1958 (Norman Rockwell cover)	19.00	21.00	20.00

	Current Price Range		C/Y Avg.

☐ November 8, 1958 (Norman Rockwell cover) **14.00 16.00 15.00**

☐ October 24, 1959 (Norman Rockwell cover) **19.00 21.00 20.00**

☐ February 13, 1960 (Norman Rockwell cover; Rockwell's own story with repros) **37.50 42.50 40.00**

☐ September 17, 1960 (Norman Rockwell cover; Pittsburgh Bucs) **14.00 16.00 15.00**

☐ October 29, 1960 (J. F. Kennedy portrait by Norman Rockwell on cover) **22.50 27.50 25.00**

☐ November 5, 1960 (Richard Nixon portrait by Norman Rockwell on cover) ... **20.00 25.00 22.50**

☐ January 13, 1962 (Norman Rockwell cover; "Shirley Jones" by Peter Martin) **14.00 16.00 15.00**

☐ January 19, 1963 (Norman Rockwell cover of Nehru) **14.00 16.00 15.00**

☐ March 2, 1963 (Norman Rockwell cover of Jack Benny) **14.00 16.00 15.00**

☐ May 25, 1963 (Norman Rockwell cover of Nasser) **14.00 16.00 15.00**

☐ July 17, 1965 (Sean Connery cover and article) **11.00 13.00 12.00**

☐ July 30, 1966 (Bob Dylan cover and article) **11.00 13.00 12.00**

☐ August 27, 1966 (Beatles cover and article) **22.50 27.50 25.00**

SATURDAY REVIEW OF LITERATURE
☐ August 5, 1944 (20th Anniversary Issue) **14.00 16.00 15.00**
☐ August 6, 1949 (25th Anniversary Issue) **14.00 16.00 15.00**

SCIENCE AND MECHANICS
☐ February–March 1942 ("Carve Lum and Abner," "$400 in Prizes") **10.00 12.00 11.00**
☐ April 1956 .... **2.00 3.00 2.50**

SCIENCE FICTION PLUS
☐ December 1953 ("The Triggered Dimension" by Harry Bates) **22.50 27.50 25.00**

SCRIBNER'S MAGAZINE
☐ July 1881 ("A Rainy Day With Uncle Remus VI" by Joel Chandler Harris) ... **12.00 14.00 13.00**

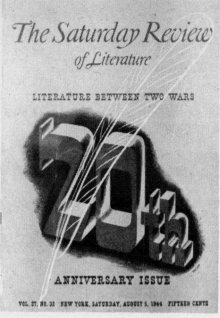

The Saturday Review of Literature, August 1944, **$14.00–$16.00.**

	Current Price Range		C/Y Avg.
☐ November 1891 ("The Wrecker, Chapters X–XI" by Robert Louis Stevenson and Lloyd Osbourne)	**10.00**	**12.00**	**11.00**
☐ January 1894 ("The Actor" by John Drew)	**8.00**	**10.00**	**9.00**
☐ February 1894 ("The Sea Island Hurricanes—The Devastation" by Joel Chandler Harris)	**8.00**	**10.00**	**9.00**
☐ November 1894 ("How Whalebone Caused a Wedding" by Joel Chandler Harris)	**8.00**	**10.00**	**9.00**
SCREEN ALBUM			
☐ Winter 1951–1952 (Doris Day on cover)	**14.00**	**16.00**	**15.00**
☐ Winter 1952–1953 (Elizabeth Taylor on cover)	**19.00**	**21.00**	**20.00**
☐ Spring 1953 (Doris Day on cover)	**14.00**	**16.00**	**15.00**
☐ Spring 1954 (Elizabeth Taylor on cover)	**19.00**	**21.00**	**20.00**

Science Fiction Plus, December 1953, $22.50–$27.50.

	Current Price Range		C/Y Avg.
SCREEN BOOK			
☐ May 1929 (Doug Fairbanks on cover) ..	45.00	55.00	50.00
☐ June 1929 (Lupe Velez on cover)	45.00	55.00	50.00
☐ July 1929	45.00	55.00	50.00
☐ December 1930 (Ann Harding on cover)	37.50	42.50	40.00
☐ March 1931 (Joan Crawford on cover)	40.00	45.00	42.50
☐ November 1933 (Helen Hayes on cover)	32.50	37.50	35.00
☐ April 1934 (Heather Angel on cover) ...	32.50	37.50	35.00
☐ October 1934 (Anna Sten on cover) ...	32.50	37.50	35.00
☐ December 1934 (Marlene Dietrich on cover)	32.50	37.50	35.00
☐ August 1935 (Greta Garbo on cover)	32.50	37.50	35.00
☐ March 1936 (Jean Harlow on cover) ...	32.50	37.50	35.00
☐ July 1937 (Olivia deHavilland on cover)	32.50	37.50	35.00
☐ September 1937 (Alice Faye on cover)	32.50	37.50	35.00
☐ November 1937 (Marlene Dietrich on cover)	32.50	37.50	35.00

		Current Price Range		C/Y Avg.
☐ May 1939 (Bette Davis on cover)		25.00	30.00	27.50
☐ June 1939 (Virginia Bruce on cover) . . .		25.00	30.00	27.50

SCREEN HITS ANNUAL

☐ 1949 (June Allyson on cover)		12.50	17.50	15.00
☐ 1952 (June Allyson on cover) . . . . . , . . .		10.00	15.00	12.50

SCREEN GUIDE

☐ June 1939 (Bette Davis on cover)		25.00	30.00	27.50
☐ January 1941 (Ginger Rogers on cover)		25.00	30.00	27.50
☐ March 1941 (Judy Garland on cover) . . .		25.00	30.00	27.50
☐ June 1941 (Paulette Goddard on cover)		18.00	20.00	19.00
☐ July 1942 (Carole Landis on cover)		18.00	20.00	19.00
☐ March 1943 (Ingrid Bergman on cover)		18.00	20.00	19.00
☐ August 1943 (Alexis Smith on cover) . . .		18.00	20.00	19.00
☐ June 1945 (Maureen O'Hara on cover)		15.00	17.00	16.00
☐ September 1948 (Ava Gardner on cover)		10.00	12.00	11.00
☐ August 1950 (Elizabeth Taylor on cover)		10.00	12.00	11.00
☐ August 1951 (Tony Curtis on cover)		8.00	10.00	9.00

SCREENLAND

☐ August 1924 (Anna Q. Nilsson on cover)		22.50	27.50	25.00
☐ March 1926 (Dorothy MacKaill on cover)		20.00	25.00	22.50
☐ January 1927 (Vilma Banky on cover) . .		18.00	20.00	19.00
☐ October 1931 (Joan Crawford on cover)		25.00	30.00	27.50
☐ April 1932 (Marlene Dietrich on cover)		25.00	30.00	27.50
☐ December 1932 (Joan Crawford on cover)		25.00	30.00	27.50
☐ April 1933 (Kay Francis on cover)		19.00	21.00	20.00
☐ May 1933 (Joan Crawford on cover) . . .		19.00	21.00	20.00
☐ June 1933 (Constance Bennett on cover)		19.00	21.00	20.00
☐ May 1934 (Katharine Hepburn on cover)		19.00	21.00	20.00
☐ July 1934 (Loretta Young on cover)		19.00	21.00	20.00
☐ November 1934 (Anna Sten on cover)		19.00	21.00	20.00
☐ April 1935 (Joan Crawford on cover) . . .		19.00	21.00	20.00
☐ July 1935 (Ginger Rogers on cover) . . .		19.00	21.00	20.00
☐ October 1935 (Carole Lombard on cover)		19.00	21.00	20.00
☐ November 1935 (Greta Garbo on cover)		19.00	21.00	20.00
☐ May 1939 (Bette Davis on cover)		16.00	18.00	17.00
☐ April 1942 (Olivia de Havilland on cover)		14.00	16.00	15.00
☐ November 1943 (Rita Hayworth on cover)		14.00	16.00	15.00
☐ February 1944 (Alexis Smith on cover)		14.00	16.00	15.00

	Current Price Range		C/Y Avg.
☐ July 1944 (Carole Landis on cover)	14.00	16.00	15.00
☐ March 1945 (Claudette Colbert on cover)	14.00	16.00	15.00
☐ January 1947 (Tyrone Power on cover)	12.00	14.00	13.00
☐ March 1947 (Rita Hayworth on cover) ..	12.00	14.00	13.00
☐ April 1947 (Olivia de Havilland on cover)	12.00	14.00	13.00
☐ September 1948 (Bogart/Bacall on cover)	12.00	14.00	13.00
☐ October 1951 (Betty Grable on cover) ..	8.00	10.00	9.00
☐ February 1952 (Hedy Lamarr on cover)	8.00	10.00	9.00
☐ August 1952 (Marilyn Monroe on cover)	35.00	40.00	37.50
☐ October 1953 (Ava Gardner on cover)	7.00	9.00	8.00
☐ September 1965 (Mia Farrow on cover)	2.00	3.00	2.50

SCREEN LIFE

☐ February 1941 (Judy Garland on cover)	13.00	15.00	14.00
☐ November 1941 (Gene Tierney on cover)	12.00	14.00	13.00
☐ September 1953 (Pier Angeli on cover)	7.00	9.00	8.00
☐ November 1953 (Marilyn Monroe on cover)	35.00	40.00	37.50
☐ March 1956 (Janet Leigh on cover)	5.00	7.00	6.00
☐ September 1964 (Taylor/Burton on cover)	3.00	5.00	4.00
☐ July 1968 (Monkees on cover)	7.00	9.00	8.00

SCREEN PLAY

☐ April 1936 (Jean Harlow on cover)	30.00	35.00	32.50
☐ April, 1937 (Virginia Bruce on cover) ...	27.50	32.50	30.00
☐ May 1937 (Jean Harlow on cover)	30.00	35.00	32.50
☐ August 1937 (Shirley Temple on cover)	35.00	40.00	37.50

SCREEN ROMANCES

☐ November 1934 (Joan Crawford on cover)	35.00	40.00	37.50
☐ April 1935 (Irene Dunne on cover)	35.00	40.00	37.50
☐ January 1936 (Jean Harlow on cover) ..	35.00	40.00	37.50
☐ March 1936 (Marlene Dietrich on cover)	35.00	40.00	37.50
☐ September 1936 (Myrna Loy and Warner Baxter on cover)	30.00	35.00	32.50
☐ February 1937 (Myrna Loy and William Powell on cover)	27.50	32.50	30.00
☐ April 1937 (Carole Lombard and Fred MacMurray on cover)	27.50	32.50	30.00

	Current Price Range		C/Y Avg.

☐ May 1937 (Fred Astaire and Ginger Rogers on cover) **27.50** **32.50** **30.00**

☐ August 1937 (Simone Simon on cover) **25.00** **30.00** **27.50**

☐ March 1938 (Katharine Hepburn on cover) **22.50** **27.50** **25.00**

☐ April 1938 (Robert Taylor and Maureen O'Sullivan on cover) **22.50** **27.50** **25.00**

☐ June 1938 (Loretta Young on cover) ... **22.50** **27.50** **25.00**

☐ August 1938 (Alice Faye and Tyrone Power on cover) **22.50** **27.50** **25.00**

SCREEN STARS

☐ November 1946 (Guy Madison on cover) **14.00** **16.00** **15.00**

☐ June 1952 (Lana Turner on cover) **8.00** **10.00** **9.00**

☐ April 1953 (Ava Gardner on cover) **8.00** **10.00** **9.00**

☐ December, 1953 (Doris Day on cover) .. **8.00** **10.00** **9.00**

☐ May 1955 (Grace Kelly on cover) **11.00** **13.00** **12.00**

☐ May 1957 (Kim Novak on cover) **5.00** **7.00** **6.00**

SCREEN STORIES

☐ June 1948 (Deanna Durbin and Dick Haymes on cover) **12.00** **14.00** **13.00**

☐ March 1950 (Jane Wyman on cover) ... **10.00** **12.00** **11.00**

☐ June 1955 (Doris Day on cover) **8.00** **10.00** **9.00**

☐ January 1957 (Debbie Reynolds on cover) **6.00** **8.00** **7.00**

☐ July 1965 (Carroll Baker on cover) **2.00** **4.00** **3.00**

☐ September 1952 (Elizabeth Taylor on cover) **11.00** **13.00** **12.00**

☐ May 1954 (Elizabeth Taylor on cover) .. **10.00** **12.00** **11.00**

☐ March 1955 (Reynolds/J. Powell on cover) **8.00** **10.00** **9.00**

☐ August 1956 (Marilyn Monroe on cover) **20.00** **25.00** **22.50**

☐ September 1957 (Kim Novak on cover) **8.00** **10.00** **9.00**

☐ February 1958 (Doris Day on cover) ... **7.00** **9.00** **8.00**

☐ July 1959 (Rock Hudson on cover) **20.00** **25.00** **22.50**

☐ November 1959 (Janet Leigh on cover) **4.00** **6.00** **5.00**

☐ June 1972 (Elizabeth Taylor on cover) **2.00** **3.00** **2.50**

SHADOPLAY

☐ October 1933 (Ginger Rogers on cover) **27.50** **32.50** **30.00**

☐ April 1935 (George Raft and Carole Lombard on cover) **25.00** **30.00** **27.50**

	Current Price Range		C/Y Avg.

SENSATION
- ☐ January 1954 .... 3.50 4.50 4.00
- ☐ March 1954 .... 1.75 2.25 2.00

SEXOLOGY
- ☐ May 1952 .... 1.00 2.00 1.50
- ☐ June 1952 .... 1.00 2.00 1.50
- ☐ August 1954 .... 1.00 2.00 1.50
- ☐ September 1954 .... 1.00 2.00 1.50
- ☐ October 1954 .... 1.00 2.00 1.50
- ☐ December 1966 .... 1.00 2.00 1.50
- ☐ January 1967 .... 1.00 2.00 1.50
- ☐ November 1967 .... 1.00 2.00 1.50

SIGHT AND SOUND
- ☐ October–December, 1954 (Judy Garland and James Mason on cover) 8.00 10.00 9.00

SNAPPY
- ☐ May 1956 .... 2.00 3.00 2.50
- ☐ July 1956 .... 2.00 3.00 2.50
- ☐ September 1956 .... 2.00 3.00 2.50
- ☐ March 1957 .... 2.00 3.00 2.50
- ☐ May 1957 .... 2.00 3.00 2.50
- ☐ July 1957 .... 2.00 3.00 2.50
- ☐ September 1957 (Ward cover) 5.00 6.00 5.50
- ☐ March 1958 (Ward cover) 5.00 6.00 5.50
- ☐ May 1960 .... 1.50 2.50 2.00
- ☐ July 1960 .... 1.50 2.50 2.00

SILVER SCREEN
- ☐ June 1939 (Ginger Rogers on cover) ... 20.00 25.00 22.50
- ☐ May 1942 (Carole Landis on cover) 13.00 15.00 14.00
- ☐ August 1948 (Judy Garland on cover) .. 15.00 17.00 16.00
- ☐ August 1949 (Jane Russell on cover) .. 13.00 15.00 14.00
- ☐ May 1953 (Rita Hayworth on cover) 11.00 13.00 12.00
- ☐ August 1953 (Doris Day on cover) 11.00 13.00 12.00
- ☐ October 1953 (Marilyn Monroe on cover) 30.00 35.00 32.50
- ☐ April 1954 (Marilyn Monroe on cover) .. 27.50 32.50 30.00
- ☐ August 1964 (Paul McCartney on cover) 19.00 21.00 20.00
- ☐ October 1964 (Ringo Starr on cover) ... 16.00 18.00 17.00

Silver Screen, May 1942, $13.00–$15.00.

	Current Price Range		C/Y Avg.

STAGE

☐ November 1935 (Alfred Lunt and Lynn Fontaine in "Taming of the Shrew" on cover) . . . .

☐ August 1936 (Miss Billie Burke on cover)

☐ October 1937 (Lynn Fontaine and Alfred Lunt; Amphitryon 38) . . . .

☐ November 1937 ("Utopia '37" by Howard Brubaker) . . . .

	Current Price Range		C/Y Avg.
November 1935	25.00	30.00	27.50
August 1936	22.50	27.50	25.00
October 1937	20.00	25.00	22.50
November 1937	20.00	25.00	22.50

STARTLING DETECTIVE

Issues during the 1930s were filled with great "inside" human interest stories where criminals and their associates told their own stories.

	Current Price Range		C/Y Avg.
☐ December 1931 (Ponzi, Bluebeard Powers)	11.00	13.00	12.00
☐ October 1933 (Hamm kidnapping)	9.00	11.00	10.00
☐ December 1936 (Rattlesnake James)	9.00	11.00	10.00

Stage, October 1937, **$20.00–$25.00.**

	Current Price Range		C/Y Avg.
☐ March 1938 (New York gang wars)	**11.00**	**13.00**	**12.00**
☐ January 1957 (Chester Gillette case) ...	**6.00**	**8.00**	**7.00**
THE STRAND MAGAZINE			
☐ February 1900 (To the Poles by Ice-Breaking Steamer)	**10.00**	**12.00**	**11.00**
STOP			
☐ Summer 1949	**1.75**	**2.25**	**2.00**
SUNSET			
☐ October 1905 (Where Nature Stores Her Jewels—A Study of San Diego, California)	**14.00**	**16.00**	**15.00**
TAB			
☐ April 1952	**1.75**	**2.25**	**2.00**
☐ November 1952	**1.75**	**2.25**	**2.00**
☐ May 1953	**1.75**	**2.25**	**2.00**

Sunset, October 1905, $14.00–$16.00.

	Current Price Range		C/Y Avg.
☐ July 1953	1.75	2.25	2.00
☐ May 1954	1.75	2.25	2.00
☐ February 1962	1.75	2.25	2.00
☐ August 1966 (Sophia Loren topless) ...	4.00	6.00	5.00

TECHNICAL WORLD MAGAZINE

☐ May 1908 (The Romance of Transmission; Frog Farming; Boat To Beat the Lusitania)	11.00	13.00	12.00

TELL

☐ October 1953 (first issue)	3.50	4.50	4.00
☐ November 1954	1.75	2.25	2.00

TEMPO

☐ June 8, 1953 (first issue)	7.00	9.00	8.00
☐ June 29, 1953	1.75	2.25	2.00
☐ July 6, 1953	1.75	2.25	2.00
☐ August 7, 1956	1.75	2.25	2.00

	Current Price Range		C/Y Avg.

THE THEATRE
☐ March 1910 (Miss Julie Opp on cover)   27.50   32.50   30.00
☐ October 1913 (Miss Valli Valli on cover)   25.00   30.00   27.50
☐ February 1914 (Miss Alexandra Carlisle
   on cover) 25.00   30.00   27.50

THEATRE MAGAZINE
☐ September 1925 (A Ziegfield Beauty on
   cover) 30.00   35.00   32.50
☐ October 1926 (photo of Miss Helen
   Gahagan on cover) 20.00   25.00   22.50

THIS WAS HOLLYWOOD
☐ 1955 (annual publication—John Gilbert
   and Greta Garbo on cover, articles on
   Charles Chaplin and Rudolph Valentino)   25.00   30.00   27.50

Theatre Magazine, September 1925, *$30.00–$35.00.*

	Current Price Range		C/Y Avg.

THREE D MOVIE

☐ 1953 No. 2 (3-D; value stated is for copy with glasses)	45.00	55.00	50.00

TIME

☐ March 28, 1932 (Gabby Street on cover)	8.00	10.00	9.00
☐ October 7, 1935 (Mickey Cochrane on cover)	6.00	8.00	7.00
☐ December 25, 1939 (Vivien Leigh as Scarlet O'Hara on cover, three page article on "Gone With the Wind")	25.00	30.00	27.50
☐ July 2, 1945 (Mel Ott on cover)	4.00	6.00	5.00
☐ August 13, 1956	1.50	2.50	2.00
☐ July 4, 1960	1.50	2.50	2.00
☐ September 14, 1962 (Senator Dirksen)	1.50	2.50	2.00
☐ March 25, 1966	1.00	2.00	1.50

TRUE DETECTIVE

This magazine has maintained the highest standards in terms of writing and content of any of its competition for the last 60 years. Issues published before 1942 averaged more than 120 pages.

☐ December 1924	14.00	16.00	15.00
☐ December 1925 (features installments on Bluebeard Watson)	14.00	16.00	15.00
☐ February 1927 (Gerald Chapman)	14.00	16.00	15.00
☐ March 1928 (Capture of D'Autremont brothers)	14.00	16.00	15.00
☐ July 1929 (Jack the Ripper, Northcott)	17.00	19.00	17.00
☐ December 1929 (I Saw Hickman Hanged, Chapman, G-Man Murdered)	17.00	19.00	18.00
☐ June 1930 (I Saw Dr. Snook Die, Kid McCoy)	14.00	16.00	15.00
☐ November 1939 (Snyder-Gray Murder, Arnold Rothstein)	14.00	16.00	15.00
☐ April 1931 (Lingle Murder Capture, Burns, St. Valentine's Day Massacre)	14.00	16.00	15.00
☐ December 1933 (Pretty Boy Floyd, Kansas City Massacre)	17.00	19.00	18.00
☐ June 1934 (Dillinger Gang Caught; Bonnie & Clyde, Hickman Case; Gerald Chapman's Hanging)	19.00	21.00	20.00

	Current Price Range		C/Y Avg.

☐ December 1934 (Dillinger Story; San Quentin Escape Plot)	17.00	19.00	18.00
☐ January 1935 (Dillinger, Lindberg Kidnapper Captured)	19.00	21.00	20.00
☐ July 1936 (Hauptmann Execution)	14.00	16.00	15.00
☐ September 1938 (Jesse James)	11.00	13.00	12.00
☐ July 1940 (Murder, Inc.)	14.00	16.00	15.00
☐ April 1942 (Willie Bioff; Hitler)	9.00	11.00	10.00
☐ February 1944 (Al Capone Story)	9.00	11.00	10.00
☐ May 1958 (Starkweather; Peter Manuel)	9.00	11.00	10.00
☐ October 1960 (John Dillinger)	9.00	11.00	10.00
☐ August 1961 (Al Capone)	9.00	11.00	10.00

TRUE STORY

☐ January 1938 (Blonde Hussy or Gossip's Martyr?)	12.00	14.00	13.00

TV

☐ May 1954 (Jack Webb, Eve Arden and Julius LaRosa on cover)	10.00	12.00	11.00

TV AND MOVIE SCREEN

☐ May 1954 (Doris Day on cover, articles on Dinah Shore, Lucille Ball, Eddie Fisher, Mark Stevens, Terry Moore, Red Skelton, Elizabeth Taylor, Roy Rogers)	15.00	17.00	16.00

TV WESTERN

☐ March 1958 (James Arness on cover, articles on Will Hutchins, Roy Rogers, Hugh O'Brian, Gene Autry, Michael Ansara, James Garner, Ward Bond, Richard Boone, Cliff Robertson, Clayton Moore)	25.00	30.00	27.50

TV GUIDE

Old *TV Guides* are a shining example—one of many among collectibles—of something published in huge quantities, which nevertheless became scarce and sought-after. *TV Guide* is the most widely-read magazine in America, printed in around 30 million copies per issue. In earlier years, not that many were printed, but its circulation was always among the largest. You'd never guess this by the prices they now fetch on the backdate magazine market, with some special issues going for

$50 and even more. *TV Guides* rank right along with *Playboys* as the most valuable modern magazines—even though *Playboy* was printed in smaller quantities and carried a much higher cover price.

Why they became scarce is obvious. Hardly anybody saved them! Since they consisted mostly of program listings, they were considered useless when the issue expired.

Their high values today are not just the result of scarcity, however. There's growing hobbyist interest in the early years of TV—its development, shows, stars, programming, etc. Vintage *TV Guides* document the history of TV better than any other printed source. There's also plenty of nostalgia wrapped up in them, reading about shows and stars you enjoyed 10, 15, 20 or more years ago.

To some extent, the selling prices depend on who's featured on the cover, as well as articles carried in the issue. Photos and/or articles on the more popular stars result in a higher price. "Popular" in this context relates to popularity among collectors, which can be quite different than overall public popularity.

As a rule, subscription copies are worth slightly less because of the mailing label attached to the front cover. When someone has attempted to remove the mailing label and torn the cover, this means a bigger reduction in price.

TV Guide was originally a regional publication put out in various areas of the country. After Volume 6, #13, March 27–April 2, 1953 edition, *TV Guide* became a national publication with a new numbering system (#1, April 3–9, 1953). The New York editions are considered the most desirable.

	Current Price Range		C/Y Avg.
1950			
☐ August 5–12, 1950, volume 3, #31 (Fred Allen and Jack Haley on cover)	37.00	42.00	39.50
☐ August 12–18, 1950, volume 3, #32 (Grace Kelly on cover)	50.00	60.00	55.00
☐ September 2–8, 1950, volume 3, #35 (Howdy Doody on cover)	60.00	70.00	65.00
☐ September 16–22, 1950, volume 3, #37 (Jimmy Durante, Kate Smith, Groucho Marx, Frank Sinatra, Jack Benny and Fred Allen on cover)	32.00	37.00	34.50
☐ September 30–October 6, 1950, volume 3, #39 (football scene on cover)	30.00	35.00	32.50
☐ October 14–20, 1950, volume 3, #41 (Miss TV of 1950 on cover)	35.00	40.00	37.50

	Current Price Range		C/Y Avg.
☐ November 11–17, 1950, volume 3, #45 (Dean Martin and Jerry Lewis on cover)	35.00	40.00	37.50
☐ November 25–December 1, 1950, volume 3, #47 (Howdy Doody, Rootie Tootie [later to be Rootie Kazootie] on cover)	60.00	70.00	65.00
☐ December 9–15, 1950, volume 3, #49 (Walter Winchell on cover)	30.00	35.00	32.50
☐ December 30, 1950–January 5, 1951, volume 3, #52 (model named Marie Dube on cover)	30.00	35.00	32.50

1951

	Current Price Range		C/Y Avg.
☐ January 20–26, 1951, volume 4, #3 (Sheriff Bob Dixon cover)	22.50	27.50	25.00
☐ January 27–February 2, 1951, volume 4 (Jerry Lester on cover)	15.00	17.00	16.00
☐ February 3–8, 1951, volume 4, #5 (cast of "Leave It To The Girls" on cover) . .	15.00	17.00	16.00
☐ February 17–23, 1951, volume 4, #7 (Lilli Palmer on cover)	20.00	25.00	22.50
☐ March 3–9, 1951, volume 4, #9 (Jack Carter on cover)	25.00	30.00	27.50
☐ March 10–16, 1951, volume 4, #10 (Sid Caesar on cover)	27.50	32.50	30.00
☐ March 24–30, 1951, volume 4, #12 (Arthur Godfrey on cover)	22.50	27.50	25.00
☐ April 14–20, 1951, volume 4, #15 (Joe DiMaggio and eight other famous ball players on cover)	15.00	17.00	16.00
☐ May 12–18, 1951, volume 4, #19 (Perry Como on cover)	22.50	27.50	25.00
☐ May 19–25, 1951, volume 4, #20 (Ken Murray on cover)	25.00	30.00	27.50
☐ May 26–June 1, 1951, volume 4, #21 (Frank Sinatra on cover)	30.00	35.00	32.50
☐ June 9–15, 1951, volume 4, #23 (Groucho Marx on cover)	35.00	40.00	37.50
☐ June 16–22, 1951, volume 4, #24 (Milton Berle on cover)	22.50	27.50	25.00
☐ July 14–20, 1951, volume 4, #28 (unknown infant on cover)	17.50	19.50	18.50

	Current Price Range		C/Y Avg.

☐ July 28–August 3, volume 4, #30 (Buster Crabbe on cover) **30.00** **35.00** **32.50**

☐ August 24–30, 1951, volume 4, #34 (Jerry Lester on cover) **27.50** **32.50** **30.00**

☐ August 31–September 6, 1951, volume 4, #35 (Howdy Doody and other TV kid show characters on cover) **45.00** **50.00** **47.50**

☐ September 21–27, volume 4, #38 (Arthur Godfrey on cover) **20.00** **25.00** **22.50**

☐ October 5–11, 1951, volume 4, #40 (Jimmy Durante on cover) **15.00** **17.00** **16.00**

☐ October 26–November 1, 1951, volume 4, #43 (Bert Parks and Betty Ann Grove on cover) **27.50** **32.50** **30.00**

☐ November 9–15, 1951, volume 4, #45 (Jackie Gleason on cover) **22.50** **27.50** **25.00**

☐ November 30–December 6, 1951, volume 4, #48 (unknown caveman and woman on cover) **10.00** **12.00** **11.00**

☐ December 7–13, 1951, volume 4, #49 (Jerry Lester and Agathon on cover) .. **17.50** **19.50** **18.50**

☐ December 14–20, 1951, volume 4, #50 (Cathy Hild on cover) **15.00** **17.00** **16.00**

1952

☐ January 4–10, 1952, volume 5, #1 (Sid Caesar, Ed Sullivan, Arthur Godfrey, Milton Berle, Perry Como and Grouch Marx on cover) **40.00** **45.00** **42.50**

☐ January 25–31, 1952, volume 5, #4 (Lucille Ball and Desi Arnez on cover) **20.00** **25.00** **22.50**

☐ February 15–21, 1952, volume 5, #7 (Harry Truman, Ike Eisenhower, Estes Kefauver and Robert Taft on cover) ... **20.00** **25.00** **22.50**

☐ March 14–20, 1952, volume 5, #11 (Martin and Lewis on cover) **55.00** **65.00** **60.00**

☐ April 18–24, 1952, volume 5, #16 (Jimmy Durante on cover) **17.50** **19.50** **18.50**

☐ May 16–22, 1952, volume 5, #20 (Gene Autry on cover) **40.00** **45.00** **42.50**

	Current Price Range		C/Y Avg.

☐ June 20–26, 1952, volume 5, #25 (Pictures of previous *TV Guide* covers on cover) **25.00 30.00 27.50**

☐ June 27–July 3, 1952, volume 5, #26 (Paul Winchell and Jerry Mahoney on cover) **15.00 17.00 16.00**

☐ July 4–10, 1952, volume 5, #27 (Bob Hope on cover) **15.00 17.00 16.00**

☐ July 25–31, 1952, volume 5, #30 (Sandra Spence of "Phantomime Quiz" on cover) **35.00 40.00 37.50**

☐ August 1–7, 1952, volume 5, #31 (Don Russell and Lee Joyce of "Cavalcade of Stars" on cover) **10.00 12.00 11.00**

☐ August 15–21, 1952, volume 5, #33 (cast of "What's My Line" on cover) **14.00 16.00 15.00**

☐ August 22–28, 1952, volume 5, #34 (Perry Como and Dinah Shore on cover) **22.50 27.50 25.00**

☐ September 12–18, 1952, volume 5, #37 (Milton Berle and Lucille Ball on cover) **17.50 19.50 18.50**

☐ October 3–9, 1952, volume 5, #40 (Marie Wilson on cover) **15.00 17.00 16.00**

☐ October 10–16, 1952, volume 5, #41 (L'il Abner characters and Al Capp on cover) **50.00 60.00 55.00**

☐ October 17–23, 1952, volume 5, #42 (Arthur Godfrey on cover) **27.50 32.50 30.00**

☐ November 21–27, 1952, #47 (Howdy Doody and Rootie Kazootie on cover) **27.50 32.50 30.00**

☐ November 28–December 4, 1952, volume 5, #48 (Eddie Fisher, Perry Como, Julius LaRosa and Patti Page on cover) **22.50 27.50 25.00**

☐ December 12–18, 1952, volume 5, #50 (Arthur Godfrey and Haleloke on cover) **25.00 30.00 27.50**

☐ December 26, 1952–January 1, 1953, volume 5, #52 (Jack Russell, Judy Johnson, Bill Hayes and Marguerite Piazza on cover) **10.00 12.00 11.00**

1953

☐ January 2–8, 1953, volume 6, #1 (Jackie Gleason on cover) **35.00 40.00 37.50**

	Current Price Range		C/Y Avg.

☐ January 23–29, 1953, volume 6, #4 (Marilyn Monroe on cover) **35.00 40.00 37.50**

☐ February 6–12, 1953, volume 6, #6 (Roxanne on cover) **20.00 25.00 22.50**

☐ February 13–19, 1953, volume 6, #7 (Kukla, Fran and Ollie on cover) **25.00 30.00 27.50**

☐ March 6–12, 1953, volume 6, #10 (Jimmy Durante on cover) **25.00 30.00 27.50**

☐ March 13–19, 1953, volume 6, #11 (Janette Davis on cover) **15.00 17.00 16.00**

☐ March 20–26, 1953, volume 6, #12 (Lucy's neighbors, the Mertz's, on cover) **17.50 19.50 18.50**

☐ March 27–April 2, 1953, volume 6, #13 (Charlton Heston, John Newland, John Forsythe and John Baragrey on cover) **25.00 30.00 27.50** (This is the last regional edition of *TV Guide.* The next issue was for nationwide distribution and the numbering system was started again from #1.)

☐ April 3–9, 1953, issue #1 (photo of Lucille Ball's baby on cover with small photo of Lucy in upper right corner, headline "Lucy's $50,000,000 Baby." This referred to the fact that many episodes of "I Love Lucy" in late 1952 and early 1953 were built around Lucy's pregnancy, and the fact that the baby, "Little Ricky", became an instant TV star. Though the issue is labeled #1, it was actually not the first issue of *TV Guide,* as regional issues had been published previously; it was the first coast-to-coast issue, and the first with a glossy cover.) **145.00 170.00 147.50**

☐ April 10–16, 1953, issue #2 (Jack Webb on cover) **50.00 60.00 55.00**

☐ April 17–23, 1953, issue #3 (caricatures of Lucille Ball, Arthur Godfrey, Milton Berle, Sid Caesar and Imogene Coca on cover) **20.00 25.00 22.50**

☐ April 24–30, 1953, issue #4 (Ralph Edwards on cover) **22.50 27.50 25.00**

	Current Price Range		C/Y Avg.

☐ May 1–7, 1953, issue #5 (Eve Arden on cover) **36.00 41.00 38.50**

☐ May 8–14, 1953, issue #6 (Arthur Godfrey on cover) **25.00 30.00 27.00**

☐ May 22–28, 1953, issue #8 (Red Buttons on cover) **20.00 25.00 22.50**

☐ June 12–18, 1953, issue #11 (Eddie Fisher on cover) **15.00 17.00 16.00**

☐ June 19–25, 1953, issue #12 (Ed Sullivan on cover)....................... **10.00 12.00 11.00**

☐ July 3–9, 1953, issue #14 (Perry Como on cover) **8.00 10.00 9.00**

☐ July 17–23, 1953, issue #16 (Lucille Ball and Desi Arnez on cover) **25.00 30.00 27.50**

☐ July 24–30, 1953, issue #17 (caricature of Groucho Marx on cover) **25.00 30.00 27.50**

☐ August 14–20, 1953, issue #20 (Patti Page on cover) **15.00 17.00 16.00**

☐ August 21–27, 1953, issue #21 (Mary Hartline and Claude Kirchner of "Super Circus" on cover) **25.00 30.00 27.50**

☐ August 28–September 3, 1953, issue #22 (Jane and Audrey Meadows on cover) **12.50 14.50 13.50**

☐ October 2–8, 1953, issue #27 (Red Skelton on cover) **17.00 19.00 18.00**

☐ October 16–22, 1953, issue #29 (TV beauty contestants on cover) **10.00 12.00 11.00**

☐ October 23–29, 1953, issue #30 (Arthur Godfrey on cover) **14.00 16.00 15.00**

☐ October 30–November 5, 1953, issue #31 (Beulah Witch, Kukla and Ollie on cover) **15.00 17.00 16.00**

☐ November 6–12, 1953, issue #32 (Warren Hull on cover) **15.00 17.00 16.00**

☐ November 20–26, 1953, issue #34 (Dorothy McGuire and Julius LaRosa on cover) **25.00 30.00 27.50**

☐ November 27–December 3, 1953, issue #35 (Lugene Sanders on cover) **10.00 12.00 11.00**

☐ December 4–10, 1953, issue #36 (Loretta Young on cover) **10.00 12.00 11.00**

	Current Price Range		C/Y Avg.

☐ December 25–31, 1953, issue #39 (Perry Como, Patti Page and Eddie Fisher on cover) **10.00** **12.00** **11.00**

1954

☐ March 19–25, 1954, issue #51 (Groucho Marx on cover) **36.00** **41.00** **38.50**

☐ May 14–20, 1954, issue #59 (Frank Sinatra on cover with headline, "Can Frank Sinatra Make Good in TV?") **32.00** **37.00** **34.50**

☐ June 25–July 1, 1954, issue #65 (Howdy Doody and Bob Smith on cover) **45.00** **50.00** **47.50**

☐ August 14–20, 1954, issue #72 (Martin and Lewis on cover) **22.50** **27.50** **25.00**

☐ October 23–29, 1954, issue #82 (Walt Disney, Mickey Mouse, Donald Duck, Pluto, Goofy and Dopey on cover) **35.00** **40.00** **37.50**

☐ December 24–31, 1954, issue #91 (Nelson family on cover, before Ricky Nelson launched pop music career) **45.00** **50.00** **47.50**

1955

☐ January 15–21, 1955, issue #94 (Gary Moore on cover, and an article on Johnny Carson) **16.00** **18.00** **17.00**

☐ March 5–11, 1955, issue #101 (Liberace on cover; he was doing a daily late-afternoon show) **15.00** **17.00** **16.00**

☐ October 22–28, 1955, issue #134 (George Gobel on cover) **9.00** **11.00** **10.00**

☐ December 17–23, 1955, issue #142 (Robert Montgomery on cover) **14.00** **16.00** **15.00**

1956

☐ January 21–27, 1956, issue #147 (Lawrence Welk on cover) **7.00** **9.00** **8.00**

☐ April 14–20, 1956, issue #159 (Grace Kelly wedding issue) **22.00** **27.00** **24.50**

☐ April 28–May 4, 1956, issue #161 (Red Skelton on cover) **5.00** **7.00** **6.00**

	Current Price Range		C/Y Avg.

☐ August 11–17, 1956, issue #176, Democratic National Convention issue (Adlai Stevenson was to oppose President Eisenhower) **7.00 9.00 8.00**

☐ September 8–14, 1956 issue #180 (Elvis Presley on cover, first *TV Guide* cover of Elvis; he had just hit the big time via appearances on the Jackie Gleason show) **80.00 90.00 85.00**

☐ December 1–7, 1956, issue #192 (caricature of George Burns on cover) **22.00 27.00 24.50**

1957

☐ January 19–25, 1957, issue #199 (Jerry Lewis on cover) **9.00 11.00 10.00**

☐ February 23–March 1, 1957, issue #204 (Charles van Doren on cover; he was a national sensation after winning a fortune on Jack Barry's "21" quiz program) ... **9.00 11.00 10.00**

☐ May 11–17, 1957, issue #215 (James Arness on cover, article on Rod Serling of "Twilight Zone") **32.00 37.00 34.50**

☐ August 31–September 6, 1957, issue #231 (Clint Walker on cover) **32.00 37.00 34.50**

☐ November 23–29, 1957, issue #243 (Mary Martin on cover, Larry Hagman's mother) **7.00 9.00 8.00**

1958

☐ February 8–14, 1958, issue #254 (Tab Hunter on cover) **14.00 16.00 15.00**

☐ April 5–11, 1958, issue #262 (Gale Storm on cover) **8.00 10.00 9.00**

☐ April 19–25, 1958, issue #264 (Polly Bergen on cover) **11.00 12.00 10.00**

☐ October 4–10, 1958, issue #288 (Dick Clark on cover) **22.00 27.00 24.50**

☐ November 8–14, 1958, issue #293 (Loretta Young on cover) **7.00 9.00 8.00**

☐ November 22–28, 1958, issue #295 (Ronald Reagan on cover; he was host of a show called "Death Valley Days") **60.00 70.00 65.00**

	Current Price Range		C/Y Avg.

1959

☐ January 10–16, 1959, issue #302 (Milton Berle on cover) **14.00 16.00 15.00**

☐ February 7–13, 1959, issue #306 (Chuck Conners on cover) **27.00 32.00 29.50**

☐ March 21–27, 1959, issue #312 (Ann Southern on cover) **17.00 19.00 18.00**

☐ June 27–July 3, 1959, issue #326 (Lloyd Bridges on cover, with article on the death of George Reeves who had played "Superman" on TV) **32.00 37.00 34.50**

☐ November 7–13, 1959, issue #345 (Jack Benny on cover) **10.00 12.00 11.00**

☐ December 12–18, 1959, issue #350 (Danny Thomas on cover) **7.00 9.00 8.00**

1960

☐ January 9–15, 1960, issue #354 (Jane Wyatt on cover) **17.00 19.00 18.00**

☐ February 27–March 4, 1960, issue #361 (Robert Stack on cover) **14.00 16.00 15.00**

☐ May 7–13, 1960, issue #371 (Elvis Presley on cover) **40.00 50.00 45.00**

☐ June 11–17, 1960, issue #376 (cast of "Bachelor Father" on cover) **14.00 16.00 15.00**

☐ August 13–19, 1960, issue #385 (Nick Adams on cover) **14.00 16.00 15.00**

☐ October 15–21, 1960, issue #394 (Carol Burnett on cover) **17.00 19.00 18.00**

1961

☐ January 28–February 3, 1961, issue #409 (Ron Howard on cover as young boy—pre-"Happy Days") **17.00 19.00 18.00**

☐ May 27–June 3, 1961, issue #426 (Ronald Reagan on cover) **27.00 32.00 29.50**

☐ July 1–7, 1961, issue #431 (The Flintstones on cover) **22.00 27.00 24.50**

☐ October 7–13, 1961, issue #445 (Walter Cronkite on cover) **7.00 9.00 8.00**

☐ December 16–22, 1961, issue #455, (Richard Chamberlain on cover) **6.00 8.00 7.00**

	Current Price Range		C/Y Avg.

1962

☐ January 6–12, 1962, issue #458 (Vince Edwards on cover) **6.00** **8.00** **7.00**

☐ March 10–16, 1962, issue #467 (Jack Paar on cover; he hosted "The Tonight Show" before Johnny Carson) **6.00** **8.00** **7.00**

☐ April 21–27, 1962, issue #473 (Connie Stevens on cover) **6.00** **8.00** **7.00**

☐ November 10–16, 1962, issue #502 (Beverly Hillbillies on cover) **7.00** **9.00** **8.00**

1963

☐ January 12–18, 1963, issue #511 (Arnold Palmer on cover) **6.00** **8.00** **7.00**

☐ February 9–15, 1963, issue #515 (Ernest Borgnine on cover) **6.00** **8.00** **7.00**

☐ February 16–22, 1963, issue #516 (Princess Grace of Monaco on cover) **10.00** **12.00** **11.00**

☐ June 8–14, 1963, issue #532 (Johnny Carson on cover) **9.00** **11.00** **10.00**

☐ October 5–11, 1963, issue #549 (Phil Silvers on cover) **6.00** **8.00** **7.00**

☐ October 19–25, 1963, issue #551 (Judy Garland on cover) **9.00** **11.00** **10.00**

☐ November 30–December 6, 1963, issue #557 (George C. Scott on cover) **6.00** **8.00** **7.00**

1964

☐ February 1–7, 1964, issue #566 (Danny Kaye on cover) **6.00** **8.00** **7.00**

☐ April 18–24, 1964, issue #577 (James Franciscus on cover, coverage of Beatles on "Ed Sullivan Show") **10.00** **12.00** **11.00**

☐ September 5–11, 1964, issue #597 (Lucille Ball on cover) **8.00** **10.00** **9.00**

☐ October 17–23, 1964, issue #603 (Lassie on cover) **5.00** **7.00** **6.00**

☐ December 12–18, 1964, issue #611 (Julie Newmar on cover) **5.00** **7.00** **6.00**

1965

☐ January 2–8, 1965, issue #614 (The Munsters on cover) **7.00** **9.00** **8.00**

	Current Price Range		C/Y Avg.

☐ March 6–12, 1965, issue #623 (David Janssen on cover) **5.00**   **7.00**   **6.00**

☐ September 11–17, 1965, issue #650, Fall Preview issue (these are always a premium item for collectors) **20.00**   **25.00**   **22.50**

☐ October 16–22, 1965, issue #655 (Red Skelton on cover) **5.00**   **7.00**   **6.00**

☐ November 13–19, 1965, issue #659 (Joey Heatherton on cover) **5.00**   **7.00**   **6.00**

☐ December 11–17, 1965, issue #663 (F Troop on cover) **5.00**   **7.00**   **6.00**

1966

☐ January 1–7, 1966, issue #666 (Carol Channing on cover) **5.00**   **7.00**   **6.00**

☐ January 15–21, 1966, issue #668 (Bill Cosby on cover, article on Ronald Reagan) **15.00**   **17.00**   **16.00**

☐ February 5–11, 1966, issue #671 (Larry Hagman on cover; he was starring in "I Dream of Jeannie") **8.00**   **10.00**   **9.00**

☐ March 26–April 1, 1966, issue #678 (Adam West ["Batman"] on cover) **10.00**   **12.00**   **11.00**

☐ May 7–13, 1966, issue #684 (Lyndon Johnson on cover) **9.00**   **11.00**   **10.00**

☐ May 14–20, 1966, issue #685 (Frank Sinatra on cover) **5.00**   **7.00**   **6.00**

☐ September 10–16, 1966, issue #702 (Fall Preview issue) **18.00**   **20.00**   **19.00**

☐ October 29–November 4, 1966, issue #709 (Bruce Lee on cover) **10.00**   **12.00**   **11.00**

1967

☐ January 21–27, 1967, issue #721 (Diana Rigg on cover) **8.00**   **10.00**   **9.00**

☐ March 4–10, 1967, issue #727 (Leonard Nimoy and William Shatner on cover; this issue ranks as a "Star Trek" collector's item) **25.00**   **30.00**   **27.50**

☐ May 13–19, 1967, issue #737 (Elizabeth Montgomery on cover) **5.00**   **7.00**   **6.00**

☐ August 12–18, 1967, issue #750 (Mike Douglas on cover) **5.00**   **7.00**   **6.00**

	Current Price Range		C/Y Avg.

☐ November 18–24, 1967, issue #764 (Leonard Nimoy and William Shatner on cover; this issue ranks as a "Star Trek" collector's item) **25.00 30.00 27.50**

1968

☐ January 6–12, 1968, issue #771 (Robert Conrad on cover) **4.00 6.00 5.00**

☐ June 29–July 5, 1968, issue #796 (Robert Wagner on cover) **4.00 6.00 5.00**

☐ August 31–September 6, 1968, issue #805 (caricature of Johnny Carson on cover) **6.00 8.00 7.00**

☐ October 19–25, 1968, issue #812 (Jim Nabors on cover) **4.00 6.00 5.00**

☐ November 30–December 6, 1968, issue #818 (Ann-Margaret on cover) **4.00 6.00 5.00**

1969

☐ April 5–11, 1969, issue #836 (Smothers Brothers on cover) **5.00 7.00 6.00**

☐ June 14–20, 1969, issue #846 (Glen Campbell on cover) **4.00 6.00 5.00**

☐ December 6–12, 1969, issue #871 (Doris Day on cover) **4.00 6.00 5.00**

1970

☐ January 3–9, 1970, issue #875 ("WELCOME TO THE SEVENTIES") **4.00 6.00 5.00**

☐ January 10–16, 1970, issue #876 (Fred MacMurray and Beverly Garland on cover, article on Henry Fonda) **3.00 5.00 4.00**

☐ January 17–23, 1970, issue #877 (Raymond Burr on cover) **3.00 5.00 4.00**

☐ January 24–30, 1970, issue #878 (Tom Jones on cover, article on Bette Davis) **3.00 5.00 4.00**

☐ January 31–February 6, 1970, issue #879 (Debbie Reynolds on cover) **3.00 5.00 4.00**

☐ February 7–13, 1970, issue #880 (Elizabeth Montgomery on cover) **3.00 5.00 4.00**

☐ February 14–20, 1970, issue #881 (Bracken's Girls on cover) **3.00 5.00 4.00**

	Current Price Range		C/Y Avg.

☐ February 21–27, 1970, issue #882 (cast of "Medical Center" on cover) **3.00 5.00 4.00**

☐ February 28–March 6, 1970, issue #883 (cast of "Mod Squad" on cover) **4.00 6.00 5.00**

☐ March 7–13, 1970, issue #884 (cast of "HeeHaw" on cover) **3.00 5.00 4.00**

☐ March 14–20, 1970, issue #885 (Diahann Carroll on cover) **3.00 5.00 4.00**

☐ March 21–27, 1970, issue #886 (Jackie Gleason on cover) **3.00 5.00 4.00**

☐ March 28–April 3, 1970, issue #887 (Rowan and Martin on cover) **4.00 6.00 5.00**

☐ April 4–10, 1970, issue #888 (cast of "Brady Bunch" on cover) **3.00 5.00 4.00**

☐ April 11–17, 1970, issue #889 (Carol Burnett on cover) **3.00 5.00 4.00**

☐ April 18–24, 1970, issue #890 (The Bold Ones on cover) **3.00 5.00 4.00**

☐ April 25–May 1, 1970, issue #891 (Raquel Welch and John Wayne on cover, article on Leonard Nimoy of "Star Trek") **8.00 10.00 9.00**

☐ May 2–8, 1970, issue #892 (Glen Campbell on cover) **3.00 5.00 4.00**

☐ May 9–15, 1970, issue #893 (David Frost on cover) **3.00 5.00 4.00**

☐ May 16–22, 1970, issue #894 (Rockwell portrait of Spiro Agnew on cover) **15.00 17.00 16.00**

☐ May 23–29, 1970, issue #895 (Tricia Nixon on cover) **4.00 6.00 5.00**

☐ May 30–June 5, 1970, issue #896 (Julie Sommars on cover) **3.00 5.00 4.00**

☐ June 6–12, 1970, issue #897 (Robert Young on cover) **3.00 5.00 4.00**

☐ June 13–19, 1970, issue #898 (Johnny Cash on cover) **3.00 5.00 4.00**

☐ June 20–26, 1970, issue #899 (To Rome with Love on cover) **3.00 5.00 4.00**

☐ June 27–July 3, 1970, issue #900 (Liza Minnelli on cover) **4.00 6.00 5.00**

☐ July 4–10, 1970, issue #901 (cast of "Eddie's Father" on cover) **3.00 5.00 4.00**

	Current Price Range		C/Y Avg.
☐ July 11–17, 1970, issue #902 (The Beverly Hillbillies on cover)	5.00	7.00	6.00
☐ July 18–24, 1970, issue #903 (Golddiggers on cover)	3.00	5.00	4.00
☐ July 25–31, 1970, issue #904 (Mayberry RFD on cover)	4.00	6.00	5.00
☐ August 1–7, 1970, issue #905 (Chet Huntley on cover)	3.00	5.00	4.00
☐ August 8–14, 1970, issue #906 (Ted Bessell on cover)	3.00	5.00	4.00
☐ August 15–21, 1970, issue #907 (Norman Rockwell portrait of Johnny Carson on cover)	15.00	17.00	16.00
☐ August 22–28, 1970, issue #908 ("Gunsmoke" cast on cover)	5.00	7.00	6.00
☐ August 29–September 4, 1970, issue #909 (Eddie Albert on cover)	3.00	5.00	4.00
☐ September 5–11, 1970, issue #910 (Elizabeth Taylor and Richard Burton on cover)	5.00	7.00	6.00
☐ September 12–18, 1970, issue #911 (Fall Preview)	15.00	17.00	16.00
☐ September 19–25, 1970, issue #912 (Mary Tyler Moore on cover)	5.00	7.00	6.00
☐ September 26–October 2, 1970, issue #913 (Room 222 on cover)	3.00	5.00	4.00
☐ October 3–9, 1970, issue #914 (Red Skelton on cover)	3.00	5.00	4.00
☐ October 10–16, 1970, issue #915 (Hershall Bernardi on cover)	3.00	5.00	4.00
☐ October 17–23, 1970, issue #916 (The Partridge Family on cover)	3.00	5.00	4.00
☐ October 24–30, 1970, issue #917 (Don Knotts on cover)	3.00	5.00	4.00
☐ October 31–November 6, 1970, issue #918 (Mike Conners on cover)	3.00	5.00	4.00
☐ November 7–13, 1970, issue #919 (cast of "Nancy" on cover)	3.00	5.00	4.00
☐ November 14–20, 1970, issue #920 (Christopher George on cover)	3.00	5.00	4.00

	Current Price Range		C/Y Avg.

☐ November 21–27, 1970, issue #921 (Sally Marr on cover; probably least known person ever on a *TV Guide* cover, still this issue brings a slight premium) — **3.00 5.00 4.00**

☐ November 28–December 4, 1970, issue #922 (John Wayne on cover) .... — **5.00 7.00 6.00**

☐ December 5–11, 1970, issue #923 (Dick Cavett on cover) .... — **3.00 5.00 4.00**

☐ December 12–18, 1970, issue #924 (Ed Sullivan on cover) .... — **4.00 6.00 5.00**

☐ December 19–25, 1970, issue #925 (Christmas issue) .... — **3.00 5.00 4.00**

☐ December 26–January 1, 1971, issue #926 (cast of "Julia" on cover) .... — **3.00 5.00 4.00**

1971

☐ January 2–8, 1971, issue #927 (review of 1970) .... — **3.00 5.00 4.00**

☐ January 9–15, 1971, issue #928 (Andy Griffith on cover) .... — **4.00 6.00 5.00**

☐ January 16–22, 1971, issue #929 (Johnny Cash and June Carter on cover) — **4.00 6.00 5.00**

☐ January 23–29, 1971, issue #970 (Flip Wilson on cover) .... — **3.00 5.00 4.00**

☐ January 30–February 5, 1970, issue #931 (James Arness on cover) .... — **4.00 6.00 5.00**

☐ February 6–12, 1971, issue #932 (Jack Klugman on cover) .... — **3.00 5.00 4.00**

☐ February 13–19, 1971, issue #933 (Goldie Hawn on cover) .... — **4.00 6.00 5.00**

☐ February 20–26, 1971, issue #934 (Doris Day on cover) .... — **3.00 5.00 4.00**

☐ February 27–March 5, 1971, issue #935 (Hal Holbrook on cover) .... — **3.00 5.00 4.00**

☐ March 6–12, 1971, issue #936 (Broderick Crawford on cover) .... — **3.00 5.00 4.00**

☐ March 13–19, 1971, issue #937 (Robert Stack on cover) .... — **3.00 5.00 4.00**

☐ March 20–26, 1971, issue #938 (Harry Reasoner on cover) .... — **3.00 5.00 4.00**

☐ March 27–April 2, 1971, issue #939 (cast of "Bonanza" on cover) .... — **5.00 7.00 6.00**

	Current Price Range		C/Y Avg.
☐ April 3–9, 1971, issue #940 (Cable TV issue)	3.00	5.00	4.00
☐ April 10–16, 1971, issue #941 (Bob Hope on cover)	4.00	6.00	5.00
☐ April 17–23, 1971, issue #942 (Paul Newman on cover)	5.00	7.00	6.00
☐ April 24–30, 1971, issue #943 (Marcus Welby on cover)	3.00	5.00	4.00
☐ May 1–7, 1971, issue #944 (Mary Tyler Moore on cover)	4.00	6.00	5.00
☐ May 8–14, 1971, issue #945 (Henry Fonda on cover)	4.00	6.00	5.00
☐ May 15–21, 1971, issue #946 (Report on TV journalism)	3.00	5.00	4.00
☐ May 22–28, 1971, issue #947 (David Cassidy on cover)	3.00	5.00	4.00
☐ May 29–June 4, 1971, issue #948 (All in the Family on cover)	6.00	8.00	7.00
☐ June 5–11, 1971, issue #949 (Rowan and Martin on cover)	4.00	6.00	5.00
☐ June 12–18, 1971, issue #950 (Lucille Ball on cover)	4.00	6.00	5.00
☐ June 19–25, 1971, issue #951 (cast of "Eddie's Father" on cover)	3.00	5.00	4.00
☐ June 26–July 2, 1971, issue #952 (Adam-12 on cover)	3.00	5.00	4.00
☐ July 3–9, 1971, issue #953 (Mod Squad on cover)	4.00	6.00	5.00
☐ July 10–16, 1971, issue #954 (Kermit the Frog on cover)	5.00	7.00	6.00
☐ July 17–23, 1971, issue #955 (Chad Everett on cover)	3.00	5.00	4.00
☐ July 24–30, 1971, issue #956 (Lefty of Ding-a-Ling Lynx on cover)	3.00	5.00	4.00
☐ July 31–August 6, 1971, issue #957 (Henry VIII's Six Wives)	3.00	5.00	4.00
☐ August 7–13, 1971, issue #958 (As the World Turns on cover)	3.00	5.00	4.00
☐ August 14–20, 1971, issue #959 (Bonanza on cover)	4.00	6.00	5.00
☐ August 21–27, 1971, issue #960 (Henry Fonda on cover)	4.00	6.00	5.00

	Current Price Range		C/Y Avg.

☐ August 28–September 3, 1971, issue #961 (Howard Cosell, Don Meredith and Frank Gifford on cover) **3.00 5.00 4.00**

☐ September 4–10, 1971, issue #962 (Jack Lord on cover) **3.00 5.00 4.00**

☐ September 11–17, 1971, issue #963 (Fall Preview) **13.00 15.00 14.00**

☐ September 18–24, 1971, issue #964 (Sandy Duncan on cover) **3.00 5.00 4.00**

☐ September 25–October 1, 1971, issue #965 (Shirley MacLaine on cover) **4.00 6.00 5.00**

☐ October 2–8, 1971, issue #966 (James Stewart on cover) **4.00 6.00 5.00**

☐ October 9–15, 1971, issue #967 (Dick Van Dyke on cover) **3.00 5.00 4.00**

☐ October 16–22, 1971, issue #968 (Mia Farrow on cover) **3.00 5.00 4.00**

☐ October 23–29, 1971, issue #969 (James Franciscus on cover) **3.00 5.00 4.00**

☐ October 30–November 5, 1971, issue #970 (Larry Hagman on cover [this was after "Jeannie" and before "Dallas"—he was starring in "The Good Life"]) **3.00 5.00 4.00**

☐ November 6–12, 1971, issue #971 (William Conrad on cover) **3.00 5.00 4.00**

☐ November 13–19, 1971, issue #972 (The Partners on cover, article on Ann-Margaret) **3.00 5.00 4.00**

☐ November 27–December 3, 1971, issue #974 (Joanne Woodward on cover) ... **3.00 5.00 4.00**

☐ December 4–10, 1971, issue #975 (Bob Hope, John Wayne and others on cover) **5.00 7.00 6.00**

☐ December 11–17, 1971, issue #976 (James Garner on cover) **3.00 5.00 4.00**

☐ December 18–24, 1971, issue #977 (The Partridge Family on cover) **3.00 5.00 4.00**

☐ December 25–31, 1971, issue #978 (Christmas issue) **3.00 5.00 4.00**

1972

☐ January 1–7, 1972, issue #979 (review of 1971) **3.00 5.00 4.00**

	Current Price Range		C/Y Avg.

☐ January 8–14, 1972, issue #980 (Flip Wilson on cover) 3.00 5.00 4.00

☐ January 15–21, 1972, issue #981 (America out of Focus on cover) 3.00 5.00 4.00

☐ January 22–28, 1972, issue #982 (Mission Impossible on cover) 8.00 10.00 9.00

☐ January 29–February 4, 1972, issue #983 (David Janssen on cover) 3.00 5.00 4.00

☐ February 5–11, 1972, issue #984 (Raymond Burr on cover) 3.00 5.00 4.00

☐ February 12–18, 1972, issue #985 (Arthur Hill on cover, article on Sonny and Cher) 3.00 5.00 4.00

☐ February 19–25, 1972, issue #986 (Richard Nixon on cover) 6.00 8.00 7.00

☐ February 26–March 3, 1972, issue #987 (Mary Tyler Moore on cover) 4.00 6.00 5.00

☐ March 4–10, 1972, issue #988 (Johnny Carson on cover) 4.00 6.00 5.00

☐ March 11–17, 1972, issue #989 (Marcus Welby on cover) 3.00 5.00 4.00

☐ March 18–24, 1972, issue #990 (Sonny and Cher on cover)................. 3.00 5.00 4.00

☐ March 25–31, 1972, issue #991 (Peter Falk on cover) 3.00 5.00 4.00

☐ April 1–7, 1972, issue #992 (Glenn Ford on cover) 3.00 5.00 4.00

☐ April 8–14, 1972, issue #993 (political coverage by TV) 3.00 5.00 4.00

☐ April 15–21, 1972, issue #994 (astronauts on cover) 5.00 7.00 6.00

☐ April 22–28, 1972, issue #995 (Don Rickles on cover) 3.00 5.00 4.00

(NOTE: Following this issue, a new numbering system was adopted which made the next issue #496. Since there had already been an issue #496—in 1962—this is confusing unless you check the date. In September, 1973, the old numbering system was reinstated.)

	Current Price Range		C/Y Avg.
☐ April 29–May 5, 1972, issue #496 (Mc-Millan and Wife on cover)	8.00	10.00	9.00
☐ May 6–12, 1972, issue #497 (Sandy Duncan on cover)	3.00	5.00	4.00
☐ May 13–19, 1972, issue #498 (Redd Foxx on cover)	3.00	5.00	4.00
☐ May 20–26, 1972, issue #499 (Efrem Zimbalist, Jr. on cover)	3.00	5.00	4.00
☐ May 27–June 2, 1972, issue #500 (All in the Family on cover)	6.00	8.00	7.00
☐ June 3–9, 1972, issue #501 (Rod Sterling on cover)	3.00	5.00	4.00
☐ June 10–16, 1972, issue #502 (Doris Day on cover)	3.00	5.00	4.00
☐ June 17–23, 1972, issue #503 (Julie London on cover)	3.00	5.00	4.00
☐ June 24–30, 1972, issue #504 (Mike Conners on cover)	3.00	5.00	4.00
☐ July 1–7, 1972, issue #505 (Carol Burnett on cover)	3.00	5.00	4.00
☐ July 8–14, 1972, issue #506 (Merv Griffin on cover)	3.00	5.00	4.00
☐ July 15–21, 1972, issue #507 (David Cassidy on cover)	3.00	5.00	4.00
☐ July 22–28, 1972, issue #508 (Adam 12 on cover)	3.00	5.00	4.00
☐ July 29–August 4, 1972, issue #509 (Love American Style on cover)	3.00	5.00	4.00
☐ August 5–11, 1972, issue #510 (War and Peace on cover)	3.00	5.00	4.00
☐ August 12–18, 1972, issue #511 (Leonardo DaVinci on cover)	3.00	5.00	4.00
☐ August 19–25, 1972, issue #512 (Chad Everett on cover)	3.00	5.00	4.00
☐ August 26–September 1, 1972, issue #513 (Olympic games on cover)	6.00	8.00	7.00
☐ September 2–8, 1972, issue #514 (Jack Klugman and Tony Randall on cover) ..	3.00	5.00	4.00
☐ September 9–15, 1972, issue #515 (Fall Preview)	11.00	13.00	12.00
☐ September 16–22, 1972, issue #516 (Anna and the King on cover)	3.00	5.00	4.00

	Current Price Range		C/Y Avg.
☐ September 23–29, 1972, issue #517 (George Peppard on cover)	3.00	5.00	4.00
☐ September 30–October 6, 1972, issue #518 (Bridget Loves Bernie on cover)	3.00	5.00	4.00
☐ October 7–13, 1972, issue #519 (Bonanza on cover, article on Groucho Marx)	4.00	6.00	5.00
☐ October 14–20, 1972, issue #520 (Robert Conrad on cover)	3.00	5.00	4.00
☐ October 21–27, 1972, issue #521 (Carroll O'Connor and Cloris Leachman on cover)	3.00	5.00	4.00
☐ October 28–November 3, 1972, issue #522 (Charlie Brown on cover)	5.00	7.00	6.00
☐ November 4–10, 1972, issue #523 (John Wayne on cover—"He learned to love TV")	5.00	7.00	6.00
☐ November 11–17, 1972, issue #524 (Alistair Cooke on cover)	3.00	5.00	4.00
☐ November 18–24, 1972, issue #525 (Bea Arthur on cover)	3.00	5.00	4.00
☐ November 25–December 1, 1972, issue #526 (cast of "Search" on cover)	3.00	5.00	4.00
☐ December 2–8, 1972, issue #527 (Mike Douglas on cover)	3.00	5.00	4.00
☐ December 9–15, 1972, issue #528 (Julie Andrews)	3.00	5.00	4.00
☐ December 16–22, 1972, issue #529 (Duke and Duchess of Windsor)	3.00	5.00	4.00
☐ December 23–29, 1972, issue #530 (Christmas issue)	3.00	5.00	4.00
☐ December 30–January 5, 1973, issue #531 (Barbara Walters on cover)	3.00	5.00	4.00

1973

	Current Price Range		C/Y Avg.
☐ January 6–12, 1973, issue #532 (review of 1972)	3.00	5.00	4.00
☐ January 13–19, 1973, issue #533 (China issue)	3.00	5.00	4.00
☐ January 20–26, 1973, issue #534 (Bob Newhart on cover)	3.00	5.00	4.00
☐ January 27–February 2, 1973, issue #535 (The Rookies on cover)	3.00	5.00	4.00

	Current Price Range		C/Y Avg.
☐ February 3–9, 1973, issue #536 (Bill Cosby on cover)	5.00	7.00	6.00
☐ February 10–16, 1973, issue #537 (Paul Lynde on cover)	3.00	5.00	4.00
☐ February 17–23, 1973, issue #538 (Rock Hudson on cover)	8.00	10.00	9.00
☐ February 24–March 2, 1973, issue #539 (M ★ A ★ S ★ H on cover)	6.00	8.00	7.00
☐ March 3–9, 1973, issue #540 (William Conrad on cover)	3.00	5.00	4.00
☐ March 10–16, 1973, issue #541 (Marlo Thomas on cover)	3.00	5.00	4.00
☐ March 17–23, 1973, issue #542 (Redd Foxx on cover)	3.00	5.00	4.00
☐ March 24–30, 1973, issue #543 (Ann-Margaret on cover)	3.00	5.00	4.00
☐ March 31–April 6, 1973, issue #544 (Lu-cille Ball on cover)	7.00	9.00	8.00
☐ April 7–13, 1973, issue #545 (children's shows issue)	3.00	5.00	4.00
☐ April 14–20, 1973, issue #546 (Shelly Fabares on cover)	3.00	5.00	4.00
☐ April 21–27, 1973, issue #547 (Raymond Burr on cover)	3.00	5.00	4.00
☐ April 28–May 4, 1973, issue #548 (The Waltons on cover)	5.00	7.00	6.00
☐ May 5–11, 1973, issue #549 (Peter Falk on cover)	3.00	5.00	4.00
☐ May 12–18, 1973, issue #550 (Shirley Booth on cover)	3.00	5.00	4.00
☐ May 19–25, 1973, issue #551 (Mary Tyler Moore on cover)	4.00	6.00	5.00
☐ May 26–June 1, 1973, issue #552 (Streets of San Francisco on cover) ...	3.00	5.00	4.00
☐ June 2–8, 1973, issue #553 (Carroll O'Connor on cover)	3.00	5.00	4.00
☐ June 9–15, 1973, issue #554 (Richard Widmark on cover)	3.00	5.00	4.00
☐ June 16–22, 1973, issue #555 (Bea Ar-thur on cover)	3.00	5.00	4.00
☐ June 23–29, 1973, issue #556 (David Carradine on cover)	3.00	5.00	4.00

	Current Price Range		C/Y Avg.
☐ June 30–July 6, 1973, issue #557 (Dennis Weaver on cover)	3.00	5.00	4.00
☐ July 7–13, 1973, issue #558 (Dick Cavett on cover)	3.00	5.00	4.00
☐ July 14–20, 1973, issue #559 (Sonny and Cher on cover)	3.00	5.00	4.00
☐ July 21–27, 1973, issue #560 (Marcus Welby on cover)	3.00	5.00	4.00
☐ July 28–August 3, 1973, issue #561 (sex movie scare)	3.00	5.00	4.00
☐ August 4–9, 1973, issue #562 (Adam 12 on cover)	3.00	5.00	4.00
☐ August 10–17, 1973, issue #563 (Roy Clark on cover)	3.00	5.00	4.00
☐ August 18–24, 1973, issue #564 (Robert Fuller on cover)	3.00	5.00	4.00
☐ August 25–31, 1973, issue #565 (Buddy Ebsen on cover)	3.00	5.00	4.00
☐ September 1–7, 1973, issue #566 (Miss America pageant on cover)	3.00	5.00	4.00
☐ September 8–14, 1973, issue #567 (Fall Preview)	10.00	12.00	11.00
(NOTE: Following this issue, the original numbering system was resumed, making the next issue #1068.)			
☐ September 15–21, 1973, issue #1068 (Football preview)	3.00	5.00	4.00
☐ September 22–28, 1973, issue #1069 (James MacArthur on cover)	3.00	5.00	4.00
☐ September 29–October 5, 1973, issue #1070 (Vietnam War on cover)	3.00	5.00	4.00
☐ October 6–12, 1973, issue #1071 (Diana Rigg on cover)	3.00	5.00	4.00
☐ October 13–19, 1973, issue #1072 (Does TV go too far?)	3.00	5.00	4.00
☐ October 20–26, 1973, issue #1073 (Telly Savalas on cover)	3.00	5.00	4.00
☐ October 27–November 2, 1973, issue #1074 (Adam's Rib on cover)	3.00	5.00	4.00
☐ November 3–9, 1973, issue #1075 (Needles and Pins on cover)	3.00	5.00	4.00

	Current Price Range		C/Y Avg.

☐ November 10–16, 1973, issue #1076 (preview of week) **3.00 5.00 4.00**

☐ November 17–23, 1973, issue #1077 (Frank Sinatra on cover) **4.00 6.00 5.00**

☐ November 24–30, 1973, issue #1078 (Jacques Cousteau on cover) **3.00 5.00 4.00**

☐ December 1–7, 1973, issue #1079 (Bill Bixby on cover) **3.00 5.00 4.00**

☐ December 8–14, 1973, issue #1080 (Mary Tyler Moore and others on cover) **4.00 6.00 5.00**

☐ December 15–21, 1973, issue #1081 (Katharine Hepburn on cover) **4.00 6.00 5.00**

☐ December 22–28, 1973, issue #1082 (Christmas issue) **3.00 5.00 4.00**

☐ December 29–January 4, 1974, issue #1083 (Mason Reese on cover) **3.00 5.00 4.00**

1974

☐ January 5–11, 1974, issue #1084, review of 1973 .... **3.00 5.00 4.00**

☐ January 12–18, 1974, issue #1085 (cast of "Maude" on cover) **3.00 5.00 4.00**

☐ January 19–25, 1974, issue #1086 (Bob Hope on cover) **4.00 6.00 5.00**

☐ January 26–February 1, 1974, issue #1087 (David Carradine on cover) **3.00 5.00 4.00**

☐ February 2–8, 1974, issue #1088 (Dom Deluise on cover) **3.00 5.00 4.00**

☐ February 9–15, 1974, issue #1089 (M ★ A ★ S ★ H on cover).............. **4.00 6.00 5.00**

☐ February 16–22, 1974, issue #1090 (Streets of San Francisco on cover) ... **3.00 5.00 4.00**

☐ February 23–March 1, 1974, issue #1091 (Richard Boone on cover) **3.00 5.00 4.00**

☐ March 2–8, 1974, issue #1092 (James Stewart on cover) **4.00 6.00 5.00**

☐ March 9–15, 1974, issue #1093 (news analysis issue) **3.00 5.00 4.00**

☐ March 16–22, 1974, issue #1094 (Carol Burnett and Vicki Lawrence on cover) **3.00 5.00 4.00**

☐ March 23–29, 1974, issue #1095 (James Franciscus on cover) **3.00 5.00 4.00**

	Current Price Range		C/Y Avg.
☐ March 30–April 5, 1974, issue #1096 (cast of "Toma" on cover)	3.00	5.00	4.00
☐ April 6–12, 1974, issue #1097 (Norman Lear and others on cover)	3.00	5.00	4.00
☐ April 13–19, 1974, issue #1098 (The Waltons on cover)	5.00	7.00	6.00
☐ April 20–26, 1974, issue #1099 (Peter Falk on cover)	3.00	5.00	4.00
☐ April 27–May 3, 1974, issue #1100 (QB VII on cover)	3.00	5.00	4.00
☐ May 4–10, 1974, issue #1101 (cast of "The Rookies" on cover)	3.00	5.00	4.00
☐ May 11–17, 1974, issue #1102 (Bob Newhart on cover)	3.00	5.00	4.00
☐ May 18–24, 1974, issue #1103 (Lee Majors on cover)	3.00	5.00	4.00
☐ May 25–31, 1974, issue #1104 (Dennis Weaver on cover)	3.00	5.00	4.00
☐ June 1–7, 1974, issue #1105 (Sonny and Cher on cover)	3.00	5.00	4.00
☐ June 8–14, 1974, issue #1106 (Marilyn Baker on cover)	3.00	5.00	4.00
☐ June 15–21, 1974, issue #1107 (Happy Days on cover)	5.00	7.00	6.00
☐ June 22–28, 1974, issue #1108 (John Chancellor on cover)	3.00	5.00	4.00
☐ June 29–July 5, 1974, issue #1109 (cast of "Good Times" on cover)	3.00	5.00	4.00
☐ July 6–12, 1974, issue #1110 (Lucille Ball on cover)	5.00	7.00	6.00
☐ July 13–19, 1974, issue #1111 (Johnny Carson on cover)	5.00	7.00	6.00
☐ July 20–26, 1974, issue #1112 (film report issue)	3.00	5.00	4.00
☐ July 27–August 2, 1974, issue #1113 (Apple's Way on cover)	3.00	5.00	4.00
☐ August 3–9, 1974, issue #1114 (Emergency on cover)	3.00	5.00	4.00
☐ August 10–16, 1974, issue #1115 (article on Gary Burghoff)	3.00	5.00	4.00
☐ August 17–23, 1974, issue #1116 (Police Story on cover)	3.00	5.00	4.00

	Current Price Range		C/Y Avg.

☐ August 24–30, 1974, issue #1117 (Susan Blakely on cover)	3.00	5.00	4.00
☐ August 31–September 6, 1974, issue #1118 (Telly Savalas on cover)	3.00	5.00	4.00
☐ September 7–13, 1974, issue #1119 (Fall Preview)	9.00	11.00	10.00
☐ September 14–20, issue #1120 (more on new shows)	3.00	5.00	4.00
☐ September 21–27, 1974, issue #1121 (football issue)	3.00	5.00	4.00
☐ September 28–October 4, 1974, issue #1122 (Paul Sand on cover)	3.00	5.00	4.00
☐ October 5–11, 1974, issue #1123 (Sanford and Son on cover)	3.00	5.00	4.00
☐ October 12–18, 1974, issue #1124 (Valerie Harper on cover)	3.00	5.00	4.00
☐ October 19–25, 1974, issue #1125 (Chico and The Man on cover)	5.00	7.00	6.00
☐ October 26–November 1, 1974, issue #1126 (The Waltons on cover)	5.00	7.00	6.00
☐ November 2–8, 1974, issue #1127 (M★A★S★H on cover)	5.00	7.00	6.00
☐ November 9–15, 1974, issue #1128 (Sophia Loren on cover)	3.00	5.00	4.00
☐ November 16–22, 1974, issue #1129 (The Godfather on cover)	4.00	6.00	5.00
☐ November 23–29, 1974, issue #1130 (preview of week)	3.00	5.00	4.00
☐ November 30–December 6, 1974, issue #1131 (Teresa Graves on cover)	3.00	5.00	4.00
☐ December 7–13, 1974, issue #1132 (Michael Landon on cover)	3.00	5.00	4.00
☐ December 14–20, 1974, issue #1133 (Good Times on cover)	3.00	5.00	4.00
☐ December 21–27, 1974, issue #1134 (Christmas issue)	3.00	5.00	4.00
☐ December 28–January 3, 1975, issue #1135 (Bowl Games issue)	4.00	6.00	5.00

1975

☐ January 4–10, 1975, issue #1136 (Angie Dickinson on cover)	3.00	5.00	4.00

	Current Price Range		C/Y Avg.

☐ January 11–17, 1975, issue #1137 (David Janssen on cover) **2.00 4.00 3.00**

☐ January 18–24, 1975, issue #1138 (That's My Mama on cover) **2.00 4.00 3.00**

☐ January 25–31, 1975, issue #1139 (Today show on cover) **2.00 4.00 3.00**

☐ February 1–7, 1975, issue #1140 (James Garner on cover) **2.00 4.00 3.00**

☐ February 8–14, 1975, issue #1141 (Mary Tyler Moore and others on cover) **3.00 5.00 4.00**

☐ February 15–21, 1975, issue #1142 (The Rookies on cover) **2.00 4.00 3.00**

☐ February 22–28, 1975, issue #1143 (Telly Savalas on cover) **2.00 4.00 3.00**

☐ March 1–8, 1975, issue #1144 (Chico and The Man on cover) .... **4.00 6.00 5.00** (NOTE: This issue should have carried the date of March 1–7. The error was not noticed until too late, and to compensate for it the next issue was dated March 8–14.)

☐ March 8–14, 1975, issue #1145 (Chad Everett on cover) **2.00 4.00 3.00**

☐ March 15–21, 1975, issue #1146 (Karen Valentine on cover) **2.00 4.00 3.00**

☐ March 22–28, 1975, issue #1147 (Streets of San Francisco on cover) ... **2.00 4.00 3.00**

☐ March 29–April 4, 1975, issue #1148 (Bea Arthur on cover) **2.00 4.00 3.00**

☐ April 5–11, 1975, issue #1149 (baseball issue) **4.00 6.00 5.00**

☐ April 12–18, 1975, issue #1150 (Cher on cover) **3.00 5.00 4.00**

☐ April 19–25, 1975, issue #1151 (Movin' On on cover) **3.00 5.00 4.00**

☐ April 26–May 2, 1975, issue #1152 (Dennis Weaver on cover) **3.00 5.00 4.00**

☐ May 3–9, 1975, issue #1153 (Rhoda on cover) **3.00 5.00 4.00**

☐ May 10–16, 1975, issue #1154 (Muhammad Ali on cover) **4.00 6.00 5.00**

	Current Price Range		C/Y Avg.

☐ May 17–23, 1975, issue #1155 (Barry Newman on cover) **3.00** **5.00** **4.00**

☐ May 24–30, 1975, issue #1156 (Jason Robards on cover) **3.00** **5.00** **4.00**

☐ May 31–June 6, 1975, issue #1157 (Bob Newhart on cover) **3.00** **5.00** **4.00**

☐ June 7–13, 1975, issue #1158 (Little House on the Prairie on cover) **4.00** **6.00** **5.00**

☐ June 14–20, 1975, issue #1159 (violence on TV issue) **3.00** **5.00** **4.00**

☐ June 21–27, 1975, issue #1160 (The Jeffersons on cover) **3.00** **5.00** **4.00**

☐ June 28–July 4, 1975, issue #1161 (Bicentennial issue) **5.00** **7.00** **6.00**

☐ July 5–11, 1975, issue #1162 (Tony Orlando on cover) **4.00** **6.00** **5.00**

☐ July 12–18, 1975, issue #1163 (Apollo spacecraft on cover) **5.00** **7.00** **6.00**

☐ July 19–25, 1975, issue #1164 (Barney Miller on cover) **4.00** **6.00** **5.00**

☐ July 26–August 1, 1975, issue #1165 (Howard K. Smith on cover) **2.00** **4.00** **3.00**

☐ August 2–8, 1975, issue #1166 (Mike Douglas on cover) **2.00** **4.00** **3.00**

☐ August 9–15, 1975, issue #1167 (Buddy Ebsen on cover) **2.00** **4.00** **3.00**

☐ August 16–22, 1975, issue #1168 (Emergency on cover) **2.00** **4.00** **3.00**

☐ August 23–29, 1975, issue #1169 (The Waltons on cover) **4.00** **6.00** **5.00**

☐ August 30–September 5, 1975, issue #1170 (Carroll O'Connor on cover) ... **4.00** **6.00** **5.00**

☐ September 6–12, 1975, issue #1171 (Fall Preview) **7.00** **9.00** **8.00**

☐ September 13–19, 1975, issue #1172 (football issue) **3.00** **5.00** **4.00**

☐ September 20–26, 1975, issue #1173 (Barbara Walters on cover) **2.00** **4.00** **3.00**

☐ September 27–October 3, 1975, issue #1174 (Howard Cosell on cover) **2.00** **4.00** **3.00**

☐ October 4–10, 1975, issue #1175 (Lee Remick on cover) **2.00** **4.00** **3.00**

	Current Price Range		C/Y Avg.

☐ October 11–17, 1975, issue #1176 (The Family Holvak on cover) **2.00 4.00 3.00**

☐ October 18–24, 1975, issue #1177 (article on "Six Million Dollar Man") **2.00 4.00 3.00**

☐ October 25–31, 1975, issue #1178 (Cloris Leachman on cover) **2.00 4.00 3.00**

☐ November 1–7, 1975, issue #1179 (Lloyd Bridges on cover) **2.00 4.00 3.00**

☐ November 8–14, 1975, issue #1180 (Rhoda on cover) **2.00 4.00 3.00**

☐ November 15–21, 1975, issue #1181 (Starsky and Hutch on cover, article on "Star Trek" conventions) **2.00 4.00 3.00**

(NOTE: By error, the following issue was also numbered 1181. The error was not noticed until four issues later, when it was finally corrected by omitting the number 1185 and skipping from #1184 to #1186. Thus, no issue of TV Guide exists with the number 1185.)

☐ November 22–28, 1975, issue #1181 (review of week) **2.00 4.00 3.00**

☐ November 29–December 5, 1975, issue #1182 (Tony Curtis on cover) **2.00 4.00 3.00**

☐ December 6–12, 1975, issue #1183 (article on "Harry O." [David Janssen]) **2.00 4.00 3.00**

☐ December 13–19, 1975, issue #1184 (cast of "Switch" on cover) **2.00 4.00 3.00**

☐ December 20–26, 1975, issue #1186 (Christmas issue) **2.00 4.00 3.00**

☐ December 27–January 2, 1976, issue #1187 (Robert Blake on cover) **2.00 4.00 3.00**

1976

☐ January 3–9, 1976, issue #1188 (Telly Savalas on cover) **2.00 4.00 3.00**

☐ January 10–16, 1976, issue #1189 (Henry Winkler on cover) **3.00 5.00 4.00**

☐ January 17–23, 1976, issue #1190 (Police Woman on cover) **2.00 4.00 3.00**

	Current Price Range		C/Y Avg.

☐ January 24–30, 1976, issue #1191 (M ★ A ★ S ★ H on cover) 4.00 6.00 **5.00**

☐ January 31–February 6, 1976, issue #1192 (Steve Forrest on cover) 2.00 4.00 **3.00**

☐ February 7–13, 1976, issue #1193 (Barney Miller on cover) 2.00 4.00 **3.00**

☐ February 14–20, 1976, issue #1194 (Redd Foxx on cover) 2.00 4.00 **3.00**

☐ February 21–27, 1976, issue #1195 (William Conrad on cover) 2.00 4.00 **3.00**

☐ February 28–March 5, 1976, issue #1196 (Bob Hope on cover) 4.00 6.00 **5.00**

☐ March 6–12, 1976, issue #1197 (James Garner on cover) 2.00 4.00 **3.00**

☐ March 13–19, 1976, issue #1198 (Chico and The Man on cover) 5.00 7.00 **6.00**

☐ March 20–26, 1976, issue #1199 (Danny Thomas on cover) 2.00 4.00 **3.00**

☐ March 27–April 2, 1976, issue #1200 (Jack Palance on cover) 2.00 4.00 **3.00**

☐ April 3–9, 1976, issue #1201 (baseball issue) 3.00 5.00 **4.00**

☐ April 10–16, 1976, issue #1202 (Police Story on cover) 3.00 5.00 **4.00**

☐ April 17–23, 1976, issue #1203 (Welcome Back Kotter on cover; no John Travolta) 2.00 4.00 **3.00**

☐ April 24–30, 1976, issue #1204 (Bea Arthur on cover) 2.00 4.00 **3.00**

☐ May 1–7, 1976, issue #1205 (George Kennedy on cover) 2.00 4.00 **3.00**

☐ May 8–14, 1976, issue #1206 (Bionic Woman on cover) 2.00 4.00 **3.00**

☐ May 15–21, 1976, issue #1207 (On the Rocks on cover) 2.00 4.00 **3.00**

☐ May 22–28, 1976, issue #1208 (Laverne and Shirley on cover) 3.00 5.00 **4.00**

☐ May 29–June 4, 1976, issue #1209 (Little House on the Prairie on cover) 3.00 5.00 **4.00**

☐ June 5–11, 1976, issue #1210 (Sonny and Cher on cover) 2.00 4.00 **3.00**

	Current Price Range		C/Y Avg.
☐ June 12–18, 1976, issue #1211 (Harry O. on cover)	2.00	4.00	3.00
☐ June 19–25, 1976, issue #1212 (Louise Lasser on cover)	3.00	5.00	4.00
☐ June 26–July 2, 1976, issue #1213 (Mary Tyler Moore on cover)	3.00	5.00	4.00
☐ July 3–9, 1976, issue #1214 (Bicentennial issue)	8.00	10.00	9.00
☐ July 10–16, 1976, issue #1215 (coverage of political convention)	6.00	8.00	7.00
☐ July 17–23, 1976, issue #1216 (Olympics issue)	5.00	7.00	6.00
☐ July 24–30, 1976, issue #1217 (Bonnie Franklin on cover)	2.00	4.00	3.00
☐ July 31–August 6, 1976, issue #1218 (article on Beach Boys)	2.00	4.00	3.00
☐ August 7–13, 1976, issue #1219 (Marie and Donnie Osmond on cover)	2.00	4.00	3.00
☐ August 14–20, 1976, issue #1220 (Columbo on cover)	2.00	4.00	3.00
☐ August 21–27, 1976, issue #1221 (The Waltons on cover)	3.00	5.00	4.00
☐ August 28–September 3, 1976, issue #1222 (Bionic Man on cover)	2.00	4.00	3.00
☐ September 4–10, 1976, issue #1223 (football issue)	3.00	5.00	4.00
☐ September 11–17, 1976, issue #1224 (Bob Dylan on cover)	4.00	6.00	5.00
☐ September 18–24, 1976, issue #1225 (Fall Preview)	6.00	8.00	7.00
☐ September 25–October 1, 1976, issue #1226 (Charlie's Angels on cover)	8.00	10.00	9.00
☐ October 2–8, 1976, issue #1227 (David Birney on cover)	8.00	10.00	9.00
☐ October 9–15, 1976, issue #1228 (Richard Crenna on cover)	8.00	10.00	9.00
☐ October 16–22, 1976, issue #1229 (World Series issue)	8.00	10.00	9.00
☐ October 23–29, 1976, issue #1230 (Linda Lavin on cover)	8.00	10.00	9.00

	Current Price Range		C/Y Avg.

☐ October 30–November 5, 1976, issue #1231 (Jimmy Carter and Gerald Ford on cover) **6.00** **8.00** **7.00**

☐ November 6–12, 1976, issue #1232 (Clark Gable on cover) **8.00** **10.00** **9.00**

☐ November 13–19, 1976, issue #1233 (Dorothy Hamill on cover) **2.00** **4.00** **3.00**

☐ November 20–26, 1976, issue #1234 (50th anniversary of NBC) **3.00** **5.00** **4.00**

☐ November 27–December 3, 1976, issue #1235 (Starsky and Hutch on cover) .. **2.00** **4.00** **3.00**

☐ December 4–10, 1976, issue #1236 (Tony Randall on cover) **2.00** **4.00** **3.00**

☐ December 11–17, 1976, issue #1237 (Valerie Harper on cover) **2.00** **4.00** **3.00**

☐ December 18–24, 1976, issue #1238 (David Brinkley on cover) **2.00** **4.00** **3.00**

☐ December 25–31, 1976, issue #1239, (Christmas issue) **2.00** **4.00** **3.00**

1977

☐ January 1–7, 1977, issue #1240 (John Travolta on cover) **4.00** **6.00** **5.00**

☐ January 8–14, 1977, issue #1241 (Super Bowl issue) **3.00** **5.00** **4.00**

☐ January 15–21, 1977, issue #1242 (inauguration of President Carter) **5.00** **7.00** **6.00**

☐ January 22–28, 1977, issue #1243 (Roots on cover) **8.00** **10.00** **9.00**

☐ January 29–February 4, 1977, issue #1244 (Wonder Woman on cover) **3.00** **5.00** **4.00**

☐ February 5–11, 1977, issue #1245 (Barbara Walters on cover) **2.00** **4.00** **3.00**

☐ February 12–18, 1977, issue #1246 (Kojak on cover) **2.00** **4.00** **3.00**

☐ February 19–25, 1977, issue #1247 (Nancy Walker on cover) **2.00** **4.00** **3.00**

☐ February 26–March 4, 1977, issue #1248 (Rock Hudson on cover) **8.00** **10.00** **9.00**

☐ March 5–11, 1977, issue #1249 (Liv Ullman on cover) **2.00** **4.00** **3.00**

	Current Price Range		C/Y Avg.
☐ March 12–18, 1977, issue #1250 (Lauren Hutton on cover)	2.00	4.00	3.00
☐ March 19–25, 1977, issue #1251 (Mary Tyler Moore on cover)	3.00	5.00	4.00
☐ March 26–April 1, 1977, issue #1252 (Jack Klugman on cover)	2.00	4.00	3.00
☐ April 2–8, 1977, issue #1253 (Dinah Shore on cover)	2.00	4.00	3.00
☐ April 9–15, 1977, issue #1254 (baseball issue)	3.00	5.00	4.00
☐ April 16–22, 1977, issue #1255 (Frank Sinatra on cover)	3.00	5.00	4.00
☑ April 23–29, 1977, issue #1256 (Sixty Minutes on cover)	2.00	4.00	3.00
☐ April 30–May 6, 1977, issue #1257 (Richard Nixon on cover)	4.00	6.00	5.00
☐ May 7–13, 1977, issue #1258 (One Day at a Time on cover)	2.00	4.00	3.00
☐ May 14–20, 1977, #1259 (Tom Brokaw on cover)	2.00	4.00	3.00
☐ May 21–27, 1977, issue #1260 (Farrah Fawcett on cover)	4.00	6.00	5.00
☐ May 28–June 3, 1977, issue #1261 (Robert Blake on cover)	2.00	4.00	3.00
☐ June 4–10, 1977, issue #1262 (Alan Alda on cover)	2.00	4.00	3.00
☐ June 11–17, 1977, issue #1263 (Grizzly Adams on cover)	2.00	4.00	3.00
☐ June 18–24, 1977, issue #1264 (Laverne and Shirley on cover)	3.00	5.00	4.00
☐ June 25–July 1, 1977, issue #1265 (The Waltons on cover)	3.00	5.00	4.00
☐ July 2–8, 1977, issue #1266 (Linda Lavin on cover)	2.00	4.00	3.00
☐ July 9–15, 1977, issue #1267 (C.P.O. Sharkey on cover)	2.00	4.00	3.00
☐ July 16–22, 1977, issue #1268 (Barney Miller on cover)	2.00	4.00	3.00
☐ July 23–29, 1977, issue #1269 (Public TV issue)	2.00	4.00	3.00
☐ July 30–August 5, 1977, issue #1270 (Johnny Carson on cover)	3.00	5.00	4.00

	Current Price Range		C/Y Avg.
☐ August 6–12, 1977, issue #1271 (The Muppets on cover)	4.00	6.00	5.00
☐ August 13–19, 1977, issue #1272 (David Soul on cover)	2.00	4.00	3.00
☐ August 20–26, 1977, issue #1273 (James Garner on cover).............	2.00	4.00	3.00
☐ August 27–September 2, 1977, issue #1274 (violence on TV)	2.00	4.00	3.00
☐ September 3–9, 1977, issue #1275 (Washington Behind Closed Doors)	2.00	4.00	3.00
☐ September 10–16, 1977, issue #1276 (Fall Preview)	6.00	8.00	7.00
☐ September 17–23, 1977, issue #1277 (football issue)	3.00	5.00	4.00
☐ September 24–30, 1977, issue #1278 (Betty White on cover)	2.00	4.00	3.00
☐ October 1–7, 1977, issue #1279 (Rosetti and Ryan on cover)	2.00	4.00	3.00
☐ October 8–14, 1977, issue #1280 (Osmonds on cover)	2.00	4.00	3.00
☐ October 15–21, 1977, issue #1281 (Ed Asner on cover).....................	2.00	4.00	3.00
☐ October 22–28, 1977, issue #1282 (Welcome Back Kotter on cover)	2.00	4.00	3.00
☐ October 29–November 4, 1977, issue #1283 (We've Got Each Other)	2.00	4.00	3.00
☐ November 5–11, 1977, issue #1284 (Hardy Boys on cover)	2.00	4.00	3.00
☐ November 12–18, 1977, issue #1285 (The Godfather)	2.00	4.00	3.00
☐ November 19–25, 1977, issue #1286 (Frank Sinatra on cover)	2.00	4.00	3.00
☐ November 26–December 2, 1977, issue #1287 (cast of "Soap" on cover)	2.00	4.00	3.00
☐ December 3–9, 1977, issue #1288 (Pat Duffy on cover)	2.00	4.00	3.00
☐ December 10–16, 1977, issue #1289 (censorship in TV)	2.00	4.00	3.00
☐ December 17–23, 1977, issue #1290 (One Day at a Time on cover)	2.00	4.00	3.00
☐ December 24–30, 1977, issue #1291 (Christmas issue)	2.00	4.00	3.00

	Current Price Range		C/Y Avg.

☐ December 31–January 6, 1978, issue #1292 (cast of "Kojak" on cover) **2.00** **4.00** **3.00**

1978

☐ January 7–13, 1978, issue #1293 (cast of "Happy Days" on cover) **4.00** **6.00** **5.00**

☐ January 14–20, 1978, issue #1294 (Super Bowl issue) **3.00** **5.00** **4.00**

☐ January 21–27, 1978, issue #1295 (cast of "Family" on cover) **2.00** **4.00** **3.00**

☐ January 28–February 3, 1978, issue #1296 (Grizzly Adams on cover) **2.00** **4.00** **3.00**

☐ February 4–10, 1978, issue #1297 (The Love Boat on cover) **2.00** **4.00** **3.00**

☐ February 11–17, 1978, issue #1298 (Jack Klugman on cover) **2.00** **4.00** **3.00**

☐ February 18–24, 1978, issue #1299 (Charlie's Angels on cover) **5.00** **7.00** **6.00**

☐ February 25–March 3, 1978, issue #1300 (cast of "M ★ A ★ S ★ H" on cover) **5.00** **7.00** **6.00**

☐ March 4–10, 1978, issue #1301 (cast of "On Our Own" on cover) **2.00** **4.00** **3.00**

☐ March 11–17, 1978, issue #1302 (Carter Country on cover) **2.00** **4.00** **3.00**

☐ March 18–24, 1978, issue #1303 (Bionic Woman on cover) **2.00** **4.00** **3.00**

☐ March 25–31, 1978, issue #1304 (Mary Tyler Moore on cover) **3.00** **5.00** **4.00**

☐ April 1–7, 1978, issue #1305 (baseball issue) **3.00** **5.00** **4.00**

☐ April 8–14, 1978, issue #1306 (Linda Lavin on cover) **2.00** **4.00** **3.00**

☐ April 15–21, 1978, issue #1307 (Holocaust on cover) **2.00** **4.00** **3.00**

☐ April 22–28, 1978, issue #1308 (Changing the Shape of TV) **2.00** **4.00** **3.00**

☐ April 29–May 5, 1978, issue #1309 (Laverne and Shirley on cover) **3.00** **5.00** **4.00**

☐ May 6–12, 1978, issue #1310 (Buddy Ebsen on cover) **3.00** **5.00** **4.00**

	Current Price Range		C/Y Avg.
☐ May 13–19, 1978, issue #1311 (Little House on the Prairie on cover)	3.00	5.00	4.00
☐ May 20–26, 1978, issue #1312 (Three's Company on cover)	3.00	5.00	4.00
☐ May 27–June 2, 1978, issue #1313 (Phil Donahue on cover)	2.00	4.00	3.00
☐ June 3–9, 1978, issue #1314 (Starsky and Hutch on cover)	2.00	4.00	3.00
☐ June 10–16, 1978, issue #1315 (television coverage of UFOs)	3.00	5.00	4.00
☐ June 17–23, 1978, issue #1316 (Valerie Harper on cover)	2.00	4.00	3.00
☐ June 24–30, 1978, issue #1317 (ratings analysis)	1.00	3.00	2.00
☐ July 1–7, 1978, issue #1318 (Fantasy Island on cover)	1.00	3.00	2.00
☐ July 8–14, 1978, issue #1319 (Young and the Restless on cover)	1.00	3.00	2.00
☐ July 15–21, 1978, issue #1320 (Robert Conrad on cover)	1.00	3.00	2.00
☐ July 22–28, 1978, issue #1321 (Gavin McLeod on cover)	1.00	3.00	2.00
☐ July 29–August 4, 1978, issue #1322 (Saturday Night Live on cover)	6.00	8.00	7.00
☐ August 5–11, 1978, issue #1323 (The Jeffersons on cover)	1.00	3.00	2.00
☐ August 12–18, 1978, issue #1324 (David Hartman on cover)	1.00	3.00	2.00
☐ August 19–25, 1978, issue #1325 (sports issue)	1.00	3.00	2.00
☐ August 26–September 1, 1978, issue #1326 (Cheryl Ladd on cover)	2.00	4.00	3.00
☐ September 2–8, 1978, issue #1327 (football issue)	1.00	3.00	2.00
☐ September 9–15, 1978, issue #1328 (Fall Preview)	5.00	7.00	6.00
☐ September 16–22, 1978, issue #1329 (Battlestar Galactica on cover)	5.00	7.00	6.00
☐ September 23–29, 1978, issue #1330 (Mary Tyler Moore on cover)	2.00	4.00	3.00
☐ September 30–October 6, 1978, issue #1331 (Centennial on cover)	1.00	3.00	2.00

	Current Price Range		C/Y Avg.
☐ October 7–13, 1978, issue #1332 (World Series issue)	3.00	5.00	4.00
☐ October 14–20, 1978, issue #1333 (Robert Ulrich on cover)	1.00	3.00	2.00
☐ October 21–27, 1978, issue #1334 (WKRP in Cincinnati on cover)	1.00	3.00	2.00
☐ October 28–November 3, 1978, issue #1335 (Mork and Mindy on cover)	2.00	4.00	3.00
☐ November 4–10, 1978, issue #1336 (John Travolta on cover)	2.00	4.00	3.00
☐ November 11–17, 1978, issue #1337 (Ron Leibman on cover)	1.00	3.00	2.00
☐ November 18–24, 1978, issue #1338 (Foreign Lobbyists Manipulate TV)	1.00	3.00	2.00
☐ November 25–December 1, 1978, issue #1339 (Suzanne Somers on cover) ...	1.00	3.00	2.00
☐ December 2–8, 1978, issue #1340 (Benji on cover)	1.00	3.00	2.00
☐ December 9–15, 1978, issue #1341 (Ed Asner on cover)	1.00	3.00	2.00
☐ December 16–22, 1978, issue #1342 (Eight is Enough on cover)	1.00	3.00	2.00
☐ December 23–29, 1978, issue #1343 (Christmas cover)	1.00	3.00	2.00
☐ December 30–January 5, 1979, issue #1344 (Dick Clark on cover)	2.00	4.00	3.00

1979

	Current Price Range		C/Y Avg.
☐ January 6–12, 1979, issue #1345 (All in the Family on cover, caricature by Hirschfeld)	3.00	5.00	4.00
☐ January 13–19, 1979, issue #1346 (Network News Chiefs on cover)	1.00	3.00	4.00
☐ January 20–26, 1979, issue #1347 (Super Bowl XIII on cover)	2.00	4.00	3.00
☐ January 27–February 2, 1979, issue #1348 (Katharine Hepburn on cover)	1.00	3.00	2.00
☐ February 3–9, 1979, issue #1349 (CHIPS on cover)	1.00	3.00	2.00
☐ February 10–16, 1979, issue #1350 (William Shakespeare on cover)	2.00	4.00	3.00

	Current Price Range		C/Y Avg.

☐ February 17–23, 1979, issue #1351 (Roots II on cover) **2.00** **4.00** **3.00**

☐ February 24–March 2, 1979, issue #1352 (James Arness on cover) **1.00** **3.00** **2.00**

☐ March 3–9, 1979, issue #1353 (Gary Coleman on cover) **1.00** **3.00** **2.00**

☐ March 10–16, 1979, issue #1354 (Sixty Minutes on cover) **1.00** **3.00** **2.00**

☐ March 17–23, 1979, issue #1355 (Alan Alda on cover) **1.00** **3.00** **2.00**

☐ March 24–30, 1979, issue #1356 (Ricardo Montalban on cover) **1.00** **3.00** **2.00**

☐ March 31–April 6, 1979, issue #1357 (baseball issue) **2.00** **4.00** **3.00**

☐ April 7–13, 1979, issue #1358 (Battlestar Galactica on cover) **3.00** **5.00** **4.00**

☐ April 14–20, 1979, issue #1359 (Quincy on cover) **1.00** **3.00** **2.00**

☐ April 21–27, 1979, issue #1360 (Walter Cronkite on cover) **1.00** **3.00** **2.00**

☐ April 28–May 4, 1979, issue #1361 (Judd Hirsch and Danny DeVito on cover) ... **2.00** **4.00** **3.00**

☐ May 5–11, 1979, issue #1362 (John Houseman on cover) **1.00** **3.00** **2.00**

☐ May 12–18, 1979, issue #1363 (What Viewers Hate About TV) **1.00** **3.00** **2.00**

☐ May 19–25, 1979, issue #1364 (Laverne and Shirley on cover) **2.00** **4.00** **3.00**

☐ May 26–June 1, 1979, issue #1365 (Ken Howard on cover) **1.00** **3.00** **2.00**

☐ June 2–8, 1979, issue #1366 (James Garner on cover) **1.00** **3.00** **2.00**

☐ June 9–15, 1979, issue #1367 (Donna Pescow on cover) **1.00** **3.00** **2.00**

☐ June 16–22, 1979, issue #1368 (Victoria Principal on cover) **2.00** **4.00** **3.00**

☐ June 23–29, 1979, issue #1369 (Johnny Carson on cover) **2.00** **4.00** **3.00**

☐ June 30–July 7, 1979, issue #1370 (Dukes of Hazzard on cover) **2.00** **4.00** **3.00**

☐ July 7–13, 1979, issue #1371 (Barney Miller on cover) **2.00** **4.00** **3.00**

	Current Price Range		C/Y Avg.

☐ July 14–20, 1979, issue #1372 (Little House on the Prairie on cover) **1.00**   **3.00**   **2.00**

☐ July 21–27, 1979, issue #1373 (BJ and the Bear on cover) **1.00**   **3.00**   **2.00**

☐ July 28–August 3, 1979, issue #1374 (Bill Bixby and Lou Ferringo on cover)   **1.00**   **3.00**   **2.00**

☐ August 4–10, 1979, issue #1375 (Joyce DeWitt on cover) **1.00**   **3.00**   **2.00**

☐ August 11–17, 1979, issue #1376 (Rod Arrants on cover) **1.00**   **3.00**   **2.00**

☐ August 18–24, 1979, issue #1377 (Lou Grant on cover) **1.00**   **3.00**   **2.00**

☐ August 25–31, 1979, issue #1378 (Pro Football '79 issue) **2.00**   **4.00**   **3.00**

☐ September 1–7, 1979, issue #1379 (Miss America on cover) **1.00**   **3.00**   **2.00**

☐ September 8–14, 1979, issue #1380 (Fall Preview issue) **4.00**   **6.00**   **5.00**

☐ September 15–21, 1979, issue #1381 (Robert Guillaume on cover) **1.00**   **3.00**   **2.00**

☐ September 22–28, 1979, issue #1382 (Carroll O'Connor on cover) **1.00**   **3.00**   **2.00**

☐ September 29–October 5, 1979, issue #1383 (Pope John Paul II on cover) . .   **2.00**   **4.00**   **3.00**

☐ October 6–12, 1979, issue #1384 (World Series issue) **3.00**   **5.00**   **4.00**

☐ October 13–19, 1979, issue #1385 (Tom Snyder on cover) **1.00**   **3.00**   **2.00**

☐ October 20–26, 1979, issue #1386 (WKRP in Cincinnati on cover) **1.00**   **3.00**   **2.00**

☐ October 27–November 2, 1979, issue #1387 (Muhammad Ali on cover) **1.00**   **3.00**   **2.00**

☐ November 3–9, 1979, issue #1388 (Stephanie Powers and Robert Wagner on cover) **1.00**   **3.00**   **2.00**

☐ November 10–16, 1979, issue #1389 (BeeGees on cover) **3.00**   **5.00**   **4.00**

☐ November 17–23, 1979, issue #1390 (The Associates on cover) **1.00**   **3.00**   **2.00**

☐ November 24–30, 1979, issue #1391 (Pernell Roberts on cover) **1.00**   **3.00**   **2.00**

	Current Price Range		C/Y Avg.

☐ December 1–7, 1979, issue #1392 (Barbara Walters on cover) **1.00** **3.00** **2.00**

☐ December 8–14, 1979, issue #1393 (talk show hosts on cover) **1.00** **3.00** **2.00**

☐ December 15–21, 1979, issue #1394 (Henry Winkler on cover) **1.00** **3.00** **2.00**

☐ December 22–28, 1979, issue #1395 (Christmas cover) **1.00** **3.00** **2.00**

☐ December 29–January 4, 1980, issue #1396 (Charlie's Angels on cover) **3.00** **5.00** **4.00**

1980

☐ January 5–11, 1980, issue #1397 (M ★ A ★ S ★ H on cover) **3.00** **5.00** **4.00**

☐ January 12–18, 1980, issue #1398 (Eric Estrada on cover) **1.00** **3.00** **2.00**

☐ January 19–25, 1980, issue #1399 (Super Bowl '80) **2.00** **4.00** **3.00**

☐ January 26–February 1, 1980, issue #1400 (cast of "Soap" on cover) **1.00** **3.00** **2.00**

☐ February 2–8, 1980, issue #1401 (Different Strokes on cover) **1.00** **3.00** **2.00**

☐ February 9–15, 1980, issue #1402 (Winter Olympics on cover) **2.00** **4.00** **3.00**

☐ February 16–22, 1980, issue #1403 (Barnaby Jones on cover) **1.00** **3.00** **2.00**

☐ February 23–29, 1980, issue #1404 (Presidential campaign coverage) **3.00** **5.00** **4.00**

☐ March 1–7, 1980, issue #1405 (Fantasy Island on cover) **1.00** **3.00** **2.00**

☐ March 8–14, 1980, issue #1406 (Larry Hagman on cover) **4.00** **6.00** **5.00**

☐ March 15–21, 1980, issue #1407 (cast of "Family" on cover) **1.00** **3.00** **2.00**

☐ March 22–28, 1980, issue #1408 (Misadventures of Sheriff Lobo on cover) **1.00** **3.00** **2.00**

☐ March 29–April 4, 1980, issue #1409 (Archie Bunker's Place on cover) **2.00** **4.00** **3.00**

☐ April 5–11, 1980, issue #1410 (baseball issue) **3.00** **5.00** **4.00**

☐ April 12–18, 1980, issue #1411 (Olivia Newton-John on cover) **2.00** **4.00** **3.00**

	Current Price Range		C/Y Avg.

☐ April 19–25, 1980, issue #1412 (Linda Lavin on cover) **1.00 3.00 2.00**

☐ April 26–May 2, 1980, issue #1413 (cast of "United States" on cover) **1.00 3.00 2.00**

☐ May 3–9, 1980, issue #1414 (Mork and Mindy on cover) **1.00 3.00 2.00**

☐ May 10–16, 1980, issue #1415 (One Day At A Time on cover) **1.00 3.00 2.00**

☐ May 17–23, 1980, issue #1416 (The Jeffersons on cover) **1.00 3.00 2.00**

☐ May 24–30, 1980, issue #1417 (Situation Comedies: Better or Worse?) **1.00 3.00 2.00**

☐ May 31–June 6, 1980, issue #1418 (Vega$ on cover) **1.00 3.00 2.00**

☐ June 7–13, 1980, issue #1419 (Knots Landing on cover) **1.00 3.00 2.00**

☐ June 14–20, 1980, issue #1420 (Lynn Redgrave on cover) **1.00 3.00 2.00**

☐ June 21–27, 1980, issue #1421 (Hart to Hart on cover) **1.00 3.00 2.00**

☐ June 28–July 4, 1980, issue #1422 (Trapper John, M.D. on cover) **1.00 3.00 2.00**

☐ July 5–11, 1980, issue #1423 (Little House on the Prairie on cover) **1.00 3.00 2.00**

☐ July 12–18, 1980, issue #1424 (Dukes of Hazzard on cover) **1.00 3.00 2.00**

☐ July 19–25, 1980, issue #1425 (Love Boat on cover) **1.00 3.00 2.00**

☐ July 26–August 1, 1980, issue #1426 (Judd Hirsch on cover) **1.00 3.00 2.00**

☐ August 2–8, 1980, issue #1427 (Real People on cover) **1.00 3.00 2.00**

☐ August 9–15, 1980, issue #1428 (Children's Television) **1.00 3.00 2.00**

☐ August 16–22, 1980, issue #1429 (Eric Estrada and others on cover) **1.00 3.00 2.00**

☐ August 23–29, 1980, issue #1430 (Genie Francis on cover) **1.00 3.00 2.00**

☐ August 30–September 5, 1980, issue #1431 (football issue) **1.00 3.00 2.00**

☐ September 6–12, 1980, issue #1432 (Richard Chamberlain on cover) **1.00 3.00 2.00**

	Current Price Range		C/Y Avg.

☐ September 13–19, 1980, issue #1433 (Fall Preview issue) **4.00** **6.00** **5.00**

☐ September 20–26, 1980, issue #1434 (Priscilla Presley on cover) **3.00** **5.00** **4.00**

☐ September 27–October 3, 1980, issue #1435 (Cosmos on cover) **1.00** **3.00** **2.00**

☐ October 4–10, 1980, issue #1436 (Ed Asner on cover) **1.00** **3.00** **2.00**

☐ October 11–17, 1980, issue #1437 (World Series issue) **2.00** **4.00** **3.00**

☐ October 18–24, 1980, issue #1438 (Sophia Loren on cover) **1.00** **3.00** **2.00**

☐ October 25–31, 1980, issue #1439 (Barney Miller on cover) **1.00** **3.00** **2.00**

☐ November 1–7, 1980, issue #1440 (Ronald Reagan and Jimmy Carter on cover) **4.00** **6.00** **5.00**

☐ November 8–14, 1980, issue #1441 (Polly Holliday on cover) **1.00** **3.00** **2.00**

☐ November 15–21, 1980, issue #1442 (Larry Hagman on cover) **2.00** **4.00** **3.00**

☐ November 22–28, 1980, issue #1443 (Pam Dawber on cover) **1.00** **3.00** **2.00**

☐ November 29–December 5, 1980, issue #1444 (Monday Night Football on cover) **1.00** **3.00** **2.00**

☐ December 6–12, 1980, issue #1445 (Gary Coleman on cover) **1.00** **3.00** **2.00**

☐ December 13–19, 1980, issue #1446 (I'm A Big Girl Now on cover) **1.00** **3.00** **2.00**

☐ December 20–26, 1980, issue #1447 (Christmas cover) **1.00** **3.00** **2.00**

☐ December 27–January 2, 1981, issue #1448 (Tom Selleck on cover) **2.00** **4.00** **3.00**

1981

☐ January 3–9, 1981, issue #1449 (Too Close For Comfort on cover) **1.00** **3.00** **2.00**

☐ January 10–16, 1981, issue #1450 (David Hartman on cover) **1.00** **3.00** **2.00**

☐ January 17–23, 1981, issue #1451 (Ronald Reagan on cover) **4.00** **6.00** **5.00**

	Current Price Range		C/Y Avg.

☐ January 24–30, 1981, issue #1452 (Super Bowl '81) **3.00** **5.00** **4.00**

☐ January 31–February 6, 1981, issue #1453 (Johnny Carson, Bob Hope and George Burns on cover) **2.00** **4.00** **3.00**

☐ February 7–13, 1981, issue #1454 (Jane Seymour on cover) **1.00** **3.00** **2.00**

☐ February 14–20, 1981, issue #1455 (Loni Anderson on cover) **1.00** **3.00** **2.00**

☐ February 21–27, 1981, issue #1456 (Faye Dunaway as Eva Peron on cover) **1.00** **3.00** **2.00**

☐ February 28–March 6, 1981, issue #1457 (Hollywood's Cocaine Connection) **1.00** **3.00** **2.00**

☐ March 7–13, 1981, issue #1458 (Dukes of Hazzard on cover) **1.00** **3.00** **2.00**

☐ March 14–20, 1981, issue #1459 (Suzanne Somers on cover) **1.00** **3.00** **2.00**

☐ March 21–27, 1981, issue #1460 (Lynn Redgrave on cover) **1.00** **3.00** **2.00**

☐ March 28–April 3, 1981, issue #1461 (Johnny Carson on cover) **2.00** **4.00** **3.00**

☐ April 4–10, 1981, issue #1462 (baseball issue) **2.00** **4.00** **3.00**

☐ April 11–17, 1981, issue #1463 (Ed Asner on cover) **1.00** **3.00** **2.00**

☐ April 18–24, 1981, issue #1464 (Ted Koppel on cover) **1.00** **3.00** **2.00**

☐ April 25–May 1, 1981, issue #1465 (Alan Alda on cover) **1.00** **3.00** **2.00**

☐ May 2–8, 1981, issue #1466 (That's Incredible on cover) **1.00** **3.00** **2.00**

☐ May 9–15, 1981, issue #1467 (Larry Hagman on cover) **2.00** **4.00** **3.00**

☐ May 16–22, 1981, issue #1468 (Hart to Hart on cover) **1.00** **3.00** **2.00**

☐ May 23–29, 1981, issue #1469 (Barbara Eden on cover) **1.00** **3.00** **2.00**

☐ May 30–June 5, 1981, issue #1470 (Dan Rather on cover) **1.00** **3.00** **2.00**

☐ June 6–12, 1981, issue #1471 (Judd Hirsch on cover) **1.00** **3.00** **2.00**

	Current Price Range		C/Y Avg.

☐ June 13–19, 1981, issue #1472 (Trapper John, M.D. on cover) **1.00** **3.00** **2.00**

☐ June 20–26, 1981, issue #1473 (Real People on cover) **1.00** **3.00** **2.00**

☐ June 27–July 3, 1981, issue #1474 (Linda Evans on cover) **1.00** **3.00** **2.00**

☐ July 4–10, 1981, issue #1475 (Gary Coleman on cover) **1.00** **3.00** **2.00**

☐ July 11–17, 1981, issue #1476 (Prime Time Vixens) **1.00** **3.00** **2.00**

☐ July 18–24, 1981, issue #1477 (BJ and the Bear on cover) **1.00** **3.00** **2.00**

☐ July 25–31, 1981, issue #1478 (Prince Charles and bride on cover) **5.00** **7.00** **6.00**

☐ August 1–7, 1981, issue #1479 (Miss Piggy on cover) **2.00** **4.00** **3.00**

☐ August 8–14, 1981, issue #1480 (Carroll O'Conner on cover) **1.00** **3.00** **2.00**

☐ August 15–21, 1981, issue #1481 (The Day Elvis Died) **8.00** **10.00** **9.00**

☐ August 22–28, 1981, issue #1482 (Ann Jillian on cover) **1.00** **3.00** **2.00**

☐ August 29–September 4, 1981, issue #1483 (football issue) **2.00** **4.00** **3.00**

☐ September 5–11, 1981, issue #1484 (Miss America issue) **1.00** **3.00** **2.00**

☐ September 12–18, 1981, issue #1485 (Fall Preview issue) **4.00** **6.00** **5.00**

☐ September 19–25, 1981, issue #1486 (Kate Mulgrew on cover) **1.00** **3.00** **2.00**

☐ September 26–October 2, 1981, issue #1487 (The Battle for Northern Ireland) **1.00** **3.00** **2.00**

☐ October 3–9, 1981, issue #1488 (Valerie Bertinelli on cover) **1.00** **3.00** **2.00**

☐ October 10–16, 1981, issue #1489 (Jaclyn Smith on cover) **1.00** **3.00** **2.00**

☐ October 17–23, 1981, issue #1490 (World Series issue) **2.00** **4.00** **3.00**

☐ October 24–30, 1981, issue #1491 (Middle East News Coverage) **1.00** **3.00** **2.00**

☐ October 31–November 6, 1981, issue #1492 (Hill Street Blues on cover) **2.00** **4.00** **3.00**

	Current Price Range		C/Y Avg.

☐ November 7–13, 1981, issue #1493 (The Two of Us on cover) **1.00**   **3.00**   **2.00**

☐ November 14–20, 1981, issue #1494 (Loretta Lynn on cover) **1.00**   **3.00**   **2.00**

☐ November 21–27, 1981, issue #1495 (John Lennon on cover) **8.00**   **10.00**   **9.00**

☐ November 28–December 4, 1981, issue #1496 (Merlin Olsen on cover) **1.00**   **3.00**   **2.00**

☐ December 5–11, 1981, issue #1497 (Lorna Patterson on cover) **1.00**   **3.00**   **2.00**

☐ December 12–18, 1981, issue #1498 (Video Games) **4.00**   **6.00**   **5.00**

☐ December 19–25, 1981, issue #1499 (Christmas cover) **1.00**   **3.00**   **2.00**

☐ December 26–January 1, 1982, issue #1500 (Henry Fonda on cover) **3.00**   **5.00**   **4.00**

1982

☐ January 2–8, 1982, issue #1501 (Tom Selleck on cover) **1.00**   **3.00**   **2.00**

☐ January 9–15, 1982, issue #1502 (Michael Landon on cover) **1.00**   **3.00**   **2.00**

☐ January 16–22, 1982, issue #1503 (Bending the Rules in Hollywood) **1.00**   **3.00**   **2.00**

☐ January 23–29, 1982, issue #1504 (Super Bowl) **2.00**   **4.00**   **3.00**

☐ January 30–February 5, 1982, issue #1505 (CHIPS on cover) **1.00**   **3.00**   **2.00**

☐ February 6–12, 1982, issue #1506 (Sherman Helmsley on cover) **1.00**   **3.00**   **2.00**

☐ February 13–19, 1982, issue #1507 (TV's Holocaust Films) **1.00**   **3.00**   **2.00**

☐ February 20–26, 1982, issue #1508 (Sixty Minutes on cover) **1.00**   **3.00**   **2.00**

☐ February 27–March 5, 1982, issue #1509 (Joan Collins on cover) **3.00**   **5.00**   **4.00**

☐ March 6–12, 1982, issue #1510 (Love Sidney on cover) **1.00**   **3.00**   **2.00**

☐ March 13–19, 1982, issue #1511 (Three's Company on cover) **1.00**   **3.00**   **2.00**

☐ March 20–26, 1982, issue #1512 (Ronald Reagan on cover) **4.00**   **6.00**   **5.00**

	Current Price Range		C/Y Avg.
☐ March 27–April 2, 1982, issue #1513 (Larry Hagman on cover)	3.00	5.00	4.00
☐ April 3–9, 1982, issue #1514 (baseball issue)	2.00	4.00	3.00
☐ April 10–16, 1982, issue #1515 (Tom Brokaw on cover)	1.00	3.00	2.00
☐ April 17–23, 1982, issue #1516 (Happy Days on cover)	2.00	4.00	3.00

WESTERN STARS

☐ February 1949 (first issue; Roy Rogers on cover)	20.00	25.00	22.50
☐ Summer 1950 (Charles Starrett on cover)	15.00	17.00	16.00
☐ Winter 1950 (Gene Autry on cover)	22.50	27.50	25.00

WESTERN STORY

☐ April 17, 1943 ("A Corral Full of Action Tales of the Old West" by Allan Vaughn Elston)	10.00	12.00	11.00

WOMAN'S HOME COMPANION

☐ December 1900 (Christmas Issue; "The Queen Who Writes Fairy Tales" by George T.B. Davis)	17.00	19.00	18.00
☐ April 1901 (England's New Queen and Her Hobbies; American Girls as Brides)	17.00	19.00	18.00
☐ November 1904 ("The Challenge" by Alice Brown)	16.00	18.00	17.00
☐ December 1904 ("The Greatest Christmas Charity in the World" by Commander Booth-Tucker)	16.00	18.00	17.00
☐ July 1906 ("Child Slaves of the Slums" by John Spargo)	14.00	16.00	15.00

WOMAN'S HOME COMPANION

☐ April 1914 (cover artwork by T.K. Hanna)	8.00	10.00	9.00
☐ November 1914 ("The American Girl" by Anne Morgan)	8.00	10.00	9.00
☐ April 1939 (50 Smart Spring Fashions)	5.00	7.00	6.00
☐ November 1941 (Five Superb Short Stories)	3.00	5.00	4.00

	Current Price Range		C/Y Avg.

THE WOMAN'S MAGAZINE

☐ May 1903 ("The House of the Seven Shadows" by Fitz Mac) **6.00   8.00   7.00**

THE YOUTH'S COMPANION

☐ December 8, 1904 (The Robert Treat Paine Statue on cover) **6.00   8.00   7.00**

☐ Autumn 1913 (cover artwork by Chase Emerson) **5.00   7.00   6.00**

☐ April 1929 (articles by Paul Waner, Herb Pennock, Mickey Cochrane) **4.00   6.00   5.00**

GLOSSARY

ACID DAMAGE. Nearly all paperbacks and magazines have been printed on paper containing some acid content. As the item ages, the acid can cause staining, changes in color, or other problems, depending on the acid level and method of storage.

ADULTS ONLY. Dealers selling explicit paperbacks or magazines sometimes include "adults only" in their terms of business. The purchaser should include, in his order, a signed statement that he is over 18 years of age. There is no prohibition against mailing such material, so long as it can be shown that it was not mailed to a minor.

ALL NEW. When this appeared as a magazine cover "blurb," it indicated that the content was not an anthology of previously published material but was appearing for the first time.

ANNOTATED EDITION. Annotated editions are usually confined to great works of literature, especially very old ones. The editor has supplied his own footnotes, either along with those already existing from a previous edition (if any), or in place of them. Works like Pepys' *Diary* and Boswell's *Life of Johnson* have been annotated so often that an edition carrying all the annotations would be the size of an encyclopedia. Strange though it may seem, it is not easy to write good annotations. Often the necessary information cannot be found, or one is doubtful about what the reader really wants to know.

ANTHOLOGY. Books containing works by more than one author, usually republished from magazines.

ART PAPER. Glossy paper used in printing better-grade magazines, especially those with numerous color photographs: *National Geographic, Scientific American,* and almost all of the men's magazines are printed on art paper.

ARTWORK. This always refers to a picture created by the medium of drawing or painting. It is never used in connection with a photograph.

AS IS. Something is wrong with the item. The dealer is sure that a customer ordering the item will want to return it, so he points out that this is impossible.

AUTHORIZED BIOGRAPHY. Biography approved by the subject. Not necessarily compiled in collaboration with the subject, but supposedly reviewed by him to correct errors or omissions of fact. Its meaning is more potent in the legalistic and commercial sense. Once the subject has authorized the biography, he cannot bring any actions against the publisher. Also, the words "authorized biography" on a book tend to generate more sales. This is rather an enigma, as unauthorized biographies often contain controversial material that would never be included in an authorized one.

BAXTER PAPER. High-quality paper used in printing deluxe magazines. Also used in printing fine books.

B.C.G. Back cover gone.

BEST SELLER. Numerous paperbacks carry the words "best seller" in the advertising matter appearing on their front or back covers. This may mean (a) the work was a best seller when published in hardcover, (b) it was previously published in paperback and achieved best seller status, (c) the publisher expects it to be a best seller.

BI-MONTHLY. Magazine published once every two months. While this is the standard American interpretation, some European bi-monthlies are published *twice* a month.

BLURB. This refers to wording on the cover of a paperback which attempts to catch the eye of bookshop browsers. It may be set over or under the title, on a banner or bullet, in any of various styles; and it can be lengthy or just a single word. Blurbs are still used in the paperback trade and in the view of some publishers are as valuable a sales tool as the title or author's name.

BONDAGE COVER. Used on paperbacks and pulp magazines (also comic books, which we do not list in this book): cover, usually painted but sometimes photographic, showing a woman chained, tied with rope, or otherwise bound. Very popular during the 1930s and 1940s, and popular today among specialist collectors.

B.P.M. Blank page missing (usually the front or rear flyleaf of a paperback, torn out by a previous owner who had written his name and address on it and wanted to remain anonymous when selling the book).

B.W. (or B/W). Black and white. Mostly used in reference to magazine covers by famous artists, which a customer is likely to order in the expectation of receiving color covers. Prior to 1920, quite a few magazines habitually ran black and white covers. The British expression is "monochrome."

CASE NUMBER. Magazine collectors will occasionally encounter bound volumes that carry a case number on the spine, in addition to the Dewey decimal number applied by a public library. Case numbers are used mainly in small rural libraries and indicate the bookcase, or shelf stack, to which it should be returned after use.

CHIP. When a small piece is missing from the cover of a paperback, it is often referred to as a chip. This is almost always the result of the cover being creased, the paper weakening at the crease and eventually coming loose.

CONCORDANCE. Reference book designed to serve as a glossary to a special subject or to another book (such as *Concordance to the Bible*). Many are author concordances, giving information about every character, subject, etc., appearing in the works of a given author.

COPYRIGHT. Legal protection of published works against their unauthorized use. The first international copyright laws were drawn up in Switzerland in 1886. In the U.S., initial copyright lasts for 28 years and may be renewed for an additional 28 years, making a limitation of 56. The assumption is that the author or creator would no longer be alive after 56 years and thus his work is protected in his lifetime. There have been many instances, however, of authors surviving their earliest books by more than 56 years. This happened in the cases of George Bernard Shaw, Bertrand Russel, and Sir Winston Churchill.

COPYRIGHT DATE. Most paperbacks carry a copyright date, though it will often go unmentioned in a dealer's list. The copyright date is not always the same as the actual year of printing. A paperback can go through various editions over a period of years without the copyright being renewed. Usually there will be no copyright renewal unless the book has been materially changed in some way. Thus you could have a book with a 1945 copyright which was printed in 1950. Check to see whether the notice "first printing," "second printing," etc., is included. If "first printing" is indicated, the book was printed in the copyright year, or perhaps at the close of the preceding year for distribution in the copyright year.

COVER FADED. This is almost always the result of the item being displayed for a long time in a dealer's shop window. Today the majority of shops catering to collectors (as opposed to readers) have shaded windows and leave all valuable items on the shelves.

COVER LOOSE. A confusing term, as it can mean (a) the cover is completely loose (separated), (b) not as tight as it should be.

COVER PRICE. The price at which the paperback or magazine was originally sold, as printed on the cover. In the case of foreign imports, the U.S. price might not be printed but rather stamped or hand written. It will always be more than the exchange rate, as the cost of importation is added.

COVERS REGLUED. Refers to magazine covers which have been reattached by gluing. It is seldom correct in the technical sense, as the great majority of magazine covers were not glued in the first place but attached by staples only.

DISBOUND. A term found only in the lists of dealers who are very well acquainted with the language of book collecting. A disbound magazine was once bound, presumably along with other issues of the same title, in hard covers. For some reason it was removed. Any disbound magazine will show clear evidence of its past. At the very least there will be small holes near the spine, running entirely through from cover to cover, where the stitching was done. There may be glue stains and (worse) missing covers and missing ad pages.

DOUBLE ISSUE. In the era of weekly magazines, which have dwindled down to a very few, it was a common practice to publish "double issues" at least once a year. *Life* magazine traditionally did this at Christmas; its annual double issue arrived on the newsstands the week before Christmas and no issue was published in the week between Christmas and New Year's Day. The basic motive behind double issues was to allow for employee holidays. Most double issues carried a higher than normal cover price, though not necessarily double (nor was the issue necessarily twice as large).

ERRORS. So far the paperback and magazine hobbies have not developed any special appreciation for freaks and errors, unlike many other areas of collecting. Paperbacks and magazines are sometimes found with pages bound upside down and other oddities, but there is apparently no willingness at this point to pay premiums for such copies. Quite the reverse, they are flatly rejected by nearly all buyers.

EX LIBRIS. An inscription, often used on bookplates, stating the owner's name of the book.

FASHION PLATE. In the language of collecting (which is often different than that of everyday life), this means a full-page illustration, usually colored, of fashions for women, men or children. It is generally used only in reference to illustrations printed by engraving or lithography, not to photographic plates. The magazine best known for its fashion plates (in the U.S., at any rate) was *Godey's Lady's Book.*

FIRST ISSUE COLLECTING. Restricting oneself exclusively to magazines identified as Volume 1, Number 1. Most first issues are slightly more expensive than later issues, and this is apparently the direct result of competition from the "first issue" collectors. Some collectors firmly believe that first issues have a special quality, insofar as publishers strove to make a great impression with them. But this is not necessarily the case, as numerous first issues were published on low budgets under the worst conditions. Quality-wise, most magazines tend to improve with age, and this is certainly the case with all of those which become commercially successful.

FINAL ISSUE. Unless the magazine is a great favorite of collectors, or its final issue was special in some way, it will not command a premium price solely on account of being the last issue published.

FIRST PAPERBACK EDITION. First appearance in paperback of a work which previously was published in hardcover. This is different than a first edition paperback, which is the first appearance of the work in any form.

FLAT SPINE. There are two ways to bind a magazine. The pages (attached in sets) can be laid one inside the other with a pair of staples passing through the spine and locking at the centerfold. This creates a so-called "wedge spine." Method number two is to lay the gatherings one on top of another, instead of one inside another. Magazines bound in this fashion are still stapled, but the staples are not visible from the outside as they are applied *under* the cover. The cover is then glued in place, and a flat spine is achieved.

FOXED. Brown splotches on the paper, which look like rust but are really caused by a type of lice which thrives on paper fibre.

FULL ISSUE. In reading dealers' lists of very old magazines, such as *Harper's Weekly* of the 1800s, you will occasionally find the note "full issue." This indicates that other offerings on the list are *not* full issues, but are loose covers or illustration plates. Be sure before ordering.

GATEFOLD COVER. Cover of a magazine which is approximately twice the size of the magazine. Half the cover is folded under, and when unfolded forms a long continuous picture. Covers of this type are not confined to men's magazines and in fact have seldom been used by them. *Life* used gatefold covers during the 1950s for its "The World We Live In" series.

HACKER. Term used in the days of pulp magazines, referring to authors from whom the editors bought stories in large quantities without much consideration for quality. It was more important for a hacker to be quick and productive than to be a first rate writer. However, many outstanding authors got their start as hackers. The enormous quantity of pulps published in the 1930s left most editors short on stories and they were in no position to be fussy. Some resorted to writing their own stories, or filling up blank pages with artwork. It was not unusual for a hard-working hacker to sell 50 or more stories per year.

HARDBOUND MAGAZINE. Very few magazines have been published with hard, booklike bindings. These have included *Horizon, American Heritage,* and the ill-fated (but very valuable to collectors) *Eros* published by Ralph Ginsburg. Hard bindings not only add considerably to the cost of publication but also to the cost of distribution and mailing, and are unpopular with most readers anyway.

HEADINGS BLED. When magazines are bound into hard covers it is customary for the binder to trim their edges, to make all the pages even. If the trimming goes too deep, some headings may be touched or cut into. This is known as "headings bled." You may also see "page numbers bled," "side notes bled," or (worst of all) "text bled."

IMPRESSION. An impression of a paperback (as in sixth impression) is different than an edition (as in first edition). There can be several— sometimes a great many—impressions of the same edition. The difference between a new edition and new impression is that nothing changes in the new impression. It is the identical book with the identical cover. The publisher has simply run low on his stock, and ordered a fresh batch of copies from his printer.

INCREMENT. The amount by which an auction bid is raised over the next highest bid. If you bid $50 for the sake of topping a $40 bid, you have bid a $10 increment. Try to determine what sort of increments the auctioneer accepts. You could easily end up bidding more than is necessary. In the example just given, most auctioneers would accept an increment of $5. But if the bid is $1000, a $5 increment won't work. If you have to proceed by guesswork, never use an increment of more than 10% of the bid amount.

INDEX ISSUE. Magazine containing an index for all articles, etc., published in all issues of that volume. Normally the index issue is the final issue for the volume, but in some cases the index does not appear until the first issue of the next volume. Magazines which publish indexes (few do) always number their pages consecutively throughout the volume. If the last numbered page in Volume 1, Number 1 was 132, the first numbered page in the next issue will be 133.

INFINITY COVER. Found mainly on science fiction and fantasy paperbacks, and not too common even on those: a cover painting in which the scene repeats itself many times, diminishing in size until it finally disappears. A typical infinity cover is a person holding the book, which pictures the person holding the book, which pictures . . . well, you get the idea.

INSERT. Whenever something has been inserted into a magazine— such as a foldout poster, phonograph record, etc.—intended to be removed for use, most copies will lack it. Always check to see if the insert is present. Inserts normally give the issue a higher value than other issues.

LAMINATED COVER. Paperback cover with protective cellophane atop it, as issued. Most paperback covers are laminated. The purpose was not just protection but to make the cover glossy.

LIMITATION NOTICE. Statement appearing in a paperback, usually on the reverse side of the title page, to the effect that only X number of copies have been printed. This qualifies the book as a limited edition, though if the number is high (say 20,000 or more) it is hardly limited in the actual sense.

LOOSE BINDER. A binder (more correctly called a holder) for magazines, in which the issues are held in place by rods and can be removed at will. Used both by public libraries and magazine collectors. Some magazines sell loose binders specifically designed for that particular publication. These are always preferable when available, as there will be no problem with fit.

LOOSELY INSERTED. This refers to business reply cards, coupons, or anything included in a magazine which can be removed without tugging, tearing or cutting. In very few instances are these loosely inserted items to be found in secondhand copies.

MAGAZINE BOX. There are several types of magazine storage boxes available. By far the best is shaped like a book and has the magazine's title stamped on the spine. These boxes are expensive but make a very neat appearance on bookcase shelves, and do a good storage job in terms of protection. Fiberboard boxes of various sizes are also used to store magazines. These have a lid at the top and cutouts at the sides by which they can be carried. They are often referred to as "comic book boxes," as they are extensively used by comics collectors.

MIXED CONDITION. When used by a seller in reference to a batch of magazines or paperbacks, beware. If there are a hundred items in the lot, the presence of just one in reasonable shape could result in a "mixed condition" designation. Likewise if all are damaged, some more than others, the condition is mixed.

MONOCHROME. Term used by British book and magazine dealers, referring to black and white (or one-color) illustrations.

MYLAR. A special type of acid-free plastic, in which paper items can be stored for long periods of time without deterioration. Mylar is a registered trademark of the Du Pont Co.

N.B.C. No back cover.

NEW TRANSLATION. Commonly found in paperback editions of the writings of ancient Greek and Roman poets, historians, etc. New translations of these works are made frequently. The newest translation is not necessarily the best, and in fact is very likely not to be, as one of the major objectives in translating is to avoid duplicating a previous translation (which could have been a really good one). Generally speaking, each new translation brings the work further and further from the way its author designed it.

NEWSPRINT. A low quality pulp paper, used in printing newspapers and, in the early days of the paperback industry (when prices were 10 cents), paperbacks as well. Because of its high wood fibre content, it contains a great deal of moisture, and as this moisture dries out the paper becomes stiff and brittle.

N.S. No spine: a paperback with spine missing. Also referred to as S.M. (spine missing) and in a variety of other ways.

OFFPRINT. Separate printing of an article that appeared in a magazine. It must indeed *be* a printing, not a xerox copy, and certainly not pages torn from the magazine. Most offprints are scholarly articles from technical journals. Offprint is always spelled as one word. Offprints originated as a means by which poor publishers could offer their writers something in payment, other than money.

ONE SHOT. Magazine of which only one issue was published. Used only in reference to those for which no further issues were planned, as opposed to magazines that were unsuccessful and terminated after one issue.

OUT OF SERIES ISSUE. Special issue of a magazine, not published as part of the regular series. It may or may not be dated and/or numbered. Out of series issues are very infrequent in magazine publishing. One example was *Life*'s Kennedy Memorial issue published shortly after the events of November 1963. It was not sent to subscribers but sold on newsstands only.

PAGES PLUS ADS. In the earlier days of magazine publishing it was a standard practice to group advertisements and place them at the back. These ad pages were seldom numbered so that they could be discarded before binding a run of issues and therefore achieve a less clumsy volume. Dealers will often note that a magazine contains "128 pages plus ads," sometimes stating the number of ad pages (but rarely, because that means counting them).

PAINTED COVER. Cover of a paperback or magazine which features a reproduction of an oil painting rather than a watercolor sketch or some other type of artwork.

PAPERBACK RACK. Some collectors like to store and display their paperbacks on revolving wire racks, as are used in bookshops. These can be bought directly from the manufacturers and often at secondhand shops at a much lower price (a fresh paint job makes them look new).

One drawback is that they take up more space, in relation to the number of books stored, than conventional shelving.

PHOTO COVER. Paperback cover which has been reproduced from a photograph. These started coming into vogue in the 1950s and are still seen today, but have never been used as extensively as drawn or painted covers.

POSTER INSERT. Generally a poster insert in a magazine will be attached by staples, and should be in place just as it was originally for the full market value to be achieved.

PRIZE NOVEL. Novel which won a writing competition, usually one sponsored by the publishing company. The prize is normally modest and the purpose of a writing contest is to encourage new authors to submit manuscripts to the publisher. A clause in the rules always states that the publisher has the option to publish any of the manuscripts, including the losers.

READING COPY. Paperback or magazine in poor condition, suitable for reading but not collecting. A reading copy should at least be complete.

REPRINT. Correctly speaking a reprint is a later edition brought out by a different publisher. If the work is issued again by the same publisher this is normally called a reissue.

REVIEW COPY. Copy of a paperback sent to book review editors of magazines, as well as any other persons who might give it publicity. Sometimes finished copies are sent out for review, differing in no respect from those shipped to bookstores. They simply have a card inserted requesting two copies of the review, if one is published. But some review copies, depending on the publisher's practice, are trial copies with blank covers or other variations from the bookstore copies. It was once a common approach to send out uncorrected galleys for review, to be sure of getting the review published early. This is rarely done anymore.

RUN. A run of magazines is a batch of consecutive issues, anything from a few to hundreds. The run may not start from number one, and may not carry up to the final issue published. When a run is completed it is normally called a "set," or at least "complete run."

SCARCE. This can usually be taken to mean the item is scarce in the opinion of the person making the statement. Many expensive paperbacks and magazines are not really scarce, but are expensive because of their popularity with collectors.

SEPIA COVER. Many magazines published before 1920 utilized sepia covers. These were photographic covers in which the photo was printed in a dark reddish-brown tone.

SERIAL NUMBER. More than 99 percent of paperbacks carry serial numbers. Most of those which do not are either very early ones, or titles published by companies which had no intention of issuing more than a few. While serial numbers are often overlooked by general readers, they play an important role in the paperback hobby.

The serial number is the number assigned to a paperback by its publisher. It appears on the book, either on the front cover or spine (frequently both), and is used by distributors and retailers in ordering the book. Its purpose is to identify the book and the *edition* without the need for writing out author, title, date and other information. Each paperback publisher sets its own rules on how its serial numbering system will operate. There is no hard and fast tradition. Some take the obvious approach and number their first book #1, their second #2, and so on. There are certain disadvantages in doing this, however. Some customers, seeing very low serial numbers, will presume the books are inferior because they are published by a new company. So instead of starting with No. 1, many new publishers will call their first book No. 101, or even No. 1001.

If the company intends to publish titles in various subject categories, it may elect to use a separate serial numbering system for each group. For example, its mysteries may be given serial numbers beginning with the prefix letter M, westerns W, romances R, and so forth. Or the identifying letter may be placed behind the number as a suffix rather than prefix. If fiction and non-fiction are being published simultaneously, they will almost always have separate serial numbers, and the non-fiction may likewise be identified by letters: H for history, A for art, B for biography.

Serial numbering systems such as these are too simplistic to suit the tastes of some publishers, so you will find much more complex examples in the world of paperbacks. It is not unusual for publishers to devise serial numbering systems in which not only the book but its publisher is identified. The Vintage paperbacks have serial numbers beginning with V, which tells a distributor or retailer that he is dealing with a Vintage book. Of course he must be aware of Vintage's practice of doing this, otherwise he might easily mistake it for a *Vantage* paperback.

Normally, but not invariably, one digit will change in each new serial number, regardless of the number of digits or digits and letters comprising it. If the previous serial number used by the publisher was 117H, the next title will be 118H, assuming it falls in the same subject group. If the previous number was 503467, the next should be 503468. Serial numbers are assigned chronologically in the order in which the books are published. This does not provide an absolute guarantee that 117H reached the bookshops before 118H, since they might have been published simultaneously; or delays in printing or shipping could have resulted in 118H getting to the bookshops long before 117H. But, generally speaking, one can rely on the chronological evidence supplied by serial numbers, and to a collector this is important evidence indeed. Some paperbacks are not dated, and the serial numbers become the only means of assigning a rough date to them. For example, if you have a book from the XYZ publishing company dated 1967 with a serial number of 332, this tells you quite a bit about its dateless books. If 332 was published in 1967, most likely 330 was too and probably 325. If they were not published in 1967, you could not be wrong by more than a year for assigning dates in this fashion. By the same token, if you come across an XYZ book dated 1961 with a serial number of 115, you can do some mathematics and discover approximately how many titles that company published each year. It took them six years to get from 115 to 332, a difference of 217. That would be a yearly average of 36 titles. Thus, if you find one of their books with a serial number above 115 but below 200, it should belong to 1962 or 1963. You will not get infallible results this way, but you can make fairly good guesses. The company might have published twice as many books in one year as it did in another, but still your calculations will be close, much closer than you could come by estimating age on the basis of literary style or cover artwork. The most *that* will do is bring you into the right decade, and sometimes not. The cover price is not even a great aid in estimating age, unless you know precisely when the publisher changed its prices.

There is another very positive accomplishment in studying serial numbers. If you have two editions of the same book by the same publisher, the serial numbers tell you which is the earlier—and the earlier one will almost always be more valuable. Signet's later editions of the James Bond novels can be instantly distinguished by their high serial numbers.

Serial numbers are sometimes referred to as code numbers, series numbers, or by various other terms.

SIXTIES SLEAZE. Paperbacks with racy covers, but normally far less racy content, published during the 1960s. While works of this nature appeared before the 1960s, and in vast profusion thereafter, collectors often specialize in titles from that decade exclusively. One reason is that the cover artists included many whose works are very popular. It is also the opinion of some collectors that sleaze novels reached their pinnacle as an art form during the 1960s.

SPICY. The word "spicy" was used in the titles of numerous magazines in the 1920s, 1930s, and 1940s. Mostly these were pulp fiction magazines with a few illustrations and sported painted or drawn covers. Though tame by later standards, they were not publicly displayed by most newsdealers and had to be requested.

SPINE ROLL. Used in connection with paperbacks and magazines, but more prevalent on magazines. A condition in which the spine is out of shape, usually as the result of the item being improperly stored over a long period of time. Instead of "tight," the spine is curved inward or outward from the book or magazine. In the case of a thick paperback, the two edges of the spine may be almost meeting each other. Spine roll can be corrected, or at least lessened, by a paper restorations expert, but it is expensive work and most paperbacks and magazines are not worth the effort.

SUBSCRIPTION COPY. Magazine which has an address label on the front cover, and (usually) an unattractive crease down the center as the result of being jammed into a letterbox.

SUPPLIED IN XEROX. This note, when found in a magazine dealer's list, means a page (or more) is missing but a photocopy has been provided. If the dealer has two copies of the magazine, he will photocopy the missing page and loosely insert it. This is really done only as a favor to the customer, as it does not increase the sales value.

TAPE. When the description of a paperback or magazine in a dealer's list mentions "tape," without further explanation, one should presume the item has been heavily repaired with cellophane tape (covers and interior).

THE BEST OF. . . . Whenever a collection of writings is published as "The Best of . . . ," one can usually assume that the author's best known works will be included. Whether these were indeed his best is open to conjecture.

TIGHT SPINE. The spine of a paperback or magazine is in the same condition as when issued, showing no evidence of fatigue or careless storage.

TIPPED IN. Some early magazines, notably *Camera Work,* did not print their photographs directly on the magazine's pages but separately, then attached them in place with glue. This is always the sign of a high quality magazine, as the photos are printed on regular photographic paper and are sharper than they would otherwise be. It was more expensive to do this, as every photo in every copy had to be glued individually by hand. Look especially for missing ones. Tipped in photos are still to be found in art books, but no longer in magazines. The name refers to the fact that glue was applied to the very tips of the photos only, where creasing (if it occurred) would not be disfiguring.

T.S. Tape stain, the result of making a repair with cellophane tape. As the tape ages it deteriorates and leaves a brownish sludge on the paper, while the cellophane itself becomes brittle and falls away.

UNCENSORED. A favorite cover-word in the magazine industry during the 1930s and 1940s. It almost always referred to photos or stories that contained nothing worth censoring, but it helped sell magazines.

UNCOVERED MAGAZINE. Some dealers will (incorrectly) call a magazine "uncovered" if its covers are printed on the same paper stock as its interior pages. But a cover is always a cover, regardless of the material.

UNPUBLISHED ISSUES. Before assuming that your set of a monthly publication lacks an issue, because it skips from June to August, check the issue number to determine if there was indeed an issue published for that month. In earlier days it was quite a common practice (and still is among many foreign magazines) to miss one or two summer months. This was done intentionally and the subscription notices read, "One year—10 months." In the magazine business a year does not necessarily comprise twelve months. Of course a publisher could easily alleviate the confusion by calling his June issue June/July, but this is not invariably done.

VOLUME. For magazines, a volume may comprise a month's issues, half a year, or an entire year. It varies depending on (a) the frequency of publication, (b) the thickness of each issue. The basic object in assigning volume numbers is to assist public libraries in binding the issues into hard covers, which many libraries automatically do. If twelve issues would make too thick and clumsy a book, the volume numbering will include six issues only. In the case of quarterly magazines (four times a year), a volume is almost always a year's worth.

INDEX

The HOUSE OF COLLECTIBLES Series

☐ Please send me the following price guides—
☐ I would like the most current edition of the books listed below.

THE OFFICIAL PRICE GUIDES TO:

☐ 753-3	American Folk Art (ID) 1st Ed.	$14.95
☐ 199-3	American Silver & Silver Plate 5th Ed.	11.95
☐ 513-1	Antique Clocks 3rd Ed.	10.95
☐ 283-3	Antique & Modern Dolls 3rd Ed.	10.95
☐ 287-6	Antique & Modern Firearms 6th Ed.	11.95
☐ 755-X	Antiques & Collectibles 9th Ed.	11.95
☐ 289-2	Antique Jewelry 5th Ed.	11.95
☐ 362-7	Art Deco (ID) 1st Ed.	14.95
☐ 447-X	Arts and Crafts: American Decorative Arts, 1894–1923 (ID) 1st Ed.	12.95
☐ 539-5	Beer Cans & Collectibles 4th Ed.	7.95
☐ 521-2	Bottles Old & New 10th Ed.	10.95
☐ 532-8	Carnival Glass 2nd Ed.	10.95
☐ 295-7	Collectible Cameras 2nd Ed.	10.95
☐ 548-4	Collectibles of the '50s & '60s 1st Ed.	9.95
☐ 740-1	Collectible Toys 4th Ed.	10.95
☐ 531-X	Collector Cars 7th Ed.	12.95
☐ 538-7	Collector Handguns 4th Ed.	14.95
☐ 748-7	Collector Knives 9th Ed.	12.95
☐ 361-9	Collector Plates 5th Ed.	11.95
☐ 296-5	Collector Prints 7th Ed.	12.95
☐ 001-6	Depression Glass 2nd Ed.	9.95
☐ 589-1	Fine Art 1st Ed.	19.95
☐ 311-2	Glassware 3rd Ed.	10.95
☐ 243-4	Hummel Figurines & Plates 6th Ed.	10.95
☐ 523-9	Kitchen Collectibles 2nd Ed.	10.95
☐ 080-6	Memorabilia of Elvis Presley and The Beatles 1st Ed.	10.95
☐ 291-4	Military Collectibles 5th Ed.	11.95
☐ 525-5	Music Collectibles 6th Ed.	11.95
☐ 313-9	Old Books & Autographs 7th Ed.	11.95
☐ 298-1	Oriental Collectibles 3rd Ed.	11.95
☐ 761-4	Overstreet Comic Book 18th Ed.	12.95
☐ 522-0	Paperbacks & Magazines 1st Ed.	10.95
☐ 297-3	Paper Collectibles 5th Ed.	10.95
☐ 744-4	Political Memorabilia 1st Ed.	10.95
☐ 529-8	Pottery & Porcelain 6th Ed.	11.95
☐ 524-7	Radio, TV & Movie Memorabilia 3rd Ed.	11.95
☐ 081-4	Records 8th Ed.	16.95
☐ 763-0	Royal Doulton 6th Ed.	12.95
☐ 280-9	Science Fiction & Fantasy Collectibles 2nd Ed.	10.95
☐ 747-9	Sewing Collectibles 1st Ed.	8.95
☐ 358-9	Star Trek/Star Wars Collectibles 2nd Ed.	8.95
☐ 086-5	Watches 8th Ed.	12.95
☐ 248-5	Wicker 3rd Ed.	10.95

THE OFFICIAL:

☐ 760-6	Directory to U.S. Flea Markets 2nd Ed.	5.95
☐ 365-1	Encyclopedia of Antiques 1st Ed.	9.95
☐ 369-4	Guide to Buying and Selling Antiques 1st Ed.	9.95
☐ 414-3	Identification Guide to Early American Furniture 1st Ed.	9.95
☐ 413-5	Identification Guide to Glassware 1st Ed.	9.95

☐ 412-7	Identification Guide to Pottery & Porcelain 1st Ed.	$9.95
☐ 415-1	Identification Guide to Victorian Furniture 1st Ed.	9.95

THE OFFICIAL (SMALL SIZE) PRICE GUIDES TO:

☐ 309-0	Antiques & Flea Markets 4th Ed.	4.95
☐ 269-8	Antique Jewelry 3rd Ed.	4.95
☐ 085-7	Baseball Cards 8th Ed.	4.95
☐ 647-2	Bottles 3rd Ed.	4.95
☐ 544-1	Cars & Trucks 3rd Ed.	5.95
☐ 519-0	Collectible Americana 2nd Ed.	4.95
☐ 294-9	Collectible Records 3rd Ed.	4.95
☐ 306-6	Dolls 4th Ed.	4.95
☐ 762-2	Football Cards 8th Ed.	4.95
☐ 540-9	Glassware 3rd Ed.	4.95
☐ 526-3	Hummels 4th Ed.	4.95
☐ 279-5	Military Collectibles 3rd Ed.	4.95
☐ 764-9	Overstreet Comic Book Companion 2nd Ed.	4.95
☐ 278-7	Pocket Knives 3rd Ed.	4.95
☐ 527-1	Scouting Collectibles 4th Ed.	4.95
☐ 494-1	Star Trek/Star Wars Collectibles 3rd Ed.	3.95
☐ 088-1	Toys 5th Ed.	4.95

THE OFFICIAL BLACKBOOK PRICE GUIDES OF:

☐ 092-X	U.S. Coins 27th Ed.	4.95
☐ 095-4	U.S. Paper Money 21st Ed.	4.95
☐ 098-9	U.S. Postage Stamps 11th Ed.	4.95

THE OFFICIAL INVESTORS GUIDE TO BUYING & SELLING:

☐ 534-4	Gold, Silver & Diamonds 2nd Ed.	12.95
☐ 535-2	Gold Coins 2nd Ed.	12.95
☐ 536-0	Silver Coins 2nd Ed.	12.95
☐ 537-9	Silver Dollars 2nd Ed.	12.95

THE OFFICIAL NUMISMATIC GUIDE SERIES:

☐ 254-X	The Official Guide to Detecting Counterfeit Money 2nd Ed.	7.95
☐ 257-4	The Official Guide to Mint Errors 4th Ed.	7.95

SPECIAL INTEREST SERIES:

☐ 506-9	From Hearth to Cookstove 3rd Ed.	17.95
☐ 504-2	On Method Acting 8th Printing	6.95

TOTAL		

SEE REVERSE SIDE FOR ORDERING INSTRUCTIONS

FOR IMMEDIATE DELIVERY

VISA & MASTER CARD CUSTOMERS
ORDER TOLL FREE!
1-800-733-3000

This number is for orders only; it is not tied into the customer service or business office. Customers not using charge cards must use mail for ordering since payment is required with the order—sorry, no C.O.D's.

OR SEND ORDERS TO

THE HOUSE OF COLLECTIBLES
201 East 50th Street
New York, New York 10022

_____ POSTAGE & HANDLING RATES _____

First Book $1.00

Each Additional Copy or Title $0.50

Total from columns on order form. Quantity_____ $_____

☐ Check or money order enclosed $_____ (include postage and handling)

☐ Please charge $_____to my: ☐ MASTERCARD ☐ VISA

Charge Card Customers Not Using Our Toll Free Number
Please Fill Out The Information Below

Account No. _____Expiration Date_____
(All Digits)

Signature_____

NAME (please print)_____PHONE_____

ADDRESS_____APT. # _____

CITY_____STATE_____ZIP_____